תלמוד בבלי

KOREN TALMUD BAVLI

THE NOÉ EDITION

נזיר

NAZIR

Daf 2a through Daf 20b

COMMENTARY BY

Rabbi Adin Even-Israel Steinsaltz

EDITOR-IN-CHIEF

Rabbi Dr Tzvi Hersh Weinreb

SENIOR CONTENT EDITOR

Rabbi Dr Shalom Z Berger

EXECUTIVE EDITOR

Rabbi Joshua Schreier

STEINSALTZ CENTER

KOREN PUBLISHERS JERUSALEM

Supported by the Matanel Foundation

Koren Talmud Bavli, The Noe Edition
Vol. 17a: Tractate Nazir, Daf 2a through Daf 20b
Paperback, ISBN, 978-965-7765-80-7

First Hebrew/English paperback edition, 2021

Koren Publishers Jerusalem Ltd.
PO Box 4044, Jerusalem 91040, ISRAEL
PO Box 8531, New Milford, CT 06776, USA
www.korenpub.com

Steinsaltz Center

Steinsaltz Center is the parent organization of institutions established by Rabbi Adin Even-Israel Steinsaltz

PO Box 45187, Jerusalem 91450 ISRAEL
Telephone: +972 2 646 0900, Fax +972 2 624 9454
www.steinsaltz-center.org

This book was published in cooperation with the Israel Institute for Talmudic Publications.

Koren Talmud Bavli
THE NOÉ EDITION

NAZIR

Steinsaltz Center

KOREN

הִנֵּה יָמִים בָּאִים, נְאֻם אֲדֹנָי יֱהֹוִה, וְהִשְׁלַחְתִּי רָעָב בָּאָרֶץ,
לֹא־רָעָב לַלֶּחֶם וְלֹא־צָמָא לַמַּיִם, כִּי אִם־לִשְׁמֹעַ אֵת דִּבְרֵי יהוה.

Behold, days are coming – says the Lord God – I will send a hunger to the land, not a hunger for bread nor a thirst for water, but to hear the words of the Lord. (AMOS 8:11)

The Noé edition of the Koren Talmud Bavli
with the commentary of Rabbi Adin Even-Israel Steinsaltz
is dedicated to all those who open its covers
to quench their thirst for Jewish Knowledge,
in our generation of Torah renaissance.

This beautiful edition is for the young, the aged,
the novice and the savant alike,
as it unites the depth of Torah knowledge
with the best of academic scholarship.

Within its exquisite and vibrant pages,
words become worlds.

It will claim its place in the library of classics,
in the bookcases of the Beit Midrash,
the classrooms of our schools,
and in the offices of professionals and business people
who carve out precious time to grapple with its timeless wisdom.

For the Student and the Scholar

DEDICATED BY LEO AND SUE NOÉ

Steinsaltz Center

Executive Director, Steinsaltz Center

Rabbi Meni Even-Israel

Managing Editor

Rabbi Jason Rappoport

Senior Content Editor

Rabbi Dr. Shalom Z. Berger

Editors

Rabbi Dr. Joshua Amaru, *Coordinating Editor*
Rabbi Avishai Magence, *Content Curator*
Menucha Chwat
Rabbi Yehoshua Duker
Betzalel Philip Edwards
Rabbi Yonatan Shai Freedman
Catriel Lev
Elisha Loewenstern
Adina Luber
Yedidya Naveh
Rabbi Eli Ozarowski
Noam Shapiro
Rabbi Michael Siev
Rabbi David Strauss
Rabbi Binyamin Zimmerman

Copy Editors

Aliza Israel, *Coordinator*
Bracha Hermon
Ita Olesker
Debbie Ismailoff
Shira Finson
Ilana Sobel
Deena Nataf
Eliana Kurlantzick Yorav
Erica Hirsch Edvi
Nava Wieder

Language Consultants

Dr. Stephanie E. Binder, *Greek & Latin*
Rabbi Yaakov Hoffman, *Arabic*
Dr. Shai Secunda, *Persian*
Shira Shmidman, *Aramaic*

KOREN

Design & Typesetting

Dena Landowne Bailey, *Typesetting*
Tani Bayer, *Jacket Design*
Raphaël Freeman, *Design & Typography*

Images

Eliahu Misgav, *Illustration & Image Acquisition*
Daniel Gdalevich, *Illustration & Image Acquisition*

Introduction by the Publisher

The Talmud has sustained and inspired Jews for thousands of years. Throughout Jewish history, an elite cadre of scholars has absorbed its learning and passed it on to succeeding generations. The Talmud has been the fundamental text of our people.

Beginning in the 1960s, Rabbi Adin Even-Israel Steinsaltz שליט״א created a revolution in the history of Talmud study. His translation of the Talmud, first into modern Hebrew and then into other languages, as well the practical learning aids he added to the text, have enabled millions of people around the world to access and master the complexity and context of the world of Talmud.

It is thus a privilege to present the *Koren Talmud Bavli*, an English translation of the talmudic text with the brilliant elucidation of Rabbi Steinsaltz. The depth and breadth of his knowledge are unique in our time. His rootedness in the tradition and his reach into the world beyond it are inspirational.

Working with Rabbi Steinsaltz on this remarkable project has been not only an honor, but a great pleasure. Never shy to express an opinion, with wisdom and humor, Rabbi Steinsaltz sparkles in conversation, demonstrating his knowledge (both sacred and worldly), sharing his wide-ranging interests, and, above all, radiating his passion. I am grateful for the unique opportunity to work closely with him, and I wish him many more years of writing and teaching.

Our intentions in publishing this new edition of the Talmud are threefold. First, we seek to fully clarify the talmudic page to the reader – textually, intellectually, and graphically. Second, we seek to utilize today's most sophisticated technologies, both in print and electronic formats, to provide the reader with a comprehensive set of study tools. And third, we seek to help readers advance in their process of Talmud study.

To achieve these goals, the *Koren Talmud Bavli* is unique in a number of ways:

- The classic *tzurat hadaf* of Vilna, used by scholars since the 1800s, has been reset for great clarity, and opens from the Hebrew "front" of the book. Full *nikkud* has been added to both the talmudic text and Rashi's commentary, allowing for a more fluent reading with the correct pronunciation; the commentaries of *Tosafot* have been punctuated. Upon the advice of many English-speaking teachers of Talmud, we have separated these core pages from the translation, thereby enabling the advanced student to approach the text without the distraction of the translation. This also reduces the number of volumes in the set. At the bottom of each *daf*, there is a reference to the corresponding English pages. In addition, the Vilna edition was read against other manuscripts and older print editions, so that texts which had been removed by non-Jewish censors have been restored to their rightful place.
- The English translation, which starts on the English "front" of the book, reproduces the *menukad* Talmud text alongside the English translation (in bold) and commentary and explanation (in a lighter font). The Hebrew and Aramaic text is presented in logical paragraphs. This allows for a fluent reading of the text for the non-Hebrew or non-Aramaic reader. It also allows for the Hebrew reader to refer easily to the text alongside. Where the original text features dialogue or poetry, the English text is laid out in a manner appropriate to the genre. Each page refers to the relevant *daf*.

- Critical contextual tools surround the text and translation: personality notes, providing short biographies of the Sages; language notes, explaining foreign terms borrowed from Greek, Latin, Persian, or Arabic; and background notes, giving information essential to the understanding of the text, including history, geography, botany, archaeology, zoology, astronomy, and aspects of daily life in the talmudic era.
- Halakhic summaries provide references to the authoritative legal decisions made over the centuries by the rabbis. They explain the reasons behind each halakhic decision as well as the ruling's close connection to the Talmud and its various interpreters.
- Photographs, drawings, and other illustrations have been added throughout the text – in full color in the Standard and Electronic editions, and in black and white in the Daf Yomi edition – to visually elucidate the text.

This is not an exhaustive list of features of this edition, it merely presents an overview for the English-speaking reader who may not be familiar with the "total approach" to Talmud pioneered by Rabbi Steinsaltz.

Several professionals have helped bring this vast collaborative project to fruition. My many colleagues are noted on the Acknowledgments page, and the leadership of this project has been exceptional.

RABBI MENACHEM EVEN-ISRAEL, DIRECTOR OF THE STEINSALTZ CENTER, was the driving force behind this enterprise. With enthusiasm and energy, he formed the happy alliance with Koren and established close relationships among all involved in the work.

RABBI DR. TZVI HERSH WEINREB שליט״א, EDITOR-IN-CHIEF, brought to this project his profound knowledge of Torah, intellectual literacy of Talmud, and erudition of Western literature. It is to him that the text owes its very high standard, both in form and content, and the logical manner in which the beauty of the Talmud is presented.

RABBI JOSHUA SCHREIER, EXECUTIVE EDITOR, assembled an outstanding group of scholars, translators, editors, and proofreaders, whose standards and discipline enabled this project to proceed in a timely and highly professional manner.

RABBI MEIR HANEGBI, EDITOR OF THE HEBREW EDITION OF THE STEINSALTZ TALMUD, lent his invaluable assistance throughout the work process, supervising the reproduction of the Vilna pages.

RAPHAËL FREEMAN, EXECUTIVE EDITOR OF KOREN, created this Talmud's unique typographic design which, true to the Koren approach, is both elegant and user friendly.

It has been an enriching experience for all of us at Koren Publishers Jerusalem to work with the Steinsaltz Center to develop and produce the *Koren Talmud Bavli*. We pray that this publication will be a source of great learning and, ultimately, greater *avodat Hashem* for all Jews.

Matthew Miller, Publisher
Koren Publishers Jerusalem
Jerusalem 5772

Contents

For the vocalized Vilna Shas layout, please open as a Hebrew book.

Introduction to **Nazir**

Tractate *Nazir* is located in the order of *Nashim*, usually after tractate *Nedarim* and before tractate *Sota*.[1] The content of the tractate is not directly related to the order of *Nashim*, and the Gemara (2a) discusses this problem. However, since the passage in the Torah that speaks of the nazirite (Numbers, chapter 6) is juxtaposed to the passage in the Torah that speaks of a woman suspected by her husband of having been unfaithful [*sota*] (Numbers, chapter 5), tractate *Nazir* was similarly placed next to tractate *Sota* in the Mishna. The entire tractate deals with the *halakhot* of a nazirite and with some of the *halakhot* of vows, offerings, and ritual purity and impurity.

A nazirite vow is a special form of a vow that one accepts upon himself. It obligates him in the rules and regulations established for a nazirite in the Torah. As with other types of vows, one might take a nazirite vow for a variety of reasons, e.g., to be absolved of a sin or to express gratitude to God for His kindness. Alternatively, one might take a nazirite vow in order to merit divine favor as one makes a request of God, or one might take the vow out of anger or spite. At its best, when accepted with pure intentions, naziriteship is considered a way to achieve holiness, as the Torah states: "All the days of his naziriteship he is holy to the Lord" (Numbers 6:8).

The term nazirite [*nazir*] refers to one who abstains [*mitnazer*] from certain actions. It also alludes to the uncut hair of the nazirite, which is comparable to a crown [*nezer*] (see Numbers 6:7). Although the Torah never establishes a general prohibition against becoming ritually impure or drinking wine, abstaining from these actions is considered a prerequisite for holiness, as demonstrated by the fact that it is prohibited for one to enter the Temple courtyard after drinking wine or while in a state of ritual impurity. Additionally, because of their inherent sanctity, priests are prohibited from becoming impure through contact with a corpse. A nazirite, who voluntarily accepts these prohibitions, is considered to have temporarily elevated himself to a status similar to that of a priest.[2]

A nazirite is called "a nazirite of God" (Judges 13:5), and the verse praises the Jewish people by saying (Amos 2:11): "And I raised up of your sons for prophets, and of your young men for nazirites" (see Rambam *Sefer Hafla'a, Hilkhot Nezirut* 10:14). The Rabbis differ with regard to their appraisal of naziriteship. Though according to all it is considered praiseworthy to abstain from contracting impurity and from inebriation, according to some it is considered a transgression to entirely prohibit oneself from becoming impure or from drinking wine. Additionally, sometimes people became nazirites due to ulterior motives or out of spite, and at times nazirites would regret ever having taken a nazirite vow. Under these circumstances, the observance of naziriteship is not considered praiseworthy.

The main *halakhot* of a nazirite are stated explicitly in the Torah. A nazirite is prohibited from cutting his hair, eating or drinking anything originating from a grapevine, and becoming ritually impure through contact with a corpse. When he completes the term of his naziriteship, he brings a sheep as a burnt-offering, a ewe as a sin-offering, and a ram as a peace-offering, along with unleavened loaves and unleavened wafers. Afterward, he is released from the restrictions of naziriteship. If a nazirite became impure through contact with a corpse during his term of naziriteship, then after completing the standard purification process of sprinkling on the third and seventh days and immersing in a ritual bath, he shaves his hair and on the eighth day brings two doves or pigeons, one for a sin-offering and the other for a burnt-offering, and a sheep in its first year as a guilt-offering. He then must begin his term of naziriteship anew.

As with most of the *halakhot* recorded in the Torah, even the *halakhot* that are explicitly delineated in the Torah with regard to naziriteship do not provide guidance for every scenario that could arise when one attempts to implement these *halakhot* practically. This tractate attempts to explain and clarify the *halakhot* of naziriteship as they apply in practice.

One of the main topics of this tractate is the clarification of the ways in which the *halakhot* of naziriteship conform to or deviate from the general *halakhot* of vows. As explained earlier, acceptance of naziriteship is a form of a vow. There is no obligation to become a nazirite, and naziriteship takes effect only when one willingly takes a nazirite vow. However, unlike a standard vow, the guidelines that pertain to one who takes this vow are not up to the discretion of the individual. The rules that apply to a nazirite have already been determined by the Torah. Therefore, one who takes a nazirite vow is bound by all of the *halakhot* incumbent upon a nazirite, even if he states that he is accepting only some of them. However, the duration of the period for which he becomes a nazirite is up to his discretion, provided that it is no less than thirty days.

Tractate *Nazir* also addresses the language that effects a nazirite vow. When one accepts naziriteship using clear and precise language, the *halakha* is clear. However, sometimes the wording that one uses is so ambiguous and confusing that it must be clarified whether the statement is considered a nazirite vow and how long the term of naziriteship will last. Sometimes, one takes a vow using substitutes for the language of nazirite vows, e.g., by saying the word *nazik* instead of *nazir*, or using intimations of nazirite vows. In these cases, it must be clarified which expressions obligate the speaker in a nazirite vow. Similarly, the implication of one's statement must be determined in cases where it is not clear whether the speaker accepted upon himself a nazirite vow or a different vow, or where he accepted upon himself a partial term of naziriteship. Sometimes, one accepts a nazirite vow conditionally, because of a mistake, as a result of outside intervention, or to demonstrate that he is telling the truth in a different context. In all of these cases, it is necessary to determine whether one has become a nazirite.

Although the Torah explicitly states the restrictions that apply to a nazirite, there are *halakhot* pertaining to naziriteship that were transmitted via oral tradition. One of these traditions is that an unspecified term of naziriteship lasts for thirty days, which is the minimum term of naziriteship. Another is that one can become a permanent nazirite, in which case he is a nazirite forever but may trim his hair once a year. Additionally, one can become a nazirite like the judge Samson, whereby one is a nazirite for his entire life but with unique *halakhot*. It is permitted for him to become impure through contact with a corpse but prohibited for him ever to cut his hair or drink wine.

These *halakhot* lead to questions concerning one who took a nazirite vow obligating himself in partial periods of naziriteship, e.g., half of a term of naziriteship or naziriteship for one hour. They also lead to questions pertaining to a situation where one took several nazirite vows simultaneously. Additionally, the Gemara must clarify the practical differences between a permanent nazirite; one who takes upon himself a term of naziriteship that will, in practice, last for the duration of his lifetime; and one who takes a vow whereby he is obligated in continuous, consecutive terms of naziriteship.

Another unique *halakha* of nazirite vows relates to minors. The *halakha* is that a father, and only a father, can obligate his son in a vow of naziriteship. Additionally, a minor who is close to the age of majority can take a nazirite vow and become a nazirite.

The prohibitions specified in the Torah as pertaining to a nazirite require elaboration and explanation. The Torah specifies that "all the days of his vow of naziriteship no razor shall come upon his head" (Numbers 6:5). However, it must be clarified whether this prohibition applies only to one who shaves off all his hair with a razor, as with the prohibition against removing one's beard, or if it applies to any removal of hair. Similarly, it is necessary to clarify how much hair one must remove in order to be liable to receive lashes. The tractate clarifies the circumstances in which one is liable to receive lashes, and whether it is only the nazirite who is liable or also one who cuts the nazirite's hair. Additionally, a variety of circumstances could result in the nazirite's hair being cut. This could occur because the nazirite intentionally or accidentally had his hair cut or because he was obligated for a separate reason to shave his hair. The question then becomes whether a nazirite can complete his term of naziriteship with his hair shaven.

It is prohibited for a nazirite to eat anything that is "made of the grapevine" (Numbers 6:4), although the prohibition primarily applies to drinking wine. This is supported by the language of the Torah: "He shall abstain from wine and strong drink" (Numbers 6:3), and: "And after that the nazirite may drink wine" (Numbers 6:20). It is necessary to clarify whether this prohibition applies to all or only parts of the grape and what quantity the nazirite has to ingest of each part or combination of different parts of the grape to violate this prohibition. Another question that arises is with regard to the status of a mixture of grape products and other foods.

It is prohibited for a nazirite to contract ritual impurity from a corpse. If he does become impure, whether intentionally or unintentionally, the days of his term of naziriteship that he already observed are void and he must begin his term anew. Ritual impurity is imparted not only through touching a corpse, but also from carrying a corpse without direct contact or by standing under the same structure as a corpse. Even parts of an incomplete corpse, such as limbs, bones, blood, and skin, impart ritual impurity. An individual also becomes impure by touching certain items after they have made contact with a corpse. The Gemara clarifies when a nazirite becomes impure in a manner that negates his term of naziriteship and when his term is not negated despite his impurity. Additionally, the Gemara discusses whether there are unique circumstances where even a nazirite is obligated to become ritually impure from a corpse.

It is explained in the Torah that if a nazirite becomes ritually impure, the days of naziriteship that he has already observed are negated. The Gemara discusses whether or not this *halakha* is equally true throughout the entire term of naziriteship. The Gemara also discusses whether this is unique to the prohibition against becoming impure from a corpse, or whether it also applies to one who violates the other prohibitions of naziriteship. There is also a discussion concerning one who becomes impure after his term of naziriteship is completed but before he has brought the requisite offerings, which release him from nazirite restrictions. The Gemara also raises a question as to whether one who is ritually impure can take a nazirite vow and when such a vow would take effect. The Gemara also discusses the *halakha* in situations where a nazirite violates one of the prohibitions of naziriteship multiple times.

For a variety of reasons, a situation could arise where a nazirite never completed his term of naziriteship. This could occur if a husband nullified the nazirite vow of his wife, or a nazirite vow was dissolved by a Sage, or if the nazirite died before completing his term of naziriteship. In these situations, if the nazirite had already designated money or animals for his offerings, many questions arise with regard to the status of these items. The many *halakhot* in these cases are dependent on the manner in which the nazirite set aside his offering, whether he set aside only money or the animals themselves, and if he set aside animals, whether he specified which offering each animal was intended for or if he set them aside without specification. Additionally, the Gemara discusses whether a nazirite may use animals for his offerings after they were designated by another nazirite for his offerings.

This tractate addresses the principle *halakhot* of the offerings brought by both a nazirite who became impure and a nazirite who completed his term of naziriteship. However, many of the details relevant to the offerings are discussed in tractates *Zevaḥim* and *Menaḥot*, which deal more generally with the *halakhot* of offerings.

It should be noted that the commentary printed on the inside column of the Vilna Talmud for tractate *Nazir* is not the commentary of Rashi but a commentary of unknown authorship, which is referred to here as the Commentary on *Nazir*.

Tractate *Nazir* contains nine chapters. Some of the chapters deal with one clearly defined topic. Others deal with several issues, some of which are spread out over several chapters.

Chapter One deals with the language of nazirite vows, including substitutes for nazirite vows, intimations of nazirite vows, nazirite vows for unspecified lengths of time, and vows that specify short or extensive periods of naziriteship. It also addresses the *halakhot* of a permanent nazirite and a nazirite like Samson. The chapter also addresses manners in which one can take a vow by extending the forbidden status of a forbidden item.

Chapter Two discusses the level of intent that is required to accept naziriteship upon oneself, cases where it is uncertain if the vow is considered a nazirite vow, and situations where different terms of naziriteship overlap.

Chapter Three deals primarily with how impurity negates naziriteship. It discusses when ritual impurity obliterates the entire period observed by the nazirite, when it prevents naziriteship from taking effect, and the negation of a term of naziriteship because of the impurity decreed upon lands outside of Eretz Yisrael.

Chapter Four discusses taking a nazirite vow by extending the prohibition of particular items that are already forbidden. It also addresses the dissolution of a nazirite vow and the question of what is done with animals that a nazirite designated as offerings but that were never sacrificed. The chapter also discusses the *halakha* that a father can obligate his son in a vow of naziriteship and the *halakha* that a son inherits the nazirite offerings of his father.

Chapter Five deals with statements that constitute nazirite vows or that declare items consecrated, when the statements were made mistakenly, conditionally, or due to uncertainty.

Chapter Six compares and contrasts the different prohibitions incumbent upon a nazirite, primarily the prohibitions against drinking wine and becoming impure from a corpse. It also compares and contrasts the *halakhot* of the process whereby a nazirite shaves and brings offerings at the completion of his term of naziriteship to those of the process by which he shaves and brings offerings if he becomes impure from a corpse.

Chapter Seven deals with the *halakhot* of ritual impurity imparted by a corpse, as pertains to a nazirite.

Chapter Eight deals with individuals whose status as a nazirite is uncertain and discusses how they fulfill their vows.

Chapter Nine discusses who can become a nazirite and uncertainties that exist with regard to different types of ritual impurity.

NOTES

1. The Meiri places it after tractate *Sota*, in accordance with the order of the passages in the Torah.
2. See the mishna on 47a, which compares a nazirite to a priest.

Introduction to **Perek I**

Speak to the children of Israel and say to them: When either a man or a woman shall clearly utter a vow, the vow of a nazirite, to consecrate himself to the Lord.

(Numbers 6:2)

In order for a nazirite vow to take effect, one must "clearly utter a vow, the vow of a nazirite, to consecrate himself to the Lord." This chapter identifies problems that arise with terminology used in making such declarations. The many details in this chapter can be divided into two categories: First, issues related to clarifying the terms one might use to take a nazirite vow; and second, the meaning of different expressions used to describe the duration of the term of naziriteship or to accept multiple terms of naziriteship at once.

With regard to the first issue, it is clear that one becomes a nazirite if he says: I am hereby a nazirite. The Gemara considers other, less direct ways that one can express his desire to become a nazirite, both by using substitutes for nazirite vows and by using intimations of nazirite vows. The Gemara discusses situations where these less direct expressions are effective, as well as situations where the speaker's statement does not give clear expression to this intent, and he is not a nazirite even if his intention was to take a nazirite vow.

The second issue concerns setting the duration of the term of naziriteship. It is clear that when one explicitly states the duration or the number of terms of naziriteship that he accepts, he becomes a nazirite for the period that he articulated. The difficulty facing the Gemara is establishing the duration of a term of naziriteship in a situation where he used vague expressions of length or when it is unclear whether he accepted a single term or multiple terms of naziriteship.

The Sages established that the minimum time frame for a term of naziriteship is thirty days, and one who does not specify the length of his term of naziriteship becomes a nazirite for this amount of time. The Gemara investigates the source for this principle and questions whether the term of naziriteship ends at the end of the twenty-ninth day or only after the thirtieth day.

These issues and related questions comprise the subject matter of this chapter.

מתני׳ כָּל כִּינּוּיֵי נְזִירוּת כִּנְזִירוּת.

MISHNA One becomes a nazirite by taking a nazirite vow, in which he simply declares himself a nazirite, as detailed in the Torah (Numbers 6:1–21). Additionally, **all substitutes** for the language **of nazirite vows**[N] **are like nazirite vows**[H] and are binding. Furthermore, intimations of nazirite vows, i.e., incomplete statements that are understood from context to be meant as nazirite vows, are considered binding nazirite vows.

הָאוֹמֵר ״אֱהֵא״ – הֲרֵי זֶה נָזִיר, אוֹ ״אֱהֵא נָאֶה״ – נָזִיר. ״נָזִיק״, ״נָזִיחַ״, ״פָּזִיחַ״ – הֲרֵי זֶה נָזִיר. ״הֲרֵינִי כָּזֶה״, ״הֲרֵינִי מְסַלְסֵל״, ״הֲרֵינִי מְכַלְכֵּל״, ״הֲרֵי עָלַי לְשַׁלַּח פֶּרַע״ – הֲרֵי זֶה נָזִיר.

Consequently, **one who says: I will be,**[H] without further clarification, **is a nazirite,** as this is his implied intention. **Or,** if he said: **I will be beautiful,** he is **a nazirite.** The substitutes for the language of nazirite vows are as follows: If one says: I will be a ***nazik***,[N] a ***nazi'aḥ***, or a ***pazi'aḥ***, **he is a nazirite.** If one says: **I am hereby like this,**[N] **I am hereby** a hair curler,[N] **I am hereby growing** my **hair**; or: **It is** incumbent **upon me to grow long hair, he is a nazirite.**

״הֲרֵי עָלַי צִיפּוֹרִים״. רַבִּי מֵאִיר אוֹמֵר: נָזִיר, וַחֲכָמִים אוֹמְרִים: אֵינוֹ נָזִיר.

If one says: An obligation **is hereby** incumbent **upon me** with regard to **birds,**[H] **Rabbi Meir says: He is a nazirite.** A nazirite brings two bird-offerings if he inadvertently becomes ritually impure from a corpse (Numbers 6:10), and it is understood that the individual used this indirect phrase to take a vow of naziriteship. **And the Sages say: He is not a nazirite.**

גמ׳ מִכְּדִי תַּנָּא בְּסֵדֶר נָשִׁים קָאֵי, מַאי טַעְמָא תָּנֵי נָזִיר?

GEMARA The Gemara begins by clarifying why this tractate appears in the order of *Nashim* within the six orders of the Mishna. **Now, the *tanna* is engaged in** the study of **the order of *Nashim*,** which discusses laws concerning marriage and the resulting obligations as well as with forbidden sexual relations. **What** then **is the reason** that he **teaches** the laws of **the nazirite**[N] here?

HALAKHA

All substitutes for the language of nazirite vows – כָּל כִּינּוּיֵי נְזִירוּת כִּנְזִירוּת: All substitutes for the language of nazirite vows are like nazirite vows. For example, in a place where a nazirite is called a *nazik*, *nazi'ah*, or *pazi'aḥ*, one who uses one of those terms in a vow is a nazirite (Rambam *Sefer Hafla'a*, *Hilkhot Nezirut* 1:8).

One who says, I will be, etc. – הָאוֹמֵר אֱהֵא וכו׳: If one says: I will be, or: I will be beautiful, he is a nazirite, subject to the conditions specified in the Gemara below (2b). The same applies to the other substitute terms mentioned in the mishna (Rambam *Sefer Hafla'a*, *Hilkhot Nezirut* 1:6).

An obligation is hereby incumbent upon me with regard to birds – הֲרֵי עָלַי צִיפּוֹרִים: If one says: An obligation is hereby incumbent upon me with regard to birds, his statement is of no consequence, even if a nazirite is passing before him, and even if he intends to become a nazirite (Rambam *Sefer Hafla'a*, *Hilkhot Nezirut* 1:7).

NOTES

All substitutes for the language of nazirite vows – כָּל כִּינּוּיֵי נְזִירוּת: The biblical source for the *halakha* that substitutes for the language of vows are considered vows is discussed at the beginning of tractate *Nedarim* (3a). The Gemara there explains that the verses that discuss naziriteship use the same word repetitively: "When a man or a woman shall clearly utter a vow [*lindor neder*], the vow of a nazirite, to consecrate himself [*nazir lehazir*] to the Lord" (Numbers 6:2). The doubled term *nazir lehazir* teaches that one can become a nazirite not only through a direct vow, but also through substitute expressions. The doubled term *lindor neder* indicates that the same is true for other types of vows.

***Nazik*, etc. – נָזִיק וכו׳:** The Gemara in tractate *Nedarim* (10a) relates that Rabbi Yoḥanan and Reish Lakish debate the explanation of these terms. The same dispute is found in the Jerusalem Talmud, where the opinions attributed to each *amora* are reversed. According to one opinion, these substitute terms are words in other languages, while according to the other opinion they are special terms invented by the Sages to prevent situations from arising where one might utter the name of God in vain.

Tosafot raise difficulties with each opinion: If these are simply words in other languages, what new *halakha* is being taught? One can declare a vow in any language. They answer that if one takes a vow in a foreign language it is necessary for him to understand the words that he is saying, whereas if one vows by using one of the terms listed in the mishna, the naziriteship takes effect even if he does not know the meaning of the words, because they are similar in pronunciation to the term *nazir* used in the Torah. It is noted in the Commentary on *Nazir* that these words are also similar to the word *nazir* in their spelling. Even according to the opinion of *Tosafot* that the person taking the vow of naziriteship using these terms need not know precisely what they mean, he must intend to take a nazirite vow in order for it to take effect.

With regard to the second opinion, that these substitute terms are expressions invented by the Sages, *Tosafot* ask: If the Sages invented these terms, how does naziriteship take effect by Torah law when they are used? If the vow does not take effect by Torah law, how can the nazirite offer the sacrifices that mark the end of naziriteship? They explain that since the Sages established these particular terms, the person taking the vow intends to use these terms in order to accept naziriteship, and therefore the vow takes effect. The Jerusalem Talmud offers a similar resolution of this problem. Some commentaries claim that the dispute about the origin of these terms is only with regard to those used for ordinary vows. In the case of naziriteship, everyone agrees that these terms come from other languages and therefore take effect by Torah law (Rabbeinu Todros, cited in *Shita Mekubbetzet*).

Others argue that even according to the opinion that these terms come from other languages, they are not words in use in any specific language. Rather, gentiles, who did not know how to pronounce the word *nazir* properly, used these terms, and their corrupted versions in turn influenced some Jews (Rambam *Sefer Hafla'a*, *Hilkhot Nedarim* 1:16, and see Radbaz there; Meiri).

I am hereby like this – הֲרֵינִי כָּזֶה: *Tosafot* cite the Gemara (3a), which explains that a nazirite was walking by when the person made this statement. They add that the novelty of this ruling is that a vow is not effective if one merely says: I am hereby. Rabbeinu Azriel, cited in *Shita Mekubbetzet*, argues that the statement: I am hereby, certainly indicates naziriteship. He adds that this is explicitly stated in the Jerusalem Talmud (*Nazir* 1:2). The novel aspect of this *halakha* is that the phrase: I am hereby like this, is also considered a vow of naziriteship (see Rashash).

I am hereby a hair curler, etc. – הֲרֵינִי מְסַלְסֵל וכו׳: *Tosafot* point out that these expressions are not intimations, which is why they are not listed when the mishna gives an example of an intimation. This is because they are not partial statements, but rather full statements that do not explicitly mention naziriteship, although the intention of the individual taking the vow is clear from context.

What is the reason he teaches the topic of nazirite – מַאי טַעְמָא תָּנֵי נָזִיר: Some commentaries had a version of the order of *Nashim* in which tractate *Sota* precedes tractate *Nazir*. They had a different version of the Gemara text here, which states: Since the *tanna* has finished with the *halakhot* of a heifer whose neck is broken, which appears at the end of tractate *Sota*, what is the reason that he now teaches tractate *Nazir* (Meiri)?

Tosafot reinforce the idea that *Nazir* does not belong in the order of *Nashim* by pointing out that since the nazirite must bring offerings, this tractate ostensibly belongs in the order of *Kodashim*. Rabbeinu Azriel, cited in *Shita Mekubbetzet*, adds to the Gemara's question by stating that tractate *Nazir* could have followed tractate *Karetot*, which deals with the prohibition barring priests serving in the Temple from drinking wine, a prohibition parallel to the prohibition against a nazirite's drinking wine (*Shita Mekubbetzet*).

תַּנָּא אַקְּרָא קָאֵי: ״וְהָיָה אִם לֹא תִמְצָא חֵן בְּעֵינָיו כִּי מָצָא בָהּ עֶרְוַת דָּבָר״. וְהָכִי קָאָמַר: מִי גָּרַם לָהּ לַעֲבֵירָה – יַיִן, וְקָאָמַר: כָּל הָרוֹאֶה סוֹטָה בְּקִלְקוּלָהּ – יַזִּיר עַצְמוֹ מִן הַיַּיִן.

The Gemara answers: **The *tanna* is engaged in** the study of **the verse**[N] pertaining to divorce: **"Then it comes to pass, if she finds no favor in his eyes, because he has found some unseemly matter about her"** (Deuteronomy 24:1). **And this is what he is saying: What caused** the woman **to** commit the **transgression** of adultery, alluded to in the verse by the phrase "unseemly matter"? It was **wine. And** the *tanna* **is saying: Anyone who sees a *sota* in her disgrace should abstain from wine.**[H] Consequently, tractate *Nazir* is placed in the order of *Nashim*, immediately preceding tractate *Sota*, which is about a woman suspected by her husband of having been unfaithful, and tractate *Gittin*, which discusses divorce.

פָּתַח בְּכִינּוּיִין וּמְפָרֵשׁ יָדוֹת!

§ The Gemara asks a question with regard to the mishna's presentation of the different topics it addresses: The *tanna* **began with** the statement that all **substitutes** for the language of nazirite vows are considered nazirite vows, **but** then it **explains** the *halakha* of **intimations** of nazirite vows by providing examples of intimations rather than examples of substitutes for nazirite vows. Why didn't the Gemara provide examples of substitutes immediately after stating the *halakha* concerning substitutes?

אֲמַר רָבָא וְאִיתֵּימָא כְּדִי: חַסּוֹרֵי מִיחַסְּרָא, וְהָכִי קָתָנֵי: כָּל כִּינּוּיֵי נְזִירוּת כִּנְזִירוּת, וִידוֹת נְזִירוּת כִּנְזִירוּת; וְאֵלּוּ הֵן יָדוֹת: הָאוֹמֵר ״אֱהֵא״ – הֲרֵי זֶה נָזִיר.

Rava said, and some say this statement **without attribution** [*kedi*]:[L] The mishna **is incomplete**[N] **and is teaching the following: All substitutes** for the language **of nazirite vows are like nazirite vows. And** similarly, all **intimations of nazirite vows are like nazirite vows. And these are** examples of **intimations: One who says: I will be, is a nazirite.**

וְלִפְרוֹשׁ כִּינּוּיֵי בְּרֵישָׁא! תַּנָּא מֵהַהוּא דְּסָלֵיק הַהוּא מְפָרֵשׁ בְּרֵישָׁא. כִּדְתְנַן: בַּמֶּה מַדְלִיקִין וּבַמֶּה אֵין מַדְלִיקִין, וּמְפָרֵשׁ ״אֵין מַדְלִיקִין״ בְּרֵישָׁא.

The Gemara asks: **But** nevertheless, **let** the *tanna* **explain** the cases of **substitutes first**, before providing examples of intimations, as the *halakha* of substitutes is mentioned before the *halakha* of intimations. The Gemara answers: The ***tanna*** employs the general style of the Mishna, which is that **the** subject **with which it concludes is the one that it explains first, as we learned** in a mishna (*Shabbat* 20b): **With what may one light** the Shabbat lamp **and with what may one not light** it? **And** the mishna **explains** the details of what **one may not light first,** before providing examples of fuel that may be used to light the Shabbat lamp.

בַּמֶּה טוֹמְנִין וּבַמֶּה אֵין טוֹמְנִין, וּמְפָרֵשׁ ״אֵין טוֹמְנִין״ בְּרֵישָׁא.

Similarly, another mishna (*Shabbat* 47b) states: **In what may one insulate** a pot of cooked food on Shabbat eve, **and in what may one not insulate** it? **And** the mishna **explains** the cases of material in which **one may not insulate** it **first,** before providing examples of materials in which one may insulate a pot of cooked food.

בַּמֶּה אִשָּׁה יוֹצְאָה וּבַמֶּה אֵינָהּ יוֹצְאָה, וּמְפָרֵשׁ ״לֹא תֵּצֵא אִשָּׁה״ בְּרֵישָׁא.

A third example of this style is in the following mishna (*Shabbat* 57a): **With what** items **may a woman go out** into the public domain on Shabbat **and with what** items **may she not go out? And** the mishna **explains** the items with which **a woman may not go out first,** before providing examples of items with which she may go out.

HALAKHA

Should abstain from wine – יַזִּיר עַצְמוֹ מִן הַיַּיִן: It is proper for one to distance himself from levity, drunkenness, and flirtatious behavior, since all of these lead to sin (Rambam *Sefer Kedusha, Hilkhot Issurei Bia* 22:21; *Shulḥan Arukh, Even HaEzer* 25:1).

LANGUAGE

Without attribution [*kedi*] – כְּדִי: There are various opinions as to the meaning of this word. Rashi in several places suggests two possibilities: One explanation is that it is the name or nickname of a Sage (Maharatz Ḥayyut). Alternatively, it is a word used to introduce an unattributed statement. This appears to be the explanation of the *ge'onim*, who maintain that the word is an abbreviation of *kedehi*, meaning: As it is, i.e., without attribution.

NOTES

The *tanna* is engaged in the study of the verse – תַּנָּא אַקְּרָא קָאֵי: The Gemara in tractate *Sota* (2a) explains that tractate *Nedarim*, literally, vows, appears in the order of *Nashim* due to its connection to tractate *Ketubot*, which deals with the *halakhot* of one who imposes a vow on his wife. *Nazir* then follows *Nedarim*, as a central issue in *Nazir* is the nazirite vow. This explanation is ostensibly deemed insufficient by the Gemara here. However, Rashi is cited in *Sefer HaYashar* (*Ḥiddushim* 65) as explaining that the text of the entire discussion in the Gemara here has been corrupted and should be omitted, as there is already a satisfactory account of the order and placement of this tractate.

Another way to resolve the contradiction between the Gemara in tractate *Sota* and the Gemara here is to note that while the Gemara in tractate *Sota* explains the order of the tractates, it does not offer a suitable answer as to why tractate *Nazir* appears in the order of *Nashim* at all. It should have been placed in the order of *Kodashim*, and then tractate *Nedarim* would have been taught there as well, due to its connection with this tractate (Rabbeinu Tam; *Tosafot*; Rabbeinu Todros, cited in *Shita Mekubbetzet*).

Is incomplete, etc. – חַסּוֹרֵי מִיחַסְּרָא וכו׳: The early commentaries ask: Since the Gemara is inserting a ruling about intimations into the mishna, it should have simply inserted this ruling before the mishna's ruling about substitute expressions. This would have resolved the Gemara's upcoming question, which is why the mishna provides examples of intimations before it provides examples of substitute expressions, when the ruling about substitute expressions comes first in the mishna. They answer that there was a tradition that the tractate begins with the ruling about substitute terms, and therefore the Sages could not claim that the missing words actually comprised the opening line of the tractate (*Shita Mekubbetzet*).

וְהָתְנַן: בַּמֶּה בְּהֵמָה יוֹצְאָה וּבַמֶּה אֵינָהּ יוֹצְאָה, וּמְפָרֵשׁ ״יוֹצֵא גָּמָל״ בְּרֵישָׁא!

The Gemara challenges this explanation: **But didn't we learn** in a mishna (*Shabbat* 51b): **With what may an animal go out** into the public domain on Shabbat, **and with what may it not go out? And it explains** the items with which **a camel may go out first,** before providing examples of items with which it may not go out.

יֵשׁ נוֹחֲלִין וּמַנְחִילִין, נוֹחֲלִין וְלֹא מַנְחִילִין, מַנְחִילִין וְלֹא נוֹחֲלִין, לֹא נוֹחֲלִין וְלֹא מַנְחִילִין, וּמְפָרֵשׁ ״אֵלּוּ נוֹחֲלִין וּמַנְחִילִין״ בְּרֵישָׁא!

Similarly, it is taught in another mishna (*Bava Batra* 108a): **There are** some relatives who **inherit and bequeath,** e.g., a father and son, who are heirs to each other; some who **inherit but do not bequeath;** some **bequeath but do not inherit;** and some **do not inherit and do not bequeath. And** the mishna **explains** the cases of **those** who both **inherit and bequeath first,** before providing examples of the other categories that were mentioned later in the opening clause of the mishna.

אֶלָּא, לְעוֹלָם תָּנֵי הָכִי וְתָנֵי הָכִי.

Rather, the mishna **actually teaches** in **this** manner at times, **and** it **teaches** in **that** manner at other times. There are instances where the *tanna* begins by elaborating on the first principle mentioned in the mishna, while on other occasions he first elaborates upon the last principle mentioned.

אֶלָּא, הָתָם דְּאִיסּוּרָא דְּנַפְשֵׁיהּ הוּא – מְפָרֵשׁ אִיסּוּרָא דְּנַפְשֵׁיהּ בְּרֵישָׁא. גַּבֵּי בְּהֵמָה דְּאִיסּוּרָא אַיְּידֵי בְּהֵמָה הוּא דְּאָתֵי – מְפָרֵשׁ הֶיתֵּירָא בְּרֵישָׁא.

However, there is a rationale as to when the *tanna* employs each style. **There,** in the passages concerning the fuels one may use to light the Shabbat lamp, the materials one may use to insulate a pot on Shabbat eve, and the items with which a woman may go out on Shabbat to the public domain, **where it is** the individual's **own prohibition**[N] that is being discussed, the *tanna* **explains** the cases pertaining to the individual's **own prohibition first.** By contrast, **with regard to** the mishna that addresses **an animal** carrying into the public domain on Shabbat, **where the prohibition comes by means of the animal,** the *tanna* **explains** what is **permitted first.**

NOTES

There, where it is the individual's own prohibition, etc. – הָתָם דְּאִיסּוּרָא דְּנַפְשֵׁיהּ וכו׳: Some commentaries explain that a prohibition that one violates himself is more severe than a prohibition that one violates through the behavior of his animal (Commentary on *Nazir*; *Tosafot*). Alternatively, since one must let his animals rest on Shabbat, it should be prohibited to allow one's animal to go to the public domain carrying anything at all. Consequently, the *halakha* that one's animal may enter the public domain while carrying certain items is of greater novelty than the *halakha* that it is prohibited to allow one's animal to enter the public domain while carrying other items, and the *tanna* discusses first the case that contains the greater novelty (Rabbeinu Azriel, cited in *Shita Mekubbetzet*).

Perek **I**
Daf **2** Amud **b**

גַּבֵּי ״יֵשׁ נוֹחֲלִין״ נַמִי, מְפָרֵשׁ עִיקַּר נַחֲלָה בְּרֵישָׁא.

Similarly, **with regard to** the mishna that teaches that **there are** some relatives who **inherit** and bequeath, the *tanna* **also** had a reason for initially providing examples from the first category: He thereby **explains the principal** case of the Torah's *halakhot* of **inheritance**[N] **first.**

אֶלָּא [הָכָא], לִפְרוֹשׁ כִּינּוּיֵי בְּרֵישָׁא! אֶלָּא, הַיְינוּ טַעַם: יָדוֹת, הוֹאִיל וְאָתְיָין לֵיהּ מִדְּרָשָׁא – חֲבִיבִין לֵיהּ.

The Gemara now returns to its question: **But here, let** the *tanna* **explain** the cases of **substitutes first.**[N] The Gemara explains: **Rather, this is the reason: Since intimations are derived from** the **exposition** of verses and are not explicitly mentioned in the Torah, they are **dear to** the *tanna* and he therefore mentions them first.

וְלִיפְתַּח בְּהוֹן בְּרֵישָׁא! תַּנָּא כִּי מַתְחִיל – מַתְחִיל בְּעִיקַּר קָרְבָּן, וּלְעִנְיַן פֵּירוּשֵׁי – מְפָרֵשׁ יָדוֹת בְּרֵישָׁא.

The Gemara asks: **But** if that is so, then **let him begin with them first** in the opening clause of the mishna as well. The Gemara answers: **When the** *tanna* **begins, he begins with the main offering** of the nazirite, i.e., with the *halakha* that has a basis in the Torah. **But with regard** to the **explanation** of these *halakhot*, **he explains** the cases of **intimations first,** as he favors that topic.

״הָאוֹמֵר אֱהֵא הֲרֵי זֶה נָזִיר״. דִּלְמָא ״אֱהֵא בְּתַעֲנִית״ קָאָמַר! אָמַר שְׁמוּאֵל: כְּגוֹן שֶׁהָיָה נָזִיר עוֹבֵר לְפָנָיו.

§ The mishna taught: **One who says: I will be, is a nazirite.** The Gemara asks: **Perhaps he is saying: I will be fasting,**[N] i.e., his intention is to take a vow that will obligate himself to fast rather than to be a nazirite. The Gemara answers that **Shmuel said:** The mishna is describing a case **where a nazirite was passing before him,**[H] so that it is clear that he is taking a nazirite vow.

HALAKHA

Where a nazirite was passing before him – כְּגוֹן שֶׁהָיָה נָזִיר עוֹבֵר לְפָנָיו: One who says: I will be, when a nazirite is passing before him becomes a nazirite, as stated by Shmuel (Rambam *Sefer Hafla'a*, *Hilkhot Nezirut* 1:6).

NOTES

The principal case of the Torah's *halakhot* of inheritance – עִיקַּר נַחֲלָה: The principal paradigm of inheritance is the category of relatives who both inherit and bequeath, meaning that there is a two-way relationship whereby each individual is an heir to the other. An example of this is fathers and sons. Sons inherit from their father and, if they do not have sons of their own, bequeath to their father. This is also the first case of inheritance mentioned in the Torah's passage on the topic (see Numbers 27:8 and *Bava Batra* 108b).

But here let the *tanna* explain the cases of substitutes first – אֶלָּא הָכָא לִפְרוֹשׁ כִּינּוּיֵי בְּרֵישָׁא: The Rosh explains the Gemara's question in the following manner: Just as the mishna in *Bava Batra* explains the principal case of inheritance first, the mishna here should first provide examples of substitute language of vows, as they are a more primary manner of expressing a vow than employing an intimation of a vow.

Perhaps he is saying I will be fasting – דִּלְמָא אֱהֵא בְּתַעֲנִית קָאָמַר: The Rosh elaborates on the Gemara's question: If the intention of the person who takes the vow is unclear, as he could be merely taking a vow to fast, then the mishna should not rule that he is a nazirite and compel him to bring the offerings at the conclusion of his nazariteship, as doing so is prohibited if he is not in fact a nazirite. Furthermore, there is a principle that one is lenient in cases of naziriteship, which the mishna seems to ignore.

Some commentaries wonder why one does not simply ask the individual whether he intended to accept upon himself naziriteship or a fast. They answer that this is a case where the individual says that he himself did not have a particular intention. His intention was to accept upon himself whatever vow the Sages determine applies to one who says: I will be (*Shita Mekubbetzet*).

לֵימָא קָסָבַר שְׁמוּאֵל יָדַיִם שֶׁאֵינָן מוֹכִיחוֹת לָא הָוְויָין יָדַיִם? אָמְרִי: בִּזְמַן שֶׁנָּזִיר עוֹבֵר לְפָנָיו – לֵיכָּא לְסְפוּקָא בְּמִילְּתָא אַחֲרִינָא, אֲבָל וַדַּאי אֵין הַנָּזִיר עוֹבֵר לְפָנָיו – אָמְרִינַן: דִּלְמָא "אֱהֵא בְּתַעֲנִית" קָאָמַר.

The Gemara asks: **Shall we say** that **Shmuel holds** as a principle that **ambiguous intimations**[HN] **are not** considered **intimations,**[N] i.e., they are not considered vows? The Gemara rejects this suggestion: **Say** that **when**[N] **a nazirite is passing before him, there is no** reason **to doubt** his intention. There is no possibility that he is referring **to another matter,** and therefore his statement is definitely an intimation of naziriteship. **However,** it is **certainly** the case that when **a nazirite is not passing before him,** and he states: I will be, **we say** that **perhaps he is saying: I will be fasting.** It is only in the latter case, where one's intimation is so ambiguous that it offers no evidence whatsoever of his intentions, that Shmuel holds that one's statement is not considered a vow.

וְדִלְמָא לְפוֹטְרוֹ מִן קָרְבְּנוֹתָיו קָאָמַר. דְּקָאָמַר בְּלִבּוֹ.

The Gemara asks: **But** even if he made his statement when a nazirite was passing before him, **perhaps he was saying** that he intends to purchase the animals the nazirite will need for his offerings and thereby **exempt** the nazirite **from** paying for **his** own **offerings.** The Gemara answers: This is a case **where he said in his heart**[HN] that he accepts upon himself a nazirite vow.

HALAKHA

Ambiguous intimations – יָדַיִם שֶׁאֵינָן מוֹכִיחוֹת: Intimations of vows are considered vows as long they give some indication as to the intention of the speaker. For example, if one person says to another: I vow about you that I will eat not of yours, the vow is effective. However, intimations that are entirely ambiguous are not considered intimations (*Shulḥan Arukh, Yoreh De'a* 206:1).

Where he said in his heart – דְּקָאָמַר בְּלִבּוֹ: In order to accept upon oneself naziriteship, it is not necessary to make an explicit statement that everyone would understand to be the acceptance of naziriteship. Rather, as long as one intends to become a nazirite and vocalizes that intent in some way, and in a context in which that is the likely interpretation, he becomes a nazirite even if his words in themselves do not indicate that he is taking a nazirite vow (Rambam *Sefer Hafla'a, Hilkhot Nezirut* 1:5).

NOTES

Ambiguous intimations – יָדַיִם שֶׁאֵינָן מוֹכִיחוֹת: Rabbeinu Todros and *Tosafot* (on *Nedarim* 5b) quote Rabbeinu Tam's opinion that there are two types of ambiguous intimations. One type is so ambiguous that it offers no evidence of the speaker's intention whatsoever. The other type is only mildly ambiguous, so that there is some indication as to the speaker's intention, although he did not clearly articulate that intention.

Are not considered intimations – לָא הָוְויָין יָדַיִם: The suggestion that Shmuel holds that ambiguous intimations are not valid vows is based upon the fact that even when no nazirite is passing before him, it is more likely that the expression: I will be, is referring to naziriteship than to a fast. This is because the language indicates the immediate acceptance of a vow, which is possible in the case of naziriteship, but not usually in the case of a fast, as once the day has begun one cannot accept upon himself a fast for that day. The later commentaries also point out that one must accept a vow to fast in the afternoon of the day before one intends to fast. Therefore, it is more likely that his intention was to accept a nazirite vow (*Tosafot*; *Shita Mekubbetzet*).

Say that when, etc. – אָמְרִי בִּזְמַן וכו׳: There are two explanations of this answer. Some claim that the Gemara's conclusion is that, according to Shmuel, ambiguous intimations are considered intimations. However, if a nazirite is not passing by when the individual makes this statement, his statement is not even considered an ambiguous intimation, as it is not at all clear what he means to say (Commentary on *Nazir*; Rosh).

Conversely, according to the first explanation of *Tosafot* and Rabbeinu Tam, the Gemara's conclusion is that according to Shmuel, ambiguous intimations are not considered intimations. However, if a nazirite is passing by when the individual makes this statement, it is obvious that his statement is meant as a nazirite vow, and the vow takes effect. *Tosafot* point out that according to this interpretation, the Gemara's introduction of the question with the phrase: Shall we say, is imprecise, as this phrase usually indicates a suggestion that will be rejected, which is not the case here. However, the language in tractate *Nazir* in general is different from that of standard Gemara usage, and *Tosafot* provide an example from elsewhere in the tractate where this expression is used in a similar manner.

There is another opinion, based on a variant version of the text, in which the Gemara states: Shall we say that Shmuel holds that ambiguous intimations are considered intimations? According to this reading, the Gemara suggests that Shmuel holds that even if a nazirite is not passing before him at that precise moment, he becomes a nazirite. The Gemara concludes that there is a distinction between a person who says: I will be, at the exact moment when a nazirite is passing in front of him, and one who makes such a statement a little while later. In the latter case, the speaker does not become a nazirite, as ambiguous intimations are not considered intimations (Meiri).

Where he said in his heart – דְּקָאָמַר בְּלִבּוֹ: This is effective only when there was also a nazirite passing before him when he said: I will be. This is because the verse pertaining to naziriteship states that it applies when one "shall clearly utter a vow" (Numbers 6:2). Consequently, one must articulate his acceptance of naziriteship. The point in the Gemara is that if one says: I will be, while a nazirite is passing by and his intention is: I will be like that nazirite, his statement is considered an articulation of a nazirite vow (*Tosafot*). The Rid writes that, in general, intentions that are not articulated are inconsequential as far as the *halakha* is concerned, unless there is some action proving one's intention. Other commentaries disagree, claiming that in certain cases intention and thought alone are of consequence.

אִי הָכִי מַאי לְמֵימְרָא? מַהוּ דְּתֵימָא: בָּעֵינַן פִּיו וְלִבּוֹ שָׁוִין, קָא מַשְׁמַע לַן.

The Gemara asks: **If that is so,** then **what** is the purpose **of stating** this *halakha*? Isn't it obvious that he becomes a nazirite? The Gemara answers: It is necessary to state this *halakha*, **lest you say** that **we require his mouth and heart** to be **identical.**[N] If that were the case, then if one did not clearly articulate his nazirite vow, he would not become a nazirite even if he intended to become one. Therefore, the mishna **teaches us**[N] that since his words can be interpreted as referring to a nazirite vow, and that was his intention, he becomes a nazirite.

"אֶהֱא נָאֶה נָזִיר". וְדִלְמָא אֶנָּאֶה לְפָנָיו בְּמִצְוֹת? כִּדְתַנְיָא: "זֶה אֵלִי וְאַנְוֵהוּ" – אֶנָּאֶה לְפָנָיו בְּמִצְוֹת. אֶעֱשֶׂה לְפָנָיו סוּכָּה נָאָה, לוּלָב נָאֶה, צִיצִית נָאָה, אֶכְתּוֹב לְפָנָיו סֵפֶר תּוֹרָה נָאֶה, וְאֶכְרְכֶנּוּ בְּשִׁירָאִין נָאִים!

§ The mishna taught that if one says: **I will be beautiful** [*na'e*], he is **a nazirite.** The Gemara asks: **But perhaps** when he said: I will be beautiful, he meant: **I will be beautiful**[N] **before Him in mitzvot? As it is taught** in a *baraita*: **"This is my God and I will glorify Him** [*anvehu*]**"** (Exodus 15:2). *Anvehu* has the same root as the word *na'e*; therefore, the verse means: **I will be beautiful before Him in mitzvot.**[H] How is this done? **I will make before Him a beautiful** ***sukka*****, a beautiful** ***lulav*****, beautiful ritual fringes. I will write before Him a beautiful Torah scroll, and I will wrap it in beautiful silk cloths** [***shira'in***].[L]

אָמַר שְׁמוּאֵל: שֶׁתָּפוּס בִּשְׂעָרוֹ, וְאָמַר "אֶנָּאֶה".

The Gemara answers that **Shmuel said:** The mishna is referring to a case **where one is holding his hair**[HN] **and says: I will be beautiful.** This clearly indicates that he is referring to naziriteship.

נְזִירָא מִילְּתָא דַּעֲבֵירָה, וְאָמְרִינַן לֵיהּ "נָאֶה"?

The Gemara asks: Since **naziriteship** is **a matter of transgression,**[N] can **we say about** a nazirite that he is **beautiful?**

HALAKHA

I will be beautiful before Him in mitzvot – אֶנָּאֶה לְפָנָיו בְּמִצְוֹת: One should perform all mitzvot in the most beautiful manner possible. One should write a Torah scroll with correct, fine letters; one's phylacteries should be elegant; and likewise with regard to all the mitzvot. Some authorities state that if one has a choice between two *etrogim*, he should take the more beautiful one if its cost does not exceed the other by more than one-third (Rambam *Sefer Ahava, Hilkhot Sefer Torah* 7:4; *Shulḥan Arukh, Oraḥ Ḥayyim* 32:4, 656:1).

Where one is holding his hair – שֶׁתָּפוּס בִּשְׂעָרוֹ: One who said while holding his hair: I will be beautiful, or: I will hereby be a hair curler, or: I am hereby accepting upon myself to tend to my hair, or: It is hereby incumbent upon me to grow my hair, is a nazirite, provided his intent was to take a nazirite vow (Rambam Sefer *Hafla'a, Hilkhot Nezirut* 1:6).

LANGUAGE

Silk cloths [*shira'in*] – שִׁירָאִין: From the Greek σηρικόν, *sērikon*, meaning silk.

NOTES

His mouth and heart to be identical – פִּיו וְלִבּוֹ שָׁוִין: It is not enough for there to be no contradiction between one's statement and his thoughts. He must express what he has in mind, and if he fails to do so in a clear manner, the naziriteship does not take effect (Commentary on *Nazir*).

The mishna teaches us – קָא מַשְׁמַע לַן: The conclusion is that one does not need to fully articulate everything he is thinking. However, it is still necessary to give some verbal expression to one's thoughts. Consequently, one becomes a nazirite only if he said: I will be, while a nazirite was passing by (Commentary on *Nazir*).

Perhaps he meant I will be beautiful, etc. – וְדִלְמָא אֶנָּאֶה וכו׳: The Rosh explains that although he could have been referring to naziriteship, it is not clear that this was his intention, and therefore he cannot be considered a nazirite, because one is lenient in cases of doubt concerning naziriteship. The Jerusalem Talmud derives the *halakha* that one who says: I will be beautiful, is a nazirite by *a fortiori* inference, as one who merely says: I will be, is considered a nazirite. The mishna is presumably not referring to a *halakha* that can be derived independently. Therefore, it must be referring to a case where one says, while a nazirite is passing by: No one is as beautiful as this individual. The mishna's point is that this statement should be interpreted as praise and as an acceptance of naziriteship rather than as a critique.

Where one is holding his hair – שֶׁתָּפוּס בִּשְׂעָרוֹ: In this case, the fact that a nazirite was passing before him is insufficient, as he could be understood to be saying that he intends to beautify himself by performing other mitzvot, just as the nazirite beautifies himself by means of his mitzva of naziriteship (*Tosafot*). The Rosh and Rabbeinu Todros add that if one takes hold of his hair, not only is it unnecessary for a nazirite to be passing before him, but he does not even require a definitive intention of naziriteship, since his statement is self-evident. The Rambam, however, maintains that even in this case he must fully intend to become a nazirite.

Naziriteship is a matter of transgression – נְזִירָא מִילְּתָא דַּעֲבֵירָה: The Gemara's question is as follows: The Gemara in tractate *Nedarim* (9a) establishes that a nazirite vow is considered a vow of the wicked. Consequently, acceptance of naziriteship is a kind of transgression, and the Gemara asks how it can be initiated by the statement: I will be beautiful (Commentary to *Nazir*). Rabbeinu Todros, cited in *Shita Mekubbetzet*, offers a different interpretation of the question, according to which the Gemara is asking rhetorically: Is naziriteship undertaken in order to beautify oneself? *Tosafot* and other early commentaries cite an alternative version of the text. Instead of: Naziriteship is a matter of transgression [*da'aveira*], it reads: Is naziriteship a matter that is done [*de'avida*], such that a nazirite may be called beautiful? In other words, is it recommended to take on naziriteship *ab initio*?

Rabbeinu Azriel, cited in *Shita Mekubbetzet*, cites this alternative version of the text. However, he reads it not as a question but as the continuation of Shmuel's statement, so that it reads: The case is where one is holding his hair and says: I will be beautiful, as naziriteship is matter that one ought to do; it is a mitzva, and as such it is beautiful.

אִין, דַּאֲפִילּוּ לְרַבִּי אֶלְעָזָר הַקַּפָּר דְּאָמַר: נָזִיר חוֹטֵא, הָנֵי מִילֵּי גַּבֵּי נָזִיר טָמֵא, דְּאַיְּידֵי דְּבָעֵי מִיסְתַּר, דְּאָמַר רַחֲמָנָא ״וְהַיָּמִים הָרִאשֹׁנִים יִפְּלוּ כִּי טָמֵא נִזְרוֹ״. הָתָם הוּא דִּלְמָא אָתֵי לְמִיעֲבַר עַל נְזִירוּתֵיהּ, אֲבָל נָזִיר טָהוֹר – לָאו חוֹטֵא קָרֵי בֵּיהּ.

The Gemara answers: **Yes, as even according to Rabbi Elazar HaKappar, who said** that **a nazirite is a sinner, that applies** only **with regard to a ritually impure nazirite.**[N] This is **because it is necessary** for him **to void** the days of his vow that have been observed and to begin his term anew, **as the Merciful One states** in the Torah: **"But the first days will be void, because his consecration was defiled"** (Numbers 6:12). **It is there** that Rabbi Elazar HaKappar called the nazirite a sinner, because **perhaps** he will **come to transgress**[N] **his naziriteship** now that he is a nazirite for a longer period than he originally intended. **However,** with regard to **a ritually pure nazirite,** Rabbi Elazar HaKappar **does not call him a sinner.**[H]

״הֲרֵינִי כָּזֶה״. נְהִי נַמִּי דְּתָפוּס בִּשְׂעָרוֹ, ״הֲרֵינִי כָּזֶה״ לָא אֲמַר! אָמַר שְׁמוּאֵל: כְּגוֹן שֶׁהָיָה נָזִיר עוֹבֵר לְפָנָיו.

§ The mishna taught that one who says: **I am hereby like this,**[H] is a nazirite. The Gemara asks: **Though** this is **indeed** a case **where he is holding his hair** at the time, since **he did not say: I am hereby like this,**[N] how can this statement constitute an acceptance of naziriteship? **Shmuel said:** It is a case **where a nazirite was passing**[N] **before him** when he made his statement. His intention was to declare himself a nazirite like the individual passing before him, and his statement therefore constitutes a nazirite vow.

״הֲרֵינִי מְסַלְסֵל״. מִמַּאי דְּהָדֵין סִלְסוּל שַׂעֲרָא? כְּדַאֲמַרָה לֵיהּ הַהִיא אַמְתָּא דְּבֵי רַבִּי לְהַהוּא גַּבְרָא: עַד מָתַי אַתָּה מְסַלְסֵל בִּשְׂעָרְךָ?

The mishna rules that one who says: **I am hereby a hair curler** is a nazirite. The Gemara asks: **From where** is it known **that this** term is referring to the **curling** [*silsul*][L] **of hair** by allowing it to grow? The Gemara answers: **As that maidservant of the house of Rabbi** Yehuda HaNasi[P] **said to a certain man** who grew his hair long: **Until when will you curl** [*mesalsel*] **your hair?** This shows that *mesalsel* means to grow hair.

אֵימָא תּוֹרָה, דִּכְתִיב ״סַלְסְלֶהָ וּתְרוֹמְמֶךָּ״! אֲמַר שְׁמוּאֵל: הָכָא נַמִּי שֶׁתָּפוּס בִּשְׂעָרוֹ.

The Gemara suggests: **Say** that the word *mesalsel* is referring to the study of **Torah, as it is written** with regard to Torah: **"Extol her** [*salseleha*] **and she will exalt you"** (Proverbs 4:8). The Gemara responds that **Shmuel said: Here too,** the case is **where he was holding his hair**[N] at the time of his pronouncement.

HALAKHA

However with regard to a ritually pure nazirite Rabbi Elazar HaKappar does not call him a sinner – אֲבָל נָזִיר טָהוֹר לָאו חוֹטֵא קָרֵי בֵּיהּ: One who undertakes a vow of naziriteship as an act of dedication to God is considered holy and praiseworthy (Rambam *Sefer Hafla'a, Hilkhot Nezirut* 10:14).

I am hereby like this – הֲרֵינִי כָּזֶה: If one said: I am hereby like this, as a nazirite passed before him, he is a nazirite, as stated by Shmuel (Rambam *Sefer Hafla'a, Hilkhot Nezirut* 2:4).

PERSONALITIES

That maidservant of the house of Rabbi Yehuda HaNasi – הַהִיא אַמְתָּא דְּבֵי רַבִּי: The maidservant of the house of Rabbi Yehuda HaNasi is mentioned here and in several other contexts. Because she used the purest, most ancient form of the Hebrew language, including words that the Sages themselves were no longer familiar with, it seems that she was no ordinary servant and was possibly even raised among the family of the *Nasi*. Her conduct and the witty, wise manner of speech that she would employ are recounted in the Gemara. It appears that she may have served as Rabbi Yehuda HaNasi's housekeeper.

LANGUAGE

Curling [*silsul*] – סִלְסוּל: Although this word is found in the Bible, its primary meaning is unclear. Some claim that it refers mainly to raising or elevating, as this is one of the meanings of the root *samekh, lamed, lamed*. This is plausible based on the continuation of the verse in Proverbs cited in the Gemara, and this is how it is explained by several commentaries. The term also has the connotation of decorating or beautifying, which could be its meaning both in the verse in Proverbs and in the Gemara here. *Silsul* also means making things round, perhaps like the words *sal* and *salsala*, which both mean basket. This meaning can also pertain to styling hair.

NOTES

That applies only with regard to a ritually impure nazirite – הָנֵי מִילֵּי גַּבֵּי נָזִיר טָמֵא: The early commentaries point out that this appears to contradict the Gemara (19a) that states that according to Rabbi Elazar HaKappar, even a pure nazirite is a sinner. They answer that although the pure nazirite is considered a sinner to a certain extent because of the discomfort he causes himself by abstaining from wine, the mitzva of naziriteship and its sanctity nevertheless override this sin, and therefore he can be called beautiful (see *Tosafot* on 2b). Rabbeinu Todros, cited in *Shita Mekubbetzet*, attributes a similar opinion to Rabbeinu Tam. Among other possibilities, it is suggested in the Meiri that this might be one of those variant talmudic discussions in which the opinion of the Gemara is not consistent, especially as tractate *Nedarim* and tractate *Nazir* differ from other tractates in many ways.

Perhaps he will come to transgress, etc. – דִּלְמָא אָתֵי לְמִיעֲבַר וכו׳: The Gemara later in the tractate (19a) explains that an impure nazirite is considered a sinner because by becoming impure he is forced to undergo a second period of naziriteship and thereby repeat his initial sin of becoming a nazirite. The Gemara here does not cite this reason because this reason assumes that naziriteship is inherently sinful, whereas that is not the opinion of the Gemara here (Rabbeinu Azriel, cited in *Shita Mekubbetzet*).

It is explained in the Commentary on *Nazir* that an impure nazirite is called a sinner because he might regret his vow over the course of time. Regret is the basis for dissolving a vow, and therefore, since there was basis for dissolving his nazirite vow, when the nazirite brings his offering at the conclusion of his term of naziriteship, it is somewhat similar to sacrificing non-consecrated animals in the Temple. Other commentaries maintain that there are two separate reasons why an impure nazirite is called a sinner, both of which relate to the fact that he must begin his term of naziriteship anew: He might come to transgress his vow due to the unanticipated length of time it is taking to complete it, and alternatively he might regret his vow and bring offerings that are similar to the sacrifice of non-sacred animals (Rosh).

He did not say, I am hereby like this – הֲרֵינִי כָּזֶה לָא אֲמַר: Many early commentaries found this statement puzzling, as the mishna explicitly states that he said: I am hereby like this. For this reason, *Tosafot* dismiss this version of the text as a scribal error and cite an alternate version, which reads: He did not say: I am hereby a nazirite.

The Rosh and Rabbeinu Azriel hold that the correct version of the text states: Although this is a case where he was holding his hair at the time, he did not say anything that indicated a nazirite vow. Another version of the text is cited by Rabbi Avraham min HaHar: He did not say: I am hereby in this. According to this version, had he said: I am hereby in this, while holding his hair, his statement would be interpreted to mean: I am hereby a nazirite in regard to this hair I am holding. It is therefore considered an intimation of a nazirite vow, which is binding. This is the version of the text that is recorded by the author of the *Mishne LaMelekh*, and it appears in some older editions of the Talmud.

Where a nazirite was passing, etc. – שֶׁהָיָה נָזִיר עוֹבֵר וכו׳: *Tosafot* explain that according to this answer, since one said: I am hereby like this, when a nazirite was passing before him, he becomes a nazirite even if he was not holding his hair when he made this statement. The Rosh wonders why it was necessary to mention that a statement such as this constitutes a nazirite vow. He explains that one might have thought that the individual meant to say that he is like the nazirite with regard to beauty or wisdom rather than naziriteship. Therefore, it was necessary for the mishna to state that this constitutes a nazirite vow. The Meiri explains that the novelty is not that this statement constitutes a nazirite vow, but that if one says only: I am hereby, he is not considered a nazirite even if a nazirite is walking by at that moment.

Here too, the case is where he was holding his hair, etc. – הָכָא נַמִּי שֶׁתָּפוּס בִּשְׂעָרוֹ וכו׳: The early commentaries explain that the terms *mesalsel* and *mekhalkel* are insufficient when said alone, even if a nazirite was passing before him, since these words do not on their own indicate naziriteship (Rosh; Rabbeinu Azriel, cited in *Shita Mekubbetzet*; Meiri). These statements are effective only if one was holding his hair at the time. Conversely, the explanation of the *Shita Mekubbetzet* is that the Gemara could have said that this is a situation where a nazirite was passing in front of him, but it preferred to explain the mishna as referring to the simpler case of one who was holding his hair.

״הֲרֵינִי מְכַלְכֵּל״. מִמַּאי דְּהָהֵין כִּילְכּוּל שְׂעָרוֹ הוּא? כִּדְתְנַן: סִיד, רַבִּי יְהוּדָה אוֹמֵר: כְּדֵי לָסוּד כִּילְכּוּל. וְאָמַר רַב: בַּת צִידְעָא.

The mishna rules that one who says: **I am hereby growing** my **hair** is a nazirite. The Gemara asks: **From where is it known that this** term **is a reference to growing** [***kilkul***][L] **his hair?** The Gemara answers: **As we learned** in a mishna (*Shabbat* 78b): With regard to the measure that determines liability for carrying out **lime** on Shabbat from a private to a public domain, **Rabbi Yehuda says:** The measure is **equivalent** to that which is used **to spread**[B] on one's ***kilkul*****. And Rav said:** This is referring to the hair that grows on **the areas beneath the temple.**[N]

אֵימָא מֵיזַן עֲנִיֵּי, כְּדִכְתִיב ״וַיְכַלְכֵּל יוֹסֵף אֶת אָבִיו וְאֶת אֶחָיו״! אֲמַר שְׁמוּאֵל: הָכָא נַמִי שֶׁתָּפוּס בִּשְׂעָרוֹ.

The Gemara suggests: Say that he vowed to **sustain the poor, as it is written: "And Joseph sustained** [***vaykhalkel***] **his father and his brethren"** (Genesis 47:12). The Gemara responds that **Shmuel said: Here too,** in the mishna, the case is one **where the individual was holding his hair**[H] when he made his pronouncement, so that it was clear that he was referring to growing his hair.

״הֲרֵי עָלַי לְשַׁלֵּחַ פֶּרַע הֲרֵי זֶה נָזִיר״. מִמַּאי דְּהָהֵין שִׁלּוּחַ רִיבּוּיָא הוּא? דִּכְתִיב ״שְׁלָחַיִךְ פַּרְדֵּס רִמּוֹנִים״.

The mishna rules that with regard to one who says: **It is incumbent upon me to grow** [***leshale'aḥ***] **long hair, he is a nazirite.** The Gemara asks: **From where** is it known **that this** term ***shilu'aḥ***, which is a different form of the word *leshale'aḥ*, is an expression of **increase** and growth? The Gemara answers: **As it is written: "Your tresses** [***shelaḥayikh***] **are a park of pomegranates"** (Song of Songs 4:13).[N]

אֵימָא מִידֵּי דְּעַבּוּרֵי, כְּדִכְתִיב ״וְשֹׁלֵחַ מַיִם עַל פְּנֵי חוּצוֹת״!

The Gemara suggests: **Say** that it is referring to **a matter** involving **transfer,**[N] **as it is written: "And sends** [***shole'aḥ***] **water upon the earth"** (Job 5:10), where the word *shole'aḥ* is referring to the transport of water from one place to another. Here too, the individual taking the vow might mean that he intends to transfer, i.e., to remove, his hair.

תַּנָּא ״פֶּרַע״ ״פֶּרַע״ יָלֵיף. כְּתִיב הָכָא ״קָדֹשׁ יִהְיֶה גַּדֵּל פֶּרַע״. וּכְתִיב הָתָם גַּבֵּי כֹּהֵן הֶדְיוֹט ״וּפֶרַע לֹא יְשַׁלֵּחוּ״.

The Gemara answers: The ***tanna***[N] **derives** the meaning of this term based upon a verbal analogy of the term **long locks** [***pera***] written with regard to a nazirite and the term **long locks** [***pera***] written with regard to a priest. **It is written here,** with regard to a nazirite: **"He shall be holy, he shall let the** hair of his head **grow** [***gadel***] **long locks** [***pera***]**"** (Numbers 6:5). **And it is written there, with regard to a common priest** serving in the Temple: **"And they will not let their locks grow long** [***pera lo yeshaleḥu***]**"** (Ezekiel 44:20). Just as the word *pera* with regard to a nazirite indicates growing long hair, so too, in the case of a priest it is referring to growing long hair. This proves that the term *shilu'aḥ* means letting one's hair grow.

וְאִיבָּעֵית אֵימָא: הַאי ״שׁוֹלֵחַ מַיִם״ נַמִי רִיבּוּי הוּא, (כְּדִמְתַרְגֵּם רַב יוֹסֵף: דְּכַד מַשְׁקִין לֵיהּ מַיָּא לְפֵירָא וְרַבִּי.

The Gemara offers an alternate answer: **And if you wish,** say that the meaning of the word *shole'aḥ* in **that** phrase: **Sends** [***shole'aḥ***] **water, is also increase** and growth, **as Rav Yosef translated**[N] this verse into Aramaic in the following manner: **When one waters produce,**[N] **it grows.** Consequently, the verse is referring to growth by means of water.

LANGUAGE

Growing [*kilkul*] – כִּלְכּוּל: This word is found in several places in the Mishna. In Syriac, it means a full head of hair. Its precise definition in the Mishna is the hair growing on the temples. The word *kilkul* is also used to describe excessive hair growth on different parts of the body (see *Nidda* 52b).

BACKGROUND

To spread – לָסוּד: For many generations, women have considered body hair an aesthetic blemish and have used different methods to remove it. One method, employed mostly by women who could not afford expensive materials, was to dissolve the hair by plastering the specific area with lime, found in chalk deposits. One needed to be particularly careful about this treatment, since the lime could cause serious burns on the skin. In a few cases described in the Talmud, it even caused fatal injuries.

Chalk deposit in the Negev

HALAKHA

Where he was holding his hair – שֶׁתָּפוּס בִּשְׂעָרוֹ: If one said: I am hereby a hair curler, or: I am hereby growing my hair, or: It is hereby incumbent upon me to grow long hair, and when he made this statement he was holding his hair and intended to become a nazirite, his statement is considered a nazirite vow (Rambam *Sefer Hafla'a*, *Hilkhot Nezirut* 1:6).

NOTES

The areas beneath the temple – בַּת צִידְעָא: *Tosafot*, on *Nidda* 52b, cite a different version of the Gemara, which states: The temple and the areas beneath the temple. This version of the text is consistent with the Gemara in *Shabbat* (80b), where Rav says that *kilkul* is referring to the hair on the temple itself. According to this understanding, the phrase: The areas beneath the temple, is not the definition of the word *kilkul*, and it is cited here only because it appears in that passage in *Shabbat* in addition to the word *kilkul* (*Oraḥ Mishor*).

Your tresses are a park of pomegranates – שְׁלָחַיִךְ פַּרְדֵּס רִמּוֹנִים: See the Commentary on *Nazir*. Rabbi Avraham min HaHar explains, citing Rashi, that the verse should be understood as follows: The hairs that grow on your head are like an orchard of pomegranates.

Say that it is referring to a matter involving transfer, etc. – אֵימָא מִידֵּי דְּעַבּוּרֵי וכו׳: It is explained in the Commentary on *Nazir* that, according to the conclusion of the Gemara, even if *shilu'aḥ* means transfer, the phrase: It is incumbent upon me *leshale'aḥ* long hair, is still understood as referring to naziriteship. The individual is understood to be saying: It is incumbent upon me to remove the long hair from my head after growing it for the thirty days of naziriteship.

The *tanna*, etc. – תַּנָּא וכו׳: *Tosafot* explain that this is not a reference to the *tanna* of the mishna here, but rather the *tanna* cited in *Sanhedrin* 22b, who states that a priest must cut his hair every thirty days. The Gemara there explains that this is because thirty days' growth is considered long locks, as derived from a verbal analogy based on the verse concerning a priest and the one pertaining to a nazirite. The Gemara here also cites this verbal analogy as proof of the meaning of the term *shiluaḥ*. However, the Rosh maintains that the Gemara here is referring to the *tanna* of the mishna here, who derived from the verbal analogy that just as the term *shiluaḥ* in the context of priests is referring to growing long hair, so too with regard to a nazirite.

As Rav Yosef translated – כִּדְמְתַרְגֵּם רַב יוֹסֵף: The early commentaries prove that the Aramaic translation of the book of Job existed already in the time of the *tanna'im* (see *Tosafot* on *Shabbat* 115a). Consequently, Rav Yosef is not the author of the translation, and the statement is attributed to him because he would often cite it. The Maharatz Ḥayyut notes that the Aramaic translation that is currently extant does not render the verse in the manner cited here in the Gemara. It is therefore possible that this was actually Rav Yosef's own translation.

When one waters produce, etc. – דְּכַד מַשְׁקִין לֵיהּ מַיָּא וכו׳: *Tosafot* point out that even if the verse in Job is explained as referring to growth, the usual meaning of the word *shilu'aḥ*, when it appears in the Torah, is transfer rather than growth (see Deuteronomy 22:7). They explain that the Gemara's question is: Perhaps there is no source at all that the word could mean growth, and the verse in Song of Songs should be understood differently. For this reason, the Gemara demonstrates that the verse in Job may be understood to use this word to mean growth. Consequently, it is reasonable to assume that when an individual employs the term *leshale'aḥ* in reference to his hair, he is using the word in the sense of growth and intends to become a nazirite (*Tosafot*; Rabbeinu Todros, cited in *Shita Mekubbetzet*). It is explained in the *Shita Mekubbetzet* that although *shilu'aḥ* is often used in the Torah to mean removal, that is the case when the word is used in the context of living creatures. The discussion here pertains to the word *shiluaḥ* when it is used in other contexts.

"הֲרֵי עָלַי צִיפֳּרִין רַבִּי מֵאִיר אוֹמֵר נָזִיר". מַאי טַעְמָא דְּרַבִּי מֵאִיר? אֲמַר רֵישׁ לָקִישׁ: צִיפֳּרִין סְמוּכִין לְשֵׂיעָר קִיבֵּל עָלָיו, דִּכְתִיב "עַד דִּי שַׂעְרֵיהּ כְּנִשְׁרִין רְבָה וְטִפְרוֹהִי כְצִפְּרִין".

§ The mishna taught that if one says: An obligation **is hereby** incumbent **upon me** with regard to **birds,**[N] **Rabbi Meir says: He is a nazirite,** and the Sages say: He is not a nazirite. The Gemara asks: **What is the reason** for the opinion **of Rabbi Meir? Reish Lakish said: He accepted upon himself** an obligation with regard to the **birds** that are **juxtaposed** in a verse **to hair,**[N] **as it is written: "Until his hair was grown like eagles' feathers, and his nails like birds' claws"** (Daniel 4:30). Since the verse juxtaposes birds with growing hair, it is understood that when this individual accepted an obligation with regard to birds, he was referring to growing his hair as a nazirite.

רַבִּי מֵאִיר סָבַר: מַתְפִּיס אִינִישׁ בְּמִידֵּי דִּסְמִיךְ לֵיהּ,

The Gemara explains the basis of the dispute: **Rabbi Meir holds** that **a person associates** the object of his vow with **something that is juxtaposed** to it in a verse, so that when he says that it is incumbent upon him to bring birds, he means that it is incumbent upon him to grow his hair.

NOTES

An obligation is hereby incumbent upon me with regard to birds [*tzipporin*] – הֲרֵי עָלַי צִפּוֹרִין: Rav Natan *Av HaYeshiva* cites an alternative version of the text in his commentary to the mishna: An obligation is hereby incumbent upon me with regard to nails [*tzippornayyim*]. According to this version, the speaker has vowed to grow his nails long. The idea is similar to that of the common version of the Gemara text: Since the verse mentions growing nails right next to growing hair, the implication of his statement is that he intends to grow his hair long as a nazirite. However, it is difficult to reconcile this version of the text with the continuation of the Gemara.

The birds that are juxtaposed in a verse to hair – צִיפֳּרִין סְמוּכִין לְשֵׂיעָר: In the Jerusalem Talmud, it is Rabbi Yoḥanan who explains that the statement is considered a nazirite vow due to the placement of the word "birds" in the verse in Daniel. The word "eagles" is a substitute term for a nazirite vow, as hair is compared to eagles in the verse: "Until his hair was grown like eagles' feathers." Since the verse continues and mentions birds, stating: "And his nails like birds' claws," birds are viewed a substitute for the original substitute term, which is eagles.

Tosafot claim that Reish Lakish's explanation is based not only on the juxtaposition of the words in the verse but on a combination of that juxtaposition and the fact that an impure nazirite must bring birds for his purification. According to the Commentary on *Nazir*, the Gemara is referring to a case where one took this vow as a nazirite was passing before him or as he was holding his hair (see Rosh).

Perek I
Daf 3 Amud b

וְרַבָּנַן סָבְרִי: לָא מַתְפִּיס אִינִישׁ בְּמִידֵּי דִּסְמִיךְ לֵיהּ.

And the Rabbis hold that **a person does not associate** the object of his vow with **something that is juxtaposed to it** in a verse, and the individual did not mean to take a nazirite vow.

רַבִּי יוֹחָנָן אֲמַר: דְּכוּלֵּי עָלְמָא לָא מַתְפִּיס. אֶלָּא הַיְינוּ טַעְמָא דְּרַבִּי מֵאִיר: דְּחָיְישִׁינַן שֶׁמָּא צִפּוֹרֵי נָזִיר טָמֵא קִיבֵּל עָלָיו.

Rabbi Yoḥanan said: Everyone agrees that one **does not associate** the object of his vow with something juxtaposed to it in a verse. **Rather, this is the reason of Rabbi Meir: We are concerned** that **perhaps he accepted upon himself the birds of an impure nazirite.**[B] Since an impure nazirite must bring two birds as offerings if he inadvertently becomes impure from a corpse (Numbers 6:10), when the individual accepts upon himself an obligation pertaining to birds, he means that he is becoming a nazirite and will be responsible for bringing an offering of birds if he becomes impure.

מִכְּדִי חָיְישִׁינַן קָאָמַר, דִּלְמָא צִפּוֹרֵי נְדָבָה קִיבֵּל עָלָיו! אִם כֵּן "הֲרֵי עָלַי קֵן" מִבָּעֵי לֵיהּ.

The Gemara asks: **Since** Rabbi Yoḥanan **said** that, even according to Rabbi Meir, **we are concerned**[N] that the individual intended to become a nazirite, but it is not clear that this was his intention, it can be argued that **perhaps he accepted upon himself a gift** offering of birds as a burnt-offering. Consequently, why is he considered a nazirite? The Gemara answers: **If** it was **so,** that his intention was to bring a gift offering, **he should have** said: **It is hereby** incumbent **upon** me to bring **a nest,**[N] which is the common expression used to accept an obligation to bring a gift offering of birds.

NOTES

We are concerned, etc. – חָיְישִׁינַן קָאָמַר וכו׳: The Gemara's question is as follows: According to Rabbi Yoḥanan, his vow is not necessarily a nazirite vow. Rather, it is uncertain whether he intended to take a nazirite vow or a different vow. Since a nazirite vow must be expressed clearly, as explained in the Gemara (34a), why is this considered a nazirite vow (Commentary on *Nazir*)?

Another explanation of the Gemara's question is: Since a nazirite vow includes many more stringencies than a vow to bring a gift offering, it should be assumed that he meant to accept the less stringent vow (*Tosafot*). Alternatively, there is a principle that one is lenient in cases of uncertainty with regard to naziriteship (Rosh).

Other commentaries explain the question in the following manner: Since it is not clear from his statement whether he intended to become a nazirite or to bring gift offerings, he should be required to fulfill both of the vows (*Shita Mekubbetzet*; Meiri; see Rosh).

It is hereby incumbent upon me to bring a nest, etc. – הֲרֵי עָלַי קֵן וכו׳: The term nest was typically used in reference to voluntary bird offerings, which is why the tractate that deals with this topic is called *Kinnim*, which means nests. If the individual intended to obligate himself to bring a voluntary bird offering, he would have used the standard term (*Tosafot*). The Rosh adds that since there is a principle that vows are interpreted according to the vernacular, and people generally call voluntary bird offerings nests, it cannot be assumed that he was referring to a voluntary bird offering when he did not use that term. It is explained in the Jerusalem Talmud that the Rabbis, who disagree with Rabbi Meir in the mishna, maintain that although the individual cannot be assumed to have been referring to a voluntary bird offering, it may be assumed that he meant to donate birds to the Temple treasury. This is in accordance with the principle found in the Jerusalem Talmud that vows are interpreted according to the language of the Torah (*Tziyyun Yerushalayim*).

BACKGROUND

The birds of an impure nazirite – צִפּוֹרֵי נָזִיר טָמֵא: According to the Torah (Numbers 6:9–12), when a nazirite becomes ritually impure through contact with a corpse, whether intentionally or not, he must first purify himself. He then brings two pigeons to the Temple as offerings, one as a sin-offering and the other as a burnt-offering, as well as a lamb as a guilt-offering. Afterward, he must start his term of naziriteship over again.

וְדִלְמָא "הֲרֵי עָלַי צִפּוֹרֵי מְצוֹרָע" קָאָמַר! כְּגוֹן שֶׁהָיָה נָזִיר עוֹבֵר לְפָנָיו. וְדִלְמָא נָזִיר טָמֵא, וּלְפוֹטְרוֹ מִן קָרְבְּנוֹתָיו קָאָמַר! כְּגוֹן שֶׁהָיָה נָזִיר טָהוֹר עוֹבֵר לְפָנָיו.

The Gemara asks further: **But perhaps he** was **saying: It is** incumbent **upon me** to bring the **birds of a leper,**[BN] rendering himself liable to bring a leper's offerings on a leper's behalf (see Leviticus 14:4). The Gemara answers: This is a case **where a nazirite was passing before him** when he spoke, and he clearly had naziriteship in mind. The Gemara asks: **But perhaps** it was **an impure nazirite, and he** was **saying** that he accepts the obligation **to exempt** the nazirite **from his offerings** by sacrificing them on the nazirite's behalf. The Gemara answers: This is a case **where a pure nazirite was passing before him.**[N]

מַאי בֵּינַיְיהוּ?

The Gemara asks: **What is** the difference **between** the opinions of Reish Lakish and Rabbi Yoḥanan? After all, according to both explanations it is necessary to say that this is a case where a nazirite was passing before him.

אִיכָּא בֵּינַיְיהוּ כְּגוֹן דַּאֲמַר "צִיפֳּרִין הַסְּמוּכִין לְשֵׂעָר עָלַי". לְרַבִּי יוֹחָנָן, אַף עַל גַּב דַּאֲמַר הָכִי, אִי נָזִיר עוֹבֵר לְפָנָיו – אִין, אִי לָא – לָא. לְרַבִּי שִׁמְעוֹן בֶּן לָקִישׁ – אַף עַל גַּב דְּאֵין נָזִיר עוֹבֵר לְפָנָיו.

The Gemara answers: **There is** a practical difference **between them** in a case **where he** explicitly **said:** An obligation is hereby incumbent **upon me** with regard to **the birds juxtaposed** in the verse **to hair. According to Rabbi Yoḥanan, although he said this, if a nazirite was passing before him, yes,** Rabbi Meir considers it a nazirite vow; **if not, no,** it is not considered a nazirite vow. Conversely, **according to Rabbi Shimon ben Lakish, although no nazirite was passing before him,** Rabbi Meir considers it a nazirite vow, as he holds that according to Rabbi Meir, one associates the object of his vow with something juxtaposed to it in a verse.

מִי אִיכָּא לְמַאן דְּאָמַר לָא מַתְפִּיס אִינִישׁ בְּמִילְּתָא דִּסְמִיךְ לֵיהּ? וְהָתַנְיָא: הָאוֹמֵר "יָמִין" – הֲרֵי זוֹ שְׁבוּעָה. מַאי טַעֲמָא – לָאו מִשּׁוּם דִּכְתִיב "וַיָּרֶם יְמִינוֹ וּשְׂמֹאלוֹ אֶל הַשָּׁמַיִם וַיִּשָּׁבַע בְּחֵי הָעוֹלָם"?

The Gemara asks: **Is there,** in fact, **anyone who says** that **a person does not associate** the object of his vow with **something juxtaposed to it** in a verse? **Isn't it taught** in a *baraita* that in the case of **one who says: Right** [*yamin*],[L] **that is** an expression of **an oath? What is the reason** for this? Is it **not because it is written: "When he lifted up his right hand and his left hand unto heaven, and swore by Him that lives forever"** (Daniel 12:7)? It seems evident that the term "right" indicates an oath merely because in the verse it is juxtaposed to an oath.

אָמְרִי: לָא, מִשּׁוּם דְּיָמִין גּוּפֵיהּ אִיקְּרֵי שְׁבוּעָה. דְּתַנְיָא: מִנַּיִין לָאוֹמֵר "יָמִין" שֶׁהִיא שְׁבוּעָה – שֶׁנֶּאֱמַר "נִשְׁבַּע ה' בִּימִינוֹ". וּמִנַּיִין לָאוֹמֵר "שְׂמֹאל" שֶׁהִיא שְׁבוּעָה – שֶׁנֶּאֱמַר "וּבִזְרוֹעַ עוּזּוֹ".

The Gemara rejects this: **Say no,** it is **because** the **right** hand **itself is called an oath, as it is taught** in a *baraita*: **From where** is it derived **that** in the case of **one who says: Right, that it is an oath?** It is derived from the verse where it **is stated: "The Lord has sworn by His right hand"** (Isaiah 62:8).[N] **And from where** is it derived **that** in the case of **one who says: Left,**[H] **that it is an oath?** It is derived from the continuation of that verse, where it **is stated: "And by the arm of His strength"** (Isaiah 62:8). Since this is the complementary phrase for the right hand, it must refer to the left hand. It is clear from here that both right and left are themselves expressions of an oath and do not indicate an oath merely because they are juxtaposed in a verse to an expression of an oath.

BACKGROUND

The birds of a leper – **צִפּוֹרֵי מְצוֹרָע**: The Torah prescribes the use of two birds in the purification ceremony undergone by a cured leper or by the owner of a previously leprous house (see Leviticus 14:4–7, 49–53). Both these birds must be alive, unblemished, non-domesticated, and from a kosher species. The general practice was to use a kind of sparrow. One of the birds is slaughtered over an earthenware vessel filled with springwater, and its blood is drained into the water in this vessel. This mixture is sprinkled on the cured leper or house. The other bird is dipped in the mixture of blood and water and set free. The second bird is not considered sacred. If it is captured after being set free, it may be slaughtered and eaten or used for any other purpose.

LANGUAGE

Right [*yamin*] – **יָמִין**: Apparently, the connotation is influenced by the root of the word, since the root *yud, mem, nun* is similar to the root *alef, mem, nun*, which indicates faith, trustworthiness, and proper conduct. The connection between right and righteous is also found in other languages. In light of this, one who merely employs the word *yamin* in accepting an obligation has thereby expressed an oath, as this term connotes acceptance with faith.

HALAKHA

That in the case of one who says: Right…one who says: Left – **לָאוֹמֵר יָמִין...לָאוֹמֵר שְׂמֹאל**: One who uses the term right has uttered an oath, and the same applies to one who uses the term left. The Rema writes, citing the *Tur*, and in accordance with the opinion of the Ra'avad, that this is the case only if one had in mind the right hand and left hand mentioned in the verse "God has sworn by His right hand" (Rambam *Sefer Hafla'a, Hilkhot Shevuot* 2:6; *Shulḥan Arukh, Yoreh De'a* 237:8).

NOTES

Birds of a leper, etc. – **צִפּוֹרֵי מְצוֹרָע וכו׳**: One explanation of the Gemara's question is that he might have intended to bring two birds and offer them in the manner of the leper's purification ritual (Commentary on *Nazir*). However, most commentaries maintain that he meant to obligate himself to bring bird offerings in order to exempt a leper from having to bring his own birds (*Tosafot*; Meiri). Some explain that the Gemara is not suggesting that he should be required to bring only an offering of leper's birds. Rather, in addition to becoming a nazirite, he should be required to bring an offering of birds (see Rosh).

Where a pure nazirite was passing before him – **כְּגוֹן שֶׁהָיָה נָזִיר טָהוֹר עוֹבֵר לְפָנָיו**: *Tosafot* ask: Even if a pure nazirite passed by, the speaker might have intended to bring the bird offerings in place of the nazirite, in the event that the nazirite became impure. They answer that this is a case where the speaker explains that he meant to accept naziriteship upon himself. This raises a further difficulty: If the speaker is asked to clarify his intention, why is it necessary for a nazirite to be passing before him when he mentions birds? *Tosafot* answer that one's statement must accurately reflect one's intention when he accepts naziriteship. However, *Tosafot* also cite the opinion of Rabbeinu Peretz, who contends that the answer cannot be that the speaker is asked to clarify what he meant, since this requirement is not mentioned in the Gemara. Rather, it is not assumed that he would be referring to the birds the nazirite would have to offer if he were to become impure, since one does not accept upon himself an obligation that does not yet exist. This is not similar to the discussion concerning the birds of a leper, since there it can be assumed that there is a leper somewhere who is already in need of them.

The Lord has sworn by His right hand – **נִשְׁבַּע ה׳ בִּימִינוֹ**: In other words, it is as though God has sworn by something that can be used in an oath, His right hand. This is considered a sacred article, like one who swears by the Torah or any other sacred item. The Ra'avad learns from here that if one takes an oath using the words: By the right, without intending to refer to God's right hand, the oath is not effective. Other commentaries maintain that the term right itself indicates an oath, even if one does not intend to refer to God's right hand.

HALAKHA

I am hereby a nazirite and therefore will refrain from grape seeds, etc. – **הֲרֵינִי נָזִיר מִן הַחַרְצַנִּים וכו׳**: If one said: I am a nazirite and therefore will refrain from grape seeds, or: I am a nazirite and therefore will refrain from grape skins, or: I am a nazirite and therefore will refrain from impurity, or: I am a nazirite and therefore will refrain from shaving, then he is a nazirite, and all the *halakhot* of naziriteship apply to him. Even if he intended to accept only one of the prohibitions of naziriteship, he becomes a nazirite in every sense (Rambam *Sefer Hafla'a*, *Hilkhot Nezirut* 1:9).

Kiddush* and *havdala – **קְדוּשְׁתָּא וְאַבְדַּלְתָּא**: A nazirite is prohibited from drinking wine in the performance of a mitzva. Consequently, it is prohibited for him to drink the wine from *kiddush* or *havdala* (Rambam *Sefer Hafla'a*, *Hilkhot Nezirut* 7:11).

מתני׳ ״הֲרֵינִי נָזִיר מִן הַחַרְצַנִּים״ וּ״מִן הַזַּגִּים״ וּ״מִן הַתִּגְלַחַת״ וּ״מִן הַטּוּמְאָה״ – הֲרֵי זֶה נָזִיר, וְכׇל דִּקְדּוּקֵי נְזִירוּת עָלָיו.

MISHNA If one said: **I am hereby a nazirite** and therefore will refrain **from grape seeds,**[H] **or:** I am hereby a nazirite and therefore will refrain **from** grape **skins, or: From shaving, or: From impurity, he is a nazirite. And all details of naziriteship** are incumbent **upon him.**[N] Not only does the prohibition he mentioned take effect, he is bound by all of the strictures of naziriteship.

גמ׳ מַתְנִיתִין דְּלָא כְּרַבִּי שִׁמְעוֹן. דְּתַנְיָא, רַבִּי שִׁמְעוֹן אוֹמֵר: אֵינוֹ חַיָּיב עַד שֶׁיִּדּוֹר מִכּוּלָּם, וְרַבָּנַן אָמְרִי: אֲפִילּוּ לֹא נָזַר אֶלָּא בְּאֶחָד מֵהֶן הָוֵי נָזִיר.

GEMARA The Gemara comments: **The mishna is not in accordance with** the opinion of **Rabbi Shimon,**[N] **as it is taught** in a *baraita* that **Rabbi Shimon says:** One **is not obligated**[N] as a nazirite **until he vows** that **all** items and actions forbidden to a nazirite are forbidden **to** him. **And the Rabbis say: Even if he vowed** to abstain **from only one of them, he is a nazirite.**

מַאי טַעְמָא דְּרַבִּי שִׁמְעוֹן? אָמַר קְרָא ״מִכֹּל אֲשֶׁר יֵעָשֶׂה מִגֶּפֶן הַיַּיִן מֵחַרְצַנִּים וְעַד זָג״. וְרַבָּנַן מַאי טַעְמָא? אָמַר קְרָא ״מִיַּיִן וְשֵׁכָר יַזִּיר״.

The Gemara explains: **What is the reason** for the opinion **of Rabbi Shimon? The verse states** with regard to a nazirite: "All the days of his naziriteship he shall not eat **from anything that is made of the grapevine, from pits to grape skin"** (Numbers 6:4),[N] which indicates that his vow of naziriteship must include all the prohibitions of a nazirite. The Gemara continues to clarify: **And** according to **the Rabbis, what is the reason** that he becomes a nazirite even if he specified only one of the prohibitions of a nazirite? **The verse states: "He shall abstain from wine and strong drink"** (Numbers 6:3). This implies that even if one vows to abstain only from wine and strong drink, all of the *halakhot* of a nazirite take effect.

וְרַבִּי שִׁמְעוֹן נַמִי, הָכְתִיב ״מִיַּיִן וְשֵׁכָר יַזִּיר״! הַהוּא מִיבְּעֵי לֵיהּ לֶאֱסוֹר יֵין מִצְוָה כְּיֵין הָרְשׁוּת.

The Gemara asks: **And also** according to **Rabbi Shimon, isn't it written "he shall abstain from wine and strong drink"?** The Gemara answers: Rabbi Shimon **requires that** verse **to prohibit** a nazirite from drinking **wine** that is consumed for **a mitzva** just **as** he is prohibited from drinking **wine** whose consumption is **optional.**

מַאי הִיא – קְדוּשְׁתָּא וְאַבְדַּלְתָּא?

The Gemara asks: **What is** wine that is consumed for a mitzva? Is it the wine of ***kiddush* and *havdala*?**[H]

NOTES

And all details of naziriteship are incumbent upon him – **וְכׇל דִּקְדּוּקֵי נְזִירוּת עָלָיו**: The commentaries write that it was necessary for the mishna to specify this because the mishna on 4a discusses the *halakhot* of a permanent nazirite and a nazirite like Samson, and not all the details of naziriteship apply to the latter. The mishna here therefore states that in the case under discussion, all of the *halakhot* of a nazirite are in effect, despite the fact that one mentioned only one aspect of the *halakhot* of naziriteship (*Tosafot*; Rosh).

The mishna is not in accordance with the opinion of Rabbi Shimon – **מַתְנִיתִין דְּלָא כְּרַבִּי שִׁמְעוֹן**: Rabbeinu Todros explains that Rabbi Shimon similarly disagrees with the Rabbis concerning one who says: I am hereby a hair curler, since he is referring only to the prohibition against cutting hair. Most commentaries disagree, however, and hold that one who says: I am hereby a hair curler, intends to accept standard naziriteship. Since he does not say that he will curl his hair, but that he is becoming a hair curler, his point is that he intends to be like a nazirite, who is someone who curls his hair. Rabbi Shimon disagrees only in a case where one explicitly states that he is accepting upon himself just a single aspect of naziriteship. This is also indicated by the Jerusalem Talmud (Rosh; *Shita Mekubbetzet*).

One is not obligated – **אֵינוֹ חַיָּיב**: Some commentaries explain that Rabbi Shimon does not hold that the statement is entirely meaningless. Rather, the speaker has taken a regular vow to render grape seeds forbidden. This vow takes effect, but it is not a nazirite vow (Meiri; see Rabbi Avraham min HaHar).

From pits to grape skin – **מֵחַרְצַנִּים וְעַד זָג**: Once the verse states: "From anything that is made of the grapevine," the phrase "from pits to grape skin" is unnecessary. Rabbi Shimon derives from this seemingly unnecessary phrase that just as one is a nazirite only if he accepts all the prohibitions associated with grape products, one is a nazirite only if he accepts all the prohibitions of naziriteship. However, one does not have to specify all the relevant prohibitions, as one who says simply: I am a nazirite, is bound by all aspects of naziriteship. It is only in a case where one goes into detail that he must specify all the prohibitions of a nazirite (Rosh).

הֲרֵי מוּשְׁבָּע וְעוֹמֵד עָלָיו מֵהַר סִינַי!

He is already sworn[N] **and obligated about it from Mount Sinai,** i.e., he is obligated by Torah law to keep the *halakhot* of naziriteship, and therefore it is obvious that he may not drink wine from *kiddush* or *havdala*, as drinking the wine is required by rabbinic law (Rambam).

אֶלָּא כִּי הָא דַּאֲמַר רָבָא: ״שְׁבוּעָה שֶׁאֶשְׁתֶּה״ וְחָזַר וַאֲמַר ״הֲרֵינִי נָזִיר״ אָתְיָא נְזִירוּת חָיְילָא עַל שְׁבוּעָה.

Rather, it is **like that**[N] **which Rava said:** If one said: I hereby take **an oath that I will drink** wine, **and he then said:**[H] **I am hereby a nazirite,** the **naziriteship comes and applies**[N] **to the** subject of his **oath.** Although drinking wine is a mitzva for him due to his oath, his naziriteship supersedes the previous oath and renders it prohibited for him to drink wine.

וְרַבָּנַן נַמִי, הָא מִיבָּעֵי לֵיהּ לֶאֱסוֹר יֵין מִצְוָה כְּיֵין רְשׁוּת! אִם כֵּן לֵימָא קְרָא ״מִיַּיִן״. מַאי ״וְשֵׁכָר״ – שָׁמְעַתְּ מִינָּהּ תַּרְתֵּי.

The Gemara asks: **And** according to **the Rabbis also, isn't** the verse **needed to prohibit** to a nazirite **wine** that is consumed as a **mitzva,** just **like wine** whose consumption is **optional?** The Gemara answers: **If** that is **so, let the verse say** only "he shall abstain **from wine**" (Numbers 6:3). **What** is the purpose of the additional phrase **"and strong drink"? Learn from it** that the verse teaches **two** *halakhot*, that one is a full-fledged nazirite even if he accepted only one of the prohibitions of naziriteship, and that a nazirite is prohibited from drinking wine even when its consumption is a mitzva.

וְרַבִּי שִׁמְעוֹן: הַיְינוּ טַעְמָא דִּכְתַב ״שֵׁכָר״ – לְאַלּוֹפֵי ״שֵׁכָר״ ״שֵׁכָר״ לַמִּקְדָּשׁ. דִּכְתִיב ״יַיִן וְשֵׁכָר אַל תֵּשְׁתְּ אַתָּה וּבָנֶיךָ אִתָּךְ״, מַה גַּבֵּי נָזִיר יַיִן הוּא דְּלִיתְסַר, אֲבָל שְׁאָר מַשְׁקִין – לָא. אַף גַּבֵּי מִקְדָּשׁ נַמִי, יַיִן הוּא דְּלִיתְסַר, אֲבָל שְׁאָר מַשְׁקִין הַמְּשַׁתַּכְּרִין – לָא.

The Gemara explains: **And Rabbi Shimon** could respond to this argument as follows: **This is the reason that** the verse **writes "strong drink"**: It is **to teach** a verbal analogy between "**strong drink**" written here and "**strong drink**" written **with regard to** entering and performing service in **the Temple, as it is written** that Aaron the priest was commanded: "**Do not drink wine or strong drink, you nor your sons with you,** when you go into the Tent of Meeting" (Leviticus 10:9). This teaches: **Just as with a nazirite, it is wine alone that is forbidden**[H] **but other** beverages are **not** forbidden, **so too, with regard to the Temple,**[N] **it is wine that is forbidden** to priests, **but other intoxicating beverages** are **not** forbidden to them.

HALAKHA

An oath that I will drink wine, and he then said, etc. – שְׁבוּעָה שֶׁאֶשְׁתֶּה, וְחָזַר וְאָמַר וכו׳: If one takes an oath that he will drink wine today and subsequently takes a nazirite vow, the nazirite vow takes effect and supersedes the oath, and it is therefore prohibited for him to drink wine (Rambam *Sefer Hafla'a*, *Hilkhot Nezirut* 7:11).

It is wine alone that is forbidden – יַיִן הוּא דְּלִיתְסַר: It is prohibited for a nazirite to consume wine or any product that contains grape derivatives. However, it is permitted for him to drink strong drinks made from figs or other produce (Rambam *Sefer Hafla'a*, *Hilkhot Nezirut* 5:1).

NOTES

He is already sworn, etc. – הֲרֵי מוּשְׁבָּע וכו׳: This version of the Gemara text is difficult. The plain meaning of the Gemara seems to indicate that one is obligated from Mount Sinai to drink the wine from *kiddush* and *havdala* (Commentary on *Nazir*). This fits well with the version of the *She'iltot* that states that there is a mitzva by Torah law to mention Shabbat over wine at its beginning, in *kiddush*, and at its end, during *havdala*. According to this opinion, the Gemara refutes the possibility that the verse teaches that a nazirite is prohibited from drinking *kiddush* and *havdala* wine, and the early authorities of Ashkenaz ruled accordingly. A different interpretation, also based on this version of the text, is that just as the Gemara states that a nazirite cannot be viewed as beautiful if his naziriteship involves a transgression (2b), the Torah would likewise have refrained from praising a nazirite if his vow meant he could not drink the wine of *kiddush* and *havdala* (*Tosefot Rabbeinu Peretz*).

However, most commentaries reject these opinions, since it is evident from other sources that although *kiddush* is a mitzva by Torah law, the use of wine is by rabbinic law. This is certainly the case with regard to reciting *havdala* over wine. Furthermore, since one can recite *kiddush* over bread or fulfill the mitzva by listening to the *kiddush* of another individual, the drinking of *kiddush* wine cannot be seen as an act that is incumbent on one from Mount Sinai and that should therefore be permitted to a nazirite. Consequently, many commentaries accept a different version of the text, attributed to Rabbeinu Tam, according to which the Gemara asks rhetorically: Is he already sworn from Mount Sinai? In other words, it is obvious that a nazirite may not drink the wine from *kiddush* or *havdala*, as there is no mitzva by Torah law to drink this wine. The Rosh and most commentaries explain the text in this manner.

The Rambam, in his Responsa (120), explains the Gemara differently: It is obvious that the mitzva of *kiddush* over wine is by rabbinic law. The words: He is already sworn about it from Mount Sinai, refer not to the mitzvot of *kiddush* and *havdala* over wine, but to the prohibitions of naziriteship. The Gemara is then saying: If you say that this *halakha* teaches that a nazirite is prohibited from drinking *kiddush* wine, that is not a novelty, since *kiddush* is a rabbinic mitzva, whereas a nazirite is sworn by Torah law to uphold his vow of naziriteship.

Rather it is like that, etc. – אֶלָּא כִּי הָא וכו׳: This version of the text does not make sense according to the commentaries who explain that the nazirite is considered to have sworn from Mount Sinai to perform *kiddush* and *havdala* with wine. The Rosh explains that according to that opinion, the word: Rather, should be omitted, as Rava's statement is a continuation of the previous argument. The Gemara is then providing proof that the prohibitions of naziriteship take precedence over the mitzva wine of *kiddush* and *havdala*, by demonstrating that the prohibitions of naziriteship take precedence over an oath to drink wine. However, others explain that according to these commentaries, although a nazirite is not prohibited from drinking the wine of *kiddush* and *havdala*, he is prohibited from drinking wine that he took an oath to drink (Meiri, citing Rashi; Commentary on *Nazir*; see Rashba).

Naziriteship comes and applies, etc. – אָתְיָא נְזִירוּת חָיְילָא וכו׳: The Rashba, in his Responsa (4:109), explains the Gemara in the following manner: A nazirite vow prohibits the nazirite from consuming wine, and also takes effect with regard to the wine itself and causes the wine to be considered a forbidden item vis-à-vis the nazirite. In this regard, a nazirite vow is similar to other vows, which render an item forbidden. By contrast, oaths create an obligation or a prohibition that applies to the person who took it (see *Nedarim* 2b). Consequently, even if the individual has already obligated himself to drink wine, since the wine itself becomes a forbidden item due to his nazirite vow, he may not fulfill his oath by drinking the wine. However, it is explained in the Meiri that a nazirite vow is like an oath in that it applies only to the individual, prohibiting him from consuming wine, but does not affect the status of the wine itself. The verse teaches that naziriteship overrides one's earlier oath, as it is more inclusive and powerful than a regular oath.

So too with regard to the Temple, etc. – אַף גַּבֵּי מִקְדָּשׁ נַמִי וכו׳: This does not mean that a priest is permitted to perform the service when he is drunk from some other intoxicating beverage, since the Torah's prohibition applies to all intoxicating drinks. Rather, one who drinks other beverages and proceeds to serve in the Temple is not liable to death at the hand of Heaven, which is the punishment reserved for one who performs the Temple service while drunk from wine (*Shita Mekubbetzet*).

HALAKHA

Ate a dried fig from Ke'ila, etc. – **אָכַל דְּבֵילָה קְעִילִית וכו׳**: A priest who becomes drunk from any intoxicating beverage is prohibited from entering the Temple. If he performed service in the Temple after drinking an intoxicating beverage other than wine, he is liable to receive lashes, though his service is valid. If he performed a service after drinking wine, his service is invalid and he is liable to death at the hand of Heaven. The *halakha* is in accordance with Rabbi Yehuda (Rambam *Sefer Avoda, Hilkhot Biat HaMikdash* 2:1).

The verse taught that the prohibitions of a nazirite combine with each other – **לִימֵּד עַל אִיסּוּרֵי נָזִיר שֶׁמִּצְטָרְפִים זֶה עִם זֶה**: All of the different types of grapes that are forbidden to a nazirite combine with each other to make up one measurement. For example, if a nazirite ate moist grapes with dried ones, unripe ones, grape seeds, or grape skins, and if he ate a total volume of an olive-bulk, he is liable to receive lashes. Similarly, if a nazirite drank a quarter-*log* of a mixture of wine and of vinegar made of wine, he receives lashes (Rambam *Sefer Hafla'a, Hilkhot Nezirut* 5:3).

BACKGROUND

A dried fig from Ke'ila – **דְּבֵילָה קְעִילִית**: This refers to dried figs from the town of Ke'ila in Judea. Apparently, the figs in this area contained a high level of sugar. Other places in the Talmud tell of how honey would drip from the figs and ferment, turning into alcohol.

Even without fermentation, ingesting a large amount of sugar can cause mild poisoning. This may be due to an inability of the liver to process a large amount of sugar fast enough. This causes feelings of nausea and dizziness similar to what one might feel after drinking hard liquor.

וּלְאַפּוּקֵי מִדְּרַבִּי יְהוּדָה. דְּתַנְיָא, רַבִּי יְהוּדָה אוֹמֵר: אָכַל דְּבֵילָה קְעִילִית, וְשָׁתָה דְּבַשׁ וְחָלָב, וְנִכְנַס לַמִּקְדָּשׁ – חַיָּיב.

And this is to the exclusion of the opinion **of Rabbi Yehuda, as it is taught** in a *baraita* **that Rabbi Yehuda says:** If one **ate a dried fig from Ke'ila,**[HB] **and** similarly if one **drank honey or** if one drank **milk,** which can dull the senses, **and entered the Temple, he is liable** for violating the prohibition against strong drink.

אִיבָּעֵית אֵימָא: רַבִּי שִׁמְעוֹן לֵית לֵיהּ אִיסּוּר חָל עַל אִיסּוּר.

The Gemara suggests a different reason for the inclusion of the term "strong drink," according to Rabbi Shimon. **If you wish, say** instead that it is necessary because **Rabbi Shimon does not** generally **accept** the principle that **a prohibition takes effect upon** a preexisting **prohibition.**[N]

דְּתַנְיָא, רַבִּי שִׁמְעוֹן אוֹמֵר: הָאוֹכֵל נְבֵילָה בְּיוֹם הַכִּפּוּרִים – פָּטוּר.

As it is **taught** in a *baraita* that **Rabbi Shimon says: One who eats an animal carcass**[N] **on Yom Kippur is exempt** from the punishment of *karet* for eating on Yom Kippur. It is prohibited to eat an animal carcass, and therefore the additional prohibition against eating on Yom Kippur does not take effect with regard to it. The inclusion of the term "strong drink" alludes to the fact that with regard to naziriteship, a second prohibition does take effect. Consequently, if one took an oath not to drink wine and afterward vowed to be a nazirite, both prohibitions apply.

וּלְרַבָּנַן נַמִּי, הָכְתִיב ״מִכֹּל אֲשֶׁר יֵעָשֶׂה מִגֶּפֶן הַיַּיִן״! אָמְרִי לָךְ רַבָּנַן: הָתָם לִימֵּד עַל אִיסּוּרֵי נָזִיר שֶׁמִּצְטָרְפִים זֶה עִם זֶה.

The Gemara asks: **And also** according to **the Rabbis, isn't it written: "Anything that is made of the grapevine"** (Numbers 6:4), which seems to indicate, as stated by Rabbi Shimon, that one becomes a nazirite only if he vows to accept all the prohibitions of a nazirite? The Gemara answers: **The Rabbis** could have **said to you: There** the verse **taught** that **the prohibitions of a nazirite combine with each other.**[H] In other words, if a nazirite eats less than an olive-bulk of both grape skins and grape seeds, but together they amount to an olive-bulk, he receives lashes for transgressing a Torah prohibition.

וְרַבִּי שִׁמְעוֹן לֵית לֵיהּ צֵירוּף. דְּתַנְיָא, רַבִּי שִׁמְעוֹן אוֹמֵר: כָּל שֶׁהוּ לְמַכּוֹת, לֹא אָמְרוּ כַּזַּיִת אֶלָּא לְעִנְיַן קָרְבָּן.

The Gemara explains: **And Rabbi Shimon** does not interpret the verse in this manner because **he does not hold** that there is a need for the **combination** of quantities of different foods in order to render one liable to receive lashes, **as it is taught** in a *baraita* that **Rabbi Shimon says:** Even **the smallest quantity** of forbidden food is sufficient to render one liable **to receive lashes.** The Sages **stated** the measurement of **an olive-bulk only with regard to** the obligation to bring **an offering.** Consequently, in the case of a nazirite, who is not obligated to bring a sin-offering if he inadvertently eats grape products, there is no need for a special verse to teach that the different foods add up to the measurement of an olive-bulk. Therefore, the purpose of the verse must be to teach about the nature of a nazirite vow.

NOTES

Does not generally accept the principle that a prohibition takes effect upon a preexisting prohibition – **לֵית לֵיהּ אִיסּוּר חָל עַל אִיסּוּר**: The commentaries struggle to account for the relevance of this principle to the discussion. The Rid even concludes that the text of this entire section has been corrupted.

It is explained in the Commentary on *Nazir* that the discussion in the Gemara is referring to Rabbi Shimon's opinion in the mishna. The Gemara is explaining that once one is prohibited by a vow from eating grape seeds, then a nazirite vow, which also prohibits him from eating such seeds, cannot take effect.

Tosafot maintain that the Gemara is offering an alternative explanation as to what Rabbi Shimon learns from the term "strong drink." According to this explanation, although Rabbi Shimon generally holds that a prohibition does not take effect where another prohibition already exists, the extra term in the verse indicates that naziriteship is an exception to this principle. Consequently, if one took an oath not to drink wine, and then took a nazirite vow, and then drank wine, he is punished with lashes twice (Rabbeinu Peretz and Rabbeinu Azriel, cited in *Shita Mekubbetzet*).

The Rosh attributes an opposing explanation to Rabbeinu Tam: Rabbi Shimon learns from the term "strong drink" that if a nazirite drinks wine on Yom Kippur he is liable only for transgressing his vow of naziriteship but not for eating on Yom Kippur. This serves as the source for Rabbi Shimon's opinion that one prohibition does not take effect when there is a preexisting prohibition.

One who eats an animal carcass, etc. – **הָאוֹכֵל נְבֵילָה וכו׳**: The commentaries explain that this *halakha* applies only if the animal died before Yom Kippur, in which case the prohibition against eating an animal carcass took effect before the prohibition of eating on Yom Kippur took effect. If, however, it died on Yom Kippur itself, then he is liable for eating on Yom Kippur (*Shita Mekubbetzet*).

מתני׳ ״הֲרֵינִי כְּשִׁמְשׁוֹן״ ״כְּבֶן מָנוֹחַ״. ״כְּבַעַל דְּלִילָה״ ״כְּמִי שֶׁעָקַר דַּלְתוֹת עַזָּה״ ״כְּמִי שֶׁנִּקְּרוּ פְלִשְׁתִּים אֶת עֵינָיו״ – הֲרֵי זֶה נְזִיר שִׁמְשׁוֹן.

MISHNA If one said: **I am hereby like Samson,**[H] **like the son of Manoah, like the husband of Delilah, like the one who tore off**[N] **the doors of Gaza, like the one whose eyes were gouged out by the Philistines, he is a nazirite** like **Samson,** whose *halakhot* are explained in the next mishna (see Judges, chapters 13–16).

גמ׳ לָמָּה לִי לְמִיתְנָא כָּל הָלֵין? צְרִיכִי; דְּאִי אֲמַר ״הֲרֵינִי כְּשִׁמְשׁוֹן״ – הֲוָה אָמִינָא שִׁמְשׁוֹן אַחֲרִינָא, קָא מַשְׁמַע לָן ״כְּבֶן מָנוֹחַ״.

GEMARA The Gemara asks: **Why do I** need the *tanna* **to teach all these** cases? It should be enough to state only the *halakha* where one says: Like Samson. The Gemara answers: These specifications **are necessary because if one said** only: **I am hereby like Samson,**[N] **I would say** he was referring to **another Samson,** and this is not a nazirite vow. The *tanna* therefore **teaches us** that he adds: **Like the son of Manoah,** which shows he is referring to the biblical Samson.

וְאִי תְּנָא ״כְּבֶן מָנוֹחַ״ – הֲוָה אָמִינָא: אִיכָּא דְּמִיתְקְרֵי הָכִי, קָא מַשְׁמַע לָן ״כְּבַעַל דְּלִילָה״ וּ״כְמִי שֶׁנִּקְּרוּ פְלִשְׁתִּים אֶת עֵינָיו״.

And if the *tanna* had **taught** that he said he would be: **Like the son of Manoah, I would say there is** some person **who is called that** name, Samson, son of Manoah, and this is not a reference to the biblical Samson and is not an acceptance of naziriteship. The *tanna* therefore **teaches us** that he adds: **Like the husband of Delilah,** or: Like the one who tore off the doors of Gaza, **or: Like the one whose eyes were gouged out by the Philistines.** It is therefore clear that he is referring to the biblical figure and that his statement is a vow of naziriteship.

מתני׳ מַה בֵּין נְזִיר עוֹלָם לִנְזִיר שִׁמְשׁוֹן? נְזִיר עוֹלָם – הִכְבִּיד שְׂעָרוֹ מֵיקֵל בְּתַעַר, וּמֵבִיא שָׁלֹשׁ בְּהֵמוֹת, וְאִם נִטְמָא – מֵבִיא קָרְבַּן טוּמְאָה.

MISHNA **What is** the difference **between a permanent nazirite**[N] **and a nazirite** like **Samson,** both of whom remain nazirites forever? In the case of **a permanent nazirite,**[H] if **his hair grows** too **heavy** for him, **he lightens** it by cutting some hair **with a razor,**[N] **and he** then **brings three animals**[N] as a sin-offering, a burnt-offering, and a peace-offering, like one who completes his term of naziriteship. **And if he becomes ritually impure, he brings** the **offering** for **impurity** brought by a regular nazirite who became impure.

נְזִיר שִׁמְשׁוֹן – הִכְבִּיד שְׂעָרוֹ אֵינוֹ מֵיקֵל, וְאִם נִטְמָא – אֵינוֹ מֵבִיא קָרְבַּן טוּמְאָה.

By contrast, in the case of **a nazirite** like **Samson, if his hair grows heavy he may not lighten** it, since he is entirely prohibited from cutting his hair. **And if he becomes impure, he does not bring an offering** for **impurity.**

HALAKHA

I am hereby like Samson, etc. – **הֲרֵינִי כְּשִׁמְשׁוֹן וכו׳**: If one says: I am hereby a nazirite like Samson, or: I am like Delilah's husband, or: I am like the son of Manoah, or: I am like the one who tore the doors off Gaza, or: I am like the one whose eyes were gouged out by the Philistines, he is a nazirite. Some authorities (Commentary on *Nazir*; *Tosafot*; *Likkutei Halakhot*) claim that one becomes a nazirite only if he said: I am like Samson, or: I am like Samson ben Manoah, and added a modifier, for example: Like the one who tore the doors off Gaza (Rambam *Sefer Hafla'a*, *Hilkhot Nezirut* 3:15).

Permanent nazirite – **נְזִיר עוֹלָם**: One who vowed to be a permanent nazirite may shave his hair once every twelve months if his hair gets too heavy. He then brings three animals as offerings. If he becomes impure he must bring an offering for his impurity and shave his head like a regular nazirite (Rambam *Sefer Hafla'a*, *Hilkhot Nezirut* 3:12).

NOTES

Like the one who tore off – **כְּמִי שֶׁעָקַר**: *Tosafot* explain that one who says that he will be like Samson or like the son of Manoah must add an additional identifying feature in order to clarify that he is referring to the Samson of the Bible, such as: The husband of Delilah, or: The one who tore off the doors of Gaza, or: The one whose eyes were gouged out by the Philistines. Rabbeinu Tam slightly emended the text of the mishna to reflect this point.

Because if one said only: I am hereby like Samson – **דְּאִי אֲמַר הֲרֵינִי כְּשִׁמְשׁוֹן**: This indicates that one who says: I am like Samson, or even: I am like Samson, son of Manoah, without further specification, is not a nazirite unless he identified the biblical figure beyond any possible doubt. One doesn't have to mention all the examples listed in the mishna; any one of them suffices (Commentary on *Nazir*; Rabbeinu Tam).

According to the Rid, if one simply said: I am like Samson, he is a nazirite like Samson. However, if he then explains that he had another Samson in mind, the court cannot compel him to adhere to the *halakhot* of a nazirite, whereas if he clearly identified the Samson of the Bible, then he is definitely a nazirite. The Rambam's ruling indicates a similar understanding. By contrast, the Meiri slightly adjusts the text of the Gemara and explains that anyone who intended to become a nazirite and employed any one of the terms mentioned in the mishna has thereby taken a nazirite vow. This opinion is supported by the Jerusalem Talmud, where it is explained that not only does the explicit mention of Samson [*Shimshon*] entail naziriteship, but the same is true even of substitute languages of his name, e.g., *Shimshor* and *Shimshutz*.

What is the difference between a permanent nazirite, etc. – **מַה בֵּין נְזִיר עוֹלָם וכו׳**: The early commentaries point out that the *tanna* could have added another difference, i.e., that a vow of a nazirite like Samson cannot be dissolved, as explained below (14a). *Tosafot* explain that the *tanna* did not mention this difference because he was dealing with differences that apply specifically to nazirites, and a nazirite whose vow has been dissolved is not a nazirite (see Rabbeinu Todros, cited in *Shita Mekubbetzet*).

He lightens it by cutting some hair with a razor – **מֵיקֵל בְּתַעַר**: Some commentaries explain that a permanent nazirite may trim his hair but may not completely shave it off. Their proof is the fact that Absalom, who is the paradigm of a permanent nazirite, was hung by his hair. This shows that his hair was not shaved off (*Tosafot*; *Shita Mekubbetzet*; Meiri). The Meiri adds that he may use only a razor but not scissors, so that he cuts it in an unusual manner. However, Rabbeinu Todros, cited in the *Shita Mekubbetzet*, says, citing Rabbi Eliezer of Metz that he may even shave his hair entirely, and the Rambam seems to agree. Needless to say, he must be careful not to transgress the prohibition against rounding off the corners of the head. Some commentaries hold that he may trim his hair once every thirty days (Commentary on *Nazir*), but the Rambam rules that he may do so only once every twelve months.

And he then brings three animals – **וּמֵבִיא שָׁלֹשׁ בְּהֵמוֹת**: *Tosafot* explain that a support for this *halakha* can be seen in the case of Absalom, as it is written that Absalom said that he was going to Hebron to "pay my vow" (II Samuel 15:7), which implies the sacrifice of offerings. However, the *halakha* itself was transmitted to Moses from Sinai. Other commentaries write that this *halakha* cannot be derived from Absalom, since the verses can be explained in a manner that has no connection to naziriteship.

גמ׳ נְזִיר עוֹלָם מַאן דְּכַר שְׁמֵיהּ? חַסּוּרֵי מִיחַסְּרָא, וְהָכִי קָתָנֵי: הָאוֹמֵר ״הֲרֵינִי נְזִיר עוֹלָם״ – הֲרֵי זֶה נָזִיר. מַה בֵּין נְזִיר עוֹלָם לִנְזִיר שִׁמְשׁוֹן? נְזִיר עוֹלָם – הִכְבִּיד שְׂעָרוֹ מֵיקֵל בְּתַעַר, וּמֵבִיא שָׁלֹשׁ בְּהֵמוֹת, וְאִם נִטְמָא – מֵבִיא קָרְבַּן טוּמְאָה. נְזִיר שִׁמְשׁוֹן – הִכְבִּיד שְׂעָרוֹ אֵינוֹ מֵיקֵל בְּתַעַר,

GEMARA The Gemara asks: **Who mentioned anything about a permanent nazirite?** Since the mishna has not yet mentioned this concept, how can it analyze the differences between it and a nazirite like Samson? The Gemara answers: The mishna **is incomplete and is teaching the following:**[B] In the case of **one who says: I am hereby a permanent nazirite,**[N] **he is** a permanent **nazirite. What is the** difference **between a permanent nazirite and a nazirite like Samson?** In the case of **a permanent nazirite,** if **his hair grows** too **heavy** for him, **he lightens** it **with a razor and he** then **brings three animals** for offerings. **And if he becomes ritually impure, he brings** the **offering** for **impurity.** In the case of **a nazirite** like **Samson, if his hair grows heavy he may not lighten it with a razor,**

BACKGROUND

The mishna is incomplete and is teaching the following – חַסּוּרֵי מִיחַסְּרָא וְהָכִי קָתָנֵי: This phrase, which appears extensively in the Gemara, does not indicate a proposal to emend the text of the mishna. Rather, the addition mentioned in the Gemara is an elaboration upon that which is written in the mishna, which is unclear as written. The addition facilitates understanding of the mishna.

NOTES

One who says: I am hereby a permanent nazirite – הָאוֹמֵר הֲרֵינִי נְזִיר עוֹלָם: Some commentaries add that one is also a permanent nazirite if he says that he will be like Absalom, son of David. The Gemara does not mention this case because not everyone knows that Absalom was a permanent nazirite, whereas Samson is famous for his naziriteship (Rabbeinu Azriel, cited in *Shita Mekubbetzet*; see Meiri).

Perek **I**
Daf **4** Amud **b**

וְאֵינוֹ מֵבִיא קָרְבַּן טוּמְאָה.

but he does not bring the **offering** for **impurity.**

קָרְבָּן הוּא דְּלָא מַיְיתֵי, אֲבָל נְזִירוּת – חַיְילָא עֲלֵיהּ.

The Gemara comments: From the words: But if he becomes impure he does not bring an offering for impurity, one can infer that **it is the offering that he does not bring. However,** all of the prohibitions of **naziriteship apply**[N] **to him,** and it is prohibited for him to become impure from a corpse.

מַנִּי מַתְנִיתִין? לָא רַבִּי יְהוּדָה, וְלָא רַבִּי שִׁמְעוֹן. דְּתַנְיָא, רַבִּי יְהוּדָה אוֹמֵר: נְזִיר שִׁמְשׁוֹן מוּתָּר לִיטַּמֵּא לַמֵּתִים, שֶׁכֵּן מָצִינוּ בְּשִׁמְשׁוֹן שֶׁנִּטְמָא. רַבִּי שִׁמְעוֹן אוֹמֵר: הָאוֹמֵר ״נְזִיר שִׁמְשׁוֹן״ – לֹא אָמַר כְּלוּם, שֶׁלֹּא מָצִינוּ בְּשִׁמְשׁוֹן שֶׁיָּצָאת נְזִירוּת מִפִּיו.

This leads to the following question: **Whose** opinion is expressed in **the mishna?** It is **not** the opinion of **Rabbi Yehuda and not** the opinion of **Rabbi Shimon, as it is taught** in a *baraita*: **Rabbi Yehuda says: A nazirite** like **Samson is permitted to become impure from a corpse**[H] *ab initio*, **as we find with Samson that he became impure. Rabbi Shimon says: One who says** he will be **a nazirite** like **Samson has not said anything, since we do not find with Samson that** an utterance of a vow of **naziriteship left his mouth.** Samson never took a vow to be a nazirite. He received his status from the angel's instructions to his mother (see Judges 13:5). Consequently, Rabbi Shimon holds that one who vows to be a nazirite like Samson is not considered to have taken a nazirite vow.

מַנִּי? אִי רַבִּי יְהוּדָה – הָאָמַר אֲפִילּוּ לְכַתְּחִילָּה, וּמַתְנִיתִין קָתָנֵי ״אִם נִטְמָא״. אִי רַבִּי שִׁמְעוֹן – הָאָמַר לָא חָיְילָא עֲלֵיהּ נְזִירוּת כְּלָל!

The Gemara explains the question: **Whose** opinion is expressed in the mishna? **If** it is the opinion of **Rabbi Yehuda, didn't he say** that it is permitted for a nazirite of this kind to become impure from a corpse **even** *ab initio*, **but the mishna teaches: If he becomes impure,** which indicates that he is prohibited from doing so *ab initio*? However, **if** you say that the mishna is according to the opinion of **Rabbi Shimon, didn't he say** that **naziriteship does not apply to him at all?**

לְעוֹלָם רַבִּי יְהוּדָה הִיא, וְאַיְּידֵי דְּקָתָנֵי גַּבֵּי נְזִיר עוֹלָם ״אִם נִטְמָא״ – תְּנָא נַמִּי גַּבֵּי נְזִיר שִׁמְשׁוֹן ״אִם נִטְמָא״.

The Gemara answers: **Actually,** the mishna **is** in accordance with the opinion of **Rabbi Yehuda,** and a nazirite like Samson may become impure from a corpse even *ab initio*. **And since it teaches with regard to a permanent nazirite: If he becomes impure,** as it is prohibited for a permanent nazirite to become impure from a corpse *ab initio*, the *tanna* **also taught** the same expression **with regard to a nazirite** like **Samson** and used the expression: **If he becomes impure.**

NOTES

The prohibitions of naziriteship apply – נְזִירוּת חָיְילָא: A similar question appears in the parallel discussion in the Jerusalem Talmud. The Gemara there infers from the mishna that although a nazirite like Samson does not have to bring an offering if he becomes impure from a corpse, he is liable to receive lashes.

HALAKHA

A nazirite like Samson is permitted to become impure from a corpse – נְזִיר שִׁמְשׁוֹן מוּתָּר לִיטַּמֵּא לַמֵּתִים: It is prohibited for a nazirite like Samson to drink wine and to cut his hair, but he may become impure from a corpse. This *halakha* is learned by tradition, in accordance with the opinion of Rabbi Yehuda (Rambam *Sefer Hafla'a*, *Hilkhot Nezirut* 3:13).

לֵימָא בִּפְלוּגְתָּא דְּהָנֵי תַּנָּאֵי קָמִיפַּלְגִי, דִּתְנַן: ״הֲרֵי עָלַי כִּבְכוֹר״. רַבִּי יַעֲקֹב אוֹסֵר וְרַבִּי יוֹסֵי מַתִּיר.

§ The Gemara suggests: **Let us say that** Rabbi Yehuda and Rabbi Shimon **disagree with regard to** the issue that is the subject of **the dispute between these *tanna'im*, as we learned** in a *baraita*: If one says: This object **is hereby** forbidden **to me like a firstborn,**[HB] **Rabbi Ya'akov prohibits** the individual from deriving benefit from the object, as he holds that a vow of this sort is valid. **And Rabbi Yosei permits** it, because the sanctity of a firstborn is not the result of a vow or sanctification. Rather, it is sacred of its own accord, and therefore its forbidden status cannot be extended by means of a vow to other items.

מַאי לָאו, רַבִּי יְהוּדָה סָבַר לָהּ כְּרַבִּי יַעֲקֹב, דְּאָמַר: לָא בָּעֵינַן דָּבָר הַנִּידָּר, וְרַבִּי שִׁמְעוֹן סָבַר לָהּ כְּרַבִּי יוֹסֵי, דְּאָמַר: בָּעֵינַן דָּבָר הַנִּידָּר?

What, is it not the case that **Rabbi Yehuda holds in accordance with** the opinion of **Rabbi Ya'akov, who said** that in order for a vow to take effect, **we do not require** one to extend the forbidden status of **an item** rendered forbidden by means of **a vow?** Consequently, just as one can render an object forbidden by extending to it the sanctity of a firstborn animal, one can become a nazirite by accepting upon himself the status of Samson, whose prohibitions were not established by a vow. **And Rabbi Shimon holds in accordance with** the opinion of **Rabbi Yosei, who said** that in order for a vow to take effect, **we do require** one to extend the forbidden status of **an item** rendered forbidden by means of **a vow.** Consequently, one cannot become a nazirite by accepting upon himself the status of Samson.

לָא, דְּכוּלֵּי עָלְמָא בָּעֵינַן דָּבָר הַנִּידָּר, וְשָׁאנֵי גַּבֵּי בְּכוֹר דִּכְתִיב בֵּיהּ ״לַה׳״ לְרַבּוֹת אֶת הַבְּכוֹר.

The Gemara responds: **No,** it can be explained **that everyone** agrees[N] that **we require** one to extend the forbidden status of **an item** rendered forbidden by means of **a vow.**[H] **And** according to Rabbi Ya'akov, the *halakha* **is different with regard to a firstborn, as it is written about** this in the verse pertaining to vows: "When a man vows a vow **to the Lord**" (Numbers 30:3). This comes **to include the firstborn** and teach that since the firstborn is consecrated, its status is comparable to animals designated as offerings by means of a vow, and one can extend its forbidden status to another item.

וְרַבִּי יוֹסֵי אָמַר לָךְ: הַהוּא ״לַה׳״ מִיבָּעֵי לֵיהּ לְרַבּוֹת חַטָּאת וְאָשָׁם.

And Rabbi Yosei could have **said to you** in response that **he needs** that expression: **"To the Lord," to include a sin-offering and a guilt-offering.** One may not obligate himself to bring these offerings by means of a vow. They are brought only when one becomes liable due to a transgression. Nevertheless, one can take a vow by extending to another item the forbidden status of a sin-offering or guilt-offering.

וּמָה רָאִיתָ לְרַבּוֹת חַטָּאת וְאָשָׁם וּלְהוֹצִיא אֶת הַבְּכוֹר? מְרַבֶּה אֲנִי חַטָּאת וְאָשָׁם – שֶׁכֵּן מַתְפִּיסָן בְּנֶדֶר, וּמוֹצִיא אֲנִי אֶת הַבְּכוֹר, שֶׁאֵין מַתְפִּיסוֹ בְּנֶדֶר.

The Gemara questions Rabbi Yosei's explanation: **And what did you see** that indicated to you **to include a sin-offering and a guilt-offering and to exclude a firstborn?** The Gemara answers: **I include a sin-offering and a guilt-offering,**[H] **as one grants** consecrated status to the animals designated for these offerings **by** means **of a vow,** i.e., the act of designating specific animals for these offerings is comparable to taking a vow. **And I exclude a firstborn, as one does not grant it** consecrated status **by** means **of a vow.**

וְרַבִּי יַעֲקֹב אָמַר לָךְ: בְּכוֹר נַמִי מַתְפִּיסוֹ בְּנֶדֶר הוּא. דְּתַנְיָא: שֶׁל בֵּית רַבֵּינוּ אָמְרוּ: מִנַּיִן לְנוֹלָד לוֹ בְּכוֹר בְּתוֹךְ עֶדְרוֹ שֶׁמִּצְוָה עָלָיו לְהַקְדִּישׁוֹ – שֶׁנֶּאֱמַר ״הַזָּכָר תַּקְדִּישׁ״.

And Rabbi Ya'akov could have **said to you** in response: **Also** in the case of **a firstborn, one grants it** consecrated status **by** means **of a vow, as it is taught** in a *baraita*: The Sages **of the house of our Rabbi,** i.e., Rabbi Yehuda HaNasi, **said: From where** is it derived **that when a firstborn** male animal **is born in one's herd,**[H] there is **a mitzva for him to consecrate it,** although it is consecrated from the time it is born? **As it is stated:** "All firstborns **males** that are born to your herd and to your flock **you shall sanctify**" (Deuteronomy 15:19).

וְרַבִּי יוֹסֵי אָמַר לָךְ: נְהִי דְּמִצְוָה לְהַקְדִּישׁוֹ, אִי לָא מַקְדִּישׁ לֵיהּ, מִי לָא קָדוֹשׁ?

And Rabbi Yosei could have **said to you** in response: **Granted that** there is **a mitzva to consecrate it.** But **if he does not consecrate it, is it not consecrated** of its own accord? Since a firstborn is forbidden principally because of its inherent sanctity and not because of a vow, one cannot express a vow by extending a firstborn's forbidden status to another item.

HALAKHA

This object is hereby prohibited to me like a firstborn – הֲרֵי עָלַי כִּבְכוֹר: If one declares an object forbidden to himself like a firstborn animal, it is permitted for him to use the object. The forbidden status of a firstborn cannot be extended to other items because its forbidden status is not initiated by man. This is consistent with the principle that the *halakha* is in accordance with Rabbi Yosei's opinion when he disagrees with a colleague (Rambam *Sefer Hafla'a*, *Hilkhot Nedarim* 1:13).

We require one to extend the forbidden status of an item rendered forbidden by a vow – בָּעֵינַן דָּבָר הַנִּידָּר: The basic vow stated in the Torah refers to a statement through which one renders an item forbidden to himself by extending to it the forbidden status of another item that is already forbidden by a vow. An example is in the case of one who says: This is forbidden to me like an offering, as the process of consecrating an animal as an offering is a type of vow (Rambam *Sefer Hafla'a*, *Hilkhot Nedarim* 1:9; *Shulḥan Arukh*, *Yoreh De'a* 204:1–2).

I include a sin-offering and a guilt-offering – מְרַבֶּה אֲנִי חַטָּאת וְאָשָׁם: If one says: This food is like a sin-offering to me, or: This food is like a guilt-offering to me, the food is forbidden to him. A sin-offering and guilt-offering are comparable to items forbidden by a vow. Although one cannot voluntarily vow to bring these offerings, he can render himself liable to bring them by vowing to be a nazirite. All the more so can one can take a vow by extending the forbidden status of other offerings, such as a burnt-offering or a peace-offering, which one can volunteer to bring via a vow (Rambam *Sefer Hafla'a*, *Hilkhot Nedarim* 1:10).

When a firstborn animal is born in one's herd, etc. – לְנוֹלָד לוֹ בְּכוֹר בְּתוֹךְ עֶדְרוֹ וכו׳: It is a mitzva to pronounce one's firstborn kosher animal to be consecrated, in accordance with the opinion of Rabbi Yehuda HaNasi. However, if one failed to consecrate his firstborn animal, it is consecrated automatically (Rambam *Sefer Korbanot*, *Hilkhot Bekhorot* 1:4; *Shulḥan Arukh*, *Yoreh De'a* 306:1).

BACKGROUND

Firstborn – בְּכוֹר: The firstborn male offspring of a cow, sheep, or goat belonging to a Jew is consecrated from birth. It must be given to a priest to be sacrificed on the altar in the Temple, and its meat is then eaten by the priests and their families (Numbers 18:17–18). If a firstborn animal develops a physical blemish that disqualified it from being sacrificed as an offering, it may be slaughtered and eaten like any other non-sacred kosher animal. Nevertheless, it still has to be given to a priest.

It is prohibited to intentionally inflict a disqualifying blemish on a firstborn animal, and it may not be used for any mundane purpose even if it is blemished. It is prohibited to work the animal, and its fleece may not be used. Since the destruction of the Second Temple, a firstborn animal continues to be considered consecrated. However, since it cannot be sacrificed in the Temple and it may be slaughtered only if it has a marked disqualifying blemish, various halakhic devices are employed to restrict the classification of animals as firstborn and to permit their slaughter as non-sacred animals after they acquire disqualifying blemishes.

NOTES

That everyone agrees, etc. – דְּכוּלֵּי עָלְמָא וכו׳: Two explanations of this passage are offered by the Meiri. According to one opinion, the term everyone includes all the Sages mentioned in this passage, i.e., Rabbi Yehuda, Rabbi Shimon, Rabbi Ya'akov, and Rabbi Yosei. This assumes that Samson is considered to have been rendered a nazirite through a vow (*Tosafot*; Rabbeinu Peretz; Rosh; Rabbeinu Azriel, cited in *Shita Mekubbetzet*). Alternatively, everyone includes only Rabbi Ya'akov and Rabbi Yosei. However, Rabbi Yehuda, who argues that a vow takes effect if one declares that he will be a nazirite like Samson, holds that one can extend the forbidden status of an item whose own forbidden status was not caused by a vow (*Shita Mekubbetzet*).

גַּבֵּי נָזִיר נַמִי, הָכְתִיב ״לַה׳״.

The Gemara asks: Both Rabbi Ya'akov and Rabbi Yosei agree that the phrase "to the Lord" indicates that one can take a vow by associating the object of his vow with an item whose prohibition does not stem from a vow. **With regard to a nazirite as well,**[N] **isn't it written:** "Shall clearly utter a vow, the vow of a nazirite, to consecrate himself **to the Lord**" (Numbers 6:2)? Why doesn't Rabbi Shimon derive from this verse that one can become a nazirite by accepting the naziriteship of Samson, despite the fact that Samson did not accept his naziriteship by means of a vow?

הַהוּא מִיבָּעֵי לֵיהּ לְכִדְתַנְיָא: אָמַר שִׁמְעוֹן הַצַּדִּיק: מִיָּמַי לֹא אָכַלְתִּי אֲשַׁם נָזִיר טָמֵא, חוּץ מֵאָדָם אֶחָד שֶׁבָּא אֵלַי מִן הַדָּרוֹם, יְפֵה עֵינַיִם וְטוֹב רוֹאִי, וּקְווּצּוֹתָיו סְדוּרוֹת לוֹ תַּלְתַּלִּים. אָמַרְתִּי לוֹ: בְּנִי, מָה רָאִיתָ לְשַׁחֵת שֵׂעָר נָאֶה זֶה?

The Gemara answers: **That** phrase **is required by him for that which is taught in a** ***baraita*****: Shimon HaTzaddik**[P] **said: In all my days** as a priest, **I never ate the guilt-offering of a ritually impure nazirite,**[N] apart from the offering of **one man who came to me from the South,**[B] who had **beautiful eyes and a fine countenance, and his locks were arranged in curls. I said to him: My son, what did you see** to become a nazirite, which would force you **to destroy this beautiful hair,** as a nazirite must cut off all his hair at the conclusion of his term?

אָמַר לִי: רוֹעֶה הָיִיתִי לְאָבִי בְּעִירִי, וְהָלַכְתִּי לִשְׁאוֹב מַיִם מִן הַמַּעְיָין, וְנִסְתַּכַּלְתִּי בַּבָּבוּאָה שֶׁלִּי, וּפָחַז יִצְרִי עָלַי וּבִיקֵּשׁ לְטוֹרְדֵנִי מִן הָעוֹלָם. אָמַרְתִּי לוֹ: רֵיקָה. מִפְּנֵי מָה אַתָּה מִתְגָּאֶה בְּעוֹלָם שֶׁאֵינוֹ שֶׁלְּךָ, שֶׁסּוֹפְךָ לִהְיוֹת רִמָּה וְתוֹלֵעָה? הָעֲבוֹדָה שֶׁאֲגַלֵּחֲךָ לַשָּׁמַיִם.

He said to me: I was a shepherd for my father in my town, and I went to draw water from the spring, and I looked at my reflection in the water. **And my evil inclination quickly rose against me and sought to drive me**[N] **from the world. I said to** my evil inclination: **Empty one! For what reason are you proud in a world that is not yours, as your end is to be maggots and worms** when you die. I swear by **the Temple service that I will** become a nazirite and **shave you for the sake of Heaven.**

עָמַדְתִּי וּנְשַׁקְתִּיו עַל רֹאשׁוֹ. אָמַרְתִּי לוֹ: כְּמוֹתְךָ יִרְבּוּ נְזִירִים בְּיִשְׂרָאֵל, עָלֶיךָ הַכָּתוּב אוֹמֵר: ״אִישׁ...כִּי יַפְלִא לִנְדֹּר נֶדֶר נָזִיר לְהַזִּיר לַה׳״.

Shimon HaTzaddik relates: When I heard his response, **I arose and kissed him on his head,** and **said to him: May there be more nazirites like you in Israel,**[H] whose intentions are noble, and who would not regret their vow of naziriteship even if they became impure. **With regard to you the verse states: "When either a man** or a woman **shall clearly utter a vow, the vow of a nazirite, to consecrate himself to the Lord"** (Numbers 6:2). The verse speaks of a vow that is not undertaken out of anger or spite, but purely for the sake of God. The phrase "to the Lord" in this context means: For the sake of Heaven. It cannot be used to teach that if one declares his intention to become a nazirite like Samson, his statement constitutes a nazirite vow.

וְשִׁמְשׁוֹן לָאו נָזִיר הֲוָה? וְהָכְתִיב ״כִּי נְזִיר אֱלֹהִים יִהְיֶה הַנַּעַר מִן הַבָּטֶן״! הָתָם מַלְאָךְ הוּא דְּקָאָמַר.

The Gemara challenges the assumption that Samson's naziriteship was not accepted through a vow: **And was Samson not a nazirite**[N] whose naziriteship was accepted by a vow? **Isn't it written: "For the child shall be a nazirite**[N] **of God from the womb"** (Judges 13:5)? The Gemara answers: **There it was the angel who spoke.** Samson's nazirite status did not stem from a vow uttered by a human being.

NOTES

With regard to a nazirite as well, etc. – גַּבֵּי נָזִיר נַמִי וכו׳: The Gemara's question is as follows: Since the verse states "to the Lord," why is it necessary for one to extend the forbidden status of an item forbidden by a vow (Commentary on *Nazir*)? According to this opinion, the Gemara's question applies to both Rabbi Ya'akov and Rabbi Yosei. *Tosafot* explain that the question is referring to Rabbi Ya'akov's opinion, and just as he holds that the phrase "to the Lord," written with regard to a regular vow, includes a firstborn, here too, it should include a nazirite like Samson with regard to naziriteship.

I never ate the guilt-offering of a ritually impure nazirite – לֹא אָכַלְתִּי אֲשַׁם נָזִיר טָמֵא: The reason for this policy was that he was concerned that many people who took nazirite vows did so impetuously. In the case of one who became impure and would therefore have to start his term of naziriteship from the beginning, there was even greater concern that he would regret his initial vow. Since regret can serve as a basis for nullifying a vow, Shimon HaTzaddik considered the nazirite vow as though it were almost nullified, in which case the offering would be unnecessary and invalid.

And sought to drive me, etc. – וּבִיקֵּשׁ לְטוֹרְדֵנִי וכו׳: It is explained in the Meiri on tractate *Nedarim* (9b) that once the youth realized how beautiful he was, his evil inclination tempted him with lust for women. The explanation found in the *Arukh* is that the evil inclination tempted him to engage in homosexual relations. According to the Maharsha on tractate *Nedarim* (9b), when this person perceived his own beauty, he considered it beneath his dignity to continue working as a lowly shepherd, despite the fact that abandoning this work would cause dishonor to his parents. By contrast, some commentaries maintain that he was tempted to worship himself, as a form of idolatry (Rabbeinu Azriel and Ritz, cited in *Shita Mekubbetzet*).

And was Samson not a nazirite – וְשִׁמְשׁוֹן לָא הֲוָה נָזִיר: In other words, although Samson himself did not take a nazirite vow, perhaps his father understood from the angel that he must declare his son a nazirite, as the Gemara (28b) explains that one can take a nazirite vow on behalf of his son (*Tosafot*). Alternately, perhaps Samson decided to accept his naziriteship upon himself in the form of a vow (Rabbeinu Azriel, cited in *Shita Mekubbetzet*).

For the child shall be a nazirite, etc. – כִּי נְזִיר אֱלֹהִים יִהְיֶה הַנַּעַר וכו׳: Some commentaries claim that Rabbeinu Azriel had a slightly different version of this text, in which the Gemara cites a verse spoken by Samson himself: "For I am a nazirite to God" (Judges 16:17). This indicates that he was a proper nazirite. These commentaries reject this explanation however, since here too, Samson is not uttering a vow but merely recounting what the angel said to his mother.

BACKGROUND

The South – הַדָּרוֹם: This is a reference to the southern part of Eretz Yisrael. In the time of Shimon HaTzaddik, when most of the Jewish population of Eretz Yisrael was in Judea, the South was a term for the southern part of that region, south of Hebron and adjacent to the northern border of Edom.

PERSONALITIES

Shimon HaTzaddik – שִׁמְעוֹן הַצַּדִּיק: Shimon HaTzaddik, or Shimon the righteous, is the first Sage mentioned in the chain of transmission in tractate *Avot* (1:2). He is described there as one of the remnants of the Great Assembly. According to Josephus, his full name was Shimon ben Ḥonyo ben Yadua. Based on the few mentions of him in the Talmud, it seems that he was the High Priest during the beginning of Greek rule in Eretz Yisrael and was the one who received Alexander of Macedon when he came to conquer Eretz Yisrael. Several tales are told about him in Josephus's *Antiquities*, and he is praised at the end of the book of Ben Sira. It is possible that ben Sira had contact with Shimon HaTzaddik. That book also describes how Shimon HaTzaddik came out of the Holy of Holies on Yom Kippur, a description later inserted into the liturgy of Yom Kippur. Ben Sira further relates how Shimon HaTzaddik rebuilt the ruins of Jerusalem and initiated the building of the walls of the Temple. He is lauded in the Jerusalem Talmud for his righteousness and piety, and the *Tosefta* (*Sota* 13:8) states that after him the priests in the Temple would no longer say God's ineffable name in the priestly blessing, since the Sages did not think that the people were worthy of it.

HALAKHA

May there be more nazirites like you in Israel, etc. – כְּמוֹתְךָ יִרְבּוּ נְזִירִים וכו׳: If one undertakes a vow in order to improve his character and correct his ways, it is considered praiseworthy. Examples of this include: A glutton who renders meat forbidden to him, a drunkard who takes a vow rendering wine forbidden to him, and one who is proud of his beauty and undertakes naziriteship. However, it is inadvisable to take many vows. It is preferable to improve one's character without the use of a vow (Rambam *Sefer Hafla'a*, *Hilkhot Nedarim* 13:23–24; *Shulḥan Arukh*, *Yoreh De'a* 203:7).

וּמְנָלַן דְּאִיטַּמֵּי לְמֵתִים? אִילֵימָא מִדִּכְתִיב "בִּלְחִי הַחֲמוֹר הִכֵּיתִי אֶלֶף אִישׁ" – דִּילְמָא גְּרוּיֵי גָּרֵי בְּהוּ, וְלָא נָגַע בְּהוּ!

The Gemara asks: **And from where do we** derive **that** Samson **became impure from corpses? If we say** it is **from** the fact **that it is written:** "And Samson said: **With the jawbone of an ass,**[N] **I smote a thousand men"** (Judges 15:16), **perhaps he thrust** the jawbone **at them**[N] **but did not touch them,** and he remained pure.

אֶלָּא מֵהָכָא "וַיַּךְ מֵהֶם שְׁלֹשִׁים אִישׁ וַיִּקַּח אֶת חֲלִיצוֹתָם". דִּילְמָא אַשְׁלַחִינוּן בְּרֵישָׁא וַהֲדַר קַטְלִינַן? "וַיַּךְ...וַיִּקַּח" כְּתִיב.

Rather, it is derived **from here: "And he smote thirty men of them, and took their garments"** (Judges 14:19). Since he stripped the clothes off the dead he must have come into contact with them. The Gemara counters: **Perhaps he stripped them first and afterward killed them.** The Gemara responds: **It is written: "And he smote…and took,"** in that order, indicating that first he killed them and then he took their clothing.

וְדִילְמָא גּוֹסְסִין שַׁוְּינַן! אֶלָּא, גְּמָרָא גְּמִירִי לַהּ.

The Gemara asks: **But perhaps** he mortally wounded them and thereby **caused them** to be in the process of **dying,**[N] and he then took their clothes before they died so that he would not touch their corpses. **Rather,** it must be concluded that **it is learned as a tradition**[N] that Samson would become impure from corpses.

וְנָזִיר עוֹלָם הֵיכָא כְּתִיב. דְּתַנְיָא, רַבִּי אוֹמֵר: אַבְשָׁלוֹם נְזִיר עוֹלָם הָיָה, שֶׁנֶּאֱמַר "וַיְהִי מִקֵּץ אַרְבָּעִים שָׁנָה וַיֹּאמֶר אַבְשָׁלוֹם אֶל הַמֶּלֶךְ אֵלְכָה נָּא וַאֲשַׁלֵּם אֶת נִדְרִי אֲשֶׁר נָדַרְתִּי לַה׳ בְּחֶבְרוֹן". וּמְגַלֵּחַ אֶחָד לִשְׁנֵים עָשָׂר חֹדֶשׁ – שֶׁנֶּאֱמַר "וַיְהִי מִקֵּץ יָמִים לְיָמִים".

§ The Gemara clarifies a *halakha* taught in the mishna: **And where is the concept of a permanent nazirite written?**[N] **As it is taught** in a *baraita*: **Rabbi** Yehuda HaNasi **says: Absalom was a permanent nazirite, as it is stated: "And it came to pass at the end of forty years, that Absalom said to the king: I pray to you, let me go and pay my vow,**[N] **which I have vowed to the Lord, in Hebron"**[N] (II Samuel 15:7). **And he cut** his hair **once** every **twelve months, as it is stated:** "And when he polled his head, **now it was at every year's [*yamim*] end** that he polled it; because the hair was heavy on him" (II Samuel 14:26).

NOTES

With the jawbone of an ass, etc. – **בִּלְחִי הַחֲמוֹר וכו׳**: The Rosh explains that this suggestion can easily be countered by saying that since Samson acted in self-defense, as the Philistines came to kill him, he was certainly permitted to become impure. He explains that the Gemara raises this possibility only as an introduction to the second, more persuasive answer.

He thrust [*garuyei garei*] the jawbone at them – **גְּרוּיֵי גָּרֵי בְּהוּ**: Samson did not kill them through direct contact but by throwing the bone at each one like an arrow, as the Aramaic word for arrow, *geira*, is very similar to the phrase here, *garuyei garei* (*Tosafot*). Others, following an alternative version of the text, explain that he cut them with the jawbone (Commentary on *Nazir*) or he struck them with it but did not touch them (*Arukh*).

Caused them to be in the process of dying – **גּוֹסְסִין שַׁוְּינַן**: Even according to the opinion that it is prohibited for a nazirite to touch someone who is dying, it is possible to explain that the Gemara here does not mean that the Philistines were actually in the final stages of dying when Samson touched them. It is also possible to differentiate between someone who is dying at the hands of a man and someone who is dying from natural causes, and perhaps a nazirite is prohibited from touching only the latter (Rosh; see *Tosafot*).

It is learned as a tradition – **גְּמָרָא גְּמִירִי לַהּ**: *Tosafot* explain that it is a tradition that Samson actually killed the Philistines before removing their garments. Alternatively, the Maharatz Ḥayyut explains that there is a tradition that it was permitted for Samson to become impure from the dead. This is also implied by the Rambam.

And where is the concept of a permanent nazirite written – **וְנָזִיר עוֹלָם הֵיכָא כְּתִיב**: The basic concept of a permanent nazirite does not require a source. Just as one can undertake a vow of naziriteship for a particular length of time, he can vow to be a nazirite forever. Rather, the verses cited by the Gemara serve to teach the details of the *halakhot* of this type of nazirite. It is explained in the Commentary on *Nazir* that the Gemara is asking about the source for the *halakha* that a permanent nazirite can cut his hair and bring offerings even while he is a nazirite. According to Rabbeinu Peretz, the Gemara is discussing the fact that a permanent nazirite may shorten his hair. This is different from a regular nazirite, who may not cut his hair at all during the term of his naziriteship, and when his term is completed he must shave off all of his hair.

My vow – **אֶת נִדְרִי**: *Tosafot* explain that according to Rabbi Yehuda HaNasi, a generic vow refers to a nazirite vow, which is especially logical in light of the fact that Absalom grew his hair. Another explanation is that the Sages apparently had a tradition that this vow of Absalom's was that of a permanent nazirite (Meiri).

In Hebron – **בְּחֶבְרוֹן**: The plain meaning of the verse is that he went to Hebron to fulfill his vow. The Gemara (*Temura* 14b) asks how he could have gone to Hebron to bring offerings. The conclusion of the Gemara there is that this was during the period when it was permitted to bring offerings on private altars.

וְיָלֵיף ״יָמִים״ ״יָמִים״ מִבָּתֵּי עָרֵי חוֹמָה, מָה הָתָם שְׁנֵים עָשָׂר חוֹדֶשׁ – אַף כָּאן שְׁנֵים עָשָׂר חוֹדֶשׁ.

And Rabbi Yehuda HaNasi **derives** the meaning of the term *yamim* stated with regard to Absalom based upon a verbal analogy from the word ***yamim*** that appears in the context **of houses of walled cities,** where it states: "For a full year [*yamim*] he shall have the right of redemption" (Leviticus 25:29). **Just as there,** in the case of walled cities, the term *yamim* means **twelve months,** as the verse states immediately afterward: "Within the space of a full year" (Leviticus 25:30), **so too here,** in the case of Absalom, the term *yamim* means **twelve months.**[H]

רַבִּי נְהוֹרַאי אוֹמֵר: מְגַלֵּחַ אַחַת לִשְׁלֹשִׁים יוֹם. רַבִּי יוֹסֵי אוֹמֵר: מְגַלֵּחַ מֵעֶרֶב שַׁבָּת לְעֶרֶב שַׁבָּת, שֶׁכֵּן מָצִינוּ בִּבְנֵי מְלָכִים שֶׁמְּגַלְּחִים מֵעֶרֶב שַׁבָּת לְעֶרֶב שַׁבָּת.

Rabbi Nehorai says: Absalom **cut** his hair **once** every **thirty days.**[N] **Rabbi Yosei says: He cut** his hair **from one Shabbat eve to** another **Shabbat eve, as we find that the sons of kings**[N] **cut** their hair **from one Shabbat eve to** another **Shabbat eve.**

מַאי טַעְמָא דְּרַבִּי – יָלֵיף מִבָּתֵּי עָרֵי חוֹמָה, וְהָא רַבִּי הוּא דְּאָמַר: אֵין ״יָמִים״ פְּחוּתִין מִשְּׁנַיִם!

The Gemara asks: **What is the reasoning of Rabbi** Yehuda HaNasi? He **derives** the meaning of the verse concerning Absalom **from** the verse concerning **houses of walled cities. But isn't it Rabbi** Yehuda HaNasi himself **who said** that one may not redeem his house until it has been in the buyer's possession for at least two days, as the word *yamim* does **not** refer to **fewer than two** days? This demonstrates that Rabbi Yehuda HaNasi understands the word *yamim* in the case of walled city houses as referring to a period of two days rather than a year. How then can he employ a verbal analogy from houses of walled cities to derive that the word *yamim* in the case of Absalom indicates a period of twelve months?

הַאי גְּזֵירָה שָׁוָה מִשּׁוּם כּוֹבֶד גָּמֵיר, וּבִשְׁנֵי יָמִים לֵיכָּא כּוֹבֶד.

The Gemara answers: **He learned this verbal analogy**[B] because the verse states that Absalom would trim his hair **due to** its **weight** (II Samuel 14:26), **and in two days there is no** significant **weight** added to the hair. Consequently, the term *yamim* cannot be understood to mean two days in the case of Absalom.

וְאֵימָא שְׁתֵּי שָׁנִים, דִּכְתִיב ״וַיְהִי מִקֵּץ שְׁנָתַיִם יָמִים״! דָּנִין ״יָמִים״ שֶׁאֵין עִמָּהֶן שָׁנִים מִ״יָּמִים״ שֶׁאֵין עִמָּהֶן שָׁנִים, וְאַל יוֹכִיחַ זֶה שֶׁיֵּשׁ עִמּוֹ שָׁנִים.

The Gemara asks: **But say** that *yamim* means **two years, as it is written: "And it came to pass at the end of two years of days** [*yamim*]" (Genesis 41:1). The Gemara rejects this: **We derive** the meaning of the term *yamim* in a case **where it does not have** the term **years** mentioned **with it,** as in the case of Absalom, **from** another usage of the term ***yamim* that does not have** the term **years** mentioned **with it,** i.e., the verse about houses of walled cities. **And this** usage of the term *yamim* **that does have** the term **years** mentioned **with it will not prove** otherwise.

וְאֵימָא שְׁלֹשִׁים יוֹם, דִּכְתִיב ״עַד חֹדֶשׁ יָמִים״! דָּנִין ״יָמִים״ שֶׁאֵין עִמָּהֶם חֳדָשִׁים מִ״יָּמִים״ שֶׁאֵין עִמָּהֶם חֳדָשִׁים, וְאַל יוֹכִיחַ זֶה שֶׁיֵּשׁ עִמּוֹ חֳדָשִׁים.

The Gemara asks: **But say** that *yamim* means **thirty days, as it is written: "But a month of days** [*yamim*]" (Numbers 11:20). The Gemara rejects this: **We derive** the meaning of the term ***yamim*** in a case **where it does not have** the term **months** mentioned **with it from** another usage of the term ***yamim* that does not have** the term **months** mentioned **with it. And this** usage of the term *yamim* **that does have** the term **months** mentioned **with it will not prove** otherwise.

וְאֵימָא מֵהָכָא ״מִיָּמִים יָמִימָה״ וגו׳! דָּנִין ״יָמִים״ מִ״יָּמִים״. וְאֵין דָּנִין ״יָמִים״ מִ״יָּמִימָה״.

The Gemara asks: **But say** that Rabbi Yehuda HaNasi should have derived the meaning of the term *yamim* **from here:** "The daughters of Israel went **from time to time** [*yamim yamima*] to lament the daughter of Jephthah the Gileadite four days in a year" (Judges 11:40). This teaches that the daughters of Israel would go four times a year, each time for one day, to lament her, in which case *yamim yamima* means once every three months. The Gemara rejects this: **We derive** the meaning of the term ***yamim*** **from** another usage of the term ***yamim*,** **and we do not derive** the meaning of the term ***yamim*** **from** a case where the word *yamim* is used in conjunction with the term ***yamima*.**

HALAKHA

So too here, the term *yamim* means twelve months – אַף כָּאן שְׁנֵים עָשָׂר חוֹדֶשׁ: A permanent nazirite may trim his hair with a razor once every twelve months if it becomes too heavy for him, as derived from the case of Absalom (Rambam *Sefer Hafla'a*, *Hilkhot Nezirut* 3:12).

NOTES

Once every thirty days – אַחַת לִשְׁלֹשִׁים יוֹם: Some explain that the dispute cited in the *baraita* pertains only to the conduct of Absalom. However, with regard to the *halakha* itself, they all agree that a permanent nazirite may cut his hair once a month (Commentary on *Nazir*). Others explain that it is unlikely that they would have argued only about the case of Absalom. Rather, the dispute pertains to the *halakhot* of a permanent nazirite in general, and the case of Absalom is cited only as evidence (*Mishne LaMelekh*). The statement of Rabbi Yehuda HaNasi in the Jerusalem Talmud seems to support this conclusion.

As we find that the sons of kings – שֶׁכֵּן מָצִינוּ בִּבְנֵי מְלָכִים: In other words, it is known that the custom of princes is to have their hair cut on a weekly basis. Rabbeinu Azriel, cited in *Shita Mekubbetzet*, points out that this is referring only to the king's sons, whereas the king himself cuts his hair every day. Other commentaries add that although the verse states that his hair was heavy for him, and hair does not grow that much in a week, since a prince is used to cutting his hair every week, if he were to fail to do so his hair would feel heavy to him.

BACKGROUND

Verbal analogy – גְּזֵירָה שָׁוָה: This is a fundamental talmudic principle of biblical interpretation, appearing in all standard lists of exegetical principles. If the same word or phrase appears in two places in the Torah, and a certain *halakha* is explicitly stated in one of these places, it may be inferred on the basis of a verbal analogy that the same *halakha* must apply in the other case as well. Consequently, the inferences drawn on the basis of verbal analogy rely on verbal identity rather than on conceptual similarity. For example, the Torah states, concerning those convicted of certain types of sorcery: "Shall surely be put to death; they shall stone them with stones; their blood shall be upon them" (Leviticus 20:27). Since this verse uses the expression "their blood shall be upon them" when speaking of death by stoning, the Talmud infers by verbal analogy that in all cases where this expression is used, capital punishment is to be inflicted by stoning. Generally, inferences are drawn through verbal analogy only if the same word or phrase appears in both of the verses being compared, although a verbal analogy is occasionally drawn even if the words being compared are not identical, provided that their meanings are similar.

וּמַאי נָפְקָא מִינָּהּ? וְהָא תָּנָא דְּבֵי רַבִּי יִשְׁמָעֵאל: "וְשָׁב הַכֹּהֵן", "וּבָא הַכֹּהֵן" – זוֹ הִיא שִׁיבָה זוֹ הִיא בִּיאָה!

The Gemara raises a difficulty: **And what is the difference** between *yamim* and *yamima*? **Didn't the school of Rabbi Yishmael teach** a verbal analogy with regard to leprosy of houses between the words **"and the priest shall return [*veshav*]"** (Leviticus 14:39) and the words **"and the priest shall come [*uva*]"** (Leviticus 14:44)? It is derived from this that just as **this is** the *halakha* with regard to **returning,** i.e., the priest returns after seven days, **this is** the *halakha* with regard to **coming,** which is also after seven days. Just as the Hebrew words *veshav* and *uva* can be used in a verbal analogy, certainly two words with a less pronounced variation, i.e., *yamim* and *yamima,* can be used to teach a verbal analogy.

הָנֵי מִילֵּי – הֵיכָא דְּלֵיכָּא דְּדָמֵי לֵיהּ, אֲבָל הֵיכָא דְּאִיכָּא דְּדָמֵי לֵיהּ – מִדְּדָמֵי לֵיהּ יָלְפִינַן.

The Gemara responds: **This applies** only **where there are no** terms **that are identical to it. However, where there are** terms **that are identical to it, we derive** the meaning of a term **from** the usage of terms **that are identical to it** rather than from the usage of terms that are merely similar.

אִיכָּא דְּאָמְרִי: מְנָא יָדְעִינַן דְּכָל תְּלָתָא יַרְחִין חַד זִימְנָא? דִּילְמָא אַרְבָּעָה זִימְנֵי בְּשַׁתָּא, (אִי נַמִי,) אַרְבָּעָה יַרְחִין חַד זִימְנָא, תְּרֵין יַרְחִין בְּחַד זִימְנָא.

Some say that the reason the *halakha* is not derived from *yamim yamima* is because the time period to which it refers is unclear: **From where do we know that** they would lament Jephthah's daughter **once every three months,** at fixed intervals? **Perhaps** they would lament her **four times a year,** in irregular intervals. **Alternatively,** it might have taken place in regular but uneven intervals, e.g., after **four months** they would visit **one time,**[N] and then after **two months** they would visit **one time,** and then they would visit again after a four-month interval and again after a two-month interval.

רַבִּי נְהוֹרַאי אוֹמֵר מְגַלֵּחַ אַחַת לִשְׁלֹשִׁים יוֹם. מַאי טַעְמָא גַּבֵּי כֹּהֲנִים – מִשּׁוּם דְּאִיכָּא כּוֹבֶד, הָכָא נַמִי אִיכָּא כּוֹבֶד.

It was taught in the *baraita* that **Rabbi Nehorai says** that Absalom **cut** his hair **once every thirty days.** The Gemara explains the basis for this opinion: **What is the reason** that **with regard to priests,**[N] the *halakha* is that they must cut their hair every thirty days? It is **because** after that interval **there is** noticeable **weight** to the hair. **Here, too,** in the case of Absalom, **there is** noticeable **weight** after this period of time has passed, and it is clear that Absalom cut his hair due to its weight, as it is stated: "Because the hair was heavy on him, therefore he polled it" (II Samuel 14:26).

רַבִּי יוֹסֵי אוֹמֵר: מְגַלֵּחַ מֵעֶרֶב שַׁבָּת לְעֶרֶב שַׁבָּת. מַאי אִיכָּא בֵּינֵיהּ לִשְׁאָר אֲחוֹהִי?

It was taught in the *baraita* that **Rabbi Yosei says:** Absalom **cut** his hair **from one Shabbat eve to** another **Shabbat eve,** as the sons of kings would cut their hair every Shabbat eve. The Gemara asks: If so, **what** difference **is there between** Absalom, who was a nazirite, **and the rest of his brothers,**[N] King David's sons, who also cut their hair once a week?

NOTES

After four months they would visit one time – אַרְבָּעָה יַרְחִין חַד זִימְנָא: The logic here is that they would travel more frequently in the summer, since it is harder to leave the house during the winter months (*Leket HaKotzerim*). Some manuscripts and other sources do not contain this sentence.

What is the reason that with regard to priests, etc. – מַאי טַעְמָא גַּבֵּי כֹּהֲנִים וכו׳: The early commentaries point out that the *halakha* that priests must cut their hair once a month is not explicitly stated in the Bible, which merely says: "And they will not let their locks grow long" (Ezekiel 44:20). Rather, it is derived through a verbal analogy between a verse pertaining to a priest and one concerning a nazirite (see *Ta'anit* 17a): Since an unspecified term of naziriteship is thirty days, it is derived that a priest cuts his hair every thirty days. That being the case, why does the Gemara derive that a permanent nazirite cuts his hair every thirty days based upon the *halakha* that applies to a priest, rather than deriving this *halakha* directly from its source, which is the case of an unspecified term of naziriteship?

Tosafot answer that Rabbi Nehorai preferred to derive the *halakhot* of a permanent nazirite from the case of a priest, whose sanctity is also permanent, rather than from the temporary sanctity of an ordinary nazirite. Other commentaries explain that this *halakha* cannot be derived from a regular nazirite, since he cuts his hair only because his term of naziriteship is completed. Rabbi Nehorai must derive the *halakha* from the case of priests, who cut their hair every month despite the fact that they retain their sanctity for longer than a month (Rosh; Rabbeinu Peretz; Rabbeinu Azriel, cited in *Shita Mekubbetzet*). Another reason given is that cutting the hair of a permanent nazirite resembles cutting the hair of a priest, since neither of them entirely shave off their hair. A regular nazirite, however, must shave his entire head (Rabbeinu Todros, cited in *Shita Mekubbetzet*).

What difference is there between Absalom and the rest of his brothers – מַאי אִיכָּא בֵּינֵיהּ לִשְׁאָר אֲחוֹהִי: *Tosafot* point out that there is an obvious difference between them, as only Absalom was required to bring offerings when he cut his hair. They answer that this question is referring to a difference with regard to cutting hair, as the Torah indicates that Absalom grew his hair longer than most people grew their hair. The Rosh notes that there were other differences even in the manner in which they were permitted to cut their hair, as Absalom was permitted to use only a razor while they were permitted to use scissors. Furthermore, he was allowed only to trim his hair, whereas they were allowed to cut it all off if they so desired. He explains that the Gemara is referring to his brothers' usual manner of cutting their hair, since they customarily used a razor and did not cut off all their hair. With regard to the observation of *Tosafot,* that an obvious difference is that only Absalom brought offerings when he cut his hair, the Rosh and Rabbeinu Azriel explain that when the Gemara states that Absalom was permitted to cut his hair only in the evening, it means to say that he was permitted to cut his hair only if he had already brought his offerings.

יוֹם טוֹב שֶׁחָל לִהְיוֹת בְּאֶמְצַע שַׁבָּת, דַּאֲחוּהִי מְגַלְּחִין, הוּא לָא מְגַלַּח. אִי נַמִי, לְגַלּוּחֵי מִן צַפְרָא דְּמַעֲלֵי שַׁבְּתָא; אֲחוּהִי מְגַלְּחִין, אִיהוּ לָא מְגַלַּח עַד פַּנְיָא.

The Gemara answers: There is a difference between them with regard to a **Festival that occurs in the middle of the week, as his brothers** would **cut** their hair in honor of the Festival, whereas **he** would **not cut** his hair. **Alternatively,** the difference between them concerns **cutting** hair **on the morning of Shabbat eve. His brothers would cut** their hair at that hour, whereas **he** would **not cut** his hair **until the evening,** shortly before Shabbat.

הָנֵי אַרְבָּעִים שָׁנָה מַאי עֲבִידְתַּיְיהוּ? רַבִּי נְהוֹרַאי אוֹמֵר מִשּׁוּם רַבִּי יְהוֹשֻׁעַ: לְקֵץ אַרְבָּעִים שָׁנָה שֶׁשָּׁאֲלוּ לָהֶן מֶלֶךְ. תָּנָא: אוֹתָהּ שָׁנָה שֶׁשָּׁאֲלוּ לָהֶן מֶלֶךְ הִיא שְׁנַת עֶשֶׂר לִשְׁמוּאֵל הָרָמָתִי.

Having mentioned in 4b the verse "and it came to pass at the end of forty years, that Absalom said unto the king" (II Samuel 15:7), the Gemara asks: With regard to **these forty years, what is their purpose** in this discussion,[N] i.e., to what time period do they refer? The Gemara answers: **Rabbi Nehorai says in the name of Rabbi Yehoshua:** It is referring **to the end of forty years,** since the Jewish people **requested for themselves a king**[N] in the days of Samuel (see I Samuel, chapter 8). It was **taught: That year when they requested for themselves a king was the tenth year** of the leadership **of Samuel the Ramathite.**

מתני׳ סְתַם נְזִירוּת שְׁלֹשִׁים יוֹם.

MISHNA In the case of **unspecified naziriteship,** where one does not state how long he wishes to be a nazirite, the term lasts for **thirty days.**[H]

גמ׳ מְנָהָנֵי מִילֵּי? אֲמַר רַב מַתָּנָא: אָמַר קְרָא "קָדוֹשׁ יִהְיֶה". "יִהְיֶה" בְּגִמַטְרִיָּא תְּלָתִין הָווּ.

GEMARA The Gemara asks: **From where are these matters** derived,[N] that an unspecified naziriteship is thirty days? In answer to this question, **Rav Mattana**[P] **said: The verse states** with regard to a nazirite: **"He shall be [*yihye*] holy"** (Numbers 6:5), and **the numerical value [*gimatriyya*]**[L] **of** the letters of the word ***yihye***[N] **is thirty.**

בַּר פַּדָּא אָמַר: כְּנֶגֶד "נָזִיר", "נִזְרוֹ" הָאֲמוּרִים בַּתּוֹרָה, שְׁלֹשִׁים חָסֵר אַחַת.

Bar Padda[P] **said:** The number of days of an unspecified naziriteship **corresponds** to the number of appearances of the words **"nazirite," "his naziriteship,"**[N] and similar terms **that are stated in the Torah** in the chapter of naziriteship (Numbers, chapter 6): **Thirty less one** times. So too, an unspecified term of naziriteship is twenty-nine days.

וְרַב מַתָּנָא נַמִי, נֵילַף מִ"נָּזִיר" "נִזְרוֹ"!

The Gemara asks: **And Rav Mattana should also derive from** the number of times that the words **"nazirite"** and **"his naziriteship"** appear, to conclude like bar Padda that an unspecified naziriteship lasts for twenty-nine days.

HALAKHA

Unspecified naziriteship lasts for thirty days – סְתַם נְזִירוּת שְׁלֹשִׁים יוֹם: One who takes a nazirite vow without further specification becomes a nazirite for thirty days (Rambam *Sefer Hafla'a, Hilkhot Nezirut* 1:1).

PERSONALITIES

Rav Mattana – רַב מַתָּנָא: Rav Mattana was among the second generation of *amora'im* in Babylonia. He was one of the important disciples of Shmuel, as we find his teacher asking him for help understanding a certain point. Rav Mattana also quotes teachings in the name of Rav. For a while he lived in the city of Paponya, where he occupied himself with the dissemination of Torah. Third-generation *amora'im* quote halakhic and aggadic teachings in his name, and there are also teachings in his name in the *midrashim* from Eretz Yisrael.

Bar Padda – בַּר פַּדָּא: Bar Padda is the Sage Rabbi Yehuda bar Pedaiah, the son of bar Kappara's sister. He was among Rabbi Yehuda HaNasi's younger disciples. Rabbi Yehuda bar Pedaiah was among the Sages of the South, living in the region of Judea. He may have lived in the town of Lod. All of the great second- and third-generation *amora'im* in Eretz Yisrael studied under his tutelage, and some of his teachings are quoted by Sages such as Rabbi Yehoshua ben Levi, Rabbi Yoḥanan, and Reish Lakish. His contributions to *halakha* and *aggada* are found throughout both the Babylonian Talmud and the Jerusalem Talmud and in *midrashim.*

LANGUAGE

Numerical value [*gimatriyya*] – גִּמַטְרִיָּא: Derived from the Greek γεωμετρία, *geometria*, which means measurement or calculation in general, although the term was later designated for a specific type of calculation, geometry. In rabbinic literature, it also refers to mathematical calculations in general, although it most commonly refers to tabulating the numerical values of the letters in a word.

NOTES

These forty years, what is their purpose in this discussion – הָנֵי אַרְבָּעִים שָׁנָה מַאי עֲבִידְתַּיְיהוּ: The verse cannot mean forty years from the start of David's reign, since David reigned for a total of only forty years, and it is clear that he continued to reign for a few years after Absalom's rebellion (see II Samuel, chapter 21). The *tanna'im* in *Seder Olam* disagree about the precise date of the rebellion. The Gemara in tractate *Temura* (14b–15a) states that David had reigned for thirty-seven years before Absalom's rebellion, but the early commentaries cite manuscripts of that Gemara that state that he had reigned for thirty-six years (see Commentary on *Nazir* and *Tosafot*).

Requested for themselves a king – שֶׁשָּׁאֲלוּ לָהֶן מֶלֶךְ: The verse mentions this date because Absalom knew that his father was destined to reign for forty years, as he did, but he mistakenly thought that these forty years should be counted from the inception of the monarchy among the Jewish people (Commentary on *Nazir*). Other early commentaries explain that the Jewish people's request for a king constituted a rebellion against God, or a rebellion against the rule of Samuel the prophet, who served as a judge over the Jewish people. Consequently, the verse links Absalom's revolt with the original rebellion of the Jewish people (Rosh; Rabbeinu Peretz). Alternatively, the verse dates the rebellion against the king from the time of the inception of the institution of Jewish monarchy (Rabbeinu Peretz, citing *Tosafot*).

From where are these matters derived – מְנָהָנֵי מִילֵּי: Only Rav Mattana provides an answer to the Gemara's question, since bar Padda's opinion that an unspecified term of naziriteship is twenty-nine days contradicts the *halakha* stated in the mishna. Other explanations of the mishna's ruling are offered in the Jerusalem Talmud. One explanation links the *yamim* stated with regard to a nazirite to the *yamim* stated in the context of a beautiful captive woman (Deuteronomy 21:13), which refers to thirty days. Alternatively, it might be derived from the verse that states with regard to a nazirite: "On the day when the days of his consecration are complete" (Numbers 6:13), since only a month can be called "complete" in days, and a month can be either thirty or twenty-nine days in the Jewish calendar (see 6b).

The numerical value of the letters of the word *yihye* – יִהְיֶה בְּגִמַטְרִיָּא: In the Rambam's Commentary on the Mishna, it is explained that according to Rav Mattana, this *halakha* is learned through a tradition transmitted to Moses from Sinai, and he is merely providing support for it with a hint from the word's numerical value. The Rosh likewise explains that this proof is merely a support, since calculating the numerical value of words is not included in the list of the thirteen exegetical principles through which *halakhot* are derived from the Torah. It is only one of the thirty-two exegetical principles that Rabbi Eliezer, son of Rabbi Yosei, uses to learn *aggada*. See Rabbi Yoshiya's comments cited in the Gemara on 6b.

Nazirite, his naziriteship, etc. – נָזִיר, נִזְרוֹ וכו׳: It is explained in the Commentary on *Nazir* that this list includes not only the words "nazirite" and "his naziriteship," but also the terms "vow" and "his vow" whenever they appear in this chapter. The full list of these terms is mentioned in the Commentary on *Nazir* and in greater detail in the Meiri. These terms actually appear thirty times in the chapter, but the verse "because his consecration [*nezer*] to God is upon his head" (Numbers 6:7) is not included in the list, since its meaning in context is crown and not naziriteship, as seen in the *Targum Onkelos* (Commentary on *Nazir*; *Tosafot*). The fact that these terms appear thirty times is also raised in the Jerusalem Talmud, where it is explained that one usage of the term nazirite is needed in order to state that the chapter is referring to a nazirite, and all of the other times that it appears are to teach the length of an unspecified term of naziriteship.

אָמַר לָךְ: הַהוּא לִדְרָשָׁה: "מִיַּיִן וְשֵׁכָר יַזִּיר" – לֶאֱסוֹר יֵין מִצְוָה כְּיֵין רְשׁוּת. "כִּי יַפְלִא לִנְדּוֹר נֶדֶר נָזִיר לְהַזִּיר" – מְלַמֵּד שֶׁהַנְּזִירוּת חָלָה עַל נְזִירוּת.

The Gemara answers: Rav Mattana could have **said to you: That** word is needed **for** a specific **exposition.** The words: **"He shall abstain [*yazir*] from wine and strong drink"** (Numbers 6:3), comes **to prohibit** a nazirite from drinking **wine** that is consumed for **a mitzva** just as he is prohibited from drinking **wine** whose consumption is **optional.** Likewise, the words: "When either man or woman **shall clearly utter a vow, the vow of a nazirite, to consecrate himself"** (Numbers 6:2), **teach that** one vow of **naziriteship takes effect where** another vow of **naziriteship** already exists.[H] For example, if one takes a vow by stating: I will be a nazirite today, and then repeats the vow, he must observe two periods of naziriteship. Consequently, since sometimes the word nazirite, in its different forms, appears in order to serve as the source of a particular exposition, the number of times it occurs does not indicate the length of an unspecified term of naziriteship.

HALAKHA

That one vow of naziriteship takes effect where another vow of naziriteship already exists – שֶׁהַנְּזִירוּת חָלָה עַל הַנְּזִירוּת: One who takes two nazirite vows must observe a term of naziriteship for thirty days, whereupon he cuts his hair, brings his offerings, and then proceeds with his second term of naziriteship. This is the case whether he declared his two vows on one occasion or at separate times (Rambam *Sefer Hafla'a, Hilkhot Nezirut* 1:6; 10).

Perek **I**
Daf **5** Amud **b**

וּבַר פַּדָּא אָמַר לָךְ: לֵיכָּא חַד מִינַּיְהוּ דְּלָאו לִדְרָשָׁא? אֶלָּא, מִדְּהַהוּא לְמִנְיָינָא – כּוּלְּהוּ נַמִי לְמִנְיָינָא.

And bar Padda could have **said to you** that although some of these verses are required for an exposition, is **there not** at least **one of them**[N] **that is not** used **for an exposition? Rather, since that** usage of the term nazirite is stated **to** indicate **the number** of days in an unspecified term of naziriteship, **all of** the other usages of the term **are also** stated **to** indicate **the number** of days[N] in an unspecified term of naziriteship in addition to the specific *halakhot* that are derived from them.

תְּנַן: סְתַם נְזִירוּת שְׁלֹשִׁים יוֹם. בִּשְׁלָמָא לְרַב מַתָּנָא – נִיחָא, אֶלָּא לְבַר פַּדָּא קַשְׁיָא!

The Gemara analyzes the opinions of Rav Mattana and bar Padda in light of the mishna and relevant *baraitot*. **We learned** in the mishna: An **unspecified naziriteship** lasts for **thirty days. Granted,** according **to Rav Mattana it works out well. However, according to bar Padda it is difficult,** since in his opinion the mishna should have stated that an unspecified naziriteship lasts for twenty-nine days.

אָמַר לָךְ בַּר פַּדָּא: אַיְּידֵי דְּאִיכָּא יוֹם תְּלָתִין, דִּמְגַלֵּחַ וּמֵבִיא קָרְבְּנוֹתָיו – מִשּׁוּם הָכִי תְּנָא שְׁלֹשִׁים.

The Gemara answers: **Bar Padda** could have **said to you:** The principal days of naziriteship are twenty-nine days. However, **since there is the thirtieth day, when** the nazirite **shaves** his hair **and brings his offerings,** and the prohibitions of naziriteship remain in effect on that day until he has brought these offerings, **due to that** reason the *tanna* **teaches** that an unspecified naziriteship lasts for **thirty** days.

תְּנַן: מִי שֶׁאָמַר "הֲרֵינִי נָזִיר" – מְגַלֵּחַ יוֹם שְׁלֹשִׁים וְאֶחָד. בִּשְׁלָמָא לְרַב מַתָּנָא – נִיחָא, אֶלָּא לְבַר פַּדָּא קַשְׁיָא!

The Gemara asks: **We learned** in a mishna (16a): **One who said: I am hereby a nazirite, shaves** his hair on **the thirty-first day. Granted,** according **to Rav Mattana** this **works out well,** since one must finish his term of naziriteship, which lasts for thirty days, before he can shave his hair. **However,** according **to bar Padda,** it is **difficult.** Why doesn't he shave his hair on the thirtieth day?

אָמַר לָךְ בַּר פַּדָּא, אֵימָא סֵיפָא: אִם גִּילַּח לְיוֹם שְׁלֹשִׁים – יָצָא. אֶלָּא סֵיפָא מְסַיְּיעָא לֵיהּ, רֵישָׁא – נַעֲשָׂה כְּאוֹמֵר "שְׁלֵימִין".

The Gemara answers: **Bar Padda** could have **said to you** in response: **Say the latter clause** of that mishna: **If he shaved** his hair **on the thirtieth day, he has fulfilled** his obligation. This indicates that the naziriteship itself lasts only twenty-nine days. **Rather, the latter clause** of that mishna certainly **supports his** opinion. As for **the first clause,** the reason a nazirite must wait until the thirty-first day in order to shave his hair *ab initio* is as follows: Since one who specifies that he is becoming a nazirite for thirty complete days may shave his hair only on the thirty-first day, the Sages ruled that even one who did not specify a time period **becomes like one who said** explicitly that he will be a nazirite for thirty **complete** days.[N] Consequently, he may shave his hair *ab initio* only after thirty days have passed.

NOTES

Is there not at least one of them – לֵיכָּא חַד מִינַּיְהוּ: Although *halakhot* are derived from some occurrences of the words nazirite and naziriteship, there is at least one occurrence that does not teach any *halakha*, and it can therefore be assumed that just as that word presumably appears in order to teach the number of days in a period of unspecified naziriteship, even the words that serve as the source of other *halakhot* also indicate the length of an unspecified naziriteship (*Tosafot*). Rabbeinu Peretz explains that since the expositions for all of the terms are not known, it is unreasonable to assume that all the words are used for derivations but those derivations are not currently known. It is far more plausible to assume that some of these words appear in order to indicate the number of days in an unspecified naziriteship. It is also impossible to count only the superfluous words, since one or more of them might be expounded in a manner unknown to us. Therefore, all the words must be included.

All of the other usages of the term are also stated to indicate the number of days – כּוּלְּהוּ נַמִי לְמִנְיָינָא: Similar disputes are recorded elsewhere (see *Sukka* 6b) with regard to the question of whether a word in the Torah that is needed to convey a *halakha* through its straightforward meaning can also be counted along with other, seemingly unnecessary usages of the word, so that the total number of times the word appears can be used to teach a *halakha*.

Becomes like one who said explicitly that he will be a nazirite for thirty complete days – נַעֲשָׂה כְּאוֹמֵר שְׁלֵימִין: Nevertheless, since he himself did not say that he was accepting naziriteship for thirty complete days, if he shaves his hair on the thirtieth day, he fulfills his obligation (Commentary on *Nazir*). *Tosafot* and the Rosh explain that according to bar Padda, who does not accept the principle that part of the day is like the entire day, even if one said that he is accepting naziriteship for thirty days, and he did not specify thirty complete days, he may shave his hair only on the thirty-first day by Torah law. The Gemara mentions the case of one who said he will be a nazirite for thirty complete days only so that it can give the same answer on behalf of Rav Mattana in the continuation of this discussion.

The Rosh explains that the reason for the rabbinic decree is that people are more accustomed to using round numbers, such as thirty, rather than twenty-nine. Similarly, the Torah speaks of forty lashes and counting fifty days of the *omer*, although the precise number is one less than that (*Leket HaKotzerim*). Consequently, people are likely to accept thirty-day terms of naziriteship. In order to avoid confusion, the Sages decreed that anyone who accepts an unspecified term of naziriteship or a twenty-nine-day term must observe a thirty-day term of naziriteship (see Commentary on *Nazir*).

HALAKHA

The legal status of part of the day is like that of an entire day – מִקְצָת הַיּוֹם כְּכוּלּוֹ: With regard to various *halakhot*, the legal status of part of a day is like that of an entire day. For example, with regard to the seventh day of mourning, once the mourner has observed the *halakhot* of mourning for the beginning of the day, it is as though he observed them for the entire day. He is not required to observe the *halakhot* of mourning for the duration of the day. The same is true with regard to the single day of mourning that must be observed when one receives the news that his relative died more than thirty days earlier (Rambam *Sefer Shofetim*, *Hilkhot Evel* 7:2–3, 10:5; *Shulḥan Arukh*, *Yoreh De'a* 402:1, 6).

וּלְרַב מַתָּנָא קַשְׁיָא סֵיפָא! קָסָבַר: מִקְצָת הַיּוֹם כְּכוּלּוֹ.

The Gemara asks: **And for Rav Mattana, the latter clause** of the mishna is **difficult,** since it states that one who shaves his hair on the thirtieth day has fulfilled his obligation, whereas Rav Mattana claims that his naziriteship is not yet complete at that time. The Gemara answers: He **holds** that the legal status of **part of the day is like** that **of an entire** day.[HN] Although the term of naziriteship is thirty days, once the thirtieth day begins it is as though it has been completed, and a nazirite who shaves his hair on that day has fulfilled his obligation.

תְּנַן: ״הֲרֵינִי נָזִיר שְׁלֹשִׁים יוֹם״. אִם גִּילַּח יוֹם שְׁלֹשִׁים – לֹא יָצָא! בְּאוֹמֵר ״שְׁלֵימִין״.

The Gemara asks further: **We learned** in that same mishna: In the case of one who says: **I am hereby a nazirite** for **thirty days, if he shaved** his hair on the **thirtieth day, he has not fulfilled** his obligation. This appears to contradict the opinion of Rav Mattana, who holds that part of the day is like an entire day. The Gemara answers: This is referring **to** one who **says** that he will be a nazirite for thirty **complete** days,[N] in which case he certainly does not fulfill his obligation by shaving his hair on the thirtieth day itself.

תְּנַן: מִי שֶׁנָּזַר שְׁתֵּי נְזִירוֹת, מְגַלֵּחַ אֶת הָרִאשׁוֹנָה יוֹם שְׁלֹשִׁים וְאֶחָד, וְהַשְּׁנִיָּה לְיוֹם שִׁשִּׁים וְאֶחָד. בִּשְׁלָמָא לְרַב מַתָּנָא – נִיחָא,

The Gemara asks further: **We learned** in that mishna: **One who accepted two** terms of **naziriteship**[N] **shaves** his hair for **the first** naziriteship on the **thirty-first day, and** he shaves his hair for **the second** term **on the sixty-first day. Granted,** according **to Rav Mattana** this **works out well,**[N] since he shaves his head for the first naziriteship after a full thirty days have passed. The second term of naziriteship then commences on that day, which is the thirty-first day since he took his vows. He then shaves for the second time on the thirty-first day of his second naziriteship, which is the sixty-first day since he took his vows.

NOTES

The legal status of part of the day is like that of an entire day – מִקְצָת הַיּוֹם כְּכוּלּוֹ: The commentaries ask: Since bar Padda and Rav Mattana agree that the nazirite must cut his hair on the thirty-first day *ab initio* but if he did so on the thirtieth day he has fulfilled his obligation, what is the practical difference between their opinions?

Rabbeinu Peretz explains that there is no need to find a practical difference, as they are merely arguing over the source of the *halakha*. Other commentaries explain that they differ with regard to a nazirite who became impure on the thirtieth day before bringing his offerings. According to bar Padda, he does not negate the days of his naziriteship since he became impure after the completion of his term, whereas Rav Mattana holds that he must start his naziriteship anew (Commentary on *Nazir*). Alternatively, bar Padda holds that he must start his naziriteship again by rabbinic law, whereas Rav Mattana holds that he must begin his naziriteship anew by Torah law. Additionally, they disagree with regard to one who explicitly stated that he will be a nazirite for twenty-nine days. According to bar Padda, in this case he may cut his hair on the thirtieth day *ab initio*, whereas according to Rav Mattana this is a case of one who takes a nazirite vow for a shorter period than the minimum amount, and he must complete the thirty days (Commentary on *Nazir*).

Tosafot add another difference: Since they disagree about whether the legal status of part of a day is like that of the entire day, in any case where one specifies a term of naziriteship of a particular number of days, Rav Mattana holds that one can shave his hair on the last day of that term and bar Padda holds that one must wait until the following day. It should be noted that an opinion is cited in the Jerusalem Talmud that claims that according to Rav Mattana, one who takes upon himself an unspecified term of naziriteship and cuts his hair on the thirtieth day has not fulfilled his obligation.

This is referring to one who says that he will be a nazirite for thirty complete days – בְּאוֹמֵר שְׁלֵימִין: Since he said so explicitly, he does not fulfill his obligation if he cuts his hair earlier (Commentary on *Nazir*). *Tosafot* explain that the question cited here in the Gemara does not present a difficulty for the opinion of bar Padda, because he holds that part of a day is not like an entire day. Consequently, since the individual specified that his term of naziriteship was to last thirty days, he did not fulfill his obligation if he shaved his hair on the thirtieth day.

Tosafot explain further that, according to Rav Mattana, even if the individual did not explicitly state that his term of naziriteship would last thirty complete days, that is implied by his statement that his term would last thirty days. Otherwise it would have been unnecessary for him to specify that his term was for thirty days, as an unspecified term of naziriteship is also thirty days. The Rosh cites an alternative version of the Gemara text that states: It is as though he said that his term would be thirty complete days.

Two terms of naziriteship – שְׁתֵּי נְזִירוֹת: The Rosh explains simply that he said he is accepting upon himself two terms of naziriteship. Rabbeinu Azriel, cited in *Shita Mekubbetzet*, claims that the same *halakha* applies to one who made two consecutive statements, such as: I am hereby a nazirite, I am a nazirite.

According to Rav Mattana this works out well – לְרַב מַתָּנָא נִיחָא: This is because he maintains that the thirty-first day from the beginning of the first naziriteship is the first day of the second term, and therefore on both occasions the nazirite shaves his hair on the thirty-first day (Commentary on *Nazir*).

אֶלָּא לְבַר פַּדָּא קַשְׁיָא!

However, according to bar Padda this is difficult.[N] Why doesn't he shave his hair on the thirtieth day of each term of naziriteship?

אָמַר לָךְ בַּר פַּדָּא, אֵימָא סֵיפָא: וְאִם גִּילֵּחַ אֶת הָרִאשׁוֹנָה לְיוֹם שְׁלֹשִׁים – מְגַלֵּחַ אֶת הַשְּׁנִיָּה לְיוֹם שִׁשִּׁים. אֶלָּא, סֵיפָא – מְסַיְּיעָא לֵיהּ, רֵישָׁא – בְּאוֹמֵר "שְׁלֵימִים".

The Gemara answers: **Bar Padda** could have **said to you: Say the latter clause** of the mishna: **And if he shaved** his hair for **the first** term **on the thirtieth day, he shaves** his hair for **the second** term **on the sixtieth day.** This demonstrates that the periods of naziriteship really last only twenty-nine days. **Rather, the latter clause** of the mishna **supports his** opinion, whereas the **earlier clause** of the mishna, which teaches that he shaves his hair on the thirty-first and sixty-first days, is referring **to one who says** that his naziriteship will be for thirty **complete** days.[N]

וּלְרַב מַתָּנָא קַשְׁיָא סֵיפָא! אָמַר לָךְ רַב מַתָּנָא, כִּדְקָתָנֵי סֵיפָא: יוֹם שְׁלֹשִׁים עוֹלֶה לְכָאן וּלְכָאן.

The Gemara now asks: **And according to Rav Mattana, the latter clause** of the mishna is **difficult.** The Gemara answers that **Rav Mattana** could have **said to you that** it is **as the latter clause teaches: The thirtieth day counts for** both **this and that,** i.e., it is considered both the last day of the first term of naziriteship, as well as the first day of the second term.

מַאי הִיא – מִקְצָת הַיּוֹם כְּכוּלּוֹ? הָא אָמְרָה חֲדָא זִימְנָא! מַהוּ דְּתֵימָא: הָנֵי מִילֵּי לְעִנְיַן חֲדָא נְזִירוּת, אֲבָל לִשְׁתֵּי נְזִירוּת – לָא, קָא מַשְׁמַע לַן.

The Gemara asks: **What is** the novelty of the latter clause of the mishna? Is it that the legal status of **part of the day is like** that of **an entire** day? **But didn't he** already **say this once**[N] in an earlier clause in that mishna, as explained above? The Gemara answers: The latter clause was necessary; **lest you say** that **this** principle **applies** only **with regard to one** term of **naziriteship, but** with regard **to two** terms of **naziriteship, no,**[N] this principle does not apply, the *tanna* therefore **teaches us** that part of the day is like that of an entire day, even to allow counting the beginning of the day as the last day of one term of naziriteship and the end of the day as the first day of another term of naziriteship.

NOTES

However according to bar Padda this is difficult – אֶלָּא לְבַר פַּדָּא קַשְׁיָא: Since bar Padda holds that an unspecified term of naziriteship lasts only twenty-nine days, the nazirite should be permitted to shave his hair on the thirtieth day. The remainder of that day would then count as the first day of his second term, and he should be permitted to shave his hair again on the thirtieth day of that term, which is the fifty-ninth day since the onset of his first term of naziriteship (Commentary on *Nazir*). Rabbeinu Azriel, cited in *Shita Mekubbetzet*, explains that the difficulty stems from the *halakha* that he shaves his hair for the first term of naziriteship on the thirty-first day. Although bar Padda holds that the Sages decreed that one must wait until the thirty-first day to shave his hair *ab initio*, this decree should not apply in this case, in order not to postpone the beginning of the second term of naziriteship (*Leket HaKotzerim*).

Is referring to one who says that his naziriteship will be for thirty complete days – בְּאוֹמֵר שְׁלֵימִים: An alternative version of the text reads: He is considered like one who says that his naziriteship will be for thirty complete days. The difference between the two versions is that if the individual explicitly stated that he would be a nazirite for thirty complete days, he is prohibited from shaving his hair before the thirty-first day by Torah law. If it is considered as though he made this statement, he is prohibited to do so by rabbinic decree.

But didn't he already say this once – הָא אָמְרָה חֲדָא זִימְנָא: The commentaries point out that according to bar Padda as well, this statement of the mishna does not seem to teach anything new, as he already explained (5b) that the case in the mishna is where the individual stated that he was becoming a nazirite for thirty complete days. *Tosafot* explain the novelty for bar Padda as follows: Although he does not accept the principle that part of a day is like the entire day with regard to the end of naziriteship, as far as the beginning of naziriteship is concerned, even he agrees that part of the day is like an entire day. Consequently, after the nazirite shaves his hair upon concluding his first term of naziriteship, the remainder of the day counts as the first day of his second term. This is similar to any case where one takes a nazirite vow, as the day on which the vow is taken is considered the first day of naziriteship, even if one took the vow after the day began.

But with regard to two terms of naziriteship, no – לִשְׁתֵּי נְזִירוּת לָא: The logic here is that once part of the day is considered like the entire day, the entire day is counted toward a particular term of naziriteship, and ostensibly it cannot be counted again for a second term of naziriteship.

NOTES

I too rely on this – אֲנָא נַמִי אַהָא סָמְכִי: When the mishna states that the thirtieth day counts as part of his tally, it means that it is counted as part of the second term of naziriteship. Consequently, it is clear that the first term lasted only twenty-nine days. It is obvious to bar Padda that one cannot use the principle that part of a day is like an entire day and count one day for both terms of naziriteship (*Tosafot*; Rosh).

Granted according to Rav Mattana it works out well – בִּשְׁלָמָא לְרַב מַתָּנָה נִיחָא: The early commentaries ask: Doesn't this mishna also present a difficulty with regard to the opinion of Rav Mattana? If he maintains that part of the day is like the entire day, the naziriteship should be considered completed after the beginning of the day. Why, then, would the nazirite have to start his term again? They answer that although part of a day is like the entire day, so that a nazirite can bring his offerings and shave his hair on the thirtieth day, the naziriteship is not considered to have ended until he actually brings his offerings. The case here is one where the nazirite became impure before he brought his offerings (*Tosafot*; Rosh; see Meiri).

Rabbeinu Todros, cited in *Shita Mekubbetzet*, indicates that even Rav Mattana agrees that the *halakha* that one who becomes impure on the thirtieth day must start his naziriteship anew is by rabbinic law, but not by Torah law. It is explained in the Commentary on *Nazir* that Rav Mattana stated that part of a day is like the entire day only according to the opinion of Rabbi Eliezer (see 6b). The first *tanna* in the mishna, who disagrees with Rabbi Eliezer, does not accept this principle.

תְּנַן: אִם גִּילַּח יוֹם שִׁשִּׁים חָסֵר אֶחָד – יָצָא, שֶׁיּוֹם שְׁלֹשִׁים עוֹלֶה לוֹ מִן הַמִּנְיָן. בִּשְׁלָמָא לְרַב מַתָּנָא – נִיחָא, אֶלָּא לְבַר פַּדָּא לָמָּה לִי? הָא אֲמַר שְׁלֹשִׁים חָסֵר אֶחָד!

The Gemara raises another question. **We learned** in the mishna (16a): **If he shaved** his hair on **day sixty less one,** i.e., on the fifty-ninth day after he vowed to observe two consecutive terms of naziriteship, **he has fulfilled** his obligation, **as the thirtieth day counts** as part **of his tally. Granted,** according **to Rav Mattana** this **works out well,** since the mishna is stating that the thirtieth day can be counted for both terms of naziriteship due to the principle that part of a day is like an entire day. **However, according to bar Padda, why do I need** the mishna to state that the thirtieth day counts in his tally? **Didn't he say** that an unspecified term of naziriteship is for **thirty** days **less one?** It is obvious that the thirtieth day counts for the second term of naziriteship.

אָמַר לָךְ: אֲנָא נַמִי אַהָא סָמְכִי.

The Gemara answers: Bar Padda could have **said to you: I too rely on this.**[N] This is my proof for the principle that an unspecified naziriteship lasts for twenty-nine days.

תְּנַן: מִי שֶׁאָמַר ״הֲרֵינִי נָזִיר״. נִטְמָא יוֹם שְׁלֹשִׁים – סוֹתֵר אֶת הַכֹּל. בִּשְׁלָמָא לְרַב מַתָּנָא – נִיחָא, אֶלָּא לְבַר פַּדָּא קַשְׁיָא!

The Gemara continues to ask: **We learned** in the mishna (16a): In the case of **one who said: I am hereby a nazirite,** if he **became ritually impure** on the **thirtieth day, it negates the entire** tally, and he must start his naziriteship afresh. **Granted,** according **to Rav Mattana** it **works out well,**[N] since he became impure before the conclusion of his naziriteship. **However, according to bar Padda** it is **difficult,** as the term of naziriteship ended at the conclusion of the twenty-ninth day, and one who becomes impure after completing his term does not have to observe a new term of naziriteship.

Perek **I**
Daf **6** Amud **b**

אָמַר לָךְ בַּר פַּדָּא, אֵימָא סֵיפָא: רַבִּי אֱלִיעֶזֶר אוֹמֵר: אֵינוֹ סוֹתֵר אֶלָּא שִׁבְעָה. אִי סָלְקָא דַּעְתָּךְ שְׁלֹשִׁים בָּעֵינַן – נִסְתּוֹר כּוּלְּהוּ.

The Gemara answers: **Bar Padda** could have **said to you: Say the latter clause** of that mishna: **Rabbi Eliezer says:**[N] **It negates only seven days.**[N] **If it enters your mind** that **we require thirty** days for a term of naziriteship, the nazirite **should negate all of them,** since he is still in the middle of his naziriteship. This proves that an unspecified naziriteship is only twenty-nine days long.

קָסָבַר רַבִּי אֱלִיעֶזֶר: מִקְצַת הַיּוֹם כְּכוּלּוֹ.

The Gemara responds that Rav Mattana can explain Rabbi Eliezer's opinion as follows: This does not prove that an unspecified term of naziriteship is less than thirty days, as **Rabbi Eliezer holds** that the legal status of **part of the day is like** that **of an entire day,** and it is viewed as though the nazirite has completed his term of naziriteship at the start of the thirtieth day.

NOTES

Say the latter clause of that mishna: Rabbi Eliezer says, etc. – אֵימָא סֵיפָא, רַבִּי אֱלִיעֶזֶר אוֹמֵר וכו׳: The early commentaries ask: This seemingly indicates that bar Padda holds in accordance with the minority opinion of Rabbi Eliezer. Why would he accept the minority opinion rather than the opinion of the majority of the Rabbis? They answer that, according to bar Padda, the Rabbis agree with Rabbi Eliezer that an unspecified naziriteship lasts twenty-nine days. They disagree only with regard to the *halakha* of one who becomes impure on the thirtieth day. According to the Rabbis, there is a rabbinic decree requiring the nazirite to begin his term anew, lest there be confusion in a case of one who accepts a term of thirty complete days of naziriteship, in which case if he becomes impure on the thirtieth day he must begin his term again by Torah law (*Tosafot*). Rav Mattana is of the opinion that, according to the Rabbis, the nazirite must start his term anew according to Torah law.

It negates only seven days – אֵינוֹ סוֹתֵר אֶלָּא שִׁבְעָה: In other words, none of the days of his naziriteship are invalidated, but he must wait seven additional days until the completion of his term. Two explanations for this are offered in the Commentary on *Nazir*. One explanation is that since he must shave his hair due to his impurity, he must wait another seven days for his hair to grow a little so that the end of one hair can be bent over to the root of another, to enable him to shave his hair for the completion of his term. The second explanation is that the nazirite cannot bring his offerings during these seven days because he is impure. He must therefore wait seven days until he becomes pure and can bring his offerings. This second explanation is also cited by *Tosafot*, the Rosh, and the Meiri. The Rosh and the Meiri add that although an impure person can have someone else bring his offerings on his behalf, this is not possible in the case of a nazirite because the verse states: "And he shall put them upon the hands of the nazirite" (Numbers 6:19). This indicates that the nazirite must bring his offerings himself, which he cannot do when he is impure.

Rabbi Eliezer uses the word negates, although none of the days of naziriteship are actually negated. Rabbeinu Peretz explains that this is in order to parallel the word choice employed by the first *tanna*. Alternatively, since he must keep the *halakhot* of naziriteship for an extra seven days, in practice it is as though the last seven days of naziriteship were invalidated.

תְּנַן: ״הֲרֵינִי נָזִיר מֵאָה יוֹם״. נִטְמָא יוֹם מֵאָה – סוֹתֵר אֶת הַכֹּל, רַבִּי אֱלִיעֶזֶר אוֹמֵר: אֵינוֹ סוֹתֵר אֶלָּא שְׁלֹשִׁים יוֹם. וְאִי סָלְקָא דַּעְתָּךְ סָבַר רַבִּי אֱלִיעֶזֶר מִקְצָת הַיּוֹם כְּכוּלּוֹ – נִסְתּוֹר שִׁבְעָה, וְאִי לָא סָבַר מִקְצָת הַיּוֹם כְּכוּלּוֹ – לִיסְתּוֹר כּוּלְּהוּ!

The Gemara raises a difficulty with Rabbi Eliezer's opinion. **We learned** in the mishna (16a): If one says: **I am hereby a nazirite** for **one hundred days,** if **he became impure** on the **one hundredth day, it negates the entire** tally. He must bring offerings for having become impure, and he then begins his term of naziriteship anew. **Rabbi Eliezer says: It negates only thirty days.** The Gemara comments: **And if it enters your mind** that **Rabbi Eliezer holds**[N] that the legal status of **part of the day is like** that of **an entire** day, the nazirite **should negate seven** days because it is considered as though he became impure after completing his term of naziriteship. **And if he does not hold** that **part of the day is like an entire** day, **he should negate all of** the days, since he became impure during his naziriteship.

לְעוֹלָם לָא אָמְרִינַן מִקְצָת הַיּוֹם כְּכוּלּוֹ. אִי הָכִי לִיסְתּוֹר כּוּלְּהוּ! אָמַר רֵישׁ לָקִישׁ: הַיְינוּ טַעְמָא דְּרַבִּי אֱלִיעֶזֶר: אָמַר קְרָא ״זֹאת תּוֹרַת הַנָּזִיר בְּיוֹם מְלֹאת יְמֵי נִזְרוֹ״ הַתּוֹרָה אָמְרָה: נִטְמָא בְּיוֹם מְלֹאת – תֵּן לוֹ תּוֹרַת נָזִיר.

The Gemara answers: **Actually, we do not say** that the legal status of **part of the day is like** that **of an entire** day. The Gemara asks: **If that is so,** then **let him negate all of** the days. **Reish Lakish said** that **this is the reason of Rabbi Eliezer: The verse states: "This is the law of the nazirite, on the day when the days of his consecration are complete"** (Numbers 6:13). **The Torah stated:** If **he became impure on the day of the completion**[N] of his term of naziriteship, **give him the *halakha* of** an unspecified **nazirite,** and he must recount an unspecified term of naziriteship, which is thirty days.

לֵימָא כְּתַנָּאֵי: ״עַד מְלֹאת הַיָּמִם״.

§ Until this point the Gemara has been attempting to prove whether the *halakha* is in accordance with the opinion of Rav Mattana or bar Padda. The Gemara now suggests: **Let us say** that this is **parallel to** a dispute between ***tanna'im,*** as it is taught in a *baraita*: The verse states: **"Until the days are complete,"** in which he consecrated himself to the Lord, he shall be holy, he shall let the locks of the hair of his head grow long" (Numbers 6:5).

שׁוֹמְעַנִי מִיעוּט ״יָמִים״ שְׁנַיִם – תַּלְמוּד לוֹמַר ״קָדוֹשׁ יִהְיֶה גַּדֵּל פֶּרַע״. אֵין גִּידּוּל שֵׂעָר פָּחוֹת מִשְּׁלֹשִׁים, דִּבְרֵי רַבִּי יֹאשִׁיָּה.

I hear from this: The **least** amount of days that the plural **"days"** can indicate is **two,** implying that one can become a nazirite for a term of two days. Therefore, **the verse states: "He shall be holy, he shall let** the locks of the hair of his head **grow long,"** and **there is no** significant **growth of hair**[N] in **less than thirty** days. This is **the statement of Rabbi Yoshiya.**

רַבִּי יוֹנָתָן אוֹמֵר: אֵינוֹ צָרִיךְ, הֲרֵי הוּא אוֹמֵר ״עַד מְלֹאת הַיָּמִם״. אֵי אֵלּוּ הֵן יָמִים שֶׁצְּרִיכִין לְמַלְּאוֹת – הֱוֵי אוֹמֵר שְׁלֹשִׁים.

Rabbi Yonatan says: This proof is **not needed,** as the verse **says: "Until the days are complete." What are the days that require completion? You must say** this is referring to the days of a month. Since a lunar cycle lasts for approximately twenty-nine and a half days, some months are twenty-nine days, whereas full months are **thirty** days. This demonstrates that a term of naziriteship must be at least one month.

מַאי לָאו, רַב מַתָּנָא דְּאָמַר כְּרַבִּי יֹאשִׁיָּה, וּבַר פַּדָּא דְּאָמַר כְּרַבִּי יוֹנָתָן?

The Gemara suggests: **What, is it not** the case that **Rav Mattana said in accordance with** the opinion of **Rabbi Yoshiya,** who derives the minimum length of a term of naziriteship from the phrase "he shall be holy, he shall let his hair grow long," and therefore a term of naziriteship lasts thirty days, **and bar Padda said in accordance with** the opinion of **Rabbi Yonatan,** who derives this *halakha* from the length of a month, and since a month can be twenty-nine days, the minimum length of a term of naziriteship is also twenty-nine days?

אָמַר לָךְ רַב מַתָּנָא: כּוּלֵּי עָלְמָא שְׁלֹשִׁים בָּעֵינַן, וְהָכָא בְּ״עַד״ וְעַד בִּכְלָל פְּלִיגִי. רַבִּי יֹאשִׁיָּה סָבַר: ״עַד״ וְלֹא עַד בִּכְלָל, וְרַבִּי יוֹנָתָן סָבַר: ״עַד״ וְעַד בִּכְלָל.

The Gemara responds: **Rav Mattana** could have **said to you: Everyone**[N] agrees that **we require** a term of naziriteship to last at least **thirty** days, **and here they disagree with regard to** whether **"until"** means **until and including. Rabbi Yoshiya holds** that **"until** the days are complete" indicates that a term of naziriteship must last **until, but not** necessarily **including,** the thirtieth day of a full month. Consequently, he derives the minimum length of a term of naziriteship from the phrase "he shall let the locks of the hair of his head grow long." **And Rabbi Yonatan holds** that the term **"until"** means **until and including** the thirtieth day of a full month, and he derives the minimum length of a term of naziriteship from the phrase "until the days are complete."

NOTES

And if it enters your mind that Rabbi Eliezer holds, etc. – וְאִי סָלְקָא דַּעְתָּךְ סָבַר רַבִּי אֱלִיעֶזֶר וכו׳: The Gemara can be understood as challenging the opinions of both Rav Mattana and bar Padda. According to Rav Mattana, Rabbi Eliezer holds that part of the day is like the entire day. Consequently, Rabbi Eliezer should hold that the nazirite must keep the *halakhot* of naziriteship for only seven more days. According to bar Padda, Rabbi Eliezer holds that part of the day is not like the entire day. Therefore, Rabbi Eliezer should hold that the entire term of naziriteship is negated (*Tosafot*). However, the Meiri explains that this is a question directed solely against Rav Mattana. It is possible that the Meiri had a different version of the Gemara text.

He became impure on the day of the completion, etc. – נִטְמָא בְּיוֹם מְלֹאת וכו׳: This answer apparently adopts the opinion of bar Padda that Rabbi Eliezer denies that part of a day is like the entire day. Conversely, according to Rav Mattana, since Rabbi Eliezer holds that part of a day is like the entire day, the nazirite should not have to keep any additional days of naziriteship. Some explain that according to Rav Mattana, the case is where the individual explicitly stated that his term of naziriteship would last one hundred complete days (*Tosafot*; Rosh). Alternatively, since there is a verse that indicates that one who becomes impure on the day of the completion of his naziriteship must keep an additional thirty days of naziriteship, this applies even according to Rav Mattana, despite the fact that part of a day is like the entire day (*Tosafot*, citing Rabbeinu Peretz).

There is no significant growth of hair, etc. – אֵין גִּידּוּל שֵׂעָר וכו׳: The Rosh explains that Rabbi Yoshiya expounds the verse in precisely the same manner as does Rav Mattana and derives that a significant growth of hair takes thirty days. This is based upon the first part of the verse: "He shall be [*yihye*] holy," as the numerical value of the word *yihye* is thirty (see 5a). However, it is explained in the *Likkutei Halakhot* that the *halakha* is derived from the phrase "let the locks of the hair of his head grow long," and it is logical that this is referring to a period of at least thirty days.

Rav Mattana could have said to you, everyone, etc. – אָמַר לָךְ רַב מַתָּנָא, כּוּלֵּי עָלְמָא וכו׳: According to bar Padda, however, there is no choice but to say that the minimum term of naziriteship is a matter of dispute between *tanna'im*, and he agrees with the opinion of Rabbi Yonatan (*Tosafot*). The commentaries ask: How can bar Padda agree with Rabbi Yonatan when the latter himself said that the verse is referring to thirty days? Rabbeinu Azriel, cited in *Shita Mekubbetzet*, answers that according to Rabbi Yonatan the nazirite must shave his hair on the thirtieth day, upon the completion of his twenty-nine-day term of naziriteship. Rabbeinu Peretz explains that according to bar Padda's understanding of the opinion of Rabbi Yonatan, the term of naziriteship lasts twenty-nine complete days and continues on the thirtieth day, until the nazirite shaves his hair and brings his offerings (Rabbeinu Peretz).

אָמַר מָר: אִי אֵלּוּ הֵן יָמִים שֶׁצְּרִיכִין לְמַלְאוֹת – הֱוֵי אוֹמֵר שְׁלֹשִׁים. וְאֵימָא שַׁבָּת! שַׁבָּת מִי אִיכָּא חַסִּירוּתָא?

The Gemara now analyzes the *baraita* that cites the opinions of Rabbi Yoshiya and Rabbi Yonatan. **The Master,** Rabbi Yonatan, **said: What are the days that require completion? You must say** this is referring to the **thirty** days of a full month. The Gemara asks: **But say** it is referring to the seven days of **a week.**[N] The Gemara responds: In the case of **a week, is there** ever a week that is **lacking?** All weeks are seven days. Conversely, since some months are twenty-nine days and others are thirty days, it can be said that the thirtieth day completes that which was lacking.

NOTES

But say it is referring to the seven days of a week – **וְאֵימָא שַׁבָּת:** Since there are six weekdays and then the week is completed by Shabbat, it can be said that a week requires completion (*Tosafot*; Rosh).

Perek **I**
Daf **7** Amud **a**

וְאֵימָא שָׁנָה! מִי מָנֵינַן לְיוֹמֵי? וְהָא רַבָּנַן דְּקֵיסָרִי אָמְרִי: מִנַּיִן שֶׁאֵין מוֹנִין יָמִים לְשָׁנִים? שֶׁנֶּאֱמַר "לְחָדְשֵׁי הַשָּׁנָה" – חֳדָשִׁים מְחַשְּׁבִין לְשָׁנִים, וְלֹא יָמִים לְשָׁנִים.

The Gemara asks further: **But say** it is referring to **a year,**[N] which can also be full or lacking. The Gemara responds: **Do we count** years **by days? Didn't the Sages of Caesarea say: From where** is it derived **that one does not count days toward years,**[H] but that years are calculated according to months? **As it is stated: "Of the months of the year"** (Exodus 12:2). This teaches that **months are calculated to comprise years,**[N] **but days are not** counted **toward years.** Therefore, only a month can be described as being completed by a particular day.

מתני׳ אָמַר "הֲרֵינִי נָזִיר אַחַת גְּדוֹלָה", "הֲרֵינִי נָזִיר אַחַת קְטַנָּה", אֲפִילּוּ "מִכָּאן וְעַד סוֹף הָעוֹלָם" – נָזִיר שְׁלֹשִׁים יוֹם.

MISHNA If **one said: I am hereby a nazirite** for **one long** term, or: **I am hereby a nazirite** for **one short** term,[NH] or **even**[H] if one said: I am hereby a nazirite **from now until the end of the world,** in all these cases he is **a nazirite** for **thirty days.**

גמ׳ אַמַּאי? וְהָא "מִכָּאן וְעַד סוֹף הָעוֹלָם" קָאָמַר! הָכִי קָאָמַר: אֲרִיכָא לִי הָדָא מִילְּתָא כְּמִכָּאן וְעַד סוֹף הָעוֹלָם.

GEMARA The mishna taught that even one who said: I am hereby a nazirite from now until the end of the world, becomes a nazirite for thirty days. The Gemara asks: **Why** does he become a nazirite for only thirty days? **Didn't he say: From now until the end of the world?** The Gemara answers: **This is what he is saying:** Because of the difficulties it entails, it is as though **this matter** of naziriteship **were as lengthy**[N] **for me as the** time **from now until the end of the world.**

תְּנַן: "הֲרֵינִי נָזִיר מִכָּאן עַד מָקוֹם פְּלוֹנִי" – אוֹמְדִים כַּמָּה יָמִים מִכָּאן וְעַד מָקוֹם פְּלוֹנִי, פָּחוֹת מִשְּׁלֹשִׁים יוֹם – נָזִיר שְׁלֹשִׁים יוֹם, וְאִם לָאו – נָזִיר כְּמִנְיַן הַיָּמִים. וְאֵימָא הָכָא נַמִי: אֲרִיכָא לִי הָא מִילְּתָא כְּמִכָּאן וְעַד מָקוֹם פְּלוֹנִי!

The Gemara raises a difficulty: **We learned** in the mishna (8a): If one says: **I am hereby a nazirite from here until such and such a place,**[H] **one estimates how many days** it takes to walk **from here until such and such a place.** If it is a distance of **less than thirty days,** he is **a nazirite** for **thirty days,** since this is the minimum term of naziriteship. **And if not,** i.e., if it takes more than thirty days to walk that distance, he is **a nazirite in accordance with the number of days** it takes to walk to that place. **But here too,** in that mishna, **say** that the individual intends to accept only a thirty-day term of naziriteship, and he means to say: **This matter** of naziriteship **is as lengthy for me as** the time it would take me to walk **from here until such and such a place.**

NOTES

But say it is referring to a year – **וְאֵימָא שָׁנָה:** The length of a regular year in the Jewish calendar can vary between 353 days and 355 days, depending upon how many months in the year are comprised of twenty-nine or thirty days.

Months are calculated to comprise years – **חֳדָשִׁים מְחַשְּׁבִין לְשָׁנִים:** *Tosafot* explain that even when the lunar year is lengthened in order to keep it balanced with the solar year, it is one month that is added rather than a particular number of days. Since the verse states: "Until the days are complete," it must be referring to a period of time that is measured in days. Others explain that if one takes a vow for a year, his vow remains in effect until the same day of the same month the following year, regardless of whether this period of time is longer or shorter than the 365 days of a solar year (Rosh; Rashi on *Megilla* 5a).

One short term – **אַחַת קְטַנָּה:** This can be explained in a manner similar to the Gemara's interpretation of: One long term, i.e., he is referring to the term as short because it is not bothersome for him (*Tosafot*).

This is what he is saying: It is as though this matter of naziriteship were as lengthy, etc. – **הָכִי קָאָמַר אֲרִיכָא וכו׳:** *Tosafot* explain that since it takes five hundred years to walk across the world, had the individual intended to become a nazirite for the amount of time it takes to walk across the world, he would have specified five hundred years. Consequently, it is clear that this individual was referring to the level of difficulty involved in his naziriteship. The Rosh maintains that since his statement can be interpreted in multiple ways, the most lenient interpretation is adopted, in accordance with the general principle that one is lenient with regard to naziriteship. It is explained in the *Mishne LaMelekh* that the answer of *Tosafot* is meant to apply even according to Rabbi Shimon, who holds that one must always be stringent with regard to naziriteship.

The commentaries also disagree with regard to the details of the case under discussion. *Tosafot* explain that the individual said: I am herby a nazirite from here until the end of the world. However, it is explained in the Commentary on *Nazir* that this is a case where one said: I am hereby a nazirite for one long term from here until the end of the world. If he did not specify: One long term, he would in fact be a nazirite forever. This issue likely depends on the text of the mishna. According to the version cited in *Tosafot*, the mishna first mentions the case of one who accepts a long term of naziriteship, then the case of one who accepts a short term, and then it mentions one who says he will be a nazirite from now until the end of the world. The version of the text cited in the Commentary on *Nazir* first mentions the case of one who accepts a short term of naziriteship, then the case of one who accepts a long term, and then the case of one who says he will be a nazirite from now until the end of the world.

HALAKHA

One does not count days toward years – **אֵין מוֹנִין יָמִים לְשָׁנִים:** When the lunar year falls approximately thirty days behind the solar year, the year is declared a leap year. Only a full month may be added to a year to make it a leap year (Rambam *Sefer Zemanim, Hilkhot Kiddush HaḤodesh* 1:2).

I am hereby a nazirite for one short term – **הֲרֵינִי נָזִיר אַחַת קְטַנָּה:** If one specifies that he will be a nazirite for less than thirty days, e.g., he says: I am hereby a nazirite for one day, or: I am hereby a nazirite for ten days, he is a nazirite for thirty days, since the minimum term of naziriteship is thirty days (Rambam *Sefer Hafla'a, Hilkhot Nezirut* 3:2).

Even, etc. – **אֲפִילּוּ וכו׳:** Even if one says: I am hereby a nazirite for an extremely long term, he is a nazirite for only thirty days (Rambam *Sefer Hafla'a, Hilkhot Nezirut* 3:1).

I am hereby a nazirite from here until such and such a place, etc. – **הֲרֵינִי נָזִיר מִכָּאן עַד מָקוֹם פְּלוֹנִי וכו׳:** If one said: I am hereby a nazirite from here until such and such a place, if he had not yet set out on his journey, then he is a nazirite for thirty days. If he had set out on his journey and the place he mentioned is less than thirty days' walk away, he is a nazirite for thirty days. If the place is farther away than that, he observes one term of naziriteship lasting as long as the number of days of travel (Rambam *Sefer Hafla'a, Hilkhot Nezirut* 3:5).

אָמַר רָבָא: שֶׁהֶחֱזִיק בַּדֶּרֶךְ. וְלֶיהֱוֵי כֹּל פַּרְסָה וּפַרְסָה! אֲמַר רַב פַּפָּא: בְּאַתְרָא דְּלָא מָנֵי פַּרְסֵי.

Rava said: That mishna is referring to one **who had** already **set out on the way,**[N] so that it is apparent that his intention is to be a nazirite until he reaches his destination. The Gemara asks: Why is it assumed that he means to accept a single term of naziriteship that is the length of time it takes to travel to a certain destination? **And let each and every parasang** [***parsa***][LN] be understood to refer to a separate term of naziriteship, such that the individual is understood to have accepted a separate term of naziriteship for each parasang that he must travel. **Rav Pappa said:** The mishna deals **with a place where** people **do not measure** distances in **parasangs.**[N]

וְלֶיהֱוֵי כָּל אַוָּונָא וְאַוָּונָא. מִי לָא תְּנַן: ״הֲרֵינִי נָזִיר כַּעֲפַר הָאָרֶץ״ וְ״כִשְׂעַר רֹאשִׁי״ וּ״כְחוֹל הַיָּם״ – הֲרֵי זֶה נְזִיר עוֹלָם, וּמְגַלֵּחַ אֶחָד לִשְׁלֹשִׁים יוֹם.

The Gemara asks further: **And let each and every way station** [***avvana***],[LN] where travelers lodge at night, be understood to refer to a separate term of naziriteship, such that the individual is understood to have accepted a separate term of naziriteship for each station that he passes along the way. **Didn't we learn** in a mishna (8a): If one says: **I am hereby a nazirite like the dust of the earth,**[H] **or: Like the hair of my head, or: Like the sand of the sea, he is a nazirite forever,** as it is understood that he accepted upon himself terms of naziriteship in accordance with the number of his hairs, or grains of dust, or sand, **and he shaves once** every **thirty days?**

כָּל מִילְּתָא דְּאִית בֵּיהּ קִיצּוּתָא לָא קָתָנֵי.

The Gemara responds: **Everything that has a fixed amount is not taught** in this clause, which states that one is a nazirite forever. When one declares that he will be a nazirite for a length of time corresponding to an item that people consider infinite, e.g., the dust of the earth, his intention is not to define the length of a single term of naziriteship, as it is unknown how many grains of dust there are. However, when one mentions something that does have a fixed number, e.g., the number of days it takes to walk to a certain place, his intention is to define the length of a single term of naziriteship.

וְהָתַנְיָא: ״הֲרֵינִי נָזִיר כָּל יְמֵי חַיַּי״, ״הֲרֵינִי נְזִיר עוֹלָם״ – הֲרֵי זֶה נְזִיר עוֹלָם. אֲפִילּוּ ״מֵאָה שָׁנָה״ אֲפִילּוּ ״אֶלֶף שָׁנִים״ – אֵין זֶה נְזִיר עוֹלָם אֶלָּא נָזִיר לְעוֹלָם.

And similarly, **it is taught** in a *baraita*: If one says: **I am hereby a nazirite all the days of my life,**[H] or: **I am hereby a permanent nazirite, he is a permanent nazirite.**[N] However, if he said that he is a nazirite for a fixed period of time, **even** for **one hundred years** or **even** for **one thousand years, he is not a permanent nazirite. Rather,** he is a regular **nazirite forever,** since he will not live long enough to complete his term of naziriteship. This demonstrates that there is a difference between a naziriteship that lasts for a fixed time and a naziriteship that is unlimited.

LANGUAGE

Parasang [*parsa*] – **פַּרְסָא:** This is the word in the ancient world for a Persian mile, a measurement that was adopted in a number of languages, including Greek, Syriac, and in this case, Judeo-Aramaic. The form of the word in this passage comes from Middle Iranian frasax. In the talmudic system of measurement, one *parsa* equals four *mil*.

Way station [*avvana*] – **אַוָּונָא:** This word is of ancient Syriac-Aramaic origin and means a way station or a wayside inn. Some linguists have connected it to the Greek **εὐνή**, *eunē*, meaning a bed or a place to sleep.

HALAKHA

I am hereby a nazirite like the dust of the earth, etc. – הֲרֵינִי נָזִיר כַּעֲפַר הָאָרֶץ וכו׳: If one says: I am hereby a nazirite like the dust of the earth, or: Like the hair of my head, or: Like the sand of the sea, it is as though he said: I am obligated in terms of naziriteship corresponding to the number of hairs on my head and the like. Consequently, he must shave his hair and start a new term of naziriteship every thirty days for the rest of his life (Rambam *Sefer Hafla'a*, *Hilkhot Nezirut* 3:18).

I am hereby a nazirite all the days of my life – הֲרֵינִי נָזִיר כָּל יְמֵי חַיַּי: The Rambam rules that if one says: I am hereby a nazirite forever, or: I am hereby a nazirite all the days of my life, he is a nazirite forever. However, if one specified a fixed period, even if it was a thousand years, he is a nazirite for a fixed period, despite the fact that the term exceeds his life span. It appears that this ruling is based upon a version of the Gemara text that is consistent with the *Tosefta* and the Jerusalem Talmud but is not consistent with the text printed in the Vilna Talmud (*Kesef Mishne*; Rambam *Sefer Hafla'a*, *Hilkhot Nezirut* 3:11; see Meiri and Ra'avad).

NOTES

Who had already set out on the way – שֶׁהֶחֱזִיק בַּדֶּרֶךְ: Two explanations are offered in the Commentary on *Nazir*. According to the first opinion, the fact that one has set out on his way proves that he does not consider the journey insurmountable, and it cannot be described as a case where one accepted naziriteship from now until the end of the world. The second explanation, which is also the explanation of *Tosafot* and the Rosh, is that it can be assumed that this person intended to be a nazirite while he was on the road in order to merit divine protection from harm on his travels.

And let each and every parasang – וְלֶיהֱוֵי כֹּל פַּרְסָה וּפַרְסָה: The commentaries disagree about which mishna the Gemara is challenging with this question. It is explained in the Commentary on *Nazir* that the Gemara's question pertains to the mishna cited from 8a, which states that the individual is understood to have accepted a single term of naziriteship, whose duration is the number of days it takes to complete the journey he mentioned. *Tosafot* explain that the question pertains to the mishna here, which states that one who accepts naziriteship from now until the end of the world is a nazirite for only thirty days. According to both commentaries, the question is why each parasang is not viewed as representing an independent term of naziriteship. The Meiri mentions both explanations.

The mishna deals with a place where people do not measure distances in parasangs – בְּאַתְרָא דְּלָא מָנֵי פַּרְסֵי: According to the opinion that the Gemara's question is referring to the mishna here, the answer is as follows: Since in that place they do not have a definitive method of measuring the distance to the end of the world, he must have accepted upon himself a single term of naziriteship, which feels to him as lengthy as the distance from here until the end of the world (Meiri).

Way station – אַוָּונָא: One explanation of this word is that it means a county or district. The Gemara's question is why each county is not counted as a separate unit, which would mean that he has accepted upon himself as many periods of naziriteship as there are counties between the two places he specified (Commentary on *Nazir*). The explanation found in the *Arukh* is that it means a station along the way that serves as an inn for travelers. According to this opinion, the Gemara is saying that the days it would take to get from here to the end of the world can be determined by counting the number of rest stations along the way. The Meiri cites a version of the text in which this question is resolved by the Gemara saying that the reference is to a place where they have no way stations. However, he himself rejects this version.

He is a permanent nazirite – הֲרֵי זֶה נְזִיר עוֹלָם: This does not just mean that he is a nazirite forever. He is a particular type of nazirite known as a permanent nazirite (see 4a), like Absalom. This type of nazirite may periodically cut his hair and bring offerings (Rosh; see 4b–5a).

HALAKHA

I am hereby a nazirite and one day, etc. – **הֲרֵינִי נָזִיר וְיוֹם אֶחָד וכו׳**: If one says: I am hereby a nazirite and one day, or: I am hereby a nazirite and one hour, or: I am a nazirite for one and a half, he must observe two consecutive terms of naziriteship (Rambam *Sefer Hafla'a*, *Hilkhot Nezirut* 3:8).

רַבָּה אָמַר: שָׁאנֵי שְׂעָרוֹת, הוֹאִיל וּמוּבְדָּלוֹת זוֹ מִזּוֹ.

Rabba said another reason for the distinction between one who accepts naziriteship based on the distance between places and one who accepts naziriteship based on the number of hairs on his head or the dust of the earth. **Hairs are different, since they are separated from each other.** Consequently, one who says: Like the hair of my head, is referring to distinct terms of naziriteship.

גַּבֵּי יוֹמֵי נַמִי, הָא כְּתִיב ״וַיְהִי עֶרֶב וַיְהִי בֹקֶר יוֹם אֶחָד״!

The Gemara asks: **Also with regard to days, isn't it written: "And there was evening and there was morning, one day"** (Genesis 1:5), which indicates that each day is a separate unit? Consequently, one who vows to be a nazirite: From here until such and such a place, should be considered to have accepted upon himself distinct terms of naziriteship corresponding to the number of days it takes to travel to the designated destination.

הָתָם לָאו דְּמִפְסְקִי מֵהֲדָדֵי הוּא. מַאי קָאָמַר – יְמָמָא וְלֵילְיָא חַד יוֹמָא הוּא, וּלְעוֹלָם לָא מִפְסְקִי מֵהֲדָדֵי.

The Gemara answers: The meaning of the verse **there is not that** days **are separated from each other,**[N] because time is continuous. Rather, **what it is saying** is that the period of **day and night is one** calendar **day, but actually** days **are not separate from each other.**

רָבָא אָמַר: לָמָּה לָךְ אַקְשׁוּיֵי כּוּלֵּי הַאי? שָׁאנֵי הָתָם, דְּהָא קָתָנֵי ״הֲרֵינִי נָזִיר אַחַת״.

The discussion above stemmed from the difficulty with the mishna's case where one accepted naziriteship from now until the end of the world. **Rava said: Why do you raise all these difficulties? It is different there, as it teaches** that the individual said: **I am hereby a nazirite** for **one** long term.[N] Since he specified that he is accepting one term of naziriteship, his statement is interpreted accordingly and is not interpreted as a reference to multiple terms of naziriteship.

מתני׳ ״הֲרֵינִי נָזִיר וְיוֹם אֶחָד״. ״הֲרֵינִי נָזִיר וְשָׁעָה אַחַת״. ״הֲרֵינִי נָזִיר אַחַת וּמֶחֱצָה״ – הֲרֵי זֶה נָזִיר שְׁתַּיִם.

MISHNA If one said: **I am hereby a nazirite and one day,**[H] or: **I am hereby a nazirite and one hour,** or: **I am hereby a nazirite** for **one and a half, he** becomes a **nazirite** for **two** consecutive terms of naziriteship. When he says: I am hereby a nazirite, he accepts upon himself one thirty-day term of naziriteship. When he subsequently adds an additional amount of time, e.g., an extra day, he thereby accepts upon himself an additional term of naziriteship, and the minimal term of naziriteship is thirty days.

גמ׳ לָמָּה לִי לְמִיתְנָא כָּל הָנֵי? צְרִיכִי, דְּאִי תְּנָא ״הֲרֵינִי נָזִיר וְיוֹם אֶחָד״ – הָכָא הוּא דְּאָמְרִינַן אֵין נְזִירוּת לְיוֹם אֶחָד, אִמְּטוּ לְהָכִי קָמָנֵי תַּרְתֵּין. אֲבָל ״הֲרֵינִי נָזִיר וְשָׁעָה אַחַת״ – לִימְנֵי שְׁלֹשִׁים וְאֶחָד יוֹם, קָא מַשְׁמַע לָן.

GEMARA The Gemara asks: **Why do I** need the mishna **to teach all these** cases rather than giving just one example of the mishna's principle? The Gemara explains: All the cases **are necessary, as,** if the mishna had **taught** only the case where one said: **I am hereby a nazirite and one day,** one might have thought: **It is here that we say**[N] that **there is no naziriteship for one day,** and **therefore he must count two** terms of naziriteship. **However,** if he said: **I am hereby a nazirite and one hour, let him count thirty-one days.** The mishna therefore **teaches us** that even in this latter case he must keep two terms of naziriteship.

NOTES

The meaning of the verse there is not that days are separated from each other – **הָתָם לָאו דְּמִפְסְקִי מֵהֲדָדֵי הוּא**: In other words, although the verse is referring to an evening and morning as "one day," this does not mean that days are divided from one another. Rather, the verse marks a period of time as a calendar day, although night and day merge into one another without any clear demarcation (Commentary on *Nazir*). The Maharatz Ḥayyut adds that in actual fact, the days on earth are not separated from each other, because when it is night in one place it remains daytime elsewhere.

As it teaches that the individual said, I am hereby a nazirite for one long term – **דְּהָא קָתָנֵי הֲרֵינִי נָזִיר אַחַת**: Although the word one appears in the mishna only in the cases of one who accepts one long term or one short term, it is understood that this word is also included in the case where one declares himself a nazirite from now until the end of the world (*Tosafot*). Consequently, it is clear that the individual intended to accept a single term of naziriteship rather than multiple terms. Had he simply said: I am hereby a nazirite from now until the end of the world, he might be understood to be accepting many terms of naziriteship. This is explained similarly in the Jerusalem Talmud.

It is here that we say – **הָכָא הוּא דְּאָמְרִינַן**: When he said: I am hereby a nazirite, he accepted upon himself a standard thirty-day term of naziriteship. When he then said: And a day, he intended to accept an additional one-day term of naziriteship. However, since the minimal term of naziriteship is thirty days, he must keep the second term for thirty days. Conversely, if he said: I am hereby a nazirite and one hour, since terms of naziriteship are not measured in hours, it is not clear that he meant to add a separate term of naziriteship. He may have intended to accept a single term of naziriteship for thirty days and part of the thirty-first day, in which case he should have to keep a thirty-one-day term of naziriteship, as naziriteship does not end in the middle of a day (Rosh). The author of *Birkat Rosh* explains that since, in practice, one must continue to observe the restrictions of naziriteship until he brings his offerings on the day following the conclusion of his term of naziriteship, when one says: I am hereby a nazirite and one hour, he may have been referring to the time before he brings his offerings on the day following his term of naziriteship.

וְאִי תְּנָא ״שָׁעָה אַחַת״ – מִשּׁוּם דְּלָא נָחֵית לְדַוְקָא, אֲבָל ״אַחַת וּמֶחֱצָה״ דְּנָחֵית לְדַוְקָא – אֵימָא לָא לִימְנֵי תַּרְתֵּי, קָמַשְׁמַע לַן: כּוּלְּהוּ נָזִיר שְׁתַּיִם.

And if the mishna **taught** only the case where one said: I am hereby a nazirite and **one hour,** one might have said that he is obligated in two periods of naziriteship **because he did not go into specific detail** [*davka*].[LN] He merely stated that he accepts upon himself some part of a second term of naziriteship, and therefore he must observe a full second term of naziriteship. **However,** in the case of one who says he will be a nazirite for **one and a half, where** he **does go into specific detail,** one might **say he should not** have to **count two** full terms of naziriteship but rather forty-five days of naziriteship. The mishna therefore **teaches us** that in **all** these cases **he is a nazirite** for **two** full terms of naziriteship.

מתני׳ ״הֲרֵינִי נָזִיר שְׁלֹשִׁים יוֹם וְשָׁעָה אַחַת״ – נָזִיר שְׁלֹשִׁים וְאֶחָד יוֹם, שֶׁאֵין נְזִירוּת לְשָׁעוֹת.

MISHNA One who says: **I am hereby a nazirite** for **thirty days and one hour,**[HN] becomes a **nazirite** for **thirty-one days, as there is no naziriteship for hours** but only for full days.

גמ׳ אָמַר רַב: לֹא שָׁנוּ אֶלָּא דְּאָמַר ״שְׁלֹשִׁים וְאֶחָד יוֹם״ אֲבָל אָמַר ״שְׁלֹשִׁים [יוֹם] וְיוֹם אֶחָד״ – נָזִיר שְׁתַּיִם.

GEMARA **Rav said: They taught** that he is a nazirite for thirty-one days **only**[N] **when he said: Thirty-one days.**[HN] **But if he said: Thirty days and one day,**[H] he is **a nazirite for two** terms of naziriteship, since the thirty days are considered one term of naziriteship, and the additional day is the start of an additional term.

LANGUAGE

Specific detail [*davka*] – דַּוְקָא: From the root *dalet, vav, kuf* or *dalet, yud, kuf,* meaning to be precise. Sometimes *davka* means: It is exactly that way and is not to be changed. At other times, as here, it indicates that something has been ascertained or expressed precisely, intentionally.

HALAKHA

I am hereby a nazirite for thirty days and one hour – הֲרֵינִי נָזִיר שְׁלֹשִׁים יוֹם וְשָׁעָה אַחַת: If one says: I am hereby a nazirite for thirty days and one hour, he is a nazirite for thirty-one days, since naziriteship does not take effect when established in terms of hours rather than days (Rambam *Sefer Hafla'a, Hilkhot Nezirut* 3:4).

When he said thirty-one days – דְּאָמַר שְׁלֹשִׁים וְאֶחָד יוֹם: If one vowed to be a nazirite for longer than thirty days, e.g., he said: I am hereby a nazirite for thirty-one days, he is a nazirite for the period specified (Rambam *Sefer Hafla'a, Hilkhot Nezirut* 3:3).

He said thirty days and one day – אָמַר שְׁלֹשִׁים יוֹם וְיוֹם אֶחָד: One who said: I am hereby a nazirite for thirty days and one day, is a nazirite for one term of naziriteship lasting thirty-one days. The *halakha* is not in accordance with Rav (Rambam *Sefer Hafla'a, Hilkhot Nezirut* 3:8).

NOTES

He did not go into specific detail – לָא נָחֵית לְדַוְקָא: In other words, his statement was not precise, since naziriteship does not take effect for hours (Commentary on *Nazir*). Alternatively, since he specified a term that is halakhically infeasible, there is no choice but to add on to his words and say he vowed an additional term of naziriteship (*Tosafot*).

Thirty days and one hour – שְׁלֹשִׁים יוֹם וְשָׁעָה אַחַת: The mishna employed this specific example because the last case in the previous mishna was about one who accepted the obligation to become: A nazirite and one hour, and the *tanna* wanted to stress that if he adjusted his wording and said: Thirty days and one hour, he is a nazirite for thirty-one days. The same is true if he said: Thirty and one days, rather than: I am hereby a nazirite and one day (*Tosafot*). As for the reason for this difference, the commentaries explain that when one says: I am hereby a nazirite, he has accepted a thirty-day term of naziriteship. When he then adds extra time, he thereby adds an additional term of naziriteship. Conversely, one who says: Thirty days and one hour, has merely accepted a term of naziriteship that is longer than thirty days. Since a term of naziriteship cannot include a part of a day, he is a nazirite for thirty-one days (Rabbeinu Peretz; Rabbeinu Azriel, cited in *Shita Mekubbetzet*).

Rav said, they taught that he is a nazirite for thirty-one days only, etc. – אָמַר רַב, לֹא שָׁנוּ אֶלָּא וכו׳: Rav's statement is also cited in the Jerusalem Talmud, where his opinion is rejected based on a *baraita* that explicitly states that in this case Rabbi Akiva and Rabbi Yishmael agree that only one term of naziriteship takes effect. The two disagree only with regard to one who says: I am hereby a nazirite for thirty days and one more day, in which case Rabbi Akiva holds that two periods of naziriteship take effect.

When he said thirty-one days – דְּאָמַר שְׁלֹשִׁים וְאֶחָד יוֹם: Rav clearly did not mean to say that these were his exact words, as the mishna states that this is a case where he said: Thirty days and one hour. The point is that his statement is understood as though he said: Thirty-one days (Rosh). *Tosafot* explain that the case in the mishna is similar to one of the cases in the mishna on 7a, and it can be inferred that in a case where one said: Thirty-one days, which is a different formulation of one of the other cases in the mishna on 7a, one would also observe only one term of naziriteship. According to the text in the Radbaz's version of the Gemara, however, the mishna here explicitly states that if one says: I am hereby a nazirite for thirty days and one day, he is a nazirite for one term of thirty-one days. Another version of the text, cited in the Meiri, reads: They taught this only with regard to one who said: Thirty and one hour, but if he said: Thirty days and one hour, he is obligated in two terms of naziriteship.

BACKGROUND

Cistern – דוּת: A cistern is a place built for gathering water or produce. A pit and cistern have the same purpose, but a cistern is a structure built from stones above the ground, whereas a pit is dug into the earth or rock.

רַב סָבַר לָהּ כְּרַבִּי עֲקִיבָא, דְּדָרֵישׁ לִישָּׁנָא יְתֵירָא.

The Gemara comments: In this regard, **Rav holds in accordance with** the opinion of **Rabbi Akiva, who derives** meaning from **superfluous language.**[N] Rabbi Akiva believes that if one uses unnecessary words, it is inferred that he intended to add something. In this case, since the individual said: Thirty days and one day, without combining them into one amount, he intended to accept an additional term of naziriteship.

דִּתְנַן: לֹא אֶת הַבּוֹר וְלֹא אֶת הַדּוּת, אַף עַל פִּי שֶׁכָּתַב לוֹ ״עוּמְקָא וְרוּמָא״. וְצָרִיךְ לִיקַּח לוֹ דֶּרֶךְ, דִּבְרֵי רַבִּי עֲקִיבָא.

As we learned in a mishna (*Bava Batra* 64a): According to Rabbi Akiva, if one sold his house to another without specification, he has sold **neither the pit nor the cistern** [*dut*][B] with it, **although he wrote to him** in the document of sale: With **its depth and its height.**[H] This is because anything that is not part of the house, e.g., pits and cisterns, must be explicitly mentioned in the contract. **And** the seller **must purchase a path**[NH] through the property he sold along with the house in order to reach the pit or cistern that he kept for himself. This is **the statement of Rabbi Akiva.**

וַחֲכָמִים אוֹמְרִים: אֵינוֹ צָרִיךְ לִיקַּח לוֹ דֶּרֶךְ. וּמוֹדֶה רַבִּי עֲקִיבָא בִּזְמַן שֶׁאָמַר לוֹ ״חוּץ מֵאֵלּוּ״ שֶׁאֵינוֹ צָרִיךְ לִיקַּח לוֹ דֶּרֶךְ.

And the Rabbis say: He does not need to purchase a path, as it is assumed that just as he maintained his rights to the pit or cistern, he also maintained the right to walk through the rest of the property in order to access the pit or cistern. **And Rabbi Akiva concedes that when he says to him** in the document of sale: **Apart from these,**[H] i.e., the pit and cistern, **that he does not need to purchase a path.** Rabbi Akiva's reasoning is this: Since the seller unnecessarily stressed that the pit and cistern are not included in the sale, he must have intended to thereby reserve for himself the right of access. This proves that, according to Rabbi Akiva, if one adds a superfluous clause he must have had a specific meaning in mind, and something must be derived from his statement. Rav follows a similar line of reasoning with regard to the case of a nazirite.

NOTES

Who derives meaning from superfluous language – דְּדָרֵישׁ לִישָּׁנָא יְתֵירָא: The Rosh explains that Rabbi Akiva is not alone in this opinion, as even the Rabbis, who disagree with Rabbi Akiva in the case of a pit and cistern, accept this principle. They simply do not apply the principle to that particular case because they assume that a seller does not want to include in the sale anything he did not explicitly mention. The Gemara attributes to Rabbi Akiva the principle of deriving meaning from superfluous language only because he clearly applies this principle in the case mentioned. Consequently, Rav can be presented as accepting this principle despite the fact that he does not apply it to the case of the pit and cistern, with regard to which he rules in accordance with the Rabbis.

However, Rabbi Avraham min HaHar contends that the Rabbis disagree with Rabbi Akiva with regard to the legitimacy of expounding superfluous language, and the *halakha* is in accordance with their opinion and not the opinion of Rabbi Akiva and Rav. The Rambam rules in accordance with Rabbi Akiva concerning a sale but rules against Rav's opinion in the case of a nazirite. The Meiri explains that, according to the Rambam, Rabbi Akiva might not agree with Rav's ruling here. This is because in the case of a sale the words are clearly superfluous, which is not true in the case of the nazirite. Alternatively, it can be explained that the Rambam follows the ruling of the Jerusalem Talmud, in which Rav's opinion is rejected. As a general rule, whenever the Babylonian Talmud does not provide a clear halakhic ruling, the Rambam follows the Jerusalem Talmud.

And the seller must purchase a path – וְצָרִיךְ לִיקַּח לוֹ דֶּרֶךְ: The Gemara in *Bava Batra* (64b) explains that Rabbi Akiva holds that it may be assumed that a seller is generous and includes all rights to the property he sells, except where the contract stipulates otherwise. Consequently, one who sells his property has not maintained for himself even the right to pass through it in order to draw water from his pit, and he must purchase this right or otherwise obtain permission to pass through from the buyer. The Rabbis, however, hold that it may be assumed that a seller intends to retain all rights that he does not explicitly agree to relinquish.

HALAKHA

Although he wrote to him, with its depth and its height – אַף עַל פִּי שֶׁכָּתַב לוֹ עוּמְקָא וְרוּמָא: One who sells a house without specification has not sold the pit or cistern that is there, even if he wrote in the document of sale: With its depth and height (Rambam *Sefer Kinyan, Hilkhot Mekhira* 25:2; *Shulḥan Arukh, Ḥoshen Mishpat* 214:2).

And the seller must purchase a path – וְצָרִיךְ לִיקַּח לוֹ דֶּרֶךְ: One who sells a house without specification retains the pit or cistern that is there, but he must purchase the right of access to them from the buyer if he wishes to use them. He is not considered to have reserved a path for himself so that he can gain access to them. The *halakha* is in accordance with Rabbi Akiva's opinion that a seller acts generously, as concluded by the Gemara in *Bava Batra* 65a (Rambam *Sefer Kinyan, Hilkhot Mekhira* 25:4; *Shulḥan Arukh, Ḥoshen Mishpat* 214:2; 215:5).

When he says to him, apart from these – בִּזְמַן שֶׁאוֹמֵר לוֹ, חוּץ מֵאֵלּוּ: If one sold his house and specified that he was not selling the pit and cistern, he does not have to purchase access to the pit and cistern from the buyer (Rambam *Sefer Kinyan, Hilkhot Mekhira* 25:3; *Shulḥan Arukh, Ḥoshen Mishpat* 214:2, 215:5).

מתני׳ ״הֲרֵינִי נָזִיר כִּשְׂעַר רֹאשִׁי״. וְ״כַעֲפַר הָאָרֶץ״ וּ״כְחוֹל הַיָּם״ – הֲרֵי זֶה נְזִיר עוֹלָם, וּמְגַלֵּחַ אַחַת לִשְׁלֹשִׁים יוֹם.

MISHNA If one says: **I am hereby a nazirite like the hair of my head,**[H] **or: Like the dust of the earth, or: Like the sand of the sea, he is a nazirite forever.** He has accepted a separate term of naziriteship for every hair or particle of dust or sand, which in practice means that he will be a nazirite forever. **And he shaves** his hair **once** every **thirty days.**

רַבִּי אוֹמֵר: אֵין זֶה מְגַלֵּחַ אַחַת לִשְׁלֹשִׁים יוֹם. וְאֵיזֶהוּ מְגַלֵּחַ אַחַת לִשְׁלֹשִׁים – הָאוֹמֵר ״הֲרֵי עָלַי נְזִירוֹת כִּשְׂעַר רֹאשִׁי״, וְ״כַעֲפַר הָאָרֶץ״ וּ״כְחוֹל הַיָּם״.

Rabbi Yehuda HaNasi **says: This** nazirite **does not shave** his hair **once** every **thirty days,**[N] as he has accepted upon himself one long term of naziriteship lasting for as many days as there are hairs or particles of dust or sand. **And who is** the nazirite who **shaves** his hair **once** every **thirty** days? One **who says: It is hereby** incumbent **upon** me to observe **naziriteships like the hair of my head, or: Like the dust of the earth, or: Like the sand of the sea.** Since he used the plural term naziriteships, it is clear that he is accepting distinct terms of naziriteship.

״הֲרֵינִי נָזִיר מְלֹא הַבַּיִת״ אוֹ ״מְלֹא הַקּוּפָּה״ – בּוֹדְקִין אוֹתוֹ. אִם אָמַר: אַחַת גְּדוֹלָה נָזַרְתִּי – נָזִיר שְׁלֹשִׁים יוֹם. וְאִם אָמַר: סְתָם נָזַרְתִּי – רוֹאִין אֶת הַקּוּפָּה כְּאִילּוּ הִיא מְלֵאָה חַרְדָּל, וְנָזִיר כָּל יָמָיו.

If one says: **I am hereby a nazirite** in accordance with **the capacity of the house,**[HN] **or: The capacity of the basket, one checks with him**[N] what he had in mind. **If he said:** My intention was to take a nazirite vow for **one long** term of naziriteship, he is **a nazirite** for only **thirty days,** in accordance with the ruling of the mishna that the words long or short are of no account when used in a nazirite vow (7a). **And if he said: I took a nazirite vow without specification,**[N] it is assumed that he meant to accept upon himself terms of naziriteship corresponding to the number of items that fit into the basket, and the smallest items normally placed in baskets are used for this evaluation. Consequently, one **views the basket as though** it were **full of mustard**[B] seeds, which are extremely small, **and he is a nazirite** for **his entire life.**

BACKGROUND

Mustard – חַרְדָּל: Mustard is produced from several plants, including the white mustard plant, *Sinapis nigra*, and the black mustard plant, *Brassica nigra*. Often, seeds from different plants are mixed together. These plants all come from the Brassicaceae family and grow wild in Eretz Yisrael. Black mustard has tangled branches and grows in bunches of large, crowded flowers. The condiment mustard is produced from its seeds. Black mustard is the largest plant in the Brassicaceae family, normally reaching anywhere from 0.5–2 m in height, and in some uncommon cases growing to up to 5 m. Mustard seeds are small, around 1.5–2 mm in width, and they are therefore used as an example of something very small, as in the Gemara here.

Above: White mustard plant
Left: Black mustard plant

Seeds of black and white mustard plants

HALAKHA

I am hereby a nazirite like the hair of my head, etc. – הֲרֵינִי נָזִיר כִּשְׂעַר רֹאשִׁי וכו׳: One who says: I am hereby a nazirite like the hair of my head, or: Like the dust of the earth, is considered to have accepted upon himself terms of naziriteship corresponding to the number of hairs on his head. He must therefore shave his hair and bring offerings every thirty days for the rest of his life (Rambam *Sefer Hafla'a, Hilkhot Nezirut* 3:18).

I am hereby a nazirite in accordance with the capacity of the house, etc. – הֲרֵינִי נָזִיר מְלֹא הַבַּיִת וכו׳: If one says: I am hereby a nazirite in accordance with the capacity of the house, or: In accordance with the capacity of the basket, he is asked to clarify what he meant. If he explains that he meant to accept one term of naziriteship, he is a nazirite for thirty days. If he says he vowed to be a nazirite without any specific intention, the basket is seen as though it were full of mustard seeds, and consequently he is a nazirite forever and cuts his hair once every twelve months. This is in accordance with the decision cited in the Jerusalem Talmud (Rambam *Sefer Hafla'a, Hilkhot Nezirut* 3:17).

NOTES

This nazirite does not shave his hair once every thirty days – אֵין זֶה מְגַלֵּחַ אַחַת לִשְׁלֹשִׁים יוֹם: The commentaries disagree as to the status of this individual according to Rabbi Yehuda HaNasi. Some say he has the status of a permanent nazirite, who trims his hair and brings offerings once every twelve months (Rambam's Commentary on the Mishna; Meiri). This is the explanation cited in the Jerusalem Talmud. Others maintain that according to Rabbi Yehuda HaNasi, his status is like one who accepts a one-hundred-year term of naziriteship (see 7a), and he may never cut his hair (Commentary on *Nazir*; *Tosafot*; Rosh).

The capacity of the house – מְלוֹא הַבַּיִת: The refers to the capacity of a house or a basket that is currently empty (*Tosafot*). If the house or basket was filled with items, he would be obligated to observe a term of naziriteship for each item in the house or basket.

One checks with him, etc. – בּוֹדְקִים אוֹתוֹ וכו׳: Rabbeinu Todros, cited in *Shita Mekubbetzet*, asks why one checks with the individual in this case but not in the first case in the mishna, where one accepted naziriteship like the hairs of his head. Is it not possible that in the earlier case as well, one intended to accept a single term of naziriteship that seemed large and daunting to him? He answers that a basket is a single unit, and therefore the intention must be clarified. Conversely, the hairs on one's head are many separate units, and therefore one who uses this language has accepted many terms of naziriteship.

I took a nazirite vow without specification – סְתָם נָזַרְתִּי: The Rosh explains that he says that he had no particular intention in mind and relied on the Sages to clarify his statement (see *Tosefot Yom Tov*).

"הֲרֵינִי נָזִיר מִכָּאן עַד מָקוֹם פְּלוֹנִי" – אוֹמְדִין כַּמָּה יָמִים מִכָּאן עַד מָקוֹם פְּלוֹנִי, אִם פָּחוֹת מִשְּׁלֹשִׁים יוֹם – נָזִיר שְׁלֹשִׁים יוֹם, וְאִם לָאו – נָזִיר כְּמִנְיַן הַיָּמִים.

If one says: **I am hereby a nazirite from here until such and such a place,**[H] **one estimates how many days** it takes to walk **from here until such and such a place. If it is less than thirty days,** he is a **nazirite** for **thirty days,** since this is the minimum term of naziriteship. **And if not,** i.e., if it takes more than thirty days to walk that distance, he is **a nazirite in accordance with the number of days** it takes to walk to that place.

"הֲרֵינִי נָזִיר כְּמִנְיַן יְמוֹת הַחַמָּה" – מוֹנֶה נְזִירוּת כְּמִנְיַן יְמוֹת הַחַמָּה. אָמַר רַבִּי יְהוּדָה: מַעֲשֶׂה הָיָה, כֵּיוָן שֶׁהִשְׁלִים – מֵת.

If one says: **I am hereby a nazirite in accordance with the number of days in a solar year,**[H] he **counts** 365 consecutive **naziriteships, in accordance with the number of days in a solar year. Rabbi Yehuda said: There was an incident** where someone took this vow and observed 365 consecutive terms of naziriteship. **Once he completed** all these terms of naziriteship, **he died.**[N]

גמ׳ "רוֹאִין אֶת הַקּוּפָּה כְּאִילּוּ מְלֵאָה חַרְדָּל וְנָזִיר כָּל יָמָיו". וְאַמַּאי? וְלִיחְזְיֵיהּ כְּאִילּוּ מְלֵאָה קִישּׁוּאִין וּדְלוּעִין, וְתֶיהֱוֵי לֵיהּ תַּקַּנְתָּא!

GEMARA The mishna taught that if one said: I am hereby a nazirite in accordance with the capacity of the basket, and he did not specifically intend to accept one term of naziriteship, one **views the basket as though** it were **full of mustard** seeds, **and he is a nazirite** for **his entire life.** The Gemara asks: **But why** does one view the basket as though it were full of mustard seeds? **Let us view it as though** it were **full of cucumbers**[N] **or gourds,** which are much larger. The basket would consequently hold fewer of them, **and there would be a remedy for him,** i.e., he would be able to complete his terms of naziriteship and resume living as a non-nazirite.

אָמַר חִזְקִיָּה: בְּמַחֲלוֹקֶת שְׁנוּיָה, וְרַבִּי שִׁמְעוֹן הִיא, דְּאָמַר: אָדָם מַכְנִיס אֶת עַצְמוֹ לְדָבָר שֶׁסְּפֵיקוֹ חָמוּר מִוַּדַּאי.

In response to this question, **Ḥizkiyya said:** This issue **is taught** as **a dispute** between *tanna'im*, **and** the mishna **is** in accordance with the opinion of **Rabbi Shimon, who said: A person places himself**[N] **in a state where** the resulting **uncertainty is more stringent than** if there were **certainty,**[N] i.e., an individual willingly accepts conditions that are ambiguous although this may cause him to have to keep more stringent *halakhot* if the uncertainty is not clarified.

דְּתַנְיָא: "הֲרֵינִי נָזִיר עַל מְנָת שֶׁיְּהֵא בִּכְרִי זֶה מֵאָה כּוֹר" וְהָלַךְ וּמְצָאוֹ שֶׁנִּגְנַב אוֹ שֶׁאָבַד, רַבִּי שִׁמְעוֹן אוֹסֵר, שֶׁסְּפֵק נְזִירוּת לְהַחְמִיר.

This is **as it is taught** in a *baraita*: With regard to one who says: **I am hereby a nazirite on the condition that this pile** of grain **will** be found to contain at least **one hundred *kor*,**[H] **and he went** to measure the pile **and found that it was stolen**[N] **or lost,** making it impossible to determine whether it contained one hundred *kor*, **Rabbi Shimon prohibits** him to drink wine or cut his hair, **as** he holds that in a case of **uncertain naziriteship** one is required **to** act **stringently.** Similarly, in the case in the mishna, since it is not known whether one intended to accept naziriteship according to the number of mustard seeds in the basket or according to the number of gourds there, he must act stringently.

HALAKHA

I am hereby a nazirite from here until such and such a place – הֲרֵינִי נָזִיר מִכָּאן עַד מָקוֹם פְּלוֹנִי: If one said: I am hereby a nazirite from here until such and such a place, if he has not yet set out on his way, then he is a nazirite for thirty days. If he has set out on his journey and the place is less than thirty days' walk away, he is a nazirite for thirty days. If the place is farther away than that, he observes one term of naziriteship lasting as long as the number of days of travel remaining on his journey. This is in accordance with the explanation cited in the Gemara on 7a (Rambam *Sefer Hafla'a, Hilkhot Nezirut* 3:5).

I am hereby a nazirite in accordance with the number of days in a solar year – הֲרֵינִי נָזִיר כְּמִנְיַן יְמוֹת הַחַמָּה: If one says: I am hereby a nazirite in accordance with the number of days in a year, he must observe 354 terms of naziriteship, each lasting thirty days. This corresponds to the number of days of a non-leap year in the Jewish calendar, as that is what people generally mean when they refer to a year. However, if one explicitly referred to a solar year, he must observe 365 terms of naziriteship (Rambam *Sefer Hafla'a, Hilkhot Nezirut* 3:7).

On the condition that this pile will be found to contain one hundred *kor* – עַל מְנָת שֶׁיְּהֵא בִּכְרִי זֶה מֵאָה כּוֹר: If one says: I am a nazirite if this pile will be found to contain at least one hundred *kor*, and it turns out that the pile has been stolen or lost and cannot be measured, he is not a nazirite. A case of uncertain naziriteship is treated leniently, in accordance with the opinion of Rabbi Yehuda (Rambam *Sefer Hafla'a, Hilkhot Nezirut* 2:9).

NOTES

Once he completed all these terms of naziriteship he died – כֵּיוָן שֶׁהִשְׁלִים מֵת: Rabbi Yehuda HaNasi is cited in the Jerusalem Talmud as explaining that the individual was blessed with a long life so that he could complete his terms of naziriteship.

As though it were full of cucumbers – כְּאִילּוּ מְלֵאָה קִישּׁוּאִין: *Tosafot* point out that the Gemara could have said: Full of dough, or any other substance that would fill the basket entirely. They explain that since the mishna mentioned mustard seeds, the Gemara gives an example involving larger produce, but the question allows for the possibility that one be obligated in only one term of naziriteship as well (see *Keren Ora*).

A person places himself, etc. – אָדָם מַכְנִיס אֶת עַצְמוֹ וכו׳: Naziriteship is accepted with a vow, and there is a principle with regard to vows that when the vow is expressed ambiguously, it is interpreted based upon the intentions of the individual who took the vow. The dispute between Rabbi Shimon and Rabbi Yehuda is about whether the speaker meant to take the vow even when it was impossible to determine some details pertaining to the vow, and this lack of certainty entails stringency, or if it is assumed that he certainly did not intend to accept the vow under these circumstances. In the *Tosefta*, it is explained that they differ with regard to whether one who unwittingly takes a nazirite vow must observe naziriteship. Rabbi Shimon maintains that such a naziriteship takes effect, whereas Rabbi Yehuda believes that a mistaken naziriteship does not take effect.

Where the resulting uncertainty is more stringent than if there were certainty – שֶׁסְּפֵיקוֹ חָמוּר מִוַּדַּאי: One explanation of this phrase, as it applies to the case in the mishna, is that the stringency arises because of the ambiguous statement. Had he been clearer, he would be obligated to be a nazirite only for the duration that he explicitly stated (Rabbi Avraham min HaHar). However, most early commentaries explain that since it is unclear how many terms of naziriteship he intended to accept, once he has completed terms of naziriteship corresponding to the number of cucumbers or gourds that could fit into the house or basket, he has the status of an uncertain nazirite. The *halakhot* that apply to an uncertain nazirite are more stringent than those that apply to one who definitely accepted terms of naziriteship according to the number of mustard seeds that can fit into the house or basket. If he was a definite nazirite, he would shave his hair and bring offerings every thirty days. An uncertain nazirite can never shave his hair, due to the prohibition against rounding off the corners of the head, which he would transgress if he was not really a nazirite (Meiri). He is also unable to bring the offerings of a nazirite, in case he is not a nazirite and will thereby be bringing non-consecrated animals into the Temple courtyard. He cannot even bring the offerings on a voluntary basis since they include a sin-offering, which cannot be brought on a voluntary basis.

And he went and found that it was stolen – וְהָלַךְ וּמְצָאוֹ שֶׁנִּגְנַב: In this case, the individual's uncertain status as a nazirite requires him to act more stringently than if he were certainly a nazirite. Due to the possibility that he is not a nazirite, he cannot bring the offerings a nazirite must bring at the conclusion of his term of naziriteship. However, due to the possibility that he is a nazirite, he cannot cut his hair or drink wine without having brought the offerings. Therefore, he must refrain from cutting his hair and drinking wine indefinitely. The solution for such an individual is to state: If I am not a nazirite due to my previous statement, I hereby accept naziriteship. That would cause him to certainly be a nazirite, and thirty days later he may bring the offerings and conclude his naziriteship. However, if he became impure due to a corpse before he made the second statement, he cannot bring the offerings of an impure nazirite and must observe the restrictions of naziriteship indefinitely (*Tosafot*; Rosh).

רַבִּי יְהוּדָה מַתִּיר, שֶׁסְּפֵק נְזִירוּת לְהָקֵל.

Conversely, **Rabbi Yehuda permits** him to drink wine or cut his hair, **as** he holds that in a case of **uncertain naziriteship** one is permitted **to** act **leniently.** The naziriteship does not take effect, since the pile might have contained less than one hundred *kor*.

רַבִּי יוֹחָנָן אָמַר: אֲפִילּוּ תֵּימָא רַבִּי יְהוּדָה, הָתָם – לָא נָחֵית לֵיהּ לִנְזִירוּת, הָכָא – נָחֵית לֵיהּ לִנְזִירוּת, בְּמַאי לְסַלּוֹקֵיהּ מִינֵּיהּ!

Rabbi Yoḥanan said: You can **even say** that the mishna is in accordance with the opinion of **Rabbi Yehuda** because the cases in the mishna and in the *baraita* are not comparable. **There,** in the case discussed in the *baraita,* **he does not** necessarily even **enter** a state of **naziriteship,**[N] as it is unclear whether the pile contained a *kor* of grain. Consequently, he retains his previous status and is not considered a nazirite. Conversely, in the case discussed **here** in the mishna, **he** certainly **enters** a state of **naziriteship,** since he undoubtedly vowed to be a nazirite for some period of time. Consequently, **how** is it possible **to remove** the state of naziriteship **from him** when it is uncertain when his terms end? Therefore, even Rabbi Yehuda would agree that he remains a nazirite indefinitely.

אַמַּאי לָא? לִיחַזְיַיהּ לַקּוּפָּה כְּאִילּוּ מְלֵאָה קִישּׁוּאִין וּדְלוּעִין, וְתֶיהֱוֵי לֵיהּ תַּקַּנְתָּא, הָא סָלְקָא דַּעְתִּין נְזִירוּת הוּא דְּקַבֵּיל עִילָּוֵיהּ!

The Gemara asks: **Why** is it **not** possible to remove from him the status of naziriteship? **Let us view the basket as though** it were **full of cucumbers or gourds,** as he has accepted at least as many terms of naziriteship as the number of cucumbers or gourds that can fit in the basket, **and** in this way **there will be a remedy for him. It entered our minds**[N] to say that **it is** distinct **naziriteships that he accepted upon himself,** and so once he has completed the minimal number of naziriteships, he should no longer be considered a nazirite unless it can be determined that he accepted more than this number of terms of naziriteship.

NOTES

He does not necessarily even enter a state of naziriteship – לָא נָחֵית לֵיהּ לִנְזִירוּת: Since it is uncertain whether or not he accepted naziriteship, he is not considered a nazirite. This is because it is assumed that he did not want to enter into naziriteship with an ambiguous statement (Rosh). Rabbeinu Peretz explains that the speaker merely stated his intention to clearly accept naziriteship upon measuring the pile. Rabbeinu Azriel, cited in *Shita Mekubbetzet*, explains that since he was not yet a nazirite when he made his statement, he is presumed to maintain his prior status until it can be proven otherwise. In the case in the mishna, however, one certainly accepted naziriteship and the question pertains to the number of terms he accepted. Consequently, he must remain a nazirite until it is clear that his terms are complete.

It entered our minds, etc. – הָא סָלְקָא דַּעְתִּין וכו׳: *Tosafot* and Rabbeinu Peretz explain that this sentence concludes the Gemara's question and is read as follows: Since the individual has accepted a separate term of naziriteship for each item that can fit into the house or basket, once he has observed a single term, he brings the offerings for concluding that term. At that point, since it is not clear whether he accepted additional terms, Rabbi Yehuda should exempt him from naziriteship, just as he is quoted in the *baraita* as exempting one who never clearly accepted naziriteship. According to this explanation, the wording of the Gemara at the beginning of the following page must be adjusted slightly. Alternatively, it is explained in the Commentary on *Nazir* that this statement is the start of the Gemara's answer and is read as follows: The speaker did not accept separate terms of naziriteship, as Rabbi Yehuda agrees with Rabbi Yehuda HaNasi that he has accepted one long term of naziriteship. Consequently, since it is unclear when that term ends, he can never bring the offerings brought at the conclusion of naziriteship and he must observe the restrictions of naziriteship indefinitely. According to this explanation, the wording of the Gemara here must be adjusted slightly.

Perek **I**
Daf **8** Amud **b**

דְּרַבִּי יְהוּדָה סָבַר לָהּ כְּרַבִּי. דִּתְנַן, רַבִּי אוֹמֵר: אֵין זֶה מְגַלֵּחַ אַחַת לִשְׁלֹשִׁים יוֹם. וְאֵיזֶהוּ שֶׁמְּגַלֵּחַ אַחַת לִשְׁלֹשִׁים יוֹם – הָאוֹמֵר "[הֲרֵי] עָלַי נְזִירוֹת כִּשְׂעַר רֹאשִׁי" וְ"כַעֲפַר הָאָרֶץ" וּ"כְחוֹל הַיָּם".

The Gemara answers: This is not possible, **as Rabbi Yehuda holds in accordance with** the opinion of **Rabbi** Yehuda HaNasi, **as we learned** in the mishna (8a) with regard to one who vows: I am hereby a nazirite like the hair of my head, **Rabbi** Yehuda HaNasi **says: This** nazirite **does not shave** his hair **once** every **thirty days,** as he is considered to have accepted one long term of naziriteship. **And who is** the nazirite **who** has accepted distinct terms of naziriteship and therefore **shaves** his hair **once** every **thirty days?** One **who says: It is** incumbent **upon me** to observe **naziriteships like the hair of my head, or: Like the dust of the earth, or: Like the sand of the sea.** Since Rabbi Yehuda agrees with Rabbi Yehuda HaNasi, he holds that one who uses a formulation similar to that used in the first case in the mishna and says: I am hereby a nazirite according to the capacity of the basket, has accepted one long term of naziriteship.

וְרַבִּי יְהוּדָה מִי סָבַר לָהּ כְּרַבִּי? וְהָתְנַן: "הֲרֵינִי נָזִיר כְּמִנְיַן יְמוֹת הַחַמָּה" וכו׳, אָמַר רַבִּי יְהוּדָה: מַעֲשֶׂה הָיָה וְכֵיוָן שֶׁהִשְׁלִים מֵת.

The Gemara asks: **And does Rabbi Yehuda hold in accordance with** the opinion of **Rabbi** Yehuda HaNasi? **But didn't we learn** in the mishna that if one says: **I am hereby a nazirite in accordance with the number of days** in **a solar** year, he counts 365 consecutive naziriteships, in accordance with the number of days in a solar year. **Rabbi Yehuda said: There was an incident** where someone took this vow and observed 365 consecutive terms of naziriteship. **Once he completed** all these terms of naziriteship, **he died.**

אִי אָמְרַתְּ בִּשְׁלָמָא נְזִירוּת קָא מְקַבֵּל עֲלֵיהּ – הַיְינוּ טַעֲמָא דְּכֵיוָן דְּהִשְׁלִים מֵת. אֶלָּא אִי אָמְרַתְּ חֲדָא נְזִירוּת קִבֵּל עִילָּוֵיהּ – מִי הָוֵי הַשְׁלָמָה כְּלָל?

The Gemara explains its question: **Granted, if you say** that **he accepts upon himself** many **nazariteships, that is the reason** for his statement **that once he completed** all these terms of naziriteship **he died. However, if you say** that Rabbi Yehuda does not agree with the unattributed opinion of the mishna and holds that **he accepted upon himself one** term of **naziriteship** lasting 365 days, **is there completion**[N] here **at all?** Rabbi Yehuda would not have used this terminology in reference to the mishna's previous statement if he himself holds that the individual accepted only one term of naziriteship.

וְעוֹד, מִי סָבַר לַהּ כְּרַבִּי? וְהָא תַּנְיָא, רַבִּי יְהוּדָה אוֹמֵר: "הֲרֵינִי נָזִיר מִנְיַן הֶילְקְטֵי קַיִץ" וּ"מִנְיַן שִׁבֳּלֵי שְׁמִיטָּה" – מוֹנֶה נְזִירוּת כְּמִנְיַן הֶילְקְטֵי קַיִץ, וּכְמִנְיַן שִׁבֳּלֵי שְׁמִיטָּה.

And furthermore, does Rabbi Yehuda **hold in accordance with** the opinion of **Rabbi** Yehuda HaNasi? **But isn't it taught** in a *baraita* that **Rabbi Yehuda says:** If one says: **I am hereby a nazirite** like **the number of piles** [*helketei*][L] **of figs** [*kayitz*][L] left to dry, **or:** Like **the number of sheaves of the Sabbatical Year,**[N] he must **count** as many **naziriteships as the number of piles of figs or as the number of sheaves of the Sabbatical Year?** This proves that Rabbi Yehuda does not hold that the individual accepts only one long term of naziriteship.

"מִנְיָן" שָׁאנֵי.

The Gemara responds: This does not prove that Rabbi Yehuda does not agree with Rabbi Yehuda HaNasi, since one who specifies: Like the **number, is different,** as even Rabbi Yehuda HaNasi would agree that he is referring to distinct terms of naziriteship rather than one long term of naziriteship.

וּמִי שָׁאנֵי לֵיהּ לְרַבִּי "מִנְיָן"? וְהָתַנְיָא: "הֲרֵינִי נָזִיר כְּמִנְיַן יְמוֹת הַחַמָּה" – מוֹנֶה נְזִירוּת כְּמִנְיַן יְמוֹת הַחַמָּה: "כִּימֵי הַלְּבָנָה" – מוֹנֶה כִּימֵי הַלְּבָנָה, רַבִּי אוֹמֵר: עַד שֶׁיֹּאמַר "נְזִירוּת עָלַי כְּמִנְיַן יְמוֹת הַחַמָּה" וּ"כְמִנְיַן יְמוֹת הַלְּבָנָה"!

The Gemara asks: **And is** the case of one who says: Like the **number, different** according **to Rabbi** Yehuda HaNasi? **But isn't it taught** in a *baraita* that if one says: **I am hereby a nazirite like the number of days** in a **solar** year, **he counts naziriteships** corresponding **to the number of days in a solar** year. If one says: **Like the days** in **a lunar** year, i.e., a year comprised of twelve lunar months, **he counts** terms of naziriteship corresponding **to the days** in **a lunar** year. **Rabbi** Yehuda HaNasi **says:** He is assumed to have accepted one term of naziriteship **until he says:** It is incumbent **upon me** to observe **naziriteships like the number of days** in **a solar** year, **or: Like the number of days** in **a lunar** year. This demonstrates that if one did not explicitly use the plural term naziriteships, he is assumed to have accepted a single term of naziriteship even if he said: Like the number.

NOTES

Is there completion – מִי הָוֵי הַשְׁלָמָה: It is explained in the Commentary on *Nazir* that according to Rabbi Yehuda HaNasi, the individual has not undertaken 365 terms of naziriteship, each of which lasts for thirty days. Rather, each term lasts for 365 days. Alternatively, the statement is understood to refer to one term of naziriteship for as long as the sun shines, i.e., forever. Either way, it is impossible for the individual to complete his term of naziriteship.

Other commentaries hold that, according to Rabbi Yehuda HaNasi, the individual has accepted one term of naziriteship lasting 365 days. Accordingly, the Rid explains that if Rabbi Yehuda agreed with this opinion he would not have noted that there was an incident in which an individual completed this term and then died, as one year is not a very long time. *Tosafot* and the Rosh explain that a mishna will typically cite an incident in support of a previously stated ruling. Consequently, Rabbi Yehuda's statement is understood to be providing support for the opinion of the first, anonymous *tanna*, who disagrees with Rabbi Yehuda HaNasi. Rabbeinu Peretz and an alternative answer of *Tosafot* claim that the word completion is unsuitable for a single term of naziriteship and applies only to one who vowed to observe several consecutive periods of naziriteship.

Sheaves of [*shibbolei*] the Sabbatical Year – שִׁבֳּלֵי שְׁמִיטָּה: It is explained in the Commentary on *Nazir* that since fields are not sown in the Sabbatical Year, the only produce that grows are aftergrowths of plants from the previous year. Consequently, they grow in sparse patches that can be counted. However, most commentaries, e.g., the *Arukh*, had a text of the Gemara that included the word *shevilei*, paths, instead of *shibbolei*. According to this version, a consequence of the fact that fields are not sown in the seventh year is that their owners do not mind if people walk through them, which leads to the formation of many paths. This version of the text is also cited in the Commentary on *Nazir*.

LANGUAGE

Piles [*helketei*] – הֶילְקְטֵי: There are many opinions as to the source of this word. Some assert that it comes from the Greek ἑλικτός, *heliktos*, meaning something bent and rounded, like a kind of bracket. According to this explanations, the term *helketei* is used here to refer to piles of figs left out to dry. Others claim that *helketei* is derived from the Greek ὁλκός, *holkos*, meaning a trail or path. Accordingly, the term is used here because when figs are laid out to dry they are arranged with paths between them in order to allow the owner to attend to the figs.

Figs [*kayitz*] – קַיִץ: A biblical word for figs that are left out to dry. The ends [*katzot*] of the figs were cut to allow some of the latex, the milky substance found in figs, to flow out, and then they were left in the sun to dry. Additionally, during the summer [*kayitz*], the fields were filled with mounds of drying figs.

Figs with dripping latex left out to dry

רַבִּי יְהוּדָה סָבַר לָהּ כְּוָתֵיהּ בַּחֲדָא, וּפָלֵיג עֲלֵיהּ בַּחֲדָא, סָבַר לָהּ כְּוָתֵיהּ בַּחֲדָא – נְזִירוּת קַבֵּיל עִילָּוֵיהּ, וּפָלֵיג עֲלֵיהּ בַּחֲדָא – דְּאִילּוּ רַבִּי יְהוּדָה שָׁנֵי לֵיהּ מוֹנֶה, וְרַבִּי לָא שָׁנֵי לֵיהּ מוֹנֶה.

The Gemara answers: **Rabbi Yehuda holds in accordance with** Rabbi Yehuda HaNasi's opinion **in one** case **and disagrees with him in one** case. **He holds in accordance with his** opinion **in one** case, as follows: If one says: I am hereby a nazirite like the hairs of my head, he has **accepted upon himself** one term of **naziriteship** for as many days as the number of hairs on his head. **And he disagrees with him in one** case, **as** according to **Rabbi Yehuda,** the case of one who **counts** is **different**[N] from the previous case, and so one who states: Like the number of hairs of my head, is considered to have accepted many distinct terms of naziriteship. However, according to **Rabbi** Yehuda HaNasi, one who **counts is not different.** He is assumed to have accepted a single term of naziriteship unless he explicitly uses the plural term naziriteships.

תָּנוּ רַבָּנַן: ״הֲרֵינִי נָזִיר כָּל יְמֵי חַיַּי״, ״הֲרֵינִי נְזִיר עוֹלָם״ – הֲרֵי זֶה נְזִיר עוֹלָם, אֲפִילּוּ ״מֵאָה שָׁנָה״ אֲפִילּוּ ״אֶלֶף שָׁנִים״ – אֵין זֶה נְזִיר עוֹלָם אֶלָּא נָזִיר לְעוֹלָם.

§ **The Sages taught:** If **one says: I am hereby a nazirite all the days of my life,**[H] or: **I am hereby a permanent nazirite, he is a permanent nazirite** and he trims his hair on a yearly basis like Absalom. However, in the case of one who accepts upon himself naziriteship for a fixed amount of time, **even** if he says: **One hundred years**[N] or **even: One thousand years, he is not** the specific type of nazirite known as **a permanent nazirite. Rather,** he is a regular **nazirite forever,** and he may never cut his hair.

תָּנוּ רַבָּנַן: ״הֲרֵינִי נָזִיר וְאַחַת״ – מוֹנֶה שְׁתַּיִם. ״וְעוֹד״ – מוֹנֶה שָׁלֹשׁ. ״וְשׁוּב״ – מוֹנֶה אַרְבַּע. פְּשִׁיטָא! מַהוּ דְּתֵימָא: ״וְשׁוּב״ כִּי כּוּלְּהוּ, וְהָוְיָא לֵיהּ שִׁית, קָא מַשְׁמַע לָן דְּלָא.

§ **The Sages taught** in a *baraita*: If one said: **I am hereby a nazirite and one,**[H] **he counts two** terms of naziriteship, since he first took a nazirite vow and then accepted an additional term of naziriteship. If one said: I am hereby a nazirite and one **and more, he counts three** terms of naziriteship. If he added to that statement: **And again, he counts four.** The Gemara asks: **Isn't** this last *halakha* **obvious?** The Gemara answers: It is necessary to teach this *halakha*. **Lest you say** that the words **and again** are referring to terms of naziriteship **equal** in number to **all the** terms[N] he has already accepted, **and he has** therefore accepted **six** terms of naziriteship altogether, the *baraita* therefore **teaches us that** this is **not** the correct interpretation of his statement.

תָּנוּ רַבָּנַן: ״הֲרֵינִי נָזִיר״. סוּמָכוֹס אוֹמֵר: ״הֵין״ – אַחַת, ״דִּיגוֹן״ – שְׁתַּיִם, ״טְרִיגוֹן״ – שָׁלֹשׁ, ״טֶטְרָגוֹן״ – אַרְבַּע, ״פּוּנְטִיגוֹן״ חָמֵשׁ.

The Sages taught in a *baraita*: If one said: **I am hereby a nazirite, Sumakhos says:** If he then added the word *hen*, which means one in Greek, he has accepted **one**[N] term of naziriteship. If one said: ***Digon,***[L] which means two sides in Hebraicized Greek, he must observe **two** terms of naziriteship. If one said: ***Trigon,*** which means triangle in Hebraicized Greek, then he has accepted three terms of naziriteship. If he said: ***Tetragon,*** quadrilateral in Hebraicized Greek, then he has accepted **four** terms, and if he said: ***Puntigon,*** pentagon in Hebraicized Greek, then he has accepted **five** terms of naziriteship.

HALAKHA

I am hereby a nazirite all the days of my life, etc. – הֲרֵינִי נָזִיר כָּל יְמֵי חַיַּי וכו׳: If one says: I am hereby a nazirite all the days of my life, or: I am hereby a permanent nazirite, he becomes a permanent nazirite. If he stipulates a fixed time in his vow, he is a nazirite for that period of time, even if it is longer than the human life span (Rambam *Sefer Hafla'a, Hilkhot Nezirut* 3:11).

I am hereby a nazirite and one, etc. – הֲרֵינִי נָזִיר וְאַחַת וכו׳: If one says: I am hereby a nazirite and one, he is obligated to observe two terms of naziriteship. If he says: I am hereby a nazirite and one and another, he is obligated to observe three terms of naziriteship, and if he adds: And again, he is a nazirite for four terms, as stated in the *baraita* (Rambam *Sefer Hafla'a, Hilkhot Nezirut* 3:8).

LANGUAGE

Digon, etc. – דִּיגוֹן וכו׳: From the Greek δίγονον, *digonon*, meaning having two sides, and related to δίγονος, *digonos*, meaning again, another time. Similarly, τρίγωνον, *trigonon*, means a triangle, and τρίγωνος, *trigonos*, means a third time. *Tetragon* comes from the Greek τετράγωνον, *tetragonon*, meaning with four equal angles, rectangular, or square. *Puntigon* comes from the Greek πεντάγωνον, *pentagonon*, meaning five sided, and it is used here to mean a fifth time.

NOTES

According to Rabbi Yehuda one who counts is different – רַבִּי יְהוּדָה שָׁנֵי לֵיהּ מוֹנֶה: According to this explanation, there are three distinct opinions cited in the mishna: According to the Rabbis, one who takes a vow to be a nazirite by mentioning something that divides into a number of distinct units is obligated to observe terms of naziriteship corresponding to that number. Rabbi Yehuda HaNasi holds that unless one explicitly mentions the plural term naziriteships, one who vows in this manner intends to observe a single term of naziriteship lasting as many days as those units. According to both these opinions, there is no difference whether or not the speaker mentions the word number. According to Rabbi Yehuda, if one mentions the word number, e.g., he says: Like the number of hairs of my head, he intends to accept separate terms of naziriteship. However, if he does not use this term he intends to accept a single term of naziriteship (see Rosh).

Even one hundred years – אֲפִילּוּ מֵאָה שָׁנָה: Any fixed number is considered a single unit, and therefore this statement is an acceptance of a single term of naziriteship.

The words and again are referring to terms of naziriteship like all the terms – וְשׁוּב כִּי כּוּלְּהוּ: The Rosh explains that the Gemara could have said that one might have thought that the words: And more, imply the same as the previous total, but it preferred to address the last phrase mentioned in the *baraita*.

If he then added the word *hen* he has accepted one, etc. – הֵין אַחַת וכו׳: Most commentaries explain that the novelty of Sumakhos's teaching is that one can accept naziriteship in any language. The Rosh indicates that the novelty is that if one says: I am hereby *hen*, or: I am hereby *digon*, he has accepted one or two terms of naziriteship, respectively. This is because the phrase: I am hereby, serves as an intimation of naziriteship. Additionally, the words of Greek origin mentioned here are not numbers but rather refer to shapes with certain numbers of sides, and the novelty is that despite the imprecision of his language, it is understood that one is referring to terms of naziriteship.

The Gemara cites another *baraita* dealing with these same expressions: **The Sages taught: A round house,**[H] **a two-sided** house, **a triangle**-shaped house, and **a pentagon**-shaped house **cannot become impure with leprosy,** whereas a house shaped like **a quadrilateral** can **become impure with leprosy.**[B] **What is the reason** for this? In the verse **below it states,** when referring to **a wall,** the plural term **walls:**[N] "And, behold, if the plague has spread in the walls of the house" (Leviticus 14:39). Additionally, in the verse **above it states,** when referring to **a wall,** the plural term **walls:** "And behold, if the plague be in the walls of the house" (Leviticus 14:37). These plural terms are unnecessary, and it is therefore understood that **there are four** walls mentioned **here** in order to indicate that a house can become impure through leprosy only if it has four sides.

תָּנוּ רַבָּנַן: בַּיִת עָגוֹל, דִּיגוֹן, טְרִיגוֹן, פּוּנְטִיגוֹן – אֵינוֹ מִטַּמֵּא בִּנְגָעִים. טֶטְרָגוֹן מִטַּמֵּא בִּנְגָעִים. מַאי טַעְמָא? לְמַטָּה הוּא אוֹמֵר "קִיר" "קִירוֹת". לְמַעְלָה הוּא אוֹמֵר "קִיר" "קִירוֹת" – הֲרֵי כָּאן אַרְבַּע.

הדרן עלך כל כינויי

HALAKHA

A round house, etc. – בַּיִת עָגוֹל וכו׳: Only a house with four walls can become impure with leprosy. If the house is round or has three or five walls, it cannot become impure (Rambam *Sefer Tahara, Hilkhot Tzara'at* 14:6).

BACKGROUND

Leprosy of the house – נִגְעֵי בָתִּים: By Torah law (see Leviticus 14:33–57), if leprous spots appear on a house, all the objects in the house are removed in order to prevent them from becoming ritually impure, after which a priest is brought to examine the house. If the priest confirms that there is evidence of leprosy, the house is quarantined for a week, after which it is reexamined by the priest. If the leprous spots have darkened or disappeared, the house is declared ritually pure. If the spots have remained unchanged, the house is quarantined for a second week. If the spots then darken, the house is declared ritually pure after undergoing a purification process. However, if the spots remain unchanged or have spread, the affected parts of the house are removed and replaced with new materials, after which the house is quarantined for a third week. If the spots reappear, the entire house must be destroyed, and its stones are disposed of in a ritually impure place.

A leprous house renders people and objects inside it ritually impure, with the exception of objects in hermetically sealed earthenware containers. If the house is declared free of leprosy, it is purified by a process involving birds, cedarwood, and red thread, parallel to the purification process of a leprous person.

NOTES

It states, when referring to a wall, the plural term walls, etc. – הוּא אוֹמֵר קִיר, קִירוֹת וכו׳: It is noted in the Commentary on *Nazir* that the *baraita* does not expound every instance where the word wall appears in the verses pertaining to leprosy on a house, as the verse also states: "And its appearance be lower than the wall" (Leviticus 14:37). Rather, the *baraita* expounds only the instances in which the plural walls is used unnecessarily instead of the singular term wall.

The early commentaries ask why the plural terms are considered unnecessary, given that the Gemara derives from these terms that a house is considered to be afflicted with leprosy only if a symptom appears on a corner of the house, such that a single, unbroken spot appears on two walls (*Sanhedrin* 71a). The Rosh answers that only one of the plural terms is necessary for that derivation, and the other usage serves as the source for the *halakha* that only a four-sided house can be afflicted with leprosy. Alternatively, Rabbeinu Peretz states that if the plural term were used only in order to teach that the symptom must appear on a corner of the house, the Torah would have used the same term throughout.

Summary of **Perek I**

In this chapter the Gemara established the following: Commonly used substitute terms for the language of nazirite vows and substitute terms that were set by the Sages are effective expressions to use when accepting upon oneself a nazirite vow. Similarly, intimations of nazirite vows that clearly express one's intent to become a nazirite are effective nazirite vows, although they are incomplete statements. Occasionally, the meaning of a statement is understood from its context. For example, if one takes a vaguely articulated vow while a nazirite is passing by or while holding on to one's hair, his statement is considered a nazirite vow. Additionally, one who accepts upon himself some of the restrictions of a nazirite becomes a full-fledged nazirite. However, expressions that are themselves only substitutes for substitute terms of nazirite vows, and ambiguous intimations of nazirite vows that are completely obscure are not considered nazirite vows. They do not obligate the speaker to become a nazirite.

The Gemara determined that the minimum duration of a term of naziriteship is thirty days. If one takes a nazirite vow without specifying the duration of the naziriteship, he becomes a nazirite for thirty days. This is true even if he says that he will be a nazirite for one large period, or for one small period, without specifying the precise length of the period. If he accepts upon himself a period of a naziriteship and a half, he is obligated to observe two thirty-day periods, unless it was clear that he intended to accept upon himself one term of naziriteship that would last longer than the duration of an unspecified term of naziriteship. If one compares the number of naziriteship periods that he is accepting upon himself with separate, distinct items, he becomes obligated in multiple, consecutive terms, equal to the number of items with which he compared his naziriteship.

This chapter discussed the three different ways that one can become a nazirite for the duration of his lifetime and the different *halakhot* that apply to each type of lifelong nazirite. One who accepts upon himself consecutive terms of naziriteship or a single term of naziriteship that will last longer than his life span is a nazirite forever. In the case of consecutive terms, the nazirite treats each period as a separate term of naziriteship. He shaves his hair and brings offerings at the conclusion of each term. One who takes a nazirite vow and specifies that it applies for the duration of his life is also a nazirite forever. In this case, the individual is known as a permanent nazirite and is obligated in one long term of naziriteship that lasts for the duration of his lifetime. However, once a year he trims his hair and brings the nazirite offerings. Finally, some Sages explain that it is possible to vow to be a nazirite like Samson. This type of naziriteship lasts for the duration of one's life but differs from a permanent nazirite in that the individual is permitted to become impure from a corpse but is prohibited from ever cutting his hair.

Introduction to **Perek II**

This chapter addresses instances where unusual terminology is employed in uttering vows of naziriteship. This chapter discusses statements that can be interpreted in multiple ways, vows of naziriteship that are made with a variety of stipulations or vows made in circumstances that complicate their implementation.

The first issue the Gemara considers is a situation in which the language or context of a statement might indicate an acceptance of naziriteship or might be a different vow altogether. A second set of problems concerns instances where an individual takes a vow of naziriteship without a full understanding of its *halakhot* or without the willingness to accept all of the restrictions involved in naziriteship.

One is able to vow to pay for the offerings of a nazirite rather than to become one himself. The Gemara addresses the extent of the obligations incurred by one who states such a vow, and the obligations incurred by one who obligates himself to pay for only a part of the nazirite offerings.

Another discussion in this chapter examines a naziriteship vow made conditional on the speaker having a child. The Gemara addresses whether he meant to become a nazirite both if he had a boy or a girl, or perhaps only if he had a boy.

This chapter also discusses the *halakha* in a case where one vowed to observe a term of naziriteship that would begin on a certain day or when a certain event occurs, and then accepts another vow of naziriteship whose term will interfere with the implementation of the previous vow.

מתני׳ ״הֲרֵינִי נָזִיר מִן הַגְּרוֹגָרוֹת וּמִן הַדְּבֵילָה״. בֵּית שַׁמַּאי אוֹמְרִים: נָזִיר, וּבֵית הִלֵּל אוֹמְרִים: אֵינוֹ נָזִיר. אָמַר רַבִּי יְהוּדָה: אַף כְּשֶׁאָמְרוּ בֵּית שַׁמַּאי – לֹא אָמְרוּ אֶלָּא בְּאוֹמֵר ״הֲרֵי הֵן עָלַי קָרְבָּן״.

MISHNA If one says: **I am hereby a nazirite** and therefore will refrain **from dried figs**[H] **and from cakes of dried figs, Beit Shammai say:** His statement renders him a full-fledged **nazirite,** and his addition: From dried figs, is insignificant, as this fruit is not included in the prohibitions of a nazirite, which include only products of the grapevine. **And Beit Hillel say: He is not a nazirite,** since he did not accept naziriteship upon himself. **Rabbi Yehuda said: Even when Beit Shammai said** that this vow takes effect, **they said** that **only in** a case **where** one **said** that he meant: **They are hereby** forbidden **to me**[N] as **an offering.** In that case it is as though he took a vow rendering the figs forbidden to him. However, Beit Shammai concede that although the vow takes effect, it is not a vow of naziriteship.

גמ׳ ״הֲרֵינִי נָזִיר מִן הַגְּרוֹגָרוֹת וּמִן הַדְּבֵילָה״. בֵּית שַׁמַּאי אוֹמְרִים: נָזִיר. וְאַמַּאי? ״מִכֹּל אֲשֶׁר יֵעָשֶׂה מִגֶּפֶן הַיַּיִן״ אָמַר רַחֲמָנָא! בֵּית שַׁמַּאי סָבְרִי לָהּ כְּרַבִּי מֵאִיר, דְּאָמַר: אֵין אָדָם מוֹצִיא דְּבָרָיו לְבַטָּלָה.

GEMARA It is stated in the mishna that if one says: **I am hereby a nazirite** and therefore will refrain **from dried figs and from cakes of dried figs, Beit Shammai say:** He is a **nazirite.** The Gemara asks: **But why? The Merciful One states** in the Torah in the passage dealing with naziriteship: **"From anything that is made of the grapevine**…he shall not eat" (Numbers 6:4). In naziriteship, only the fruit of the vine is prohibited. The Gemara answers: **Beit Shammai hold in accordance with** the opinion of **Rabbi Meir, who says: A person does not utter a statement for naught.** In other words, if one utters a statement that cannot be fulfilled as stated, his statement is interpreted in a manner that renders it relevant. Here too, Beit Shammai say that he misspoke and actually intended to take a vow of naziriteship.

וּבֵית הִלֵּל סָבְרִי לָהּ כְּרַבִּי יוֹסֵי, דְּאָמַר: בִּגְמַר דְּבָרָיו אָדָם נִתְפָּס. וְהַאי נֶדֶר וּפִתְחוֹ עִמּוֹ הוּא.

And Beit Hillel hold in accordance with the opinion of **Rabbi Yosei, who says: A person** is also **held accountable for the conclusion of his statement.** If one states two irreconcilable clauses, e.g., this animal is a substitute for a burnt-offering, a substitute for a peace-offering; the second clause is not disregarded, and the animal assumes both statuses. **And this is a vow with its** inherent **opening,** i.e., reason for dissolution. Although he said: I am hereby a nazirite, by adding the words: From dried figs and from cakes of dried figs, he indicated that his intention was that the naziriteship would not take effect.

וּבֵית שַׁמַּאי נַמִי, נֶדֶר וּפִתְחוֹ עִמּוֹ הוּא.

The Gemara asks: **And** according to **Beit Shammai too,**[N] **it is a vow with its** inherent **opening,** and since they certainly agree that a vow of this kind does not take effect, why do they hold that this vow takes effect?

HALAKHA

I am hereby a nazirite from dried figs, etc. – **הֲרֵינִי נָזִיר מִן הַגְּרוֹגָרוֹת וכו׳**: The Rambam writes that if one says: I am hereby a nazirite and therefore will refrain from dried figs, or: From cakes of dried figs, or any statement of this kind, it is prohibited for him to derive benefit from them due to his vow, but he is not rendered a nazirite. This ruling is in accordance with the opinion of Beit Hillel. The Ra'avad disagrees with the Rambam, claiming that the Gemara indicates that according to the opinion of Beit Hillel one is not prohibited from deriving benefit even from dried figs. *Tosefot Yom Tov* and *Likkutei Halakhot* offer additional explanations of this matter (Rambam *Sefer Hafla'a, Hilkhot Nezirut* 1:10).

NOTES

In a case where one said: They are hereby forbidden to me, etc. – **בְּאוֹמֵר הֲרֵי הֵן עָלַי וכו׳**: Many commentaries (Rabbeinu Peretz, citing Rosh; Rid) explain that although the first term he used explicitly referred to naziriteship, he actually intended to state a standard vow of prohibition. The Rid even has a variant reading: Like one who said, instead of: In a case of one who said. *Tosafot* explain that although the word nazirite has a specific meaning, it can refer to separation in general, and therefore it can be used as an expression of a vow. An alternative approach, cited by Rabbeinu Peretz and Rabbeinu Azriel, is that he was actually asked about his intention afterward, and he clarified that he intended to vow that dried figs were forbidden to him. The Commentary on *Nazir*, according to some later authorities, and Rabbi Avraham min HaHar claim that the case under discussion is one in which one explicitly stated: They are hereby forbidden to me like an offering, in addition to his initial statement of: I am hereby a nazirite and therefore will refrain from dried figs.

An entirely different approach is presented in the Rambam's Commentary on the Mishna. He contends that even according to Rabbi Yehuda, Beit Shammai hold that the individual becomes a nazirite, since the usage of the word: Offering, indicates that he wishes to be a nazirite, as offerings are an integral part of naziriteship. If he does not mention an offering, his words are meaningless even according to Beit Shammai.

And Beit Shammai too – **וּבֵית שַׁמַּאי נַמִי**: The Rid points out that the logic of this claim is in fact the opposite of that which was previously attributed to Beit Shammai, as earlier the Gemara explained that the second statement is not to be understood as a clarification of the first. He therefore explains that the Gemara is suggesting an alternative formulation, whose initial assumption is that this is a vow with its inherent opening to broach dissolution, and then explains that Beit Shammai holds in accordance with the opinion of Rabbi Meir. See *Tosafot* for a different explanation.

אֶלָּא, בֵּית שַׁמַּאי סָבְרִי לָהּ כְּרַבִּי מֵאִיר, דְּאָמַר: אֵין אָדָם מוֹצִיא דְּבָרָיו לְבַטָּלָה. וְכֵיוָן דְּאָמַר ״הֲרֵינִי נָזִיר״ – הֲוָה לֵיהּ נָזִיר, כִּי קָאָמַר ״מִן הַגְּרוֹגָרוֹת וּמִן הַדְּבֵילָה״ – לְאִיתְּשׁוּלֵי הוּא דְּקָאָתֵי. וּבֵית שַׁמַּאי לְטַעֲמַיְיהוּ, דְּאָמְרִי: אֵין שְׁאֵלָה בְּהֶקְדֵּשׁ. וְכֵיוָן דְּאֵין שְׁאֵלָה בְּהֶקְדֵּשׁ – אֵין שְׁאֵלָה בִּנְזִירוּת.

The Gemara explains the dispute: **Rather, Beit Shammai hold in accordance with** the opinion of **Rabbi Meir, who said: A person does not utter a statement for naught, and once he said: I am hereby a nazirite, he is** immediately rendered **a nazirite. When he then says:** And therefore I will refrain **from dried figs and from cakes of dried figs, he is coming to request**[N] that a halakhic authority dissolve his vow, as he regrets having taken the vow and is now seeking to dissolve it. **And Beit Shammai follow their** standard line of **reasoning, as they say:** One **cannot request** that a halakhic authority dissolve a vow **of consecrated** property,[H] which one can do for vows of prohibition. **And since** one **cannot request** that a halakhic authority dissolve a vow **of consecrated** property, likewise one **cannot request** that a halakhic authority dissolve a vow **of naziriteship,**[NH] as the legal status of a vow of naziriteship is like that of a vow of consecrated property in this regard.

וּבֵית הִלֵּל סָבְרִי כְּרַבִּי שִׁמְעוֹן, דִּתְנַן: וְרַבִּי שִׁמְעוֹן פּוֹטֵר, שֶׁלֹּא הִתְנַדֵּב כְּדֶרֶךְ הַמִּתְנַדְּבִים.

And Beit Hillel hold in accordance with the opinion of **Rabbi Shimon,**[N] **as we learned** in a mishna (*Menaḥot* 103a): If one vows to bring a meal-offering from barley, since voluntary meal-offerings are brought only from wheat, the Rabbis say: He must bring a meal-offering from wheat, **and Rabbi Shimon exempts** him entirely, **as he did not donate in the manner** typical **of donors.** Since he donated an offering that cannot be sacrificed, his vow is meaningless. Here too, since he took a vow of naziriteship stating that he therefore will refrain from dried figs rather than from wine, his statement is meaningless.

NOTES

He is coming to request – לְאִיתְּשׁוּלֵי הוּא דְּקָאָתֵי: The early commentaries point out that the wording here is imprecise, as he has not actually appeared before a halakhic authority to request the dissolution of his vow. Rather, it means that he regrets taking the vow, and this is comparable to one who goes to request dissolution (*Tosafot*).

One cannot request of a halakhic authority to dissolve a vow of naziriteship – אֵין שְׁאֵלָה בִּנְזִירוּת: The Commentary on *Nazir* explains that naziriteship is compared to consecration in the verse: "He shall be holy" (Numbers 6:5), as the same Hebrew word, *kadosh*, is used for both consecration and the holiness of a nazirite. *Tosafot* and other early commentaries offer similar explanations. Maharit Algazi and the Netziv suggest that a vow of naziriteship is considered like consecration because it includes the offerings brought by the nazirite upon the completion of his term. One who seeks to have his naziriteship dissolved is effectively asking for the dissolution of the requirement to bring these offerings. The language of the Gemara offers some support for this interpretation.

And Beit Hillel hold in accordance with the opinion of Rabbi Shimon – וּבֵית הִלֵּל סָבְרִי כְּרַבִּי שִׁמְעוֹן: Beit Hillel do not even address the issue of whether one can rescind consecrated property because they hold that one who does not formulate his statement properly has not consecrated the item at all (*Tosafot*). The following question is posed by some early commentaries: Why doesn't the Gemara simply say that according to Beit Hillel, rescinding is possible in the case of consecrated property, as they do in fact hold? On the following page, *Tosafot* answer that this explanation would not account for the fact that in this situation Beit Hillel do not even prohibit one from benefiting from dried figs. Others suggest that the Gemara preferred an explanation that applies even according to the opinion that there is no rescinding of consecrated items (*Shita Mekubbetzet*), or that it wanted to suggest an answer that also suits Rabbi Yehuda's explanation of the opinion of Beit Shammai (Rabbeinu Todros).

HALAKHA

Request dissolution of a vow of consecrated property – שְׁאֵלָה בְּהֶקְדֵּשׁ: The *halakha* is not in accordance with the opinion of Beit Shammai; rather, one may rescind a donation of consecrated property and dissolve vows of consecration, just as one may dissolve standard vows. However, it is a mitzva to fulfill one's dedications to the Temple, and one should seek to dissolve those vows only in cases of extreme necessity (Rambam *Sefer Hafla'a, Hilkhot Nedarim* 4:7, 13:25; *Shulḥan Arukh, Yoreh De'a* 203:3, 258:1).

Request dissolution of a vow of naziriteship – שְׁאֵלָה בִּנְזִירוּת: One who takes a vow of naziriteship and regrets his vow may request that a halakhic authority dissolve his naziriteship in the same manner as standard vows are dissolved (Rambam *Sefer Hafla'a, Hilkhot Nezirut* 2:1).

מתניתין דלא כי האי תנא. דתניא, רבי נתן אומר: בית שמאי אומרים: נדור ונזיר, ובית הלל אומרים: נדור ואין נזיר. בית שמאי סברי לה כרבי מאיר וכרבי יהודה, ובית הלל סברי לה כרבי יוסי.

§ The Gemara comments: **The mishna is not in accordance with** the opinion of **this** ***tanna*****. As it is taught** in a *baraita*: **Rabbi Natan says** that if one says: I am hereby a nazirite and therefore will refrain from dried figs, **Beit Shammai say:** He has rendered dried figs **forbidden** to himself **by a vow, and** he is also **a nazirite; and Beit Hillel say:** He has rendered dried figs **forbidden** to himself **by a vow, but** he is **not a nazirite.**[H] According to Rabbi Natan, **Beit Shammai hold in accordance with** the opinion of **Rabbi Meir** that a person does not utter statements for naught and that he becomes a nazirite as soon as he says: I am hereby a nazirite; **and** he explains the opinion of Beit Shammai **as Rabbi Yehuda** does, i.e., that one in this situation has vowed that dried figs are forbidden to him, since the rest of his statement also has significance. **And Beit Hillel hold in accordance with** the opinion of **Rabbi Yosei**[N] that one is held to the conclusion of his statement, and he has therefore vowed that dried figs are forbidden to him.

לישנא אחרינא אמרי לה: רבי נתן אומר, בית שמאי אומרים: נדור ואינו נזיר, ובית הלל אומרים: לא נדור ולא נזיר. בית שמאי – כרבי יהודה, ובית הלל – כרבי שמעון.

Some say a different version[N] of the *baraita*: **Rabbi Natan says** that **Beit Shammai say:** He has rendered dried figs **forbidden** to himself **by a vow and he is not a nazirite; and Beit Hillel say:** He has **not** rendered dried figs **forbidden** to himself **by a vow, and** he is **not a nazirite.** According to this version, the opinion of **Beit Shammai is as Rabbi Yehuda** explained in the mishna, **and Beit Hillel hold in accordance with** the opinion of **Rabbi Shimon,** who maintains that a donation not performed in the manner typical of donors is not a donation.

תנן התם: האומר "הרי עלי מנחה להביא מן השעורים" – יביא מן החיטים: "קמח" – יביא סולת: "שלא בשמן ולבונה" – יביאנה בשמן ולבונה: "חצי עשרון" – יביא עשרון שלם: "עשרון ומחצה" – יביא שנים. רבי שמעון פוטר, שלא התנדב כדרך המתנדבים.

§ The Gemara discusses a case mentioned earlier. **We learned** in a mishna **there** (*Menaḥot* 103a): With regard to **one who says: It is** incumbent **upon me to bring a meal-offering**[B] **from barley,**[H] since voluntary meal-offerings are made only with wheat **he must bring** a meal-offering **from wheat.** If one vows to bring a meal-offering from **flour,** since a standard meal-offering is made from fine flour **he must bring** one from **fine flour.** If one vows to bring a meal-offering **without oil and frankincense, he must bring it with oil and frankincense,** in accordance with the *halakha*. If one vows to bring a meal-offering with **half of a tenth** of an ephah of fine flour, **he must bring** a meal-offering with **a full tenth,** since a meal-offering cannot have less than one-tenth of an ephah of flour. If one vows to bring a meal-offering with **a tenth and a half, he brings two** units of a tenth of an ephah in his meal-offering. Since half of one-tenth of an ephah is the minimum, his vow is increased to two full tenths. **Rabbi Shimon exempts** him entirely in all these cases, **as he did not donate in the manner** typical **of donors.**

מאן תנא, דכי אמר "הרי עלי מנחה מן השעורים" – מביא מן החיטים? אמר חזקיה: במחלוקת שנויה, ובית שמאי היא. לאו אמרי בית שמאי כי אמר "מן הגרוגרות ומן הדבילה" הוי נזיר – הכי נמי, כי אמר "מן השעורין" – מביא מן החיטים.

The Gemara asks: **Who is the** *tanna* who **taught that when one said: It is** incumbent **upon me** to bring **a meal-offering from barley, he brings** a meal-offering **from wheat? Ḥizkiyya said** that this *halakha* **is taught as a dispute** between *tanna'im*, **and it is** the opinion of **Beit Shammai.** He explains: **Didn't Beit Shammai say that when one said:** I am hereby a nazirite and therefore will refrain **from dried figs and from cakes of dried figs, he is a nazirite,** indicating that he is held to only the first part of his statement, and the conflicting details are ignored? **So too, when he said** that he will bring a meal-offering **from barley, he brings** it **from wheat,** and the same analysis applies to the other cases listed in this mishna.

ורבי יוחנן אמר: אפילו תימא דברי הכל, באומר "אילו הייתי יודע שאין נודרין כך – לא נדרתי כך אלא כך".

And Rabbi Yoḥanan said: You can **even say** that **all,** including Beit Hillel, **agree** with the opinion of the Rabbis of the mishna, as the mishna may be stated **with regard to one who** later **says,** to clarify his earlier statement: **Had I known that one cannot vow in this manner,** that one cannot bring a voluntary meal-offering from barley, **I would not have vowed that way, only this way,** to bring a meal-offering from wheat. Mentioning barley was an error on his part rather than a condition, and he actually meant to bring a standard meal-offering. In this case even Beit Hillel, who maintain in the mishna here that there is no vow at all, deem him liable to bring a proper meal-offering.

HALAKHA

Forbidden by a vow, but he is not a nazirite, etc. – **נדור ואין נזיר וכו׳**: The Rambam rules that if one says: I am hereby a nazirite and therefore will refrain from dried figs, or any similar statement, then dried figs are forbidden to him due to his vow, however naziriteship does not take effect. The Ra'avad objects to the Rambam's ruling, as the Gemara indicates that the mishna is not in accordance with the opinion of Rabbi Natan, and therefore one should not even be bound by a vow. The *Kesef Mishne* states that the Rambam's version of the text probably read: The mishna is in accordance with Rabbi Natan. Other commentaries reconcile Rambam's ruling without emending the text, since they maintain that this is the opinion of Beit Hillel as presented in the mishna (Rambam *Sefer Hafla'a*, *Hilkhot Nezirut* 1:10).

It is incumbent upon me to bring a meal-offering from barley, etc. – **הרי עלי מנחה להביא מן השעורים וכו׳**: If one says: It is incumbent upon me to bring a meal-offering of barley, or: A meal-offering of half a tenth, or: A meal-offering of no oil or frankincense, he is exempt, since he has not donated in the manner typical of donors. If he says: It is incumbent upon me to bring a meal-offering from barley, or: From lentils, and the like, he is questioned about his intentions. If he thought that there was such a meal-offering, and had he known that meal-offerings must comprise a full tenth of fine wheat flour with oil and frankincense he would not have vowed as he did, he is exempt. If he says that had he known, he would have vowed in the proper manner, he is obligated to bring a standard meal-offering. The *Kesef Mishne* explains that the ruling of the Rambam is in accordance with the opinion of Rabbi Yoḥanan, as well as in accordance with the opinion of Ze'eiri in tractate *Menaḥot*, who differentiate between one who says: A meal-offering of, and one who says: A meal-offering from (Rambam *Sefer Avoda*, *Hilkhot Ma'aseh HaKorbanot* 17:9).

NOTES

And Beit Hillel hold in accordance with the opinion of Rabbi Yosei – **ובית הלל סברי לה כרבי יוסי**: *Tosafot* and other early commentaries have a variant reading of the text: Hold in accordance with the opinion of Rabbi Yehuda. In other words, the opinion of Beit Hillel in the *baraita* is the same as Rabbi Yehuda's explanation of Beit Shammai in the mishna, i.e., that there is only a vow and no naziriteship.

A different version – **לישנא אחרינא**: This version is exactly the same as that of Rabbi Yehuda in the mishna. The only difference is the Gemara's addition that Beit Hillel hold in accordance with the opinion of Rabbi Shimon that if one did not express his donation in the typical manner it does not take effect.

BACKGROUND

Meal-offering – **מנחה**: There are a variety of offerings of flour or bread that were brought in the Temple. The Gemara here is discussing a vow to bring a voluntary meal-offering, which may be brought in one of four ways: Mixed with oil, baked in an oven, fried on a griddle, or in a pan (see Leviticus 2:1–13). All of these offerings were made of fine wheat flour.

אָמַר חִזְקִיָּה: לֹא שָׁנוּ אֶלָּא שֶׁאָמַר "מִן הַשְּׂעוֹרִים". אֲבָל אָמַר "מִן הָעֲדָשִׁים" – לָא מַיְיתֵי וְלָא כְּלוּם.

With regard to this ruling **Ḥizkiyya says: They taught** that he must bring a meal-offering from wheat **only if he said** that he will bring a meal-offering **from barley. But** if **he said** he will bring a meal-offering **from lentils,**[B] **he does not bring anything.** The difference is that the meal-offerings of the *omer* and of a *sota* are made from barley, so if he said: From barley, he may have mistakenly believed that a voluntary meal-offering can be prepared from barley as well. As everyone knows that no meal-offering is made from lentils, his statement demonstrates that he never intended to bring a meal-offering.

מִכְּדִי חִזְקִיָּה כְּמַאן מוֹקִים לַהּ לְמַתְנִיתִין – כְּבֵית שַׁמַּאי, וְהָא עֲדָשִׁים לְגַבֵּי מִנְחָה כִּגְרוֹגָרוֹת לְגַבֵּי נָזִיר דָּמוּ, וְקָאָמְרִי בֵּית שַׁמַּאי הָוֵי נָזִיר! הֲדַר בֵּיהּ חִזְקִיָּה.

The Gemara asks: **Now** consider, **in accordance with whose** opinion **does Ḥizkiyya establish the mishna** in *Menaḥot*? It is **in accordance with** the opinion of **Beit Shammai. But lentils relative to a meal-offering are comparable to dried figs relative to a nazirite,** as everyone is likewise aware that one cannot be a nazirite and therefore refrain from figs, **and** yet **Beit Shammai say he is a nazirite.** Why not say that one who vows to bring a meal-offering from lentils is obligated to bring a standard meal-offering? The Gemara answers: **Ḥizkiyya retracted**[N] **from it** and no longer holds that the mishna in *Menaḥot* is in accordance with the opinion of Beit Shammai.

וְאַמַּאי הֲדַר בֵּיהּ? אָמַר רָבָא: מַתְנִיתִין קַשִׁיתֵיהּ, מַאי אִירְיָא דְּתָנֵי "מִן הַשְּׂעוֹרִים"? לִיתְנֵי "מִן הָעֲדָשִׁים". אֶלָּא סָבַר חִזְקִיָּה: כִּי קָאָמְרִי בֵּית שַׁמַּאי הָתָם – כְּרַבִּי יְהוּדָה.

The Gemara asks: **And why did he** in fact **retract from it? Rava said:** The **mishna caused him difficulty** and demonstrated his error. If the mishna is in accordance with Beit Shammai's opinion with regard to a nazirite, **why does** the *tanna* **specifically teach** the case of one who says that he will bring a meal-offering **from barley? Let him teach** a greater novelty, i.e., that even one who vowed to bring a meal-offering **from lentils** is obligated to bring a meal-offering made from wheat. **Rather, Ḥizkiyya holds** that **when Beit Shammai stated** their opinion **there,** i.e., in the mishna with regard to a nazirite, their intention was **as** explained by **Rabbi Yehuda,** that one's statement is interpreted to be meaningful and it can have the meaning of creating a vow that dried figs are forbidden to him. In the case of the meal-offering, even they agree that since one's vow has no meaning, as there cannot be a meal-offering made of lentils, no vow takes effect.

וְרַבִּי יוֹחָנָן אָמַר: אֲפִילּוּ מִן הָעֲדָשִׁים. וְהָא רַבִּי יוֹחָנָן הוּא דְּאָמַר: בְּאוֹמֵר "אִילּוּ הָיִיתִי יוֹדֵעַ שֶׁאֵין נוֹדְרִין כָּךְ – לֹא נָדַרְתִּי כָּךְ אֶלָּא כָּךְ"! לְדִבְרָיו דְּחִזְקִיָּה הוּא דְּקָאָמַר:

And Rabbi Yoḥanan said: Even one who vowed to bring a meal-offering **from lentils** must bring a meal-offering from wheat. The Gemara asks: **But Rabbi Yoḥanan is he who said** that the mishna is referring to a case of one **who says: Had I known that one cannot vow in this manner, I would not have vowed that way, only this way?** In the case of the lentils, it is not reasonable to say that he erred in thinking that one may vow to bring a meal-offering from lentils. The Gemara answers: **He stated** this ruling **in accordance with the statement of Ḥizkiyya.** Rabbi Yoḥanan was not stating his own opinion; he was challenging the ruling of Ḥizkiyya.

אַתְּ מַאי טַעְמָא קָא הָדְרַתְּ בָּךְ – מִשּׁוּם דְּלָא קָתָנֵי "מִן הָעֲדָשִׁים". דִּלְמָא לָא מִיבַּעְיָא קָאָמַר; לָא מִיבַּעְיָא כִּי אָמַר "מֵעֲדָשִׁים" – דְּמַיְיתֵי מִנְחָה מְעַלַּיְיתָא, דְּאִיכָּא לְמֵימַר מִיהְדַּר הוּא דַּהֲדַר בֵּיהּ, וְתִפּוֹס לָשׁוֹן רִאשׁוֹן. אֶלָּא כִּי אָמַר "מִן הַשְּׂעוֹרִין" וַדַּאי דְּהָכִי קָאָמַר: אִי קְדֻשָּׁה כְּמִנְחַת הָעוֹמֶר,

The Gemara explains his challenge: **What is the reason you retracted** your earlier opinion that the mishna is in accordance with the opinion of Beit Shammai? You did so **because it does not teach: From lentils.** That is not conclusive, as **perhaps it is speaking** utilizing the style of: **It is not necessary,** as follows: **It is not necessary** to say that **when one says:** It is incumbent upon me to bring a meal-offering **from lentils, that he brings a proper meal-offering** of wheat. In that situation **it can be said** that by saying: From lentils, **he is retracting** his first statement and now wants to rescind his vow. **And** yet Beit Shammai hold that he is **held to the first** part of his **statement,** and they do not allow the rescinding of a vow of consecration. **But if he said:** It is incumbent upon me to bring a meal-offering **from barley,** since it is possible to explain that **certainly this is what he said: If** this meal-offering that I have vowed to bring from barley **is consecrated like the *omer* meal-offering,**[B]

BACKGROUND

Lentils – עֲדָשִׁים: Lentils, *Lens culinaris*, are a type of legume that grows on a bushy plant with purple flowers. The plant is about 40 cm tall, and the seeds grow in pods. The color of the seeds can be orange, green, yellow, brown, or black. There is evidence that lentils were consumed by people throughout the world since antiquity.

Lentil bush and flowers

Lentils of different colors

The *omer* meal-offering – מִנְחַת הָעוֹמֶר: The *omer* is a measure of grain, one-tenth of an ephah. This term is used to refer to the measure of barley offered in the Temple on the sixteenth of Nisan, the second day of Passover. The offering was brought irrespective of whether the sixteenth of Nisan was a Shabbat or a weekday. The *omer* was harvested on the night following the first day of Passover from the newly ripe barley and was prepared as roasted flour. A handful was burned on the altar; the rest was eaten by the priests. In addition to the *omer*, a male sheep was sacrificed as a burnt-offering, together with a wine libation and two-tenths of an ephah of wheat flour as a meal-offering. Once the *omer* had been offered, grain from the new harvest could be eaten.

NOTES

Ḥizkiyya retracted – הֲדַר בֵּיהּ חִזְקִיָּה: *Tosafot* explain that Ḥizkiyya retracted his opinion that the mishna in tractate *Menaḥot* is in accordance with the opinion of Beit Shammai. Instead, he now agrees with Rabbi Yoḥanan that it is referring to one who says he vowed in error. Accordingly, *Tosafot* omit the following sentence from the Gemara: Rather, Ḥizkiyya holds that when Beit Shammai stated their opinion there, their intention was as explained by Rabbi Yehuda. This sentence likewise does not appear in the parallel discussion in *Menaḥot*. Others claim that Ḥizkiyya did not retract his statement about the mishna in *Menaḥot*. They contend that Ḥizkiyya in fact retracted his understanding of the opinion of Beit Shammai in the mishna here. He is no longer of the opinion that Beit Shammai's opinion is as stated by the unattributed mishna, and he agrees with Rabbi Yehuda that according to Beit Shammai one is bound by a vow but is not a nazirite (Commentary on *Nazir*; Meiri).

אוֹ כְּמִנְחַת סוֹטָה – תִּקְדּוֹשׁ, אִי לָא – לָא. קָא מַשְׁמַע לַן דְּמַיְיתֵי מִן הַחִיטִּים.

or like the meal-offering of a ***sota*****,**[B] both of which are made of barley, **it should become consecrated,** and **if** it is **not** possible to volunteer a meal-offering from barley, it should **not** be a meal-offering at all. The mishna therefore **teaches us that one** nevertheless **brings** a meal-offering made **from wheat.** Rabbi Yoḥanan holds that the difficulty raised by Ḥizkiyya against his own explanation is inconclusive, and he need not have retracted it.

מתני׳ אָמַר: ״אָמְרָה פָּרָה זוֹ הֲרֵינִי נְזִירָה אִם עוֹמֶדֶת אֲנִי״. ״אוֹמֵר הַדֶּלֶת הַזֶּה הֲרֵינִי נְזִירָה אִם נִפְתַּח אֲנִי״. בֵּית שַׁמַּאי אוֹמְרִים: נָזִיר, וּבֵית הִלֵּל אוֹמְרִים: אֵינוֹ נָזִיר. אָמַר רַבִּי יְהוּדָה: אַף כְּשֶׁאָמְרוּ בֵּית שַׁמַּאי לֹא אָמְרוּ אֶלָּא בְּאוֹמֵר ״הֲרֵי פָּרָה זוֹ עָלַי קָרְבָּן אִם עוֹמֶדֶת הִיא״.

MISHNA If one **said: This cow said:**[H] **I am hereby a nazirite if I stand up;** or if he said: **This door says: I am hereby a nazirite if I am opened, Beit Shammai say** he is **a nazirite, and Beit Hillel say** he is **not a nazirite. Rabbi Yehuda said:**[N] **Even when Beit Shammai say** that the vow is effective, **they say** so **only** with regard to **one who said: This cow is hereby** forbidden **to me** as **an offering if it stands up.** In that case it is as if he took a vow that the cow is forbidden. However, Beit Shammai concede that although the vow takes effect, it is not a vow of naziriteship.

גמ׳ פָּרָה מִי קָא מִישְׁתַּעְיָא? אָמַר רָמִי בַּר חָמָא: הָכָא בְּמַאי עָסְקִינַן – כְּגוֹן שֶׁהָיְתָה פָּרָה רְבוּצָה לְפָנָיו, וְאָמַר: כִּסְבוּרָה פָּרָה זוֹ אֵינָהּ עוֹמֶדֶת – הֲרֵינִי נָזִיר מִבְּשָׂרָהּ אִם עָמְדָה מֵאֵלֶיהָ. וְעָמְדָה מֵאֵלֶיהָ. וְהָלְכוּ בֵּית שַׁמַּאי לְשִׁיטָתָן, וּבֵית הִלֵּל לְשִׁיטָתָן.

GEMARA The Gemara asks: **Does a cow speak?** What is the meaning of the statement: A cow said: I am hereby a nazirite? **Rami bar Ḥama said: With what are we dealing here?** We are dealing with a case **where there was a prone cow before him,** and he tried, without success, to cause it to stand, **and he said: This cow thinks** it will **not stand; I am hereby a nazirite** and therefore will refrain **from its flesh if it stands of its own accord, and** in fact **it stood of its own accord. Beit Shammai follow their** standard **approach and Beit Hillel follow their** standard **approach.**

בֵּית שַׁמַּאי דְּאָמְרִי: ״מִן הַגְּרוֹגָרוֹת וּמִן הַדְּבֵילָה״ הָוֵי נָזִיר – הָכָא נַמִי, כִּי אָמַר ״מִבְּשָׂרָהּ״ – הָוֵי נָזִיר. וּבֵית הִלֵּל אוֹמְרִים: לָא הָוֵי נָזִיר.

The Gemara explains: **Beit Shammai, who say** that one who vows to be a nazirite and therefore will refrain **from dried figs and from cakes of dried figs is a nazirite,** say that **here too, when he says: I am hereby a nazirite** and therefore will refrain **from its flesh, is a nazirite.** Since one does not utter a statement for naught, he is held to the first part of his statement: I am hereby a nazirite, and the words: And therefore will refrain from its flesh, are disregarded. **And Beit Hillel say: He is not a nazirite.**

וְהָא אָמְרוּהָ בֵּית שַׁמַּאי חֲדָא זִימְנָא. אָמַר רָבָא: תַּרְתֵּי תְּלָת. וְכֵן תָּנֵי רַבִּי חִיָּיא תַּרְתֵּי תְּלָת. וְכֵן אָמַר רַבִּי אוֹשַׁעְיָא תַּרְתֵּי תְּלָת.

The Gemara raises a difficulty: **But** if Rami bar Ḥama is correct, **didn't Beit Shammai** already **say this** ***halakha*** **one time?** According to Rami bar Ḥama's explanation, this mishna and the previous one differ only with regard to the examples provided, but the principle is identical. **Rava said:** It is normal for the Sages to cite **two** or **three** examples from different cases that offer novel perspectives, although they essentially reflect the same principle. **And Rabbi Ḥiyya also taught two** or **three** examples with regard to this same issue. **And Rabbi Oshaya also said two** or **three** examples.

וּצְרִיכִי; דְּאִי אִיתְּמַר בְּהָא, גְּרוֹגָרוֹת וּדְבֵילָה – הָתָם הוּא דְּאָמְרִי בֵּית שַׁמַּאי הָוֵי נָזִיר, מִשּׁוּם דְּמִיחַלְּפָן בַּעֲנָבִים. אֲבָל בָּשָׂר בַּעֲנָבִים – לָא מִיחַלַּף. וְאִי אִיתְּמַר בָּשָׂר – הָכָא הוּא דְּאָמְרִי בֵּית שַׁמַּאי הָוֵי נָזִיר בְּבִישְׂרָא וְחַמְרָא, אֲבָל גְּרוֹגָרוֹת וּדְבֵילָה – לָא, קָא מַשְׁמַע לַן.

And all these cases **are necessary, as, if it were stated** only that he is a nazirite **in this** case of **dried figs and cakes of dried figs,** it could have been said that it is only **there that Beit Shammai say he is a nazirite, since** figs **are confused with grapes,** and it is reasonable to assume that he had grapes in mind. **But meat is** certainly **not confused with grapes,** and it could be that in the case of the mishna he is not a nazirite even according to Beit Shammai. **And if it were stated** only that he is a nazirite where he vowed that **meat** was forbidden to him, it could have been said that **it is here that Beit Shammai say he is a nazirite** because he was referring to the often-paired **meat and wine,** and it is reasonable to assume that he might have had wine in mind. **But dried figs and cakes of dried figs** are not paired with wine, so he should **not** be a nazirite. To counter that claim, the mishna **teaches us** that he is a nazirite in both cases.

BACKGROUND

Meal-offering of a ***sota*** **– מִנְחַת סוֹטָה:** This is the meal-offering brought by a suspected adulteress [*sota*] (Numbers 5:11–31). A suspected adulteress, whose husband brings her to the Temple to undergo the biblical procedure to test her faithfulness to him, is required to bring a meal-offering of barley flour, unlike most meal-offerings, which are brought from wheat flour. No oil or incense is added to it (Numbers 5:15). A handful of flour is removed from this offering, and the remainder of it is eaten by the priests (Numbers 5:25–26).

HALAKHA

This cow said, etc. – אָמְרָה פָּרָה זוֹ וכו׳: Some authorities cite this mishna as proof that if one makes his vow dependent on an event that he does not expect to occur, as is the case here, it still is a vow, despite the fact that this is considered a stipulation of surety (*Shulḥan Arukh*, *Oraḥ Ḥayyim* 562:13 and *Ḥoshen Mishpat* 207:19; see *Beur HaGra* there).

NOTES

Rabbi Yehuda said, etc. – אָמַר רַבִּי יְהוּדָה וכו׳: The Commentary on *Nazir* writes on the next page that Rabbi Yehuda certainly agrees with regard to the case of: The door said, that it cannot be comparing a door to an offering, since a door cannot be described in terms of an offering. However, Rabbeinu Todros writes that in that case one might render the wood of a door forbidden to himself by a vow, in the manner of a standard vow of prohibition, where an item is rendered forbidden by one comparing the item to an offering.

וְאִי אִיתְּמַר הָנֵי תַּרְתֵּי – הָנֵי הוּא דְּקָאָמְרִי בֵּית שַׁמַּאי, אֲבָל דֶּלֶת – אֵימָא מוֹדוּ לְהוּ לְבֵית הִלֵּל. וְאִי תְּנָא דֶּלֶת – בְּהָא קָאָמְרִי בֵּית הִלֵּל, אֲבָל בְּהַנְךְ תַּרְתֵּי – אֵימָא מוֹדוּ לְהוּ לְבֵית שַׁמַּאי, קָמַשְׁמַע לָן דְּלָא.

And if it were stated only that he is a nazirite with regard to **these two** cases of figs and meat, it could be said: It is in **these** cases **that Beit Shammai say** he is a nazirite, **but** in the case of **a door, I will say they concede to Beit Hillel** that such a statement certainly does not constitute a vow of naziriteship. Therefore, this case had to be stated as well. **And** conversely, **if it taught** only the case of **a door,** the opposite could be said, i.e., that it is **in this** case that **Beit Hillel say** there is no naziriteship, **but in these two** earlier cases **I will say they concede to Beit Shammai** that the individual has taken a vow of naziriteship. The *tanna* therefore **teaches us that** this is **not** the case; in fact, Beit Shammai hold that he is a nazirite in all three cases, and Beit Hillel hold that he is not.

אֲמַר רָבָא: מִי קָתָנֵי "אִם עָמְדָה מֵאֵלֶיהָ"? אֶלָּא אֲמַר רָבָא: כְּגוֹן שֶׁהָיְתָה פָּרָה רְבוּצָה לְפָנָיו, וְאָמַר "הֲרֵי עָלַי קָרְבָּן". בִּשְׁלָמָא פָּרָה – בַּת קָרְבָּן הִיא, אֶלָּא דֶּלֶת בַּת קָרְבָּן הִיא? אֶלָּא אֲמַר רָבָא: כְּגוֹן שֶׁהָיְתָה פָּרָה רְבוּצָה לְפָנָיו,

After providing the answer to one difficulty raised against Rami bar Ḥama's explanation, Rava presents another problem. **Rava said: Is** the mishna **teaching: If it stood of its own accord?** The mishna states: If it stands, and does not mention the condition of: On its own accord. **Rather, Rava said:** The mishna is referring to a case **where there was a prone cow before him, and he said: It is** incumbent **upon me to bring** it as a nazirite **offering,**[N] and in this way the individual accepts naziriteship upon himself. The Gemara raises a difficulty: **Granted, a cow** can **be an offering, but** can **a door be an offering?** How can his vow that a door should be an offering be considered an acceptance of naziriteship? **Rather, Rava said** it means the following: It is a case **where there was a prone cow before him** refusing to stand,

NOTES

And he said: It is incumbent upon me to bring it as a nazirite offering – וְאָמַר הֲרֵי עָלַי קָרְבָּן: This is not the conclusion of Rava's statement, as he has yet to explain the mishna. The Gemara interrupts his statement to clarify how his approach fits with the case of a door. Once it clarifies this point, the Gemara returns and quotes Rava's explanation in full (Commentary on *Nazir*; *Tosafot*).

וְאָמַר "הֲרֵינִי נָזִיר מִיַּיִן אִם לֹא עָמְדָה". וְעָמְדָה מֵאֵלֶיהָ; בֵּית שַׁמַּאי סָבְרִי: תּוּרְפֵּיהּ דְּהַאי גַּבְרָא מִשּׁוּם אוֹקְמַהּ בִּידֵיהּ הוּא, וְהָא לָא אוֹקְמַהּ. וּבֵית הִלֵּל סָבְרִי: מִשּׁוּם דִּרְבִיעָא הוּא, וְהָא קָמַת.

and he said: I am hereby a nazirite and therefore will refrain **from wine**[N] **if it does not stand,** since I will force it to do so, **and it stood of its own accord,** without him causing it to stand. **Beit Shammai hold: This man's intention** [*turpeih*][NL] **is based upon him having it stand by his own hand, and he did not have it stand.** Since he did not cause it to stand, his vow of naziriteship takes effect. **And Beit Hillel hold:** His intention **is based upon** the fact **that it was prone, and now it has stood.** Since the cow stood up it does not matter what caused it to stand, and his vow of naziriteship does not take effect.

אִי הָכִי, אֵימָא סֵיפָא: אָמַר רַבִּי יְהוּדָה: אַף כְּשֶׁאָמְרוּ בֵּית שַׁמַּאי לֹא אָמְרוּ אֶלָּא בְּאוֹמֵר "הֲרֵי הֵן עָלַי קָרְבָּן". פָּרָה מִי קָא מַתְפִּיס בָּהּ מִידֵּי?

The Gemara asks: **If so, say the latter clause** of the mishna as follows: **Rabbi Yehuda said: Even when Beit Shammai said** the vow is effective **they said** so **only** with regard **to one who said: They are hereby** forbidden **to me as an offering.** But **does he** take a vow and **extend any** prohibition **to the cow?** Since according to this approach, he explicitly mentions naziriteship, the cow is not rendered forbidden but is merely the subject of a condition of the vow, so why does Rabbi Yehuda speak of a prohibition on the cow?

אֶלָּא, כְּגוֹן דְּאָמַר "הֲרֵינִי נָזִיר מִבְּשָׂרָהּ אִם לֹא עָמְדָה" וְעָמְדָה מֵאֵלֶיהָ; בֵּית שַׁמַּאי סָבְרִי: תּוּרְפֵּיהּ דְּהַהוּא גַּבְרָא מִשּׁוּם אוֹקְמַהּ בִּידֵיהּ הוּא, וְהָא לָא אוֹקְמַהּ. וּבֵית הִלֵּל סָבְרִי: תּוּרְפֵּיהּ דְּהַאי גַּבְרָא מִשּׁוּם דִּרְבִיעָא, וְהָא קָמַת.

The Gemara offers another explanation: **Rather,** the mishna is referring to a case **where he said: I am hereby a nazirite** and therefore will refrain **from its flesh if it does not stand, and it stood of its own accord. Beit Shammai hold: That man's intention is based upon him having it stand by his own hand, and he did not have it stand.** Since he did not cause it to stand, his vow of prohibition takes effect. **And Beit Hillel hold: This man's intention is based** upon the fact **that it was prone, and now it has stood,** so his vow does not take effect.

וּבֵית הִלֵּל סָבְרִי אִי לָא קָמַת הָוֵי נָזִיר? וְהָאָמְרִי "מִבְּשָׂרָהּ" לָא הָוֵי נָזִיר.

The Gemara asks: **And do Beit Hillel hold** that **if** the cow **does not stand he will be a nazirite? But didn't they say** that if one states: I am hereby a nazirite and therefore will refrain **from** the cow's **flesh, he is not a nazirite,** just as they ruled in a case where one states that he is a nazirite from dried figs?

NOTES

And he said: I am hereby a nazirite from wine – וְאָמַר הֲרֵינִי נָזִיר מִיַּיִן: *Tosafot* ask: After questioning Rami bar Ḥama for adding to the mishna the phrase: Of its own accord, how can Rava himself adjust the wording of the mishna by adding the word: Not? They answer that a mishna may be deemed incomplete if there is no other explanation. The criticism of Rami bar Ḥama was that he was adding a phrase in a case where it was not needed for the explanation of the mishna, as the dispute of Beit Shammai and Beit Hillel does not depend upon the precise wording of the condition. The Commentary on *Nazir* maintains that the words attributed to the cow do not serve as his precise vow but merely express his general intention. In this case, the individual says: It is as though the cow says it will be a nazirite if it stands, which indicates that the man himself will be a nazirite if it does not stand.

This man's intention [*turpeih*] – תּוּרְפֵּיהּ דְּהַאי גַּבְרָא: Some commentaries explain that *turpeih* means revealed, i.e., the revealed aspect of his intention (*Tosafot*). It is therefore similar to the *toref* of a document, which refers to the part of a document that explicitly summarizes its conditions. The *Arukh* cites the slightly different explanation (see Commentary on *Nazir*) that *turpeih* means the main part of his statement, just as the *toref* of a document is its most important section. The Rosh combines these two interpretations.

LANGUAGE

Intention [*turpeih*] – תּוּרְפֵּיהּ: Some commentaries explain that *turpeih* in this context means: His main desire. Others assert that it comes from the Greek τροπή, *tropē*, meaning tendency or direction (see *Arukh* and *Tosafot*).

לְטַעֲמַיְיהוּ דְּבֵית שַׁמַּאי קָאָמְרִי: לְדִידָן – אֲפִילּוּ לָא קָמַת נַמִּי לָא הָוֵי נָזִיר, לְדִידְכוּ דְּאָמְרִיתוּ הָוֵי נָזִיר – אוֹדוּ לָן מִיהַת דְּתוּרְפֵּיהּ דְּהָדֵין גַּבְרָא מִשּׁוּם דִּרְבִיעָא, וְהָא קָמַת. וּבֵית שַׁמַּאי: לָאו תּוּרְפֵּיהּ דְּהַאי גַּבְרָא מִשּׁוּם אוֹקְמַהּ בִּידֵיהּ הוּא – וְהָא לָא אוֹקְמַהּ.

The Gemara answers: **They stated** their opinion **in accordance with the reasoning of Beit Shammai: According to our** opinion, **even** if the cow **does not stand he is also not a nazirite,** since naziriteship takes effect only if he vowed that products of the vine are forbidden to him. However, **according to your** reasoning **that you say he is a nazirite, in any event concede to us that this man's intention is based upon** the fact **that** the cow **was prone, and it has stood,** so the naziriteship should not take effect. **And Beit Shammai** hold: **Isn't this man's intention based upon** him **having it stand by his own hand, and he did not have it stand?** Since his condition was not fulfilled, the naziriteship does not take effect.

Perek **II**
Daf **11** Amud **a**

מתני׳ מָזְגוּ לוֹ אֶת הַכּוֹס, וְאָמַר "הֲרֵינִי נָזִיר מִמֶּנּוּ" – הֲרֵי זֶה נָזִיר. מַעֲשֶׂה בְּאִשָּׁה אַחַת שֶׁהָיְתָה שִׁיכּוֹרָה, וּמָזְגוּ לָהּ אֶת הַכּוֹס, וְאָמְרָה "הֲרֵינִי נְזִירָה מִמֶּנּוּ". אָמְרוּ חֲכָמִים: לֹא נִתְכַּוְּונָה זוֹ אֶלָּא לוֹמַר "הֲרֵי הוּא עָלַי קָרְבָּן".

MISHNA **If they poured one a cup**[H] of wine **and he said: I am hereby a nazirite** and therefore will refrain **from it, he is a** full-fledged **nazirite** who must observe all the *halakhot* of naziriteship. **An incident** occurred **with regard to a certain woman who was intoxicated**[N] from wine, **and they poured a cup for her and she said: I am hereby a nazirite** and therefore will refrain **from it. The Sages said: This** woman **did not intend** to accept naziriteship **but** rather, meant **to say: It is hereby** forbidden **to me** as **an offering.** She vowed against deriving benefit from that cup alone, since she did not want to drink any more.

גמ׳ מַעֲשֶׂה לִסְתּוֹר?! אָמְרַתְּ רֵישָׁא "הֲרֵי זֶה נָזִיר". וַהֲדַר תָּנֵי "מַעֲשֶׂה בְּאִשָּׁה אַחַת". אַלְמָא בְּהַאי הוּא דְּאָסוּר, הָא יֵינָא אַחֲרִינָא – שָׁרֵי!

GEMARA The Gemara asks: Was **an incident** cited **to contradict** the previous ruling? **You said in the first clause** of the mishna that if one said that he is hereby a nazirite and therefore will refrain from a cup that was poured for him, then **he is a nazirite. And the** *tanna* **then teaches: An incident** occurred **with regard to a certain woman** who said: I am hereby a nazirite and therefore will refrain from it, which the Sages interpreted as a vow rendering the cup forbidden to her like an offering. **Apparently it is** only **with regard to this** cup of wine **that is forbidden** to her; **consequently,** any **other wine is permitted,** and she is not a nazirite.

חַסּוּרֵי מִיחַסְּרָא וְהָכִי קָתָנֵי: מָזְגוּ לוֹ אֶת הַכּוֹס וְאָמַר "הֲרֵינִי נָזִיר מִמֶּנּוּ" – הֲרֵי זֶה נָזִיר. וְאִם שִׁיכּוֹר הוּא, וְאָמַר "הֲרֵינִי נָזִיר מִמֶּנּוּ" – אֵינוֹ נָזִיר; מַאי טַעֲמָא – כְּמַאן דְּאָמַר "הֲרֵי עָלַי קָרְבָּן" הוּא. וְכִי תֵּימָא: לֵימָא הָכִי – סָבַר: מַיְיתִין לִי אַחֲרִינָא וּמְצַעֲרָן לִי, אֵימָא לְהוּ הָא מִילְּתָא דִּפְסִיקָא לְהוּ; וּמַעֲשֶׂה נַמִּי בְּאִשָּׁה אַחַת.

The Gemara answers: The mishna **is incomplete and is teaching the following: If they poured a cup** of wine **for one and he said: I am hereby a nazirite** and therefore will refrain **from it, he is a nazirite. And if he is intoxicated** and they pour a cup of wine for him **and he said: I am hereby a nazirite** and therefore will refrain **from it, he is not a nazirite. What is the reason** for this? **He is** considered to be **like one who said:** This cup is forbidden **to me** like **an offering.** The Gemara asks: **And if you would say** that this was his meaning, **let him say so** explicitly; why would he say: I am hereby a nazirite and therefore will refrain from it? The reason is because **he maintains:** If I specify this cup, **they will bring me another**[N] cup **and aggravate me** with it. It is better that **I say to them this statement, which is definitive to them,** and they will understand that I do not want to drink any more wine. The mishna continues: **And an incident also** occurred **with regard to a certain woman** who was intoxicated[H] and took this vow, and the Sages explained her statement accordingly.

מתני׳ "הֲרֵינִי נָזִיר עַל מְנָת שֶׁאֱהֵא שׁוֹתֶה יַיִן וּמִיטַּמֵּא לַמֵּתִים" – הֲרֵי זֶה נָזִיר, וְאָסוּר בְּכוּלָּן.

MISHNA If one says: **I am hereby a nazirite on the condition that I will** be allowed to **drink**[H] **wine and may become** ritually **impure from corpses,** i.e., he wishes to be a nazirite only with respect to the growth of his hair, **he is a** full-fledged **nazirite and is prohibited from** engaging in **all of the** behaviors forbidden to a nazirite, including consuming products of the vine and contracting impurity from a corpse.

HALAKHA

If they poured one a cup, etc. – **מָזְגוּ לוֹ אֶת הַכּוֹס וכו׳**: If a cup of wine was poured for an individual and he said: I am hereby a nazirite and therefore will abstain from it, he is a nazirite (Rambam *Sefer Hafla'a, Hilkhot Nezirut* 1:11).

And an incident also occurred with regard to a certain woman – **וּמַעֲשֶׂה נַמִּי בְּאִשָּׁה אַחַת**: If one was depressed or a mourner, and when his friends attempted to persuade him to drink to relieve his misery he said: I am hereby a nazirite and therefore will abstain from it, only that cup is forbidden to him, and he is not a nazirite. Similarly, if one was intoxicated and, when a cup of wine was poured for him, said: I am hereby a nazirite and therefore will abstain from it, only that cup is forbidden to him. If he was completely intoxicated, like Lot, his statement is entirely disregarded (Rambam *Sefer Hafla'a, Hilkhot Nezirut* 1:11–12).

I am hereby a nazirite on the condition that I will drink, etc. – **הֲרֵינִי נָזִיר עַל מְנָת שֶׁאֱהֵא שׁוֹתֶה וכו׳**: If one said: I am hereby a nazirite on the condition that I may drink wine, or: That I may become impure from corpses, he is a nazirite, and all of the prohibitions of naziriteship apply to him, since he cannot stipulate counter to what is written in the Torah (Rambam *Sefer Hafla'a, Hilkhot Nezirut* 1:13).

NOTES

Who was intoxicated [*shikkora*] – **שֶׁהָיְתָה שִׁיכּוֹרָה**: A variant version of the text reads: *Shikolet*, instead of: *Shikkora*, meaning that she did not want to drink wine because she was bereaved [*shekula*]. This reading is followed in the Rambam's Commentary on the Mishna (see Rav Kapaḥ's version), and the Rambam similarly rules in the *Mishne Torah* that if one was in mourning or otherwise in despair, and upon being offered wine to assuage his pain said: I am hereby a nazirite and therefore will abstain from it, he meant to render only this cup forbidden to himself, and he is not a nazirite.

They will bring me another – **מַיְיתִין לִי אַחֲרִינָא**: The Rosh and other commentaries explain that it is common for people to pressure an intoxicated person to drink more. This person therefore forces them to stop offering him more to drink. Conversely, a sober person who is not being pressured by anyone to drink would state that he is a nazirite only if he actually wanted to be a nazirite. If he wanted to vow that only the cup before him is forbidden to him, he would word his statement in the following manner: It is forbidden to me like an offering.

״יוֹדֵעַ אֲנִי שֶׁיֵּשׁ נְזִירוּת אֲבָל אֵינִי יוֹדֵעַ שֶׁהַנָּזִיר אָסוּר בְּיַיִן״ – הֲרֵי זֶה אָסוּר, וְרַבִּי שִׁמְעוֹן מַתִּיר. ״יוֹדֵעַ אֲנִי שֶׁהַנָּזִיר אָסוּר בְּיַיִן, אֲבָל סָבוּר הָיִיתִי שֶׁחֲכָמִים מַתִּירִין לִי מִפְּנֵי שֶׁאֵין אֲנִי יָכוֹל לִחְיוֹת אֶלָּא בְּיַיִן״ אוֹ ״מִפְּנֵי שֶׁאֲנִי קוֹבֵר אֶת הַמֵּתִים״ – הֲרֵי זֶה מוּתָּר, וְרַבִּי שִׁמְעוֹן אוֹסֵר.

If one stated a vow of naziriteship and then said: **I know that there is naziriteship,**[H] **but I do not know that a nazirite is prohibited from wine, he is prohibited** in all the prohibitions of naziriteship. **But Rabbi Shimon permits** him, since he holds that naziriteship takes effect only if the person accepts all the relevant prohibitions. If one said: **I know that a nazirite is prohibited from wine, but I thought that the Sages would permit me**[H] to drink wine **because I cannot live without wine, or:** I thought that the Sages would allow me to contract impurity from corpses **because I bury the dead, he is permitted** and the vow of naziriteship does not take effect, **but Rabbi Shimon prohibits** him.

גמ׳ וְלִפְלוֹג נַמִי רַבִּי שִׁמְעוֹן בְּרֵישָׁא! אָמַר רַבִּי יְהוֹשֻׁעַ בֶּן לֵוִי: חָלוּק הָיָה רַבִּי שִׁמְעוֹן אַף בְּרֵישָׁא.

GEMARA In the second case of the mishna, where one states that he did not know that the prohibitions of naziriteship include wine, Rabbi Shimon says that the naziriteship does not take effect because he did not include all of the prohibitions in his vow. The Gemara therefore asks: **Let Rabbi Shimon disagree** with the first *tanna* **in the first clause** in the mishna **as well,** where one said: I am hereby a nazirite on the condition that I may drink wine. **Rabbi Yehoshua ben Levi said:** In fact, **Rabbi Shimon disagrees even** with the first *tanna* **in the first clause** of the mishna, and the mishna's statement: Rabbi Shimon permits him, is referring to both clauses.

רָבִינָא אֲמַר: בְּרֵישָׁא לָא פָּלֵיג רַבִּי שִׁמְעוֹן; מַאי טַעֲמָא – מִשּׁוּם דַּהֲוָה לֵיהּ מַתְנֶה עַל מַה שֶּׁכָּתוּב בַּתּוֹרָה, וְכָל הַמַּתְנֶה עַל מַה שֶּׁכָּתוּב בַּתּוֹרָה – תְּנָאוֹ בָּטֵל. וְרַבִּי יְהוֹשֻׁעַ בֶּן לֵוִי אָמַר לָךְ: [הַאי] ״עַל מְנָת״ – כְּ״חוּץ״ דָּמֵי.

Ravina said: Rabbi Shimon does not disagree with the first *tanna* **in the first clause** of the mishna. **What is the reason** for that? It is **because one was stipulating counter to that which is written in the Torah** by attempting to limit an explicit Torah law, **and** with regard to **anyone who stipulates counter to that which is written in the Torah,**[H] **his stipulation is void.** The statement: I am hereby a nazirite, remains valid, and he is therefore a nazirite in all regards. Conversely, **Rabbi Yehoshua ben Levi** could have **said to you: This** phrase: **On the condition,** does not mean he accepts upon himself all the *halakhot* of naziriteship and then adds a stipulation counter to that which is written in the Torah; rather, it is **considered like** he said: **Apart** from. It is as though he stated from the outset that he will be a nazirite apart from one particular aspect. According to Rabbi Yehoshua ben Levi, Rabbi Shimon holds that since he is not trying to stipulate alternative *halakhot* for full naziriteship but is instead accepting a partial naziriteship, his vow takes effect.

תַּנְיָא כְּוָותֵיהּ דְּרָבִינָא: אָמַר ״הֲרֵינִי נָזִיר עַל מְנָת שֶׁאֱהֵא שׁוֹתֶה יַיִן וּמִיטַּמֵּא לַמֵּתִים״ – הֲרֵי זֶה נָזִיר, וְאָסוּר בְּכוּלָּן, מִפְּנֵי שֶׁהוּא מַתְנֶה עַל מַה שֶּׁכָּתוּב בַּתּוֹרָה, וְכָל הַמַּתְנֶה עַל מַה שֶּׁכָּתוּב בַּתּוֹרָה – תְּנָאוֹ בָּטֵל.

The Gemara comments: It **is taught** in the *Tosefta* (*Nazir* 2:2) **in accordance with** the opinion **of Ravina.** If one **said: I am hereby a nazirite on the condition that I will be allowed to drink wine and may become** ritually **impure from corpses, he is a nazirite and is prohibited from all of them because he stipulates counter to that which is written in the Torah, and** with regard to **anyone who stipulates counter to that which is written in the Torah, his stipulation is void.**

״יוֹדֵעַ אֲנִי שֶׁהַנָּזִיר אָסוּר בְּיַיִן״. וְהָאָמַרְתְּ רֵישָׁא: אָסוּר, וְרַבִּי שִׁמְעוֹן מַתִּיר! אֵימָא נַמִי: הֲרֵי זֶה אָסוּר, וְרַבִּי שִׁמְעוֹן מַתִּיר. וְאִיבָּעֵית אֵימָא: לְעוֹלָם לָא תֵּיפוֹךְ, הָתָם

§ The final clause of the mishna teaches that if one says: **I know that a nazirite is prohibited from** drinking **wine** but I thought that the Sages would permit me to drink, the Rabbis say that the vow is void, but Rabbi Shimon disagrees. The Gemara asks: **But didn't you say in the earlier clause** of the mishna that with regard to one who says: But I did not know that a nazirite is prohibited from wine, the first *tanna* holds that he is **prohibited and Rabbi Shimon permits** him? What is the difference between the two cases? The Gemara answers: Emend the text and **say** in the final clause **as well: He is prohibited, and Rabbi Shimon permits** him. **And if you wish, say** instead: **Actually, do not reverse** the opinions, and leave the text as it is. Instead, distinguish between the two cases, as **there**

HALAKHA

I know that there is naziriteship, etc. – **יוֹדֵעַ אֲנִי שֶׁיֵּשׁ נְזִירוּת וכו׳**: If one vows to be a nazirite and then says he did not know that a nazirite is prohibited from drinking wine, contracting impurity from corpses, or cutting his hair, he is nevertheless a nazirite and is bound by all of these prohibitions (Rambam *Sefer Hafla'a, Hilkhot Nezirut* 1:14).

I thought that the Sages would permit me, etc. – **סָבוּר הָיִיתִי שֶׁחֲכָמִים מַתִּירִין לִי וכו׳**: If one vowed to be a nazirite and was aware of the relevant prohibitions but thought that the Sages would permit him to drink wine because he needs to, or that they would permit him to contract impurity from corpses because he earns his living by burying the dead, he is not a nazirite, as it is considered an unwitting vow (Rambam *Sefer Hafla'a Hilkhot Nezirut* 1:15; see Ra'avad and *Kesef Mishne* there).

Stipulates counter to that which is written in the Torah – **הַמַּתְנֶה עַל מַה שֶּׁכָּתוּב בַּתּוֹרָה**: If one stipulates a condition that contradicts a mitzva of the Torah, the condition is entirely disregarded (Rambam *Sefer Nashim, Hilkhot Ishut* 6:8–10, 12:7; *Sefer Hafla'a, Hilkhot Nezirut* 1:13; *Sefer Zera'im, Hilkhot Mattenot Aniyyim* 5:8; and *Sefer Zera'im, Hilkhot Bikkurim* 9:11; *Shulḥan Arukh, Yoreh De'a* 61:29; *Even HaEzer* 38:5, 69:6; and *Ḥoshen Mishpat* 26:3–4, 61:6, 97:28).

רֵישָׁא – כְּגוֹן דְּנָדַר מֵחֲדָא; לְרַבָּנַן דְּאָמְרִי דַּאֲפִילּוּ לֹא נָזַר אֶלָּא מֵאַחַת מֵהֶן – הָוֵי נָזִיר, וְאָסוּר. לְרַבִּי שִׁמְעוֹן דְּאָמַר עַד שֶׁיַּזִּיר מִכּוּלָּם – מוּתָּר.

in **the earlier clause,** where one said: I did not know that a nazirite is prohibited from drinking wine, that is a case **where he vowed naziriteship** with regard to only **one** of the prohibitions. The difference of opinion is as follows: **According to the Rabbis, who say that even if he vowed naziriteship** with regard to **only one of the** prohibitions of naziriteship **he is** nevertheless **a nazirite,** in that case **he is prohibited** by all of them, despite not knowing about the prohibition against consuming wine. **According to Rabbi Shimon** who **said** he is not a nazirite **unless he takes a vow of naziriteship** with regard to **all of them,** he **is permitted.**

סֵיפָא – דְּנָדַר מִכּוּלְּהוּ וְאִיתְשִׁיל מֵחֲדָא;

Conversely, **the last clause** addresses one who **vowed** naziriteship with regard to **all of them,** thereby accepting upon himself all the *halakhot* of naziriteship, **and** now wishes **to request** dissolution **of one** of the prohibitions, thinking that a halakhic authority can dissolve one aspect of his naziriteship.

לְרַבָּנַן דְּאָמְרִי אֲפִילּוּ לֹא נָזַר אֶלָּא מֵאַחַת מֵהֶן הָוֵי נָזִיר, כִּי מִתְשִׁיל מֵחֲדָא מִינַּיְיהוּ – אִישְׁתְּרֵי. לְרַבִּי שִׁמְעוֹן דְּאָמַר עַד שֶׁיַּזִּיר מִכּוּלָּם, כִּי מִתְשִׁיל נַמִי מֵהַהוּא – עַד דְּמִתְשִׁיל מִכּוּלְּהוּ, מִשּׁוּם הָכִי קָתָנֵי: וְרַבִּי שִׁמְעוֹן אוֹסֵר.

The Gemara explains: **According to the Rabbis, who say that even if he vowed naziriteship** with regard to **only one of the** prohibitions of naziriteship **he is** nevertheless **a nazirite,** in that case too, **when he requests** of a halakhic authority to dissolve **one of them, he is permitted** to engage in all of the behaviors forbidden to a nazirite. Just as the acceptance of one part of naziriteship causes one to be bound by all the *halakhot* of naziriteship, dissolution of one element of naziriteship nullifies the entire naziriteship. **According to Rabbi Shimon, who said** that he is not a nazirite **unless he takes a vow of naziriteship** with regard to **all of them, when he requests** dissolution **of that** prohibition, none of the prohibitions are permitted **until he requests** dissolution **of all of** the prohibitions of naziriteship. **Due to this** the mishna **teaches: And Rabbi Shimon prohibits** him.

וְאִיבָּעֵית אֵימָא: בְּנִדְרֵי אוֹנָסִין קָא מִיפַּלְגִי, וּבִפְלוּגְתָּא דִּשְׁמוּאֵל וְרַב אַסִי. דִּתְנַן: אַרְבָּעָה נְדָרִים הִתִּירוּ חֲכָמִים: נִדְרֵי זֵירוּזִין, נִדְרֵי הֲבַאי, נִדְרֵי שְׁגָגוֹת, נִדְרֵי אוֹנָסִין.

And if you wish, say instead: The Rabbis and Rabbi Shimon **disagree with regard to vows** impeded by **circumstances beyond one's control,**[N] and their disagreement is **in the dispute between Shmuel and Rav Asi. As we learned** in a mishna (*Nedarim* 20b): **The Sages dissolved four** types of **vows**[H] without the requirement of a request to a halakhic authority. The first category is **vows of exhortation,** where one employs a vow to urge another to perform some action. The second category is **vows of exaggeration** [*havai*],[L] where one utters a vow that is dependent upon some outlandish claim, such as: I should be bound by a vow if I did not see a square snake. Since he knows that there are no square snakes, it is evident that he is not serious in taking his vow. The third category is **vows that are unintentional,** where one vows for a particular reason and later discovers he was mistaken with regard to the facts; and the fourth is **vows** whose fulfillment are impeded by **circumstances beyond one's control.**

וְאָמַר רַב יְהוּדָה אָמַר רַב אַסִי: אַרְבָּעָה נְדָרִים הַלָּלוּ צְרִיכִין שְׁאֵלָה לַחֲכָמִים. כִּי אָמְרִיתָהּ קַמֵּיהּ דִּשְׁמוּאֵל, אֲמַר לִי: תַּנָּא קָתָנֵי ״הִתִּירוּ חֲכָמִים״. וְאַתְּ אָמְרַתְּ צְרִיכִין שְׁאֵלָה לַחֲכָמִים?!

The Gemara relates the dispute between Shmuel and Rav Asi: **And Rav Yehuda said** that **Rav Asi said: These four vows require a request** made **to the halakhic authorities** to dissolve them, and the vows are not dissolved unless one does so. Rav Yehuda related: **When I stated this** *halakha* of Rav Asi **before Shmuel, he said to me: The** *tanna* **teaches** that **the Sages dissolved** them,[H] **and you say they require a request** made **to the halakhic authorities?** Shmuel holds that they are dissolved automatically.

NOTES

With regard to vows impeded by circumstances beyond one's control – בְּנִדְרֵי אוֹנָסִין: The parallel is that just as with vows impeded by circumstances beyond one's control the *halakha* is that circumstances beyond one's control release one from the vow, even though he pronounced it with the full intention of fulfilling it, here too, the inability to fulfill the vow, due to one's inability to live without wine, or due to his need to bury the dead, nullifies the naziriteship (Commentary on *Nazir*; *Tosafot*). Some early commentaries question the comparison to vows impeded by circumstances beyond one's control, as there the fulfillment of the vow was within one's power at the time of its pronouncement, and the circumstances impeding the fulfillment of the vow arose later, whereas here, the contraindicative circumstance was present from the outset. They answer (*Tosafot*, citing Rabbeinu Tam; Rosh) that here too, this is referring to a situation where the individual vowed to be a nazirite before the contraindicative circumstance began. It was only later that he weakened and required wine, or found it necessary to bury the dead in order to earn a living or because no one else was available to perform the task.

HALAKHA

The Sages dissolved four types of vows – אַרְבָּעָה נְדָרִים הִתִּירוּ חֲכָמִים: One who pronounces a vow of exhortation, a vow of exaggeration, vows that are unintentional, or a vow impeded by circumstances beyond one's control is not bound by the vow. The same applies to these types of oaths and to these types of vows of naziriteship (Rambam *Sefer Hafla'a*, *Hilkhot Shevuot* 3:1, 3, *Hilkhot Nedarim* 4:1, 3, and *Hilkhot Nezirut* 2:1; *Shulḥan Arukh*, *Yoreh De'a* 232:1).

The Sages dissolved – הִתִּירוּ חֲכָמִים: The four types of vows dissolved by the Sages do not require dissolution by a halakhic authority but are dissolved automatically (Rambam *Sefer Hafla'a*, *Hilkhot Shevuot* 3:1, 3, *Hilkhot Nedarim* 4:1, 3, and *Hilkhot Nezirut* 2:1; *Shulḥan Arukh*, *Yoreh De'a* 232:1).

LANGUAGE

Exaggeration [*havai*] – הֲבַאי: *Havai* means an insubstantial matter, words of exaggeration, or prattle.

HALAKHA

I am hereby a nazirite and it is incumbent upon me to shave, etc. – הֲרֵינִי נָזִיר וְעָלַי לְגַלֵּחַ וכו׳: If one said: I am hereby a nazirite and it is incumbent upon me to shave a nazirite, and another heard and said: And I, and it is incumbent upon me to shave a nazirite, they are both nazirites and must pay for the offerings of a nazirite. If they are perspicacious, each of them may pay for the offerings of the other. If they do not do so, they are obligated to pay for the offerings of other nazirites (Rambam *Sefer Hafla'a, Hilkhot Nezirut* 8:19).

And I, indicates acceptance of the beginning of the statement – וַאֲנִי עַל תְּחִילַּת דִּיבּוּרָא מַשְׁמַע: If one said: I am hereby a nazirite and it is incumbent upon me to shave a nazirite, and another heard and said: And I, the latter is obligated to observe naziriteship but he is not required to shave a nazirite, since his statement refers only to the vow of naziriteship (Rambam *Sefer Hafla'a, Hilkhot Nezirut* 8:19).

רַבָּנַן סָבְרִי כִּשְׁמוּאֵל, וְרַבִּי שִׁמְעוֹן כְּרַב אַסִי.

The Gemara continues its explanation: The dispute between the Rabbis and Rabbi Shimon in the last clause of the mishna is also with regard to this *halakha*. This case is referring to a kind of a vow impeded by circumstances beyond one's control, as he claims that he has no choice but to drink wine or contract impurity from corpses. **The Rabbis hold in accordance with** the opinion of **Shmuel,** and therefore the vow is dissolved automatically, without the need to request dissolution from a halakhic authority; **and Rabbi Shimon holds in accordance with** the opinion of **Rav Asi** that one must make a request to a halakhic authority to dissolve the vow, and he remains a nazirite until he does so.

מתני׳ ״הֲרֵינִי נָזִיר וְעָלַי לְגַלֵּחַ נָזִיר״. וְשָׁמַע חֲבֵירוֹ וְאָמַר ״וַאֲנִי וְעָלַי לְגַלֵּחַ נָזִיר״. אִם הָיוּ פִּקְחִים – מְגַלְּחִין זֶה אֶת זֶה, וְאִם לָאו – מְגַלְּחִין נְזִירִים אֲחֵרִים.

MISHNA If one says: **I am hereby a nazirite and it is incumbent upon me to shave**[H] **a nazirite,** meaning he will also pay for the offerings that a nazirite brings when he cuts his hair; **and another heard and said: And I** too am a nazirite **and it is** incumbent **upon me to shave a nazirite,** the other is also a nazirite and is obligated to pay for the offerings of a nazirite. **If they were perspicacious** and wish to limit their expenses, **they shave each other.** They may each pay for the other's offerings, so that their additional vows will not cost them anything. **And if not,** if this arrangement did not occur to them and each brought his own offerings, **they shave other nazirites,** i.e., they must pay for the offerings of other nazirites.

גמ׳ אִיבַּעְיָא לְהוּ: שָׁמַע חֲבֵירוֹ וְאָמַר ״וַאֲנִי״. מַהוּ? ״וַאֲנִי״ אַכּוּלֵּיהּ דִּיבּוּרָא מַשְׁמַע, אוֹ דִּלְמָא אַפַּלְגֵיהּ דְּדִיבּוּרָא מַשְׁמַע? אִם תִּמְצֵי לוֹמַר אַפַּלְגֵיהּ דְּדִיבּוּרָא מַשְׁמַע, אַרֵישָׁא אוֹ אַסֵּיפָא?

GEMARA **A dilemma was raised before** the Sages. If one said: I am hereby a nazirite and it is incumbent upon me to shave a nazirite as well, and **another heard and said** only: **And I, what is** the *halakha*? Do we say that: **And I, indicates** acceptance **of the entire statement** of the first one, which would mean he is both a nazirite and must shave a nazirite, **or perhaps it indicates** acceptance **of** only **half the statement** of the first speaker? **If you say it indicates** acceptance **of** only **half the statement,** does it indicate acceptance **of the first clause,** i.e., I am hereby a nazirite, **or the last clause,** i.e., it is incumbent upon me to shave a nazirite?

תָּא שְׁמַע: ״וַאֲנִי וְעָלַי לְגַלֵּחַ נָזִיר״ אִם הָיוּ פִּקְחִים – מְגַלְּחִין זֶה אֶת זֶה. מִדְּקָאָמַר ״וַאֲנִי וְעָלַי״ שְׁמַע מִינַּהּ ״וַאֲנִי״ אַפַּלְגֵיהּ דְּדִיבּוּרָא. אָמְרִי: אִין, אַפַּלְגֵיהּ דְּדִיבּוּרָא מַשְׁמַע, מִיהוּ אַרֵישָׁא אוֹ אַסֵּיפָא? מִינַּהּ, מִדְּקָאָמַר ״וְעָלַי לְגַלֵּחַ״ – שְׁמַע מִינַּהּ ״וַאֲנִי״ עַל תְּחִילַּת דִּיבּוּרָא מַשְׁמַע.

The Gemara suggests: **Come and hear** a proof from the mishna. If a second person said: **And I, and it is** incumbent **upon me to shave a nazirite,** then **if they are perspicacious they shave each other. From** the fact **that it says: And I, and it is** incumbent **upon me,** you can **learn from this** that: **And I, indicates** acceptance **of** only **half the statement,** as otherwise he would not need to add the second part. The Sages **say** in response to this attempted proof: **Yes,** this proves that it **indicates** acceptance **of** only **half the statement. However,** the other question still has not been answered: Is he referring **to the first** part of the original statement **or to the last** part? The Gemara answers: This can be learned **from** the mishna **itself. From** the fact **that it says: And it is** incumbent **upon me to shave** a nazirite, one can **learn from this** that: **And I, indicates** acceptance **of the beginning of the statement**[H] to become a nazirite, which is why one has to add that he must also pay for the offerings of a nazirite.

אָמַר לֵיהּ רַב הוּנָא בְּרֵיהּ דְּרַב יְהוֹשֻׁעַ לְרָבָא: מִמַּאי דְּהָכִי? לְעוֹלָם אֵימָא לָךְ ״וַאֲנִי״ אַכּוּלֵּיהּ דְּדִיבּוּרָא, וְאִי מִשּׁוּם ״וְעָלַי״. מַאי קָאָמַר – וְעָלַי בְּהָא מִילְּתָא. דְּאִי לָא תֵּימָא הָכִי, דְּקָתָנֵי סֵיפָא: ״הֲרֵי עָלַי לְגַלֵּחַ חֲצִי נָזִיר״ וְשָׁמַע חֲבֵירוֹ וְאָמַר ״וַאֲנִי עָלַי לְגַלֵּחַ חֲצִי נָזִיר״. הָתָם מִי אִיכָּא תַּרְתֵּין מִילֵּי? אֶלָּא מַאי קָאָמַר ״עָלַי״ – בְּהָא מִילְּתָא, הָכָא נַמִי כִּי קָאָמַר ״עָלַי״ – בְּהָא מִילְּתָא.

Rav Huna, son of Rav Yehoshua, said to Rava: From where do you know **that** it is **so** that the words: And I, are referring to the first part of the statement? **Actually, I will say to you** that: **And I,** is referring **to the entire statement, and if** you claim otherwise **because** he added: **And** it is incumbent **upon me,** the explanation of **what he is saying** is: **And** it is incumbent **on me** to do **this matter.** He was merely clarifying what his intention was when he said: And I. **As, if you do not say so,** then with regard to **that which is taught in the last clause,** in the following mishna, that if one said: **It is** incumbent **upon me to shave half a nazirite, and another heard** that **and said: And I, it is** incumbent **upon me to shave half a nazirite,** then **there, are there two statements?** That mishna is addressing only a single vow. **Rather, what is he saying** by using the words: **It is** incumbent **upon me?** He is referring **to that** whole **matter; here too,** in this mishna, **when he says: And it is** incumbent **upon me,** he is referring **to that** whole **matter.**

אֲמַר לֵיהּ רָבָא: הָכִי הַשְׁתָּא?! אִי אָמְרַתְּ בִּשְׁלָמָא רֵישָׁא צְרִיכָא סֵיפָא לָא צְרִיכָא, תָּנֵי סֵיפָא דְּלָא צְרִיכָא מִשּׁוּם רֵישָׁא דִּצְרִיכָא. אֶלָּא אִי אָמְרַתְּ רֵישָׁא לָא צְרִיכָא סֵיפָא לָא צְרִיכָא, תָּנֵי רֵישָׁא דְּלָא צְרִיכָא וְתָנֵי סֵיפָא דְּלָא צְרִיכָא?!

Rava said to him: How can these cases **be compared? Granted, if you say** that in **the first clause** it **is necessary** to teach both parts of the statement and in **the latter clause** it **is not necessary** to teach both parts of the statement, then it can be said that **he taught the unnecessary latter clause due to the necessary first clause,** as it is typical for a mishna to phrase both of its sections in the same style. **But if you say** that it **is not necessary** to teach both parts of the statement in **the first clause** and it is also **not necessary** to teach both parts of the statement in **the latter clause,** as one has accepted the other's entire statement by saying: And I, would the *tanna* **teach an unnecessary first clause and teach an unnecessary latter clause?** Since the addition of: And it is incumbent upon me, is not required in the latter mishna, it must be necessary in this mishna, so the inference of Rava is correct.

אָמַר רַבִּי יִצְחָק בַּר יוֹסֵף אָמַר רַבִּי יוֹחָנָן: הָאוֹמֵר לִשְׁלוּחוֹ,

§ After analyzing the mishna itself, the Gemara turns to a related issue. **Rabbi Yitzḥak bar Yosef said** that **Rabbi Yoḥanan said: One who says to his agent:**

Perek **II**
Daf **12** Amud **a**

״צֵא וְקַדֵּשׁ לִי אִשָּׁה״ סְתָם – אָסוּר בְּכָל הַנָּשִׁים שֶׁבָּעוֹלָם; חֲזָקָה שָׁלִיחַ עוֹשֶׂה שְׁלִיחוּתוֹ, וְכֵיוָן דְּלָא פָּרֵישׁ לֵיהּ – הָא לֹא יָדַע הֵי נִיהוּ קַדֵּישׁ לֵיהּ.

Go out and betroth[N] **a woman for me, without specifying** a particular woman; from that moment onward the one who appointed the agent is **forbidden to all the women**[N] **in the world** until he finds out which woman the agent betrothed. There is a **presumption** that **an agent performs his** assigned **agency**[H] and that he has betrothed a woman for him, **and since** the agent **did not clarify to him** which woman he chose, **he** therefore **does not know which** woman **is the one betrothed to him.** If he now betroths another woman, it is possible that she is the daughter, sister, or mother of the one his agent betrothed on his behalf and is therefore forbidden to him.

אֵיתִיבֵיהּ רֵישׁ לָקִישׁ לְרַבִּי יוֹחָנָן: קֵן סְתוּמָה שֶׁפָּרְחָה גּוֹזָל אֶחָד מֵהֶן לַאֲוִיר הָעוֹלָם, אוֹ שֶׁפָּרְחָה לְבֵין חַטָּאוֹת הַמֵּתוֹת, אוֹ שֶׁמֵּת אֶחָד מֵהֶן – יִקַּח זוּג לַשֵּׁנִי.

Reish Lakish raised an objection to Rabbi Yoḥanan from a mishna (*Kinnim* 2:1): With regard to an impure person who comes to undergo his purification process, and for this purpose set aside **an unspecified nest,**[B] meaning a pair of turtledoves or pigeons, to use for his offerings. One is to be a burnt-offering and one is to be a sin-offering, and he had not yet specified which bird will be used for which offering. If **one fledgling of the pair flew**[H] **away** and escaped **to the open air of the world, or if it flew among** birds invalidated for **sin-offerings that** have been left to **die,**[N] **or if one of them died,** in each of these cases the owner of the nest **purchases a partner for the second,** i.e., remaining, bird. At that point he may decide which is for a sin-offering and which is for a burnt-offering.

HALAKHA

A presumption that an agent performs his assigned agency – חֲזָקָה שָׁלִיחַ עוֹשֶׂה שְׁלִיחוּתוֹ: If one instructs his agent to perform a matter on his behalf, the latter is presumed to have fulfilled his bidding. In matters of rabbinic law, this rule applies both as a leniency and a stringency. With regard to a matter that involves Torah law, this presumption is used to create a stringency, but a forbidden matter is not permitted based on this presumption (Rambam; Rabbeinu Tam). Others (Rash; Rosh) claim that this presumption can be used to be lenient even with regard to Torah prohibitions, if the agent knew that inaction on his part might lead others to sin (Rambam *Sefer Nashim, Hilkhot Ishut* 9:6 and *Sefer Zemanim, Hilkhot Eiruvin* 6:22; *Shulḥan Arukh, Oraḥ Ḥayyim* 409:8; *Yoreh De'a* 331:34; and *Even HaEzer* 35:11).

An unspecified nest…if a fledgling flew away, etc. – קֵן סְתוּמָה שֶׁפָּרְחָה גּוֹזָל וכו׳: If one fledgling flew out of an unspecified nest and escaped, or became mingled with sin-offerings that are left to die, or if one of the fledglings died, its owner must bring a new fledgling to pair with the remaining fledgling (Rambam *Sefer Avoda, Hilkhot Pesulei HaMukdashin* 9:1).

BACKGROUND

Nest – קֵן: A pair of doves, either turtledoves or pigeons, were brought as offerings on a number of occasions. Generally one dove was brought as a burnt-offering and the other as a sin-offering by a woman after childbirth, or as part of the purification process of a woman who had experienced an unusual discharge of uterine blood (see Leviticus 12:6, 15:29). However, there are other cases where both doves were brought as burnt-offerings. Tractate *Kinnim* discusses some of the issues that arise with regard to this offering, e.g., the procedure if the birds are accidentally switched.

NOTES

Go out and betroth, etc. – צֵא וְקַדֵּשׁ וכו׳: He did not tell the agent which woman or where to find a woman to betroth (Commentary on *Nazir*), and the agent did not come back and inform him of his actions (*She'iltot deRav Aḥai Gaon*), since he either died or left the region *(Halakhot Gedolot)*. If the agent returns and claims he betrothed him to a particular woman, and this is confirmed by the woman, he is deemed credible, since one's agent is like himself and it is as though the man himself made these claims (Rivash).

He is forbidden to all the women – אָסוּר בְּכָל הַנָּשִׁים: The early commentaries question this, as, if there is a concern that the agent may have betrothed any woman to him, then no man should be allowed to betroth any woman, in case she is the one betrothed by the agent. Even if a woman was to claim that she never was betrothed to anyone, she cannot know if her father accepted betrothal on her behalf when she was a minor, at least in the case where her father is not available to clarify this.

Various suggestions have been given to answer this difficulty. *Tosafot* state that the *halakha* in this Gemara is a rabbinic penalty instituted as a disincentive against behaving irresponsibly by appointing an agent with such vague instructions. This penalty is only for the one who appointed the agent, and no one else is impacted by it. In his *Sefer HaYashar*, Rabbeinu Tam writes that the presumption that an agent performs his assigned agency, which is the basis of the prohibition, is by rabbinic law, so the penalty is also by rabbinic law and applies exclusively to the one who appointed the agent. The Rid similarly states that since there is no guarantee that the agent betrothed any woman, the Sages rendered only the one who appointed the agent forbidden, as a penalty.

Flew among birds invalidated for sin-offerings that have been left to die – שֶׁפָּרְחָה לְבֵין חַטָּאוֹת הַמֵּתוֹת: The *halakha* is that any sin-offering whose owner has achieved atonement by means of a replacement offering, or whose owner has died, must be set aside until it dies. Since this individual is unable to identify the fledgling that became mixed up with such sin-offerings, it too must be left to die.

וְאִילּוּ קֵן מְפוֹרֶשֶׁת – אֵין לוֹ תַּקָּנָה.

But if a fledgling flew away or died from **a specified nest,** after the owner had designated which bird would be used for which offering, and it is not known which bird escaped, **it has no** means of **remedy.** This is because he does not know whether the remaining fledgling is for a burnt-offering or a sin-offering.

וְאִילּוּ שְׁאָר קִינִּין בְּעָלְמָא – מִיתַּקְּנָן. וְאַמַּאי? לֵימָא כָּל חֲדָא וַחֲדָא דִּלְמָא הַאי נִיהוּ!

Reish Lakish infers: **But generally, other nests** belonging to other people are **fit;** there is no concern with regard to them. Reish Lakish states his objection to the opinion of Rabbi Yoḥanan: According to your opinion that there is a concern that each woman might be a relative of the woman the agent betrothed, **then why** should the *halakha* with regard to nests be so? **Let us** likewise **say** with regard to **each and every** fledgling bird in the world that **perhaps this is the one** that was consecrated and flew away. How can anyone ever use a bird for their own offering, as it may be the bird that flew away from someone else's nest?

אֲמַר לֵיהּ: קָאָמִינָא אֲנָא אִשָּׁה דְּלָא נָיְידָא, וְאָמְרַתְּ לִי אַתְּ אִיסּוּרָא דְּנָייד?

Rabbi Yoḥanan **said to** Reish Lakish: **I state** my opinion that there is a concern for other women only with regard to **a woman, who does not move** but is fixed in her home. An unidentified item is presumed to have the same legal status as the majority of items like it, and there is no concern that it may be forbidden, even if there are some forbidden items like it. However, if this unidentified item was fixed in its place, there is an equal presumption that it may belong to the class of similar permitted items or to the class of similar forbidden items. Consequently, all women in the world are forbidden to him, as there is an equal presumption that she may or may not be a relative of the woman that the agent betrothed to him. **And you speak to me** of **a prohibition that moves** and is not fixed. Since the fledgling bird is not fixed in one spot, the majority is followed and the minority is ignored.

וְכִי תֵּימָא: הָכָא נַמִי נָייד, אֵימוּר בְּשׁוּקָא אַשְׁכַּח וְקַדֵּישׁ – הָתָם הָדְרָא לְנִיחוּתָא, גַּבֵּי קֵן מִי הָדְרָא?

And if you would say: Here too, she **moves,** since it is possible to **say that** the agent **found** the woman **in the marketplace**[N] **and betrothed her** there to the one who appointed the agent, so the prohibited woman was not in a fixed location? Nevertheless, **there** she eventually **returns to her** place of **rest,** i.e., her home, and is therefore considered to be fixed. Conversely, **with regard to a nest, does** the fledgling **return** to a fixed place? Since it does not, the assumption is that any bird has the status of the majority of birds in the world, which have not been consecrated as offerings.

אֲמַר רָבָא: וּמוֹדֶה רַבִּי יוֹחָנָן בְּאִשָּׁה שֶׁאֵין לָהּ לֹא בַּת, וְלֹא בַּת בַּת, וְלֹא בַּת בֵּן, וְלֹא אֵם, וְלֹא אֵם אֵם, וְלֹא אֲחוֹת, וְאַף עַל פִּי שֶׁהָיְתָה לָהּ אֲחוֹת וְנִתְגָּרְשָׁה לְאַחַר מִכָּאן – דְּהַהִיא שַׁרְיָא.

Rava said: And Rabbi Yoḥanan concedes that with regard to a **woman who does not have**[H] **a daughter, nor a daughter of a daughter, nor a daughter of a son, nor a mother, nor a mother of a mother, nor a sister** who was single when he appointed the agent, that the one who appointed the agent may betroth her. There is no concern that the agent might have betrothed a relative that would now render such a woman forbidden. **And even though she had,** when he appointed the agent, a married **sister,** or daughter, or other female relative, **and she was later divorced,** Rabbi Yoḥanan concedes **that this** woman whom he wishes to now marry is **permitted.**

מַאי טַעֲמָא – דִּבְהַהִיא שַׁעְתָּא דְּקָא אֲמַר לֵיהּ, הֲוָה נְסִיבָן לְגַבְרֵי. כִּי מְשַׁוֵּי שָׁלִיחַ – בְּמִילְּתָא דְּקַיְימָא קַמֵּיהּ, בְּמִילְּתָא דְּלָא קַיְימָא קַמֵּיהּ – לָא מְשַׁוֵּי שָׁלִיחַ.

What is the reason for this? It is **that at that moment, when he told** the agent to go betroth a woman on his behalf, these women **were married to men.** There is a principle that **when one appoints an agent,** he does so only **with regard to a matter present before him.** In other words, he instructs his agent to betroth a woman who is available at that time, but **he does not appoint an agent with regard to a matter that is not present before him.** Consequently, even if the agent betrothed one of the relatives of the woman after they were divorced, the betrothal would not take effect because he was not authorized to betroth them, and therefore the one who appointed the agent is permitted to the woman.

NOTES

Say that the agent found her in the marketplace, etc. – **אֵימוּר בְּשׁוּקָא אַשְׁכַּח וכו׳**: Some commentaries explain that the one who appointed the agent should choose a woman for himself from the marketplace, since she would be considered mobile and therefore presumed to be part of the majority, and her status would be established accordingly (Commentary on *Nazir*). The Rosh states that the Gemara is suggesting the agent might have found and betrothed a woman in the marketplace, in which case the prohibition was never fixed. The question of whether the status of a prohibition being fixed is determined by the moment that the prohibition begins, or by the moment that the prohibition becomes known, is discussed at length by the later commentaries.

HALAKHA

With regard to a woman who does not have, etc. – **בְּאִשָּׁה שֶׁאֵין לָהּ וכו׳**: If one says to his agent: Go and betroth a woman for me, and the latter died before telling the one who appointed him whether he carried out his task or whom he betrothed, the presumption is that the agent performed his agency, and the one who appointed the agent is forbidden to every woman in the world who has family members, e.g., a daughter, mother, or sister, who would render her prohibited as a forbidden relative. He is permitted to marry any woman who did not have an unmarried female relative at the time when he appointed the agent. The Rema adds that the same applies if all her relatives say they never were betrothed, and then they proceed to marry others (Rambam *Sefer Nashim*, *Hilkhot Ishut* 9:6; *Shulḥan Arukh*, *Even HaEzer* 35:11).

תְּנַן: "הֲרֵינִי נָזִיר וְעָלַי לְגַלֵּחַ נָזִיר" וְשָׁמַע חֲבֵירוֹ וְאָמַר "וַאֲנִי, וְעָלַי לְגַלֵּחַ נָזִיר". אִם הָיוּ פִּקְחִין – מְגַלְּחִין זֶה אֶת זֶה, וְאִם לָאו – מְגַלְּחִין נְזִירִים אֲחֵרִים. בִּשְׁלָמָא בָּתְרָאָה אִיכָּא קַדְמָאָה קַמֵּיהּ, אֶלָּא קַדְמָאָה – מִי אִיכָּא בָּתְרָאָה קַמֵּיהּ?

The Gemara now proceeds to raise a difficulty against this last argument from the mishna: **We learned** in the mishna that if one says: **I am hereby a nazirite and it is** incumbent **upon me to shave a nazirite, and another heard** him **and said: And I** am hereby a nazirite, **and** it is incumbent **upon me to shave a nazirite, if they are perspicacious they shave each other; and if not, they shave other nazirites.** According to the reasoning that one takes into account only that which is possible at the time, the following difficulty arises: **Granted, the last** person **has the first one before him** and may have had in mind to volunteer to pay for the other's offerings; **but** with regard to **the first** person, **is the last one before him?** When the first one stated his vow, the other one was not yet a nazirite, and he could not have been taking him into account when he vowed to pay for the offerings of another. How can paying for the offerings of the second nazirite be considered a fulfillment of his vow?

אֶלָּא הָכִי קָאָמַר: אִי מַשְׁכַּחְנָא דְּהָוֵי נָזִיר – אֲגַלְּחֵיהּ. הָכָא נַמִי הָכִי קָאָמַר לֵיהּ: אִי מַשְׁכַּחַתְּ דְּמִיגָּרְשָׁה – קַדֵּישׁ לִי.

Rather, it can be explained that **this is what he is saying: If I find** someone **who becomes a nazirite, I will shave him. Here too,** in the case of betrothal, **this is what** the one who appointed the agent **is saying to** the agent: Even **if** the woman **you find** is married at this moment but when you come to her you discover that she **has** been **divorced** in the meantime, **betroth** her **to me.** If so, he would be prohibited from marrying her sister, contrary to the ruling of Rava.

אָמְרִי: לָא מְשַׁוֵּי אִינִישׁ שָׁלִיחַ אֶלָּא בְּמִילְּתָא דְּמָצֵי עָבֵיד הַשְׁתָּא, בְּמִילְּתָא דְּלָא מָצֵי עָבֵיד לֵיהּ הַשְׁתָּא – לָא מְשַׁוֵּי.

The Gemara rejects this comparison: The Sages **say** that there is a distinction between the two cases: **A person appoints an agent only for a matter that he** himself **can perform now,** at the time of the appointment, **but for a matter that he cannot perform**[N] now, **he does not appoint** an agent. Consequently, the agent cannot betroth a woman who was married at the time of his appointment. The one who appointed the agent may therefore marry the sister of the recently divorced woman, as stated by Rava.

וְלָא? תָּא שְׁמַע: הָאוֹמֵר לְאַפּוֹטְרוֹפּוֹס שֶׁלּוֹ "כׇּל נְדָרִים שֶׁתִּדּוֹר אִשְׁתִּי מִכָּאן עַד שֶׁאָבוֹא מִמָּקוֹם פְּלוֹנִי הָפֵר לָהּ" וְהֵפֵר לָהּ, יָכוֹל יְהוּ מוּפָרִין – תַּלְמוּד לוֹמַר "אִישָׁהּ יְקִימֶנּוּ וְאִישָׁהּ יְפֵרֶנּוּ" דִּבְרֵי רַבִּי יֹאשִׁיָּה, וְרַבִּי יוֹנָתָן אוֹמֵר: מָצִינוּ בְּכׇל מָקוֹם שֶׁשְּׁלוּחוֹ שֶׁל אָדָם כְּמוֹתוֹ.

The Gemara asks another question on the ruling of Rava: **And** can one **not** appoint an agent to betroth a woman in this manner? **Come and hear** a *baraita* that indicates the contrary: **One who says to the steward [*apotropos*]**[L] **of his**[H] affairs: **All vows that my wife will vow from now until I come from such and such a place, nullify for her,**[B] **and** the steward **nullified** them **for her,** one **might** have thought **they are nullified.** Therefore, **the verse states: "Her husband sustains** the vow **and her husband nullifies** the vow" (Numbers 30:14); this is **the statement of Rabbi Yoshiya.** The repetition of "husband" teaches that it is the husband alone who may nullify his wife's vows. **And Rabbi Yonatan says: We have found in all places that** the legal status of **a person's agent is like** that of **himself.**[H] Therefore, a steward, who serves as the husband's agent, may nullify the wife's vows.

BACKGROUND

Nullification of vows – **הֲפָרַת נְדָרִים**: The *halakhot* of vows and their nullification are stated in the Torah (Numbers, chapter 30) and an entire tractate, *Nedarim*, is devoted to explaining these *halakhot*. In essence, when either a young woman still under her father's auspices or a married woman takes a vow, her father or her husband, respectively, can nullify the vow on the day that he hears it if he does not approve of it. The Sages explained based on the verses that this is permitted only in certain situations. Only vows taken with regard to matters between the woman and her husband or between the young woman and her father can be nullified. Vows that do not affect the woman's relationship with her husband or father cannot be nullified.

NOTES

For a matter that he cannot perform – **בְּמִילְּתָא דְּלָא מָצֵי עָבֵיד**: The reason is that an agent cannot have more power than the one who appointed him, and since the action cannot be performed now, one cannot appoint an agent to perform it later. At this stage the action cannot be done, because it is considered to be an entity that has not yet come into the world (Rosh). As for the reason why a nazirite may shave someone who was not yet a nazirite at the time of his vow, Rabbeinu Azriel explains that since there were nazirites in the world at the time of his vow, it is not considered to be an entity that has not entered the world. The *Tosefot HaRosh* explains that there is a fundamental difference between an obligation that one accepts upon himself, which can refer to future developments as well, and the appointment of an agent, which applies only to acts that are possible at the time of the appointment.

LANGUAGE

Steward [*apotropos*] – **אַפּוֹטְרוֹפּוֹס**: From the Greek ἐπίτροπος, *epitropos*, meaning appointee.

HALAKHA

One who says to the steward of his, etc. – **הָאוֹמֵר לְאַפּוֹטְרוֹפּוֹס שֶׁלּוֹ וכו׳**: If one appoints an agent to nullify or ratify his wife's vows, the appointment is meaningless, since it is a biblical decree that only the husband can nullify or ratify his wife's vows (Rambam *Sefer Hafla'a*, *Hilkhot Nedarim* 13:9; *Shulḥan Arukh*, *Yoreh De'a* 234:30).

The legal status of a person's agent is like that of himself – **שְׁלוּחוֹ שֶׁל אָדָם כְּמוֹתוֹ**: If one instructs his agent to betroth a woman on his behalf, or to perform a business transaction for him, the agent acts in his stead, and it is considered as though the one who appointed the agent performed the deed himself, since a person's agent is like himself (Rambam *Sefer Nashim*, *Hilkhot Ishut* 3:15; *Sefer Kinyan*, *Hilkhot Sheluḥin VeShutafin* 1:1; and *Sefer Hafla'a*, *Hilkhot Shevuot* 7:6; *Shulḥan Arukh*, *Ḥoshen Mishpat* 182:1 and *Even HaEzer* 35:1).

HALAKHA

All vows that you will vow…shall be ratified – כָּל נְדָרִים שֶׁתִּדּוֹרִי...יְהוּ קַיָּימִין: If one says to his wife or daughter that all the vows that she vows from now until he returns from his travels shall be upheld, his statement is of no consequence (Rambam *Sefer Hafla'a, Hilkhot Nedarim* 13:9).

They are hereby nullified, etc. – הֲרֵי הֵן מוּפָרִין וכו׳: If one says to his wife or daughter that all vows that she vows from now until he returns shall be nullified, his words are meaningless (Rambam *Sefer Hafla'a, Hilkhot Nedarim* 13:9; *Shulḥan Arukh Yoreh De'a* 234:28).

It is incumbent upon me to shave half a nazirite, etc. – הֲרֵי עָלַי לְגַלֵּחַ חֲצִי נָזִיר וכו׳: If one says: It is incumbent upon me to shave half a nazirite, and another heard him and vowed to shave half a nazirite as well, they are each obligated to pay for half the offerings of a nazirite, in accordance with the opinion of the Rabbis (Rambam *Sefer Hafla'a, Hilkhot Nezirut* 8:20).

טַעְמָא דְּאָמַר רַחֲמָנָא ״אִישָׁהּ יְקִימֶנּוּ וְאִישָׁהּ יְפֵירֶנּוּ״. הָא לָאו הָכִי – אַפּוֹטְרוֹפּוֹס מֵיפֵר. וְאִילּוּ גַּבֵּי דִּידֵיהּ תַּנְיָא: הָאוֹמֵר לְאִשְׁתּוֹ ״כָּל נְדָרִים שֶׁתִּדּוֹרִי מִכָּאן וְעַד שֶׁאָבֹא מִמָּקוֹם פְּלוֹנִי יְהוּ קַיָּימִין״ – לֹא אָמַר כְּלוּם. ״הֲרֵי הֵן מוּפָרִין״. רַבִּי אֱלִיעֶזֶר אוֹמֵר: מוּפָר, וַחֲכָמִים אוֹמְרִים: אֵינוֹ מוּפָר.

Even according to Rabbi Yoshiya, who maintains that the steward cannot nullify her vows, **the reason is that the Merciful One states** in the Torah: **"Her husband sustains** the vow **and her husband nullifies** the vow," **but if** it were **not so,** the **steward could nullify** even the future vows of the wife. **However, with regard to** the husband **himself** it **is taught** in a mishna (*Nedarim* 75a): **One who says to his wife: All vows that you will vow from now until I come from such and such a place shall be ratified,**[H] **he has not said anything.** However, if a husband says: All vows that you will vow from now until I come from such and such a place, **they are hereby nullified,**[H] **Rabbi Eliezer says: It is nullified, and the Rabbis say: It is not nullified.**

קָא סָלְקָא דַּעְתִּין: כִּי אָמַר רַבִּי יֹאשִׁיָּה – אַלִּיבָּא דְּרַבָּנַן דְּאָמְרִי: לָא מָצֵי מֵיפֵר. וְאִי לָאו דְּאָמַר רַחֲמָנָא ״אִישָׁהּ יְקִימֶנּוּ וְאִישָׁהּ יְפֵירֶנּוּ״ – אַפּוֹטְרוֹפּוֹס הֲוָה מֵיפֵר!

The Gemara finishes the question: **It enters our mind** to say that **when Rabbi Yoshiya said** that the steward cannot nullify the vows, he spoke **in accordance with** the opinion of **the Rabbis, who say** that the husband **is not able to nullify** her vows ahead of time, **and** yet, even according to their approach, **if the Merciful One had not stated** in the Torah: **"Her husband sustains** the vow **and her husband nullifies** the vow" the **steward would** be able to **nullify** such vows. This proves that one can appoint an agent for something he himself cannot do at the time, which contradicts the statement of Rava.

וְדִלְמָא אַלִּיבָּא דְּרַבִּי אֱלִיעֶזֶר, דְּאָמַר: מָצֵי מֵיפֵר. אִי הָכִי לָמָּה לִי לְשַׁוּוֹיֵי שָׁלִיחַ? לֵיפַר לַהּ אִיהוּ! קָסָבַר: דִּלְמָא מִשְׁתַּלֵּינָא, אוֹ רַתַחְנָא, אוֹ מִיטְּרִידְנָא.

The Gemara rejects this: **And perhaps** Rabbi Yoshiya spoke **in accordance with** the opinion of **Rabbi Eliezer, who says** the husband **can nullify** the vows ahead of time, and it is for this reason that he can appoint the steward to do the same. The Gemara rejects this: **If so, why do I need to make him into an agent; let him nullify** the future vows **for her**[N] before he sets out on his journey. The Gemara answers: **He thinks, perhaps I will forget, or become angry, or be occupied** with other matters when I am about to set out on my journey. This is why he appoints an agent to nullify the vows on his behalf, and no proof can be derived from this *baraita*.

מתני׳ ״הֲרֵי עָלַי לְגַלֵּחַ חֲצִי נָזִיר״. וְשָׁמַע חֲבֵירוֹ וְאָמַר ״וַאֲנִי עָלַי לְגַלֵּחַ חֲצִי נָזִיר״ – זֶה מְגַלֵּחַ נָזִיר שָׁלֵם, וְזֶה מְגַלֵּחַ נָזִיר שָׁלֵם, דִּבְרֵי רַבִּי מֵאִיר. וַחֲכָמִים אוֹמְרִים: זֶה מְגַלֵּחַ חֲצִי נָזִיר, וְזֶה מְגַלֵּחַ חֲצִי נָזִיר.

MISHNA If one says: **It is incumbent upon me to shave half a nazirite,**[H] i.e., he is vowing to pay half the costs of a nazirite's offerings, **and another heard and said:**[N] **And I, it is incumbent upon me to shave half a nazirite, this** one **shaves a whole nazirite and that** one **shaves a whole nazirite,** i.e., each pays the full cost of a nazirite's offerings; this is **the statement of Rabbi Meir,** since there is no such entity as half a nazirite. **And the Rabbis say: This one shaves half a nazirite and that** one **shaves half a nazirite;** they may join together to pay for the offerings of one nazirite.

NOTES

Let him nullify for her – לֵיפַר לַהּ אִיהוּ: The Commentary on *Nazir* explains this as follows: Let him nullify her vows for her at this point in time. *Tosafot* maintain that the Gemara means he should nullify them upon his departure. He does not wish to nullify them now in case she utters vows before he leaves that he will want to ratify. He also does not wish to nullify now any vows that she will utter from the time that he departs, as his wife may take offense at his nullifying her vows, which could lead to quarrels between the couple before the husband's departure.

And another heard and said – וְשָׁמַע חֲבֵירוֹ וְאָמַר: The commentaries point out that this clause is superfluous since the dispute between Rabbi Meir and the Rabbis applies even to a single person who vows in this manner. This phrase was added only due to its similarity to the previous mishna (Rabbeinu Todros). The Rosh states that this clause does teach a novelty with regard to the opinion of Rabbi Meir; it is seen from this addition that even if there are two people, in which case they can together bring a complete set of nazirite offerings, Rabbi Meir still holds that each of them is obligated to pay for all the offerings of a nazirite.

גמ׳ אֲמַר רָבָא: הַכֹּל מוֹדִים כׇּל הֵיכָא דַּאֲמַר ״חֲצִי קׇרְבְּנוֹת נָזִיר עָלַי״ – חֲצִי קׇרְבָּן מַיְיתֵי; ״קׇרְבְּנוֹת חֲצִי נָזִיר עָלַי״ – כּוּלֵּיהּ קׇרְבָּן בָּעֵי אֵיתוּיֵי; מַאי טַעְמָא – דְּהָא לָא אַשְׁכַּחַן נְזִירוּת לְפַלְגָא.

GEMARA With regard to this dispute, **Rava said: All concede that whenever one said: Half of the offerings of a nazirite are** incumbent **upon me,**[H] **he brings half of the offerings,** since he vowed to pay only that amount. Also, everyone agrees that if he said: **The offerings of half a nazirite are** incumbent **upon me, he needs to bring all of the offerings** of a nazirite. **What is the reason** that he must bring all of the offerings of a nazirite? It is **that we have not found** such an entity as **half a naziriteship.** If one vowed to be half a nazirite, he is a full nazirite.

וְכִי פְּלִיגִי – בְּלִישָּׁנָא דְּמַתְנִיתִין פְּלִיגִי, רַבִּי מֵאִיר סָבַר: כֵּיוָן דַּאֲמַר ״הֲרֵי עָלַי״ – אִיחַיַּיב אַכּוּלֵּיהּ קׇרְבַּן נְזִירוּת, וְכִי קָאָמַר חֲצִי נְזִירוּת – לָאו כׇּל כְּמִינֵּיהּ. וְרַבָּנַן סָבְרִי: נֶדֶר וּפִתְחוֹ עִמּוֹ הוּא.

And when they disagree, it is only **in** a case of one who used **the** precise **wording of the mishna. Rabbi Meir holds** that once he **said:** It is incumbent **upon me, he is obligated in all of the naziriteship offerings, and when he** later **says: Half a naziriteship,** it **is not in his power** to uproot his first obligation. **And the Rabbis hold** that **it is a vow with** its inherent **opening.**[N] By saying he had only half the offerings of a nazirite in mind from the outset, he has nullified his own vow.

מתני׳ ״הֲרֵינִי נָזִיר לִכְשֶׁיִּהְיֶה לִי בֵּן״ וְנוֹלַד לוֹ בֵּן – הֲרֵי זֶה נָזִיר. נוֹלַד לוֹ בַּת, טוּמְטוּם, וְאַנְדְּרוֹגִינוֹס – אֵינוֹ נָזִיר. אִם אָמַר ״כְּשֶׁיִּהְיֶה לִי וָלָד״ – אֲפִילּוּ נוֹלַד לוֹ בַּת, טוּמְטוּם, וְאַנְדְּרוֹגִינוֹס – הֲרֵי זֶה נָזִיר.

MISHNA If one said: **I am hereby a nazirite when I will have a son,**[H] **and a son was born to him, he is a nazirite. If a daughter, a** ***tumtum*****,**[B] **or a hermaphrodite** [*androginos*][L] **is born to him, he is not a nazirite,** since a son was not born to him. However, **if he says:** I am hereby a nazirite **when I will have a child,** then **even if a daughter, a** ***tumtum*****, or a hermaphrodite is born to him, he is a nazirite.**

BACKGROUND

Tumtum – טוּמְטוּם: A *tumtum* has no visible protruding sex organ. For this reason he cannot be identified as a man, and he appears to be a woman. Yet since he bears no secondary female characteristics, he is not identified as a woman either.

LANGUAGE

Hermaphrodite [*androginos*] – אַנְדְּרוֹגִינוֹס: From the Greek ἀνδρόγυνος, *androgunos*, literally meaning man-woman, i.e., one who has both male and female reproductive organs.

HALAKHA

Half of the offerings of a nazirite are incumbent upon me – חֲצִי קׇרְבְּנוֹת נָזִיר עָלַי: If one says: It is incumbent upon me to pay for half the offerings of a nazirite, or: It is incumbent upon me to shave half a nazirite, he must cover the expenses for half the offerings of a nazirite of his choice, and that nazirite pays the rest. However, if he said: It is incumbent upon me to pay for the offerings of half a nazirite, he must pay for all the offerings of a nazirite, since there is no such thing as half a naziriteship. The Ra'avad suggests a different distinction between the expressions. He claims that if one says: It is incumbent upon me to pay for the offerings of half a nazirite, he brings only half, but if he states: The offerings of half a nazirite are incumbent upon me, he must pay for all the nazirite offerings (Rambam *Sefer Hafla'a*, *Hilkhot Nezirut* 8:18).

I am hereby a nazirite when I will have a son – הֲרֵינִי נָזִיר לִכְשֶׁיִּהְיֶה לִי בֵּן: If one says: I am hereby a nazirite when will I have a son, and a son is born to him, he is a nazirite. If he had a daughter, a *tumtum*, or a hermaphrodite, he is not a nazirite. However, if he vowed to be a nazirite when he will have a child, he is a nazirite whether he has a son, a daughter, a *tumtum*, or a hermaphrodite (Rambam *Sefer Hafla'a*, *Hilkhot Nezirut* 1:17).

NOTES

A vow with its inherent opening – נֶדֶר וּפִתְחוֹ עִמּוֹ: Some commentaries (*Tosafot*; Rabbeinu Peretz) explain that this means that the last part of his statement explains the first part, and he is therefore liable for only half the offerings of a nazirite. The Commentary on *Nazir*, as well as Rabbi Avraham min HaHar, explains that even the Rabbis agree that if one person alone says: It is incumbent upon me to shave half a nazirite, he is obligated to pay for all of the offerings. The Rabbis disagree with Rabbi Meir only with regard to two people who stated the same vow. The reason is that the circumstances show that each of them had only half an offering in mind, so they can pay for a full set of offerings together. This circumstantial evidence is what the Gemara means by: Its inherent opening. This interpretation also explains why the mishna cited a case involving two people (Rabbeinu Peretz). See *Nusḥat Rivan* in the Vilna edition, which states that even if there were no other person who vowed with him, he can approach any nazirite and offer to pay for half of his offerings.

HALAKHA

If his wife miscarried he is not a nazirite – הִפִּילָה אִשְׁתּוֹ אֵינוֹ נָזִיר: One who vowed to be a nazirite when a child is born to him is not a nazirite if his wife miscarried (Rambam *Sefer Hafla'a, Hilkhot Nezirut* 1:17).

Gave birth again – חָזְרָה וְיָלְדָה: If one vowed to be a nazirite when he will have a child, and his wife miscarried, and she later became pregnant and gave birth again, he is a nazirite (Rambam *Sefer Hafla'a, Hilkhot Nezirut* 9:13).

הִפִּילָה אִשְׁתּוֹ – אֵינוֹ נָזִיר. רַבִּי שִׁמְעוֹן אוֹמֵר: יֹאמַר ״אִם הָיָה בֶּן קַיָּימָא – הֲרֵי אֲנִי נְזִיר חוֹבָה, וְאִם לָאו – הֲרֵי אֲנִי נְזִיר נְדָבָה״.

However, if **his wife miscarried**[N] **he is not a nazirite,**[H] since his wife did not give birth to a live child. **Rabbi Shimon says:**[N] Since it is possible that the fetus was viable, in which case his vow of naziriteship takes effect, **he should say** the following: **If** this fetus **was viable** in terms of its development but died due to other causes, **I am hereby an obligatory nazirite** in fulfillment of my vow; **and if** it was **not** viable, **I am hereby a voluntary nazirite.** He then proceeds to observe naziriteship.

חָזְרָה וְיָלְדָה – הֲרֵי זֶה נָזִיר. רַבִּי שִׁמְעוֹן אוֹמֵר: יֹאמַר ״אִם הָרִאשׁוֹן בֶּן קַיָּימָא – הָרִאשׁוֹן חוֹבָה, וְזוֹ נְדָבָה. וְאִם לָאו – הָרִאשׁוֹן נְדָבָה, וְזוֹ חוֹבָה״.

If, subsequent to this, his wife **gave birth again,**[H] **he is a nazirite,** since the unattributed opinion in the mishna holds that the condition of his vow has now been fulfilled. **Rabbi Shimon says,** following his earlier ruling: He must now accept upon himself an additional naziriteship and **he should say: If the first** fetus was **viable** then my naziriteship for **the first** child was **obligatory, and this** naziriteship is **voluntary; and if** the first child was **not** viable, then the naziriteship for **the first** one was **voluntary and this** naziriteship is **obligatory.**

גמ׳ הַאי מַאי לְמֵימְרָא? מִשּׁוּם סֵיפָא: בַּת, טוּמְטוּם, וְאַנְדְּרוֹגִינוּס – אֵינוֹ נָזִיר. פְּשִׁיטָא! מַהוּ דְּתֵימָא: ״לִכְשֶׁאֶבָּנֶה״ הוּא דְּקָאָמַר, קָא מַשְׁמַע לַן דְּלָא.

GEMARA With regard to the statement of the mishna that one who vowed to be a nazirite when a son is born to him is a nazirite when his son is born, the Gemara asks: **What** is the purpose **of stating this** ruling? Of course he is a nazirite. The Gemara answers: This *halakha* is stated **due to the latter clause** of that mishna, which states that if **a daughter, a *tumtum*, or a hermaphrodite** are born to him, **he is not a nazirite.** The Gemara questions this, too: **Isn't** that **obvious,** since he specified a son? The Gemara answers: It is necessary **lest you say** he did not literally mean a son, but rather **he meant to say: When I will be built up**[N] by means of any child, including the types listed. The mishna therefore **teaches us that** this is **not** the case.

״וְאִם אָמַר כְּשֶׁיִּהְיֶה לִי וָלָד״ כו׳. פְּשִׁיטָא! מַהוּ דְּתֵימָא: וָלָד דְּמִיחֲשַׁב בֵּינֵי אֱינָשֵׁי בָּעֵינַן, קָא מַשְׁמַע לַן.

The mishna also taught: **And if he said: When I have a child,** then even if he has a daughter, a *tumtum*, or a hermaphrodite, his vow takes effect. The Gemara asks: **Isn't** it **obvious** that this is the case? The Gemara answers: It is necessary to state this **lest you say** that **we require a child** of the kind **that is considered** significant[N] **by people,** and he meant to exclude these other types of children when he vowed. The mishna therefore **teaches us** that this is not so.

NOTES

If his wife miscarried – הִפִּילָה אִשְׁתּוֹ: Even though the word miscarried usually refers to the pregnancy terminating before reaching its full term, it is difficult to accept that this is the meaning here, as the father certainly did not have a miscarried child in mind when he vowed to be a nazirite on the condition that he would have a child. Additionally, Rabbi Shimon's uncertainty that the child might have been viable appears irrelevant if it was lost before the pregnancy reached its full term. Rather, it is more reasonable to explain that the woman gave birth to a child only to see the child die before it was thirty days old. In that case, it is unclear whether the baby died because it was not properly developed or due to external factors (Rabbeinu Azriel; Rabbeinu Peretz). The *Tosefta* (2:4) indicates likewise, as it states: If a son was born to him, and it is uncertain if it is viable. Other commentaries maintain that the case is that of a child that was stillborn and that was clearly fully developed, but it is not known whether it died in its mother's womb, in which case it is certainly not considered a child, or whether it died during birth (see Responsa of the Maharshdam, *Even HaEzer* 208; *Keren Ora*, following the opinion of *Tosafot*).

Rabbi Shimon says, etc. – רַבִּי שִׁמְעוֹן אוֹמֵר וכו׳: Rabbi Shimon maintains that the *halakha* is ruled stringently in uncertain cases of naziriteship (Commentary on *Nazir*). The *Tosefta* (2:4) states that according to Rabbi Shimon a mistaken vow of naziriteship takes effect. According to the Rosh and Rabbeinu Peretz, Rabbi Shimon holds that one who vows intends to be held accountable in a situation of doubt.

When I will be built up – לִכְשֶׁאֶבָּנֶה: He may have used the word son [*ben*] in the sense of building [*binyan*], so that he means: When I build up my family by means of a child. If that was his intention, the naziriteship would take effect, as even one who has only a daughter can be considered built (*Tosafot*).

A child that is considered significant – וָלָד דְּמִיחֲשַׁב: This excludes a *tumtum* or a hermaphrodite. Since their gender and legal status are not clearly defined, they are not considered proper children (Rabbeinu Peretz). The Commentary on *Nazir* and *Tosafot* state that it may have been thought that even a daughter may not be considered a significant child in relation to a son, and all the more so a *tumtum* or a hermaphrodite.

"וְהִפִּילָה אִשְׁתּוֹ אֵינוֹ נָזִיר". מַאן קָתָנֵי לַהּ? רַבִּי יְהוּדָה דִּכְרִי הוּא.

§ The mishna taught that if **his wife miscarried he is not a nazirite,** even though it may have been a viable child. The Gemara clarifies: According to **whose** opinion **is this taught?** The Gemara answers: **It is** the opinion of **Rabbi Yehuda with regard to a heap**[N] of wheat. Rabbi Yehuda holds that if one vows to be a nazirite if a heap contains a certain amount of wheat and it is unclear whether or not his condition was fulfilled, the *halakha* is ruled leniently, and he is not a nazirite.

רַבִּי שִׁמְעוֹן אוֹמֵר: יֹאמַר "אִם הָיָה בֶּן קַיְימָא הֲרֵינִי נְזִיר חוֹבָה וְאִם לָאו הֲרֵינִי נְזִיר נְדָבָה". בְּעָא מִינֵּיהּ רַבִּי אַבָּא מֵרַב הוּנָא: "הֲרֵינִי נָזִיר לִכְשֶׁיְּהֵא לִי בֵּן" וְהִפִּילָה אִשְׁתּוֹ, וְהִפְרִישׁ קׇרְבָּן, וְחָזְרָה וְיָלְדָה, מַהוּ?

The mishna further taught that **Rabbi Shimon says** that the individual **should say: If** this fetus **was viable** in terms of its development but died due to other causes, **I am hereby an obligatory nazirite** in fulfillment of my vow; **and if** it was **not** viable, **I am hereby a voluntary nazirite.** The Gemara relates that **Rabbi Abba inquired of Rav Huna:** If one said: **I am hereby a nazirite when I will have a son, and his wife miscarried, and he separated an offering**[HN] for his naziriteship but did not sacrifice it, **and** his wife **gave birth again** to a son, **what is** the *halakha* with regard to the offering he separated?

אַלִּיבָּא דְּמַאן? אִי אַלִּיבָּא דְּרַבִּי שִׁמְעוֹן – מַאי תִּיבְּעֵי לֵיהּ? הָא אָמַר רַבִּי שִׁמְעוֹן: סְפֵק נְזִירוּת לְהַחְמִיר. וְאֶלָּא אַלִּיבָּא דְּרַבִּי יְהוּדָה, דְּאָמַר סְפֵק נְזִירוּת לְהָקֵל, מַאי? קָדוֹשׁ אוֹ לָא קָדוֹשׁ?

The Gemara asks: **In accordance with whose** opinion did Rabbi Abba pose his question? **If** he asked it **in accordance with** the opinion **of Rabbi Shimon, what dilemma is he raising? Didn't Rabbi Shimon say:** In a case of **uncertainty** with regard to **naziriteship,** the ruling is **to be stringent?** Here too, since the fetus might have been viable, he was required to separate the offerings after she miscarried, and he may not use those offerings for the naziriteship brought about by the later birth. **Rather,** one should say that the question was **in accordance with** the opinion **of Rabbi Yehuda, who said** that in a case of **uncertainty** with regard to **naziriteship,** the ruling is **to be lenient.** The question is as follows: **What** is the *halakha* in such a situation? Are the offerings already considered **consecrated** and need not be consecrated again, **or** are they **not consecrated** and therefore he must consecrate them a second time?

HALAKHA

And his wife miscarried and he separated an offering – וְהִפִּילָה אִשְׁתּוֹ וְהִפְרִישׁ קׇרְבָּן: If one says: I am hereby a nazirite when I will have a son, and he separated his nazirite offerings, and then his wife miscarried, became pregnant again, and gave birth, it is uncertain whether all of the offerings he had separated are consecrated. One may not shear them or use them for work, but he is not liable to receive lashes if he does. This case remains unresolved by the Gemara and the ruling is therefore stringent (Rambam *Sefer Hafla'a*, *Hilkhot Nezirut* 9:13).

NOTES

Rabbi Yehuda with regard to a heap – רַבִּי יְהוּדָה דִּכְרִי: Rabbi Yehuda rules that if one said he will be a nazirite if a certain heap contains one hundred *kor* of wheat and it was stolen or lost before it could be examined, preventing him from checking whether the condition was fulfilled, he is not a nazirite. The reason is either because the *halakha* is ruled leniently in questions of naziriteship (Commentary on *Nazir*), or because he holds that people do not state conditions that may result in them being left in a state of uncertainty (Rabbeinu Peretz).

And his wife miscarried and he separated an offering – וְהִפִּילָה אִשְׁתּוֹ וְהִפְרִישׁ קׇרְבָּן: As explained below, this question is relevant only according to Rabbi Yehuda, who holds that one is not obligated to observe a term of naziriteship at all in the case of a stillborn. The commentaries disagree with regard to why the animals he separated should be considered consecrated at all if he is not obligated to observe a term of naziriteship. Some commentaries claim that the case is one of a woman who miscarried and then gave birth to a child from the same pregnancy; e.g., if she gave birth to twins on the same day (Rosh; Rabbeinu Peretz). In such a situation, it may be assumed that the first child was also viable, as it had reached its full term, but it died as a result of external factors. Consequently, even Rabbi Yehuda would agree that the uncertainty in this case is stronger than in that of a standard pregnancy.

The Rid, however, prefers a variant version of the text, which is also that of Rambam: He separated an offering and his wife miscarried, and she gave birth again. In this reading, he separated the offerings before his wife miscarried. According to the Rid, the question is whether he is required to consecrate the offering a second time since it is apparent that the first sanctity did not take effect, or whether the first consecration stands. The Meiri claims that even according to the approach of the Rid, the uncertainty applies only to another child from the same pregnancy. If the case is not specifically referring to two births from the same pregnancy, as explained by the Commentary on *Nazir*, the question might be whether the original consecration is viewed as erroneous and is entirely null, or whether the fact that it later turns out to have a purpose, as another child was born to him, means that it was not an erroneous consecration (*Mishne LaMelekh*).

מאי נפקא מינה? לגיזתו ולעבוד בו. תיקו.

The Gemara asks: **What difference is there?** In any case, he is certainly obligated to observe naziriteship now, and he must separate the offerings. The Gemara answers: The question is referring **to** the issue of **its shearing and its labor.** If they are considered consecrated from the initial consecration, it is prohibited to shear their wool and use them for labor, like any other consecrated animal. But if they are not yet consecrated, it is permitted to use them. No answer was found for this question, and the Gemara concludes that the dilemma **shall stand** unresolved.

בעא מיניה בן רחומי מאביי: "הריני נזיר לכשיהא לי בן". ושמע חבירו ואמר "ועלי". מהו? אדיבוריה משמע, או אגופיה משמע?

§ With regard to one who accepted naziriteship upon himself that would begin upon the birth of his son, the Sage **ben Reḥumi**[P] **inquired of Abaye:** If one said: **I am hereby a nazirite when I will have a son, and another heard** him **and said: And it is** incumbent **upon me,**[H] **what is** the *halakha* with regard to the second person? Is **the implication** of his statement a concurrence **to the statement** of the first one, which would mean that he too accepts naziriteship upon himself when the first has a son, **or** is **the implication** of his statement meant to be understood **about himself,** i.e., that he has vowed to be a nazirite when he has a son of his own?

אם תמצי לומר אגופיה משמע, אמר "הריני נזיר לכשיהא לי בן". ושמע חבירו ואמר "ואני". מהו? אנפשיה קאמר, או דילמא הכי קאמר: רחימנא לך כוותיך? אם תמצי לומר כל באנפיה

The Gemara develops the question further: Even **if you say** that the phrase: And it is incumbent upon me, has **the implication** of meaning that it is to be understood **about himself, what is** the *halakha* if one **said: I am hereby a nazirite when**[H] **I will have a son, and another heard** him **and said: And I?**[N] What is the meaning of the second person's statement? Is it to be understood that here too, **he is speaking of himself,** meaning: I shall be a nazirite when I will have a son of my own, **or perhaps this is what he is saying: I love you as you** love **yourself;** I would be as happy as you at the birth of your son, and I too will be a nazirite when you have a son. Ben Reḥumi continues: **If you say** that **anything** he says to another **in front of him**

PERSONALITIES

Ben Reḥumi – בן רחומי: Some suggest that ben Reḥumi is not a name but the nickname of a Sage who asked a question concerning the concept of *raḥimana lei*, I am as a good friend. There are other such nicknames in various places in the Talmud. However, aside from the fact that the name Reḥumi itself is the proper name of several Sages, the name Raḥum is also found in the Bible. One Sage named Reḥumi was a disciple of Abaye, and it is possible that ben Reḥumi was the son of Rav Reḥumi, and he is called: Son of Reḥumi [*ben Reḥumi*] since he was very young when he asked his question.

HALAKHA

And another heard and said: And it is incumbent upon me, etc. – ושמע חבירו ואמר ועלי וכו׳: If one says: I am hereby a nazirite when I have a son, and another heard and said: And I, the latter becomes a nazirite immediately. The Ra'avad raises a question as to the Rambam's source for this ruling. According to the *Kesef Mishne*, the Rambam has a variant text, which replaces the phrase: And it is incumbent upon me, with: And I. Additionally, he interprets the word *aggufeih* to mean: About itself, referring to the immediate, unconditional acceptance of naziriteship. The principle of the Rambam is that whenever the Gemara introduces a dilemma with the phrase: If you say, the assumption upon which the dilemma is based is the decided *halakha*. In this case as well as the following cases, the Ra'avad holds that if both of them have sons he has no recourse but to observe two sets of naziriteship, one for the other's son and one for his own (Rambam *Sefer Hafla'a*, *Hilkhot Nezirut* 2:5).

I am hereby a nazirite when, etc. – הריני נזיר לכשיהא וכו׳: If one said to another: I am hereby a nazirite when I have a son, and the other heard him and said: And I, the latter is not a nazirite since he only meant that he loves him and wishes for him to have a son (Rambam *Sefer Hafla'a*, *Hilkhot Nezirut* 2:6).

NOTES

And another heard and said: And I – ושמע חבירו ואמר ואני: Most commentaries who accept this version of the text maintain that the difference between this question and the previous one is that the phrase: And it is incumbent upon me, indicates that he must also observe naziriteship when he has a son, whereas: And I, means: I too shall be like you and be a nazirite when you have a son (see Commentary on *Nazir* and Rosh). However, Rabbeinu Peretz questions this distinction and holds to the contrary, that saying: It is incumbent upon me, is more indicative of an acceptance of the first person's vow than saying: And I. He prefers a variant text, which is that of many early commentaries, in which one says: I am hereby a nazirite when you have a son, and another heard and said: And I. The question is whether he meant that he too will be a nazirite when he has a son of his own, or that due to his affection for the other he vows a reciprocal naziriteship when the other will have a son. Rabbeinu Peretz states, citing *Tosafot*, that according to this version the next case is referring to a situation where the first person speaks to a third party, and the second one adds: And I. The Rambam explains similarly.

כסיפא ליה מילתא, אמר "הריני נזיר לכשיהא לפלוני בן". ושמע חבירו ואמר "ואני". מהו? מי אמרינן שלא בפניו – אנפשיה קאמר, או דילמא הכי קאמר ליה: רחימנא ליה כוותיך? תיבעי.

should be understood in light of the fact that **the matter is embarrassing for him,** the second person is likely to mean that he will become a nazirite upon the birth of a child to the first person, as he will be embarrassed to seem indifferent about the birth of the child to the person standing before him, then the following question arises: If one **said: I am hereby a nazirite when so-and-so will have a son,**[H] **and another heard and said: And I, what is** the *halakha*? **Do we say** that since the second person **did not** vow **in front of** the subject of the first person's vow, he therefore **speaks of himself** when he says: And I, meaning that he will be a nazirite when he has a son of his own? **Or perhaps this is what he is saying to him: I love him as you do,** and I too will be a nazirite when he has a son. As in the previous cases, no answer was found for this question, and **the dilemma remains** unresolved.[N]

מתני׳ "הריני נזיר, ונזיר כשיהיה לי בן" התחיל מונה את שלו, ואחר כך נולד לו בן – משלים את שלו, ואחר כך מונה את של בנו. "הריני נזיר כשיהיה לי בן, ונזיר" התחיל מונה את שלו, ואחר כך נולד לו בן – מניח את שלו ומונה את של בנו, ואחר כך משלים את שלו.

MISHNA In a case where one said: **I am hereby a nazirite** now, **and** I will be **a nazirite when I will have a son,**[H] and **he began counting his** own term of naziriteship, i.e., his first vow, **and afterward** in the middle of this naziriteship period **a son was born to him,** he first **completes his own**[N] initial term of naziriteship **and afterward he counts** the term of naziriteship he vowed on the condition **of** the birth **of his son.** However, if he reversed the order and said: **I am hereby a nazirite when I will have a son, and** I am hereby **a nazirite,**[H] and he **began counting his** own term of naziriteship **and afterward,** during this period, **a son was born to him, he sets aside his** own term of naziriteship **and counts that** which he vowed on condition of the birth **of his son, and afterward** he **completes his** own term of naziriteship.

גמ׳ בעי רבא: אמר "הריני נזיר לאחר עשרים יום ומעכשיו מאה יום" מהו? כיון דהלין מאה בעשרין לא שלמין – לא חיילין, או דילמא כיון דאית ליה גידול שער לבסוף – חיילין?

GEMARA In light of the ruling of the mishna, **Rava asks:** If one **said: I am hereby a nazirite** for a standard term of thirty days and will begin observing it **after twenty days,**[H] **and** I am also a nazirite **from now** for **one hundred days, what is** the *halakha*? Should one say that **since these one hundred** days of naziriteship are **not completed within** those first **twenty** days, it could be said that the one hundred days of naziriteship **do not take effect**[N] at all until after he has completed the thirty-day naziriteship? **Or perhaps, since he** still **has** at least thirty days of **hair growth**[N] **at the end,** as after the thirty-day term he could observe an additional eighty days, therefore the one hundred days of naziriteship **take effect** from now, and he counts twenty days, pauses to observe the other term of naziriteship for thirty days, shaves, and then completes the final eighty days of the long term of naziriteship.

NOTES

The dilemma remains unresolved [*tiba'ei*] – **תיבעי:** This is equivalent to the more prevalent phrase: The dilemma shall stand [*teiku*]. The early commentaries point out that differences of this kind are characteristic of the style of this tractate, as well as tractate *Nedarim*, in contrast to other tractates.

He completes his own, etc. – **משלים את שלו וכו׳:** The early commentaries suggest two basic explanations for this statement. Some commentaries even cite both interpretations, including different versions of each (see Rabbeinu Peretz and Rabbeinu Azriel). One explanation (Commentary on *Nazir*; Rosh) is that after completing his term he does not shave, since the term of naziriteship for his son took effect during the first term of naziriteship, and he then immediately observes the term of naziriteship for his son. Upon the completion of the second term of naziriteship he shaves and brings the offerings for both terms. Alternatively, he brings only one set of offerings, as the offerings are contingent on the shaving, and he has shaved only once (Rabbeinu Azriel). The other explanation is that he completes his own term of naziriteship, shaves, and brings the offerings, and afterward begins to count a second term of naziriteship for his son. The Commentary on *Nazir* attributes this interpretation to an individual called: The teacher, which may refer to Rashi. Many early commentaries agree with this second explanation, and the Jerusalem Talmud explains likewise.

Do not take effect – **לא חיילין:** If this is the *halakha*, then one in this situation does not observe naziriteship at all during the first twenty days. He may drink wine and contract impurity from a corpse. After twenty days have passed he observes thirty days of naziriteship, shaves, and then observes a further term of one hundred days. *Tosafot* explain that although he said: From now, he meant only that he is vowing now, but it is clear from the content of his statement that he does not wish to start counting that term of naziriteship immediately. As for the difference between this *halakha* and the *halakha* of the mishna with regard to one whose term of naziriteship for his son came into effect while he was observing his own term of naziriteship, where everyone agrees that he starts his own term of naziriteship and stops it, the commentaries offer the following explanation: In the case of the mishna he does not know the precise date of his son's birth, so his own term of naziriteship begins immediately, as he might be able to complete it in time. Here, however, he knows ahead of time that twenty days are insufficient for a term of naziriteship, so it can be assumed that he did not intend for the term of naziriteship to begin immediately.

Since he has hair growth – **כיון דאית ליה גידול שער:** Some commentaries explain that since he must shave at the completion of the thirty days of the second term of naziriteship, there is a need for sufficient time for another complete term of naziriteship in order for his hair to grow, so that he can shave again at the completion of the restarted term of naziriteship. This means that at least thirty days of the initial naziriteship must remain, because one cannot shave for hair growth of less than thirty days (*Tosafot*). Others explain that as in the case of the mishna, he shaves only once, at the conclusion of the final term of naziriteship. According to this explanation, the Gemara is not referring to actual hair growth, as his hair has already grown during the intervening term, but refers to a sufficiently long period of time for the growth to occur after the intervening term has ended (see *Shita Mekubbetzet* and Meiri).

HALAKHA

When so-and-so will have a son – **לכשיהא לפלוני בן:** If one says: I am hereby a nazirite when so-and-so will have a son, and another heard him and said: And I, it is uncertain whether the second person has accepted naziriteship upon himself or whether he was merely expressing his equal affection for him. Since the *halakha* is to be lenient in uncertain cases of naziriteship, he is not a nazirite. According to the Ra'avad he remains in a state of uncertainty until he vows to observe two terms of naziriteship: One for the other's son and one for his own (Rambam *Sefer Hafla'a, Hilkhot Nezirut* 2:7).

I am hereby a nazirite, and a nazirite when I will have a son – **הריני נזיר, ונזיר כשיהיה לי בן:** If one says: I am hereby a nazirite, and I will be a nazirite when I have a son, and then a son was born to him while he was counting his naziriteship, he completes the first term of naziriteship and afterward observes the term of naziriteship he vowed for the birth of his son (Rambam *Sefer Hafla'a, Hilkhot Nezirut* 4:3).

I am hereby a nazirite when I will have a son, and I am hereby a nazirite – **הריני נזיר כשיהיה לי בן ונזיר:** If one says: I am hereby a nazirite when I will have a son and I am hereby a nazirite for a certain period of time, and a son was born to him during his term of naziriteship, he stops counting that term of naziriteship, observes the term of naziriteship for his son, and afterward completes the first term (Rambam *Sefer Hafla'a, Hilkhot Nezirut* 4:3).

I am hereby a nazirite after twenty days, etc. – **הריני נזיר לאחר עשרים יום וכו׳:** If one says: I am hereby a nazirite after twenty days, and then says: I am hereby a nazirite from now for one hundred days, he counts twenty days, pauses, and proceeds to observe the thirty days of his first vow of naziriteship. At the conclusion of those thirty days he shaves and brings the offerings. He then observes the remaining eighty days of the term of naziriteship he had started to observe, shaves, and brings the offerings. The *halakha* is in accordance with the opinion of Rava, based on the assumption of the question beginning: If you say, on the following page (Rambam *Sefer Hafla'a, Hilkhot Nezirut* 4:6).

וְתִיבְּעֵי לֵיהּ נְזִירוּת מוּעֶטֶת! חֲדָא מִגּוֹ חֲדָא קָא מִיבַּעְיָא לֵיהּ;

The Gemara asks: **And let him raise** this **dilemma** with regard to **a short** term of **naziriteship,** when fewer than thirty days would remain if he suspended the first term of naziriteship in order to observe the other. The Gemara answers: **He raises one dilemma as a result of the other.** In other words, Rava's question was an outgrowth of a different inquiry, which in turn led to his question. The full discussion is as follows:

Perek **II**
Daf **14** Amud **a**

אִם תִּמְצֵי לוֹמַר נְזִירוּת מוּעֶטֶת, כֵּיוָן דַּעֲשָׂרָה יוֹמִין הוּא דְּיָתְרִין – לָא סָלֵיק לֵיהּ הָלֵין עֲשָׂרָה; וַדַּאי נָזִיר מֵאָה יוֹם, כֵּיוָן דְּאִית לֵיהּ תְּמָנִין יוֹמִין לְבַסּוֹף – סָלְקִין לֵיהּ, אוֹ לָא?

If you say that when he accepts naziriteship upon himself after twenty days, and then vows **a short** term of **naziriteship**[H] of thirty days starting now, then **since,** if he pauses from his first term of naziriteship after twenty days, **it is only ten days that are left over** to complete after the second term of naziriteship, **those ten should not be reckoned for him** to complete a full term of naziriteship. Ten days are insufficient for hair growth. Therefore, he must observe a full thirty-day term of naziriteship after the second term of naziriteship, which means he is not a nazirite for the first twenty days. With that assumption in mind, the question arose: **Certainly** if he vows to be **a nazirite** for **one hundred days, since he has** a further **eighty days at the end,** which is sufficient time for his hair to grow, do the first twenty days **count for him** as part of the one hundred days **or not?**

וְאִם תִּמְצֵי לוֹמַר חָיְילִי, אָמַר ״הֲרֵינִי נָזִיר לְאַחַר עֶשְׂרִים יוֹם וּמֵעַכְשָׁיו נָזִיר עוֹלָם״ מַהוּ? מִי חָיְילָא עֲלֵיהּ אוֹ לָא?

This inquiry leads to yet another question: **And if you say** that the first days of naziriteship **take effect,**[N] and his term of naziriteship will be completed in the eighty days after the second term of naziriteship, then if he **said: I am hereby a nazirite after twenty**[H] **days, and from now** I am **a permanent nazirite, what is the** *halakha*? **Does** the permanent naziriteship **take effect for him** during those twenty days **or not?** Since permanent naziriteship is unlimited, he could not have intended to complete its days after the second term of naziriteship, and it is reasonable to assume that he intended for the permanent naziriteship to begin after the second term of naziriteship has been completed.

HALAKHA

A short naziriteship, etc. – נְזִירוּת מוּעֶטֶת וכו׳: If one says: I am hereby a nazirite after twenty days and a nazirite from now, he observes a term of naziriteship of thirty days, shaves, and then observes a second term of thirty days for the naziriteship that was to commence after twenty days. This is because if he counts twenty and stops for the second term of naziriteship, only ten days would remain for the completion of his first term, and there must be at least thirty days between each shaving (Rambam *Sefer Hafla'a, Hilkhot Nezirut* 4:7 and *Kesef Mishne* there).

I am hereby a nazirite after twenty, etc. – הֲרֵינִי נָזִיר לְאַחַר עֶשְׂרִים וכו׳: If one said: I am hereby a nazirite after twenty days, and then said: I am a permanent nazirite from now, the naziriteship of his first vow does not take effect (Rambam *Sefer Hafla'a, Hilkhot Nezirut* 4:8 and *Kesef Mishne* there).

NOTES

And if you say that they take effect – וְאִם תִּמְצֵי לוֹמַר חָיְילִי: At this point the Gemara expands Rava's question: Even if the previous problem is resolved by saying that a term of naziriteship that cannot be completed before the second term of naziriteship starts should nevertheless commence at once, it is possible that this is so only because both terms of naziriteship are of limited duration. Moreover, since they can be completed consecutively, the first one takes immediate effect.

If, however, one of the terms of naziriteship is unlimited, this means that once he begins it the second term of naziriteship can never take effect, and even if it could take effect, he cannot shave at its conclusion (Rabbeinu Peretz). The Rosh explains that when there are two terms of naziriteship that last for a specific period of time, neither of them is viewed as an interruption of the other, whereas a permanent naziriteship represents an entirely different category.

אִם תִּמְצֵי לוֹמַר, הָכָא כֵּיוָן דְּאֶפְשָׁר לְאִיתְשׁוּלֵי – חָיֵילָא, אָמַר "הֲרֵינִי נָזִיר שִׁמְשׁוֹן לְאַחַר עֶשְׂרִים יוֹם וּמֵעַכְשָׁיו נָזִיר סְתָם" מַהוּ? הָכָא לָא אֶפְשָׁר לְאִיתְשׁוּלֵי – מִי חָיְילָא אוֹ לָא? אָמַר "כְּמֹשֶׁה בְּשִׁבְעָה בַּאֲדָר". מַאי?

If you say: Here, with regard to cases of a standard permanent naziriteship after twenty days, since it is possible to request of a halakhic authority to dissolve the vow, which would result in the first term of naziriteship taking full effect, it therefore takes effect during those twenty days, then the following question arises: If one said: I am hereby a nazirite like Samson[NHB] after twenty days, and from now I am hereby a nazirite without specification, what is the *halakha*? Since here it is not possible to request of a halakhic authority to dissolve the vow of naziriteship like Samson, and there is no way of completing the first term of naziriteship, does the first naziriteship take effect or not? The Gemara adds another question: If one said: I am hereby like Moses on the seventh day of Adar,[N] what is the *halakha*? Is this considered an expression of naziriteship in that just as Moses passed away on that date and drank no more wine, so too, the speaker vows to be a nazirite? Alternatively, perhaps this phrase does not indicate the acceptance of naziriteship.

פְּשׁוֹט מִינַּיְיהוּ קַדְמַיְיתָא: "הֲרֵינִי נָזִיר לְאַחַר עֶשְׂרִים יוֹם וּמֵעַכְשָׁיו מֵאָה יוֹם" – מוֹנֶה עֶשְׂרִים, וְאַחַר כָּךְ מוֹנֶה שְׁלֹשִׁים, וְאַחַר כָּךְ מוֹנֶה שְׁמוֹנִים, כְּדֵי לְהַשְׁלִים נְזִירוּת רִאשׁוֹנָה.

The Gemara comments: At least resolve the first of these questions, the one raised at the beginning of the discussion, as it is stated explicitly in the *Tosefta* (2:5): If one says: I am hereby a nazirite after twenty days, and I am hereby a nazirite from now for one hundred days, he counts twenty days of his term of naziriteship immediately, after which he counts thirty days for the subsequent term of naziriteship, and afterward he counts eighty days in order to complete his first term of naziriteship.

נִטְמָא בִּימֵי בְּנוֹ, רַבִּי יוֹחָנָן אָמַר: סוֹתֵר, רֵישׁ לָקִישׁ אָמַר: אֵינוֹ סוֹתֵר.

§ The Gemara returns to its discussion of the statement of the mishna with regard to one who vowed to be a nazirite upon the birth of a son in addition to a standard term of naziriteship. The mishna ruled that he begins his term of naziriteship, and if he has a son during that term, he pauses from that term of naziriteship and starts the term for his son, after which he completes the first term. The Torah states that a nazirite who becomes impure while observing his term of naziriteship must start counting afresh, which leads to the following question: What happens if he became impure during the days of his term of naziriteship for his son?[H] Rabbi Yoḥanan says: This negates all of it, even the days he has counted for his own term of naziriteship, and he must observe two full terms of naziriteship. Reish Lakish says: This does not negate the days he observed for his own term of naziriteship, only those of the term of naziriteship for his son.

רַבִּי יוֹחָנָן אָמַר: סוֹתֵר, חֲדָא נְזִירוּת אֲרִיכְתָּא הִיא. רֵישׁ לָקִישׁ אָמַר: אֵינוֹ סוֹתֵר, נְזִירוּת דִּידֵיהּ לְחוּד, וְדִבְרֵיהּ לְחוּד.

The Gemara clarifies the two approaches: Rabbi Yoḥanan says it negates all of it, since he holds that it is one long term of naziriteship.[N] Reish Lakish says it does not negate the days he observed for his own term of naziriteship because his term of naziriteship is a discrete naziriteship, and that for his son is a discrete naziriteship.

HALAKHA

I am hereby a nazirite like Samson, etc. – הֲרֵינִי נָזִיר שִׁמְשׁוֹן וכו׳: If one said: I am hereby a nazirite like Samson after twenty days, and subsequently said: I am hereby a nazirite from now, he does not shave at the completion of the term of naziriteship observed due to his second vow, as he is then a nazirite like Samson (Rambam *Sefer Hafla'a*, *Hilkhot Nezirut* 4:9 and see *Kesef Mishne* there).

He became impure during the days of his son – נִטְמָא בִּימֵי בְּנוֹ: If one vowed to be a nazirite upon the birth of his son, and then took a vow of a standard term of naziriteship beginning immediately, he starts the latter term of naziriteship at once. If he has a son before completing his term, he observes the term of naziriteship for his son and afterward completes his term of naziriteship. These two terms of naziriteship are considered a single term, and if he became impure during the term of naziriteship for his son all of the days are negated. This is because the *halakha* is generally ruled in accordance with Rabbi Yoḥanan's opinion in opposition to Reish Lakish. If one became impure during the final days of his own term of naziriteship, after the term of naziriteship for his son was completed, he forfeits only the latter days. The Ra'avad maintains that he also forfeits the first days of his own term of naziriteship (Rambam *Sefer Hafla'a*, *Hilkhot Nezirut* 4:3).

BACKGROUND

A nazirite like Samson – נְזִיר שִׁמְשׁוֹן: According to some authorities, one who takes a vow to be a nazirite like Samson is not a nazirite at all, since Samson himself did not take a vow of naziriteship (see Judges, chapter 13); however, others set norms for a nazirite like Samson. They permit him to become ritually impure by coming in contact with dead bodies, thereby freeing him from the obligation to bring the special nazirite offerings if he becomes ritually impure, but they prohibit him from cutting his hair or drinking wine. Such a nazirite vow is permanent, and some hold that it cannot be dissolved.

NOTES

I am hereby a nazirite like Samson, etc. – הֲרֵינִי נְזִיר שִׁמְשׁוֹן וכו׳: The Sages had a tradition that one cannot request to have a naziriteship of this type dissolved (Rabbeinu Peretz). The Commentary on *Nazir* explains that this is because Samson himself never vowed to be a nazirite but rather had it imposed upon him by an angel; therefore, he could not request its dissolution. Consequently, one who vows to be a nazirite like Samson has no option of dissolution.

Like Moses on the seventh day of Adar, etc. – כְּמֹשֶׁה בְּשִׁבְעָה בַּאֲדָר וכו׳: The *Keren Ora* is puzzled by the placement of this question, which appears unrelated to the previous questions. Rabbeinu Peretz explains simply that this question is in fact unconnected to the other ones, and is mentioned here only as one of a series of unresolved questions.

The Meiri claims that this problem is related to the case of a naziriteship like Samson. In both situations one is stating a vow of naziriteship by comparing himself to someone who did not drink wine, but not as a result of a vow of naziriteship. Samson's naziriteship did not come about through a vow, and Moses' refraining from wine also was not the result of a vow. When one links his naziriteship to the behavior of a person who refrains from drinking wine due to illness or a similar reason, the vow does not take effect. The question in the Gemara is whether that *halakha* applies to the comparison to Moses, or whether the case of one who compares himself to Moses has the same *halakha* as that of a naziriteship like Samson.

With regard to what the uncertainty is when he says: The seventh of Adar, most commentaries (*Tosafot*; Rosh; Rabbeinu Todros; Rabbeinu Azriel, citing Rabbeinu Tam) explain that it is uncertain whether or not he had naziriteship in mind. On the one hand, since Moses died on the seventh of Adar, it is possible that many Jews decided to be nazirites as an expression of mourning, since, like a mourner, a nazirite may not drink wine or shave. On the other hand, the one in question might have intended to celebrate that day in honor of the birth of Moses, which occurred on the same date, and did not intend to accept upon himself naziriteship or any other prohibition. The Commentary on *Nazir* explains that just as Moses himself did not drink wine from the day of his death onward, this person vows that wine is forbidden to him as well. The Meiri suggests that Moses did not drink wine on the day of his death, as he was presumably not focused on his physical needs on that day.

It is one long term of naziriteship – חֲדָא נְזִירוּת אֲרִיכְתָּא הִיא: The early commentaries explain that this naziriteship is considered one long term, even though it contains both his own term of naziriteship as well as the one for his son, because he does not shave until the conclusion of the entire period. *Tosafot* claim that Rabbi Yoḥanan said it is a long term of naziriteship and one forfeits the entire period only if he became impure during the days of the naziriteship for his son, in which case it also negates the first period he had observed for his own term of naziriteship. However, if he became impure during the period in which he completes his term of naziriteship, after the completion of the term of naziriteship for his son, he does not forfeit the days of the term of naziriteship for his son but only the first days he had counted for his own term of naziriteship. In contrast, the Rambam rules that if one became impure during those last days, not only does it not negate the term of naziriteship for his son, but even the earlier days he observed for his own term of naziriteship remain valid. The *Keren Ora* writes that the Rambam here is consistent with his approach that one must shave after concluding the term of naziriteship for his son, which means the two parts of his own term of naziriteship are linked only by the numbering of days. They are not considered a single unit with regard to negation.

נִטְמָא בִּימֵי צָרַעְתּוֹ, רַבִּי יוֹחָנָן אָמַר: סוֹתֵר, רֵישׁ לָקִישׁ אָמַר: אֵינוֹ סוֹתֵר.

These two *amora'im* have a similar dispute in the case of one who contracted leprosy during his naziriteship and **became impure** by coming into contact with corpse **during the days of his leprosy.**[BH] Although the days of his leprosy do not negate the previous days of his naziriteship, they are not counted as part of his naziriteship either. **Rabbi Yoḥanan says:** Contraction of impurity from a corpse **negates** the days of naziriteship observed before his leprosy, which means he must start counting afresh once he is purified of leprosy. **Reish Lakish says: It does not negate** the days he has observed, and he need observe only the remaining days of his naziriteship after his purification.

רַבִּי יוֹחָנָן אָמַר: סוֹתֵר, דְּהָא בִּנְזִירוּת קָאֵי. רֵישׁ לָקִישׁ אָמַר: אֵינוֹ סוֹתֵר, צָרַעַת לְחוּד וּנְזִירוּת לְחוּד.

The Gemara clarifies their respective approaches. **Rabbi Yoḥanan says** the impurity from a corpse **negates** the days he already observed, **since he remains in** a period of **naziriteship** even when he is a leper, as his leprosy does not negate his naziriteship. **Reish Lakish says it does not negate** the days he observed, since he maintains that **leprosy is discrete and naziriteship is discrete.** One's time as a leper is not considered part of his naziriteship.

וּצְרִיכָא, דְּאִי אִיתְּמַר בְּהַךְ קַמַּיְיתָא – בְּהַהִיא אֲמַר רַבִּי יוֹחָנָן סוֹתֵר, שֵׁם נְזִירוּת אַחַת הִיא, אֲבָל בְּהָא – אֵימָא מוֹדֶה לֵיהּ לְרֵישׁ לָקִישׁ, דְּנָזִיר לְחוּד וְצָרַעַת לְחוּד.

The Gemara comments: **And** it is **necessary** to teach this dispute in both cases. **As, if it were stated in this first one,** with regard to one who became impure during his term of naziriteship for the birth of his son, one might say that it is specifically **in that** case that **Rabbi Yoḥanan said it** also **negates** the days of his standard naziriteship because **there is one label of naziriteship** that applies to both vows, **but in this** case, where the leper became impure from a corpse, one might **say he concedes to Reish Lakish** that it does not negate the days of his naziriteship that he has counted, **since a nazirite is discrete and leprosy is discrete.**

וְאִי אִיתְּמַר בְּהָא – בְּהָא קָאָמַר רֵישׁ לָקִישׁ, אֲבָל בְּהַךְ – אֵימָא מוֹדֶה לֵיהּ לְרַבִּי יוֹחָנָן, צְרִיכָא.

And conversely, **if it were stated** only **in this** case, that of the leper who contracted impurity from a corpse, one might say that it is only **in this** case that **Reish Lakish said** it does not negate his days of naziriteship, **but in that** case, where one became impure while observing the term of naziriteship for his son, one might **say he concedes to Rabbi Yoḥanan** that it negates the entire period, since they are all days of naziriteship. Therefore, it is **necessary** for the dispute to be taught in both cases.

נִטְמָא בְּיוֹם גִּידּוּל שֵׂעָר, רַב אֲמַר: אֵינוֹ סוֹתֵר; אֲפִילּוּ לְרַבִּי יוֹחָנָן דְּאָמַר סוֹתֵר – הָנֵי מִילֵּי הֵיכָא דְּקָאֵי בִּנְזִירוּת, גִּידּוּל שֵׂעָר – מִישְׁלָם נְזִירוּת הוּא.

In connection with the dispute between Rabbi Yoḥanan and Reish Lakish, the Gemara discusses the case of a nazirite **who became impure on the day of** his **hair growth.**[NH] The case is that of one who contracted leprosy during his naziriteship and then was purified from his condition and shaved, as required of him. At this point he must wait another thirty days so that his hair can grow enough for him to shave it for the end of his naziriteship. If he became impure during this additional period, **Rav said: It does not negate** the days he previously counted for his naziriteship. The Gemara explains: **Even according to Rabbi Yoḥanan, who says** that if one became impure during the days of the term of naziriteship for his son it **negates** the entire period, **this statement** applies only **where he** still **remains in** a period of **naziriteship,** but the time of **hair growth is an addition to** his period of **naziriteship** and is not considered part of the term itself.

BACKGROUND

Leprosy [*tzara'at*] **– צָרַעַת:** Traditionally rendered as leprosy, the term *tzara'at* used is the Torah is not necessarily the equivalent of the disease known by that name. The Torah term refers to symptoms that cause severe ritual impurity. The *halakhot* governing these symptoms are articulated at length in Leviticus, chapters 13–15, and in the Mishna in tractate *Nega'im*. Leprosy can be contracted on skin, hair, articles of clothing, and houses. When a symptom appears, it is examined by a priest, and only a priest is authorized to determine whether to quarantine the affected person for a certain period or to declare immediately that the symptom is or is not leprosy. Leprosy is one of the primary sources of ritual impurity, and it is particularly severe in that it imparts ritual impurity to items found in the same enclosure with it, like the impurity imparted by corpses. One afflicted with leprosy in the wilderness was sent out of the Israelite camp, and once the Jewish people entered Eretz Yisrael, out of his town or city. He must live in solitude until his affliction is cured. A cured leper undergoes certain rites outside the city and a purification ceremony in the Temple itself. He is obligated to bring specific offerings as part of his purification.

NOTES

On the day of hair growth – בְּיוֹם גִּידּוּל שֵׂעָר: There are different opinions with regard to this case. Most early commentaries explain that the Gemara is referring to a person who shaved his hair during his naziriteship either against his will or because he contracted leprosy. Although the shaving does not cause him to forfeit his previous days of naziriteship, he is nevertheless required to observe a period of thirty days so that his hair can grow enough for shaving.

Rav and Shmuel have a dispute with regard to the *halakha* of one who became impure during this additional period of hair growth. Rav maintains that Rabbi Yoḥanan and Reish Lakish would both agree that these days are not considered part of his naziriteship, since he has already counted the requisite number of days. Conversely, Shmuel argues that since these days serve to complete his naziriteship they are viewed as an integral part of it (*Tosafot*; Rosh; Rabbeinu Peretz; Rabbeinu Todros). The Commentary on *Nazir* offers an alternative explanation which suggests a similar approach. It states that the Gemara is referring to a nazirite who became impure and, after becoming pure again, began counting a new full term of naziriteship as required. He then became impure during the period added to his naziriteship due to the first impurity. In this case, Rav and Shmuel disagree over whether these days can be viewed as merely an addition to the previous naziriteship, or whether they are considered part of the naziriteship itself since the previous days were negated.

In contrast to this, some commentaries maintain that the phrase: The day of his hair growth, should be understood literally as referring to a particular day. Therefore, the Commentary on *Nazir*'s initial interpretation explains that the case is of one who vowed to be a nazirite for one hundred days, and after seventy days passed he contracted leprosy, was cured, and resumed his naziriteship. He shaved on the one hundredth day, and on the very day that he completed his term became a leper again. According to this approach, everyone agrees that he negates the last thirty days, and the dispute concerns the status of the first seventy.

In *Sefer HaYashar*, Rabbeinu Tam writes that Rav agrees with the opinion that one who became impure on the day of the completion of his term of naziriteship has to repeat only thirty days, and the words: It does not negate, mean it does not negate it all. The Meiri states that if one became impure on the day of his offerings, which occurs on the day after the completion of his naziriteship, he forfeits at least thirty days. It is the day after this that is called: The day of hair growth, and since this day is not part of his naziriteship even by rabbinic decree, Rav maintains that it does not negate his term if he became impure on that day.

HALAKHA

Became impure during the days of his leprosy – נִטְמָא בִּימֵי צָרַעְתּוֹ: A nazirite with leprosy who later contracts impurity from a corpse forfeits all his previous days of naziriteship because he is still considered a nazirite, despite the impurity of the leprosy (Rambam *Sefer Hafla'a*, *Hilkhot Nezirut* 7:10).

Became impure on the day of hair growth – נִטְמָא בְּיוֹם גִּידּוּל שֵׂעָר: If a nazirite completes his term of naziriteship and on the following day, when he may grow his hair, he becomes impure, he does not forfeit any part of his naziriteship even if he has yet to shave, since his period of naziriteship is over. The *halakha* is in accordance with Rav in opposition to Shmuel in matters of ritual law (Rambam *Sefer Hafla'a*, *Hilkhot Nezirut* 6:5 and *Kesef Mishne* there).

וּשְׁמוּאֵל אֲמַר: סוֹתֵר; אֲפִילּוּ לְרֵישׁ לָקִישׁ דְּאָמַר אֵין סוֹתֵר – הָתָם שְׁתֵּי נְזִירוּת, הָכָא חֲדָא נְזִירוּתָא.

And Shmuel said: It **negates** the earlier days. The Gemara explains: **Even according to Reish Lakish, who says** that becoming impure during the naziriteship for his son **does not negate** the days of his naziriteship, **there** it is referring to a case of **two** distinct terms of **naziriteship,** a standard one for himself and another for his son. But **here** it is **one naziriteship,** since the days he observes for the growth of his hair complete his naziriteship.

אָמַר רַב חִסְדָּא: הַכֹּל מוֹדִים שֶׁאִם קָדַשׁ שֵׂעָר בַּדָּם – אֵין לוֹ תַּקָּנָה.

§ **Rav Ḥisda said: All concede that if the hair was consecrated** during the sprinkling **of the blood, he has no** means of **remedy.** That is, if the nazirite had completed his term and brought his offerings, and the blood of the offerings was sprinkled, and he then became impure before shaving, he has no way to shave or to render wine permitted to himself. It has not been permitted through the offerings he brought because he has become impure, and he cannot bring other offerings for this purpose since one may not bring two sets of offerings for the same term of naziriteship.

אַלִּיבָּא דְּמַאן? אִי אַלִּיבָּא דְּרַבִּי אֱלִיעֶזֶר, כֵּיוָן דְּאָמַר תִּגְלַחַת מְעַכֶּבֶת – תּוֹךְ מְלֹאת הִיא, וְלִסְתּוֹר! אֶלָּא אַלִּיבָּא דְּרַבָּנַן – הָאָמְרִי תִּגְלַחַת לֹא מְעַכֶּבֶת! לְעוֹלָם אַלִּיבָּא דְּרַבָּנַן, וּמַאי "אֵין לוֹ תַּקָּנָה" – אֵין לוֹ תַּקָּנָה לְמִצְוַת גִּילּוּחַ.

The Gemara asks: **In accordance with whose** opinion did Rav Ḥisda state this *halakha*? **If** one says that it is **in accordance with** the opinion **of Rabbi Eliezer,** this cannot be, **since** Rabbi Eliezer **said** that **shaving is indispensable** to the completion of naziriteship. The impurity **is** therefore contracted **within the full term** of his naziriteship, in which case it would not make sense that he has no remedy; **but let** it instead **negate** his days of naziriteship, and he will observe them again, after which he will shave. **Rather,** perhaps Rav Ḥisda spoke **in accordance with** the opinion **of the Rabbis; didn't they say** that **shaving is not indispensable**[H] to the completion of naziriteship, which means his impurity occurred when he was no longer a nazirite? The Gemara answers: **Actually,** Rav Ḥisda ruled **in accordance with** the opinion **of the Rabbis, and what** is the meaning of: **He has no** means of **remedy?** It means: **He has no** means of **remedy for the mitzva of shaving,** i.e., he cannot fulfill the mitzva of shaving in purity as required.

אָמַר רַבִּי יוֹסֵי בְּרַבִּי חֲנִינָא: נָזִיר שֶׁכָּלוּ לוֹ יָמָיו – לוֹקֶה עַל הַטּוּמְאָה, וְאֵינוֹ לוֹקֶה עַל הַתִּגְלַחַת וְלֹא עַל הַיַּיִן. מַאי שְׁנָא טוּמְאָה דְּלָקֵי – דְּאָמַר קְרָא "כָּל יְמֵי הַזִּירוֹ לַה'" לְרַבּוֹת יָמִים שֶׁלְּאַחַר מְלֹאת כְּיָמִים שֶׁלִּפְנֵי מְלֹאת.

§ **Rabbi Yosei, son of Rabbi Ḥanina, said: A nazirite whose days** of naziriteship **are completed** but who has yet to bring his offerings **is flogged for the** contracting of **impurity**[N] if he becomes impure from a corpse, like any nazirite who becomes impure, **but he is not flogged for the** act of **shaving, nor for the** drinking of **wine.** The Gemara asks: **What is different** with regard to **impurity that he is flogged** for it? It is **as the verse states: "All the days that he has consecrated himself unto the Lord** he shall not come near to a dead body" (Numbers 6:6). The additional word "all" comes **to include** the **days after the completion** of his naziriteship and teaches that they are **like the days before** its **completion** with regard to the prohibition against contracting impurity from the dead. Therefore, he is liable to receive lashes.

אִי הָכִי אַתִּגְלַחַת נַמִי לִיחַיֵּיב, דְּהָא אָמַר רַחֲמָנָא "כָּל יְמֵי נֶדֶר נִזְרוֹ תַּעַר לֹא יַעֲבֹר עַל רֹאשׁוֹ" – לַעֲשׂוֹת יָמִים שֶׁלְּאַחַר מְלֹאת כְּיָמִים שֶׁלִּפְנֵי מְלֹאת! וְתוּ: "כָּל יְמֵי נִזְרוֹ מִכֹּל אֲשֶׁר יֵעָשֶׂה מִגֶּפֶן הַיַּיִן" – לַעֲשׂוֹת יָמִים שֶׁלְּאַחַר מְלֹאת כְּיָמִים שֶׁלִּפְנֵי מְלֹאת!

The Gemara asks: **If so, let him also be liable** to receive lashes **for shaving, since the Merciful One states** in the Torah: **"All the days of his vow of naziriteship there shall no razor come upon his head"** (Numbers 6:5). Here too, the word "all" should **render** the **days after** the **completion** of his naziriteship **like the days before** its **completion. And furthermore,** with regard to wine as well, the verse states: **"All the days of his naziriteship, from anything that is made of the grapevine,** from the pressed grapes even to the grapestone, he shall not eat" (Numbers 6:4). Once again, the word "all" should **render** the **days after** the **completion** of his naziriteship **like the days before** its **completion** with regard to drinking wine. What is the reason for the difference in *halakha* between contracting impurity on the one hand, and shaving and drinking wine on the other?

HALAKHA

Shaving is not indispensable – תִּגְלַחַת לֹא מְעַכֶּבֶת: If a nazirite has completed his days of naziriteship and brought his offerings, the fact that he has not yet shaved does not preclude the conclusion of his naziriteship. Rather, he may drink wine and contract impurity from a corpse after nightfall, in accordance with the opinion of the Rabbis (Rambam *Sefer Hafla'a, Hilkhot Nezirut* 8:5).

NOTES

He is flogged for the contracting of impurity – לוֹקֶה עַל הַטּוּמְאָה: Even Rabbi Yosei, son of Rabbi Ḥanina, agrees that one does not forfeit his period of naziriteship, since he has already counted the requisite number of days (*Tosafot*).

שָׁאנֵי הָכָא, דְּאָמַר רַחֲמָנָא ״וְטִמֵּא רֹאשׁ נִזְרוֹ״ – מִי שֶׁנְּזִרוֹ תָּלוּי לוֹ בְּרֹאשׁוֹ. מֵיתִיבִי: נָזִיר שֶׁכָּלוּ לוֹ יָמָיו – אָסוּר לְגַלֵּחַ וְלִשְׁתּוֹת יַיִן וְלִטַּמֵּא לְמֵתִים, וְאִם גִּילַּח וְשָׁתָה יַיִן וְנִטְמָא לְמֵתִים – הֲרֵי זֶה סוֹפֵג אֶת הָאַרְבָּעִים. תְּיוּבְתָּא.

The Gemara answers: **Here,** with regard to impurity, **it is different, as the Merciful One states** in the Torah: **"And he defile his consecrated head"** (Numbers 6:9), which indicates that even **one whose naziriteship is** dependent only **upon his head,** i.e., one who has completed his naziriteship other than shaving, is liable to receive lashes if he contracts impurity. The Gemara **raises an objection** to the statement of Rabbi Yosei, son of Rabbi Ḥanina, from a *baraita*: **A nazirite whose days are completed**[H] **is forbidden to shave, and** is forbidden **to drink wine, and** is forbidden **to contract impurity from corpses. And if he did shave, or drink wine, or contract impurity from corpses, he incurs the forty** lashes administered to one who violates a Torah prohibition. This *baraita* clearly states that he is flogged for any of the three prohibitions, which is a **conclusive refutation** of the statement of Rabbi Yosei, son of Rabbi Ḥanina.

מתני׳ ״הֲרֵינִי נָזִיר לִכְשֶׁיְּהֵא לִי בֵּן, וְנָזִיר מֵאָה יוֹם״. נוֹלַד לוֹ בֵּן, עַד שִׁבְעִים – לֹא הִפְסִיד כְּלוּם, לְאַחַר שִׁבְעִים – סוֹתֵר שִׁבְעִים, שֶׁאֵין תִּגְלַחַת פָּחוֹת מִשְּׁלֹשִׁים יוֹם.

MISHNA In the case of one who said: **I am hereby a nazirite when I will have a son,**[H] **and** he added: I am hereby **a nazirite** from now for **one hundred days,** and he then began observing the one hundred days of his naziriteship, if **a son is born to him up to seventy** days from the start of his naziriteship **he has not lost anything.**[N] He pauses from the observance of the naziriteship of one hundred days and observes the thirty-day term for his son. He then completes the thirty or more days left of his initial naziriteship. However, if his son is born **after seventy** days, this **negates** the first **seventy**[N] days, and he must observe a full hundred days after he completes the naziriteship for his son. The reason is that here, he is unable to merely complete the remaining days of his initial naziriteship after shaving at the completion of the naziriteship for his son, **since shaving cannot** be performed after a period of **less than thirty days.**

HALAKHA

A nazirite whose days are completed – נָזִיר שֶׁכָּלוּ לוֹ יָמָיו: If a nazirite has completed his term of naziriteship but has yet to bring his offerings, he remains bound by all the prohibitions of naziriteship and is liable to receive lashes if he transgresses any of them (Rambam *Sefer Hafla'a, Hilkhot Nezirut* 4:12).

I am hereby a nazirite when I will have a son, etc. – הֲרֵינִי נָזִיר לִכְשֶׁיְּהֵא לִי בֵּן וכו׳: If one vowed to be a nazirite when he has a son, and then stated: I am hereby a nazirite from now for one hundred days, if he has thirty or more days remaining of his naziriteship when his son is born, e.g., if the son is born on the sixtieth day of his naziriteship, he counts the term of naziriteship for his son and shaves, then completes the remaining forty days of his own term of naziriteship and shaves again. If fewer than thirty days of his term of naziriteship remain, e.g., if the son was born on the eightieth day of his naziriteship, he observes the term of naziriteship for his son, shaves, and proceeds to observe a further thirty-day term. He is a nazirite for an extra ten days so that he will be able to shave a second time (Rambam *Sefer Hafla'a, Hilkhot Nezirut* 4:4–5).

NOTES

He has not lost anything – לֹא הִפְסִיד כְּלוּם: There are two basic explanations for this clause. One approach is that if a son is born before he has observed seventy days of his own term of naziriteship, he pauses from his observance of that term of naziriteship, observes the term for his son, shaves, and then completes the remaining days of his long naziriteship (Commentary on *Nazir*; Rid; Rabbi Avraham min HaHar). An alternative opinion states that if a son is born before seventy days have passed, he need not observe a separate term for his son, since the days of naziriteship for his son are incorporated within his own term of naziriteship, as the same days may count toward both terms of naziriteship. Upon the completion of one hundred days he shaves and brings the offerings for both vows of naziriteship (*Tosafot* 13b; Rosh; Rabbeinu Peretz). The Meiri cites both approaches.

After seventy, it negates seventy, etc. – לְאַחַר שִׁבְעִים סוֹתֵר שִׁבְעִים וכו׳: The different explanations given by the commentaries for the previous stage of the Gemara continue here as well. According to the Commentary on *Nazir*, this should be understood as follows: Since the son was born with fewer than thirty days remaining to the father's vow, the father first observes the thirty-day naziriteship for his son because that vow was stated first; he then shaves and counts another full term of one hundred days for his second vow. This explanation fits well with the text of the mishna and Gemara.

Tosafot explain differently: If the son was born after seventy days, the father pauses from the observance of his own term of naziriteship and observes the naziriteship for his son, after which he completes the remaining days of his naziriteship. However, the meaning of the phrase: It negates seventy, is unclear according to this approach, since nothing is negated, and certainly not seventy days. In fact, those commentaries have a variant text that reads only: Negates, and explain that it negates the upcoming days from his term of naziriteship (Rabbeinu Peretz; Rosh, cited in *Shita Mekubbetzet*). Yet the phrase: Since shaving cannot be performed, appears out of place here because according to this approach one shaves only at the very end, so there is not a period of less than thirty days for hair growth.

There is another interpretation that claims that if one has a son after seventy days he observes the naziriteship for his son, shaves, and brings his offerings, and afterward he observes a further thirty-day period to be able to shave his hair for his own term of naziriteship (Rambam; see *Birkat Rosh* and *Oraḥ Mishor*, who explains the Jerusalem Talmud similarly; see the note interpolated in *Tosafot* on 13b). According to this interpretation, the statement: Negates seventy, does not mean the loss of all seventy days; rather, one forfeits all the days he counted beyond the first seventy. This is in accordance with the Rambam's Commentary on the Mishna, Kapaḥ edition, which reads: Negates up to seventy. This is because he must eventually repeat all the days apart from the first seventy so that a full thirty days follow his shaving for the naziriteship for his son. The statement: Since shaving cannot be performed, is understood according to this explanation.

גמ׳ אָמַר רַב: יוֹם שִׁבְעִים עוֹלֶה לְכָאן וּלְכָאן. תְּנַן: נוֹלַד לוֹ עַד שִׁבְעִים לֹא הִפְסִיד כְּלוּם. וְאִי סָלְקָא דַּעְתָּךְ עוֹלֶה לְכָאן וּלְכָאן – אִיתְגּוּרֵי מִיתְגַּר! אֶלָּא, בְּדִין הוּא דְּלָא לִיתְנֵי "עַד שִׁבְעִים". וּמִשּׁוּם דְּקָתָנֵי סֵיפָא "אַחַר שִׁבְעִים סוֹתֵר שִׁבְעִים". קָתָנֵי רֵישָׁא שִׁבְעִים.

GEMARA Rav said: The seventieth day[H] itself counts for here and for there, as the last of the seventy days of his term of naziriteship as well as the first day of the naziriteship for his son. The Gemara questions Rav's statement. We learned in the mishna: If a son is born to him up to seventy, he has not lost anything. This seems to include the seventieth day as well. And if it enters your mind that it counts for here and for there, not only has he not lost anything, but he even gains a day, so why would the mishna state: He has not lost anything? The Gemara answers: Rather, by right the mishna should not have taught: Up to seventy he has not lost anything, since if the son is born on the seventieth day he actually gains, as stated above, but due to the fact that it is taught in the last clause of the mishna: After seventy it negates seventy, in which case he does lose, the *tanna* therefore teaches the first clause with the contrasting expression: Up to seventy he has not lost anything.

תָּא שְׁמַע מִסֵּיפָא: נוֹלַד אַחַר שִׁבְעִים – סוֹתֵר שִׁבְעִים. מַאי "אַחַר" – אַחַר אַחַר.

The Gemara asks further: Come and hear a statement that contradicts Rav's opinion from the last clause of the mishna: If the son is born after seventy days, it negates the first seventy days. If, as Rav stated, one day can count for both terms, then the final day of the thirty-day term for his son also counts toward his hundred-day term, meaning that there will be thirty days remaining for a full hair growth; in that case, why should he forfeit the first days? The Gemara answers this: What is the meaning of: After? It means after, after. The mishna is referring to the second day after the seventieth, the seventy-second day, so that there do not remain thirty days for his hair to grow.

אֲבָל אַחַר מַמָּשׁ מַאי – הָכִי נַמִי דְּלָא סָתַר? אִי הָכִי, מַאי אִירְיָא דְּתָנֵי "נוֹלַד עַד שִׁבְעִים לֹא הִפְסִיד כְּלוּם"? אֲפִילּוּ אַחַר שִׁבְעִים נַמִי, הָא אָמְרַתְּ לֹא סָתַר! אֶלָּא, שְׁמַע מִינַּהּ: אַחַר מַמָּשׁ. וְכֵן מַתְנִיתִין לְרַב, שְׁמַע מִינַּהּ.

The Gemara asks: But according to this explanation, what would be the *halakha* if a son is born on the day that actually comes after the seventieth, the seventy-first day; so too, would Rav say that it does not negate the previous days, because he has thirty days remaining to grow his hair? If so, why does the *tanna* specifically teach: If he is born up to seventy he has not lost anything? The same would hold true even for a case where he was born on the day after seventy as well, as didn't you say that it does not negate? Rather, one must learn from this that: After, means the actual day after, the seventy-first day, and likewise conclude that the mishna is difficult for Rav. The Gemara concludes: Indeed, learn from this that the *tanna* of the mishna disagrees with Rav.

וְרַב, כְּמַאן אֲמָרָהּ לִשְׁמַעְתֵּיהּ? אִילֵימָא כְּאַבָּא שָׁאוּל, דִּתְנַן: הַקּוֹבֵר אֶת מֵתוֹ שְׁלֹשָׁה יָמִים קוֹדֶם לָרֶגֶל – בָּטְלָה מִמֶּנּוּ גְּזֵירַת שִׁבְעָה,

§ The Gemara asks: And Rav, in accordance with whose opinion did he say his *halakha*? Since the *tanna* of the mishna disagrees with him, which *tanna* does he follow in ruling that one day may be counted for two different observances? If we say that he stated the ruling in accordance with the opinion of Abba Shaul, as we learned in the *Tosefta* (*Mo'ed Katan* 2:9): With regard to one who buries his dead three days before a pilgrimage Festival,[H] the rabbinic decree of seven days of mourning is voided for him, i.e., once the Festival begins, he no longer observes the prohibitions and customs of the first seven days of mourning. Since he has mourned for three days, the Festival voids the remainder of the seven days.

שְׁמֹנָה יָמִים קוֹדֶם לָרֶגֶל – בָּטְלָה מִמֶּנּוּ גְּזֵירַת שְׁלֹשִׁים, וּמוּתָּר לְסַפֵּר עֶרֶב הָרֶגֶל. וְאִם לֹא סִיפֵּר עֶרֶב הָרֶגֶל – אָסוּר לְסַפֵּר אַחַר הָרֶגֶל.

The *baraita* continues: If he buried his dead eight days before a pilgrimage Festival, the rabbinic decree of the restrictions of thirty days[B] of mourning is voided for him as well. Since he already observed one day of this type of mourning he need not complete the entire period, and it is therefore permitted for him to cut his hair on the eve of the pilgrimage Festival in honor of the Festival. But if he did not cut his hair on the eve of the pilgrimage Festival, it is prohibited for him to cut his hair after the pilgrimage Festival,[N] until thirty days of mourning have passed.

NOTES

It is prohibited for him to cut his hair after the pilgrimage Festival – אָסוּר לְסַפֵּר אַחַר הָרֶגֶל: This prohibition remains in effect until thirty days of mourning have passed. The reason is that since he has shown a lack of concern for the honor of the Festival by failing to cut his hair to prepare for the Festival, his thirty days of mourning are not canceled entirely (*Tosafot*).

HALAKHA

The seventieth day – יוֹם שִׁבְעִים: If a son is born to him on the seventieth day of his term of naziriteship, he observes the term of naziriteship for his son, followed by another thirty days for the completion of his standard term of naziriteship. According to the Radbaz, the Rambam holds that the seventieth day does not count for both terms, unlike the ruling of Rav (Rambam *Sefer Hafla'a, Hilkhot Nezirut* 4:3).

Three days before a pilgrimage Festival – שְׁלֹשָׁה יָמִים קוֹדֶם לָרֶגֶל: If one buries his dead within seven days of one of the three pilgrimage Festivals, his seven days of mourning are canceled at the start of the Festival, even if he has mourned for only a single hour before the Festival. Furthermore, he is considered to have already observed seven days of mourning. The Festival itself counts as seven days toward the thirty days of mourning, even though he does not mourn on the Festival itself, and therefore he is required to complete only the remainder of the thirty days after the Festival. However, if he did not observe any mourning at all before the Festival, his mourning is not canceled, and he is considered like one who buried his relative on the Festival itself. In that case the individual must observe the entire period of mourning after the conclusion of the Festival (Rambam *Sefer Shofetim, Hilkhot Evel* 10:3; *Shulḥan Arukh, Oraḥ Ḥayyim* 548:7 and *Yoreh De'a* 399:1).

BACKGROUND

Seven days, thirty days – שִׁבְעָה, שְׁלֹשִׁים: The first seven days after the death of a close relative are days of intense mourning during which the mourner is prohibited from leaving his home, performing work, sitting on a chair of normal height, washing himself for pleasure, wearing leather shoes, or engaging in sexual relations, among other prohibitions. The thirty-day period is one in which eulogies are recited for important people (see Deuteronomy 34:8). During this period, the mourner is not allowed to wear new clothes, cut his hair, partake in festivities, or marry, nor may he repair the garment he tore as a sign of mourning. After thirty days, all mourning rites are concluded except those observed for the passing of a father or a mother. These mourning rites are not observed publicly on Shabbat, but Shabbat is counted as a day of mourning. If a Festival occurs during the seven days of mourning, the days come to an end when the Festival begins. Similarly, if a Festival occurs during the period between the end of the seven days of mourning and the end of the thirty days, the thirty-day period ends when the Festival begins.

אַבָּא שָׁאוּל אוֹמֵר: אֲפִילּוּ לֹא סִיפֵּר קוֹדֶם הָרֶגֶל – מוּתָּר לְסַפֵּר אַחַר הָרֶגֶל, שֶׁכְּשֵׁם שֶׁמִּצְוַת שְׁלֹשָׁה מְבַטֶּלֶת גְּזֵירַת שִׁבְעָה – כָּךְ מִצְוַת שִׁבְעָה מְבַטֶּלֶת גְּזֵירַת שְׁלֹשִׁים.

Abba Shaul says: Even if he did **not cut his hair before the pilgrimage Festival, it is permitted** for him **to cut his hair after the pilgrimage Festival.** His reasoning is **that just as** the **mitzva of three**[N] voids the rabbinic **decree of seven,** as was taught before; **so** the **mitzva of seven voids**[H] the rabbinic **decree of thirty.** Since he completed the observance of the seven days of mourning before the Festival, he need not observe the thirty days of mourning.

מַאי טַעֲמָא דְּאַבָּא שָׁאוּל – לָאו מִשּׁוּם דְּקָסָבַר שְׁבִיעִי עוֹלֶה לְכָאן וּלְכָאן? דִּלְמָא עַד כָּאן לָא קָאָמַר אַבָּא שָׁאוּל אֶלָּא בַּאֲבֵילוּת שִׁבְעָה דְּרַבָּנַן, אֲבָל בְּנָזִיר דְּאוֹרַיְיתָא – לָא.

The Gemara asks: **What is the rationale of Abba Shaul** for his opinion that if he observed seven days of mourning before the Festival commenced the thirty-day mourning period is voided? **Isn't it because he holds** that the **seventh** day **counts for here and there,** i.e., the seventh day is considered both the end of the seven days and the start of the thirty days of mourning, so he had already begun observing his thirty days of mourning before the start of the Festival? This ruling may be the basis for the ruling of Rav. The Gemara rejects this: This does not support Rav, since **perhaps Abba Shaul was saying** his ruling that the same day counts for both here and there **only with regard to the mourning** of **seven** days, which is **by rabbinic law,**[H] **but with regard to a nazirite,** whose obligation is **by Torah law,** he would **not** say so.

אֶלָּא, רַב דְּאָמַר כְּרַבִּי יוֹסֵי. דְּתַנְיָא, רַבִּי יוֹסֵי אוֹמֵר: שׁוֹמֶרֶת יוֹם כְּנֶגֶד יוֹם שֶׁשָּׁחֲטוּ וְזָרְקוּ עָלֶיהָ בַּשֵּׁנִי שֶׁלָּהּ,

Rather, Rav spoke in accordance with the opinion of **Rabbi Yosei, as it is taught** in a *baraita* that **Rabbi Yosei says: A woman who observes** a clean **day for** each **day**[B] she experiences a discharge is a woman who discharges blood for one or two days at a time when she does not expect her menstrual period. The case under discussion is one where she experienced a discharge for one day and **they slaughtered** a Paschal offering **and sprinkled** the blood **for her on her second** day, after she immersed in a ritual bath. At that point, it is unclear whether she will remain clean of discharges for the remainder of the day, in which case she is retroactively pure from the time she immersed and may eat the Paschal offering at night, or whether she will experience a discharge of blood during the day, in which case her immersion is retroactively invalid and she was impure the entire time.

וְאַחַר כָּךְ רָאֲתָה – הֲרֵי זוֹ אֵינָהּ אוֹכֶלֶת, וּפְטוּרָה מִלַּעֲשׂוֹת פֶּסַח שֵׁנִי.

And after that, she saw blood, thereby retroactively clarifying that at the time the Paschal offering was slaughtered she was unfit to partake of it. The *halakha* is that **she may not eat** from the Paschal lamb due to her ritual impurity, **but she is exempt from observing** the **second** ***Pesaḥ***,[B] which is observed by those who did not sacrifice the Paschal offering on the first Pesaḥ. The reason is that since she was pure when they slaughtered the Paschal offering on her behalf, she has fulfilled the obligation of the offering, despite the fact that she became impure and was unable to eat the offering.

NOTES

That just as the mitzva of three, etc. – שֶׁכְּשֵׁם שֶׁמִּצְוַת שְׁלֹשָׁה וכו׳: Just as the Rabbis agree that one who has mourned for three days before the Festival is exempt from the seven days of mourning and may bathe on the Festival, or before the Festival according to one opinion, so too, the Festival voids his partially observed thirty days of mourning (Rosh). *Tosafot* note that Abba Shaul disagrees with the Rabbis on two counts: First, he claims that the Festival voids the thirty days of mourning entirely, whether or not one cut his hair before the Festival; second, he holds that the seventh day counts for both periods.

HALAKHA

The mitzva of seven voids, etc. – מִצְוַת שִׁבְעָה מְבַטֶּלֶת וכו׳: If one buries his dead seven days before one of the three pilgrimage Festivals, Rosh HaShana or Yom Kippur, and observes mourning before the Festival, the Festival voids his thirty-day period of mourning. Even if his seventh day is the eve of the Festival, part of the day is considered like all of it, and it is therefore permitted for him to cut his hair and shower before the Festival begins. He is certainly allowed to cut his hair and shower after the Festival, in accordance with the opinion of Abba Shaul, since the *halakha* is to follow the lenient opinion with regard to mourning (Rambam *Sefer Shofetim, Hilkhot Evel* 10:5; *Shulḥan Arukh, Oraḥ Ḥayyim* 548:8 and *Yoreh De'a* 399:3).

The mourning of seven days is by rabbinic law – אֲבֵילוּת שִׁבְעָה דְּרַבָּנַן: It is a positive mitzva by Torah law to mourn a relative on the day of death and burial. The rest of the mourning period is mandated by rabbinic law, though this is an ancient practice, dating back to Moses. This applies to the seven relatives listed by the Torah, which are a father, mother, son, daughter, brother, virgin sister, and spouse; with regard to other relatives, the entire mourning ritual is by rabbinic law (*ge'onim*; Rambam). Other early commentaries (*Tosafot*; Rosh) maintain that even the first day of mourning is by rabbinic law. The custom is not to mourn for any relative on the second Festival day of the Diaspora, and the Rema explains that this is in accordance with the opinion that even the first day of mourning is by rabbinic law (Rambam *Sefer Shofetim, Hilkhot Evel* 1:1; *Shulḥan Arukh, Yoreh De'a* 398:1, 399:13).

BACKGROUND

A woman who observes a clean day for each day – שׁוֹמֶרֶת יוֹם כְּנֶגֶד יוֹם: A woman is considered to be a full-fledged *zava* only if she experiences a discharge of uterine blood on three consecutive days at a time when she does not expect her menstrual period. The biblical source is the phrase: "And if a woman have an issue of her blood many days not in the time of her impurity" (Leviticus 15:25). Nevertheless, as soon as she has even one discharge, she becomes ritually impure as a lesser *zava* and may not engage in sexual intercourse. By Torah law, she needs to wait until only one day has passed without any discharge of blood, observing a clean day for each day, in order to become pure. Even if she immerses in a ritual bath before the clean day is complete, if she does not experience a discharge for the rest of the day, she is considered retroactively pure from the time of her immersion. Today it is customary for women to follow all the *halakhot* pertaining to a full-fledged *zava* whenever they have even a slight discharge of uterine blood, and they count seven full clean days without discharge before immersing.

Second *Pesaḥ* – פֶּסַח שֵׁנִי: One who was ritually impure, on a distant journey, or failed to bring the Paschal offering at its proper time on the fourteenth of Nisan may compensate by bringing the offering on the fourteenth of Iyyar. There is a tannaitic dispute as to whether one who was not obligated to bring a Paschal offering on the fourteenth of Nisan need sacrifice a Paschal offering on the fourteenth of Iyyar. All the *halakhot* that apply to the sacrifice of the Paschal offering apply to the second *Pesaḥ*, with one exception: There is no prohibition against eating or possessing leaven on that day. However, leaven may not be eaten together with the offering itself.

מַאי טַעְמָא דְּרַבִּי יוֹסֵי – לָאו מִשּׁוּם דְּקָסָבַר מִקְצָת הַיּוֹם כְּכוּלּוֹ? מִמַּאי? וְדִלְמָא מִשּׁוּם דְּקָסָבַר מִכָּאן וּלְהַבָּא הוּא מְטַמֵּא?

The Gemara clarifies this: **What is the rationale of Rabbi Yosei** for his opinion that she is exempt from observing the second *Pesaḥ*? **Isn't it because he holds** that the legal status of **part of the day is like** that **of an entire** day? Since she was pure for part of the day, it is considered as though she was pure the entire day. The Gemara rejects this: **From where** do you know that this is the rationale? **Perhaps** it is **because** Rabbi Yosei **holds**[N] that **one becomes impure from now and onward.** He holds that the impurity of a *zava* starts only from the moment she had a discharge of blood, but she is ritually pure up to that point, so she was ritually pure when they slaughtered the offering for her.

וּמִי סָבַר רַבִּי יוֹסֵי הָכִי?

The Gemara questions this explanation: **And does Rabbi Yosei hold** in accordance with **this** ruling that she is impure only from that moment onward?

וְהָתַנְיָא, רַבִּי יוֹסֵי אוֹמֵר: זָב בַּעַל שְׁתֵּי רְאִיּוֹת שֶׁשָּׁחֲטוּ וְזָרְקוּ עָלָיו בִּשְׁבִיעִי, וְכֵן שׁוֹמֶרֶת יוֹם כְּנֶגֶד יוֹם שֶׁשָּׁחֲטוּ וְזָרְקוּ עָלֶיהָ, וְאַחַר כָּךְ רָאוּ, אַף עַל פִּי שֶׁמְּטַמְּאִין מִשְׁכָּב וּמוֹשָׁב לְמַפְרֵעַ – פְּטוּרִין מִלַּעֲשׂוֹת פֶּסַח שֵׁנִי.

But isn't it taught in a *baraita* that **Rabbi Yosei says:** With regard to **a man who experiences a gonorrhea-like discharge** [*zav*] **who has had two sightings** of discharge, **for whom they slaughtered** a Paschal offering **and sprinkled** its blood **on the seventh,** and final, day of impurity, **and similarly,** with regard to **a woman who observes** a clean **day for a day, for whom they slaughtered** a Paschal offering **and sprinkled** its blood, and **afterward they saw** their respective discharges, **although they render objects designed for lying and sitting impure retroactively,**[H] **they are exempt from observing the second *Pesaḥ*.**[H] This is proof that Rabbi Yosei holds that their ritual impurity applies retroactively, rather than from the moment of discharge onward. It must be that the reason why they are nevertheless exempt from observing the second *Pesaḥ* is that part of the day is like the entire day, and the part of the day before they became impure, during which the blood of the Paschal offering was sprinkled for them, is considered a whole clean day.

מַאי לְמַפְרֵעַ – מִדְּרַבָּנַן. הָכִי נַמִי מִסְתַּבְּרָא, דְּאִי סָלְקָא דַּעְתָּךְ מִדְּאוֹרַיְיתָא – אַמַּאי פְּטוּרִין מִלַּעֲשׂוֹת פֶּסַח שֵׁנִי?

The Gemara responds to this attempted proof: **What** is the meaning of Rabbi Yosei's statement that the ritual impurity applies **retroactively?** It means that the ritual impurity applies retroactively **by rabbinic law.** However, by Torah law, the *zav* or *zava* is impure only from the time of the new sighting and onward. The Gemara adds: **So too, it is reasonable** that this is Rabbi Yosei's opinion, as, **if it enters your mind** that they become ritually impure retroactively **by Torah law, why are they exempt from observing** the **second *Pesaḥ*** if by Torah law they were impure at the time the offering was slaughtered?

לְעוֹלָם אֵימָא לָךְ טוּמְאָה דְּאוֹרַיְיתָא, תְּהוֹם דְּזִיבָה הִתִּירוּ.

The Gemara responds: This is no proof, since **actually, I** could **say to you**[N] that this retroactive **impurity** is **by Torah law,** and the reason they are exempt from observing the second *Pesaḥ* is that the Sages **permitted** impurity of **the deep of *ziva*.** The *halakha* is that in the case of a Paschal offering, an unknown impurity of the dead, called the impurity of the deep, is permitted. In a case where one brought his offering and later became aware that he had contracted impurity from a corpse, if this source of impurity was unknown to everyone, he is not required to observe the second *Pesaḥ*. The Gemara suggests that Rabbi Yosei may hold that the same *halakha* applies to the impurity of a *zava* as well: Since the owner of the offering was pure when it was brought and could not have known that she would become impure due to discharge later that day, it is similarly considered an impurity of the deep, and she has therefore fulfilled her obligation.

וְאַף רַבִּי אוֹשַׁעְיָא סָבַר לְמַפְרֵעַ מִדְּרַבָּנַן. דְּתַנְיָא, רַבִּי אוֹשַׁעְיָא אָמַר: (אֲבָל) הָרוֹאֶה זָב בִּשְׁבִיעִי שֶׁלּוֹ סוֹתֵר אֶת שֶׁלְּפָנָיו, וְאָמַר לֵיהּ רַבִּי יוֹחָנָן: לֹא נִסְתּוֹר אֶלָּא יוֹמוֹ.

§ The Gemara points out: **And even Rabbi Oshaya holds** that, according to Rabbi Yosei, the fact that a *zav* renders objects designed for sitting or lying impure **retroactively** is only **by rabbinic law** in this circumstance. **As it is taught** in a *baraita* that **Rabbi Oshaya says:** In a case of **one who sees gonorrhea-like discharge on his seventh** clean day,[H] this **negates** the clean days **that preceded it** and starts his seven days anew. **And Rabbi Yoḥanan said to him that it should negate only its own day,** i.e., he should require only one additional clean day.

NOTES

From where…perhaps it is because he holds, etc. – מִמַּאי, וְדִילְמָא מִשּׁוּם דְּקָסָבַר וכו׳: *Tosafot* read the continuation of the discussion as follows: Isn't it because he holds that part of the day is like the entire day, and she is impure only from now onward? They claim that the rule of: From now onward, cannot come into effect unless the principle of: Part of the day is like the entire day, is accepted as well, since only if she has become pure in the first part of the day can one say that the next discharge starts a new phase of ritual impurity. Therefore, in the following stage of the Gemara, when the Gemara attempts to posit that Rabbi Yosei holds that the impurity takes effect retroactively, this is a direct attack on the supposition that he holds that part of a day is like the entire day.

Actually, I could say to you, etc. – לְעוֹלָם אֵימָא לָךְ וכו׳: The conclusion of the discussion according to the version of the text brought here is that since Rabbi Yosei maintains that one renders objects impure retroactively, part of the day is therefore considered like all of it. According to *Tosafot* the opposite holds true: There is no evidence as to Rabbi Yosei's opinion with regard to the issue of part of the day being like the entire day.

HALAKHA

They render objects designed for lying and sitting impure retroactively, etc. – שֶׁמְּטַמְּאִין מִשְׁכָּב וּמוֹשָׁב וכו׳: A *zav* or *zava* who has immersed on their seventh day should not come into contact with pure objects until the evening, because if they experience a discharge it will void their seven clean days and they will retroactively render impure any objects they lie or sit upon, but not earthenware vessels that they move, in accordance with the opinion of Rabbi Yosei (Rambam *Sefer Tahara, Hilkhot Metamei Mishkav UMoshav* 5:9).

They are exempt from observing the second *Pesaḥ* – פְּטוּרִין מִלַּעֲשׂוֹת פֶּסַח שֵׁנִי: If a *zav* who saw two sightings of discharge immersed on his seventh day, the Paschal offering is slaughtered on his behalf and he may partake of it in the evening. If he had another discharge after the sprinkling of the blood, he is exempt from observing the second *Pesaḥ*. Similarly, a woman observing a clean day for a day may immerse on that day, and the Paschal offering is slaughtered on her behalf for her to eat in the evening. If she saw a discharge after its blood was sprinkled, she is exempt from observing the second *Pesaḥ*, in accordance with the opinion of Rabbi Yosei (Rambam *Sefer Korbanot, Hilkhot Korban Pesaḥ* 6:3).

One who sees gonorrhea-like discharge on his seventh clean day – הָרוֹאֶה זָב בִּשְׁבִיעִי שֶׁלּוֹ: If a *zav* counted seven clean days and then experienced a discharge on the seventh day, it negates the entire period, and he must count another seven days. This applies even if the discharge occurred at the end of the seventh day, after his immersion. The mishna in tractate *Zavim* (1:2) rules likewise (Rambam *Sefer Korbanot, Hilkhot Meḥusrei Kappara* 3:1).

מַה נַּפְשָׁךְ; אִי סָתַר – כּוּלְּהוּ סָתַר, אִי לָא סָתַר – לָא נִסְתּוֹר וְלָא יוֹמוֹ! אֶלָּא אֵימָא: לָא נִסְתּוֹר וְלָא יוֹמוֹ.

The Gemara expresses surprise: **Whichever way you** look at Rabbi Yoḥanan's statement, it is difficult. **If** this discharge **negates** clean days just as the case of a *zav* who had a discharge during his seven days, **it should negate all** his clean days, not only the last one. **If it does not negate** clean days, since it is not considered a discharge within his seven days but rather, as the first sighting of a new *ziva*, it should **not negate** any of it, **and not** even **its own day.** What, then, is the logic of Rabbi Yoḥanan's ruling that it negates a single day? **Rather, say** instead that Rabbi Yoḥanan said as follows: It does **not negate** at all, **and not** even **its own day,** since this discharge is considered to be the first of a new series.

Perek **II**
Daf **16** Amud **a**

וַאֲמַר לֵיהּ: רַבִּי יוֹסֵי קָאֵי כְּוָתֵיךְ, דְּאָמַר: מִכָּאן וּלְהַבָּא מְטַמֵּא. וְהָא רַבִּי יוֹסֵי לְמַפְרֵעַ הוּא דְּאָמַר! מַאי לְמַפְרֵעַ – מִדְּרַבָּנַן.

And Rabbi Oshaya **said to** Rabbi Yoḥanan: **Rabbi Yosei holds in accordance with your** opinion, **as he** too **says** that in this case one **becomes impure from now and onward,** and any impurity after the start of the seventh day does not cause him to forfeit the previous clean days. The Gemara analyzes Rabbi Oshaya's statement: **But didn't Rabbi Yosei say** that the impurity is **retroactive,** as stated above? Rather, Rabbi Oshaya must certainly hold as follows: **What** is the meaning of Rabbi Yosei's ruling that he is impure **retroactively?** It means that he is rendered impure only **by rabbinic law,** but not by Torah law.

וְרַבִּי יוֹסֵי, מִכְּדִי סָבַר מִקְצָת הַיּוֹם כְּכוּלּוֹ, זָבָה גְּמוּרָה דְּמַיְיתָא קָרְבָּן הֵיכִי מַשְׁכַּחַתְּ לָהּ? כֵּיוָן דְּחַזְיָא בְּפַלְגֵיהּ דְּיוֹמָא – אִידַּךְ פַּלְגֵיהּ דְּיוֹמָא סָלֵיק לָהּ לְשִׁימּוּר. אִיבָּעֵית אֵימָא: דְּקָא שָׁפְעָה תְּלָתָא תְּלָתָא יוֹמֵי בַּהֲדֵי הֲדָדֵי, וְאִיבָּעֵית אֵימָא: דְּחַזְיָא תְּלָתָא יוֹמֵי סָמוּךְ לִשְׁקִיעַת הַחַמָּה, דְּלָא הֲוַאי שְׁהוּת דְּסָלֵיק לֵיהּ לְמִנְיָינָא.

The Gemara poses a question with regard to Rabbi Yosei's statement: **And as to Rabbi Yosei, now, he holds** that the status of **part of the day is like** that of **an entire day.**[N] **How can you find a full-fledged *zava***[N] **who brings an offering? Since she sees** a discharge **at the midpoint of the day, the other half of the day**[N] **counts for her** as a full day of **observing,** as part of the day is considered to be like all of a day. The Gemara answers: **If you wish, say that** she **continuously discharges** blood for **three days consecutively. And if you wish, say that she saw** a discharge on **three** consecutive **days close to sunset.**[N] In that case she is impure on each occasion at the end of one day and the beginning of the next, so that **there was not** any **time** to become pure on the following day so as **to be included for her counting** of a clean day corresponding to an impure one.

הדרן עלך הריני נזיר

NOTES

And as to Rabbi Yosei, now, he holds that the status of part of the day is like that of an entire day, etc. – וְרַבִּי יוֹסֵי מִכְּדִי סָבַר מִקְצָת הַיּוֹם כְּכוּלּוֹ וכו׳: Although the Gemara had concluded earlier that the reason for Rabbi Yosei's ruling was not because he holds that the legal status of part of the day is like that of an entire day but because she becomes impure only from now onward, that answer is a forced one (Commentary on *Nazir*; Rabbi Avraham min HaHar, citing Rashi). However, according to the opinion of *Tosafot* that the principle that part of a day is like all of a day is consistent with the principle that she becomes impure from here onward, the Gemara's question here is readily understood (see *Tosafot* and Rabbeinu Peretz).

A full-fledged *zava* – זָבָה גְּמוּרָה: A full-fledged *zava* is a woman who has seen blood on three consecutive days, in which case she is required to observe seven clean days and bring an offering upon her purification.

The other half of the day – אִידַּךְ פַּלְגֵיהּ דְּיוֹמָא: There are two explanations for this statement. One interpretation is that even Rabbi Yosei agrees that she is at least considered ritually impure for the rest of the day on which she saw blood. However, since the legal status of part of the day is like that of an entire day, if she were to discharge blood, for example, at noon for two consecutive days, the morning hours of the second day would be considered a clean day in between the days of impurity (Rosh). Other commentaries claim that since the legal status of part of the day is like that of an entire day, there is no difference between the beginning and the end of a day, and the hours until nightfall following her impurity would be viewed as a break between discharges (see Commentary on *Nazir*; *Tosafot*). *Tosafot* state that the different approaches result partly from alternative interpretations of the phrase: The other half of the day.

Close to sunset – סָמוּךְ לִשְׁקִיעַת הַחַמָּה: In other words, she was experiencing a discharge during the entire twilight, beginning just before sunset and continuing into the start of the night. If this occurs at the end of both the first and second days, the night of the third day is also included, and she is therefore impure for three days (*Tosafot*). The commentaries point out that in that case, the hours between the discharges cannot be viewed as a clean day, even if one holds that part of the day is like all of a day, since this principle applies only to the start of the day, or, according to some opinions, the end of a day as well. The middle of a day certainly cannot be considered like all of a day (see Meiri).

Summary of **Perek II**

This chapter discussed the terminology used upon taking a vow of naziriteship, and highlighted how distinctions in the phrasing can render one vow binding and another invalid. If an individual declares his intention to become a nazirite and therefore will refrain from an item that is in fact not forbidden to a nazirite, his statement is treated as a standard vow of prohibition and not as a vow of naziriteship. His use of the phrase: I am hereby a nazirite, is understood to mean only that he is vowing that a particular item is forbidden to him. There are even circumstances in which one may take a vow of naziriteship with regard to wine and it will be interpreted as a standard vow of prohibition, if circumstances indicate that one was merely vowing that a particular glass of wine being offered to him would be forbidden to him.

If one vows to become a nazirite on the condition that he does not accept all of the nazirite prohibitions, his condition is disregarded and he is a full-fledged nazirite. On the other hand, if he uttered a vow of naziriteship but believed that only some of its restrictions were applicable to him, either because of ignorance or due to an assumption that the Sages would grant him a dispensation because of his unique circumstances, the vow is considered to be in error and is entirely void.

If an individual vows to become a nazirite and to bring the offerings of a nazirite, his vow obligates him to observe a term of naziriteship and to pay for the offerings of another nazirite. Should two people state such a vow, each may pay for the other's offerings. If one vows to pay for the offerings of half a nazirite, his obligations are dependent upon the precise wording of his vow. He may be obligated to pay for half the offerings of a nazirite, or he might be obligated to pay for all of the offerings. In connection with this topic, the Gemara examines cases where an individual overhears someone vowing to be a nazirite and adds: And I, or: And it is incumbent upon me. Such a person becomes a nazirite despite the brevity of his statement.

If one vows to become a nazirite when he has a son, only the birth of a son causes his naziriteship to take effect. If he vows to accept naziriteship upon the birth of a child, his vow takes effect regardless of the baby's gender, even if its genitalia make its gender indeterminate. However, the vow does not take effect if the baby is stillborn.

If one utters multiple vows to observe overlapping naziriteship terms, the term about which he vowed first takes precedence, even if he needs to interrupt the term of another vow to observe his first vow. In such a situation the days of the term that was interrupted might count toward the completion of that term or they might not, depending on how many days remain at the time of the interruption. There are similar *halakhot* that address cases in which a nazirite becomes ritually impure in the middle of one of his terms.

In connection with the possibility of impurity negating the observed days of a naziriteship term, the Gemara examines related *halakhot* and concludes that if a nazirite first becomes leprous, and then contracts impurity from the dead while he is a leper, the days of his naziriteship term that he had previously observed are not negated. Similarly, his observance of the days of his term is not negated if he became impure after having finished his term but before having brought his offerings or shaved.

Introduction to **Perek III**

And if any man dies very suddenly beside him, and he defiles his consecrated head, he shall shave his head on the day of his purification, on the seventh day shall he shave it. And on the eighth day he shall bring two turtledoves, or two young pigeons, to the priest, to the door of the tent of meeting. And the priest shall prepare one for a sin-offering, and the other for a burnt-offering, and make atonement for him, for he sinned by the soul; and he shall sanctify his head on that day. And he shall consecrate to the Lord the days of his naziriteship, and he shall bring a lamb in its first year for a guilt-offering; but the first days shall be void because his consecration was ritually impure.

(Numbers 6:9–12)

This chapter addresses the issues that relate to the duration of the term of naziriteship and its precise end point. The main situations that require clarification are those that involve consecutive terms of naziriteship or when an individual's naziriteship is interrupted by his becoming ritually impure from contact with a corpse.

Unless otherwise specified, the length of a term of naziriteship is a full thirty days. However, if the nazirite shaves his hair on the thirtieth day of his term, he has fulfilled his obligation. The reason for this is subject to an amoraic dispute appearing in the first chapter of this tractate. The present chapter tries to determine how the days are counted when one is observing two terms one after the other, in light of the different opinions in the first chapter.

The Torah writes that if a nazirite comes into contact with a corpse, all the days he had observed until that point are negated, and he begins his naziriteship from the beginning after undergoing his purification process. This chapter discusses whether the entire term of naziriteship is negated if the individual becomes ritually impure on the last day of his term, before having shaved. Is he considered to be still within his term? Must he observe an additional term from the start?

Another situation examined in this chapter is one where a person states a vow of naziriteship while he is ritually impure. Does the obligation take effect immediately? When does his counting begin?

This chapter also discusses the *halakha* of one who takes a vow of naziriteship in one of the lands outside of Eretz Yisrael, which the Sages decreed are ritually impure. Finally, the Gemara considers a case where there are conflicting testimonies with regard to how long a naziriteship, or how many terms of naziriteship, one has vowed.

Some of the issues discussed in this chapter have been partially addressed in earlier chapters.

מתני׳ מִי שֶׁאָמַר ״הֲרֵינִי נָזִיר״ – מְגַלֵּחַ יוֹם שְׁלֹשִׁים וְאֶחָד, וְאִם גִּילֵּחַ לְיוֹם שְׁלֹשִׁים – יָצָא. ״הֲרֵינִי נָזִיר שְׁלֹשִׁים יוֹם״. אִם גִּילֵּחַ לְיוֹם שְׁלֹשִׁים – לֹא יָצָא.

MISHNA **One who said: I am hereby a nazirite,**[NH] without specifying how long his term of naziriteship would last, **shaves** his hair **on the thirty-first day** after the start of his naziriteship, as an unspecified term of naziriteship lasts thirty days. **And if he shaved on the thirtieth day, he has fulfilled** his obligation. If he explicitly said: **I am hereby a nazirite** for **thirty days,** then, **if he shaved on the thirtieth day, he has not fulfilled** his obligation. Since the naziriteship would have been for thirty days even without him stating: For thirty days, this addition is understood to indicate that he will observe naziriteship for a full thirty days.

מִי שֶׁנָּזַר שְׁתֵּי נְזִירוֹת – מְגַלֵּחַ אֶת הָרִאשׁוֹנָה יוֹם שְׁלֹשִׁים וְאֶחָד, וְאֶת הַשְּׁנִיָּה יוֹם שִׁשִּׁים וְאֶחָד, וְאִם גִּילֵּחַ אֶת הָרִאשׁוֹנָה יוֹם שְׁלֹשִׁים – מְגַלֵּחַ אֶת הַשְּׁנִיָּה יוֹם שִׁשִּׁים, וְאִם גִּילֵּחַ יוֹם שִׁשִּׁים חָסֵר אֶחָד – יָצָא.

One who accepted two terms of **naziriteship**[H] **shaves** at the close of **the first** naziriteship on the **thirty-first day, and** at the close of **the second** term on the **sixty-first day.** Since his second term of naziriteship begins after shaving on the thirty-first day, the sixty-first day of the first term is the thirty-first day of his second term. **And if he shaved** for **the first** term on the **thirtieth day, he shaves** for **the second** term on the **sixtieth day,** which is the thirty-first day after the start of his second term of naziriteship. **And if he shaved** for the second term on **day sixty less one, he has fulfilled** his obligation, as this is the thirtieth day of his second term.

וְזוֹ עֵדוּת הֵעִיד רַבִּי פַּפְּיָיס עַל מִי שֶׁנָּזַר שְׁתֵּי נְזִירוֹת, שֶׁאִם גִּילֵּחַ אֶת הָרִאשׁוֹנָה יוֹם שְׁלֹשִׁים – מְגַלֵּחַ אֶת הַשְּׁנִיָּה לְיוֹם שִׁשִּׁים, וְאִם גִּילֵּחַ לְיוֹם שִׁשִּׁים חָסֵר אֶחָד – יָצָא, שֶׁיּוֹם שֶׁל שְׁלֹשִׁים עוֹלֶה לוֹ מִן הַמִּנְיָן.

And this testimony was attested to by Rabbi Pappeyas,[P] who heard from his teachers **with regard to one who vowed** to observe **two** terms of **naziriteship, that if he shaved** for **the first** term on the **thirtieth day, he shaves** for **the second** term **on the sixtieth day. And if he shaved** for the second term **on the day sixty less one, he has fulfilled** his obligation, **because the thirtieth day** of the first term of naziriteship **counts** as part **of his tally** of the second term.

מִי שֶׁאָמַר ״הֲרֵינִי נָזִיר״. נִטְמָא יוֹם שְׁלֹשִׁים – סוֹתֵר אֶת הַכֹּל, רַבִּי אֱלִיעֶזֶר אוֹמֵר: אֵינוֹ סוֹתֵר אֶלָּא שִׁבְעָה. ״הֲרֵינִי נָזִיר שְׁלֹשִׁים יוֹם״. נִטְמָא יוֹם שְׁלֹשִׁים – סוֹתֵר אֶת הַכֹּל. ״הֲרֵינִי נָזִיר מֵאָה יוֹם״. נִטְמָא יוֹם מֵאָה – סוֹתֵר אֶת הַכֹּל. רַבִּי אֱלִיעֶזֶר אוֹמֵר: אֵינוֹ סוֹתֵר אֶלָּא שְׁלֹשִׁים. נִטְמָא יוֹם מֵאָה וְאֶחָד – סוֹתֵר שְׁלֹשִׁים יוֹם, רַבִּי אֱלִיעֶזֶר אוֹמֵר: אֵינוֹ סוֹתֵר אֶלָּא שִׁבְעָה.

One who said: I am hereby a nazirite, without further specification, if **he became ritually impure** through contact with a corpse on the **thirtieth day**[NH] of his term of naziriteship, **it negates the entire** tally, and he must start his naziriteship afresh. **Rabbi Eliezer says: It negates only seven**[N] days, which he must observe until his purification, after which he brings his offerings. If he said: **I am hereby a nazirite** for **thirty days,** and **he became impure** on the **thirtieth day,** everyone agrees that **it negates the entire** tally. If he said: **I am hereby a nazirite** for **one hundred days,** if **he became impure** on the **one hundredth day, it negates the entire** tally. **Rabbi Eliezer says: It negates only thirty** days, and he observes the final thirty days again. If **he became impure** on the **one hundred and first day**[H] before bringing his offerings, **it negates** only **thirty days,** but does not negate all of the observed days. **Rabbi Eliezer says: It negates only seven** days.

גמ׳ ״מִי שֶׁאָמַר הֲרֵינִי נָזִיר וְנִטְמָא יוֹם שְׁלֹשִׁים – סוֹתֵר אֶת הַכֹּל, רַבִּי אֱלִיעֶזֶר אוֹמֵר: אֵינוֹ סוֹתֵר אֶלָּא שִׁבְעָה״.

GEMARA The mishna taught: **One who said: I am hereby a nazirite,** and **became ritually impure** on the **thirtieth day, it negates the entire** tally; **Rabbi Eliezer says: It negates only seven.**

PERSONALITIES

Rabbi Pappeyas – רַבִּי פַּפְּיָיס: We know little about Rabbi Pappeyas beyond the fact that he offers firsthand testimony about the activities that took place during the Second Temple period. Almost every time he is quoted in the Mishna, *Tosefta*, and Babylonian Talmud his statements relate to the Temple and the Temple service. There is a Sage with the name Rabbi Pappeyas who is quoted in halakhic midrash as disagreeing with Rabbi Akiva, but it is likely another scholar with the same name, inasmuch as Rabbi Akiva's academy was established several generations after the destruction of the Second Temple.

NOTES

One who said I am hereby a nazirite – מִי שֶׁאָמַר הֲרֵינִי נָזִיר: There is a dispute between bar Padda and Rav Mattana with regard to the source for the *halakha* that an unspecified naziriteship is for thirty days. The Gemara there (5a) cites this mishna and interprets it in accordance with both opinions.

Became ritually impure on the thirtieth day – נִטְמָא יוֹם שְׁלֹשִׁים: According to Rav Mattana's opinion that a term of naziriteship lasts for thirty days, the previous days are voided by Torah law, and he must bring the offerings of ritually impurity. Bar Padda, who maintains that as a matter of Torah law a term of naziriteship consists of only twenty-nine days, explains that the previous days are negated due to a decree of the Sages, and he does not bring the offerings of ritually impurity (*Tosafot*).

It negates only seven – אֵינוֹ סוֹתֵר אֶלָּא שִׁבְעָה: He is not considered a ritually impure nazirite, who is required to bring certain offerings after his seven days of purification and to start his naziriteship afresh. According to Rav Mattana this is because the legal status of part of the day is like that of an entire day, and he had therefore already completed his thirty-day term before becoming impure. Bar Padda explains that Rabbi Eliezer holds that the Sages did not decree that naziriteship should be for thirty days in such a case, but rather left intact the Torah law that he is considered to have completed his term after twenty-nine days.

HALAKHA

One who said I am hereby a nazirite – מִי שֶׁאָמַר הֲרֵינִי נָזִיר: One who said: I am hereby a nazirite, shaves on the thirty-first day, and if he shaved on the thirtieth day he has fulfilled his obligation. However, if he said: I am hereby a nazirite for thirty days, he may shave only on the thirty-first day (Rambam *Sefer Hafla'a*, *Hilkhot Nezirut* 4:1).

One who accepted two terms of naziriteship – מִי שֶׁנָּזַר שְׁתֵּי נְזִירוֹת: One who vowed to undertake two terms of naziriteship shaves for the first term on the thirty-first day, and for the second on the sixty-first day. If he shaved for the first vow on the thirtieth day, he shaves for the second term on the sixtieth day. If, after having shaved on the thirtieth day, he shaved on the fifty-ninth day, he has fulfilled his obligation (Rambam *Sefer Hafla'a*, *Hilkhot Nezirut* 4:2).

Became ritually impure on the thirtieth day – נִטְמָא יוֹם שְׁלֹשִׁים: Even if a nazirite became ritually impure on the final day of his term, his entire tally is negated. He must bring the offerings of impurity and start counting his naziriteship anew, in accordance with the unattributed opinion in the mishna (Rambam *Sefer Hafla'a*, *Hilkhot Nezirut* 6:3).

Became impure on the one hundred and first day, etc. – נִטְמָא יוֹם מֵאָה וְאֶחָד וכו׳: If a nazirite became ritually impure after the final day of his term, the day on which he brings his offerings, only thirty days are negated. How should he proceed? After completing the purification process, he brings the offerings of impurity and shaves. He then observes thirty days of naziriteship in ritual purity. Then, he shaves again and brings the offerings of a regular nazirite. This is in accordance with the unattributed mishna. The Rambam holds that becoming impure on the one hundred and first day voids part of the naziriteship by Torah law, and he is therefore obligated in the offerings of impurity. Conversely, *Tosafot* and the Rosh contend that it is a decree of the Sages, which means he does not bring the offerings of a ritually impure nazirite. The *Likkutei Halakhot* explains that in their opinion, he counts thirty days after his purification and brings the offerings of a regular nazirite (Rambam *Sefer Hafla'a*, *Hilkhot Nezirut* 6:4).

קָסָבַר רַבִּי אֱלִיעֶזֶר: כָּל אַחַר מְלֹאת – שִׁבְעָה סוֹתֵר. ״הֲרֵינִי נָזִיר שְׁלֹשִׁים יוֹם״ וְנִטְמָא יוֹם שְׁלֹשִׁים – סוֹתֵר אֶת הַכֹּל. לָא פָּלֵיג רַבִּי אֱלִיעֶזֶר, דְּאָמַר ״שְׁלֵימִין״.

The Gemara explains: **Rabbi Eliezer holds** that when **anyone** becomes ritually impure **after the completion** of his term of naziriteship, but before he brought his offerings, only **seven** days are **negated**, and the thirtieth day is after the completion of his term. The mishna then teaches that one who said: **I am hereby a nazirite** for **thirty days, and became impure** on the **thirtieth day, it negates the entire** tally. **Rabbi Eliezer does not disagree** in this case, since it is an instance **where he** explicitly **said that** he accepts naziriteship on himself for **a full** thirty days,[N] and his ritual impurity therefore occurs during his naziriteship period.

״הֲרֵינִי נָזִיר מֵאָה יוֹם״ וְנִטְמָא יוֹם מֵאָה – סוֹתֵר אֶת הַכֹּל. רַבִּי אֱלִיעֶזֶר אוֹמֵר: אֵינוֹ סוֹתֵר אֶלָּא שְׁלֹשִׁים. וְכוּלָּהּ כִּדְהָוֵינַן בָּהּ אַלִּיבָּא דְּבַר פַּדָּא וְרַב מַתָּנָא.

The mishna also taught that if one said: **I am hereby a nazirite** for **one hundred days, and he became impure** on the **one hundredth day, it negates the entire tally. Rabbi Eliezer says it negates only thirty. And this entire** mishna should be explained **as we discussed it, in accordance with** the opinions **of bar Padda and Rav Mattana** earlier (5a–6b).

מתני׳ מִי שֶׁנָּזַר וְהוּא בְּבֵית הַקְּבָרוֹת, אֲפִילּוּ הָיָה שָׁם שְׁלֹשִׁים יוֹם – אֵין עוֹלִין לוֹ מִן הַמִּנְיָן, וְאֵינוֹ מֵבִיא קָרְבַּן טוּמְאָה. יָצָא וְנִכְנַס – עוֹלִין לוֹ מִן הַמִּנְיָן, וּמֵבִיא קָרְבַּן טוּמְאָה.

MISHNA **One who took a vow of naziriteship while in a cemetery,**[H] **even if he was there** for a full **thirty days** without leaving, those days he spent in the cemetery **do not count** as part **of his tally,**[N] since his naziriteship has not yet gone into effect. **And he** therefore **does not bring** the three **offerings of impurity,**[N] brought by a nazirite when rendered ritually impure by contact with a corpse, despite having been in a cemetery. If **he left** the cemetery **and entered** it again,[H] those days **do count** as part **of his tally,**[N] meaning the naziriteship takes effect, **and he does bring the offerings of impurity** for reentering the cemetery.

רַבִּי אֱלִיעֶזֶר אוֹמֵר: לֹא בּוֹ בַּיּוֹם, שֶׁנֶּאֱמַר ״וְהַיָּמִים הָרִאשׁוֹנִים יִפְּלוּ״ – עַד שֶׁיְּהוּ לוֹ יָמִים רִאשׁוֹנִים.

Rabbi Eliezer says: This *halakha* does **not** apply to one who entered the cemetery **on the very day**[N] that he left it, **as it is stated** with regard to the *halakhot* of a ritually impure nazirite: **"But the first days shall be void"** (Numbers 6:12), which indicates that he does not bring the offerings **until he will have "first days"**[H] of purity, during which he observed his naziriteship.

גמ׳ אִיתְּמַר, מִי שֶׁנָּזַר וְהוּא בְּבֵית הַקְּבָרוֹת, רַבִּי יוֹחָנָן אָמַר: נְזִירוּת חָלָה עָלָיו, וְרֵישׁ לָקִישׁ אָמַר: אֵין נְזִירוּת חָלָה עָלָיו. רַבִּי יוֹחָנָן אָמַר: נְזִירוּת חָלָה עָלָיו, סָבַר: מִיתְלָא תַּלְיָא וְקַיְימָא, כֵּיוָן דְּמַשְׁכְּחָא טָהֳרָה – חָיְילָא. וְרֵישׁ לָקִישׁ אָמַר: אֵין נְזִירוּת חָלָה עָלָיו, אִי הָדַר וְאָמַר – חָיְילָא עֲלֵיהּ, וְאִי לָא – לָא.

GEMARA **It was stated** that the *amora'im* disagree with regard to **one who vowed to be a nazirite** while **in a cemetery. Rabbi Yoḥanan said: Naziriteship takes effect for him,**[H] **and Reish Lakish said: Naziriteship does not take effect for him.** The Gemara clarifies their respective opinions: **Rabbi Yoḥanan, who said naziriteship takes effect for him, holds** that from the moment he accepts naziriteship upon himself it is **pending,** so that **when it is found** that he is in a state of **ritual purity** it **takes** immediate **effect.** The vow registers from when he states it, but it cannot take effect in practice as long as he stands in a ritually impure location. **And Reish Lakish said** that **naziriteship does not take effect for him** at all. Consequently, **if** he **again said** after leaving the cemetery that he accepts a vow of naziriteship, **it takes effect for him; but if** he does **not** repeat his vow, he is **not** a nazirite.

NOTES

Where he said that he accepts a full thirty days – **דְּאָמַר שְׁלֵימִין**: The Commentary on *Nazir* and Rabbeinu Peretz explain that this is a case where one explicitly said: A full thirty days. In such a case, he certainly may not shave before the completion of all thirty days. *Tosafot* hold that he merely said: A nazirite for thirty days. The addition of the amount of days is superfluous, as an unspecified naziriteship is for thirty days. Therefore, the use of the additional phrase: For thirty days, is viewed as if he said a full thirty days.

Do not count as part of his tally – **אֵין עוֹלִין לוֹ מִן הַמִּנְיָן**: The Rid writes that even though he is prohibited from shaving and drinking wine during this time, in accordance with the opinion of Rabbi Yoḥanan, those days do not count as part of his naziriteship term.

Offerings of impurity – **קָרְבַּן טוּמְאָה**: As detailed in the Torah (Numbers 6:10–12), a nazirite who becomes impure through contact with a corpse must bring three offerings after completing his purification process. They are two turtledoves, one as a sin-offering and one as a burnt-offering, and a sheep, brought as a guilt offering. These three offerings together are referred to as a *korban tuma*, the offerings of impurity.

Do count as part of his tally, etc. – **עוֹלִין לוֹ מִן הַמִּנְיָן וכו׳**: The days of naziriteship he observed after having left the cemetery and completing his purification process are included in his term of naziriteship. According to the unattributed opinion in the mishna, this applies even if it was only a single day. If he reenters the cemetery, he will have to bring the offerings of impurity. It does not mean that the days before reentering the cemetery will count toward the final tally of his term of naziriteship, since the subsequent ritual impurity negates all days previously counted (*Tosafot*).

The Rambam has an entirely different opinion on this mishna. He holds that since the ritual impurity of the cemetery is a lower level of impurity, which does not render a nazirite obligated to bring offerings or void the tally of the days he has counted, the mishna rules that if he reenters the cemetery after starting the observance of his naziriteship, the days he has observed in ritual purity are counted toward the final tally of his term of naziriteship. The clause: And he brings the offerings of impurity, is referring to one who became impure by a corpse, which obligates him to bring the offerings. In that case, the days counted before becoming impure would be negated.

Not on the very day – **לֹא בּוֹ בַּיּוֹם**: The early commentaries disagree over whether two full days of ritual purity are needed (Rambam), or if his partial observance of the second day is sufficient (*Tosafot*).

HALAKHA

One who took a vow of naziriteship while in a cemetery – **מִי שֶׁנָּזַר וְהוּא בְּבֵית הַקְּבָרוֹת**: If one vowed to be a nazirite while he was in a cemetery, and then stayed there for several days, this time does not count as part of the tally of his term of naziriteship. If he became ritually impure through one of the sources of ritual impurity for which a nazirite must shave and bring offerings, he does not shave or bring the offerings (Rambam *Sefer Hafla'a*, *Hilkhot Nezirut* 6:8).

Left the cemetery and entered it again – **יָצָא וְנִכְנַס**: If one accepted naziriteship while in a cemetery and then left the cemetery, completed his purification process, and subsequently observed several days of his naziriteship, those days he counted in ritual purity do count as part of his tally. If he then became ritually impure by an impurity that causes the negation of his previous days of naziriteship and renders him obligated to bring the offerings of impurity, his days of purity are negated and he must shave and bring the offerings of impurity, as explained by the Gemara below (Rambam *Sefer Hafla'a*, *Hilkhot Nezirut* 6:10).

Until he will have first days – **עַד שֶׁיְּהוּ לוֹ יָמִים רִאשׁוֹנִים**: If a nazirite became ritually impure on the first or second day of his term of naziriteship, the tally of those days is not negated. After completing his purification process and bringing the offerings of impurity, he continues to count from where he paused. If he became ritually impure on the third day or later, the days he observed are negated, and he must bring the offerings of impurity. This is in accordance with the opinion of Rabbi Eliezer, as no one disagrees with him in this matter (Rambam *Sefer Hafla'a*, *Hilkhot Nezirut* 6:6).

Naziriteship takes effect for him – **נְזִירוּת חָלָה עָלָיו**: If one was in a cemetery and vowed to be a nazirite, the naziriteship takes effect, in accordance with the opinion of Rabbi Yoḥanan (Rambam *Sefer Hafla'a*, *Hilkhot Nezirut* 6:8).

אִיתִיבֵיהּ רַבִּי יוֹחָנָן לְרֵישׁ לָקִישׁ: מִי שֶׁנָּזַר וְהוּא בְּבֵית הַקְּבָרוֹת, אֲפִילּוּ הָיָה שָׁם שְׁלֹשִׁים יוֹם – אֵין עוֹלִין מִן הַמִּנְיָן, וְאֵינוֹ מֵבִיא קׇרְבַּן טוּמְאָה. קׇרְבַּן טוּמְאָה הוּא דְּלָא מַיְיתֵי, הָא מֵיחַל חָיְילָא עֲלֵיהּ! אֲמַר לֵיהּ: אֵינוֹ בְּתוֹרַת טוּמְאָה וְאֵינוֹ בְּתוֹרַת קׇרְבָּן.

Rabbi Yoḥanan raised an objection to the opinion of Reish Lakish from the mishna: **One who took a vow of naziriteship while in a cemetery, even if he was there** for a full **thirty days** without leaving, those days he spent in the cemetery **do not count** as part **of the tally,** since his naziriteship has not yet gone into effect. **And he** therefore **does not bring the offerings of impurity** despite having been in a cemetery. Rabbi Yoḥanan infers from this: **It is the offerings of impurity that he does not bring, but** as far as the issue of the naziriteship **taking effect, it does take effect for him.** Reish Lakish **said to him:** It means **he is not** included **in the law of** prohibited **ritual impurity,** and therefore **he is not** included **in the law of the offerings.** He is not a nazirite at all.

אִיתִיבֵיהּ: מִי שֶׁהָיָה טָמֵא וְנָזַר – אָסוּר לְגַלֵּחַ וְלִשְׁתּוֹת יַיִן וְלִיטַּמֵּא לְמֵתִים. וְאִם גִּילַּח וְשָׁתָה יַיִן וְנִטְמָא לְמֵתִים – הֲרֵי זֶה סוֹפֵג אֶת הָאַרְבָּעִים. אִי אָמְרַתְּ בִּשְׁלָמָא חָיְילָא – הַיְינוּ טַעְמָא דְּסוֹפֵג אֶת הָאַרְבָּעִים, אֶלָּא אִי אָמְרַתְּ לָא חָיְילָא – אַמַּאי סוֹפֵג אֶת הָאַרְבָּעִים?

Rabbi Yoḥanan **raised an objection to** the opinion of Reish Lakish from what was taught in a *baraita* (*Tosefta* 2:14): **One who was impure and took a vow of naziriteship**[NH] must still observe the *halakhot* of a nazirite: He is **prohibited from shaving, and from drinking wine, and from becoming impure from a corpse. And if he shaved,** or if he **drank wine,** or if **he became impure from a corpse, he incurs** [*sofeg*][L] **the forty** lashes administered to one who actively transgresses a negative Torah prohibition. Rabbi Yoḥanan asks: **Granted, if you say** that naziriteship **takes effect** despite his ritual impurity, **that is the reason that he incurs the forty** lashes, similar to any nazirite who transgresses the prohibitions of naziriteship. **But if you say** the naziriteship **does not take effect** while he is ritually impure, **why does he incur the forty** lashes?

NOTES

One who was impure and took a vow of naziriteship – מִי שֶׁהָיָה טָמֵא וְנָזַר: The early commentaries prove from here that there is no difference between one who vowed to be a nazirite while in a cemetery and one who did so while in a state of ritual impurity from a corpse, as the Gemara is attempting to bring a proof from one to the other.

HALAKHA

One who was impure and took a vow of naziriteship – מִי שֶׁהָיָה טָמֵא וְנָזַר: If one took a vow of naziriteship while he was ritually impure from a corpse, the naziriteship takes effect. Therefore, if he became impure again, drank wine, or shaved, he is liable to receive lashes (Rambam *Sefer Hafla'a*, *Hilkhot Nezirut* 6:7).

LANGUAGE

Incurs [*sofeg*] – סוֹפֵג: From the Greek σπόγγος, *spongos*, meaning sponge. The word *sefog*, from the root *shin, fey, gimmel*, meant something that absorbs liquids, and was later extended to refer to anything that can absorb something else, whether to absorb financially or, in this case, to absorb the impact of the flogging.

Perek **III**
Daf **17** Amud **a**

הָכָא בְּמַאי עָסְקִינַן – בְּיוֹצֵא וְנִכְנָס.

Reish Lakish responded: **With what are we dealing here** in this *baraita*? **With one who left and entered,** meaning that after having left the cemetery and purifying himself, he then vowed again to be a nazirite and subsequently reentered the cemetery.

אִיתִיבֵיהּ: אֵין בֵּין טָמֵא שֶׁנָּזַר לְנָזִיר טָהוֹר שֶׁנִּטְמָא, אֶלָּא: טָמֵא שֶׁנָּזַר – שְׁבִיעִי שֶׁלּוֹ עוֹלֶה לוֹ לְמִנְיָן, וְנָזִיר טָהוֹר שֶׁנִּטְמָא – אֵין שְׁבִיעִי שֶׁלּוֹ עוֹלֶה לוֹ לְמִנְיָן. וְאִי סָלְקָא דַּעְתָּךְ לָא חָיְילָא – אַמַּאי עוֹלֶה לוֹ מִן הַמִּנְיָן?

Rabbi Yoḥanan **raised** another **objection to** Reish Lakish's opinion from a different source: **The difference between a ritually impure**[H] person **who took a vow of naziriteship and a ritually pure nazirite who became impure is only** the following *halakha*: If **a ritually impure** person **took a vow of naziriteship, his seventh** day of purification **counts** as part **of his tally**[N] of his term of naziriteship, since he starts counting his term of naziriteship as soon as he becomes pure. **But** with regard to **a ritually pure nazirite who became impure, his seventh** day of purification **does not count** as part **of his tally.** Rather, he starts counting his days of naziriteship from the following day, which is the day on which he brings his offerings. **And if it enters your mind** that a vow of naziriteship stated while ritually impure **does not take effect, why** does the *baraita* state that the seventh day **counts** as part **of his tally,** indicating that the naziriteship takes effect without a need for him to restate his vow?

אָמַר מָר בַּר רַב אָשֵׁי: מֵיחַל – כּוּלֵּי עָלְמָא לָא פְּלִיגִי דְּחָיְילָא, אֶלָּא כִּי פְּלִיגִי – לְמִלְקֵי; רַבִּי יוֹחָנָן סָבַר: כֵּיוָן דְּחָיְילָא – לָקֵי, וְרֵישׁ לָקִישׁ סָבַר: לָא לָקֵי, וְחָיְילָא.

As a result of this question, the Gemara offers a different interpretation of their dispute. **Mar bar Rav Ashi said:** The dispute between Rabbi Yoḥanan and Reish Lakish is not as stated above. With regard to the question of the vow of naziriteship **taking effect, everyone agrees that** it **takes effect** from the moment of his acceptance of naziriteship, even if he was in the cemetery. **Rather, when they disagree** it is with regard **to being flogged,**[N] as follows: **Rabbi Yoḥanan holds** that **since** the vow **takes effect, he is** therefore **flogged** for becoming impure, **and Reish Lakish holds that he is not flogged** for becoming impure, **but** the vow **does take effect** with regard to the prohibitions of naziriteship.

HALAKHA

The difference between a ritually impure, etc. – אֵין בֵּין טָמֵא וכו׳: If one took a vow of naziriteship while ritually impure, the seventh day of his purification process counts as part of the tally of his term of naziriteship. However, a ritually pure nazirite who became impure starts his counting only from the eighth day (Rambam *Sefer Hafla'a*, *Hilkhot Nezirut* 6:7).

NOTES

His seventh day counts as part of his tally – שְׁבִיעִי שֶׁלּוֹ עוֹלֶה לוֹ: Since he does not have to bring an offering on the eighth day, the legal status of part of the seventh day is like a that of full day, and he can therefore begin counting his naziriteship from the seventh day of his purification (Commentary on *Nazir*). Although he does not become completely ritually pure until sunset, the ritual impurity of one who has already immersed himself is weak and does not prevent his naziriteship from taking effect (*Tosafot*).

When they disagree is with regard to being flogged – כִּי פְּלִיגִי לְמִילְקֵי: Most commentaries hold that the disagreement between Rabbi Yoḥanan and Reish Lakish is only with regard to whether a nazirite is flogged for becoming ritually impure from a corpse, and Reish Lakish agrees that a nazirite is flogged if he shaved or drank wine (*Tosafot*; Rosh). Some suggest that according to Reish Lakish the naziriteship only takes effect by rabbinic decree, and he would not be flogged for violating any of the prohibitions. However, the corresponding discussion in tractate *Nedarim* indicates that this opinion is incorrect (Rabbeinu Peretz; Rabbeinu Todros).

אֵיתִיבֵיהּ רַבִּי יוֹחָנָן לְרֵישׁ לָקִישׁ: מִי שֶׁנָּזַר וְהוּא בְּבֵית הַקְּבָרוֹת, אֲפִילּוּ הָיָה שָׁם שְׁלֹשִׁים יוֹם – אֵין עוֹלִין לוֹ מִן הַמִּנְיָן, וְאֵינוֹ מֵבִיא קׇרְבַּן טוּמְאָה. קׇרְבַּן טוּמְאָה הוּא דְּלָא מַיְיתֵי, הָא מִילְקֵי לָקֵי עֲלַהּ!

According to this version of the dispute as well, **Rabbi Yoḥanan raised an objection to Reish Lakish** from the mishna, which states: **One who took a vow of naziriteship while in a cemetery, even if he was there** for a full **thirty days** without leaving, those days he spent in the cemetery **do not count** as part **of his tally,** since his naziriteship has not yet gone into effect. **And he** therefore **does not bring the offerings of impurity,** despite having been in a cemetery. Rabbi Yoḥanan infers from this: **It is the offerings of impurity** that **he does not bring, but** he **is flogged for** contracting impurity, which is not in accordance with the opinion of Reish Lakish.

בְּדִין הוּא דְּלִיתְנֵי ״אֵינוֹ לוֹקֶה״. אֶלָּא מִשּׁוּם דְּקָא בָּעֵי לְמִיתְנָא סֵיפָא ״יָצָא וְנִכְנַס עוֹלָה לוֹ מִן הַמִּנְיָן, וּמֵבִיא קׇרְבַּן טוּמְאָה״ – תְּנָא רֵישָׁא ״אֵינוֹ מֵבִיא קׇרְבַּן טוּמְאָה״.

The Gemara answers: This inference is not correct, as **by right** the mishna **should teach: He is not flogged, but due to** the fact that the *tanna* **wants to teach the latter clause** of the mishna, which states: If **he left** the cemetery **and entered** it again, those days **do count** as part **of his tally,** meaning the naziriteship takes effect, **and he does bring the offerings of impurity** for reentering the cemetery, the *tanna* therefore **taught** a similar phrasing in **the first clause** of the mishna: **He does not bring the offerings of impurity,** so this should not be seen as an indication that he is not flogged.

תָּא שְׁמַע: אֵין בֵּין טָמֵא שֶׁנָּזַר לְנָזִיר טָהוֹר שֶׁנִּטְמָא, אֶלָּא שֶׁטָּמֵא שֶׁנָּזַר – שְׁבִיעִי שֶׁלּוֹ עוֹלֶה לוֹ מִן הַמִּנְיָן, וְנָזִיר טָהוֹר שֶׁנִּטְמָא – אֵין שְׁבִיעִי שֶׁלּוֹ עוֹלֶה לוֹ מִן הַמִּנְיָן. הָא לְמַלְקוֹת – זֶה וָזֶה שָׁוִין! אֲמַר לֵיהּ: לָא, לְתִגְלַחַת זֶה וָזֶה שָׁוִין.

The Gemara suggests another proof in support of Rabbi Yoḥanan's opinion. **Come** and **hear** a proof from another *baraita*: **The difference between an impure** person **who took a vow of naziriteship and a pure nazirite who became impure is only** the following *halakha*: **That** in the case of **an impure** person **who took a vow of naziriteship, his seventh** day of purification **counts** as part **of his tally** of the term of naziriteship. **But** in the case of **a pure nazirite who became impure, his seventh** day of purification **does not count** as part **of his tally.** The Gemara infers: **But with regard to flogging, this** nazirite **and that** nazirite **are equal.** Reish Lakish **said to** Rabbi Yoḥanan: This is **not** a correct inference; rather, it is with regard **to shaving** on the seventh day of purification that **this** nazirite **and that** nazirite **are equal,**[N] since even a ritually impure person who took a vow of naziriteship must shave on that day.

אֲבָל לְעִנְיַן מַלְקוֹת מַאי – זֶה לוֹקֶה וְזֶה אֵינוֹ לוֹקֶה? לִיתְנֵייהּ! בְּתַקַּנְתֵּיהּ קָא מַיְירֵי, בְּקִלְקוּלֵיהּ לָא קָא מַיְירֵי.

The Gemara asks: **But** in that case, according to Reish Lakish, **what is the** *halakha* **with regard to flogging? This** nazirite **is flogged, and that** nazirite, who was ritually impure when he vowed, **is not flogged?** If so, **let him teach this** difference as well; why does the *baraita* state that there is only one difference between them? The Gemara answers: This *baraita* **is speaking of his remedy;**[N] **it is not speaking of** a matter that is **detrimental to him.** Consequently the *baraita* does not discuss a nazirite's punishments and discusses only the means by which he can resume his observance of naziriteship.

תָּא שְׁמַע: מִי שֶׁהָיָה טָמֵא וְנָזַר – אָסוּר לְגַלֵּחַ וְלִשְׁתּוֹת יַיִן, וְאִם גִּילֵּחַ וְשָׁתָה יַיִן וְנִטְמָא לְמֵתִים – הֲרֵי זֶה סוֹפֵג אֶת הָאַרְבָּעִים! תְּיוּבְתָּא.

The Gemara further suggests: **Come** and **hear** a proof from that which is taught in a *baraita* (*Tosefta* 2:14): **One who was ritually impure and took a vow of naziriteship** must still observe the *halakhot* of a nazirite. He is **prohibited from shaving and from drinking wine. And if he shaved,** or **if he drank wine,** or **if he became ritually impure from a corpse, he incurs the forty** lashes administered to one who actively transgresses a negative Torah prohibition. The Gemara concludes: This is **a conclusive refutation**[N] of the opinion of Reish Lakish, as explained by Mar bar Rav Ashi.

בָּעֵי רָבָא: נָזִיר וְהוּא בְּבֵית הַקְּבָרוֹת, מַהוּ? בָּעֵי שֶׁהִיָּיה לְמַלְקוֹת אוֹ לָא?

§ After concluding that one who takes a vow of naziriteship while in a cemetery is liable to receive lashes, **Rava asks: What is the** *halakha* if one took a vow to be **a nazirite while** standing **in a cemetery:** Is it **necessary** that his exit from the cemetery be **delayed** for a specific period of time for him to become liable **to** receive **lashes,**[N] just as one who becomes ritually impure while in the Temple is receives lashes only if he remains there for a specific period of time, **or** is it **not** necessary?

NOTES

With regard to shaving, this and that are equal – לְתִגְלַחַת זֶה וָזֶה שָׁוִין: The Commentary on *Nazir* understands this to be saying that just as a nazirite who became ritually impure must shave his hair on the seventh day of his purification process, so too one who took a vow of naziriteship while ritually impure must shave on the seventh day of his purification process before reaccepting his naziriteship. Although the Gemara later proves that this is not so, the Gemara here is not concerned with that proof, since this explanation of Reish Lakish is entirely discounted anyway (*Tosafot*).

Alternatively, this means that is they are both liable to receive lashes if they shave during their days of ritual impurity. *Tosafot* question this explanation because then the *baraita* should have mentioned that they are equal with regard to being flogged for drinking wine as well. The Rosh answers that shaving is merely an example of a nazirite prohibition, and the *baraita* means that they are equal with regard to being subject to being flogged for drinking wine as well.

Speaking of his remedy, etc. – בְּתַקַּנְתֵּיהּ קָא מַיְירֵי וכו׳: The *baraita* is discussing the conditions that will enable his naziriteship to take effect, rather than the transgressions that render the nazirite liable to receive lashes (Commentary on *Nazir*). *Tosafot* explain that the phrase: His remedy, is referring to one who became ritually impure unwittingly, whereas the phrase: Detrimental to him, is referring to one who became ritually impure purposefully, and is therefore liable to receive lashes. The Rosh states that this *baraita* does not discuss transgressions, but rather the fulfillment of the mitzvot of naziriteship in their proper manner.

A conclusive refutation – תְּיוּבְתָּא: The Gemara cannot answer, as it did before, that the *baraita* is discussing one who left the cemetery and reentered, because this *baraita* mentions both ritual impurity and shaving, and according to Mar bar Rav Ashi, even Reish Lakish agrees that one who shaved or drank wine before leaving the cemetery is flogged (*Tosafot*).

Is it necessary that his exit be delayed to be liable to receive lashes – בָּעֵי שֶׁהִיָּיה לְמַלְקוֹת: The Gemara is suggesting that one who becomes a nazirite while in a cemetery will be flogged only if he stays in place for as long as it takes to prostrate oneself, as is the *halakha* with regard to one who became ritually impure while in the Temple. The Meiri theorizes that the time requirement discussed in this case may differ from that of impurity in the Temple. *Tosafot* similarly suggest that the relevant period of time here may be the time it takes to leave and reenter the cemetery (*Shevuot* 17a). The reason for the comparison between the two cases is that in both situations contracting impurity occurs after one has entered a state or place of purity, either by vowing to be a nazirite or by physically entering the Temple, as will become clear from the conclusion of the Gemara here. It is therefore reasonable to assume that the nazirite should also be granted sufficient time to leave the cemetery before he is liable to receive lashes.

הֵיכִי דָּמֵי? אִילֵימָא דְּאָמְרִי לֵיהּ ״לָא תִּינְזוֹר״ – לָמָּה לִי שְׁהִיָּיה? נָזִיר מַאי טַעֲמָא לָא בָּעֵי שְׁהִיָּיה – דְּקָא מַתְרֵי בֵּיהּ, הָכָא נַמִי – קָא מַתְרֵי בֵּיהּ!

The Gemara clarifies: **What are the circumstances** in which this question is relevant? **If we say that they said to him** in warning: **Do not take a vow of naziriteship** in the cemetery, and he ignored their warning and took a vow of naziriteship, **why do I** need him to **delay** his exit? **What is the reason** that one who was already a **nazirite** when he entered a cemetery **does not need to delay** his exit in order to be liable to receive lashes? **Because they warn him** not to enter, and if he enters he has transgressed a prohibition and is flogged. **Here too, they warn him** not to take the vow, and he should therefore be liable to receive lashes if he does take the vow.

Perek **III**
Daf **17** Amud **b**

אֶלָּא כְּגוֹן שֶׁנִּכְנַס בְּשִׁידָּה תֵּיבָה וּמִגְדָּל, וּבָא חֲבֵירוֹ וּפָרַע מֵעָלָיו מַעֲזִיבָה.

Rather, Rava's question should be understood to refer to a case **where** one **entered** the cemetery **in a chest, box, or cabinet,**[B] i.e., in large wooden containers that do not contract ritual impurity. One can enter a cemetery in such a container without becoming impure. If one was carried into a cemetery inside one of these containers, then took a vow of naziriteship, **and another came and removed**[N] **the top** [*ma'aziva*][L] **from above him,**[NH] he would become ritually impure by virtue of being in the cemetery.

כִּי גְּמִירִין שְׁהִיָּיה – בְּבֵית הַמִּקְדָּשׁ, אֲבָל אַבָּרַאי – לָא, אוֹ דִּלְמָא לָא שְׁנָא? תֵּיקוּ.

If he was then warned to leave the cemetery, the question is as follows: **When we learned**[H] by tradition that one is liable to receive lashes for **delaying** his exit, does that apply only **to the Temple, but outside** the Temple, such as when a nazirite is in a cemetery, does the *halakha* **not** apply, so that he is liable to receive lashes even if he did not delay his exit? **Or perhaps it is not different,** and a nazirite in a cemetery is flogged only if he remains there for a specific period of time. The dilemma **shall stand** unresolved.

בָּעֵי רַב אַשִׁי: נָזַר וְהוּא בְּבֵית הַקְּבָרוֹת, טָעוּן גִּילּוּחַ אוֹ לֹא? כִּי בָּעֵי תִּגְלַחַת – טָהוֹר שֶׁנִּטְמָא, דְּקָא מְטַמֵּא לִנְזִירוּתֵיהּ, אֲבָל טָמֵא שֶׁנָּזַר – לָא, אוֹ דִּלְמָא לָא שְׁנָא?

§ **Rav Ashi raises a dilemma:** If one took **a vow of naziriteship while in a cemetery,** is he **required to shave** upon becoming ritually pure, before starting his term of naziriteship, **or not?** The Gemara explains the two sides of the question: **When** a ritually impure nazirite **is required to shave** before starting his tally, does that refer only to **a ritually pure** nazirite **who became impure, who has defiled his naziriteship? But a ritually impure** person **who** only **took a vow of naziriteship,** and whose naziriteship has not yet begun, is he **not** obligated to shave? **Or perhaps it is not different.**

תָּא שְׁמַע: מִי שֶׁנָּזַר וְהוּא בְּבֵית הַקְּבָרוֹת, אֲפִילּוּ הָיָה שָׁם שְׁלֹשִׁים יוֹם – אֵינוֹ עוֹלֶה לוֹ מִן הַמִּנְיָן, וְאֵינוֹ מֵבִיא קָרְבַּן טוּמְאָה. קָרְבַּן טוּמְאָה הוּא דְּלָא מַיְיתֵי, אֲבָל גַּלּוּחֵי – בָּעֵי! מַה טַּעַם קָאָמַר; מַה טַּעַם אֵינוֹ מֵבִיא קָרְבַּן טוּמְאָה – מִשּׁוּם דְּלָא בָּעֵי גַּלּוּחֵי.

The Gemara suggests: **Come** and **hear** a proof from the mishna: **One who took a vow of naziriteship while in a cemetery, even if he was there** for a full **thirty days** without leaving, those days he spent in the cemetery **do not count** as part **of his tally,** since his naziriteship has not yet gone into effect, **and he** therefore **does not bring the offerings of impurity.** The Gemara infers from this: **It is the offerings of impurity** that **he does not bring, but he is required to shave.** The Gemara rejects this proof: It is possible that the mishna **is saying: What is the reason,** as follows: **What is the reason** that **he does not bring the offerings of impurity? Because he does not require shaving.** This indicates that the naziriteship has not yet begun, therefore, he does not bring the offerings either.

BACKGROUND

Chest [*shidda*], box [*teiva*], or cabinet [*migdal*] – שִׁידָּה תֵּיבָה וּמִגְדָּל: The difference between these terms is not clarified by the early commentaries. Based on the few sources that do explain them, it seems that the *teiva* was a simple box with a covering or a door on the top. The *shidda*, however, was more complex, with several drawers. The *migdal*, apparently similar to what is now called a cabinet, was a box whose height was greater than its width with doors on its front.

NOTES

And another came and removed – וּבָא חֲבֵירוֹ וּפָרַע: This deals only with one who became ritually impure forcibly, through the actions of another. If the nazirite removed the cover himself, or asked another to do so, and was warned against it, he is certainly liable to receive lashes even if he does not delay his exit from the cemetery (*Tosafot*).

Removed the top [*ma'aziva*] from above him – וּפָרַע מֵעָלָיו מַעֲזִיבָה: Many question the precise scenario described in the Gemara, as being in an uncovered box inside a cemetery does not cause one to become ritually impure. Therefore, some commentaries explain that the word *ma'aziva* is referring to opening the bottom of the box, which causes the ritual impurity of the cemetery to penetrate from below (Rabbi Avraham min HaHar; Rosh). Others explain that the cover was removed when both he and the box were inside an enclosure together with a corpse, which would render him ritually impure. However, some commentaries maintain that it means he removed the cover from a grave while the box was within a handbreadth of it, rendering the occupant of the box ritually impure (see *Nusḥa'ot HaRivan* and Rashash).

LANGUAGE

Top [*ma'aziva*] – מַעֲזִיבָה: The word *ma'aziva* usually refers to the portion of material in the roof used to seal the holes in the roofing and to seal the room against rain. In the days of the Talmud, the *ma'aziva* was made of a combination of fine reeds and mud.

With regard to the source of the word, some contend that its meaning is connected to fixing and assistance. Here the meaning expanded to include an upper covering for other objects as well.

HALAKHA

Removed the top from above him – וּפָרַע מֵעָלָיו מַעֲזִיבָה: If a nazirite entered a cemetery in a chest, box, or cabinet, and another came and removed the top so that the nazirite became ritually impure, he is not liable to receive lashes even if he delays his exit from the cemetery. The Ra'avad disagrees, and holds that the Gemara's dilemma only concerns the issue of whether or not he must delay his exit in order to be liable to receive lashes, and one who does delay his exit is certainly flogged. The Radbaz suggests that when the Rambam rules that he is not flogged, he is referring to a case where the nazirite was not warned (Rambam *Sefer Hafla'a*, *Hilkhot Nezirut* 6:9; see 5:1ε).

When we learned, etc. – כִּי גְּמִירִין וכו׳: If a nazirite unwittingly entered a cemetery or a room with a corpse, and after realizing where he was, he was warned that he was in violation of a Torah prohibition by remaining there, if he remains in the place he is liable to receive lashes. This applies only if he delayed his exit long enough to prostrate himself, similar to the *halakha* of a person who becomes ritually impure in the Temple (Rambam *Sefer Hafla'a*, *Hilkhot Nezirut* 5:19).

תָּא שְׁמַע: אֵין בֵּין טָמֵא שֶׁנָּדַר לְנָזִיר טָהוֹר שֶׁנִּטְמָא אֶלָּא: טָמֵא שֶׁנָּדַר – שְׁבִיעִי שֶׁלּוֹ עוֹלֶה לוֹ מִן הַמִּנְיָן, וְנָזִיר טָהוֹר שֶׁנִּטְמָא – אֵין שְׁבִיעִי שֶׁלּוֹ עוֹלֶה לוֹ מִן הַמִּנְיָן. מַאי לָאו, הָא לְתִגְלַחַת – זֶה וָזֶה שָׁוִין? לָא, הָא לְמַלְקוֹת זֶה וָזֶה שָׁוִין.

The Gemara suggests another proof. **Come and hear** a proof from another *baraita*: **The difference between a ritually impure** person **who took a vow of naziriteship and a ritually pure nazirite who became impure is only** the following *halakha*: With regard to **an impure** person **who took a vow of naziriteship, his seventh** day of purification **counts** as part **of his tally** of the term of naziriteship, **but** with regard to **a pure nazirite who became impure, his seventh** day of purification **does not count** as part **of his tally.** The Gemara infers: **What, is it not** so that **with regard to shaving, this and that are equal,** and he must shave in either case? The Gemara rejects this: **No,** there is a different inference: **It is with regard to flogging** that **this and that are equal,** but one who took a vow of naziriteship while in a cemetery does not have to shave.

אֲבָל תִּגְלַחַת מַאי – זֶה מְגַלֵּחַ, וְזֶה אֵינוֹ מְגַלֵּחַ? לִיתְנֵיהּ. תְּנָא שְׁבִיעִי שֶׁלּוֹ, וְכָל מִילֵּי.

The Gemara questions this answer: **But what** is the *halakha* concerning **shaving?** Does **this** one, who became ritually impure, **shave, and that** one, who vowed while in a cemetery, **not shave?** If so, **let him teach this** difference as well. The Gemara answers: The *tanna* **taught: His seventh day, and all matters** relevant to it, including the *halakha* of shaving. Once it says that the seventh day is part of the tally of the ritually impure nazirite who became pure, it can be inferred that he does not bring the offerings of impurity on the eighth day, and therefore he does not shave on the seventh day.

תָּא שְׁמַע: אֵין לִי אֶלָּא יְמֵי טוּמְאָתוֹ שֶׁאֵין עוֹלִין לוֹ מִן הַמִּנְיָן, יְמֵי חִלּוּטוֹ מִנַּיִן? וְדִין הוּא: מַה יְּמֵי טוּמְאָתוֹ מְגַלֵּחַ וּמֵבִיא קָרְבָּן – אַף יְמֵי חִלּוּטוֹ מְגַלֵּחַ וּמֵבִיא קָרְבָּן, וּמַה יְּמֵי טוּמְאָתוֹ אֵין עוֹלִין לוֹ מִן הַמִּנְיָן – אַף יְמֵי חִלּוּטוֹ אֵין עוֹלִין לוֹ מִן הַמִּנְיָן!

The Gemara further suggests: **Come and hear** a proof from the following *baraita*: **I have** derived **only that** a nazirite's **days of ritual impurity do not count** as part **of his tally; from where** do I derive that **his days of confirmed** leprosy,[H] in a case where a nazirite became a leper during his term, do not count toward his tally of naziriteship? **And** it would seem that **by right** it should be so: **Just as** at the end of **his days of ritual impurity** the nazirite **shaves and brings offerings, so too** at the end of **his days of confirmed** leprosy the *halakha* is that he **shaves and brings offerings** for his leprosy. **And** this comparison can be extended: **Just as the days of his ritual impurity do not count** as part **of his tally, so too his days of confirmed** leprosy **do not count** as part **of his tally.**

לֹא, אִם אָמַרְתָּ בִּימֵי טוּמְאָתוֹ – שֶׁכֵּן מְבַטֵּל בָּהֶן אֶת הַקּוֹדְמִין, לְפִיכָךְ אֵין עוֹלִין לוֹ מִן הַמִּנְיָן, תֹּאמַר בִּימֵי חִלּוּטוֹ שֶׁאֵינוֹ מְבַטֵּל אֶת הַקּוֹדְמִין, לְפִיכָךְ עוֹלִין לוֹ מִן הַמִּנְיָן.

The *baraita* continues: **No, if you say** so **with regard to his days of ritual impurity,** in that case it is **because with them, the previous** days of his naziriteship observed in ritual purity **are negated. Therefore,** those days **do not count** as part **of his tally.** But will **you say** the same **with regard to his days of confirmed** leprosy, **which do not negate the previous** days?[N] If thirty days, enough time for his hair to regrow, remain in his term of naziriteship after becoming purified from his leprosy, the days before he contracted leprosy are not negated. It is **therefore** possible to argue that **they do count** as part **of his tally.**

אָמַרְתָּ: וּמַה נָּזִיר בַּקֶּבֶר, שֶׁשְּׂעָרוֹ רָאוּי לְתִגְלַחַת – אֵין עוֹלִין לוֹ מִן הַמִּנְיָן, יְמֵי חִלּוּטוֹ שֶׁאֵין רָאוּי לְתִגְלַחַת – לֹא כָּל שֶׁכֵּן שֶׁאֵין עוֹלִין לוֹ מִן הַמִּנְיָן?

The *baraita* continues: But **you can say** that **just as** with regard to a **nazirite** who was **in the grave,**[N] i.e., a cemetery, **whose hair is fit for shaving,** those days spent in the cemetery **do not count** as part **of his tally, his days of confirmed** leprosy, **which are not fit for** counting as part of the tally required for the **shaving,** since he must first shave as part of the purification process for his leprosy, is it **not all the more so that they do not count** as part **of his tally?** This concludes the *baraita*.

מַאי לָאו תִּגְלַחַת טוּמְאָה? לָא, תִּגְלַחַת טׇהֳרָה. הָכִי נָמֵי מִסְתַּבְּרָא,

The Gemara now attempts to prove from the *baraita* that one who took a vow of naziriteship while in a cemetery must shave at the close of his process of purification: **What, is it not** so that when the *baraita* mentions shaving, it is referring to **the shaving of impurity,** and it is teaching that one who took a vow of naziriteship in a cemetery must shave at the end of his purification process? The Gemara rejects this: **No,** it is referring to **the shaving of purity,** meaning the shaving done after one completes his term of naziriteship. He then will shave all of his hair, including that which grew during the time he was ritually impure due to his presence in the cemetery. The Gemara adds: **So, too, it is reasonable** to say that this is the correct interpretation,

HALAKHA

His days of confirmed leprosy, etc. – יְמֵי חִלּוּטוֹ וכו׳: If a nazirite became a confirmed leper, none of his days as a leper, nor the seven days he must count after his purification, are included in his term of naziriteship. However, the period when he is quarantined in order to determine if he is a leper does count toward his term (Rambam *Sefer Hafla'a, Hilkhot Nezirut* 7:9).

NOTES

With regard to his days of confirmed leprosy, which do not negate the previous days – בִּימֵי חִלּוּטוֹ שֶׁאֵינוֹ מְבַטֵּל אֶת הַקּוֹדְמִין: The Gemara is referring to one who undertook a lengthy term of naziriteship. He continues to count the remaining days of his term even after having shaved due to his leprosy (Commentary on *Nazir*). If it was a regular term of naziriteship, he would be required to remain a nazirite for long enough to complete thirty days of hair growth after shaving. The early commentaries note that the *halakha* that his days of confirmed leprosy do not negate his previous days of naziriteship, which is stated as obvious here, is derived by the Gemara below (44a) from a verse, which teaches that only the ritual impurity imparted by a corpse negates his previous days; no other kind of ritual impurity does so (*Tosafot*).

Just as a nazirite who was in the grave – וּמַה נָּזִיר בַּקֶּבֶר: The reason why the Gemara tries to derive the *halakha* from the unusual case of one who takes a vow of naziriteship while in a cemetery is because in a regular case of a ritually impure nazirite, his shaving serves to negate the previous days and therefore it cannot be a source for the *halakha* of a nazirite who became a confirmed leper. By contrast, the shaving of a nazirite who took his vow in a cemetery enables him to observe his naziriteship in ritual purity, and still his days before becoming purified do not count as part of his tally. This can serve as a source to teach that his days as a leper, in which the shaving that he does is not related to his naziriteship, should likewise not be counted as part of his term of naziriteship (Rabbeinu Peretz).

דְּאִי סָלְקָא דַּעְתָּךְ תִּגְלַחַת טוּמְאָה – יְמֵי חִלּוּטוֹ מִי לָא בָּעֵי תִּגְלַחַת? לָא, תִּגְלַחַת דִּנְזִירוּת קָתָנֵי.

as if it enters your mind to say that the *baraita* is discussing the **shaving** done as a result of the nazirite's **impurity,** and contrasts a nazirite with a leper, do the end of a leper's **days of confirmed** leprosy **not require shaving?** A leper must shave when he is purified from his condition, so how can he be described as unfit for shaving? Rather, the *baraita* must be referring to the nazirite's shaving of purity, as suggested above (17b). The Gemara rejects this: **No,** it could be that the *baraita* is discussing the shaving done as a result of the nazirite's impurity, and when it states that a leper is unfit for shaving, the *baraita* **is teaching** about the **shaving of naziriteship,** and the *baraita* is stating that a leper is unfit for any shaving of a nazirite, since he must first shave for his leprosy.

תָּא שְׁמַע: "וְטִמֵּא רֹאשׁ נִזְרוֹ" – בְּטָהוֹר שֶׁנִּטְמָא הַכָּתוּב מְדַבֵּר, שֶׁהוּא טָעוּן הַעֲבָרַת שֵׂעָר וַהֲבָאַת צִיפֳּרִין, וְלִפְטוֹר אֶת הַנָּזִיר בַּקֶּבֶר – שֶׁאֵין טָעוּן הַעֲבָרַת שֵׂעָר וַהֲבָאַת צִיפֳּרִין.

The Gemara suggests another proof to answer the question of whether one who vows naziriteship while in a cemetery must shave upon undergoing purification. **Come** and **hear** a *baraita*: The verse states: **"And he defiles his consecrated head,** he shall shave his head on the day of his purification, on the seventh day shall he shave it" (Numbers 6:9). The *baraita* explains: **The verse is speaking of a ritually pure** nazirite **who became impure,**[H] **who requires hair removal and the bringing of birds** as offerings. And this verse comes **to exempt a nazirite** who vowed while **in the grave,**[H] i.e., a cemetery, **that he does not require hair removal and the bringing of birds.**

וַהֲלֹא דְּבָרִים קַל וָחוֹמֶר: וּמַה טָהוֹר שֶׁנִּטְמָא – טָעוּן הַעֲבָרַת שֵׂעָר וַהֲבָאַת צִיפֳּרִין, מִי שֶׁהָיָה טָמֵא מִתְּחִלָּה אֵינוֹ דִּין שֶׁיְּהֵא טָעוּן הַעֲבָרַת שֵׂעָר וַהֲבָאַת צִיפֳּרִין?

The *baraita* continues its analysis of this *halakha*. For one might have explained differently: **And are these matters,** the ruling that such a nazirite is exempt, **not** inferred with an ***a fortiori* inference** to reach the opposite conclusion: **Just as a** nazirite who was **pure** from the outset and **who** subsequently **became impure requires hair removal and the bringing of birds, if one was impure from the outset,** as he took a vow of naziriteship while in a cemetery, **is it not logical that he should require hair removal and the bringing of birds?**

תַּלְמוּד לוֹמַר "וְטִמֵּא רֹאשׁ נִזְרוֹ" – בְּמִי שֶׁהָיָה טָהוֹר וְנִטְמָא הַכָּתוּב מְדַבֵּר, שֶׁיְּהֵא טָעוּן הַעֲבָרַת שֵׂעָר וַהֲבָאַת צִיפֳּרִין, וְלִפְטוֹר אֶת הַנָּזִיר בַּקֶּבֶר. שְׁמַע מִינָּהּ.

Therefore **the verse states: "And he defiles his consecrated head,"** indicating that **the verse speaks** only **of one who was a pure** nazirite **and** later **became impure,** and **that** only **he requires hair removal and the bringing of birds. And** the verse serves **to exempt the nazirite** who vowed while **in** a place of **a grave,** who was ritually impure from the outset. The Gemara concludes: **Learn from this** that a nazirite who was ritually impure from the outset does not have to shave; this answers the question of Rav Ashi.

מַאן תַּנָּא הָא, דְּתָנוּ רַבָּנַן: אֵין בֵּין טָמֵא שֶׁנָּזַר לְנָזִיר טָהוֹר שֶׁנִּטְמָא, אֶלָּא שֶׁטָּמֵא שֶׁנָּזַר שְׁבִיעִי שֶׁלּוֹ עוֹלֶה לוֹ מִן הַמִּנְיָן, וְנָזִיר טָהוֹר שֶׁנִּטְמָא אֵין שְׁבִיעִי שֶׁלּוֹ עוֹלֶה לוֹ מִן הַמִּנְיָן?

§ After resolving the question, the Gemara discusses additional *halakhot* involving a ritually impure person who took a vow of naziriteship. **Who is the** *tanna* who **taught this** *baraita* **that the Sages taught** in the previous discussion: **The difference between an impure** person **who took a vow of naziriteship**[N] **and a pure nazirite who became ritually impure is only** the following *halakha*: **That** with regard to **an impure** person **who took a vow of naziriteship, his seventh** day of purification **counts**[H] as part **of his tally** of the term of naziriteship. **But** with regard to **a pure nazirite who became impure, his seventh** day of purification **does not count** as part **of his tally.**

אֲמַר רַב חִסְדָּא: רַבִּי הִיא, דְּאָמַר רַבִּי: אֵין נְזִירוּת טָהֳרָה חָלָה אֶלָּא עַד שְׁמִינִי. דְּאִי תֵּימָא רַבִּי יוֹסֵי בְּרַבִּי יְהוּדָה הִיא – הָאָמַר נְזִירוּת דְּטָהֳרָה מִשְּׁבִיעִי הוּא דְּחָיְילָא.

Rav Ḥisda said: It is the opinion of **Rabbi** Yehuda HaNasi, **as Rabbi** Yehuda HaNasi **said: Naziriteship of purity takes effect only from the eighth day.** When a nazirite becomes impure during his term, he begins to count his term of observing naziriteship in purity only on the day following his purification. **For if you say it** follows the opinion of **Rabbi Yosei, son of Rabbi Yehuda, didn't he say** that the **naziriteship of purity takes effect from the seventh** day of his purification process?

HALAKHA

The verse is speaking of a ritually pure nazirite who became impure – **בְּטָהוֹר שֶׁנִּטְמָא הַכָּתוּב מְדַבֵּר**: If a nazirite became ritually impure through contact with a corpse, whether intentionally, unwittingly, or even against his will, all of his previous days of naziriteship are negated. He must perform the shaving of ritual impurity and bring the offerings of impurity before he starts counting his naziriteship anew (Rambam *Sefer Hafla'a*, *Hilkhot Nezirut* 6:3).

To exempt a nazirite who vowed while in the grave – **וְלִפְטוֹר אֶת הַנָּזִיר בַּקֶּבֶר**: If a person took a vow of naziriteship while in a cemetery and became ritually impure there, he does not shave or bring the offerings of impurity (Rambam *Sefer Hafla'a*, *Hilkhot Nezirut* 6:8).

His seventh day counts, etc. – **שְׁבִיעִי שֶׁלּוֹ עוֹלֶה לוֹ וכו׳**: If one vowed to be a nazirite while in a state of ritual impurity, once he has received the sprinkling of the ashes of the red heifer and has immersed himself on the seventh day, that day counts as the first day of his naziriteship term. However, a ritually pure nazirite who contracted impurity only begins counting anew from the eighth day of his purification process. The *halakha* follows Rabbi Yehuda HaNasi when he has a dispute with his colleagues (Rambam *Sefer Hafla'a*, *Hilkhot Nezirut* 6:7).

NOTES

The difference between an impure person who took a vow of naziriteship, etc. – **אֵין בֵּין טָמֵא שֶׁנָּזַר וכו׳**: Although there are other significant differences between them, since a nazirite who became impure must shave and bring offerings while an impure person who took a vow of naziriteship does not need to do so, by stating that the seventh day counts toward the tally for one who was ritually impure from the outset, the *tanna* indicates that he is also exempt from shaving and from bringing the offerings, as explained in the Gemara earlier (17b).

מַאי רַבִּי וּמַאי רַבִּי יוֹסֵי בְּרַבִּי יְהוּדָה. דְּתַנְיָא: ״וְקִדֵּשׁ אֶת רֹאשׁוֹ בַּיּוֹם הַהוּא״ – בְּיוֹם הֲבָאַת קָרְבְּנוֹתָיו, דִּבְרֵי רַבִּי. רַבִּי יוֹסֵי בְּרַבִּי יְהוּדָה אוֹמֵר: בְּיוֹם תִּגְלַחְתּוֹ.

The Gemara clarifies: **What is** the statement of **Rabbi** Yehuda HaNasi, **and what is** the statement of **Rabbi Yosei, son of Rabbi Yehuda,** that Rav Ḥisda referred to? **As it is taught** in a *baraita*: The verse states with regard to a ritually impure nazirite who underwent the purification rite: **"And he shall sanctify his head on that day"** (Numbers 6:11). This means that he renews the sanctity of his hair growth, i.e., begin observing his naziriteship in purity, **on the day of the bringing of his offerings,** the eighth day of his purification. This is **the statement of Rabbi** Yehuda HaNasi. **Rabbi Yosei, son of Rabbi Yehuda, says:** This means that he renews the sanctity of his hair growth **on the day of his shaving,** the seventh day of his purification.

וְהָא דִּתְנַן: נָזִיר שֶׁנִּטְמָא טוּמְאוֹת הַרְבֵּה אֵינוֹ מֵבִיא אֶלָּא קָרְבָּן אֶחָד, מַאן תְּנָא? אֲמַר רַב חִסְדָּא: רַבִּי יוֹסֵי בְּרַבִּי יְהוּדָה הִיא, דְּאָמַר: נְזִירוּת טָהֳרָה מִשְּׁבִיעִי חָיְילָא. וּמַשְׁכַּחַתְּ לָהּ כְּגוֹן שֶׁנִּטְמָא בַּשְּׁבִיעִי וְחָזַר וְנִטְמָא בַּשְּׁבִיעִי, (וּמַנִּי – רַבִּי יוֹסֵי בְּרַבִּי יְהוּדָה הִיא); כֵּיוָן דְּלֹא יָצָא שָׁעָה הָרְאוּיָה לְהָבִיא קָרְבָּן – אֵינוֹ חַיָּיב אֶלָּא קָרְבָּן אֶחָד.

§ The Gemara cites a related *halakha*: **And that which we learned** in a mishna (*Karetot* 9a): If **a nazirite became impure** by contracting **many** consecutive **impurities,**[H] **he brings only one** set of **offerings. Who taught** that? **Rav Ḥisda said: It is Rabbi Yosei, son of Rabbi Yehuda, who said** the **naziriteship of purity takes effect from the seventh** day of his purification process. **And you find this,** that he contracts ritual impurity several times consecutively, in a case **where he became ritually impure on the seventh** day **and,** after undergoing the purification process, **again became ritually impure on the seventh** day. **And whose** opinion is it? **It is** that of **Rabbi Yosei, son of Rabbi Yehuda. Since** the **appropriate time to bring an offering had not** yet **arrived,** as all agree that his offerings are only brought on the eighth day, if he became ritually impure a second time **he is obligated** to **bring only one** set of **offerings.**

דְּאִי תֵּימָא רַבִּי הִיא, אִי דְּנִטְמָא בַּשְּׁבִיעִי וְחָזַר וְנִטְמָא בַּשְּׁבִיעִי, (וְחָזַר וְנִטְמָא בַּשְּׁבִיעִי) – כּוּלְּהוּ טוּמְאָה אֲרִיכְתָּא הִיא. וְאִי דְּנִטְמָא בַּשְּׁמִינִי, וְחָזַר וְנִטְמָא בַּשְּׁמִינִי – הֲרֵי יָצְתָה שָׁעָה שֶׁרְאוּיָה לְהָבִיא קָרְבָּן.

For if you say it follows the opinion of **Rabbi** Yehuda HaNasi, how can this mishna be explained? **If** it deals with a nazirite **who became ritually impure on the seventh** day, **and,** after undergoing the purification process, **again became ritually impure on the seventh** day, **and,** after undergoing the purification process, **again became ritually impure on the seventh** day, Rabbi Yehuda HaNasi would hold that **all these** impurities **are** in fact one **long ritual impurity,** because he never reached the eighth day, which would renew his observance of naziriteship in ritual purity, so the mishna would not refer to this as a case of multiple impurities. **And if** the mishna is referring to a nazirite **who became ritually impure on the eighth** day **and,** after undergoing the purification process, **again became ritually impure on the eighth** day, the **appropriate time to bring an offering had** already **arrived,** and if he becomes ritually impure at that stage, it is not viewed as a continuation of the previous ritual impurity, and he is obligated to bring another set of offerings.

מַאי טַעֲמָא דְּרַבִּי? אָמַר קְרָא ״וְכִפֶּר עָלָיו מֵאֲשֶׁר חָטָא עַל הַנָּפֶשׁ״ וַהֲדַר ״וְקִדֵּשׁ אֶת רֹאשׁוֹ״. וְרַבִּי יוֹסֵי בְּרַבִּי יְהוּדָה: אִם כֵּן לֵימָא קְרָא ״וְקִדֵּשׁ אֶת רֹאשׁוֹ״.

The Gemara clarifies the dispute between Rabbi Yehuda HaNasi and Rabbi Yosei, son of Rabbi Yehuda: **What is the reason for Rabbi** Yehuda HaNasi's ruling that he begins counting only from the eighth day? The Gemara answers: **The verse states:** "And the priest shall prepare one for a sin-offering, and the other for a burnt-offering, **and make atonement for him, for he sinned by the soul"** (Numbers 6:11), **and** the same verse **again** states immediately afterward: **"And he shall sanctify his head."** This shows that the naziriteship of purity commences only after he has brought his offerings. **And Rabbi Yosei, son of Rabbi Yehuda,** says in response: **If so,** if the verse intended to teach us that his naziriteship starts only on the eighth day, **let the verse** merely **state: "And he shall sanctify his head,"** since that phrase addresses the bringing of his offerings, which is on the eighth.

HALAKHA

A nazirite became impure by contracting many impurities – נָזִיר שֶׁנִּטְמָא טוּמְאוֹת הַרְבֵּה: A nazirite who became ritually impure by contracting many impurities is obligated to bring only one set of offerings, even if he was warned each time he contracted impurity (Rambam *Sefer Hafla'a*, *Hilkhot Nezirut* 6:15).

״בַּיּוֹם הַהוּא״ לָמָּה לִי? אִם אֵינוֹ עִנְיָן לַשְּׁמִינִי, תְּנֵהוּ עִנְיָן לַשְּׁבִיעִי. וְרַבִּי נַמִּי, הָכְתִיב ״בַּיּוֹם הַהוּא״! אָמַר לָךְ רַבִּי: הַהוּא לְהָכִי הוּא דְּאָתָא, לוֹמַר לְךָ: אַף עַל פִּי שֶׁלֹּא הֵבִיא קָרְבְּנוֹתָיו.

Why do I need the extra phrase **"on that day"** (Numbers 6:11)? This teaches that **if it does not** apply **to the matter** of the **eighth**[N] day, since the verse is speaking of that day anyway, **apply it to the matter of** the **seventh** day, so that "on that day" means the day when he becomes ritually purified, even before he brings his offerings. The Gemara asks: **And** according to **Rabbi** Yehuda HaNasi **also, isn't it written "on that day"?** What *halakha* does he derive from these additional words? The Gemara answers: **Rabbi** Yehuda HaNasi could have **said to you: That** verse **comes for this** purpose, **to tell you** that **even though he did not** yet **bring his offerings**, he starts counting his naziriteship of purity from the eighth day. This is derived from the verse's emphasis of: "And he shall sanctify his head on that day," indicating that it depends on the day itself, rather than the bringing of the offerings.

וְרַב חִסְדָּא, מַאי דּוּחְקֵיהּ לְאוֹקְמֵיהּ כְּרַבִּי יוֹסֵי בְּרַבִּי יְהוּדָה? לוֹקְמָהּ כְּגוֹן דְּנִטְמָא דְּחַזְיָא בְּלֵיל שְׁמִינִי, וְרַבִּי הִיא!

The Gemara asks: **And what forced Rav Ḥisda to establish** this mishna **in accordance with** the opinion of **Rabbi Yosei, son of Rabbi Yehuda? Let him establish it** as referring to a case **where** one **became impure by seeing**, i.e., contracting, impurity **on the night** preceding **the eighth**[N] day each time. Even according to Rabbi Yehuda HaNasi, the naziriteship of purity begins at the start of, presumably the night preceding, the eighth day. Therefore, this case will be one of a nazirite contracting ritual impurity many times. Nevertheless, the nazirite will be obligated to bring only one set of offerings for all of them, because each case of ritual impurity occurred at night, when he is unable to bring the offerings for his previous ritual impurity, as offerings can be brought only during the day. **And** therefore **it is** in accordance with the opinion of **Rabbi** Yehuda HaNasi.

מִדְּלָא מוֹקִים לָהּ כְּרַבִּי, לֵימָא קָסָבַר לֵילְיָא לָאו מְחוּסַּר זְמָן הוּא?

The Gemara suggests: **Since he did not establish it in accordance with** the opinion of **Rabbi** Yehuda HaNasi in this way, **shall we say that** Rav Ḥisda **holds** that **night is not** considered **premature?** In other words, although he cannot in practice bring his offerings until the morning, as the Temple service was performed only in the daytime, the night is not considered a premature time, but rather it is viewed as part of the day in which it is appropriate to bring his offerings. Consequently, the *halakha* of one who becomes ritually impure on the night preceding the eighth day is the same as that of one who contracted ritual impurity on the eighth day itself, and they are both required to bring an additional set of offerings.

NOTES

If it does not apply to the matter of the eighth – אִם אֵינוֹ עִנְיָן לַשְּׁמִינִי: The exegetic method of: If it does not apply to the matter, does not propose to link two unrelated matters. Rather, it applies one verse to a similar matter whose *halakha* is not explicit in the Torah. In this case, some commentaries understand that the derivation that "on that day" refers to the seventh day is due to the fact that these words seem superfluous (*Tosafot*; Rabbeinu Peretz). Others explain that this should be understood as an application of the exegetic principle: One restrictive expression after another restrictive expression serves to amplify, as the verse says "on that day," which is a restriction, after already having stated that he must start counting from that day, another restriction. The double restriction therefore comes to include the seventh day (*Tosafot*; Rosh; Rabbeinu Peretz).

One became impure by seeing impurity on the night preceding the eighth – דְּנִטְמָא דְּחַזְיָא בְּלֵיל שְׁמִינִי: The word seeing is problematic in this context, as the only type of ritual impurity relevant to a nazirite is ritual impurity contracted by coming into contact with or close proximity to a corpse, and the word seeing, in the context of ritual impurity, is referring to one who experiences a ritually impure discharge. The early commentaries have offered various explanations for the usage of this term. The Commentary on *Nazir* states that the quotation is taken in its entirety from the parallel discussion in tractate *Karetot* (8a) that refers to the ritual impurity of a *zava*, where the term is entirely appropriate.

אָמַר רַב אַדָּא בַּר אַהֲבָה: הָא בְּהָא תַּלְיָא; אִי אָמְרַתְּ לֵילְיָא מְחוּסַּר זְמַן, אֵימַת מֶיחֱזֵי לְקׇרְבָּן – לְצַפְרָא, נְזִירוּת נַמִּי לָא חָיְילָא עַד צַפְרָא. וְאִי אָמְרַתְּ לֵילְיָא אֵינוֹ מְחוּסַּר זְמַן – נְזִירוּת טׇהֳרָה חָיְילָא מֵאוּרְתָּא.

Rav Adda bar Ahava said: This conclusion is incorrect, as even if Rav Ḥisda holds that the night is considered to be premature, he could not establish the mishna in accordance with the opinion of Rabbi Yehuda HaNasi, as the offerings and his new term of naziriteship **depend on each other: If you say night is** considered **premature, when is he fit to** bring his **offerings?** Only **in the morning.** Accordingly, **naziriteship also does not take effect until the morning. And if you say night is not** considered **premature,** and he is already obligated in his offerings at night, in that case **naziriteship of purity takes effect from the evening,** which means that the ritual impurity he suffered at night renders him obligated to bring an additional set of offerings. Consequently, the mishna does not follow the opinion of Rabbi Yehuda HaNasi, whether night is considered premature or not, and nothing can be inferred from here with regard to Rav Ḥisda's opinion in that matter.

גּוּפָא, נִטְמָא בַּשְּׁבִיעִי וְחָזַר וְנִטְמָא בַּשְּׁבִיעִי – אֵינוֹ מֵבִיא אֶלָּא קׇרְבָּן אֶחָד. נִטְמָא בַּשְּׁמִינִי וְחָזַר וְנִטְמָא בַּשְּׁמִינִי – מֵבִיא קׇרְבָּן עַל כׇּל אֶחָד וְאֶחָד. מַתְחִיל וּמוֹנֶה מִיָּד, דִּבְרֵי רַבִּי אֱלִיעֶזֶר,

§ The Gemara cites a *baraita* (*Tosefta* 4:8) concerning **the matter** of a nazirite who contracted ritual impurity many times **itself:**[N] If a nazirite became impure, and then **became impure on the seventh** day of his purification process, **and again became impure on the** following **seventh** day of his purification process, **he brings only one set of offerings. If he became impure on the eighth** day, **and again became impure on the** following **eighth** day, **he brings** a set **of offerings for each and every** time he became impure. Nevertheless, he **begins counting** his ritually pure naziriteship **immediately**[N] on the eighth day, even if he has not yet brought his offerings. This is **the statement of Rabbi Eliezer.**

וַחֲכָמִים אוֹמְרִים: קׇרְבָּן אֶחָד עַל הַכֹּל, עַד שֶׁיָּבִיא חַטָּאתוֹ. הֵבִיא חַטָּאתוֹ וְנִטְמָא, וְהֵבִיא חַטָּאתוֹ וְנִטְמָא – מֵבִיא קׇרְבָּן עַל כׇּל אֶחָד וְאֶחָד. הֵבִיא חַטָּאתוֹ וְלֹא הֵבִיא אֲשָׁמוֹ – מוֹנֶה.

And the Rabbis say: If he had not yet brought his offerings on the eighth day when he became impure, it is considered one long period of ritual impurity, and he brings **one** set of **offerings for all** the times he became impure, **until he has brought his sin-offering**[H] at the end of his period of ritual impurity. It is only then that he can begin counting his next term of naziriteship. Therefore, if he **brought his sin-offering and** then **became impure, and** again **brought his sin-offering and** then again **became impure, he brings** a set **of offerings for each and every one. If he brought his sin-offering and did not** yet **bring his guilt-offering,** he begins to **count**[H] his term of naziriteship in ritual purity.

רַבִּי יִשְׁמָעֵאל בְּנוֹ שֶׁל רַבִּי יוֹחָנָן בֶּן בְּרוֹקָה אוֹמֵר: כְּשֵׁם שֶׁחַטָּאתוֹ עִיכַּבְתּוֹ – כֵּן אֲשָׁמוֹ מְעַכְּבוֹ.

Rabbi Yishmael, son of Rabbi Yoḥanan ben Beroka, says: Just as not bringing **his sin-offering precludes him** from starting his naziriteship in ritual purity, **so too,** not bringing **his guilt-offering precludes him** from starting his naziriteship in ritual purity, and if he became impure again before he brought his guilt-offering, he only brings one set of offerings for all his impurities.

בִּשְׁלָמָא לְרַבִּי אֱלִיעֶזֶר, אָמַר קְרָא ״וְקִדֵּשׁ אֶת רֹאשׁוֹ בַּיּוֹם הַהוּא״ – אַף עַל פִּי שֶׁלֹּא הֵבִיא קׇרְבְּנוֹתָיו. וְרַבָּנַן: ״הַהוּא״ – אַף עַל פִּי שֶׁלֹּא הֵבִיא אֲשָׁמוֹ.

After having quoted the *baraita*, the Gemara proceeds to analyze the three opinions: **Granted, according to Rabbi Eliezer,** his reason is that **the verse states: "And he shall sanctify his head on that day"** (Numbers 6:11), which indicates: **Even though he has not brought his offerings,** the eighth day determines the start of his ritually pure naziriteship. **And the Rabbis** agree that the phrase "on **that** day" is extra, and it teaches that he begins counting from that day **even though he has not brought his guilt-offering,** but he does not begin counting until after bringing his sin-offering.

אֶלָּא רַבִּי יִשְׁמָעֵאל: ״הַהוּא״ לָמָּה לִי? אָמַר לָךְ: ״הַהוּא״ – אַף עַל פִּי שֶׁלֹּא הֵבִיא עוֹלָתוֹ. וְרַבָּנַן: עוֹלָה לָא בָּעֵי מִיעוּטָא, דּוֹרוֹן בְּעָלְמָא הוּא.

But according to **Rabbi Yishmael, why do I** need the phrase "on **that** day"? According to his opinion the issue depends on the offerings, not the day. The Gemara answers: Rabbi Yishmael could have **said to you:** The phrase "on **that** day" teaches that he can begin counting **even though he has not brought his burnt-offering,** as he agrees that not bringing the burnt-offering does not preclude him from counting his naziriteship. **And the Rabbis** respond to this: **A burnt-offering does not require a limitation** in the text to teach that its omission does not preclude the start of his naziriteship in ritual purity, since **it is merely a gift** and not part of his atonement process.

NOTES

The matter itself – גּוּפָא: The early commentaries are puzzled by the use of this term, which is usually used to indicate that the Gemara is returning to analyze in detail a *baraita* or mishna that was previously cited in passing. In this case the *baraita* now discussed was not quoted earlier at all. For this reason, some early commentaries (see Commentary on *Nazir* and *Tosafot*) emend the text and replace this term with: The Sages taught. However, the Rosh and others point out that the language of *Nazir* is peculiar in many respects, and it is possible that the standard text is correct, and the word here is used to mean that the Gemara is returning to analyze the topic mentioned earlier, even though this *baraita* was not quoted.

He begins counting immediately – מַתְחִיל וּמוֹנֶה מִיָּד: The Commentary on *Nazir* explains that this is referring to the eighth day, since Rabbi Eliezer holds that the time that his ritually pure naziriteship begins is dependent on the start of the day on which he can bring his offerings, rather than the bringing of the offerings in actuality. However, *Tosafot* and many other early commentaries question this explanation, since Rabbi Eliezer stated in the mishna (16b) that one is obligated to bring offerings for impurity only if he had observed more than one day of ritually pure naziriteship. If he became impure immediately after starting to count on the eighth day, he would not incur an obligation to bring an additional set of offerings. Consequently, they explain that this means that he begins counting his naziriteship on the seventh day, so that his seventh day and part of the eighth are considered his first days. Some early commentaries (see *Shita Mekubbetzet*) emend the text to read: This is the statement of Rabbi Yehuda HaNasi. This would fit with Rabbi Yehuda HaNasi's earlier opinion that he begins counting at the start of the eighth day.

HALAKHA

Until he has brought his sin-offering – עַד שֶׁיָּבִיא חַטָּאתוֹ: A nazirite who became ritually impure many times is obligated to bring only one set of offerings. This applies only if he became ritually impure the second time before he brought the sin-offering for his first instance of ritual impurity. If he contracts ritual impurity after he had already brought his sin-offering, even if he had yet to bring his guilt-offering and burnt-offering, he must bring a second set of offerings for his ritual impurity, in accordance with the opinion of the Rabbis (Rambam *Sefer Hafla'a*, *Hilkhot Nezirut* 6:15).

If he brought his sin-offering and did not yet bring his guilt-offering, he begins to count – הֵבִיא חַטָּאתוֹ וְלֹא הֵבִיא אֲשָׁמוֹ מוֹנֶה: A nazirite who became ritually impure begins counting his term of naziriteship afresh from the moment he brings his sin-offering. His guilt-offering and burnt-offering are not indispensable to the start of his new term (Rambam *Sefer Hafla'a*, *Hilkhot Nezirut* 6:12–13).

מַאי טַעֲמַיְיהוּ דְּרַבָּנַן? דְּתַנְיָא: ״וְהִזִּיר לַה׳ אֶת יְמֵי נִזְרוֹ וְהֵבִיא כֶּבֶשׂ בֶּן שְׁנָתוֹ לְאָשָׁם״ מַה תַּלְמוּד לוֹמַר? לְפִי שֶׁמָּצִינוּ שֶׁכׇּל אֲשָׁמוֹת שֶׁבַּתּוֹרָה שֶׁהֵן מְעַכְּבִין, יָכוֹל אַף זֶה מְעַכְּבוֹ,

The Gemara explains: **What is the reason of the Rabbis** for ruling that only refraining from bringing his sin-offering precludes the start of his new count of naziriteship? **As it is taught** in a *baraita*: The verse states with regard to a nazirite who became ritually impure: **"And he shall consecrate to the Lord the days of his naziriteship, and he shall bring a lamb in its first year for a guilt-offering"** (Numbers 6:12). **What does this teach?** Doesn't he wait to begin the days of his naziriteship until after he has brought all of his offerings? Rather, **since we have found that all guilt-offerings that are** mentioned **in the Torah**[H] **are indispensable** for atonement, and before he has brought his guilt-offering he is forbidden from partaking of any sacred offerings, one **might** have thought that not having brought **this** guilt-offering **also precludes him** from counting his ritually pure naziriteship,

HALAKHA

All guilt-offerings that are mentioned in the Torah – כׇּל אֲשָׁמוֹת שֶׁבַּתּוֹרָה: All guilt-offerings in the Torah are indispensable for one's atonement, apart from that of a nazirite, as ruled by the Rabbis (Rambam *Sefer Korbanot*, *Hilkhot Shegagot* 3:11).

Perek **III**
Daf **19** Amud **a**

תַּלְמוּד לוֹמַר ״וְהִזִּיר...וְהֵבִיא״ – אַף עַל פִּי שֶׁלֹּא הֵבִיא – הִזִּיר. רַבִּי יִשְׁמָעֵאל בְּנוֹ שֶׁל רַבִּי יוֹחָנָן בֶּן בְּרוֹקָה אוֹמֵר: ״וְהִזִּיר...וְהֵבִיא״. אֵימָתַי הִזִּיר – בִּזְמַן שֶׁהֵבִיא.

the verse therefore **states: "And he shall consecrate** to the Lord the days of his naziriteship, **and he shall bring**[N] a lamb in its first year for a guilt-offering," indicating: **Even though he has not brought** his guilt-offering **he has** nevertheless **consecrated** his days for the start of a new term of **naziriteship.** The opinion of **Rabbi Yishmael, son of Rabbi Yoḥanan ben Beroka,** is as follows: **The verse states: "And he shall consecrate** to the Lord the days of his naziriteship, **and he shall bring,"** which means: **When has he consecrated** his days of **naziriteship,** i.e., when does his new term of naziriteship begin? It begins **when he has** already **brought** his guilt-offering.

מַאן תְּנָא לְהָא, דְּתָנוּ רַבָּנַן: אִשָּׁה שֶׁנָּדְרָה בְּנָזִיר וְנִטְמֵאָה, וְאַחַר כָּךְ הֵפֵר לָהּ בַּעְלָהּ – מְבִיאָה חַטַּאת הָעוֹף, וְאֵינָהּ מְבִיאָה עוֹלַת הָעוֹף?

The Gemara poses a question: **Who is the** *tanna* **who taught**[N] **this that the Sages taught:** With regard to **a woman who vowed to be a nazirite**[H] **and became ritually impure,**[N] leading her to designate a bird for a sin-offering, a bird for a burnt-offering, and a sheep for a guilt-offering, **and afterward her husband nullified** her vow of naziriteship **for her, she brings the bird sin-offering and she does not bring the bird burnt-offering?**

HALAKHA

A woman who vowed to be a nazirite, etc. – אִשָּׁה שֶׁנָּדְרָה בְּנָזִיר וכו׳: If a woman who vowed to be a nazirite became ritually impure during her term of naziriteship, and afterward her husband heard of her vow and nullified it, she brings her offerings of impurity. The implication of this statement of the Rambam is that she brings all three of them: A sin-offering, a guilt-offering, and a burnt-offering. The *Mishne LaMelekh* explains that this is because the Gemara concludes (22a) that a husband severs the vow from that point onward, so her vow was in force at the time she became ritually impure (Rambam *Sefer Hafla'a*, *Hilkhot Nezirut* 9:11).

NOTES

The verse states: And he shall consecrate and he shall bring – תַּלְמוּד לוֹמַר וְהִזִּיר...וְהֵבִיא: Since the verse mentions the resumption of his naziriteship before it mentions the bringing of his offering, his naziriteship of purity resumes before he brings his guilt-offering (Commentary on *Nazir*).

Who taught, etc. – מַאן תְּנָא וכו׳: The Commentary on *Nazir* explains: Which *tanna* found it necessary to state that a woman whose vow of naziriteship was nullified before she violated it does not have to bring a burnt-offering? It is only Rabbi Yishmael, son of Rabbi Yoḥanan ben Beroka, who holds that the burnt-offering is an integral part of a nazirite's offerings, and he therefore holds that it is necessary for the *baraita* to teach that the burnt-offering need not be brought after the naziriteship has been nullified by the husband. Since the Rabbis hold that this burnt-offering is merely a gift, she certainly will not have to bring it in this case.

Conversely, *Tosafot* and others explain that according to Rabbi Yishmael, the very fact that the burnt-offering is an important part of the nazirite offerings is the reason why she cannot bring it, for she is no longer obligated in the offerings of a nazirite, so the bird is not consecrated. According to the Rabbis, by contrast, since the burnt-offering is a gift and is not integral to the naziriteship, there is no reason why she should not offer it even after her naziriteship has been nullified. The Commentary on *Nazir* also cites this opinion as an alternative explanation.

Who vowed to be a nazirite and became ritually impure – שֶׁנָּדְרָה בְּנָזִיר וְנִטְמֵאָה: *Tosafot*, the Rosh, and many other commentaries explain that this *baraita* is discussing the case of a woman who had already designated her offerings before her husband nullified her naziriteship, and the question is whether she is required to, or even can, bring them after his nullification. If she had not designated her offerings, she certainly is not obligated to bring any of them. The *Keren Ora* cites an opinion mentioned by *Tosafot* and the Ran in tractate *Nedarim* (83a) that she is obligated to bring a sin-offering even if she had not yet designated it.

HALAKHA

One who afflicts himself by abstaining from everything – **הַמְצַעֵר עַצְמוֹ מִכׇּל דָּבָר**: Although one must stay away from the pursuit of the pleasures of the world when they result from jealousy, lust, and honor, it is not proper for a person to abstain from the pleasures of the world altogether and to practice self-denial. The Sages therefore directed that one should deprive himself only of things forbidden by the Torah, and he should refrain from prohibiting permitted matters to himself by means of oaths and vows (Rambam *Sefer HaMadda*, *Hilkhot Deot* 3:1; see *Shulḥan Arukh*, *Oraḥ Ḥayyim* 571:1).

אָמַר רַב חִסְדָּא: רַבִּי יִשְׁמָעֵאל הִיא.

Rav Ḥisda said: It is the opinion of **Rabbi Yishmael,** son of Rabbi Yoḥanan ben Beroka. According to the opinion of the Rabbis, the burnt-offering is a gift, and she would bring it despite the fact that her naziriteship was nullified. According to Rabbi Yishmael, the burnt-offering is part of the atonement process, and since her naziriteship was nullified, there is no longer a need for atonement.

מַאי קָסָבַר? אִי קָסָבַר בַּעַל מִיעֲקַר עָקַר – חַטַּאת הָעוֹף נַמִי לָא לַיְיתִי, אִי קָסָבַר בַּעַל מֵיגַז גָּיֵיז – עוֹלַת הָעוֹף נַמִי לַיְיתִי! לְעוֹלָם קָסָבַר בַּעַל מִיעֲקַר עָקַר, וְרַבִּי יִשְׁמָעֵאל סָבַר לַהּ כְּרַבִּי אֶלְעָזָר הַקַּפָּר.

The Gemara asks: **What does he hold? If he holds** that the **husband uproots** a vow entirely when he nullifies it, and she is considered not to have vowed at all, **she should not bring the bird sin-offering,** as she was never a nazirite, and she does not need atonement. Conversely, **if he holds** that the **husband severs** the vow from that point onward, but it did take effect beforehand, **she should also bring the bird burnt-offering,** as she requires atonement for becoming impure while she was a nazirite. The Gemara answers: **Actually, he holds** that the **husband uproots** the vow, **and** why is she obliged to bring a sin-offering? **Rabbi Yishmael holds in accordance with** the opinion of **Rabbi Elazar HaKappar.**[N]

דְּתַנְיָא, רַבִּי אֶלְעָזָר הַקַּפָּר בְּרַבִּי אוֹמֵר: מָה תַּלְמוּד לוֹמַר ״וְכִפֶּר עָלָיו מֵאֲשֶׁר חָטָא עַל הַנָּפֶשׁ״? וְכִי בְּאֵיזוֹ נֶפֶשׁ חָטָא זֶה? אֶלָּא שֶׁצִּיעֵר עַצְמוֹ מִן הַיַּיִן. וְקַל וָחוֹמֶר: וּמָה זֶה שֶׁלֹּא צִיעֵר עַצְמוֹ אֶלָּא מִן הַיַּיִן – נִקְרָא חוֹטֵא, הַמְצַעֵר עַצְמוֹ מִכׇּל דָּבָר – עַל אַחַת כַּמָּה וְכַמָּה.

As it is taught in a *baraita*: **Rabbi Elazar HaKappar, the esteemed one, says: What** is the meaning when **the verse states** with regard to a nazirite: **"And make atonement for him, for he sinned by the soul"** (Numbers 6:11)? **And with which soul did this** person **sin**[N] by becoming a nazirite? **Rather,** in **afflicting himself** by abstaining **from wine,** he is considered to have sinned with his own soul, and he must bring a sin-offering for the naziriteship itself, for causing his body to suffer. **And** an *a fortiori* inference can be learned from this: **Just as this** person, in **afflicting himself** by abstaining **only from wine, is** nevertheless **called a sinner,** in the case of **one who afflicts himself** by abstaining **from everything,**[H] through fasting or other acts of mortification, **all the more so** is he described as a sinner. According to this opinion, Rabbi Yishmael holds that since the woman afflicted herself by abstaining from wine she must bring a sin-offering, even though, due to her husband's nullification, she did not actually become a nazirite.

NOTES

In accordance with the opinion of Rabbi Elazar HaKappar – **כְּרַבִּי אֶלְעָזָר הַקַּפָּר**: The sin-offering is brought to atone for her self-affliction of abstaining from wine during her period as a nazirite. *Tosafot* note that if she did not become ritually impure before her husband nullified her naziriteship, she does not have to bring this sin-offering. The early authorities write, based on *Nedarim* 83a, that this *halakha* refers only to the bird sin-offering, which is brought by a nazirite who becomes impure during the term of naziriteship. Since the bird sin-offering can be offered conditionally, there is no concern that she might be violating the prohibition of bringing an unconsecrated bird into the Temple courtyard. She can therefore bring it even after her vow has been nullified, as it will serve to atone for her sin of afflicting herself by abstaining from wine. If she completed her term of naziriteship, which would obligate her to bring a sheep sin-offering, and her husband nullified her naziriteship, she does not bring a sin-offering even according to the *tanna* of this *baraita*. Since an animal sin-offering cannot be brought conditionally, bringing this offering could potentially cause her to violate the prohibition of bringing an unconsecrated animal into the Temple courtyard.

And with which soul did this person sin – **וְכִי בְּאֵיזוֹ נֶפֶשׁ חָטָא זֶה**: While the straightforward meaning of the verse would seem to be referring to a nazirite who contracted impurity through contact with a corpse, the commentaries offer several explanations as to why Rabbi Elazar HaKappar interprets it in a different manner. Some explain that this verse cannot be referring to the fact that he became impure through contact with a corpse, as this had already been written earlier in the passage (Numbers 6:9). Others explain that contracting impurity through contact with a corpse does not necessarily involve a sin, since he must bring an offering even if he was made impure against his will, as the verse states: "Very suddenly" (Numbers 6:9). Therefore, Rabbi Eliezer HaKappar understands that the sin mentioned here has nothing to do with his ritual impurity, but is referring to something he did willingly (Rabbeinu Peretz).

וְהָא בְּנָזִיר טָמֵא כְּתִיב, וַאֲנַן אֲפִילּוּ נָזִיר טָהוֹר קָאָמְרִינַן. קָסָבַר רַבִּי אֶלְעָזָר הַקַּפָּר: נָזִיר טָהוֹר נַמִּי חוֹטֵא הוּא, וְהַיְינוּ טַעֲמָא דִּכְתִיב בְּנָזִיר טָמֵא – הוֹאִיל וְשָׁנָה בְּחֵטְא.

The Gemara raises a difficulty with Rabbi Elazar HaKappar's dictum: **But this** verse, labeling the nazirite a sinner, **is written with regard to an impure nazirite, and we are saying** that **even a pure nazirite** is a sinner. The Gemara answers: **Rabbi Elazar HaKappar holds** that **a pure nazirite is also a sinner. And this is the reason that** the statement that a nazirite is a sinner **is written** in reference **to an impure nazirite** rather than a pure one: **Since he repeated his sin,**[N] as his impurity causes him to start his naziriteship again, he thereby deprives himself for a longer period. He should have taken extra care to prevent this from happening.

״יָצָא וְנִכְנַס עוֹלִין לוֹ מִן הַמִּנְיָן״. קָתָנֵי ״עוֹלִין לוֹ מִן הַמִּנְיָן״. מִשּׁוּם דְּיָצָא חָל עֲלֵיהּ נְזִירוּת? אָמַר שְׁמוּאֵל: כְּגוֹן שֶׁיָּצָא וְהִזָּה, וְשָׁנָה וְטָבַל.

§ The mishna taught that if one took a vow of naziriteship while in a cemetery, **left** the cemetery, **and** then **entered** it again, the days he spent outside **do count** as part **of his tally** of his term of naziriteship, and he is obligated to bring the offerings of ritual impurity upon reentering the cemetery. The mishna **teaches: They do count** as part **of his tally.** The Gemara questions the meaning of this linkage: **Does naziriteship take effect for him because he** merely **left** the ritually impure place? He is still ritually impure and he cannot begin counting his term of naziriteship until after he has undergone the purification process. **Shmuel said:** The mishna is referring to a case **where he left and** received the **sprinkling**[H] of the ashes of the red heifer on the third day, **and he again** received the sprinkling on the seventh day **and immersed,** after which he entered the cemetery a second time. Since he is now ritually pure, his naziriteship takes effect.

אֶלָּא נִכְנַס הוּא דְּעוֹלִין לוֹ מִן הַמִּנְיָן, לֹא נִכְנַס אֵין עוֹלִין לוֹ מִן הַמִּנְיָן?! לָא מִיבַּעְיָא קָאָמַר; לָא מִיבַּעְיָא יָצָא, אֶלָּא אֲפִילּוּ נִכְנַס – עוֹלִין לוֹ מִן הַמִּנְיָן.

The Gemara poses another question: According to the precise reading of the mishna, his term of naziriteship starts only if he reentered the cemetery; **however,** is it only if he returned and **entered** the cemetery that those days **count** as part **of his tally,** but if he did **not enter,** and remained outside the cemetery, those days **do not count** as part **of his tally?** Why should the start of the naziriteship be dependent upon his reentering the cemetery? The Gemara answers: The *tanna* **is speaking** utilizing the style of: **It is not necessary,** as follows: **It is not necessary** to state this *halakha*, that those days count as part of his tally, in the case of one who **left** the cemetery and began his naziriteship, **but even if he entered** the cemetery again immediately after his purification, those days **count** as part **of his tally,** and he will be obligated to bring the offerings of ritual impurity upon his reentry.

אֲמַרוּ לֵיהּ רַב כָּהֲנָא וְרַב אַסִּי לְרַב: מַאי טַעֲמָא לָא מְפָרַשְׁתְּ לָן כְּהָלֵין מִילֵּי? אֲמַר לְהוֹן: אָמֵינָא דִּלְמָא לָא צְרִיכִיתוּ.

Rav Kahana and Rav Asi said to Rav: What is the reason you did not explain it **to us with these words** of Shmuel, as explained above? **He said to them: I said** to myself that **perhaps you do not require that** explanation, as I thought it was apparent that this is the proper explanation of the mishna.

״רַבִּי אֱלִיעֶזֶר אוֹמֵר לֹא בּוֹ בַּיּוֹם שֶׁנֶּאֱמַר: וְהַיָּמִים הָרִאשׁוֹנִים יִפְּלוּ, עַד שֶׁיִּהְיוּ יָמִים רִאשׁוֹנִים״. אָמַר עוּלָּא: לֹא אָמַר רַבִּי אֱלִיעֶזֶר אֶלָּא בְּטָמֵא שֶׁנָּזַר, אֲבָל בְּנָזִיר טָהוֹר שֶׁנִּטְמָא, אֲפִילּוּ יוֹם אֶחָד – סוֹתֵר.

§ The mishna also taught an additional *halakha*: **Rabbi Eliezer says:** This *halakha* does **not** apply to one who entered the cemetery **on that very day** that he left it, **as it is stated** with regard to the *halakhot* of an impure nazirite: **"But the first days shall be void"** (Numbers 6:12), which indicates that he does not bring the offerings **unless he had** his **"first days"** of ritual purity, during which he observed his naziriteship. **Ulla said: Rabbi Eliezer said** this *halakha*, that one day of naziriteship in purity is not sufficient to obligate him to bring offerings if he becomes impure, **only with regard to an impure** person **who took a vow of naziriteship, but a pure nazirite who became impure, even** if he was only pure for **one day** of naziriteship, **it negates** that day of his tally and he must bring the offerings of a impure nazirite.

NOTES

Since he repeated his sin – **הוֹאִיל וְשָׁנָה בְּחֵטְא**: He should have been careful to avoid becoming ritually impure, and by failing to do so he commits another sin (Commentary on *Nazir*). *Tosafot* and others state that his becoming ritually impure results in him extending his term of naziriteship, adding to the time that he is abstaining from wine and consequently repeating his earlier sin.

HALAKHA

A case where he left and received the sprinkling, etc. – **כְּגוֹן שֶׁיָּצָא וְהִזָּה וכו׳**: One who took a vow of naziriteship while in a cemetery, left, and after a while reentered, does not count the days spent outside of the cemetery in his tally. However, if he left, received the sprinkling of the ashes of the red heifer, immersed himself, began counting the days of his naziriteship, and then reentered the cemetery, those days do count as part of his tally (Rambam *Sefer Hafla'a*, *Hilkhot Nezirut* 6:10).

אֲמַר רָבָא: מַאי טַעְמָא דְּרַבִּי אֱלִיעֶזֶר – אָמַר קְרָא ״כִּי טָמֵא נִזְרוֹ״ – מִשּׁוּם דִּבְטוּמְאָה נָזַר.

Rava said: What is the reason for the opinion **of Rabbi Eliezer,** according to Ulla's explanation? **The verse states:** "But the first days shall be void **because his consecration was ritually impure"** (Numbers 6:12), which he explains as follows: Why are his first days rendered void? They are void **because he took a vow of naziriteship,** consecrating himself, **when** he was **in** a state of **ritual impurity.**

אֵיתִיבֵיהּ אַבַּיֵּי: ״הֲרֵינִי נָזִיר מֵאָה יוֹם״ וְנִטְמָא בִּתְחִלַּת מֵאָה, יָכוֹל יְהֵא סוֹתֵר? תַּלְמוּד לוֹמַר ״וְהַיָּמִים הָרִאשׁוֹנִים יִפְּלוּ״ – עַד שֶׁיְּהוּ לוֹ יָמִים רִאשׁוֹנִים, וְזֶה אֵין לוֹ רִאשׁוֹנִים.

Abaye raised an objection to Rava from a *baraita* that is not in accordance with the opinion of Ulla: One who said: **I am hereby a nazirite**[N] for **one hundred days, and he became ritually impure** immediately, **at the beginning** of the **one hundred** days, one **might** have thought **it should negate** the time he spent as a nazirite. **The verse** therefore **states: "But the first days shall be void"** (Numbers 6:12), which indicates that this *halakha* does not apply **until he will have "first days"** as a nazirite, **and** in **this** case the nazirite **does not have** his **first** days[H] completed, as he became ritually impure right away.

נִטְמָא בְּסוֹף מֵאָה, יָכוֹל יְהֵא סוֹתֵר? תַּלְמוּד לוֹמַר ״וְהַיָּמִים הָרִאשׁוֹנִים יִפְּלוּ״ – מִכְּלָל דְּאִיכָּא אַחֲרוֹנִים, וְזֶה אֵין לוֹ אַחֲרוֹנִים. נִטְמָא בְּיוֹם מֵאָה חָסֵר אַחַת, יָכוֹל לֹא יְהֵא סוֹתֵר – תַּלְמוּד לוֹמַר ״וְהַיָּמִים הָרִאשׁוֹנִים יִפְּלוּ״ – מִכְּלָל דְּאִיכָּא אַחֲרוֹנִים, וְזֶה יֵשׁ לוֹ רִאשׁוֹנִים וְאַחֲרוֹנִים.

The *baraita* continues: If one **became ritually impure at the end of one hundred** days,[N] that is, on the hundredth day, one **might** have thought **it should negate** the days he had counted. **The verse** therefore **states: "But the first days shall be void,"** indicating **by inference that there are** other days that can be called the **last** ones, **while this** nazirite **does not have last** days, as he has already completed the tally of his naziriteship. If **he became impure on the one hundredth day less one,** one **might** have thought **it should not negate** the days he had counted. **Therefore, the verse states: "But the first days shall be void,"** indicating **by inference that there are last** ones, **and this** nazirite **has first** ones **and last** ones.

וְהָא בְּטָמֵא שֶׁנָּזַר לָא מָצֵית אָמְרַתְּ, מִדְּקָתָנֵי ״הֲרֵינִי נָזִיר מֵאָה״ וְנִטְמָא בִּתְחִלַּת מֵאָה, וְקָתָנֵי: עַד שֶׁיְּהוּ לוֹ יָמִים רִאשׁוֹנִים! תְּיוּבְתָּא.

Abaye now concludes his objection to Rava: **But** with regard to **this** *halakha* of the *baraita*, **you cannot say** it is referring **to an impure** person **who took a vow of naziriteship from** the fact **that it teaches: I am hereby a nazirite** for **one hundred** days, **and he became impure** immediately **at the beginning** of the **one hundred,** indicating that it is discussing one who became impure after his term had already started. **And it** further **teaches: Until he will have "first days,"** which proves that Rabbi Eliezer states his *halakha* even with regard to a pure nazirite who later became impure. This is **a conclusive refutation** of Ulla, and his opinion is rejected.

אֲמַר לֵיהּ רַב פַּפָּא לְאַבַּיֵּי: הָלֵין יָמִים דְּקָאָמְרִינַן, דְּנָפַק חַד וּמַתְחִילִין תְּרֵין, אוֹ דִּלְמָא דְּנָפְקִין תְּרֵין וּמַתְחִילִין תְּלָתָא? לָא הֲוָה בִּידֵיהּ, אֲתָא שַׁיְילֵיהּ לְרָבָא. אֲמַר לֵיהּ: ״יִפְּלוּ״ כְּתִיב.

Rav Pappa said to Abaye: Those first **days that we said** he must observe in ritual purity according to Rabbi Eliezer, does it mean **that one day has finished and a second has started,** so that if he became impure on the second day it negates his tally, **or perhaps** it means **that two days have finished, and a third has started,** which would mean it negates his tally only if he became impure after the beginning of the third day? An answer **was not available to him,** so Rav Pappa **went to ask Rava, who said to him:** It **is written:** "But the former days **shall be void** [*yippelu*]" (Numbers 6:12)[N] in the plural, which means at least two days need to have passed.

וְאִיצְטְרִיךְ לְמִיכְתַּב ״יָמִים״ וְאִיצְטְרִיךְ לְמִיכְתַּב ״יִפְּלוּ״; דְּאִי כְּתַב רַחֲמָנָא ״יָמִים״ וְלָא כְּתַב ״יִפְּלוּ״. הֲוָה אָמֵינָא: עַד דְּנָפְקִין תְּרֵין וְעָיְילִין תְּלָתָא, כְּתַב רַחֲמָנָא ״יִפְּלוּ״. וְאִי כְּתַב ״יִפְּלוּ״ וְלֹא כְּתַב ״יָמִים״ הֲוָה אָמֵינָא: אֲפִילּוּ חַד, כְּתַב רַחֲמָנָא ״יָמִים״.

The Gemara comments: **And it was necessary** for the verse **to write "days" and it was also necessary** for it **to write "shall be void"** in the plural. **For if the Merciful One wrote** in the Torah only **"days" and had not** also **written "shall be void"**[N] in the plural, **I would say that** the *halakha* applies only **if two days have finished and a third has started. The Merciful One** therefore **wrote** in the Torah the plural form of **"shall be void." And if** the Merciful One **wrote** in the Torah **"shall be void" and had not** also **written "days," I would say even one**[N] day, that is, the *halakha* applies even if he became ritually impure on the first day. **The Merciful One** therefore **wrote** in the Torah **"days,"** indicating that he must have observed at least part of the second day.

NOTES

I am hereby a nazirite, etc. – **הֲרֵינִי נָזִיר וכו׳:** The commentaries note that even though this *baraita* is not explicitly attributed to Rabbi Eliezer, there is no other *tanna* who holds that his tally is not negated if he became impure on the first day (Rabbeinu Peretz; Rabbeinu Azriel). However, the *Kesef Mishne* writes that the Rabbis agree with the exposition of the words "and the first days," but they hold that it refers only to a pure nazirite who became impure, and not to a impure person who took a vow of naziriteship. In any case, the middle *halakha* of the *baraita*, concerning one who became impure on the hundredth day, certainly is true only according to Rabbi Eliezer, as the Rabbis hold that in this case, the entire tally is negated, as stated in an earlier mishna (16a).

If one became ritually impure at the end of one hundred days, etc. – **נִטְמָא בְּסוֹף מֵאָה וכו׳:** *Tosafot* write that this does not mean that no days are negated if he became ritually impure on the one hundredth day, but rather he is required to observe only an additional thirty days, and not a full hundred, as stated in the mishna on 16a.

It is written: Shall be void – **יִפְּלוּ כְּתִיב:** The Commentary on *Nazir* explains that the plural form of "shall be void" indicates at least two days; that is, he must have counted at least two days of his naziriteship. This explanation is in accordance with the standard text of the Gemara, which reads: I would say that the *halakha* applies only if two days have finished and a third has started. Conversely, the Rosh and others follow Rabbeinu Tam's opinion that "shall be void" indicates any number of days, even less than one. This explanation is in accordance with the variant text of the Gemara, which reads: I would say that the *halakha* applies if one day has finished and a second has started, as this can occur in less than a day, e.g., if he began his naziriteship in the afternoon.

And had not also written shall be void – **וְלָא כְּתַב יִפְּלוּ:** That is, the verse had instead written "and the first days shall be left" (Commentary on *Nazir*) or "apart from the first days" (*Tosafot*).

I would say even one – **הֲוָה אָמֵינָא אֲפִילּוּ חַד:** If this were the meaning, then the usage of the plural form of "shall be void" would be understood as a general term for all of the days he had counted, whether many, few, or even one. Alternatively, it might refer to nazirites in general, meaning that whenever this occurs to any nazirite the days they have observed are negated.

HALAKHA

And this nazirite does not have first days – **וְזֶה אֵין לוֹ רִאשׁוֹנִים:** If one became ritually impure on the first or second day of his term of naziriteship, although the Rambam rules that he must bring the offerings of impurity, it does not negate his previous days as a nazirite, and he continues to count from where he left off after he has brought his offerings. It is only if he contracted ritual impurity from the third day onward that it negates all the previous days, as the Rambam's text is like that of the Commentary on *Nazir* (*Kesef Mishne*). The *halakha* follows Rabbi Eliezer, as his opinion is discussed by the *amora'im* (Rambam *Sefer Hafla'a*, *Hilkhot Nezirut* 6:6).

מתני׳ מִי שֶׁנָּזַר נְזִירוּת הַרְבֵּה, וְהִשְׁלִים אֶת נְזִירוּתוֹ, וְאַחַר כָּךְ בָּא לָאָרֶץ, בֵּית שַׁמַּאי אוֹמְרִים: נָזִיר שְׁלֹשִׁים יוֹם, וּבֵית הִילֵּל אוֹמְרִים: נָזִיר בַּתְּחִלָּה.

MISHNA One who vowed **many** days **of naziriteship** while outside Eretz Yisrael, **and completed his naziriteship, and afterward came to Eretz** Yisrael,[H] in order to bring the offerings at the end of his naziriteship, **Beit Shammai say:** He must be **a nazirite** for **thirty days,** so that he has observed a term of naziriteship in ritual purity in Eretz Yisrael, **and Beit Hillel say:** He is **a nazirite from the beginning,** that is, he must observe his entire naziriteship again.

מַעֲשֶׂה בְּהֵילֶנֵי הַמַּלְכָּה שֶׁהָלַךְ בְּנָהּ לַמִּלְחָמָה, וְאָמְרָה: אִם יָבוֹא בְּנִי מִן הַמִּלְחָמָה בְּשָׁלוֹם – אֱהֵא נְזִירָה שֶׁבַע שָׁנִים. וּבָא בְּנָהּ מִן הַמִּלְחָמָה, וְהָיְתָה נְזִירָה שֶׁבַע שָׁנִים. וּבְסוֹף שֶׁבַע שָׁנִים עָלְתָה לָאָרֶץ, וְהוֹרוּהָ בֵּית הִלֵּל שֶׁתְּהֵא נְזִירָה עוֹד שֶׁבַע שָׁנִים אֲחֵרוֹת. וּבְסוֹף שֶׁבַע שָׁנִים נִטְמֵאת, וְנִמְצֵאת נְזִירָה עֶשְׂרִים וְאַחַת שָׁנָה. אָמַר רַבִּי יְהוּדָה: לֹא הָיְתָה נְזִירָה אֶלָּא אַרְבַּע עֶשְׂרֵה שָׁנָה.

The mishna cites a related story: **An incident** occurred **with regard to Queen Helene,**[P] **whose son had gone to war, and she said: If my son will return from war safely, I will be a nazirite** for **seven years. And her son returned** safely **from the war, and she was a nazirite** for **seven years. And at the end of seven years, she ascended to Eretz** Yisrael, **and Beit Hillel instructed her,** in accordance with their opinion, **that she should be a nazirite for an additional seven years. And at the end of** those **seven years she became ritually impure,** and was therefore required to observe yet another seven years of naziriteship, as ritual impurity negates the tally of a nazirite. **And she was found to be a nazirite** for **twenty-one years. Rabbi Yehuda said: She was a nazirite** for **only fourteen years** and not twenty-one.

גמ׳ קָתָנֵי רֵישָׁא: בֵּית שַׁמַּאי אוֹמְרִים נָזִיר שְׁלֹשִׁים יוֹם, וּבֵית הִלֵּל אוֹמְרִים: נָזִיר בַּתְּחִלָּה, לֵימָא בְּהָא קָמִיפַּלְגִי: דְּבֵית שַׁמַּאי סָבְרִי: אֶרֶץ הָעַמִּים מִשּׁוּם גּוּשָׁהּ גָּזְרוּ עָלֶיהָ,

GEMARA The **first clause** of the mishna **teaches** that **Beit Shammai say:** He must be a **nazirite** for **thirty days, and Beit Hillel say:** He is **a nazirite from the beginning.** The Gemara suggests a possible explanation of their dispute: **Let us say that they disagree about this,** that **Beit Shammai hold** that when the Sages declared that the **land of the nations**[N] outside of Eretz Yisrael is impure, **they decreed** so **with regard to its earth.**[N] In other words, they decreed that only the earth of the land of the nations is impure, but its airspace remains pure. If so, it is not a severe level of ritual impurity, and one who observed a vow of naziriteship outside of Eretz Yisrael is not considered to be impure to the extent that he would be required to start his naziriteship afresh once entering Eretz Yisrael,

PERSONALITIES

Queen Helene – הֵילֶנֵי הַמַּלְכָּה: Helene, or in Greek Ἑλένη, *Helenē*, was queen of Adiabene, a small country subjugated to the Parthian Empire. Located on the Tigris River, it was situated in what is today northern Syria. More than a generation prior to the destruction of the Second Temple, Helene and her two sons, Munbaz and Izats, converted to Judaism, apparently along with much of the local nobility.

Queen Helene and her two sons maintained strong ties to the Jewish community in Eretz Yisrael. They would send substantial gifts to the Temple and enormous sums of money to assist the poor in years of drought. It is plausible that members of the royal family of Adiabene are buried in the magnificent Graves of the Kings in Jerusalem.

As mentioned in the Talmud, Queen Helene was a righteous proselyte who accepted upon herself all elements of *halakha* as taught to her by the Sages.

Images of the remains of what is believed to be Helene's palace in Jerusalem

HALAKHA

And afterward came to Eretz Yisrael – וְאַחַר כָּךְ בָּא לָאָרֶץ: Naziriteship can be observed only in Eretz Yisrael, and one who vowed to be a nazirite outside Eretz Yisrael is obligated to ascend to Eretz Yisrael and observe his naziriteship there for the term he had specified, in accordance with the opinion of Beit Hillel. However, the vow of naziriteship itself takes effect outside Eretz Yisrael, and he is prohibited to drink wine, become ritually impure through contact with a corpse, or to shave, despite the fact that these days do not count as part of his term of naziriteship. Consequently, one who takes a vow of naziriteship nowadays must ascend to Eretz Yisrael and observe naziriteship there until his death, or until the Temple is rebuilt and he can bring his offerings. The Ra'avad claims that since all are considered ritually impure from the dead at this time, even those living in Eretz Yisrael, observing one's naziriteship in Eretz Yisrael has no advantage (Rambam Sefer *Hafla'a*, *Hilkhot Nezirut* 2:21–22).

NOTES

The land of the nations – אֶרֶץ הָעַמִּים: Although the ritual impurity of land outside of Eretz Yisrael is not by Torah law, it is a very ancient rabbinic decree. It is mentioned already in the Bible, with regard to those exiled from the Eretz Yisrael: "You shall die in an unclean land" (Amos 7:17). The Sages, however, increased the severity of this ritual impurity. As for the reason for the decree, the early authorities discuss whether it is because they were concerned about unknown burial sites of Jews, or whether it was a decree in its own right, in order to emphasize the ritual purity of Eretz Yisrael.

With regard to its earth – מִשּׁוּם גּוּשָׁהּ: If it is only its actual earth that imparts impurity through contact and the airspace is pure, then it does not have the same severity of impurity as a corpse, which renders ritually impure anything found inside a structure with it. Therefore, the Sages were not as stringent in this case as with one who takes a vow of naziriteship while in a cemetery. This is the standard version of the text, and has been accepted by several early authorities.

However, there is a variant text that reads that Beit Shammai hold that the decree was with regard to the airspace. This means that anyone who passes through the land of the nations, even if he does not come into contact with its earth, such as one who travels in a chest, a box, or a cabinet, is nevertheless ritually impure. According to this reading, this impurity is not due to the presence of graves, as graves do not impart impurity in this way; rather, it is a special form of impurity. Therefore, the *halakha* of a nazirite outside of Eretz Yisrael is not like that of one who takes a vow of naziriteship while in a cemetery, whose days in the cemetery do not count as part of his tally (Rosh; see Rabbeinu Azriel and *Tosafot* on 20a). The text of the Gemara on the following page would also be modified according to this reading.

וּבֵית הִלֵּל סָבְרִי: מִשּׁוּם אֲוִירָא גָּזְרוּ עֲלֶיהָ? לָא, דְּכוּלֵּי עָלְמָא מִשּׁוּם גּוּשָׁהּ גָּזְרוּ עֲלֶיהָ, וּבֵית שַׁמַּאי סָבְרִי: בִּסְתָם נְזִירוּת קָנֵיסְנָא, וּבֵית הִלֵּל סָבְרִי: כִּי קָנֵיסְנָא – בִּתְחִילַּת נְזִירוּת.

and Beit Hillel hold: They decreed with regard to its airspace, and it is a severe level of ritual impurity, so he must start his naziriteship from the beginning once he arrives in Eretz Yisrael. The Gemara rejects this possibility: **No,** it may be **that everyone** agrees that **they decreed** only **with regard to its earth,**[H] **and** they disagree merely over the details of the penalty. **Beit Shammai hold** that **we penalize** him **with an unspecified term of naziriteship,** which is thirty days, **and Beit Hillel hold** that **when we penalize,** we require him to return **to the beginning of** his term of **naziriteship,** and he must observe the entire term of naziriteship afresh.

״מַעֲשֶׂה בְּהֵילֶנֵי הַמַּלְכָּה״ וכו׳. אִיבַּעְיָא לְהוּ בְּשֶׁנִּטְמֵאת וְאַלִּיבָּא דְּבֵית שַׁמַּאי, אוֹ דִּלְמָא בְּשֶׁלֹּא נִטְמֵאת וְאַלִּיבָּא דְּבֵית הִלֵּל?

§ The mishna taught: **An incident** occurred **with regard to Queen Helene. A dilemma was raised before them:** What is the meaning of Rabbi Yehuda's statement? Does he hold that the case was one **where she became impure** in Eretz Yisrael, but after thirty days, and not after seven years, **and** Rabbi Yehuda spoke **in accordance with** the opinion of **Beit Shammai,** who hold that she was required to observe only a further thirty days upon her arrival in Eretz Yisrael, and due to her becoming impure she had to observe again her original term of naziriteship, for a total of fourteen years? **Or perhaps** the case is one **where she did not become impure** at the end of the seven years in Eretz Yisrael, **and** he ruled **in accordance with** the opinion of **Beit Hillel** that she had to observe an additional seven years upon her entry to Eretz Yisrael.

תָּא שְׁמַע: עָלְתָה לָאָרֶץ וְהוֹרוּהָ בֵּית הִלֵּל שֶׁתְּהֵא נְזִירָה עוֹד שֶׁבַע שָׁנִים אֲחֵרוֹת וכו׳. וְאִי סָלְקָא דַּעְתָּךְ בְּשֶׁנִּטְמֵאת וְאַלִּיבָּא דְּבֵית שַׁמַּאי, אִי הָכִי, רַבִּי יְהוּדָה אוֹמֵר לֹא הָיְתָה נְזִירָה אֶלָּא אַרְבַּע עֶשְׂרֵה שָׁנָה? אַרְבַּע עֶשְׂרֵה שָׁנָה וּשְׁלֹשִׁים יוֹם מִיבָּעֵי לֵיהּ!

The Gemara suggests: **Come** and **hear** a proof from the mishna: **She ascended to Eretz** Yisrael, **and Beit Hillel instructed her that she should be a nazirite for an additional seven years, etc. And if it enters your mind** that Rabbi Yehuda says that the case is one **where she became ritually impure** after observing thirty days of naziriteship following her arrival to Eretz Yisrael, **and** he spoke **in accordance with** the opinion **of Beit Shammai, if so,** why does **Rabbi Yehuda say she was a nazirite** for **only fourteen years? He should have** said **fourteen years and thirty days,** as even Beit Shammai obligate her to observe a thirty-day period of naziriteship in Eretz Yisrael. It must be that Rabbi Yehuda holds that she observed seven additional years, in accordance with the opinion of Beit Hillel, and says that she did not become ritually impure.

תַּנְיָא נַמִי הָכִי, רַבִּי יְהוּדָה אוֹמֵר מִשּׁוּם רַבִּי אֱלִיעֶזֶר: דְּאָמַר קְרָא ״זֹאת תּוֹרַת הַנָּזִיר״ – הַתּוֹרָה אָמְרָה: כִּי נִטְמָא בְּיוֹם מְלֹאת – תֵּן לוֹ תּוֹרַת נָזִיר.

The Gemara adds: **This is also taught** in a *baraita*, that Rabbi Yehuda's opinion cannot be established in accordance with Beit Shammai: **Rabbi Yehuda says in the name of Rabbi Eliezer that the verse states: "This is the law of the nazirite** when the days of his consecration are fulfilled" (Numbers 6:13). **The Torah states: When he becomes impure on the day of the completion** of his naziriteship, even if it was at the end of a lengthy term, **give him the law of** an unspecified **nazirite,** and he must observe a thirty-day term. Therefore, if she became impure at the end of those thirty days that Beit Shammai obligates her to observe, she should have been required to observe naziriteship for only thirty additional days, rather than a full seven years. Rather, Rabbi Yehuda certainly accepts the opinion of Beit Hillel, and claims that she did not become ritually impure.

HALAKHA

They decreed with regard to its earth, etc. – מִשּׁוּם גּוּשָׁהּ גָּזְרוּ וכו׳: The Sages initially decreed that the status of ritual impurity applied only to the earth of the land of the nations, which meant that only one who walked there or touched or carried its earth became ritually impure. Later, they also decreed that its airspace would be ritually impure, so that even one who did not touch or carry the dirt, but merely entered his head and the majority of his body into the airspace of the land of nations was considered to be ritually impure (Rambam *Sefer Tahara, Hilkhot Tumat Met* 11:1).

מתני׳ מִי שֶׁהָיוּ שְׁתֵּי כִיתֵּי עֵדִים מְעִידוֹת אוֹתוֹ, אֵלּוּ מְעִידִים שֶׁנָּזַר שְׁתַּיִם וְאֵלּוּ מְעִידִים שֶׁנָּזַר חָמֵשׁ, בֵּית שַׁמַּאי אוֹמְרִים: נֶחְלְקָה הָעֵדוּת, וְאֵין כָּאן נְזִירוּת. וּבֵית הִלֵּל אוֹמְרִים: יֵשׁ בִּכְלַל חָמֵשׁ שְׁתַּיִם, שֶׁיְּהֵא נָזִיר שְׁתַּיִם.

MISHNA In a case of one who had two sets of **witnesses testifying about him** that he had taken a vow of naziriteship for a certain period, and **these** witnesses **testify that he took a vow of naziriteship** for **two** terms, **and these** witnesses **testify that he took a vow of naziriteship** for **five** terms. **Beit Shammai say: The testimony is divided,** i.e., the testimonies contradict each other, and since the testimonies are in conflict they are both rejected entirely **and there is no naziriteship here** at all. **And Beit Hillel say:** The testimonies are not completely in conflict with each other, as **two** terms **are included in five**[H] terms, and the unanimous testimony, **that he is a nazirite** for **two** terms, is accepted.

גמ׳ מַתְנִיתִין דְּלָא כִּי הַאי תַּנָּא. דְּתַנְיָא, רַבִּי יִשְׁמָעֵאל בְּנוֹ שֶׁל רַבִּי יוֹחָנָן בֶּן בְּרוֹקָא אוֹמֵר: לֹא נֶחְלְקוּ בֵּית שַׁמַּאי וּבֵית הִלֵּל עַל שְׁתֵּי כִיתֵּי עֵדִים, אַחַת אוֹמֶרֶת שְׁתַּיִם וְאַחַת אוֹמֶרֶת חָמֵשׁ, שֶׁיֵּשׁ בִּכְלַל חָמֵשׁ שְׁתַּיִם. עַל מָה נֶחְלְקוּ – עַל כַּת אַחַת, אֶחָד אוֹמֵר שְׁתַּיִם וְאֶחָד אוֹמֵר חָמֵשׁ. שֶׁבֵּית שַׁמַּאי אוֹמְרִים נֶחְלְקָה עֵדוּתָן, וּבֵית הִלֵּל אוֹמְרִים: יֵשׁ בִּכְלַל חָמֵשׁ שְׁתַּיִם.

GEMARA The Gemara comments: **The mishna is not in accordance with** the opinion of **this** *tanna*, **as it is taught** in a *baraita* that **Rabbi Yishmael, son of Rabbi Yoḥanan ben Beroka, says: Beit Shammai and Beit Hillel did not disagree with regard to** the *halakha* in the case of **two sets of witnesses, one** of whom **says two** terms **and one** of whom **says five** terms, **that two** terms **are included in five** terms, and he must observe two terms of naziriteship. **With regard to what did they disagree?** They disagreed **with regard to one set** of two witnesses, **one** of whom **says two** terms **and one** of whom **says five** terms, and **that Beit Shammai say:** In that case **their testimony is divided,** as the two witnesses are in conflict and there is no testimony here at all. **And Beit Hillel say:** Since **two** terms **are included in five** terms, their testimony is in agreement with regard to two terms, and therefore he must observe two terms.

אָמַר רַב: הַכֹּל מוֹדִים בִּמוֹנֶה. אֲמַר לֵיהּ רַב חָמָא לְרַב חִסְדָּא: מַאי קָאָמַר? אִילֵימָא אֶחָד אוֹמֵר חָמֵשׁ וְלֹא שְׁתַּיִם, וְאֶחָד אוֹמֵר שְׁתַּיִם וְלֹא חָמֵשׁ – הָא קָא מַכְחֲשֵׁי אַהֲדָדֵי. אֶלָּא: אֶחָד אוֹמֵר אַחַת וּשְׁתַּיִם, וְאֶחָד אוֹמֵר: שָׁלֹשׁ אַרְבַּע חָמֵשׁ,

In relation to the explanation that the dispute is with regard to a single pair of witnesses, **Rav said: All concede in** a case of **counting**[N] that the testimonies contradict each other. **Rav Ḥama said to Rav Ḥisda: What is he saying;** what did Rav mean by this? **If we say that** he was referring to a case where **one** witness **says:** He vowed **five** terms **and not two** terms, **and one says:** He vowed **two** terms **and not five** terms, in such a situation **they** clearly **contradict one another,** and neither of the testimonies is reliable. **Rather,** Rav is speaking of **one** witness who **says** that he heard the person in question count out only **one and two** terms when he took a vow of naziriteship, **and one says** that he heard the person in question count out only **three, four,** and **five** terms when he took a vow of naziriteship.

HALAKHA

Two terms are included in five – יֵשׁ בִּכְלַל חָמֵשׁ שְׁתַּיִם: If one pair of witnesses testified that a person vowed to be a nazirite for two terms, while a second pair testified that he vowed to be a nazirite for five terms, he is a nazirite for two terms. This is because five includes two. The *halakha* follows Beit Hillel, but not in accordance with the explanation of Beit Hillel that is given by Rabbi Yishmael, son of Rabbi Yoḥanan ben Beroka (Rambam *Sefer Hafla'a, Hilkhot Nezirut* 3:9 and *Leḥem Mishne* there; see Rambam *Sefer Shofetim, Hilkhot Edut* 3:3; *Shulḥan Arukh, Ḥoshen Mishpat* 30:2).

NOTES

All concede in a case of counting – הַכֹּל מוֹדִים בְּמוֹנֶה: In other words, everyone agrees that the testimonies are considered divided if they say that the vow was uttered by way of counting (Rabbeinu Peretz; Rabbi Avraham min HaHar). Rabbeinu Todros explains that the witnesses counted out the numbers, therefore the assumption is that they did not make a mistake and should be seen as contradicting each other.

An opposite version is cited by the *Shita Mekubbetzet*: All agree in the case of counting that two is included in five. According to this opinion, when the witnesses stated the number with counting, all agree that the lower number is accepted, and when each set of witnesses gives a different number without counting, there is a disagreement if the lower number is accepted. Rabbi Avraham min HaHar cites a similar version of the text.

הָא לָמָּה לִי? הָשְׁתָּא יֵשׁ לוֹמַר חֲמִירְתָּא אֲמַר רַב, קִילְּתָא לָא אֲמַר?! אָמְרִי בְּמַעֲרְבָא: אֵין הַכְחָשָׁה בְּמוֹנֶה.

The Gemara asks: **Why do** I need for Rav to state **this** at all? **Now that it is** already **said** with regard to **a stringent** case, where there were two sets of witnesses who generally have full credibility yet **Rav said**[N] that the testimony is considered divided, with regard to **a lenient** case, involving a conflict within one pair of witnesses, who cannot each obligate him in naziriteship, would he **not say** that a conflict in their testimony causes it to be disregarded? Of course the testimonies are disregarded if the conflict is within the same set of witnesses. **They say in the West,**[B] Eretz Yisrael:[N] **There is no conflicting** testimony **in** a case of **counting,** as since one of them counted a smaller number and the second counted a larger number, they do not conflict at all, as the smaller number is included in the larger one.

הדרן עלך מי שאמר

NOTES

With regard to a stringent case Rav said – חֲמִירְתָּא אֲמַר רַב: This statement is difficult to understand, as Rav had not been cited previously in this discussion. The Commentary on *Nazir* explains that this stringency of Rav is referring to the statement cited in his name in the Jerusalem Talmud, that contradictory testimony of two sets of witnesses in this format is also considered to be divided. Most commentaries, however, omit the words: Rav said, and have a text that reads: Now that he said with regard to a stringency, with regard to a leniency, did he not say? In other words, if the witness who said: Three, four, and five terms, was stringent with the accused to such an extent, his testimony would certainly include the more lenient one and two terms as well (*Tosafot*; Rosh). The Meiri explains similarly, only he reads it as a suggestion made by the Gemara: Perhaps this witness stated only what he was adding to the testimony of his colleague, and did not find it necessary to repeat the number the other had already specified.

They say in the West, Eretz Yisrael – אָמְרִי בְּמַעֲרְבָא: Some commentaries explain that the statement taught in Eretz Yisrael does not refer to Rav's *halakha* in particular, but is a general statement that two witnesses who give a count are not considered to contradict one another, even if one counts a larger number than the other. This is the explanation of the Commentary on *Nazir*, and fits the standard text of the Gemara.

The parallel discussion in the Jerusalem Talmud cites a dispute of *amora'im* in this matter. Rav says that they only disagreed with regard to witnesses who state the sum total, for example, if one says two and other says five, but if they give a count everyone agrees that the larger number includes the smaller one. By contrast, Rabbi Yoḥanan claims that the dispute only concerns witnesses who count, whereas if they just state a number all agree that their testimonies conflict. The Jerusalem Talmud therefore offers support for Rav Ḥama's opinion. This also means that the Gemara is referring to the statement in the Jerusalem Talmud when it says that in Eretz Yisrael they said, citing Rav, that witnesses who count are not considered to contradict one another.

BACKGROUND

The West – מַעֲרְבָא: In the Babylonian Talmud, Eretz Yisrael is referred to as the West, since it is southwest of Babylonia. In later periods, the customs in Israel were referred to as Western, as opposed to the Eastern customs of Babylonia.

Summary of **Perek III**

In a standard term of naziriteship, the nazirite shaves on the day after the close of his term, the thirty-first day. One who shaved on the final day of his term, the thirtieth day, has fulfilled his obligation. If one vowed to observe two consecutive terms of naziriteship, he shaves for the end of the second term on the sixty-first day from the start of the first term, as that is the thirty-first day of the second term. If one shaved for the first term on the thirtieth day, then even if he shaved for the second term on the fifty-ninth day, he has fulfilled his obligation.

This chapter considered different possibilities with regard to the negation of the tally of the days of naziriteship due to ritual impurity from a corpse. If a nazirite comes into contact with a corpse during his term, the impurity negates the days he had observed of his naziriteship. After completing the purification process, the nazirite shaves and begins counting his term anew. The Gemara rules that this *halakha* applies even if one became impure on the final day of his term. On the other hand, if one contracts impurity on the day following the end of the term, before he has brought his offerings, only thirty days are negated, even if the original term was much longer.

If one who had contracted impurity from a corpse, for example one who was standing in a cemetery, took a vow of naziriteship, the naziriteship takes effect immediately with regard to the prohibition against drinking wine or cutting hair, but he begins counting the days of his term only once he completes his purification process.

A nazirite who became impure may only start to count his term again once the blood from his sin-offering has been sprinkled on the altar.

If one residing outside Eretz Yisrael vowed to observe a term of naziriteship and then observed the entire term outside of Eretz Yisrael, he must observe his term again upon arriving in Eretz Yisrael. This *halakha* applies even if the vow comprised multiple terms or a lengthy term. The reason for this is that naziriteship kept outside of Eretz Yisrael is considered to be one observed in ritual impurity.

Finally, should one vow to keep several terms of naziriteship but forget how many terms he vowed to complete, and witnesses provide conflicting reports as to what he said, the testimony of the set of witnesses who say the smaller amount is accepted.

Image **Credits**

תלמוד בבלי

— מהדורת נאה —

נזיר חלק א

Steinsaltz Center

ירושלים

KOREN

Please note that the number ranges that appear at the bottom of each daf of the Vilna pages indicate the corresponding pages of the Koren Talmud Bavli translation and commentary.

תלמוד בבלי

הוצאת קורן ירושלים

— מהדורת נאה —

מסכת נזיר
דף ב. עד דף כ:

COMMENTARY BY

Rabbi Adin Even-Israel Steinsaltz

EDITOR-IN-CHIEF

Rabbi Dr Tzvi Hersh Weinreb

EXECUTIVE EDITOR

Rabbi Joshua Schreier

STEINSALTZ CENTER

KOREN PUBLISHERS JERUSALEM

כל

אכינויי נזירות כנזירות. *בהאומר "אהא" – הרי זה נזיר, או "אהא נאה" – נזיר. ג"נזיק" "נזיח" "פזיח" – הרי זה נזיר. ד"הריני כזה" ה"הריני מסלסל" "הריני מכלכל" "הרי עלי לשלח פרע" – הרי זה נזיר "הרי עלי ציפורים", רבי מאיר אומר: נזיר, וחכמים אומרים: ואינו נזיר.§ **גמ'** מכדי תנא בסדר נשים קאי, מאי טעמא תני נזיר? – תנא אקרא קאי, °"והיה אם לא תמצא חן בעיניו כי מצא בה ערות דבר", והכי קאמר: מי גרם לה לעבירה – יין, וקאמר: *כל הרואה סוטה בקלקולה – יזיר עצמו מן היין. פתח בכינויין ומפרש ידות! אמר רבא ואיתימא כדי: חסורי מיחסרא, והכי קתני: כל כינויי נזירות כנזירות, וידות נזירות כנזירות; ואלו הן ידות: האומר "אהא" – הרי זה נזיר. *ולפרוש כינויי ברישא! תנא מההוא דסליק ההוא מפרש ברישא. כדתנן: *במה מדליקין ובמה אין מדליקין, ומפרש "אין מדליקין" ברישא. *במה טומנין ובמה אין טומנין, ומפרש "אין טומנין" ברישא. *במה אשה יוצאה ובמה אינה יוצאה, ומפרש "לא תצא אשה" ברישא. *והתנן: במה בהמה יוצאה ובמה אינה יוצאה, ומפרש "יוצא גמל" ברישא! *יש נוחלין ומנחילין, נוחלין ולא מנחילין, מנחילין ולא נוחלין, לא נוחלין ולא מנחילין, ומפרש "אלו נוחלין ומנחילין" ברישא! אלא, לעולם תני הכי ותני הכי. אלא, התם דאיסורא דנפשיה הוא – מפרש איסורא דנפשיה ברישא. גבי בהמה דאיסורא איידי בהמה הוא דאתי – מפרש היתירא ברישא. גבי

כל (א) כינויי נזירות כנזירות. כל המקבל עליו נזירות באותו לשון שבדו להן חכמים – הרי הוא נזיר כמו (ג) אם אמר "הריני נזיר" ואלו הן כינויי נזירות: ג) נזיק, נזיח, פזיח. מי שאמר "הריני נזיק", או "נזיח", או "פזיח" – הרי הוא נזיר. משום הלין טעמי, שבדו להן חכמים הן, ואית דאמרי: דהני כינויין לשון אומות הן. (א) ד) אי משום דכי מתחקת לרגל דקוף ד"נזיק", ודופן דח' ד"נזיח", וגגו דפ"א ד"פזיח" ודופן ח' שבו – משווית ליה "נזיר". **האומר אהא.** אע"פ שלא הוציא בשפתיו נזיר. **הרי זה נזיר.** דידות נזירות כנזירות. וכשם שאוחז אדם בבית יד של כלי ומגביה את הכלי עצמו, כך זה, כיון דאמר "אהא" ה) או שאמר "אהא נאה" – הרי זה נזיר. וטעמא דכולה מתניתין מפרש בגמרא. **גמ' מ"ט תני נזיר.** דמאי איריא מילי דנזיר בסדר נשים. **תנא אקרא קאי וכו'.** ובדין הוא דהוה ליה למיתנייה לבתר סוטה, אלא איידי דתנא כתובות דעיקר סדר נשים, (ב) ותנא ביה פרק "המדיר" – תנא ליה נדרים לבתר כתובות, והדר תנא נזיר ו) דמסמיך ליה קרא "לנדור נדר נזיר" וגו', והדר תנא סוטה, דאמר מר: כל הרואה סוטה בקלקולה יזיר עצמו מן היין, ז) היינו כדאמרינן בסוטה (דף ז.): "כתי, הרבה יין עושה" כו'. **פתח בכינויין.** דקתני: כל כינויי נזירות כנזירות. **ומפרש ידות.** האומר "אהא". **תנא מההוא דסליק כו'.** אורחא דתנא, מההוא דסליק מתחיל לפרושי ברישא, כדתנן כו'. **אלא לעולם תני הכי ותני הכי.** ומסתברא טעמא דהתם ח) גבי "במה בהמה יוצאה" (ג) – איידי בהמה הוא דאתי, שאסור לגמל לצאת (*באפסר), אבל הוא אינו חייב ט) בדבר שאינו ראוי לה – הלכך קלישא איסורא, ולהכי מפרש היתרא ברישא. וגבי

כל כינויי נזירות כנזירות. כל דבר שאינו עיקר שמו כן, נקרא כינוי לחול עליו נזירות לכל דבר כאילו אמר בשם העיקר, דהיינו "אהא נזיר", ומהני למיהוי נזיר כי אמר הכנויין "אהא נזיק" או "נזיח" או "פזיח", כמו בשם העיקר. והם נקראין כנויין.

האומר אהא הרי זה נזיר. ובגמרא מפרש דאיכא הוכחה, כמו שנזיר עובר לפניו. וזה נקרא ידות נזירות, שלא גמר דבורו, ומהני לחול עליו כל דיני נזירות כאילו גמר דיבורו, כאדם האוחז בבית יד של כלי ומגביהו בכך כאילו אוחז בכלי. **או** אהא נאה. גם זה נקרא ידות נזירות. ובגמרא ◦מפרש אמאי לא ערבינהו למיתנינהו לבבא אחת, וליתני הכי: האומר "אהא" או "אהא נאה" – הרי זה נזיר*.

נזיר נזיק נזיח פזיח הרי זה נזיר. לפי שרצה לפרש כל הכנויין פתח ואומר: נזיר וכו'. כלומר, "נזיר" הוא עיקר השם הכתוב בתורה, שעל ידי לשון זה חל עליו שם נזירות. וה"ה אם אמר בלשון הכנויין, כמו "נזיק", "נזיח", "פזיח". ורישא דמתניתין אתא לפרושי, דקתני: כל כינויי נזירות כנזירות. ובכינויין נחלקו אמוראים בפ"ק דנדרים (דף י.); ר' יוחנן אומר: לשון אומות הם, פירוש: שלש לשונות אלו משבעים לשונות הם. ואם תאמר: ולרבי יוחנן מאי איריא הנך ג' לשונות? בכל ע' לשונות נמי, אם קבל עליו נזירות באחד מהנך הלשונות – חייל עליה הנזירות! וי"ל: דאה"נ, דגם בשאר לשונות אם מכירם ומבינם, ומתכוין לקבל עליו נזירות – הוי נזיר. אבל מהני לישני דמתניתין, כי אמר נזרו באחד מן שלש לשונות הללו – חייל עליה נזירות (נהי) נמי כי אין מתכוין, משום דדמי טפי ללשון תורה מלשונות אחרים. ור"ל פליג התם, ואמר: לשון שבדו חכמים מלבם. והתם פריך: אמאי בדינהו ותקינהו רבנן לשון כנויין? והשיב: דזימנין דבעי למימר "לה' קרבן" ואמר "לה'" גרידא, ומפיק שם שמים לבטלה, ולכך תקנו כנויין, שלא הורגל הלשון לומר "לה' קונם". וא"ת: ור"ל איך יביא קרבן על ידי לשון שבדו חכמים? הא קמייתי חולין בעזרה! ויש לומר: כיון דמתכוין לנדור בנזיר, ויודע שלשון זה בדו חכמים לנדור בהם בנזיר – קבלה גמורה היא, כאילו אמר בלשון הכתוב בתורה. א] והר"ר יחיאל פירש: דר"ל לאו לענין קרבן קאמר, אלא לענין מלקות, דלקי אם עבר על נזירותו שקבל בלשון שבדו חכמים. **האומר** הריני כזה. בגמרא מוקי לה דנזיר עובר לפניו. ולגופיה לא איצטריך, דהא מרישא שמעינן אפילו כי לא אמר אלא "אהא" ונזיר עובר לפניו דהוי נזיר. אלא לדיוקא איצטריך: טעמא דאמר "כזה", הא האומר "הריני" אפילו נזיר עובר לפניו – ◦לא מהני, דטפי משמע "אהא כזה", מן "הריני" כי לא סיים "כזה". **הריני** מסלסל הריני מכלכל. הני לאו ידות נזירות נינהו, דאם כן ליתנינהו לעיל בהדי ידות. אלא כיון דגמר דבוריה, משמע דנזירות בא לומר, כי אמר הני לשונות ותפיס בשעריה, כדמפרש בגמרא. **מאי** טעמא תני נזיר. פירוש בסדר נשים. (ד) בסדר קדשים הוה ליה למיתנייה, שהוא הלכות קרבנות. ומשני: תנא אקרא קאי "והיה אם" וגו', מי גרם לה לעבירה – יין, כלומר מי גרם לה שזינתה – יין, הלכך (ה) תני אותה מסכתא בסדר נשים. וקאמר: כל הרואה סוטה בקלקולה יזיר עצמו מן היין – סיום הדבר שאמר תחלה: מי גרם לעבירה – יין. כלומר, ונכון הוא שתשמר עצמה מן היין, אבל לא בנדר. ושוב מוסיף לומר: שכל הרואה סוטה בקלקולה יזיר עצמו מן היין כנזיר, ולכך שנה נזיר בנשים, שגם הוא הבועל נבדק, כדאיתא בסוטה (דף כח:) שהבועל נבדק כמו הנבעלת. ובנדרים לא בעי: מ"ט תנא בנשים – משום דעיקר פרשת נדרים בפרשת אשה כתיב. ולא הוה מצ"ל טעמא כדקאמר בריש סוטה (דף ב.) כדפריך: (ו) מכדי תנא מנזיר קסליק מאי שנא דקתני סוטה, ומשני התם: איידי דתנא בכתובות פרק "המדיר את אשתו" (דף ע.) תנא נמי נדרים, ואיידי דתנא נדרים – תנא נמי נזיר דדמי ליה. א"כ ה"נ ליתני הכא דלכך שנאן בסדר נשים! וי"ל: משום דלא מיסתבר ליה דאגב נדרים לישבק לסדר קדשים שכולו קרבנות, וראוי נזיר לשנות התם טפי. ואדרבה, אגביה ה"ל למיתני נדרים התם. לכך צ"ל טעמא דתנא אקרא קאי. וקשה: דלמה לו להאריך (ז) לשונו ולומר "כל הרואה סוטה" כו' ומה ענין זה לזה? לכן נ"ל: דמאי דקאמר "תנא אקרא קאי" אינו ר"ל אקרא דכתיב בפרשה, אלא ר"ל אקרא קאי – דכתיב בסוף "המגרש" במסכת גיטין (דף צ.), דכתיב "והיה אם" וגו'. ועתה ניחא שפיר מאי דכתב נזיר בסדר נשים, דמי גרם לעבירה יין וכו'. אבל מ"מ קשה: אמאי תנא נזירות אצל סוטה? היה לו לכותבו אחר גיטין! ומשום הכי קאמר דכל הרואה סוטה בקלקולה יזיר וכו', וגם זה עבירה. ובטעמא דהכא לחוד לא סגי, דא"כ ליתני סוטה ברישא והדר נזיר כסדר הפרשה, לכך צריך טעמא דהתם דאגב "המדיר" תנא נדרים, ואגב נדרים תנא נזיר, והדר חוזר לסוטה שהוא עיקר מסדר נשים. **אלא** לעולם תני הכי והכי. וכולהו איכא טעמא. התם דאיסורא דנפשיה. פי': התלויה באדם עצמו, כגון הדלקה והטמנה ובמה אשה יוצאה – מפרש איסורו ברישא. וגבי בהמה, דאיסור דבהמה – מפרש היתר ברישא. (ח) *)**אלא** [הכא] לפרוש כנויי ברישא. כלומר, במתניתין במאי דפתח – בין הכנויין ובין הידות – איסורא דנפשיה הוא. **ידות** הואיל ואתיין מדרשא חביבא ליה. דדרשינן בפרק קמא דנדרים (דף ג.): "נזיר להזיר לה'" – לעשות ידות נזירות כנזירות. **בעיקר** קרבן. דהיינו הכנויין, שאינן צריכין לדרשה, דקבלת נזירות גמור הוא, אלא שאמר בלשון כנוי. לימא

*) מכאן שייך לע"ב

עין משפט נר מצוה

א א מיי' פ"א מהל' נזירות הל' ח סמג עשין קנו:
ב ב מיי' שם הל' ו:
ג ג מיי' שם הלכה ח:
ד ד מיי' פ"ג שם הל' ז:
ה ה מיי' שם פרק א הלכה ו:
ו ו מיי' שם הל' ו:

[עיין תוס' ע"ב ד"ה אמר שמואל]

פי' הרא"ש (א)

כל כנויי נזירות כנזירות. כל שאינו עיקר השם מיקרי כנוי כמו המכנה שם לחבירו: האומר אהא ה"ז נזיר. לאו לפרושי כנויי קא אתי אלא יד לנדר הוי כמו האוחז הכלי בבית יד שלו הכלי עולה עמו. ה"נ לאו נדר ממש הוי אלא משמעות קצת לשון נדר ורבינהו קרא למהוי נדר ממש. האומר [אהא] נאה ה"ז נזיר. אף זה נמי יד הוי וגריעא טפי מהאומר אהא בלא נאה דהאומר אהא ונזיר עובר לפניו יש במשמעותו לשון נזירות יותר מאהא (בנ') [נאה] אבל האומר אהא נאה לא מהני אם נזיר עובר לפניו דאתנאה במצות משמע ובעי' דוקא תפים בשערו כדמפרש בגמ' ומתני' לא זו אף זו קתני. ותימה אמאי לא כללינהו בהדי הדדי וליתני האו' אהא או אהא נאה ה"ז נזיר. ושמא משום דבתרי גווני איירי רישא בנזיר עובר לפניו. וסיפא בתפוס בשערו: נזיק נזיח פזיח ה"ז נזיר היינו כנויי נזירות. ובנדרים מפרש טעמא דכינויין [מהני]. הריני נזיר וכו' כולה מתני' מפרש טעמא בגמרא: **גמ'** מכדי תנא בסדר נשים קאי מ"ש תני נזיר וראוי היה לסדרו בסדר קדשים משום הבאת קרבנות ואע"ג דבפ"ק דסוטה קא יהיב טעמא אמאי תנא נזיר בתר סוטה ומפרש איידי דתנא כתובות ותנא המדיר תנא נדרים ואיידי דתנא נדרים תנא נזיר דדמיא לנדרים וקתני סוטה לכדר' כל הרואה סוטה בקלקולה וכו' אותו הטעם אינו מספיק אלא על סדר המסכתות אחר שנתברר לנו מטעם דהכא שראוי לסדרו בסדר נשים ולעקרו ממקום שהיה ראוי יותר לשנותו כגון בסדר קדשים ובמסכת נדרים לא מפרשא תלמודא טעמא אמאי סדרו בסדר נשים משום דמילתא דנפשיה היא שאין לך מקום שראוי לסדרו יותר [מכאן] משום דכתיב בנדרים בין איש לאשתו ובין אב לבתו והיה אם לא תמצא חן בעיניו כי מצא בה ערות דבר ורוב המגרשים ע"י ערות דבר מגרשים וע"י קלקול של ערות דבר חייב אדם להזיר עצמו: פתח בכנויין ומפ' ידות בנדרים נמי פריך ותו ידות אינשי שכח התנא להזכיר ידות ברישא: (לא) [אלא] התם איסורא דנפשיה וכו' משום דאיסורא דנפשיה חמיר עלויה מפ' (אסור) [איסורא] ברישא ובנדרים ליתא להך טעמא אלא מעיקרא פריך מיש נוחלין ומיש מותרות לבעליהן ומיש טעונות שמן ולבונה ומיש טעונות הגשה ומיש בכור לנחלה ומשני הני משום דאוושן מפ' ההיא דפתח ברישא והדר תו פריך מבמה בהמה:

א) פירוש זה הובא בשם הגדולים בח"א ד"ה רבינו אשר ז"ל שם ופירש על התלמוד כפי' מס' נדרים הנדפס ואני ראיתי פירושו לנזיר כתיבת יד עכ"ל.

מסורת הש"ס

קדושין ה: | דברים כד | [ברכות סג. סוטה ב.] | [נדרים כ: ע"ש] | [שבת כ:] | [שם מז:] | [שם נ.] | [שם נא.] צ"ל במטולטלת | [ב"ב קח.]

נוסחת רבינו יהודה בן רבינו נתן

א) בכ"י כתוב בתחלה כזה: הלשון פירוש מסכת נזיר לרבינו יהודה בר נתן ז"ל (ח"ש ג"ה לגבי כלהך חמוייש): ב) שלום: ג) נזיק נזיח פזיח ליתא בכ"י: ד) אי: ה) כמתן לאמר אהא חיי למר: ו) דמסמיך: ז) היינו ליתא בכ"י: ח) גבי במה מדליקין ובמה טומנין: במה אשה יוצאה: ט) בשביל הוצאה לא במזיד סקילה ולא בשוגג קרבן אלא איסורא בעלמא דנפקא בהמתו בדבר כו'.

הגהות הב"ח

(א) רש"י ד"ה כל כינויי וכו' לשון אומות הן מבוס כל"ל ותיבת אי נמחק: (ב) ד"ה תנא אקרא וכו' סדר נשים הוא ותנא: (ג) ד"ה אלא וכו' במה בהמה יוצאה איידי: (ד) תוס' ד"ה מאי טעמא וכו' בכסדר קדשים וכו': (ה) בא"ד הלכך שנאה אותה מסכתא: (ו) בא"ד כדפריך התם מכדי וכו': (ז) בא"ד להאריך בלשונו: (ח) ד"ה אלא לעולם וד"ה אלא הכא לפרוש הכ"א:

הגהות מהר"ב רנשבורג

א] בתוס' ד"ה נזיר נזיק נזיח פזיח הרי זה נזיר וכו'. והר"ר יחיאל פירש דר"ל לאו לענין קרבן קאמר אלא לענין מלקות. נ"ב וכ"ה בירושלמי דנזיר דף א ע"א וזכרוהו התוס' בנדרים דף ג ע"א בד"ה אלא למ"ד כו':

גליון הש"ס

בספר שם הגדולים להגאון מוה' חיים יוסף דוד אזולאי באות ש' כתב בשם הרב יד מלאכי דפי' נזיר אינו מרש"י: **תוס'** ד"ה או אהא נאה ובגמרא מפרש. נ"ל אפרש: **תוס'** ד"ה האומר הריני כזה כו' לא מהני. עיין ר"נ נדרים דף ע' ע"א ד"ה בשהיה:

גַּבֵּי "יֵשׁ נוֹחֲלִין" נַמִי, מְפָרֵשׁ עִיקַּר נַחֲלָה בְּרֵישָׁא. אֶלָּא [הָכָא], לִפְרוֹשׁ כִּינּוּיֵי בְּרֵישָׁא! אֶלָּא, הַיְינוּ טַעַם יָדוֹת, *הוֹאִיל וְאָתְיָין לֵיהּ מִדְּרָשָׁא — חֲבִיבִין לֵיהּ. וְלִיפְתַּח בְּהוֹן בְּרֵישָׁא! תַּנָּא כִּי מַתְחִיל — מַתְחִיל בְּעִיקַּר קָרְבָּן, וּלְעִנְיַן פֵּירוּשֵׁי — מְפָרֵשׁ יָדוֹת בְּרֵישָׁא.§ "הָאוֹמֵר אֱהֵא הֲרֵי זֶה נָזִיר". *דִּלְמָא "אֱהֵא בְּתַעֲנִית" קָאָמַר! אָמַר שְׁמוּאֵל: אכְּגוֹן שֶׁהָיָה נָזִיר עוֹבֵר לְפָנָיו. *לֵימָא קָסָבַר שְׁמוּאֵל יָדַיִם שֶׁאֵינָן מוֹכִיחוֹת בלָא הָוְויָין יָדַיִם? אָמְרִי: (א) בִּזְמַן שֶׁנָּזִיר עוֹבֵר לְפָנָיו — לֵיכָּא לְסַפּוּקָא בְּמִילְּתָא אַחֲרִינָא, אֲבָל (ב) וַדַּאי אֵין הַנָּזִיר עוֹבֵר לְפָנָיו — אָמְרִינַן: דִּלְמָא "אֱהֵא בְּתַעֲנִית" קָאָמַר. וְדִלְמָא לְפוֹטְרוֹ מִן קָרְבְּנוֹתָיו קָאָמַר! גדְּקָאָמַר בְּלִבּוֹ. אִי הָכִי מַאי לְמֵימְרָא? מַהוּ דְּתֵימָא: בָּעֵינַן פִּיו וְלִבּוֹ שָׁוִין, דקמ"ל.§ "אֱהֵא נָאֶה נָזִיר".§ וְדִלְמָא אֱנָאֶה לְפָנָיו בְּמִצְוֹת? *כִּדְתַנְיָא: "זֶה אֵלִי וְאַנְוֵהוּ" (ג) האֶנָּאֶה לְפָנָיו בְּמִצְוֹת; אֶעֱשֶׂה לְפָנָיו סוּכָּה נָאָה, לוּלָב נָאֶה, צִיצִית נָאָה, אֶכְתּוֹב לְפָנָיו סֵפֶר תּוֹרָה נָאֶה, וְאֶכְרְכֶנּוּ בְּשִׁירָאִין נָאִים! אָמַר שְׁמוּאֵל: ושֶׁתָּפוּס בִּשְׂעָרוֹ, וְאָמַר "אֱנָאֶה". נְזִירָא מִילְּתָא דַּעֲבֵירָה, וְאָמְרִינַן לֵיהּ "נָאֶה"? אִין

שמות טו

רש"י

לימא קסבר שמואל ידים שאינן מוכיחות לא הויין ידים. פי': דאי סבירא ליה דהויין ידים — למה לי' לשמואל לאוקמי מתני' בנזיר עובר לפניו? אפי' אין נזיר עובר לפניו נמי, דכשאמר "אהא" — יד מיהא הוי, דטפי משמעו אקבלת נזירות דראוי לחול לאלתר, אפי' אכל ושתה ביין כל היום — מאלי היום ואילך יכול להיות נזיר מקבלת תענית, דאם אכל כבר — לא יוכל להתענות עד למחר. ולישנא ד"אהא" משמע דאהא נזיר לאלתר, הלכך יד הוי. ואי לא בעי שמואל ידים מוכיחות — אפילו אין נזיר עובר לפניו נמי. **ה"ג** אמרי אין בזמן שהנזיר וכו'. כלומר, אין ודאי שמואל סבירא ליה: ידים שאינן מוכיחות לא הויין ידים. ובנזיר עובר לפניו ליכא לספוקי דהויין ידים מוכיחות. אבל אין נזיר עובר לפניו — דלמא "אהא בתענית" קאמר, כלומר: ולא הויין ידים מוכיחות: ויש ספרים דגרסי: אמרי לא, (ו) בזמן שאין הנזיר עובר לפניו. (ז) והכי פירושו: לעולם שמואל לא בעי ידים מוכיחות. ובזמן שנזיר עובר לפניו — ליכא ספוקי, דיד מיהא הוי. אין נזיר עובר לפניו — דלמא "אהא בתענית" קאמר, פירוש: ואפילו יד לא הוי. ולגירסא זו מסיק הכא דשמואל לא בעי ידים מוכיחות. (ח) והתם דקאמר "הרי את מקודשת" אע"ג דלא אמר "לי" הרי היא מקודשת לו, ופריך: למימרא דסבר שמואל ידים שאין מוכיחות הויין ידים? והא תנן "האומר" — אהא הרי זה נזיר, ומוקי לה שמואל אין נזיר עובר לפניו — לא, אלמא קסבר שמואל ידים שאין מוכיחות לא הויין ידים! ומשני התם: אלא באומר "מקודשת לי". אלמא מסיק התם לשמואל מהכא דידים שאינן מוכיחות לא הוין ידים. להכי גרסינן: אמרי אין. והשתא האי "לימא" אינו כשאר "לימא" שבגמרא, שכן הוא עומד. ודכוותה איכא לקמן (דף כט:): לימא הני תנאי כי הני תנאי, ועומד כן, וכדמפרש. **ודלמא** לפוטרו מקרבנותיו. המוטלין עליו להביא כשישלים נזירותו, ולא נתכוון כלל לקבל עליו על עצמו נזירות. **דקאמר** בלבו. להיות נזיר. ומ"מ, בעינא נמי דנזיר עובר לפניו, דקבלה שבלב אינו כלום, דגבי נזיר (ט) כתיב "כי יפליא" — שיפרש בפיו. אבל כי נזיר עובר לפניו ופירש בשפתיו "אהא" ובלבו חשב להיות נזיר — מחשבת הלב מהניא כאילו אמר בפיו: אהא נזיר כזה שעובר לפניו. (י) **מהו** דתימא בעינא פיו ולבו שוין קמ"ל. הכי גרסי', ולא גרסינן "דלא בעינא", דהוי משמע דלא בעינן פיו ולבו שוין. וזה אינו, דכל נדר בטעות לאו נדר הוא, דאם נתכוון לומר "מעשר" ואמר "תרומה", או איפכא, על פירות שלפניו — לא אמר כלום. ועוד קשה: למה לי עובר לפניו? הא הוי נזיר כיון דחשב בלבו, ולא בעינן פיו ולבו שוין! אלא ה"פ: מהו דתימא בעינן פיו ולבו שוין, והכא כי לא הוציא בפיו "אהא נזיר" בפירוש, אע"ג דנזיר עובר לפניו ואמר בלבו "נזיר", (כ) דאין זה פיו ולבו שוין, קמ"ל דמחשבת הלב מגלית אדיבורו ד"אהא" כי נזיר עובר לפניו — ד"אהא נזיר" קאמר, וכהאי גוונא הוי שפיר פיו ולבו שוין. **ודלמא** אהא נאה לפניו במצות. בשאר מלות, כדתני' כו', ומנלן למימר דקיבל עליו נזירות? **אמר** שמואל שתפוס בשערו. כלומר: אהא נאה במלוה התלויה בשיער, כגון נזירות. והכא ליכא לשנויי: בלא תפס בשערו ובנזיר עובר לפניו, דהכא דבור שלם קאמר: "אהא נאה", ואי לא תפס בשערו — אפי' כי נזיר עובר לפניו משתמע שפיר: אהא נאה בשאר מלות כמו אנזירות. ולעיל נמי, דפריך: ודילמא "אהא בתענית" — ליכא לשנויי בשתפס בשערו בלא נזיר עובר לפניו, דלעולם משתמע שפיר "אהא בתענית" כי אין נזיר עובר לפניו, אע"ג דתפיס בשערו. והשתא אתי שפיר, דמתניתין פלגינהו בתרי בבי: האומר אהא הרי זה נזיר, או אהא נאה, אע"ג דתרוייהו ידות נינהו — משום דמפרשי בתרי טעמי. **ואמאי** נאה הא מילתא דעבירה היא ואמרי' ליה נאה. פירוש: הנודר בנזיר עושה עבירה, וקרינן ליה "נאה"? וי"ג: מלתא עבידא. וכי מעשה הגון וכשר לעשות כן? הא עבירה היא! ומשני: אפילו לר' אלעזר הקפר כו', דילמא אתי למיעבר על נזירותו לשתות ביין כי ארכו לו הימים. אבל טהור — לא חוטא קרי ליה. וקשה: דבעלמא אייתי לר' אלעזר אפילו אנזיר טהור, על שם שליער עלמו מן היין קרי ליה חוטא! וי"ל: דטהור נמי קלת קרי ליה חוטא, ומכל מקום המלוה רבה על החטא, ולכך קרי ליה "נאה". מידי דהוה *) מתענה תענית חלום בשבת, דיש לו מלוה לבטל החלום, וקלת עבירה עשה שהתענה בשבת — שהרי לריך לישב בתענית למחרת השבת לכפר על שהתענה בשבת. אבל נזיר טמא — רחמנא קרייה חוטא, לפי שהוא סותר את נזרו ולריך לחזור לנזירתו, וכבד בעיניו המעשה, ותוהה על הראשונות *). **)**הריני** כזה נהי נמי דתפיס בשערו הרי נזיר. יש ספרים דכתיב בהן: "הריני כזה" לא אמר. אכן טעות הוא, שהרי במתני' תני בהדיא: אמר הריני כזה. ושמא הסופר טעה במאי דכתב בתר הכי: א] אמר שמואל בשנזיר כו'. פי': דס"ד דאין נזיר עובר לפניו אלא דתפיס בשעריה, דומיא דמתני' דלעיל "אהא נאה" דאוקמינן בתפיס בשעריה לחוד. ולכך פריך: "הריני כזה" לא משמע מידי דנזירות, אע"ג דתפיס בשעריה! ומשני שמואל: הכא נמי כשנזיר עובר לפניו, והשתא אין לריך לומר דתפיס בשעריה.

ממאי

*) [ועי' תוס' ב"ק לח: ד"ה אלא ותוספות תענית יח. ד"ה אמר] **) שייך לדף ג.

תוספות

וְגַבֵּי יֵשׁ נוֹחֲלִין נַמִי. מִשּׁוּם דְּעִיקַּר נַחֲלָה הוּא, מְפָרֵשׁ עִיקַּר נַחֲלָה בְּרֵישָׁא). אֶלָּא (ד) [הָכָא] לִפְרוֹשׁ כִּינּוּיֵי בְּרֵישָׁא אֶלָּא הַיְינוּ טַעְמָא. דִּמְפָרֵשׁ יָדוֹת בְּרֵישָׁא, דְּהוֹאִיל וְאָתְיָין לֵיהּ מִדְּרָשָׁא, כִּדְאָמְרִי' בְּפִרְקָא קַמָּא דִּנְדָרִים: "נָזִיר לְהַזִּיר" — לַעֲשׂוֹת כִּינּוּיֵי נְזִירוּת כִּנְזִירוּת, וִידוֹת נְזִירוּת כִּנְזִירוּת. חֲבִיבִין לֵיהּ. וְתָנֵי לְהוּ בְּרֵישָׁא. וְאִי אָמְרַתְּ: כִּינּוּיֵי נְזִירוּת נַמִי אָתְיָין לֵיהּ מִדְּרָשָׁא, ב) כִּדְקָתָנֵי עֲלָהּ: לַעֲשׂוֹת כִּנּוּיֵי נְזִירוּת כִּנְזִירוּת! הָא לָא הָוֵי, ג) מִדְּקָא הָדַר וְתָנֵי בְּהַהִיא בָּרַיְיתָא גּוּפָא דִּנְדָרִים: אֵין לִי אֶלָּא בִּנְזִירוּת, בִּנְדָרִים כו', וּמַקִּישׁ נְדָרִים לִנְזִירוּת, מַה נְּזִירוּת עָשָׂה בּוֹ יְדוֹת נְזִירוּת כִּנְזִירוּת — אַף ד) כֵּן בִּנְדָרִים, וְלָא חָשֵׁיב בַּהֲדַיְיהוּ כִּינּוּיֵי נְזִירוּת. אַלְמָא ה) בְּרֵישָׁא לָא אֲתָא אֶלָּא מִשּׁוּם יְדוֹת נְזִירוּת כִּנְזִירוּת, וְכִינּוּיֵי נְזִירוּת אַגַּב גְּרָרָא נָסְבָהּ. וְלִיפְתַּח בְּהוּ בְּרֵישָׁא. וְלִיתְנֵי: יְדוֹת נְזִירוּת כִּנְזִירוּת, וְכָל כִּינּוּיֵי נְזִירוּת כִּנְזִירוּת. תַּנָּא כִּי מַתְחִיל [מַתְחִיל] בְּעִיקַּר קָרְבָּן בְּרֵישָׁא. כְּגוֹן בְּכִינּוּיֵי נְזִירוּת, שֶׁהֵן עִנְיַן לְשׁוֹן נָזִיר, כִּדְפָרֵישְׁנָא לְעֵיל. וּלְעִנְיַן פֵּרוּשֵׁי מְפָרֵשׁ בְּרֵישָׁא יָדוֹת. דְּאָתְיָין מִדְּרָשָׁא. וּבְפ"ק דִּנְדָרִים פָּרֵיךְ: הָנִיחָא לְמ"ד כִּינּוּיִין לְשׁוֹן אוּמּוֹת הֵן, וּלְהָכִי פָּתַח בְּכִינּוּיִין בְּרֵישָׁא, דְּעִיקָּר הֵן. אֶלָּא לְמ"ד לָשׁוֹן שֶׁבָּדוּ לָהֶן חֲכָמִים לִהְיוֹת נוֹדֵר בּוֹ — מַאי אִיכָּא לְמֵימַר? לִיפְתַּח בִּידוֹת בְּרֵישָׁא, הוֹאִיל וְאָתְיָין מִדְּרָשָׁא! וּמְשַׁנֵּי: מִי קָתָנֵי יָדוֹת בְּמַתְנִיתִין כְּלָל? אֶלָּא, חַסּוּרֵי מְחַסְּרָא לָהּ וְתָנֵי יָדוֹת — לְהָא מִלְּתָא נַמִי תָּרֵיץ לָהּ, וְאַקְדֵּים נַמִי וְתָנֵי יָדוֹת בְּרֵישָׁא: כָּל יְדוֹת נְדָרִים כִּנְדָרִים, וְכָל כִּינּוּיֵי נְדָרִים כִּנְדָרִים. וּלְהָכִי מְפָרֵשׁ יָדוֹת בְּרֵישָׁא, וַהֲדַר כִּינּוּיִין: הָאוֹמֵר אֱהֵא הֲרֵי זֶה נָזִיר וְאַמַּאי דִּלְמָא אֱהֵא בְּתַעֲנִית קָאָמַר. לֵימָא דְּקָסָבַר שְׁמוּאֵל יָדַיִם שֶׁאֵין מוֹכִיחוֹת ו). כְּלוֹמַר, מִדְּקָא מוֹקִים לָהּ שְׁמוּאֵל: כְּגוֹן שֶׁהָיָה נָזִיר עוֹבֵר לְפָנָיו, הָא לָאו הָכִי — לֵיכָּא לְסַפּוּקֵי בְּנָזִיר כְּלָל, דְּקָסָבַר: יָדַיִם שֶׁאֵין מוֹכִיחוֹת לָא הָוְיָין יָדַיִם. וְהָא אִיפְּכָא שָׁמְעִינַן לֵיהּ בְּפ"ק דְּקִידּוּשִׁין, דְּאָמַר שְׁמוּאֵל: הָאוֹמֵר לְאִשָּׁה "הֲרֵי אַתְּ מְקוּדֶּשֶׁת", "הֲרֵי אַתְּ מְאוֹרֶסֶת", "הֲרֵי אַתְּ לְאִנְתּוּ" — הֲרֵי זוֹ מְקוּדֶּשֶׁת, וְאַע"ג דְּלָא אָמַר "לִי". אָמְרִי. לְעוֹלָם קָסָבַר שְׁמוּאֵל יָדַיִם שֶׁאֵין מוֹכִיחוֹת הָוְיָין יָדַיִם, ז) כְּגוֹן גַּבֵּי אֵירוּסִין וְקִידּוּשִׁין, כֵּיוָן דִּמְדַבֵּר שֵׁם אֵירוּסִין וְקִידּוּשִׁין — הָוֵי הוֹכָחָה בְּמִקְצָת. וְהָכָא הַיְינוּ טַעְמָא דְּבָעֵינַן לִהְיוֹת נָזִיר עוֹבֵר לְפָנָיו — מִשּׁוּם דְּאִיכָּא לְמֵימַר: אֱהֵא בְּתַעֲנִית קָאָמַר, ח) וְלָא הָוֵי הוֹכָחָה כְּלָל, דְּלֵיכָּא לְמֵיקַם עֲלָהּ דְּמִילְּתָא אִי אָמַר בְּתַעֲנִית אוֹ בִּנְזִירוּת. וְלָא הָוֵי נָזִיר, דְּלָא נִתְּנָה נְזִירוּת אֶלָּא לְהַפְלָאָה, עַד שֶׁיְּפָרֵשׁ, שֶׁנֶּאֱמַר (במדבר ו) "כִּי יַפְלִיא לִנְדּוֹר", וּמְתַרְגְּמִינַן: אֲרֵי יְפָרֵשׁ. [דִּילְמָא וכו']. אֲפִי' כִּי נָזִיר עוֹבֵר לְפָנָיו, אַמַּאי הָוֵי נָזִיר? וְדִילְמָא לְפוֹטְרוֹ מִקָּרְבְּנוֹתָיו קָאָמַר, וְהָכִי מַשְׁמַע: אֱהֵא אֲנִי בִּמְקוֹמוֹ לְהַקְרִיב קָרְבְּנוֹתָיו: הָכָא בְּמַאי עָסְקִינַן כְּגוֹן שֶׁאָמַר שֶׁבְּלִבּוֹ הָיָה לְקַבֵּל עָלָיו נְזִירוּת. אִי הָכִי. דְּנָזִיר עוֹבֵר לְפָנָיו, וְקָאָמַר נַמִי בְּלִבּוֹ — ט) מַאי לְמֵימְרָא? פְּשִׁיטָא, י) אַדַּעְתָּא דְּנָזִיר קָאָמַר! בָּעֵינַן שֶׁיְּהֵא פִּיו וְלִבּוֹ שָׁוִין. דְּבָעֵינַן שֶׁיְּהֵא מוֹצִיא בִּשְׂפָתָיו מַה כ) שֶּׁיְּהַרְהֵר בְּלִבּוֹ. קמ"ל. דְּלָא בָּעֵינַן וּבִלְבַד שֶׁיְּהֵא נָזִיר עוֹבֵר לְפָנָיו, הָא אִם אֵין נָזִיר עוֹבֵר לְפָנָיו, וְאַע"ג דְּאָמַר בְּלִבּוֹ, כֵּיוָן דְּלָא הוֹצִיא בִּשְׂפָתָיו — לָא הָוֵי מוּכְחָא מִילְּתָא. הָאוֹמֵר אֱהֵא נָאֶה הֲרֵי זֶה נָזִיר. דְּמַשְׁמַע ל) הָכִי קָאָמַר: שֶׁיְּהֵא שְׂעָרוֹ מְגוּדָּל וְנָאֶה: מ) נְזִירָא מִילְּתָא דַּעֲבֵירָה (ה) וְאָמְרִי' לֵיהּ נָאֶה. בִּתְמִיָּה. וְאִי אָמַר: אֱהֵא נָאֶה בְּמִילְּתֵיהּ דִּנְזִירוּת — מִי הָוְיָא נְזִירוּת מִילְּתָא דְּנוֹי, דְּאָמְרֵי' לֵי': זִיל וֶהֱיֵה נָזִיר, וְהִנָּאֶה? אִין

(ב) *) [ברכות לב:]

פי' הרא"ש

הואיל ואתיין מדרשא חביבי' ליה אבל כנויין לא אתיין מדרשא אלא כדמפ' טעמייהו בנדרים לר"י כדאית ליה ולר"ל כדאית ליה. והתם פריך הניחא למ"ד כנויין לשון אומות הם וכו' ומשני לאו חסורי מחסרא לה תני ידות ברישא כל ידות (נזיר) [נדרים] כנדרים כל כנויי נדרים כנדרים אבל הכא לא מסתבר ליה לשנויי הכי ולשבושי תחלת המסכת וניחא ליה טפי לשנויי דתנא דמתני' מתחיל בעיקר הקרבן. והתם לא (שייך) [חש] לשנויי הכי: מתחיל בעיקר הקרבן דכנויים לשון נזירות הן לר"י דאמר לשון אומות הן ולר"ל נמי כיון שתקנו חכמים להיות נודרים בהן הוי כנדר עצמו. אבל יד לא הוי עיקר הנדר שאין במשמעות לשון נדר אלא יד בעלמא: ודלמא אהא בתענית קאמר. והיכי משוית ליה נזיר ודאי להביא קרבנותיו לעזרה כיון דאיכא למימר דלתענית נתכוון. ועוד אפי' נזיר ספק לא הוי דכיון דאיכא למימר הכי והכי הא אמרינן סתם נזירות להקל: לימא קסבר שמואל ידים שאין מוכיחות לא הויין ידים דאי קסבר ידים הויין אפי' אין נזיר עובר לפניו נמי. דנהי דלא הויין ידים מוכיחות מ"מ יד לנזירות הוי דטפי משמעותיה לשון נזירות מלשון תענית דאהא משמע דקאי אגופיה לשנותו לשם חדש והיינו שיהא נקרא נזיר. אבל היושב בתענית אין שמו מתשנה: אמרי' בזמן שהנזיר עובר לפניו ליכא לספוקי במלתא אחרינא. כלומר לעולם קסבר ידים שאין מוכיחו' הויין ידים ובזמן שהנזיר עובר לפניו אכתי הוי ידים שאין מוכיחות ומ"מ מוכח טפי לנזיר מלתענית כיון דנזיר עובר לפניו הלכך ליכא לספוקי במלתא אחריתי כיון דמוכח טפי לנזיר. אבל אם היה הדבר שקול לזה כמו לזה הא אמרי' ספק נזיר להקל. אבל אם אין נזיר עובר לפניו דלמא אהא בתענית קאמר זה דבר שקול ולא הוי נזיר. ודילמא לפוטרו מקרבנותיו קאמר וה"ק אהא בחיובו של זה. מהו דתימא בעי' פיו ולבו שוין א). ועוד אי לא בעי' פיו למה לי עובר לפניו בלבו לחודיה סגי. אלא ה"פ מהו דתימא בעי' שיפרש בפיו בהדיא קמ"ל כיון דנזיר עובר לפניו קרי ביה פיו ולבו שוין אבל אם אין נזיר עובר לפניו אפי' אמר בלבו היה כך כיון דלא מוכחא מלתא לא קרי' ביה פיו ולבו שוין. ודילמא אתנאה לפניו במצות קאמר ונזיר ודאי לא הוי ואפי' ספק כדפרשתי לעיל: אמר שמואל שתפוס בשערו. אבל נזיר עובר לפניו לא מהני אלא דוקא כשאומר אהא דאיכא לספוקי או בנזיר משמע יהא גופי מתענה או נזיר. וכיון דנזיר עובר לפניו מוכח שהוא רוצה שיהיה גופו כמוהו. אבל אהא נאה דאיכא לספוקי בלשון נאה אם להתנאות בשערו ולגדלו כדין נזיר קאמר או להתנאות במצוה אם שנזיר עובר לפניו כיון דאין הספק אלא בלשון נאה אבל במה שתפוס בשערו איכא הוכחה דלהתנאות בשערו קאמר ולא בעי' שיאמר בלבו היה דהוכחה גמורה הוי מה שתפוס בשערו אבל אין תפוס בשערו אפי' יאמר בלבו היה לא מהני דלא מקרי פיו ולבו שוין כיון דליכא הוכחה כלל. הדא מילתא דעבירה ואמרי' לי' נאה. כלומר אסור הוא לנזיר כדאמרינן פ"ק דנדרים כנדרי רשעים נדר בנזיר ובקרבן כנדרי כשרים לא אמר כלום. ואית דגרסי הדא מילתא דעבידה דאמרי' ליה נאה. כלומר מי הוי דבר שרגילים לעשות וראוי לעשות דקרי ליה נאה:

א) חסר כאן וצ"ל אין הפירוש דקמ"ל דלא בעינן דולאי בעינן ועוד אי לא בעי וכו'.

עין משפט נר מצוה

ז א מיי' פ"א מהל' נזירות הלכה ו:
ח ב מיי' פ"א מהל' נדרים הל' כג סמג לאוין רמב טוש"ע יו"ד סימן רו סעיף א:
ט ג ד מיי' פ"א מהל' נזירות הלכה ה ו:
י ה מיי' פ"ז מהל' ס"ת הלכה ד ופ"ז מהל' לולב הלכה ו סמג עשין נח ולאוין שסד טוש"ע א"ח סי' תרנו:
יא ו מיי' פ"א מהל' נזירות הלכה ו:

מסורת הש"ס

[יבמות ב: וש"נ]
קדושין ה:
[שם וע"ש נדרים ה:]
שבת קלג: ע"ש סוכה יא: מכילתא פ' בשלח

נוסחת הריב"ן

א) א"נ משום דאשונו להו מילי דההוא מתני' אי מפרש מההוא דסליק ברישא משתלי ליה מאי דאמר ברישא: אלא הכא דזוטרי מילי לפרוש כנויי ברישא כו': ב) מדקתני: ג) למדקא: ד) בנדרים כן: ה) דעיקר דרשא לא אתא כו' ותיבת ברישא ליתא: ו) לא הויין ידים: ז) (כגון גבי כו' הוכחה במקצת) ליתא בכ"י: ח) ולא אמר אהא נזיר א"נ ליכא למיקם ותיבות (ולא הוי הוכחה כלל) ליתא: ט) היא: י) לאדעתא: כ) שהרהר: ל) להכי: מ) אמר שמואל כגון שתפס בשערו ואמר אי נאה. אהא נאה ונדרא דנזירות מי הויא כו' ותיבות (נזירא מלתא כו' נאה במלתיה) ליתא בכ"י:

הגהות הב"ח

(א) גמ' לא הוויין ידים אמרי אין ולאי בזמן וכו': (ב) שם אבל אין הנזיר כצ"ל ותיבת ולאי נמחק: (ג) שם ואנוהו אתנאה לפניו: (ד) רש"י ד"ה אלא התם לפרוש כינויי: (ה) ד"ה נזירא מילתא לעבירה היא ואמרינן: (ו) תוס' ד"ה ה"ג וכו' ויש ספרים דגרסי אמרי לא עובר לפניו הוויין ידים אבל בזמן: (ז) בא"ד שאין הנזיר עובר לפניו לא הוויין ידים והכי פירושו: (ח) בא"ד דשמואל לא בעי ידים מוכיחות וקשה מפ"ק דקידושין דהתם קאמר שמואל הרי את מקודשת: (ט) ד"ה ודלמא לפוטרו וכו' כתיב כי יפליא. נ"ב כפ"ג דשבועות דף כו ע"ב כתבו התוס' ... וקטועה כן הדין לצריך להוציא בשפתיו והכא דקאמר אהא לא משמע כלל לשון נזירות אם אין הנזיר עובר לפניו ולאו משום כי יפליא: (י) ד"ה ה"ג מהו דתימא בעינן פיו ולבו שוין קמ"ל ולא גרסינן דלא בעינן דהוי משמע דלא בעינן כצ"ל: (כ) בא"ד ואמר בלבו נזיר אין כצ"ל ואות ד נמחק:

הגהות מהר"ב רנשבורג א] בתוס' ד"ה הריני כזה כו' ושמא הסופר טעה במאי דכתב בתר הכי כצ"ל. נ"ב כאן הס"ד ואח"כ מה"ד אמר שמואל וכו' ועי' בספר אורח מישור פירוש לדברי התוס' ויעוב לפירוש רש"י ודפח"ח:

(א) אִין, דַּאֲפִילּוּ *לְרַבִּי אֶלְעָזָר הַקַּפָּר דְּאָמַר: נָזִיר חוֹטֵא – הָנֵי מִילֵּי גַּבֵּי נָזִיר טָמֵא, דְּאַיְּידֵי דְּבָעֵי מִיסְתַּר, דְּאָמַ' רַחֲמָנָא °"וְהַיָּמִים הָרִאשֹׁנִים יִפְּלוּ כִּי טָמֵא נִזְרוֹ" – הָתָם הוּא דִּלְמָא אָתֵי לְמִיעֲבַר עַל נְזִירוּתֵיהּ, אאֲבָל נָזִיר טָהוֹר – לָאו חוֹטֵא קָרֵי בֵּיהּ. § "הֲרֵינִי כָּזֶה". § נְהִי נַמִּי דְּתָפוּס בִּשְׂעָרוֹ, א] "הֲרֵינִי *כָּזֶה" לָא אֲמַר! אָמַר שְׁמוּאֵל: בכְּגוֹן שֶׁהָיָה נָזִיר עוֹבֵר לְפָנָיו. § "הֲרֵינִי מְסַלְסֵל". § מִמַּאי דְּהָדֵין סִלְסוּל שַׂעֲרָא? (ב) *כְּדַאֲמַרָה לֵיהּ הַהִיא אַמְתָא דְּבֵי רַבִּי לְהַהוּא גַּבְרָא: עַד מָתַי אַתָּה מְסַלְסֵל בִּשְׂעָרְךָ. אֵימָא תּוֹרָה, דִּכְתִיב °"סַלְסְלֶהָ וּתְרוֹמְמֶךָּ"! אָמַר שְׁמוּאֵל: גהָכָא נַמִּי שֶׁתָּפוּס בִּשְׂעָרוֹ. § "הֲרֵינִי מְכַלְכֵּל". § מִמַּאי דְּהָדֵין כִּילְכּוּל שְׂעָרוֹ הוּא? *כְּדִתְנַן: סִיד, ר' יְהוּדָה אוֹמֵר: כְּדֵי לָסוּד כִּילְכּוּל. וַאֲמַר רַב: בַּת צִידְעָא. (ג) אֵימָא מֵיזַן עַנְיֵי, כִּדְכְתִיב °"וַיְכַלְכֵּל יוֹסֵף אֶת אָבִיו וְאֶת אֶחָיו"! אָמַר שְׁמוּאֵל: דהָכָא נַמִּי שֶׁתָּפוּס בִּשְׂעָרוֹ. § "הֲרֵי עָלַי לְשַׁלֵּחַ פֶּרַע הֲרֵי זֶה נָזִיר". § מִמַּאי דְּהָדֵין שִׁלּוּחַ רִיבּוּיָא הוּא? דִּכְתִיב °"שְׁלָחַיִךְ פַּרְדֵּס רִמּוֹנִים". אֵימָא מִידֵי דְּעַבּוּרֵי, כִּדְכְתִיב °"וְשֹׁלֵחַ מַיִם עַל פְּנֵי חוּצוֹת"! תַּנָּא "פֶּרַע" "פֶּרַע" יָלֵיף; כְּתִיב הָכָא °"קָדֹשׁ יִהְיֶה גַּדֵּל פֶּרַע", וּכְתִיב הָתָם גַּבֵּי כֹּהֵן הֶדְיוֹט °"וּפֶרַע לֹא יְשַׁלֵּחוּ". וְאִיבָּעֵית אֵימָא: הַאי "שׁוֹלֵחַ מַיִם" נַמִּי רִיבּוּי הוּא, (כְּדִמְתַרְגֵּם רַב יוֹסֵף:) דְּכַד מַשְׁקִין לֵיהּ מַיָּא (ד) לְפֵירָא וְרַבִּי. § "הֲרֵי עָלַי צִיפֳּרִין רַבִּי מֵאִיר אוֹמֵר נָזִיר". § מַאי טַעְמָא דְּרַבִּי מֵאִיר? אָמַר רֵישׁ לָקִישׁ: צִיפֳּרִין סְמוּכִין לְשֵׂיעָר קִיבֵּל עָלָיו, דִּכְתִיב °"עַד דִּי שַׂעְרֵהּ כְּנִשְׁרִין רְבָה וְטִפְרוֹהִי כְצִפְּרִין"; רַבִּי מֵאִיר סָבַר: מַתְפִּים אִינִישׁ בְּמִידֵּי דְּסָמִיךְ לֵיהּ, וְרַבָּנַן

במדבר ו | משלי ד | בראשית מז | שיר ד | איוב ה | במדבר ו | יחזקאל מד | כת"א ל"ג | דניאל ד

אִין דַּאֲפִילּוּ לְרַבִּי אֶלְעָזָר הַקַּפָּר דְּאָמַר נָזִיר חוֹטֵא. וְלָא מִיקְרֵי נָאֶה, א) דִּכְתִיב "וְכִפֶּר עָלָיו מֵאֲשֶׁר חָטָא עַל הַנָּפֶשׁ" (במדבר ו). הָנֵי מִילֵּי גַּבֵּי נָזִיר טָמֵא. שֶׁנִּטְמָא, דְּאַיְּידֵי דְּבָעֵי מִיסְתַּר יָמִים הָרִאשׁוֹנִים, וּמִיהֲדַר וּמִימְנֵי זִימְנָא אַחֲרִינָא – אֲרִיכָא לֵיהּ מִילְּתָא. ב) דִּילְמָא אָתֵי לְמֵיעֲבַר עַל נְזִירוּתֵיהּ. כִּדְאָמַר בְּפֶרֶק קַמָּא דִּנְדָרִים (דף ט:): כְּשֶׁהֵן מִטַּמְּאִין וְרַבִּין עֲלֵיהֶם יְמֵי טוּמְאָה מִתְחָרְטִין בָּהֶן, וְנִמְצְאוּ מְבִיאִין חוּלִּין לָעֲזָרָה. אֲבָל נָזִיר טָהוֹר לָאו חוֹטֵא קָרֵינָא בֵּיהּ. וְאָמְרִי': (ה) זִיל וְתֶיהֱוֵי נָזִיר וְהַנָּאֶה. נְהִי נַמִּי. דְּמוֹקְמַתְּ לֵיהּ כְּגוֹן ג) שֶׁתָּפוּס בִּשְׂעָרוֹ, אַמַּאי הָוֵי נָזִיר? וְהָא לָא אָמַר "הֲרֵינִי ד) *כָּזֶה". דְּאִי *"כָּזֶה" אָמַר – הָכִי ה) מַשְׁמַע לְהוּ: הֲרֵינִי *כָּזֶה שֵׂיעָר לְגַדְּלוֹ. אָמַר שְׁמוּאֵל כְּגוֹן שֶׁהָיָה נָזִיר עוֹבֵר לְפָנָיו. דְּמַשְׁמַע: הֲרֵינִי בִּנְזִירוּת כָּזֶה. הֲרֵינִי מְסַלְסֵל הֲרֵינִי מְכַלְכֵּל אוֹ שֶׁאָמַר הֲרֵי עָלַי לְשַׁלֵּחַ פֶּרַע הֲרֵי זֶה נָזִיר. "הֲרֵינִי מְסַלְסֵל" מַשְׁמַע דְּלִיעֲבִיד מִידֵּי דְּלֶיהֱוֵי מְהַפֵּךְ בִּשְׂעָרוֹ ו) בְּגִידּוּל, דְּהַיְינוּ בִּנְזִירוּת. וְאֵימָא תּוֹרָה. דְּכִי אָמַר "הֲרֵינִי מְסַלְסֵל" – שֶׁמְּקַבֵּל עָלָיו לִלְמוֹד תּוֹרָה, וְקָאָמַר שֶׁיְּהֵא מְהַפֵּךְ בָּהּ כִּדְכְתִיב "סַלְסְלֶהָ וּתְרוֹמְמֶךָּ". כִּדְתְנַן. הַמּוֹצִיא סִיד בְּשַׁבָּת מֵרְשׁוּת הַיָּחִיד לִרְשׁוּת הָרַבִּים, שֶׁחַיָּיב מִשּׁוּם "לֹא תוֹצִיאוּ". כְּדֵי לָסוּד כִּילְכּוּל וַאֲמַר רַב בַּת צִידְעָא. טינפל"א בְּלַעַ"ז, ז) שֶׁמְּקַפֵּל הַשֵּׂעָר שֶׁבְּרַקָּתָהּ כְּמִין מַגְרָד, כְּדֵי לְהַעֲמִיד עַל ח) גַּבָּן כִּיפָּה שֶׁבְּרֹאשָׁהּ, שֶׁלֹּא יִפּוֹל הַשֵּׂעָר שֶׁבָּאוֹזֶן לְמַטָּה. וְאֵימָא לְמֵיזַן עַנְיֵי. קַבֵּיל עִילָּוֵיהּ. הֲרֵי עָלַי לְשַׁלֵּחַ פֶּרַע הֲרֵי זֶה נָזִיר. דְּמַשְׁמַע: הֲרֵי עָלַי לְגַדֵּל פֶּרַע. מִמַּאי דְּהָדֵין שִׁילּוּחַ רִבּוּיָא הוּא. כִּדְקָאָמְרַתְּ דִּלְגַדֵּל פֶּרַע מַשְׁמַע. דִּכְתִיב שְׁלָחַיִךְ פַּרְדֵּס רִמּוֹנִים. גִּידּוּלַיִךְ שֶׁגְּדֵלִין יִהְיוּ כְּפַרְדֵּס רִמּוֹנִים, שֶׁצּוֹמֵחַ וּמִתְגַּדֵּל. וְאֵימָא דְּשִׁילּוּחַ מִידֵּי דְּעַבּוּרֵי. הוּא, דְּמַשְׁמַע שֶׁיָּגוֹז שְׂעָרוֹ ט) כִּמְפַנֶּה מַיִם וּמַעֲבִירָן מִמָּקוֹם לְמָקוֹם, כִּדְכְתִיב "וְשׁוֹלֵחַ מַיִם" וגו'. וְהַאי נַמִּי דְּאָמַר "הֲרֵי עָלַי לְשַׁלֵּחַ פֶּרַע" – מַשְׁמַע דְּאָמַר: הֲרֵי עָלַי לְהַעֲבִיר פֶּרַע! תַּנָּא פֶּרַע פֶּרַע יָלֵיף כְּתִיב הָכָא. בְּנָזִיר "גַּדֵּל פֶּרַע", וּכְתִיב גַּבֵּי כֹּהֵן הֶדְיוֹט "וּפֶרַע לֹא יְשַׁלֵּחוּ". מַה "פֶּרַע" דִּכְתִיב גַּבֵּי כֹּהֵן הֶדְיוֹט לִישָּׁנָא דְּרִיבּוּי הוּא, כִּדְאָמְרִינַן בְּפֶרֶק "כֹּהֵן גָּדוֹל" (סנהדרין כב:): פֶּרַע לֶיהֱוֵי עַד שְׁלֹשִׁים, וּמִירְבָּא לָא לִירְבֵּי טְפֵי מִשְּׁלֹשִׁים, דְּגָמְרִינַן לֵיהּ מִנָּזִיר, דִּכְתִיב בֵּיהּ (במדבר ו) "יִהְיֶה", וְ"יִהְיֶה" בְּגִימַטְרִיָּא הָכִי הָוֵי, אַף י) "פֶּרַע" הָאָמוּר גַּבֵּי נָזִיר גִּידּוּל שֵׂיעָר כ) הָוֵי, וְהָכִי מַשְׁמַע: שֶׁיַּנִּיחֶנּוּ לְגַדֵּל עַד שֶׁיָּבֹא לִכְלַל פֶּרַע, שֶׁהֵן שְׁלֹשִׁים. וַאֲפִילּוּ ל) בָּעֵי לְמֵימַר דִּלְעוֹלָם שִׁילּוּחַ מִידֵּי דְּעַבַּר הוּא – אַכַּתִּי לָא קַשְׁיָא וְלָא מִידֵּי, דְּהָכִי מַשְׁמַע: הֲרֵי עָלַי לְשַׁלֵּחַ שֵׂיעָר מ) (וְלַהֲבִיאוֹ שֶׁיַּגִּיעַ) לִכְלַל ל' שֶׁיְּהֵא פֶּרַע. נ) דְּבֵין פֶּרַע דְּנָזִיר וּבֵין פֶּרַע דְּכֹהֵן הֶדְיוֹט אֵינָהּ פְּחוּתָה מִשְּׁלֹשִׁים. וְאִיבָּעֵית אֵימָא הַאי וְשׁוֹלֵחַ מַיִם ס) רִיבּוּי הוּא. דְּכִי מַשְׁקִין לֵיהּ מַיָּא לְאַרְעָא קָא מְרַבֵּי לְהוּ לְפֵרִי. צִיפֳּרִין הַסְּמוּכִין לְשֵׂיעָר. וְהֵיכָן הֵן לִיפָּרִין הַסְּמוּכִין לְשֵׂיעָר – כִּדְכְתִיב בְּדָנִיֵּאל "עַד דִּי שַׂעְרֵהּ כְּנִשְׁרִין רְבָה וְטִפְרוֹהִי כְּצִפְּרִין", דְּלִפָּרִין וְשֵׂיעָר בְּחַד קְרָא כְּתִיבֵי. דר"מ סָבַר מִיתְפִּים אִינִישׁ בְּמִידֵּי דְּסָמִיךְ לֵיהּ. וּלְהָכִי אָמַר לִפָּרִין, דְּבָעֵי לְקַבּוּלֵי עֲלֵיהּ גִּידּוּל שֵׂיעָר, דְּסָמִיךְ לֵיהּ לְצִפּוֹרִים. וּכְגוֹן שֶׁהָיָה נָזִיר עוֹבֵר לְפָנָיו, אוֹ תָּפוּס בִּשְׂעָרוֹ, כִּדְאָמְרִינַן לְעֵיל. וְרַבָּנַן

ממאי דהדין סילסול שערא הוא. דלשון זה נופל אהפוך שיער, דנימא נזירות קביל עליה? ואימא תורה – להפך בתורה! **הכא** נמי תפוס בשעריה. דמשמע שפיר, הריני מהפך במלוה התלויה בשיער. **שילוח** רבוי הוא. לשון גידול, כמו "שלחיך פרדס רמונים". ואימא מידי דעבורי הוא – שקיבל עליו לגלח ולהעביר השיער לכשיגדל.

תנא פרע פרע יליף. לאו אתנא דמתני' קאי, אלא אתנא דסנהדרין (דף כב:) דקאמר: כהן הדיוט צריך לגלח אחת לשלשים יום, ויליף "פרע לא ישלחו" מנזיר דכתיב "גדל פרע", מה להלן שלשים יום כמנין "יהיה" – אף בכהן הדיוט שלשים יום. וקאמר "לא ישלחו". והכא הכי פירושא: תנא פרע יליף בעלמא, אלמא דשילוח הוי לשון גידול. ואם תאמר: ולייתי מקרא דכתיב בכהן הדיוט "ופרע לא ישלחו", ואכתי ג"ש למה לי? ונראה לי: דמקרא דכהן הדיוט לא משמע, ד"לא ישלחו" הוי גידול אפילו דתרי יומי, וכיון דלא אמר בפירוש "הריני נזיר תרי יומי", אלא שילוח פרע – אין כאן קבלת נזירות. אבל כי גמרינן כהן הדיוט מנזיר, דשילוח הוי מלשון שלשים בג"ש, וקאמר "הרי [עלי] לשלח" – כאילו אמר: הרי עלי לשלח פרע שלשים יום, ומשתמע שפיר דנזירות קביל עליה, להכי מייתי ג"ש. ודווקא כי אמר "הרי עלי לשלח פרע", אבל אמר "הרי עלי פרע" בלא שילוח – לא משמע מידי, דפרע הויא לשון גילוי, כמו "ופרע ראש האשה" (במדבר ה).

משקין ליה מיא לפרי ורבי. פירוש: גדל הפרי. וקשה: דאשכחן הרבה שילוח שאינו לשון גידול אלא לשון העברה, כמו "שלח תשלח" (דברים כב) "וישלח יעקב מלאכים" (בראשית לב)! ויש לומר: דאי תותבי' מהנך קראי – הוה משני ליה כדלעיל: תנא פרע פרע יליף, ולא בא לפרש אלא למקרא דאותבינן מיניה "ושולח מים". ודוחק, דמשמע דהניח הג"ש מכל וכל, ועתה אינו צריך לה כלל. לכן נ"ל דמתחילה לא היה חושש רק שימצא לו פסוק אחד דמשמע לשון רביה, וקמייתי ליה מקרא ד"שלחיך", ודחי ליה תלמודא: דלמא ההוא גופיה לשון העברה, כמו "ושולח מים", וליכא אפילו חד קרא דלשתמע לשון רבויא. והא משני: איבעית אימא האי "שולח מים" לשון רבוי הוא, ואיכא למילף מיניה, או מקרא ד"שלחיך פרדס". ואע"ג דקראי טובא לשון העברה – שפיר ילפינן מחד קרא דהוי לשון רבויא, דמסתברא דעתו אנזירות הוא.

צפורים הסמוכין לשיער קיבל עליה. האמורין בפסוק אצל שער. כלומר, אע"פ דאמר צפורים סתמא, דהא מתני' סתמא קאמר, אפילו הכי סבירא ליה לריש לקיש דדעתיה דאיניש אצפורים הסמוכים לשיער. והכי משתמע ליה: האומר "הרי עלי צפורים" הרי זה נזיר, דכיון דצפורים סמוכין לשיער קאמר – מסתמא ה"ק: הרי עלי מצוה דשייכא ביה צפורין התלויה במצות שיער, דהיינו נזיר, שאם נטמא צריך צפורין וה"פ: מצוה התלויה בצפורין אבן אין לפרש משום סמיכות גרידא, כדמפרש תלמודא דאם כן "הרי עלי נשרין" הל"ל דהוי נזיר, דטפי סמיכי לשער. **עד** די שעריה כנשרין רבה וטפרוהי כצפרין. פסוק הוא בדניאל גבי נבוכדנצר.

*) **צפורי** נזיר **טמא** קיבל עליה. פירוש: מצות נזירות, דשייכא בהו צפורי נזיר טמא, אם יטמא. **מכדי** חיישינן קאמר ולא צפורי נזיר ודאי קאמר אלא חששא ודלמא צפורי נדבה דקביל עליה להביא עולת העוף לנדבה ולא לנזירות. דכל כמה דאיכא לפרושי דיבוריה דלאו נזירות קיבל עליה אלא נדר אחר – שפיר טפי, דלא ניחא ליה לאיניש לקבולי עליה צפורי דנזירות, דחמיר עליה, וטריחא ליה.

*) שני דבורים אלו שייכים לע"ב

הרי

פי' הרא"ש

אין ואפילו לר' אלעזר הקפר וכו' התם הוא דלמא אתי למעבר אנזירותיה שלא יוכל לסבול משך זמן דנזירות וגם תוהה על נזירותו וקרבנותיו קרובים להיות חולין בעזרה. אבל נזיר טהור אי לא דלא אמיד אנפשיה לסבול לא הוי נדר: הריני כזה נהי נמי דתפים בשערו לא אמר כלום כלומר אפי' אי מוקמת לה בתפום בשערו כההיא דאהא נאה לא מהני מידי דמשמע שיהיה כמו שערו ואין זה כלום. ומוקי לה שמואל כדאוקי (ההוא) [באהא] בשנזיר עובר לפניו. אבל אי אמר הריני ולא אמר כזה לא מהני מידי דהריני גרע מאהא. ואין לתמוה מאי קמ"ל דהריני כזה בשנזיר עובר לפניו דהוי נזיר פשיטא הא קאמר בהדיא הריני כזה. משום דלא תימא הריני כזה בעושר או ביופי או ביחוס. ומאי דהאי סלסול בשער הוא כלומר לסלסל ולגדל שער כנזיר. ואימא תורה שנדר לעסוק בתורה ולהפך בה. ה"נ שתפס בשערו אבל נזיר עובר לפניו לא מהני כיון שהספק הוא בלשון: סיד כדי לסוד כלכול שיעור הוצאת סיד להתחייב עליו המוציאו לרה"ר כדי לסוד כלכול. לשומו על שער צדעיו לטופלו ולהשירו: שלחיך פרדס רמונים גידולך נאים כפרדס של רמונים אימא מידי דעבורי שנדר לגלח ולהעביר שערו ולשלחו מעליו: תנא פרע פרע יליף. כלומר תנא דמתני' יליף האי לשלח פרע מפרע לא ישלחו דכתיב גבי כהנים מה התם גידול שער אף הכא גידול שער כי היכי דילפי' בסנהדרין פ' כהן גדול פרע דכהנים מפרע דנזיר לו' שהכהני' מגלחים לל' יום דפריך התם אימא לא לירבו כלל. ומשני אי הוה כתיב לא ישלחו פרע כדקאמרת השתא דכתיב פרע לא ישלחו ליהוי שלוחי הוא דלא לשלחו כלומר לא יגדלו יותר משיעור פרע האמור בנזיר. ואי בעית אימא האי ושולח מים נמי רבוי הוא. כלומר האי דפרכת ליה מהאי קרא דלשון העברה הוא לאו פרכא היא דמצינא לפרושי ליה לשון גידול. אבל לאו שנויא [אחרינא הוא] למימר דלא צריכנא לשנוייא קמא דכמה שלוח כתיבי בקראי דלא הוו לשון גידול: כד משקי מיא לפירא רבי וה"פ דקרא ושולח כלומר מגדל פירות ע"י מים שעל פני חוצות: אמר ר"ל צפורים סמוכים לשער קבל עליו. וא"ת אמאי נקט צפרים לימא נשרי וטפרי' דסמיכו לשער טפי מצפורי' ועק"ל לנקוט כמה תיבות הכתובים במקרא אצל שער. ופי' ר"י דר"ל אית ליה נמי טעמא דר"י דאמר חיישנן שמא צפורי נזיר טמא קבל עליו ומוקי לה גם הוא בשנזיר עובר לפניו אלא דסבר ר"ל אי לאו נמי דאיכא למימר צפורים סמוכים לשער קבל לא הוו ידים מוכיחות לנזירות וכן מוכח בתר הכי דקא בעי' מאי בינייהו אמאי לא קאמר איכא בינייהו כשאין נזיר עובר לפניו אלמא אפילו לר"ל בעי' שיהא נזיר עובר לפניו וגם א) מדקאמר לר"ל אפילו אין נזיר עובר לפניו. משמע משום דאמר בהדיא צפורים סמוכים לשער עלי אבל אמר צפורים סתם בעי ר"ל שיהא נזיר עובר לפניו. ונ"ל דאין הוכחה מהכא דאית ליה לר"ל טעמא דר"י משום דאתיא דר"ל בעי נזיר עובר לפניו בהדיה טעמא דסמוכים ב) אבל בטעם דסמוכים לחודיה לא סגי ליה ג) חיישינן שמא צפורי נזיר טמא קבל עליו והכי קאמר הרי עלי דבר שיכול לבוא לידי צפרים והיינו נזירות דנזיר שנטמא מביא אשם ושתי צפרים:

מכדי

יב א מיי' פ"א מהל' נזירות הלכה יז: יג ב מיי' שם פ"ב הלכה ז: יד ג ד מיי' שם פ"א הל' ו:

[שייך להכא דברי תוס' דלעיל ב: ד"ה הריני וכו' ועי' אורח מישור]

[לקמן יט. וש"נ]
נ"א כזה
נ"א כזה
נ"א כזה
מגילה יח. ע"ש [ר"ה כו:]
שבת פ: ע"ש

נוסחת הריב"ן
א) (דכתיב וכפר כו' הנפש במדבר ו) ליתא בכ"י: ב) ודלמא: ג) כגון שתופס בשערו ואמר האי נאה הכי אמאי הוי כו': ד) בכ"י כזה כזה וכן לקמן: ה) להוי משמע הריני כו': ו) בגידולו: ז) שמקפל: ח) גבו: ט) ונאה לה שילוח שער כמפנה כו': י) גידול פרע: כ) הכי הוי: ל) בעית: מ) ולהביא לכשיגיע: נ) פרע לנזיר: ס) נמי רבויא:

הגהות הב"ח
(א) גמ' אין דאפילו לר' אלעזר הקפר. נ"ב עיין פ"ק דנדרים דף י' ועי' בתוס' דסוטה דף טו הקשו קושיא זו ועיין גם לקמן דף יט: (ב) שם סלסול שערא הוא כדאמרה: (ג) שם ואימא מיזן עניי: (ד) שם משקין ליה מיא ורבי לפירא: (ה) רש"י ד"ה אבל נזיר וכו' ואמרינן ליה זיל ותיהוי:

נ"א ולהעבירו כשיגיע

הגהות מהר"ב רנשבורג
א] גמ' הריני כזה. נהי נמי דתפוס בשערו ואמר הריני כזה. נמחק תיבת כזה וכ"ב כזה וכל"ל גם בלשון רש"י וכן הוא בש"ס דפוס ויניציאה. וכן הגיהו בש"ס דפוס ווינא ע"פ ספר אורח מישור לסלק קושית תוס' מרש"י:

א) נ"ל וגם מדקאמר לקמן דלאו אמר צפרין הסמוכין לשער לר"ל אפילו אין נזיר וכו'. ב) נ"ל דמזה למוכח לר"ל בעי נזיר עובר לפניו אינו ראיה דאית ליה נמי טעמא דר"י ויותר נראה דנ"ל אבל י"ל דבטעם דסמוכים לחוד סגי ליה. ג) שייך לע"ב.

ורבנן סברי: לא מתפים איניש במידי דסמיך ליה. ר' יוחנן אמר: דכ"ע לא מתפים. אלא היינו טעמא דר"מ: דחיישינן שמא צפורי נזיר טמא קיבל עליו. מכדי חיישינן קאמר, דלמא צפורי נדבה קיבל עליו! א"כ "הרי עלי קן" מבעי ליה. ודלמא "הרי עלי צפורי מצורע" קאמר! כגון שהיה נזיר עובר לפניו. ודלמא נזיר טמא, ולפוטרו מן קרבנותיו קאמר! כגון שהיה נזיר טהור עובר לפניו. מאי בינייהו? איכא בינייהו כגון דאמר "ציפרין הסמוכין לשער עלי"; לרבי יוחנן, אע"ג דאמר הכי, אי נזיר עובר לפניו – אין, אי לא – לא. לרשב"ל – אע"ג דאין נזיר עובר לפניו. מי איכא למ"ד לא מתפים איניש במילתא דסמיך ליה? והתניא: *האומר "ימין" – הרי זו שבועה. מ"ט – לאו משום דכתי' °"וירם ימינו ושמאלו אל השמים וישבע בחי העולם"? אמרי: לא, משום דימין גופיה איקרי שבועה. דתניא: אמנין לאומר "ימין" שהיא שבועה – שנאמר °"נשבע ה' בימינו", ומנין בלאומר "שמאל" שהיא שבועה – שנאמר °"ובזרוע עוזו".§ **מתני'** ג"הריני נזיר מן החרצנים" ו"מן הזגים" ו"מן התגלחת" ו"מן הטומאה" – הרי זה נזיר, וכל דקדוקי נזירות עליו.§ **גמ'** מתני' דלא כר' שמעון. דתניא, ר"ש אומר: *אינו חייב עד שידור מכולם, ורבנן אמרי: *אפילו לא נזר אלא בחד מנהון הוי נזיר, מ"ט דר"ש? אמר קרא °"מכל אשר יעשה מגפן היין מחרצנים ועד זג". ורבנן מ"ט? אמר קרא °"מיין ושכר יזיר". ור'* שמעון נמי, הכתיב "מיין ושכר יזיר"! ההוא מיבעי ליה *דלאסור יין מצוה כיין הרשות. מאי היא ד – קדושתא ואבדלתא?

הרי

רש"י

ורבנן סברי לא מתפים איניש במידי דסמיך ליה. ולא אמרי' שבדעתו היה לומר גידול שער, אי לאו דמפרש בהדיא. ואע"ג דנזיר עובר לפניו. ור' יוחנן אומר דכ"ע לא מתפים. איניש במידי דסמיך ליה. אלא היינו טעמא דר"מ דחיישינן. כי אמר "הרי עלי ליפורין", דדלמא קאמר שבדעתו לקבל עליו מידי דזימנין דמייתי עליה לפורים, דהיינו נזירות, דלכי מיטמא מייתי לפרים, בנזיר טמא כתיב "וכי ימות מת עליו בפתע פתאום כו' וביום השמיני יביא שתי תורים והזיר לה' את ימי נזרו" וגו' (במדבר ו). מכדי חיישינן קאמר. כלומר, דלא הוי נזיר אלא משום דאמרי' שמא לפרי נזיר טמא קבל עליו, ואי בתר חששא א) אזלינן – ליחוש דילמא לפרי נדבה קיבל עליו, ולא ניתנה נזירות אלא להפלאה, ואמאי קאמר ר"מ דהוי נזיר כלל! א"כ. דבעי למימר לפרי נדבה – הוה אמר "הרי עלי קן", ב) דקן משמע לפרי נדבה. אבל כי אומר "הרי עלי לפורים" – לא משמע לפרי נדבה כלל. הלכך, מדקאמר "לפורין" – ליכא לספוקי אלא בלפורי נזיר. ודלמא. מקבל עליו תורת ליפורי מצורע, לטבול החיה בדם השחוטה ולשלחן ולעשותן כהלכות לפרי מצורע! והך פירכא דפרכינן השתא קא פריך בין לרבי יוחנן בין לר"ל, דמכדי "לפרים" סתם קאמר – הא איכא למיחש נמי ללפורי מצורע. ודלמא נזיר טמא. הוה, וקאמר לאיתויי לפורים ולפוטרו הוא במקומו (א). כגון שהיה נזיר טהור עובר לפניו. דלאו בר אתויי ג) הוא. והלכך, כי אמר "לפורין" – לא אמר אלא אדעתא דליהוי נזיר כמותו. מאי בינייהו. בין לרבי יוחנן בין לר"ל לא מיתרלא שמעתתא אלא כגון שנזיר טהור עובר לפניו, משום דאית ליה למיפרך בה כל הני פירוכין, ד) ותריצנא כגון דנזיר טהור עובר לפניו עסקינן – מה לי אי משום לפרין סמוכין לשיער, אי משום לפרי נזיר טמא? אי משום הכי אי משום הכי – הוה ליה נזיר! איכא בינייהו כגון דאמר צפרין סמוכין לשיער. ר' יוחנן סבר: אע"ג דאמר הכי – לא מוכחא מילתא דלקבולי עליה נזירות הוא דקאמר, אלא לקבל עליו לפרין סתם בלא נזירות, אי לאו דנזיר עובר לפניו. לריש לקיש. כיון דאמר בהדיא "לפורין סמוכין לשיער", מוכחא מילתא דמשום נזירות קאמר, ואף על גב דאין נזיר עובר לפניו, דמיתפים איניש בשיער דסמיך ליה, וכמאן דאמר: הרי עלי לגדל שיער דמי. האומר ימין. שלא אוכל ככר זה – הרי זו שבועה. מאי טעמא לאו משום דכתיב וירם ימינו ושמאלו אל השמים וישבע בחי העולם. דקא מתפים ימינו ל"ישבע" דסמיך ליה. (ב) ה) לא. "ימין שאוכל ככר זה" כאומר "שבועה שאוכל ככר זה" דמי, שנאמר "נשבע ה' בימינו" ו) בימינו אמר, ונחשב כשבועה. שנאמר ובזרוע עוזו. מדכתיב "ימינו" וכתיב "ובזרוע עוזו" – אלמא דזרועו היינו שמאלו, והכי נמי אמרי' בפרק קמא דמסכת ברכות (דף ו.): מנין שהקב"ה מניח תפילין – דכתיב "ובזרוע עוזו", ואין עוזו אלא תפילין כו', ותפילין בשמאל קיימי. **מתני'** אמר הריני נזיר מן החרצנים או שאמר הריני נזיר מן הזגין כו' הרי הוא כמי שאמר "הריני נזיר" סתם, שמקבל עליו כל דקדוקי נזירות. **גמ'** אפילו לא נזר אלא מאחד מהן. או מן חרצן או מן זג – הרי זה נזיר, וכל דקדוקי נזירות עליו. מכל אשר יעשה. ז) משמע שצריך שיהא נוזר מכל אשר יעשה, שאינו נזיר אלא א"כ נוזר מכולם. אמר קרא מיין ושכר יזיר. דמשמע דאפילו ח) דלא נזר אלא מיין לחודיה – הוי נזיר מכולם. לאסור יין מצוה כיין הרשות מאי היא קדושתא ואבדלתא ט). מי חייל עליה איסור נזירות.

והרי

תוספות

הרי עלי קן מיבעי ליה. דדרך נודבי נדבת עולת העוף לומר בלשון קן. צפורי מצורע קאמר. כלומר, להתחייב בקרבן מצורע ולהביא תחתיו לפורים, ולהצריכו לו לטהרתו. ואפילו אין מצורע עובר לפניו, דאי אפשר דליכא חד מצורע דטעון לפורים ולא נזירות, וגם דלפורי שייכי שפיר גבי מצורע. כגון שהיה נזיר עובר לפניו. והיה סבור אפילו נזיר טמא לפניו. ולהכי פריך: ודלמא לפורין דקאמר לפטור נזיר טמא העובר לפניו מקרבנותיו? ומשני: כגון שנזיר טהור עובר לפניו, ויודע זה הנודר דטהור הוא, וקאמר "הרי עלי לפורים". ואכתי קשה: נימא דלפורים דקאמר – היינו דאם יטמא זה הנזיר העובר לפניו, שיביא תחתיו לפורים! וצריך לדחות, ולומר: כגון דאמר בלבו להיות שייך למצות נזירות דשייכא ביה ליפורים אם יטמא. ולעיל, כי פריך: ודלמא לפורי מצורע קאמר – לא מצי לשנויי כגון דאמר בלבו, דדיבוריה מישתמע טפי אלפורי מצורע (טפי) מנזירות, משום דנזירות טריחא ליה וחמיר עליה לקבל. ועוד, דלשון לפורים כתובין אצל מצורע כדפרישית, ולא אצל נזיר אלא תורים. ואפי' קאמר בלבו – אין כח במחשבת הלב להכריע דיבוריה לנזירות, דאין זה פיו ולבו שוין. אבל הכא, אע"ג דנזירות חמיר עליה וטריחא ליה, כיון דנזיר שהוא עובר לפניו – *אין סברא שיקבל עליו נזירות לפורים טמא, שדבר זה אינו בעולם עדיין, והדבר שקול – לכך מהניא מחשבת הלב לומר דנזירות קביל עליה, וחשיב שפיר פיו ולבו שוין. וכן לעיל, כי אמר "אהא" – טפי משמע הלשון אנזירות, ולומר כמוהו לאלתר, אע"ג דטריחא ליה וחמיר עליה, מלומר אהא תחתיו בקרבנותיו לאחר זמן כשישלים. והדבר שקול, לכך מחשבת הלב מכרעת הדיבור לנזירות, והרי פיו ולבו שוין. וקשה: דהספר לא הזכיר כאן כלל דקאמר בלבו! לכן נראה למהר"ף דאהיה תחתיו – אין סברא לומר דאם יטמא קאמר שיתחייב בלפורין, הואיל והשתא טהור הוא, ודבר זה לא בא לעולם כלל – וא"כ סברא לומר דנזירות קביל עליה, דדבר זה מבורר לפנינו ויש בידו לקבל לאלתר אע"ג דחמיר וטריחא ליה. ולעיל כי פריך ממצורע – התם נמי הדבר מבורר לפנינו, דודאי יש מצורע בעולם הצריך לפרים. **מאי** בינייהו. כלומר, מאי בינייהו בפי' דמתני' בין לר"ל בין לר' יוחנן אליבא דר"מ? וא"ת: וליתני דאיכא בינייהו היכא דאמר לפורים סתמא קביל עליה, דלר"ל אליבא דר"מ מהא לחוד לא הוי נזיר אם לא הזכיר גם סמוכין לשיער, כדפירש ר"ל במילתיה: לפורים סמוכין לשיער קביל עליה, ולר' יוחנן דלא הזכיר במילתיה סמוכין לשיער, כשיקבל עליו לפורים סתמא, בלא סמוכין לשיער – הוי נזיר! ועוד: היא גופה תיקשי לר"ל: למה ליה סמוכין לשיער? בלפורים סתמא לחוד סגי לר"מ למיהוי נזיר, שהרי מתניתין לר"מ לא הזכיר אלא לפורין לחוד! לכ"נ לפרש: דלר"ל אליבא דר"מ בלפורין סתמא הוי נזיר כשנזיר עובר לפניו דוקא. והא דנקט ר"ל במילתיה סמוכין לשיער – להשמיענו דכי אמר לפורים סמוכין לשיער, דבלא נזיר עובר לפניו נמי הוי נזיר בהכי. וא"ת: כיון דלר"ל כשיקבל לפורים סתמא לא הוי נזיר אם לא כשנזיר עובר לפניו אליבא דר"מ – הוי ליה לתלמודא להזכיר נזיר עובר לפניו במילתיה דר"ל כמו במילתיה דרבי יוחנן! וי"ל: דלכך הזכיר טפי במילתיה דר' יוחנן ממילתיה דר"ל, משום דר' יוחנן פסיקא ליה דאף כשאמר "לפורים הסמוכין לשיער עלי" לא הוי אלא כשנזיר עובר לפניו, ולר"ל הוי נזיר כשאמר לפרים הסמוכין לשיער אפילו אין נזיר עובר לפניו. והשתא ניחא, דפריך מאי בינייהו, דלכולהו, אף בשלא הזכיר לפורין סמוכין לשיער אלא לפורים סתמא – הוי נזיר כי נזיר עובר לפניו. ואי אין נזיר עובר – בלפורים סתמא לחוד לא היה נזיר לכולהו. והשתא נמי ניחא, דלר"ל בלפורים סתמא לא מיחייב, משום דסמוכין לשיער בקרא – דא"כ ליחייב נמי כי אמר "נשרין" ו"טופרין", דסמיכי טפי לשיער בקרא מלפורים. כך שיטת הר"ף נ"ע. הגה"ה **היכא** דאמר צפורים סמוכים לשיער קביל עליה. ר"ל שקיבל עליו דבר הסמוך ללפורים, דהיינו גידול שיער. אבל כי אמר "הרי עלי לפורים", ולא אמר לפורים סמוכין לשיער – חייל עליה נזירות, משום דמשתמע שנדר דבר שיכול לבא לידי חיוב לפורים, דהיינו נזיר, כשנזיר עובר לפניו דוקא. ומשום הכי לא מהני "הרי עלי נשרין", דלישנא דנשרין לא משמע שום לשון נזירות, כן נ"ל. הגה"ה: והר"ר שבתאי כתב שיטה זאת: מאי בינייהו? כלומר, מאי בינייהו בפירוש דמתני'. דודאי נראה ליה דר"ל לא קאמר אליבא דרבי מאיר דבלפורים סתמא מיחייב בנזיר, דאיכא למיפרך כל הני פירכי דפריך לעיל לר' יוחנן. וע"כ יפרש המשנה כמו ר' יוחנן, דגם לא יוכל לפרש המשנה שאמר בפירוש "לפורים הסמוכים לשיער עלי" – דהא מתני' סתמא קאמר "לפורים עלי", הילכך ע"כ כרבי יוחנן מפרש, ובנזיר עובר לפניו והוא טהור. וע"כ פריך: מאי בינייהו בפירוש דמתני'. ונראה שנתכוון להבין כמו שפירשתי בתחילה. **האומר** ימין הרי זו שבועה. "ימין שלא אוכל ככר זה". וה"ה שמאל כדלקמן, א] פירוש התפילין, מדהזכיר ימין תחילה. **מן** החרצנים ומן הזגים. או או קתני, כדמוכח בגמרא. **וכל** דקדוקי נזירות עליו. משום דנזיר שמשון מותר ליטמא למתים קאמר הכא: וכל דקדוקי נזירות עליו.

עד

פי' הרא"ש

מכדי חיישי' קאמר ודלמא נדבה קבל עליו שנדר להביא ב' תורים נדבה. א) לכאורה משמע צפורי ולא נזיר וק' כיון דחיישי' קאמר ליחייב נמי בנזיר מיהו איכא למימר כיון דהדבר שקול לא מחייב בנזיר דספק נזיר להקל. ומיהו קשה דמשמע דלא קשה ליה אלא משום דחיישינן קאמר אבל אי הוי ודאי ניחא ליה ואמאי אדרבה כ"ש דקשה טפי ואמאי הוי ודאי דלמא נדבה קאמ' הלכך נראה לפרש דלמא צפורי נדבה קאמר ויביא מספק זה וזה כיון דחיישי' קאמר אבל אי הוה אמר ודאי לא הוה קשיא ליה שיביא שניהם וצ"ל דעל כרחי' חיישי' דקאמר לאו משום ס' דאי אפשר לעשותו נזיר מס' ולהביא קרבנותיו לעזרה ב) ומצי' כיוצא בזה חיישי' להקל דחשבי' ליה כודאי אבל לא לענין נזירות דספק נזירות להקל: א"כ הרי עלי קן מבעי ליה. שכן דרך הנודרים לומר ובנדרים הלך אחר לשון בני אדם: ודלמא צפורי מצורע קבל עליו לפטור מצורע שחייב להביא לטהרתו. לפי' קמא להתחייב ולפרושי דוקא צפורי מצורע. וק"ל אמאי שביק נזיר דקיימי' בזה ונקט צ"מ ליפרך דלמא לפטור נזיר טמא מצפורי' קאמר. ולהך פירוש דלתחייב זה בזה קאמר איכא למימר דלא ניחא ליה למימר להתחייב שתים מתורת נזיר חדא להיותו נזיר ואחת דאמר' צפורי נזיר טמא קבל עליו ועוד לפטור נזיר מקרבנותיו הלכך ניחא ליה לפרש דלפורך מצפורי מצורע. ולפי' איכא למימר דניחא ליה טפי למיפר' מצורע צפורי שמביא ב' צפורים מנזיר שמביא תורים ובני יונה: ות' לישני ג) לי הב' בלבו. וי"ל דלא מהני כיון דצפורים הוו הכי ודבי ולא מוכח טפי לנזיר: כגון שהיה נזיר טהור עובר לפניו. ואיתו לא מחייב להביא צפורים דלכך ע"כ ה"ק הרי עלי דבר שאם אטמא אתחייב להביא צפורים. ות' דלמא ה"ק הרי עלי לפטור זה מצפורים אם יטמא. וי"ל דבכי האי גוונא מהני אי אמר בלבו היה כך משום דיש לו לפרש דבריו לענין זה שחייב עצמו ודאי מהשתא. ולא שקיל עליו דבר שאם יארע במקרה שיתחייב הלכך יש לו לפרש דברי' אלא להיותו נזיר או לפטור מי שנתחייב כבר קרבנו'. לר"ל אע"ג דאין נזיר עובר לפניו. דכיון דלדידיה אהני טעמא דסמוכים (הוא) [אף] דלא פי' בהדיא להיותו נזיר אם נע"ל. אם פי' בהדיא לא בעי נע"ל. אבל לר"י סמוכים לא מהני מידי הלכך בעי' לעולם נזיר עובר לפניו: האומר ימין היא שבועה. אם אמר ימין שלא אוכל דבר זה ואכלו לוקה. לאו משום דכתיב וירם ימינו וישבע. ומנין לשמאל שהיא שבועה דכתיב ובזרוע עוזו. ומדכתיב בימינו מכלל דבזרוע עוזו היינו שמאל ואמר נמי פ"ק דברכות מנין שהקב"ה מניח תפילין דכתיב ובזרוע עוזו ואין עוז אלא תפילין דכתיב ה' עוז לעמו יתן וגו' ותפילין דשמאל הוו: הריני נזיר מן החרצנים ומן הזגים ומן התגלחת ומן הטומאה ה"ז נזיר. פי' אם אמר ה"ז נזיר וכל דקדוקי נזיר עליו כאילו אמר הריני נזיר בסתם. ומשום דבעי למתני בתר הכי דנזיר עולם ונזיר שמשון אין כל ענין נזיר עליהם תנא הכא כל דקדוקי נזירות עליו: אינו חייב עד שיזיר מכולן. פי' אם אמר נזיר בסתם ואם בא להזכיר צריך שיזכיר כולם. ומיהו מודה ר"ש בהריני מסלסל ומכלכל דהתם לא התיר כלום אע"ג דלשון גדל שער הן הוי כאילו אמר הריני כאותו שרגיל לגדל שער והוי כאילו אמר הריני נזיר בסתם: קרא מכל אשר יעשה מגפן היין מחרצנים ועד זג וכיון דכתיב מכל אשר יעשה למה לי תו למכתב מחרצנים ועד זג לומר שאם בא לפרש צריך לפרש הכל וכיון דקפיד קרא אחרצנים וזג ה"ה נמי אטומאה ותגלחת: ורבנן אמר קרא מיין ושכר יזיר. וכיון דכתיב מכל אשר יעשה מגפן היין מיין ושכר למה לי לומר לך דאפי' נזר מיין לחודיה הוי נזיר דיין ושכר חד הוא:

א) אולי צ"ל לכאורה משמע דמקשה דדילמא לפורים קיבל עליו ולא נזיר. ב) אולי צ"ל אלא הוי ודאי נזיר ומציק וכו' דחשבי' ליה כוודאי ומקשה דילמא לפורים נדבה וכו' אבל לענין נזירות. ג) אולי צ"ל לשני ליה דכך אמר בלבו.

עין משפט נר מצוה

טו א ב מיי' פ"ב מהל' שבועות הלכה ו סמג לאוין רמא טוש"ע יו"ד סימן רלט סעיף ח:

טז ג מיי' פ"א מהל' נזירות הלכה ט:

יז ד מיי' פ"ז מהל' נזירות הלכה יא סמג לאוין רנ:

מסורת הש"ס

תורה אור

דניאל יב | ישעיהו סב | שם | במדבר ו | שם

[תוס' נדרים פ"א]

לקמן יא: לח. [נדרים ז.]

[לקמן יא: נדרים ז.]

לקמן ה. מד.

גליון הש"ס

גמ' לאסור יין מצוה כיין הרשות. עי' שבועות דף כב ע"א תוס' ד"ה תומר:

נוסחת הריב"ן

א) הוא. ב) תיבות (דקן משמע לפרי נדבה כלל) ליתא בכ"י: ג) לפרין הוא: ד) וכיון דבנזיר טהור ותיבות ותריצנא כגון ליתא בכ"י: ה) מנין לאומר ימין: ו) בימינו וגו' בימינו: ז) תיבות (משמע כו' אשר יעשה) ליתא בכ"י: ח) עכ"ל: ט) כלומר קס"ד דהאי דאמר לאסור יין מצוה לקדושתא ולאבדלתא קאמר והיכי חייל כו' ותיבת מי ליתא בכ"י:

הגהות הב"ח

(א) רש"י ד"ה ודלמא נזיר וכו' במקומו הס"ד ואח"כ מ"ה כגון שהיה נזיר טהור עובר לפניו דלאו בר איתויי הוא כצ"ל והד"א: (ב) ד"ה מאי טעמא וכו' דסמיך ליה הס"ד ואח"כ מ"ה לא ימין שאוכל כו':

הגהות מהר"ב רנשבורג

א] תוס' ד"ה האומר ימין וכו' וה"ה שמאל כדלקמן עכ"ל. נ"ב כאן הס"ד ואח"כ מה"ד ובזרוע וכו' שמאל לא נמי מדלקמן ימין אי תחלה עכ"ל וכו' אורת מיעוט:

הֲרֵי מוּשְׁבָּע וְעוֹמֵד עָלָיו מֵהַר סִינַי! אֶלָּא כִּי הָא דַּאֲמַר רָבָא: א"שְׁבוּעָה שֶׁאֶשְׁתֶּה" וְחָזַר וַאֲמַר "הֲרֵינִי נָזִיר" אָתְיָא נְזִירוּת חָיְילָא עַל שְׁבוּעָה. וְרַבָּנַן נַמִּי, הָא מִיבְּעֵי לֵיהּ לֶאֱסוֹר יֵין מִצְוָה כְּיֵין רְשׁוּת! א"כ לֵימָא קְרָא "מִיַּיִן", מַאי "וְשֵׁכָר" – שְׁמַעַתְּ מִינָּהּ תַּרְתֵּי. ור"ש: הַיְינוּ טַעְמָא דִּכְתַב "שֵׁכָר" – לְאַלּוּפֵי "שֵׁכָר" "שֵׁכָר" לְמִקְדָּשׁ. דִּכְתִיב (ויקרא י) "יַיִן וְשֵׁכָר אַל תֵּשְׁתְּ אַתָּה וּבָנֶיךָ אִתָּךְ"; מַה גַּבֵּי נָזִיר ביַיִן הוּא דְּלִיתְּסַר, אֲבָל שְׁאָר מַשְׁקִין – לָא. אַף גַּבֵּי מִקְדָּשׁ נַמִּי, יַיִן הוּא דְּלִיתְּסַר, אֲבָל שְׁאָר מַשְׁקִין הַמְשַׁכְּרִין – לָא. וּלְאַפּוּקֵי מדר' יְהוּדָה. *דְּתַנְיָא, *ר' יְהוּדָה אוֹמֵר: גאָכַל דְּבֵילָה קְעִילִית, וְשָׁתָה דְּבַשׁ וְחָלָב, וְנִכְנַס לַמִּקְדָּשׁ – חַיָּיב. אִיבָּעֵית אֵימָא: ר"ש לֵית לֵיהּ אִיסּוּר חָל עַל אִיסּוּר. *דְּתַנְיָא, ר"ש אוֹמֵר: הָאוֹכֵל נְבֵילָה בְּיוֹם הַכִּפּוּרִים – פָּטוּר. וּלְרַבָּנַן נַמִּי, הָכְתִיב (במדבר ו) "מִכֹּל אֲשֶׁר יֵעָשֶׂה מִגֶּפֶן הַיַּיִן"! אָמְרִי לָךְ רַבָּנַן: הָתָם דלִימֵּד עַל אִיסּוּרֵי נָזִיר שֶׁמִּצְטָרְפִים זֶה עִם זֶה. ור"ש לֵית לֵיהּ צֵירוּף. *דְּתַנְיָא, ר"ש אוֹמֵר: (א) כָּל שֶׁהוּ לְמַכּוֹת, לֹא אָמְרוּ כַּזַּיִת אֶלָּא לְעִנְיַן קָרְבָּן.§ **מתני'** ה"הֲרֵינִי כְּשִׁמְשׁוֹן" "כְּבֶן מָנוֹחַ", "כְּבַעַל דְּלִילָה" "כְּמִי שֶׁעָקַר דַּלְתוֹת עַזָּה" "כְּמִי שֶׁנִּקְּרוּ פְּלִשְׁתִּים אֶת עֵינָיו" – הֲרֵי זֶה נְזִיר שִׁמְשׁוֹן.§ **גמ'** לָמָּה לִי לְמִיתְנָא כָּל הָלֵין? צְרִיכִי; דְּאִי אֲמַר "הֲרֵינִי כְּשִׁמְשׁוֹן" – הֲוָה אָמֵינָא שִׁמְשׁוֹן אַחֲרִינָא, קמ"ל "כְּבֶן מָנוֹחַ". וְאִי תְּנָא "כְּבֶן מָנוֹחַ" – הֲוָה אָמֵינָא: אִיכָּא דְּמִיתְקְרֵי הָכִי, קמ"ל "כְּבַעַל דְּלִילָה" וּ"כְמִי שֶׁנִּקְּרוּ פְּלִשְׁתִּים אֶת עֵינָיו".§ **מתני'** ומַה בֵּין נְזִיר עוֹלָם לִנְזִיר שִׁמְשׁוֹן? נְזִיר עוֹלָם – הִכְבִּיד שְׂעָרוֹ מֵיקֵל בְּתַעַר, וּמֵבִיא שָׁלֹשׁ בְּהֵמוֹת, וְאִם נִטְמָא – מֵבִיא קָרְבַּן טוּמְאָה. נְזִיר שִׁמְשׁוֹן – הִכְבִּיד שְׂעָרוֹ אֵינוֹ מֵיקֵל, וְאִם נִטְמָא – אֵינוֹ מֵבִיא קָרְבַּן טוּמְאָה.§ **גמ'** נְזִיר עוֹלָם מַאן דְּכַר שְׁמֵיהּ? חַסּוּרֵי מִיחַסְּרָא, וְהָכִי קָתָנֵי: הָאוֹמֵר "הֲרֵינִי נְזִיר עוֹלָם" – הֲרֵי זֶה נָזִיר. (ב) מַה בֵּין נְזִיר עוֹלָם לִנְזִיר שִׁמְשׁוֹן? נְזִיר עוֹלָם – הִכְבִּיד שְׂעָרוֹ מֵיקֵל בְּתַעַר, וּמֵבִיא שָׁלֹשׁ בְּהֵמוֹת, וְאִם נִטְמָא – מֵבִיא קָרְבַּן טוּמְאָה. נְזִיר שִׁמְשׁוֹן – הִכְבִּיד שְׂעָרוֹ אֵינוֹ מֵיקֵל בְּתַעַר, וְאֵינוֹ

א) וַהֲרֵי מוּשְׁבָּע וְעוֹמֵד ב) עָלָיו מֵהַר סִינַי הוּא. דִּכְתִיב "זָכוֹר אֶת יוֹם הַשַּׁבָּת לְקַדְּשׁוֹ" – זוֹכְרֵהוּ עַל הַיַּיִן. אֵין לִי אֶלָּא בִּכְנִיסָתוֹ, בִּיצִיאָתוֹ מִנַּיִן – ת"ל כו' (*פסחים דף קו). וְקי"ל דְּנִשְׁבָּע לְבַטֵּל אֶת הַמִּצְוָה פָּטוּר, דְּלָא חָיְילָא שְׁבוּעָה וּמְבַטְּלָה מִצְוָה. וְא"ת: הָא תְּנַן (נדרים דף טז. שבועות דף כה.): חוֹמֶר בִּנְדָרִים מִבִּשְׁבוּעוֹת, שֶׁכֵּן הַנֶּדֶר חָל עַל דְּבַר מִצְוָה כִּדְבַר הָרְשׁוּת, ד"אִישׁ כִּי יִדּוֹר נֶדֶר לַה'" כְּתִיב, אֲפִילּוּ בְּמִידֵּי דְּלַה' ג) נַמִּי! לָא קַשְׁיָא, דְּהָא לָא הָוֵי אֶלָּא כְּגוֹן דְּאָמַר "יְשִׁיבַת סוּכָּה עָלַי", דְּאוֹסֵר אוֹתָהּ עָלָיו וְאֵין מַאֲכִילִין אֶת הָאָדָם דָּבָר הָאָסוּר לוֹ. אֲבָל אִם אָמַר "קוֹנָם שֶׁלֹּא אֵשֵׁב בַּסּוּכָּה" – אֵין בִּדְבָרָיו כְּלוּם. וְהָכִי מַסְקִינַן לָהּ בִּנְדָרִים בְּפֶרֶק "וְאֵלּוּ מוּתָּרִין" (דף טז:). אֶלָּא כִּי הָא דַּאֲמַר רָבָא שְׁבוּעָה שֶׁאֶשְׁתֶּה וְחָזַר וְאָמַר הֲרֵינִי נָזִיר אָתְיָא נְזִירוּת חָיְילָא עַל שְׁבוּעָה. וְהַיְינוּ דְּקָאָמַר לֶאֱסוֹר יֵין מִצְוָה, דְּנִשְׁבָּע לִשְׁתּוֹת, כְּיֵין הָרְשׁוּת. וְכִי תֵּימָא: מַאי שְׁנָא נִשְׁבָּע מִפִּי עַצְמוֹ מִמֻּשְׁבָּע מֵהַר סִינַי? הָכִי אָמְרִינַן לֵיהּ בְּהֶדְיָא בְּמַסֶּ' שְׁבוּעוֹת (דף כט.): "שְׁבוּעָה שֶׁאוֹכַל כִּכָּר זוֹ" וְחָזַר וְאָמַר "שְׁבוּעָה שֶׁלֹּא אוֹכְלֶנָּה" – עַל הָרִאשׁוֹנָה חַיָּיב מִשּׁוּם שְׁבוּעַת בִּטּוּי, וְעַל הַשְּׁנִיָּה חַיָּיב מִשּׁוּם שְׁבוּעַת שָׁוְא. וְהָתָם מְפָרֵשׁ טַעְמָא. וּמִיהוּ, אִיכָּא לָן לְמִשְׁמַע מִינָּהּ, ד) דְּקָאָמַר חַיָּיב עַל הַשְּׁנִיָּה א] אע"ג דְּהָוֵי נִשְׁבָּע לְבַטֵּל אֶת הַמִּצְוָה, דִּנְזִירוּת נַמִּי חָיְילָא אַהַאי דְּנִשְׁבַּע לִשְׁתּוֹת יַיִן. מַאי וְשֵׁכָר ש"מ תַּרְתֵּי. לֶאֱסוֹר יֵין מִצְוָה כְּיֵין הָרְשׁוּת, וְכִי לָא נָדַר נַמִּי אֶלָּא מֵחַד מִינַּיְיהוּ – דְּהָוֵי נָזִיר מִכּוּלְּהוּ. אַף גַּבֵּי. כֹּהֵן הַבָּא לַמִּקְדָּשׁ, כִּי שָׁתָה יַיִן הוּא דְּלִיתְּסַר. אֲבָל כִּי שָׁתָה שְׁאָר מִילֵּי דְּמִשְׁכְּרִין – לָא, וּלְאַפּוּקֵי מִדְּר' יְהוּדָה כו'. קְעִילִית. שֵׁם מָקוֹם. אִיבָּעֵית אֵימָא. הַיְינוּ טַעְמָא דְּר"ש דְּאָמַר: אֵינוֹ חַיָּיב בִּנְזִירוּת עַד שֶׁיַּזִּיר מְכוּוָּן בִּסְתָם, דְּקָאָמַר "הֲרֵינִי נָזִיר". דְּר"ש לְטַעְמֵיהּ, דְּלֵית לֵיהּ אִיסּוּר חָל עַל אִיסּוּר. וְה"נ כִּי אָסַר עַצְמוֹ מִן הַחַרְצַנִּים וּמִן הַזַּגִּין ה) וְחָיְילָא עֲלֵיהּ נְזִירוּת – לָא אָתֵי אִידָךְ פַּלְגָא דְּתִגְלַחַת וְטוּמְאָה וְחָיְילָא עִילָּוֵיהּ. אִי נַמִּי, כִּי הִזִּיר עַצְמוֹ מִן הַיַּיִן – לָא אָתֵי אִיסּוּר תִּגְלַחַת וְטוּמְאָה וְחָיֵיל אַאִיסּוּר יַיִן לְשַׁוְויֵהּ נֶדֶר גָּמוּר. וּמְנָא תֵּימְרָא דְּר"ש לֵית לֵיהּ אִיסּוּר חָל עַל אִיסּוּר דְּתַנְיָא ר"ש אוֹמֵר הָאוֹכֵל נְבֵילָה בְּיוֹם הַכִּפּוּרִים וכו'. דְּלָא אָתֵי אִיסּוּר יוֹם הַכִּפּוּרִים וְחָיֵיל אַאִיסּוּר נְבֵילָה. דְּלָא אָמְרִינַן: מִיגּוֹ דַּאֲתָא יוֹם הַכִּפּוּרִים וְאִיתּוֹסַף אִיסּוּרָא לְגַבֵּי שְׁאָר מִילֵּי, אִיתּוֹסַף נַמִּי לְגַבֵּי נְבֵילָה. וְר"ש לְטַעְמֵיהּ, דְּאָמַר בְּמַסֶּכֶת כְּרֵיתוֹת (דף כג.): דְּאִיסּוּר חָמוּר לָא אָתֵי וְחָיֵיל עַל אִיסּוּר קַל. וְהָכִי ו) פָּרִישְׁנָא [בִּיבָמוֹת] (דף לג:) וּבְמַסֶּכֶת שְׁבוּעוֹת (דף כד.). לִימֵּד עַל אִיסּוּרֵי נָזִיר שֶׁמִּצְטָרְפִין זֶה עִם זֶה. לִכְזַיִת. שֶׁאִם לֹא אָכַל בֵּין הַכֹּל אֶלָּא כְּזַיִת בִּלְבַד – חַיָּיב מַלְקוֹת. וְר"ש. דְּלָא דָּרֵישׁ בֵּיהּ הַאי טַעְמָא, ז) כו' – אָזֵיל לְטַעְמֵיהּ, דְּלָא מִצְרִיךְ לֵיהּ הַאי קְרָא מִשּׁוּם צֵירוּף, דְּלֵית לֵיהּ צֵירוּף. דְּקָסָבַר ר"ש: אֲפִילּוּ לֹא אָכַל אֶלָּא כָּל שֶׁהוּא – חַיָּיב, דְּעוֹבֵר בְּלָאו הָאָמוּר בּוֹ "מֵחַרְצַנִּים וְעַד זָג לֹא יֹאכֵל". דְּתַנְיָא, ר"ש אוֹמֵר: כָּל שֶׁהוּא לְמַלְקוֹת, ט) לֹא אָמְרוּ שִׁיעוּר אֲכִילָה לְכַזַּיִת אֶלָּא לְעִנְיַן קָרְבָּן. וּלְעִנְיַן שְׁאָר אִיסּוּרִין שֶׁחַיָּיבִין עַל י) שִׁגְגָתוֹ חַטָּאת, כְּגוֹן חֵלֶב וְדָם וְחָמֵץ בְּפֶסַח. אֲבָל גַּבֵּי נָזִיר, כִּי עָבַר עַל נְזִירוּתוֹ וְאָכַל זָג אוֹ חַרְצָן – דְּמִילְקָא הוּא דְּלָקֵי, וְלָא הָוֵי חַיָּיב קָרְבָּן – בְּכָל שֶׁהוּא מְחַיֵּיב, וְלָא בָּעֵינַן בֵּיהּ צֵירוּף. הִלְכָּךְ, הוֹאִיל וְלָא מִילְּטְרִיךְ כ) מִשּׁוּם צֵירוּף – ל) מִיַּיתַּר לֵיהּ קְרָא לְהָכִי: דְּאֵינוֹ חַיָּיב עַד שֶׁיַּזִּיר מְכוּוָּן. **מתני'** הֲרֵינִי כְּשִׁמְשׁוֹן. (ג) מ) כְּבֶן מָנוֹחַ אוֹ כְּבַעַל דְּלִילָה, אוֹ שֶׁלֹּא אָמַר "כְּבַעַל דְּלִילָה" אֶלָּא אָמַר "כְּבֶן מָנוֹחַ כְּמִי שֶׁעָקַר דַּלְתוֹת עַזָּה", אוֹ שֶׁלֹּא אָמַר "דַּלְתוֹת עַזָּה" אֶלָּא אָמַר "כְּשִׁמְשׁוֹן כְּבֶן מָנוֹחַ כְּמִי שֶׁנִּקְּרוּ פְלִשְׁתִּים אֶת עֵינָיו". הֲרֵי זֶה נְזִיר שִׁמְשׁוֹן. צָרִיךְ לִנְהוֹג בְּעַצְמוֹ בִּנְזִירוּת שִׁמְשׁוֹן. וּלְקַמָּן מְפָרֵשׁ הֵיכִי הָוֵי. **גמ'** דְּאִי אָמַר כְּשִׁמְשׁוֹן וְתוּ לָא. ה"א: שִׁמְשׁוֹן אַחֲרִינָא קָאָמַר, וְלָכֵי קָאָמַר "כְּבֶן מָנוֹחַ". וְאִי הֲוָה אָמַר נַמִּי "כְּשִׁמְשׁוֹן כְּבֶן מָנוֹחַ" בִּלְבַד, ה"א: אִיכָּא אִינִישׁ אַחֲרִינָא דְּאִתְקְרֵי נַמִּי הָכִי, אוֹ בֶּן מָנוֹחַ אוֹ שִׁמְשׁוֹן אוֹ בֶּן מָנוֹחַ. לְהָכִי קָתָנֵי בַּהֲדַיְיהוּ "כְּבַעַל דְּלִילָה" אוֹ "כְּמִי שֶׁנִּקְּרוּ פְלִשְׁתִּים אֶת עֵינָיו" אוֹ "כְּמִי שֶׁעָקַר דַּלְתוֹת עַזָּה", דְּמִיגַּלְיָא מִילְּתָא דְּלָא הֲוָה אַחֲרִינָא. הֲרֵינִי נְזִיר עוֹלָם הֲרֵי זֶה נָזִיר. נ) כָּל יְמֵי חַיָּיו. דְּכִי אָמַר "הֲרֵינִי נְזִיר עוֹלָם" מַשְׁמַע דִּנְזִירוּת קִבֵּל עָלָיו עַד עוֹלָם. ס) לְפִיכָךְ כֵּיוָן שֶׁהִגִּיעַ לְל' יוֹם שֶׁיֵּשׁ לוֹ כּוֹבֶד שֵׂעָר – מֵיקֵל בְּתַעַר, ע) וּמְגַלֵּחַ כָּל ל' וְל' (ד). וּמֵבִיא. לְכָל תִּגְלַחַת וְתִגְלַחַת ג' בְּהֵמוֹת: חַטָּאת וְעוֹלָה וּשְׁלָמִים, כְּמוֹ שֶׁמֵּבִיא נְזִיר טָהוֹר. וְאִם נִטְמָא מֵבִיא קָרְבַּן טוּמְאָה. כֶּבֶשׂ בֶּן שְׁנָתוֹ לְאָשָׁם וּשְׁתֵּי תוֹרִים אוֹ שְׁנֵי בְּנֵי יוֹנָה. אֲבָל הַמְקַבֵּל עָלָיו נְזִירוּת שִׁמְשׁוֹן – הֲרֵי זֶה נְזִיר עוֹלָם, וּלְעוֹלָם אֵינוֹ מֵיקֵל בְּתַעַר. וְאִם נִטְמָא אֵינוֹ מֵבִיא קָרְבַּן טוּמְאָה. שֶׁכֵּן מָצִינוּ בְּשִׁמְשׁוֹן שֶׁנִּטְמָא לְמֵתִים, כִּדְמְפָרֵשׁ לְקַמָּן. מִפִּי

---

*)**עד** שיזיר מכוון. או יאמר סתמא, דמשמע כל מילי דנזירות קיבל עליה. ואם בא לפרש חרצן וזג – צריך לפרש כולם, גם תגלחת וטומאה.

מכל אשר יעשה מגפן היין. אלמא דמכולהו צריך להזיר. וא"ת: ואכתי תגלחת וטומאה לא שמעינן! וי"ל: כיון דגלי לן ביין – ה"ה שצריך לקבל גם תגלחת וטומאה. ונפקא לן מלישנא דקרא "מכל". **מיין** ושכר יזיר. משמע אפילו בחד הוי נזיר, דהא כבר כתיב "מכל אשר יעשה מגפן", למה לי למיכתב "מיין ושכר"? אלא לאשמועי' דאפי' לא נדר כי אם בחד מהני – דחייל נזירות עליו, ואפילו כשבא לפרש, דהכא חרצן וזג לא כתיבי. **לאסור** יין מצוה כיין הרשות. כלומר, מקרא יתירא ד"מיין ושכר יזיר". **מאי** היא קידושא ואבדלתא מושבע ועומד מהר סיני הוא. דקדוש היום דאורייתא, ואיך תחול עליו נזירות? וקשה: דאדרבה, להכי איצטריך קרא מיותר, לומר דחייל עליה נזירות! ועוד קשה: מאי משני בתר הכי: כגון שנשבע לשתות, וחזר ונדר בנזיר, דאתיא נזירות וחייל אשבועה? מ"מ תקשי לו, הרי מושבע ועומד מהר סיני, כלומר דאין מושבע ועומד גדול מזה שנשבע לשתות? ועוד קשה: דקדוש היום לאו דאורייתא הוא. דנהי נמי דכתיב "זכור" ודרשינן: זוכרהו על היין – אסמכתא הוא! ⊕לכ"נ לר"ת דגרסינן בתמיה: וכי מושבע ועומד מהר סיני? כלומר, ל"ל קרא מיותר לאסור יין מלוה, וכי מושבע וכו'? דנהי דקידושי היום דאורייתא – על היין לאו דאורייתא, ב] דזוכרהו על היין אסמכתא. והשתא משני: כגון שנשבע לשתות, וקמ"ל קרא יתירא דחייל עליה, אע"ג שנשבע לשתות*. **לאלופי** למקדש. מהכא. (ה) ואינו חייב למקדש אלא אין ושכר, ולאפוקי מרבי יהודה כו'. **ר"ש** לית ליה איסור חל על איסור. פירוש בעלמא כדתניא כו'. ואי לאו קרא הכא ה"א: היכא דנשבע שלא לשתות, ושוב הזיר בנזיר ושתה ביין – לא חייב אנזירות. קמ"ל קרא יתירא ד"מיין ושכר", דאם נשבע שלא לשתות כוס זה, ונדר בנזיר ועבר ושתה הכוס – דלקי תרתי, משום שבועתא ומשום נזירות. ולא תימא כדקאמר רבא לעיל "שבועה שאשתה", אלא תוכל לתרץ אפילו "שבועה שלא אשתה", כדפירשתי. **ורבי** שמעון לית ליה צירוף. כלומר, אין צריך יתור לצירוף, דאפי' בשאר איסורים כחלב ודם מחייב בכל שהו, ולא אמרו כזית אלא לקרבן. והכא לא שייך צירוף לקרבן, שקרבן נזיר אינו בא על ששתה יין, אלא מלקות, והקרבן בא על השלמת נדרו. **מה** בין נזיר שמשון לנזיר עולם. וא"ת: שאלה איכא בינייהו, דנזיר שמשון ליתא בשאלה, ונזיר עולם איתא בשאלה, כדאי' בפ' בתרא דמכות (דף כב.) גבי חורש תלם אחד! וי"ל: מילתא דליתא בנזירות לא קתני, ואם ישאל על נזירות – אז לא הוי נזיר. וה"ק: מה בין נזיר שמשון כו' כששניהן נזירין: ***כשמשון** כבן מנוח כבעל דלילה. אבל "כשמשון" לחודיה, או "כבן מנוח" לחודיה – לא סגי, עד שיאמר שלשתן, כדמוכח בגמ'. מכאן ואילך גרים ר"ת: וכמי שעקר דלתות עזה, בוי"ו, וכמי שנקרו פלשתים את עיניו. דאו או קאמר, כלומר: או שיאמר "כמי שעקר", או "כמי שנקרו" כו'. ג] דאי אמר "כבעל דלילה" לחוד, או "כמי שעקר דלתות עזה" לחוד, או "כמי שנקרו פלשתים את עיניו" לחוד – דהוי נזיר שמשון, דבהא ליכא למיטעי. **נזיר** עולם מיקל. ולא מגלח לגמרי, כאבשלום שלא גלח לגמרי, שהרי נתלה בשערו. **ומביא** ג' בהמות. בשעה שמיקל, הלכה למשה מסיני, ואסמכתא מאבשלום דאמר "אשלם נדרי". חטאת עולה ושלמים כנזיר טהור, קרבן טומאה – שתי תורים ואשם. קרבן

פי' הרא"ש

אלימא קדושתא ואבדלתא מושבע ועומד מהר סיני הוא דכתיב זכור את יום השבת לקדשו ודרשינן בערבי פסחים זכרהו על היין. וקשה נהי דקידוש הוי דאורייתא כדא' בברכו' נשים חייבות בקידוש היום דבר תורה מיהו קידוש על היין לאו דאורייתא דמקדשין על הפת במקום שאין יין והאי דדריש זכרהו על היין אסמכתא בעלמא הוא. ועוד אבדלתא מאי איכא למימר ע"כ לאו דאורייתא הוא. ועוד מאי קאמר אלא כי הא דאמר רבא שבועה שאשתה וכו' ואמאי חזר בו מקדושא ואבדלתא כי היכי דחל נזירו' על שבועה ה"נ חל על מצות קידוש. ונ"ל דהא ל"ק דלהך פירושא לא גרים אלא וה"ג כי הא דאמר רבא כלומר כי היכי דאמר רבא דנזירו' חלה על שבועה ה"נ חלה על מצות קידוש. ור"ת גרים קדושא ואבדלתא מושבע ועומד מהר סיני הוא בתמיה ואמאי צריך קרא למימר שנזיר נאסר ביין קידוש והבדל': ואיבעית אימא ר"ש לית ליה איסור חל על איסור פר"ת ומשכר יתירא שמעינן ליה דנזיר ששתה יין בי"ה אין חייב משום י"ה דלא אתי איסור י"ה וחיילא אאיסור נזיר. ומהכא יליף ר"ש בכל דוכתא דאין איסור חל על איסור דהכי משמע פשטא דקרא מיין ושכר יזיר ה"ק משום נזיר חייב על יין ושכר ולאו משום איסור אחר דלא אתי איסור אחר וחייל עלויה. וקשה דבפ' כל הבשר דריש שמואל דאין איסור חל על איסור מקרא דומתו בו כי יחללוהו ודריש הכא מיין ושכר דגבי נזיר חל איסור על איסור דאם אמר שבועה שלא אשתה יין ואמר הריני נזיר אתיא נזירות וחיילא אשבועה ולוקה שנים דהכי משמע פשטא דקרא: הרי

עין משפט נר מצוה

מכאן עד ד"ה מאי היא שייך לעיל ג:

יח א מיי' פ"ד מהלכות נזירות הלכה יא סמג לאוין רג:

יט ב מיי' פ"ה מהל' נזירות הלכה א סמג שם:

כ ג מיי' פ"א מהלכות ביאת מקדש הל' ג סמג לאוין שא ועש"ע בכ"מ:

כא ד מיי' פ"ה מהל' נזירות הלכה ג:

כב ה מיי' פ"ג מהלכות נזירות הלכה יב סמג לאוין רמג:

כג ו מיי' שם הל' יב:

[יומא עו.] סנהדרין ע: שבועות כג. כריתות יג: [בכורות מה:]

שבועות כב. פסחים לו. קדושין עז: [כריתות כג.]

[מעילה יח.] מכות יז. שבועות כא:

גליון הש"ס

תוד"ה מאי היא וכו' לכ"נ לר"ת. עי' סוטה דף לב ע"א תוד"ה [illegible]:

[ועי' תוס' פסחים קו. ד"ה זוכרהו וכו' ועוד מגיע למימר כו']

מסורת הש"ס

[בפסחים ליתא וגם בשאר דוכתי לא נמצא עי' במגיד משנה ריש פ' כ"ט בהל' שבת ובמגדול עוז שם]

[בכריתות מסיק הש"ס כמאן אזלא הא דתניא אכל דבילה כו' כמאן כר' יהודה וגם בבכורות לא הביא הך דר' יהודה אומר וע"ש ברש"י ועו"ק ובתוספתא דכריתות פ"א תניא ר' יהודה אומר על היין במיתה ועל המשכרין באזהרה לפיכך אם אכל דבילה קעילית או ששתה חלב ודבש הרי זה לוקה ארבעים]

נוסחת הריב"ן

א) והא: ב) תיבת עליו ליתא בכ"י: ג) דלה' הוא נמי: ד) מדקאמר: ה) חיילא: ו) פרישית: ז) (כתובות): ח) מכוון: ט) ולא: י) שגגתן: כ) אצטריך חרצנים משום: ל) דמייתר: מ) הריני כשמשון (או) כבן מנוח (או) כו' כשמשון (או) הני תיבות או ליתא בכ"י: נ) (כל ימי חייו) ליתא בכ"י: ס) לפיכך כיון שהכביד שערו כלומר כיון שהגיע כו': ע) בתער הס"ד ומה"ד מגלח כל ל' ול' ומביא כו' והד"א:

הגהות הב"ח

(א) גמ' דתניא ר"ש אומר כל שהוא. נ"ב ע"ל סוף דף ל"ו ודף ל"ח: (ב) שם הרי זה נזיר עולם מה בין: (ג) רש"י ד"ה הריני כשמשון בן מנוח כבעל דלילה או שלא אמר כשמשון בן מנוח כבעל דלילה או כו' כשמשון בן מנוח כו' כצ"ל ותיבת או נמחק ב' פעמים: (ד) ד"ה הריני נזיר עולם וכו' כל ל' ול' ומביא הכ"ל: (ה) תוס' ד"ה לאלופי למקדש מהכא לאינו חייב:

הגהות מהר"ב רנשבורג

א] רש"י ד"ה אלא כי הא דאמר רבא כו' אע"ג דהוי נשבע לבטל את המצוה. נ"ב עי' על סוגיא דש"ס בזה תורת מישור בשם [illegible]: ב] תוס' ד"ה מאי היא קידושא ואבדלתא וכו' דנהי דקידושי היום דאורייתא. נ"ב [illegible]: ג] ד"ה כשמשון וכו' דאי אמר כבעל דלילה לחוד. נ"ב עיין תוספות יו"ט ואורה מישור:

כד א מיי' פ"ג מהל' נזירות הלכה יג:
כה ב מיי' פ"א מהל' נדרים הלכה יג סמג לאוין רמב:
כו ג מיי' שם סמג שם טוש"ע יו"ד סי' רד סעיף א וסעיף ב:
כז ד מיי' שם הלכה י:
כח ה ו מיי' פ"א מהל' בכורות הלכה ד סמג עשין ריא טוש"ע יו"ד סי' שו סעיף א:
כט ז מיי' פי"ג מהל' נדרים הל' כג טור ש"ע יו"ד סי' רג סעיף ז:
ל ח מיי' פ"ג מהלכות נזירות הלכה יב:

תורה אור

וְאֵינוֹ מֵבִיא קָרְבַּן טוּמְאָה'. קָרְבָּן הוּא דְּלָא מַיְיתֵי, אֲבָל נְזִירוּת — חָיְילָא עֲלֵיהּ. מַנִּי מַתְנִי'? לָא רַבִּי יְהוּדָה, וְלָא ר"ש. דְּתַנְיָא, *ר' יְהוּדָה אוֹמֵר: נְזִיר שִׁמְשׁוֹן אמוּתָּר לִיטַּמֵּא לַמֵּתִים, שֶׁכֵּן מָצִינוּ בְּשִׁמְשׁוֹן שֶׁנִּטְמָא. ר"ש אוֹמֵר: הָאוֹמֵר "נְזִיר שִׁמְשׁוֹן" — לֹא אָמַר כְּלוּם, שֶׁלֹּא מָצִינוּ בְּשִׁמְשׁוֹן שֶׁיָּצָאת נְזִירוּת מִפִּיו. מַנִּי? אִי ר' יְהוּדָה — הָאָמַר אֲפִילּוּ לְכַתְּחִילָּה, וּמַתְנִיתִין קָתָנֵי "אִם נִטְמָא". אִי ר' שִׁמְעוֹן — הָאָמַר לָא חָיְילָא עֲלֵיהּ נְזִירוּת כְּלָל! לְעוֹלָם ר' יְהוּדָה הִיא, וְאַיְּידֵי דְּקָתָנֵי גַּבֵּי נְזִיר עוֹלָם "אִם נִטְמָא" — תְּנָא נַמִּי גַּבֵּי נְזִיר שִׁמְשׁוֹן "אִם נִטְמָא". לֵימָא בִּפְלוּגְתָּא דְּהָנֵי תַּנָּאֵי קָמִיפַּלְגִי, *דִּתְנַן: "הֲרֵי עָלַי כִּבְכוֹר", רַבִּי יַעֲקֹב אוֹסֵר וְר' יוֹסֵי במַתִּיר. מַאי לָאו, ר' יְהוּדָה סָבַר לָהּ כְּר' יַעֲקֹב, דְּאָמַר: לָא בָּעֵינַן דָּבָר הַנִּידָּר, וְר' שִׁמְעוֹן סָבַר לָהּ כְּר' יוֹסֵי, דְּאָמַר: בָּעֵינַן דָּבָר הַנִּידָּר? לָא, דְּכוּלֵּי עָלְמָא גבָּעֵינַן דָּבָר הַנִּידָּר, וְשָׁאנֵי גַּבֵּי בְּכוֹר דִּכְתִיב בֵּיהּ °"לַה'" — *לְרַבּוֹת אֶת הַבְּכוֹר. וְר' יוֹסֵי אָמַר לָךְ: הַהוּא "לַה'" מִיבָּעֵי לֵיהּ לְרַבּוֹת חַטָּאת וְאָשָׁם. וּמָה רָאִיתָ לְרַבּוֹת חַטָּאת וְאָשָׁם וּלְהוֹצִיא אֶת הַבְּכוֹר? דמְרַבֶּה אֲנִי חַטָּאת וְאָשָׁם — שֶׁכֵּן מַתְפִּיסָן בְּנֶדֶר, וּמוֹצִיא אֲנִי אֶת הַבְּכוֹר, שֶׁאֵין מַתְפִּיסוֹ בְּנֶדֶר. וְר' יַעֲקֹב אָמַר לָךְ: בְּכוֹר נַמִּי מַתְפִּיסוֹ בְּנֶדֶר הוּא. *דְּתַנְיָא: שֶׁל בֵּית רַבֵּינוּ אָמְרוּ: מִנַּיִן לְנוֹלָד לוֹ בְּכוֹר בְּתוֹךְ עֶדְרוֹ השֶׁמִּצְוָה עָלָיו לְהַקְדִּישׁוֹ — שֶׁנֶּאֱמַר °"הַזָּכָר תַּקְדִּישׁ". וְר' יוֹסֵי אָמַר לָךְ: נְהִי דְּמִצְוָה לְהַקְדִּישׁוֹ, אִי לָא מַקְדִּישׁ לֵיהּ, ומִי לָא קָדוֹשׁ? גַּבֵּי נָזִיר נַמִּי, הָכְתִיב °"לַה'"! הַהוּא מִיבָּעֵי לֵיהּ לְכִדְתַנְיָא: *אָמַר שִׁמְעוֹן הַצַּדִּיק: מִיָּמַי לֹא אָכַלְתִּי אֲשַׁם נָזִיר טָמֵא, חוּץ מֵאָדָם אֶחָד שֶׁבָּא אֵלַי מִן הַדָּרוֹם, יְפֵה עֵינַיִם וְטוֹב רוֹאִי, וּקְווּצּוֹתָיו סְדוּרוֹת לוֹ תַּלְתַּלִּים. אָמַרְתִּי לוֹ: בְּנִי, מָה רָאִיתָ לְשַׁחֵת שֵׂעָר נָאֶה זֶה? אָמַר לִי: רוֹעֶה הָיִיתִי לְאָבִי בְּעִירִי, וְהָלַכְתִּי לִשְׁאוֹב מַיִם מִן הַמַּעְיָן, וְנִסְתַּכַּלְתִּי בַּבָּבוּאָה שֶׁלִּי, וּפָחַז יִצְרִי עָלַי וּבִיקֵּשׁ לְטוֹרְדֵנִי מִן הָעוֹלָם. אָמַרְתִּי לוֹ: רֵיקָה! מִפְּנֵי מָה אַתָּה מִתְגָּאֶה בְּעוֹלָם שֶׁאֵינוֹ שֶׁלְּךָ, שֶׁסּוֹפְךָ לִהְיוֹת רִמָּה וְתוֹלֵעָה? הָעֲבוֹדָה שֶׁאֲגַלֵּחֲךָ לַשָּׁמַיִם! עָמַדְתִּי וּנְשַׁקְתִּיו עַל רֹאשׁוֹ; אָמַרְתִּי לוֹ: יכְּמוֹתְךָ יִרְבּוּ נְזִירִים בְּיִשְׂרָאֵל, עָלֶיךָ הַכָּתוּב אוֹמֵר: °"אִישׁ... כִּי יַפְלִא לִנְדֹּר נֶדֶר נָזִיר לְהַזִּיר לַה'". וְשִׁמְשׁוֹן לָאו נָזִיר הֲוָה? וְהָכְתִיב °"כִּי נְזִיר אֱלֹהִים יִהְיֶה הַנַּעַר מִן הַבָּטֶן"! הָתָם מַלְאָךְ הוּא דְּקָאָמַר. וּמְנָלַן דְּאִיטַּמִּי לַמֵּתִים? אִילֵימָא מִדִּכְתִיב °"בִּלְחִי הַחֲמוֹר הִכֵּיתִי אֶלֶף אִישׁ" — דִּילְמָא *גְּרוּיֵי גָּרֵי בְּהוּ, וְלָא נָגַע בְּהוּ! אֶלָּא מֵהָכָא °"וַיַּךְ מֵהֶם שְׁלֹשִׁים אִישׁ וַיִּקַּח אֶת חֲלִיצוֹתָם". דִּילְמָא אַשְׁלְחִינוּן בְּרֵישָׁא וַהֲדַר קַטְלִינַן? *"וַיַּךְ... וַיִּקַּח" כְּתִיב. וְדִילְמָא גּוֹסְסִין שַׁוְּינַן! אֶלָּא, גְּמָרָא גְּמִירִי לָהּ. וּנְזִיר עוֹלָם הֵיכָא כְּתִיב? דְּתַנְיָא, *רַבִּי אוֹמֵר: חאַבְשָׁלוֹם נְזִיר עוֹלָם הָיָה, שֶׁנֶּאֱמַר °"וַיְהִי מִקֵּץ אַרְבָּעִים שָׁנָה וַיֹּאמֶר אַבְשָׁלוֹם אֶל הַמֶּלֶךְ אֵלְכָה נָּא וַאֲשַׁלֵּם אֶת נִדְרִי אֲשֶׁר נָדַרְתִּי לַה' בְּחֶבְרוֹן". וּמְגַלֵּחַ אֶחָד לִשְׁנֵים עָשָׂר חֹדֶשׁ — שֶׁנֶּאֱ' °"וַיְהִי מִקֵּץ יָמִים לַיָּמִים". וְיָלֵיף

במדבר ל | דברים טו | במדבר ו | שם | שופטים יג | שם טו | שם יד | שמואל ב טו | שם יד

קרבן הוא דלא מייתי. פירוש: נזיר שמשון. אבל נזירות חייל עליה, כלומר: לענין שאסור נטמאות למתים לכתחילה. **שלא** מצינו בשמשון שיצא נזירות מפיו. כלומר, לא נזר בנזיר, אלא מבטן אמו היה נדור בנזיר ממילא. ואנן בעינן שידור בדבר הנדור, כמו "הריני כזה" שנדר בנזיר, כדדרשי' (נדרים דף יד.) "כי ידור נדר" — עד שידור בדבר הנדור. **הרי** עלי כבכור. פי': ככר זה כבכור. **לא** דכ"ע. כלומר, א] כ"ע אי אמר "כעולה וכשלמים" — הוי דבר הנדור, אבל בכור קדוש מרחם אמו. רבי יהודה סבר לה כרבי יעקב, דאמר לא בעינן דבר הנדור, ואם אמר "הריני כשמשון" — הוי נזיר, אע"ג דנזיר שמשון לאו נדור הוה, אלא קדוש מבטן אמו כבכור. **לא** דכ"ע בעינן דבר הנדור בעלמא לגבי נזירות ושאני הכא דכתיב לה'. "כי ידור נדר לה'" — לרבות את הבכור, כלומר שהוא לה' ממילא, אפילו [הכי] הוי נדור. **לרבות** את החטאת ואשם. דסד"א: עולה ושלמים הבאים נדבה — הוי דבר הנדור, אבל בחטאת ואשם הבאים בחובה — לא מיקרי דבר הנדור, קמ"ל "לה'" דמרבי כל מילי דהוי לה'. **שמצוה** לקדש. פירוש: בכור תקדיש ולומר "מוקדש בבכורה" אע"פ דקדיש מרחם. **מי** לא קדוש. הלכך לאו דבר הנדור הוא, כיון דאינו אלא מצוה בעלמא. **גבי** נזיר נמי הכתיב לה'. וכי היכי דמרבי ר' יעקב בכור מ"לה'" — ה"נ נרבה נזיר שמשון מ"לה'" דכתי' בנזיר. **לא** אכלתי אשם נזירות. אבל שאר אשמות היה אוכל. אבל אשם נזיר היה קשה בעיניו לאוכלו, לפי שאינו בא אלא בנזיר שנטמא, וכיון שנטמא — הי' דואג פן מתחרט על נדרו, שהימים הראשונים נופלין, ומביא חולין בעזרה. **עליך** הכתוב אומר להזיר לה'. כלומר, שתחילת נדרו לגמרי לש"ש, ולא היה דואג שיתחרט אע"פ שנטמא. אבל שאר נודרים — סתמא נודרי' בעת צרה, או על עבירה שבידן כדי להצטער ולכפר על עונם, וכשמתרבים הימים עליהם ממה שגמרו בדעתן — קרוב להיות תוהא על הראשונות. **שמשון** לאו נדור הוה. פירוש: לא נדור נזיר הוה. והא כתיב "כי נזיר אלהים יהיה" כו'. וקס"ד שהמלאך היה אומר לאביו שיזירנו לכשיולד, כדאמרי' לקמן (דף כח:): האיש מדיר בנו בנזיר. **התם** מלאך הוא דקאמר ליה. בנבואה, ולא יצא נזירות לא מפי אביו ולא מפי שמשון. **גרויי** גרי. לשון חצים, כלומר: מרחוק זורק בהם והרגם. **דילמא** גוססין שווינהו. לאו דוקא גוססים, כי נזיר אסור ליגע לגוסס, אלא כלומר: קרוב לגוססין. **אלא** גמר'. פירוש: דגמרי' דקטלינהו ממש והדר שלוחי שלחינן. ואפי' למאן דאמר (יבמות סא.) קברי גוים אינן מטמאין באהל — במגע מיהא מטמאין. **ונזיר** עולם היכא כתיב. כלומר, שמותר להקל. ומייתי מאבשלום שהיה מיקל, למר כדאית ליה ולמר כדאית ליה. **את** נדרי אשר נדרתי. וסתם נדר משמע ליה נזירות. ועוד, אחר שלא היה מגלח אלא מימים לימים, *משמע שהכביד עליו שערו, מכלל דנזירות נדר. אין

מַנִּי אִי רַבִּי יְהוּדָה הָא אָמַר דְּמוּתָּר לְכַתְּחִילָּה. לִיטַּמֵּא, וּמַתְנִי' קָתָנֵי "אִם נִטְמָא" — בְּדִיעֲבַד, אֲבָל לְכַתְּחִילָּה — לָא. תְּנָא נַמִּי גַּבֵּי נְזִיר שִׁמְשׁוֹן אִם (א). וְה"ה נַמִּי (א) לְכַתְּחִילָּה מוּתָּר. הֲרֵי עָלַי. כִּכָּר זוֹ כִּבְכוֹר. רַבִּי יַעֲקֹב אוֹסֵר. דְּלָא בָּעֵינַן שֶׁיְּהֵא אִיסּוּרוֹ בְּדָבָר הַנִּידָּר כְּגוֹן *(חַטָּאת) (ב) וּשְׁלָמִים, (דְּהָא כְּתִיב "אִישׁ כִּי יִדּוֹר נֶדֶר לַה'" — לְרַבּוֹת דָּבָר הָאָסוּר, כְּגוֹן בְּכוֹר). רַבִּי יְהוּדָה סָבַר לָהּ כְּר' יַעֲקֹב דְּאָמַר לָא בָּעֵינַן דָּבָר הַנָּדוּר. הָכִי נַמִּי, כִּי אָמַר "הֲרֵינִי נְזִיר שִׁמְשׁוֹן" — הָוֵי נָזִיר, וְאַע"ג דְּשִׁמְשׁוֹן לֹא יָצָא נְזִירוּת מִפִּיו. וְר"ש. דְּאוֹמֵר לָא הָוֵי נָזִיר — סָבַר לָהּ כְּר' יוֹסֵי דְּאָמַר מוּתָּר, מִשּׁוּם דְּלֹא (ג) הִתְפִּיס אֶלָּא בִּבְכוֹר, דְּלָא הָוֵי דָּבָר הַנָּדוּר, שֶׁהֲרֵי קְדוּשָּׁתוֹ מֵרֶחֶם. וְשָׁאנֵי גַּבֵּי בְּכוֹר. דְּהַיְינוּ טַעְמָא דְּרַבִּי יַעֲקֹב — מִשּׁוּם דִּכְתִיב "לַה'", "אִישׁ כִּי יִדּוֹר נֶדֶר לַה'" — לְרַבּוֹת אֶת הַבְּכוֹר. לְרַבּוֹת חַטָּאת וְאָשָׁם. דְּכִי אָמַר "כִּכָּר זֶה עָלַי כְּחַטָּאת וּכְאָשָׁם" — אָסוּר. מְרַבֶּה אֲנִי חַטָּאת וְאָשָׁם שֶׁכֵּן מַתְפִּיסָן בְּנֶדֶר. שֶׁאֵינוֹ מֵבִיא חַטָּאת וְאָשָׁם עַד שֶׁיְּהֵא מְחוּיָּב לָהֶן וְיֹאמַר "זֶהוּ לְחַטָּאתִי וְלַאֲשָׁמִי". שֶׁאֵין (ד) מַתְפִּיסוֹ אֶת הַבְּכוֹר בְּנֶדֶר. (ה) דְּנָדוּר וְעוֹמֵד מֵרֶחֶם הוּא. אֲבָל גַּבֵּי נָזִיר, דְּכוּ"ע בֵּין לְר' יַעֲקֹב בֵּין לְר' יוֹסֵי — בָּעֵינַן דָּבָר הַנָּדוּר, וְכִי אָמַר "הֲרֵינִי נְזִיר שִׁמְשׁוֹן" — לֹא אָמַר (ו) וְלֹא כְּלוּם. גַּבֵּי נָזִיר (ז) נַמִּי. בֵּין לְר' יַעֲקֹב בֵּין לְרַבִּי יוֹסֵי, אַמַּאי בָּעֵינַן דָּבָר הַנָּדוּר? הָא כְּתִיב בֵּיהּ "לַה' לְהַזִּיר"! (ח) לֹא אָכַלְתִּי [אֲשַׁם] נְזִירוּת מֵעוֹלָם. מִשּׁוּם הַהוּא טַעְמָא דְּאָמְרִי' לְעֵיל, דִּכְשֶׁהֵן (ט) מִטַּמְּאִין וְרַבִּין עֲלֵיהֶן יְמֵי טוּמְאָה הֵן מִתְחָרְטִין (י) וּמְבִיאִין חוּלִּין לָעֲזָרָה. וּפָחַז. וּמִהֵר עָלַי יִצְרִי, וֶהֱבִיאַנִי לִידֵי הִרְהוּר. לִשְׁאוֹב מַיִם מִן (כ) *)הַגִּיעַ גָּרְסִי', שֶׁכֵּן הוּא לְשׁוֹן הַמִּשְׁנָה, וּפֵי': מִן הַמַּעְיָן. עָלֶיךָ אָמַר הַכָּתוּב אִישׁ כִּי יַפְלִיא לִנְדּוֹר נֶדֶר נָזִיר לְהַזִּיר לַה'. דְּמַשְׁמַע שֶׁנּוֹדֵר לְשֵׁם שָׁמַיִם. וְשִׁמְשׁוֹן לָאו נָזִיר (ל) הֲוָא וְהָא כְּתִיב כִּי נְזִיר אֱלֹהִים (מ). וְקָא ס"ד דְּמָנוֹחַ קָאָמַר לְהָא מִילְּתָא, דַּהֲוָה לֵיהּ דָּבָר הַנָּדוּר, דְּאָדָם מַדִּיר אֶת בְּנוֹ בְּנָזִיר. מַלְאָךְ הוּא דְּקָאָמַר. "כִּי נְזִיר אֱלֹהִים יִהְיֶה הַנַּעַר מִן הַבֶּטֶן", אֲבָל מִפִּי (נ) מָנוֹחַ לֹא יָצָא. דִּילְמָא גַּרְדּוּיֵי גָּרַד לְהוּ. מִחְתַּךְ חָתַךְ בָּהֶן, אֲבָל הוּא גּוּפֵיהּ לֹא נָגַע בְּהוּ. וַיַּךְ וַיִּקַּח כְּתִיב. דְּמַשְׁמַע: וַיַּךְ, וַהֲדַר וַיִּקַּח. גּוֹסְסִין שָׁוִינְהוּ. וּבַהֲדֵי דַּהֲווּ גּוֹסְסִין אַשְׁלְחִינְהוּ, וְלֹא אִיטַּמֵּי בְּהוּ. וּנְזִיר עוֹלָם הֵיכָא כְּתִיב. שֶׁמֵּיקֵל בְּשֵׂעָר וּמֵבִיא שָׁלֹשׁ בְּהֵמוֹת. ה"ג דְּתַנְיָא רַבִּי אוֹמֵר אַבְשָׁלוֹם נְזִיר עוֹלָם הָיָה שֶׁנֶּאֱמַר וַיְהִי מִקֵּץ אַרְבָּעִים שָׁנָה (ס). וּמְגַלֵּחַ הָיָה אַבְשָׁלוֹם לִשְׁנֵים עָשָׂר חֹדֶשׁ (ע) דִּבְכָךְ הֲוָה לֵיהּ כּוֹבֶד, וּבְגָלִיר מֵהָכִי לֹא ה"ל כּוֹבֶד, דִּ"כְאִישׁ גְּבוּרָתוֹ" (שופטים ח). אֲבָל שְׁאָר (פ) נְזִירֵי עוֹלָם — מְגַלֵּחַ א' לְל' יוֹם, (צ) דַּהֲוֵי לֵיהּ בְּהָכִי כּוֹבֶד. וְיָלֵיף

*) נ"ל העין

נ"ל עולה | בס"א ל"ג | [תוספתא פ"א] | [נדרים יג. ע"ש] | [נ"ל דתניא] נדרים יב: | שם יג. ע"ש ערכין כט. | [תוספתא פ"ד ונדרים ט:] | נ"ל משום

[גירסת הערוך ערך גרד א' גורדויי גרדי בהון והוא לא נגע בהון. פי' הוא הבקיע ראשם בראש הלחי ומושך ידיו והוא טוגע בהן ועי' פרש"י]

[תוס' סוטה פ"ג ע"ש] שמואל ב טו

נוסחת הריב"ן

א) אם נטמא דיעבד: ב) או שלמים והמוסגר פה גריס ליה בכ"י: ג) התפיסו: ד) מתפים: ה) לקדוש: ו) תיבת ולא ליתא בכ"י: ז) דכ"ע: ח) להזיר לה': ט) תוהים טדרים וכשהן מטמאין: י) ונמצאו מביאין: כ) (הניע): ל) הוה: מ) יהיה הנער וגו': נ) מפיו נמי: ס) שנה וגו': ע) (דבכך הוה כו' דכאיש גבורתו) ליתא בכ"י: פ) נזיר: צ) (דהוי ליה בהכי כובד) ליתא בכ"י:

הגהות הב"ח

(א) רש"י ד"ה תנא נמי וכו' דלכתחלה מותר:

הגהות מהר"ב רנשבורג

א] בתום' ד"ה הרי עלי כבכור פי' ככר זה כבכור לא דכ"ע כלומר וכו'. נ"ב באורח מישור מוחק תיבות לא דכ"ע ועושה ממנו דבור אחד עד אבל בכור קדוש מרחם אמו ואח"כ מה"ד ר' יהודה סבירא ליה. ומיהו נלענ"ד דגם לפי הנוסחא שלפנינו כאן יהיה סוף הדבור אבל מרחם אמו ואח"כ מה"ד ר' יהודה סבירא ליה וכו' והך ד"ה רבי יהודה ס"ל הוא רק מהופך ושייך קודם ד"ה לא דכ"ע ולפ"ז אנ"ל שהוא טעות ולחנם כתב האורח מישור דהגה"ת דפוס פפד"מ שלפנינו היא טעות:

גליון הש"ס

גמ' ויך ויקח כתיב. עיין בפירוש רש"י בחומש שמות ז' כ' ולקמן דף יט ע"א:

פי' הרא"ש

הרי עלי כבכור. אם אמר הרי עלי ככר זה כבכור ר' יעקב אוסר. ס"ד דלא בעי' שיתפים בדבר הנדור. אלא אפי' התפים בדבר האסור כגון בכור שקדושתו מרחם אסור: מאי לאו ר' יהודה ס"ל כר' יעקב דשמשון נמי לא נדר בנזיר אלא ע"פ המלאך היה נזיר: לא דכו"ע בעי' דבר הנדור שאני גבי בכור דכתיב לה'. ומרבינן מיניה בכור דהוי כעין דבר הנדור דדמי לקדשים. וכן ר' יהודה נמי מרבי' לה' דכתיב גבי נזיר שמשון דדמי לשאר נזירים א"נ דר' יהודה סבר דשמשון קבל עליו נזירות כשהגיע לכלל שנותיו כי כן צוה לו המלאך. א"נ מנוח הדירו כדאמרי' האיש מדיר את בנו בנזיר: שכן מתפיסין בנדר (נזיר) דאע"פ שבאין חובה מ"מ צריך להקדישן: מימי לא אכלתי אשם נזיר טמא דמתוך שרב' עליו ימי נזירותו מתחרט וקרבנותיו קרבין להיות חולין בעזרה: מלאך הוא דקאמר אבל מנוח לא הדירו: אילימא [מדכתיב] בלחי החמור הכיתי אלף איש. נ"ל דמהאי קרא לא מייתי מידי דבאותה שעה באו עליו פלשתים והוצרך לעמוד על נפשו: ודילמא גרויי גרי בהו. כלומר זרק בהם החץ והרגם והמם כזורק חץ: *) ודילמא גוססים שוינהו ואפי' למ"ד פ' ג' מינין דנזיר אסור ליגע בגוסס. הכא לאו גוססים ממש אלא סמוכים לגוססים. ונ"ל לחלק בין גוסס בידי שמים לגוסס בידי אדם: ואשלם את נדרי אשר נדרתי וגו' היינו קרבנות נזירותו. ויליף ימים ימים מבתי ערי חומה דכתיב התם ימים תהיה גאולתו:

(זה הגהה היתה כתובה מן הצד בספר שממנו העתקנו זה). *) נראה דלמתו לחלק לגוסס בידי אדם חשוב כחי [illegible]

תורה אור

(ויקרא כה) וְיָלֵיף °"יָמִים" "יָמִים" מִבָּתֵּי עָרֵי חוֹמָה, מָה הָתָם י"ב חֹדֶשׁ – אאַף כָּאן י"ב חֹדֶשׁ. ר' נְהוֹרַאי אוֹמֵר: מְגַלֵּחַ אַחַת לל' יוֹם. רַבִּי יוֹסֵי אוֹמֵר: מְגַלֵּחַ מֵעֶרֶב שַׁבָּת לְעֶרֶב שַׁבָּת, שֶׁכֵּן מָצִינוּ בִּבְנֵי מְלָכִים שֶׁמְּגַלְּחִים מע"ש לע"ש. מַאי טַעְמָא דְּרַבִּי – יָלֵיף מִבָּתֵּי עָרֵי חוֹמָה, וְהָא רַבִּי הוּא דְּאָמַר: *אֵין "יָמִים" פְּחוּתִין מִשְּׁנַיִם! הַאי גְּזֵירָה שָׁוָה מִשּׁוּם כּוֹבֶד גָּמֵיר, וּבִשְׁנֵי יָמִים לֵיכָּא כּוֹבֶד. (בראשית מא) וְאֵימָא ב' שָׁנִים, דִּכְתִיב °"וַיְהִי מִקֵּץ שְׁנָתַיִם יָמִים"! דָּנִין "יָמִים" שֶׁאֵין עִמָּהֶן שָׁנִים מִ"יָּמִים" שֶׁאֵין עִמָּהֶן שָׁנִים, וְאַל יוֹכִיחַ זֶה שֶׁיֵּשׁ עִמּוֹ שָׁנִים. (במדבר יא) וְאֵימָא ל' יוֹם, דִּכְתִיב °"עַד חֹדֶשׁ יָמִים"! דָּנִין "יָמִים" שֶׁאֵין עִמָּהֶם חֳדָשִׁים מִ"יָּמִים" שֶׁאֵין עִמָּהֶם חֳדָשִׁים, וְאַל יוֹכִיחַ זֶה שֶׁיֵּשׁ עִמּוֹ חֳדָשִׁים. (שופטים יא) וְאֵימָא מֵהָכָא °"מִיָּמִים יָמִימָה" וגו'! דָּנִין "יָמִים" מִ"יָּמִים", וְאֵין דָּנִין "יָמִים" מִ"יָּמִימָה". וּמַאי נָפְקָא מִינַּהּ? (ויקרא יד) וְהָא *תָּנָא דְּבֵי ר' יִשְׁמָעֵאל: °"וְשָׁב הַכֹּהֵן" "וּבָא הַכֹּהֵן" – זוֹ הִיא שִׁיבָה זוֹ הִיא בִּיאָה! הָנֵי מִילֵּי – הֵיכָא דְּלֵיכָּא דְּדָמֵי לֵיהּ, אֲבָל הֵיכָא דְּאִיכָּא דְּדָמֵי לֵיהּ – מִדְּדָמֵי לֵיהּ יָלְפִינַן. (ס"א אב"א) *אִיכָּא דְּאָמְרִי: מְנָא יָדְעִינַן דְּכָל תְּלָתָא יַרְחִין חַד זִימְנָא? דִּילְמָא אַרְבָּעָה זִימְנֵי בְּשַׁתָּא, (א"נ), (ל"ג) אַרְבָּעָה יַרְחִין חַד זִימְנָא, תְּרֵין יַרְחִין בְּחַד זִימְנָא. רַבִּי נְהוֹרַאי אוֹמֵר: מְגַלֵּחַ אַחַת לִשְׁלֹשִׁים יוֹם. מַאי טַעְמָא? גַּבֵּי כֹּהֲנִים – מִשּׁוּם דְּאִיכָּא כּוֹבֶד, ה"נ אִיכָּא כּוֹבֶד. ר' יוֹסֵי אוֹמֵר: מְגַלֵּחַ מֵעֶרֶב שַׁבָּת לְעֶרֶב שַׁבָּת. מַאי אִיכָּא בֵּינֵיהּ לִשְׁאָר אֲחוּהִי? יוֹם טוֹב שֶׁחָל לִהְיוֹת בְּאֶמְצַע שַׁבָּת, דַּאֲחוּהִי מְגַלְּחִין, הוּא לָא מְגַלַּח. אִי נַמִי, לְגַלּוּחֵי מִן צַפְרָא דְּמַעֲלֵי שַׁבְּתָא; אֲחוּהִי מְגַלְּחִין, אִיהוּ לָא מְגַלַּח עַד פַּנְיָא. *הָנֵי אַרְבָּעִים שָׁנָה מַאי עֲבִידְתַּיְיהוּ? ר' נְהוֹרַאי אוֹמֵר מִשּׁוּם רַבִּי יְהוֹשֻׁעַ: לְקֵץ מ' שָׁנָה שֶׁשָּׁאֲלוּ לָהֶן מֶלֶךְ. *תָּנָא: אוֹתָהּ שָׁנָה שֶׁשָּׁאֲלוּ לָהֶן מֶלֶךְ הִיא שְׁנַת עֶשֶׂר לִשְׁמוּאֵל הָרָמָתִי.§

מתני' *בסְתַם נְזִירוּת ל' יוֹם.§

גמ' מְנָהָנֵי מִילֵּי? אָמַר רַב מַתָּנָא: (במדבר ו) אָמַר קְרָא °"קָדוֹשׁ יִהְיֶה", "יִהְיֶה" בְּגִימַטְרִיָּא תְּלָתִין הָווּ. *בַּר פַּדָּא אָמַר: כְּנֶגֶד "נָזִיר" "נִזְרוֹ" הָאֲמוּרִים בַּתּוֹרָה, ל' חָסֵר אַחַת. וְרַב מַתָּנָא נַמִי, נֵילַף מִ"נָּזִיר" "נִזְרוֹ"! – אָמַר לָךְ: (שם) הַהוּא לִדְרָשָׁה, °"מִיַּיִן וְשֵׁכָר יַזִּיר" – (שם) *לֶאֱסוֹר יֵין מִצְוָה כְּיֵין רְשׁוּת, °"כִּי יַפְלִיא לִנְדּוֹר נֶדֶר נָזִיר לְהַזִּיר" – מְלַמֵּד גשֶׁהַנְּזִירוּת חָלָה עַל נְזִירוּת.

וּבַר

רש"י

וְיָלֵיף מִבָּתֵּי עָרֵי חוֹמָה. דִּכְתִיב בְּהוּ "יָמִים תִּהְיֶה גְּאוּלָּתוֹ", מַה לְּהַלָּן י"ב חֹדֶשׁ כִּדְמְפָרֵשׁ בֵּיהּ קְרָא: "וְאִם לֹא יִגָּאֵל עַד מְלֹאת לוֹ שָׁנָה תְמִימָה". רַבִּי נְהוֹרַאי אוֹמֵר. אַבְשָׁלוֹם הָיָה מְגַלֵּחַ אַחַת לְל' יוֹם. שֶׁכֵּן מָצִינוּ בִּבְנֵי מְלָכִים. א) שֶׁכֵּן נוֹהֲגִים. וְהָא רַבִּי הוּא דְּאָמַר. בְּמַסֶּ' עֲרָכִין (דף לא.) "יָמִים תִּהְיֶה גְּאוּלָּתוֹ" אֵין יָמִים פְּחוּתִים מִשְּׁנַיִם. שֶׁאִם בָּא לִגְאָלָהּ בְּאוֹתוֹ יוֹם ב) שֶׁמְּשַׁכְּנָהּ לוֹ – אֵינוֹ יָכוֹל לִגְאָלָהּ עַד שֶׁיַּעַבְרוּ עָלָיו ב' יָמִים, לְפִי שֶׁאֵין מִקְרָא יוֹצֵא מִידֵי פְּשׁוּטוֹ. וְהָכָא נַמִי, מַאי חָזָא רַבִּי (א) מֵהַהוּא ג"ש "מַה לְּהַלָּן י"ב חֹדֶשׁ" כו'? נִגְמַר מֵהַאי טַעְמָא וְנֵימָא נַמִי דְּאַבְשָׁלוֹם מְגַלֵּחַ הָיָה לִשְׁנֵי יָמִים! הַאי ג"ש. דְּגָמֵיר מִבָּתֵּי עָרֵי חוֹמָה. מִשּׁוּם כּוֹבֶד הוּא דְּקָא גָּמֵיר ג). דִּכְתִיב בֵּיהּ בְּאַבְשָׁלוֹם "כִּי כָבֵד עָלָיו וְגִלְּחוֹ". וּבִשְׁנֵי יָמִים לֵיכָּא כּוֹבֶד. וּמִשּׁוּם הָכִי לָא גָּמֵיר מִינֵּיהּ. וְלֵימָא דִּשְׁתֵּי שָׁנִים. מַשְׁמַע הַאי "מִקֵּץ יָמִים לַיָּמִים אֲשֶׁר יְגַלֵּחַ". דִּשְׁתֵּי שָׁנִים נַמִי אִיקְרוּ "יָמִים", כִּדְכְתִיב "וַיְהִי מִקֵּץ שְׁנָתַיִם יָמִים". וְאֵימָא שְׁלֹשִׁים יוֹם. דִּשְׁלֹשִׁים ד) אִיקְרוּ "יָמִים", כִּדְכְתִיב "עַד חֹדֶשׁ יָמִים". וְאֵימָא מֵהָכָא מִיָּמִים יָמִימָה. "תֵּלַכְנָה בְּנוֹת יִשְׂרָאֵל לְתַנּוֹת לְבַת יִפְתָּח ד' יָמִים בַּשָּׁנָה", דְּהַיְינוּ יוֹם א' לִשְׁלֹשָׁה חֳדָשִׁים, הָכָא נַמִי נֵימָא דִּמְגַלֵּחַ הָיָה אַבְשָׁלוֹם לְג' חֳדָשִׁים. "לְתַנּוֹת" לְשׁוֹן "תַּאֲנִיָּה וַאֲנִיָּה" (איכה ב). וְשָׁב הַכֹּהֵן וּבָא הַכֹּהֵן זוֹ הִיא שִׁיבָה זוֹ הִיא בִּיאָה. מַה בִּיאָה מִבֵּיתוֹ שֶׁל כֹּהֵן לְבֵית הַמְנוּגָּע חוֹלֵץ וְקוֹצֶה וְטָח וְנוֹתֵן שָׁבוּעַ לְהַסְגִּירוֹ, אַף כָּאן בְּשִׁיבָה. אַף ה"נ, כֵּיוָן דִּכְתִיב "מִיָּמִים יָמִימָה" לֶיהֱוֵי נַמִי כְּמַאן דְּאָמַר "יָמִים"! א"ד. ה) לָא יָלְפִינַן מֵהַהוּא קְרָא דִּכְתִיב בְּבַת יִפְתָּח. דִּמְנָא יָדְעִינַן דְּמִתְּלָתָא יַרְחִין לִתְלָתָא יַרְחִין הָוֵי חַד זִימְנָא? דִּילְמָא. הַאי דְּקָאָמַר "ד' יָמִים בַּשָּׁנָה" הָכִי הָוֵי: לְסוֹף ד' יַרְחִין חַד זִימְנָא, וְלִתְרֵין [יַרְחִין] חַד זִימְנָא, וּלְאַרְבַּע יַרְחִין חַד זִימְנָא, וְלִתְרֵין יַרְחִין חַד זִימְנָא, דְּהַיְינוּ נַמִי אַרְבַּע זִימְנִין. וְהִילְכָּךְ, הוֹאִיל וְאִיכָּא לְמֵימַר הָכִי ו) וְאִיכָּא לְמֵימַר הָכִי, שָׁבְקִינַן הַהוּא קְרָא דְּלָא מְפָרֵשׁ וְגָמְרִינַן מִקְּרָא דִּמְפָרֵשׁ, דְּהַיְינוּ מִבָּתֵּי עָרֵי חוֹמָה. גַּבֵּי כֹּהֲנִים. הֶדְיוֹטִים. מִידֵּי הוּא טַעְמָא. דְּאָמְרִינַן דִּמְגַלְּחִין בִּשְׁלֹשִׁים יוֹם, אֶלָּא מִשּׁוּם דְּאִיכָּא כּוֹבֶד שֵׂיעָר וַהֲוָה לֵיהּ נִיווּל. הָכָא נַמִי אִיכָּא כּוֹבֶד, וּמִשּׁוּם הָכִי הָיָה אוֹמֵר רַבִּי נְהוֹרַאי דְּאַבְשָׁלוֹם הָיָה מְגַלֵּחַ לְאַחַר שְׁלֹשִׁים יוֹם. לְדִבְרֵי רַבִּי יוֹסֵי. דְּאָמַר שֶׁמְּגַלֵּחַ מֵעֶרֶב שַׁבָּת לְעֶרֶב שַׁבָּת, מַאי הֶיכֵּרָא אִיכָּא בֵּין דִּידֵיהּ דַּהֲוֵי נָזִיר לִשְׁאָר אַחִין? הָא אִינְהוּ נַמִי נוֹהֲגִין לְהִסְתַּפֵּר בְּכָךְ! אִיכָּא בֵּינַיְיהוּ בִּזְמַן שֶׁחָל יו"ט לִהְיוֹת בְּאֶמְצַע שַׁבָּת, דְּאַחִין מְגַלְּחִין בְּעֶרֶב יוֹם טוֹב וְהוּא אֵינוֹ מְגַלֵּחַ עַד עֶרֶב שַׁבָּת. וְאִי קַשְׁיָא לָךְ: וּלְרַבִּי, ז) מַאי שְׁנָא אַבְשָׁלוֹם מִשְּׁאָר נְזִירֵי עוֹלָם דְּמִסְתַּפְּרִים אַחַת לְל' יוֹם מִשּׁוּם דִּלְגַבֵּי דִּידְהוּ הָוֵי כּוֹבֶד? וְרַבִּי מְתָרֵץ לְטַעְמֵיהּ: דְּאַבְשָׁלוֹם הוֹאִיל וּבַעַל כֹּחַ הֲוָה לָא הֲוָה כּוֹבֶד לְדִידֵיהּ עַד שְׁנֵים עָשָׂר חֹדֶשׁ כִּי כָאִישׁ גְּבוּרָתוֹ. וּלְרַבִּי יוֹסֵי הוֹאִיל ח) דְּאוֹרְחַיְיהוּ דִּבְנֵי מְלָכִים לְהִסְתַּפֵּר מֵעֶרֶב שַׁבָּת לְעֶרֶב שַׁבָּת, הֲוָה לֵיהּ כּוֹבֶד כִּשְׁאָר ט) אַחִין, אֲבָל לִשְׁאָר אִינָשֵׁי לֵיכָּא כּוֹבֶד עַד ל' י). הָנֵי מ' שָׁנָה. דִּכְתִיב "וַיְהִי מִקֵּץ מ' שָׁנָה". מַאי עֲבִידְתַּיְיהוּ. וַהֲלֹא לֹא הָיוּ לְמַלְכוּת כ) בֵּית דָּוִד אֶלָּא ל"ז! לְקֵץ מ' שָׁנָה שֶׁשָּׁאֲלוּ לָהֶם מֶלֶךְ. ל) הִיא שְׁנַת עֶשֶׂר לִשְׁמוּאֵל הָרָמָתִי. שֶׁאַבְשָׁלוֹם הָיָה יוֹדֵעַ שֶׁעָתִיד דָּוִד מ) לְמַלְאוֹת מ' שָׁנָה, וּכְשֶׁנִּתְמַלְּאוּ מ' שָׁנָה שֶׁשָּׁאֲלוּ יִשְׂרָאֵל מֶלֶךְ מִיּוֹם לְיוֹם אַחַר שֶׁמָּלְכוּ שְׁמוּאֵל וְשָׁאוּל, דְּהַיְינוּ בִּתְחִלַּת הַמַּלְכוּת. וְעָלְתָה לִשְׁנֵיהֶן, לְפִי שֶׁעֲדַיִין לֹא יָצָא טִיבְעוֹ שֶׁל שָׁאוּל בָּעוֹלָם, וְאַף טִיבְעוֹ שֶׁל שְׁמוּאֵל בָּעוֹלָם שֶׁהָיָה נִקְרָא מֶלֶךְ לֹא פָּסַק. וּשְׁתַּיִם שֶׁמָּלַךְ שָׁאוּל בְּעַצְמוֹ בְּחַיֵּי שְׁמוּאֵל, כְּמוֹ שֶׁלָּמַדְנוּ [בְּסֵדֶר עוֹלָם] שֶׁלֹּא מֵת שְׁמוּאֵל לִפְנֵי נ) שָׁאוּל אֶלָּא ד' חֳדָשִׁים. וְל"ז שֶׁמָּלַךְ דָּוִד. וְטָעָה אַבְשָׁלוֹם וְאָמַר: עַכְשָׁיו הִגִּיעַ הַקֵּץ שֶׁל אַבָּא וְאֵלְכָה לְחֶבְרוֹן לְהָסֵב לִי שֵׁם הַמְּלוּכָה. וְאִם נֶפֶשׁ אָדָם לוֹמַר: מִנַּיִן אַתָּה אוֹמֵר שֶׁאוֹתָהּ שָׁנָה שֶׁמָּלְכוּ שְׁמוּאֵל וְשָׁאוּל שֶׁהָיְתָה בִּתְחִלַּת מַלְכוּת שֶׁל שָׁאוּל, וּשְׁמוּאֵל לֹא מֵת לִפְנֵי שָׁאוּל אֶלָּא ד' חֳדָשִׁים – מִכָּאן אַתָּה לָמֵד: שֶׁבְּאוֹתוֹ יוֹם שֶׁעָלְתָה חַנָּה לְשִׁילֹה, ס) דִּכְתִיב "וְעֵלִי הַכֹּהֵן יֹשֵׁב עַל הַכִּסֵּא" (שמואל א א), ע) בְּאוֹתוֹ יוֹם נִתְמַנָּה לְשׁוֹפֵט, וְהַיְינוּ דִּכְתִיב פ) "יֹשֵׁב עַל הַכִּסֵּא". וְלָמַדְנוּ שֶׁבְּאוֹתָהּ שָׁנָה נִתְעַבְּרָה חַנָּה וְיָלְדָה שְׁמוּאֵל. וְנֶאֱמַר בּוֹ בִּשְׁמוּאֵל (שם) "וְיָשַׁב שָׁם עַד עוֹלָם" – עַד עוֹלָמוֹ שֶׁל יוֹבֵל – כ' שָׁנִים, וּשְׁתֵּי שָׁנִים שֶׁגְּמָלַתּוּ אִמּוֹ, הֲרֵי לְךָ שָׁנִים שֶׁל שְׁמוּאֵל כ"ב שָׁנִים. וְעֵלִי כַּמָּה שָׁנִים נִתְמַנָּה עַל יִשְׂרָאֵל – מ' שָׁנָה, וּכְשֶׁהָיָה לוֹ לְעֵלִי אַרְבָּעִים שָׁנָה בֶּן כַּמָּה שָׁנִים הָיָה שְׁמוּאֵל – הֱוֵי אוֹמֵר בֶּן ל"ט שָׁנָה, שֶׁצָּרִיךְ אַתָּה לְהוֹצִיא שָׁנָה אַחַת לְעִיבּוּרוֹ. כַּמָּה נִשְׁתַּיְּירוּ לוֹ מִשְּׁנוֹתָיו שֶׁל שְׁמוּאֵל – י"ג. צֵא מֵהֶן עֶשֶׂר שֶׁמָּלַךְ שְׁמוּאֵל אַחַר מִיתָתוֹ שֶׁל עֵלִי, וְנִשְׁתַּיְּירוּ צ) לָהֶן ג' שָׁנִים. וְזֶה הוּא ק) שֶׁאָמְרוּ: אַחַת שֶׁמָּלַךְ שָׁאוּל וּשְׁמוּאֵל, וּשְׁתַּיִם שֶׁמָּלַךְ שָׁאוּל בְּעַצְמוֹ. בַּר פַּדָּא אָמַר כְּנֶגֶד נָזִיר נִזְרוֹ וְנֶדֶר ר) נִדְרוֹ. הָאָמוּר בַּפָּ' נָזִיר שֶׁהֵן ל' חָסֵר אַחַת: לִנְדּוֹר נֶדֶר נָזִיר לְהַזִּיר יַזִּיר נִזְרוֹ נֶדֶר נִזְרוֹ יַזִּיר הַזִּירוֹ נִזְרוֹ נִזְרוֹ וְהִזִּיר נִזְרוֹ נִזְרוֹ הַנָּזִיר נִזְרוֹ נִזְרוֹ הַנָּזִיר נִזְרוֹ הַנָּזִיר יִדּוֹר נִזְרוֹ נִדְרוֹ יִדּוֹר נִזְרוֹ – הֲרֵי ל' חָסֵר אַחַת. "נֵזֶר אֱלֹהָיו" לָא קָחָשֵׁיב, לְפִי שֶׁאֵינוֹ לְשׁוֹן נְזִירוּת אֶלָּא לְשׁוֹן עֲטָרָה, כְּמוֹ הַתַּרְגּוּם. נָזִיר לְהַזִּיר מְלַמֵּד שֶׁהַנְּזִירוּת חָלָה עַל נְזִירוּת. שֶׁאִם אָמַר "הֲרֵינִי נָזִיר אִם אוֹכַל כִּכָּר זוֹ", וְחָזַר וְאָמַר "הֲרֵינִי נָזִיר אִם אוֹכַל כִּכָּר זוֹ" וַאֲכָלָהּ – מוֹנֶה שְׁתֵּי נְזִירוּת. דְּאַף עַל גַּב דְּכִכָּר אֶחָד הוּא – חָלָה נְזִירוּת עַל נְזִירוּת. וְכֵיוָן דְּהָנֵי אָתוּ לִדְרָשָׁא וְלָא לְמִנְיָינָא, אַחֲרִינֵי נַמִי לָאו לְמִנְיָינָא אָתוּ.

וּבַר

תוספות

אין ימים פחותים משנים. דדריש מ"ימים תהיה גאולתו" שאין המוכר יכול לגאול בפחות משני ימים. (והא א"ר כו') הכי נמי דבכל ב' ימים יקל שערו! ומשני, דבב' ימים ליכא כובד. ומסתמא לא נתקבל ג"ש אהני, אלא ממשמעות ד"ימים" – דהיינו שנה, "תהיה גאולתו" – שגואל אחרי ב' ימים כל השנה, כדכתיב בתריה "ואם לא יגאל עד מלאת לו שנה תמימה" – אלמא דכל השנה גואל. **תלכנה** בנות ישראל לתנות לבת יפתח ד' ימים בשנה. ומשמע בסוף כל ג' חדשים הלכו לראות. ומשני: מנא ידעי' דמחלקין השנה בשוה? דילמא תרין ירחין בחד זמנא וד' ירחין בחד זמנא וב' ירחין בחד זמנא [וכו']. וכיון דהכי הוא לא ידעינן מהיכא נילף, דלית לן למילף ממקום שיכול להיות שאין הדבר *(עוד) – להכי ילפינן מבתי ערי חומה. **מ"ט** גבי כהנים [דאיכא] כובד. וא"ת והא כהני' עלמא ילפי' (תענית יז.) מסתם נזי' "פרע" "פרע" דמקילין אחת לשלשים יום, וא"כ נילף נזיר עולם מסתם נזיר דהוי שלשים יום! וי"ל: דלא מיסתבר ליה ללמוד קדושת עולם מקדושת שעה. ולהכי יליף מכהנים אע"ג דלמד מן הלמד, משום דכהנים נמי קדושת עולם הוו. **מאי** איכא בינייה לשאר אחוהי. וא"ת: ונימא דאיכא בינייהו קרבנות דהוא מביא ולא הן! וי"ל, דה"ק: מאי איכא ביניה בתגלחת, דקאמר קרא "ויהי מקץ ימים אשר יגלח" *משום דבתגלחת היה מאחר. **הני** (מקץ) מ' שנה למאי. פי': דליכא למימר למ' שנה (למאי) למלכות בית דוד דאז מרד אבשלום, דהא משמע קראי דהיה מלך ה' שנים אחר מעשה זה; ג' של רעב, ואחד שמנה ישראל, ואחד שהעמיד משמרות. ומשני: מקץ מ' שנה ששאלו להם מלך, (אלו) שמרדו במלכו של עולם – תלה מרידת [אבשלום בשאלתם להם מלך, א] שהיה שנת עשר] לשמואל, ובחצי י"א העמיד מלך, ומלך חצי י"א וב' שנים הרי ד' שנים לשאלה, ובתחלת ל"ו למלכות בית דוד היא שנת מ' לשאלה, ואח"כ מרד אבשלום. והשנה ההיא היה שנת רעב וגם אותה שנת מ' לשאלה. ואפי' מרד בתחלת שנת מ' לשאלה, ולאו דוקא מקץ מ' שנה. **סתם** נזירות שלשים יום. ובגמרא מפרש טעמא.

בר פדא אמר כנגד נזירות האמורין בתורה שהן ל' חסר אחת. פירוש: כתובים בפרשת נזיר, וכנגדן מושך סתם

פי' הרא"ש

מה להלן י"ב חדש דכתיב עד מלאת לו שנה תמימה. והא [רבי הוא] דאמר התם בערכין אין ימים פחותים משנים שאין המוכר יכול לגאול תוך ב' ימים. ודריש ימים כפשטיה לתחלת גאולה. ודריש לי' שנה לסוף גאולה משום דכתיב עד מלאת לו שנה תמימה גאולה. א) ד' ימים בשנה והיינו מג' חדשים לג' חדשים: זו היא שיבה זו היא ביאה. מה ביאה חולץ וקוצה וטח ונותן לו שבוע אף שיבה חולץ וקוצה [וטח] ונותן לו שבוע אע"ג דלא דמו תיבות להדדי כיון דמשמעותן חד קא דריש ליה בג"ש: דילמא ד' ירחי חד זימנא ותרי ירחי חד זימנא. ב' ימים הראשונים היו מארבע חדשים לד' חדשים וב' האחרונים מב' חדשים לב' חדשים. הלכך שבקינן קרא דלא מפרש וילפי' מקרא דמפרש: מ"ט גבי כהנים משום דאיכא כובד וכו' וכהנים גופיי' ילפי' פרע [פרע] מנזיר דמגלחים לל' יום בסנהדרין פ' כ"ג והא דלא יליף נזיר עולם מסתם נזיר משום דהתם דין הוא דמגלח משום דשלמו ימי נזירותו הלכך יליף מכהן דלא פסקה כהונתו ומגלח: מאי איכא בינייהו לשאר (דחוקי) [אחוהי] הוה מצ"ל דאינהו מצו לגלחו במספריים ואיהו דוקא בתער. ואיהו דוקא מיקל והם יכולים לגלח הכל. אלא בסתם גילוח שרגילין בני מלכים לגלח קא בעיא מאי בינייהו ואין דרכם לגלח הכל וגם במספריים. והא דלא קאמר שהוא מביא ג' בהמות כשהוא רוצה לגלח כדין סתם נזיר שאינו מגלח אלא בשעת הבאת קרבנותיו איכא למימ' דהיינו האי דקא' מגלח עד פניא. ולאו דוקא פניא אלא דלא מגלח עד הבאת קרבנותיו: מאי עבידתיהו מאיזה חשבון היתה המרידה: לקץ מ' ששאלו להם המלך. מרדות של אבשלום וישראל שמרדו במלכות בית דוד מנה ממרדות ישראל שמרדו במלכות של עולם ושאלו להם מלך: סתם נזירות ל' יום. אם אמר הריני נזיר בסתם ולא פי' כמה צריך לנהוג נזירות ל' יום ובגמ' מפרש מנ"ל: הריני נזיר אחת גדולה וכו'. בין שאמר הריני נזיר גדולה ובין שאמר הריני נזיר קטנה ובין שאמר הריני נזיר מכאן ועד סוף העולם נוהג נזירות ל' יום. ולא אמרי' כשאמר אחת גדולה ינהוג נזיר יותר מל' וכשאמר נזיר קטנה ינהוג פחות מל'. וכן כשאמר מכאן ועד סוף העולם [יהיה נזיר עולם]: יהיה בגימטריא תלתין הוו. יראה דגמרא גמירי לה ואסמכוה אקרא גימט' דלאו מי"ג מדות היא שהתורה נדרשת בהן: כנגד נזיר נדרו נזרו יזיר וכו' ול' חסר א' הם לבד מנזר אלהיו על ראשו דלא קחשיב דלשון כתר ונזר הוא כדמתרגמינן כלילא: ורב מתנא נילף מנזיר נזרו דמסתברא טפי דכלהו איכתבי למניינא מלמדרש ג' מלה: הנהו נזיר נזרו לדרשא אתא. קצת מינייהו ודרשינן להו הלכך לאו למניינא איכתיבו: ב) מדהנהו למניינא כולהו למניינא דהנהו לאו לדרשא מגלי על אינך דכמו דהנך למניינא אינך נמי למניינא ותרתי שמעי' מינייהו:

אלא

עין משפט נר מצוה

לא א מיי' פ"ג מהל' נזירות הלכה יב:

לב ב מיי' שם הל' א סמג לאוין רמג:

לג ג מיי' שם הל' ז והל' י:

מסורת הש"ס

[ערכין לא.]

עירובין נא. מכות יג: חולין פה. יבמות יז: נדה כב: יומא ב: הוריות ח: מנחות ז. מה. בכורות לב.

תמורה יג:

שם וסדר עולם פי"ד

לקמן לט. נדרים ד: תענית יז. סנהדרין כב. מ"ק יט.

[עי' תוספות תמורה י. ד"ה איתמר]

לעיל ג: וש"נ

הגהות מהר"ב רנשבורג

א] תוס' ד"ה הני (מקץ) ארבעים שנה למאי וכו' תלה מרידת [אבשלום בשאלת להם מלך]. נ"ב כאן הס"ד ואח"כ מה"ד שהיא [שנת יוד] א"מ:

גליון הש"ס

תוס' ד"ה מ"ט גבי כהנים. וא"כ ניליף וכו'. ק"ל הא פשיטא דאין ללמוד נ"ע מנזיר סתם דסתם פסק נזירתו ונ"ע עדיין נזירתו שלם אלא דילפינן תחלה כהן מנזיר פרע פרע לגבי כהן שיעור ל' יום ואמרי' הטעם גבי כהן משום כובדו וידעי' דשיעור כובד ל' יום וזהו העיקר מה דרלינו למילף שיעורא דכובד כמה הוי ומה שייכות למילף ענין זה מנזיר סתם:

נוסחת הריב"ן

א) כלומר שכן: ב) יום עלמו: ג) גמיר לה כדכתיב: ד) דשלשים יום: ה) להכי לא: ו) (ואיכא למימר הכי) ליתא בכ"י: ז) ולר' יוסי: ח) ואורחייהו: ט) אחיו: י) ל' יום: כ) (בית) ליתא בכ"י: ל) שהיא: מ) למלוך: נ) לפני מות שאול: ס) לשילה ועלי יושב על כס"ל: ע) שבאותו: פ) יושב: צ) (להן) ליתא בכ"י: ק) שאמרנו: ר) נזרו:

הגהות הב"ח

(א) רש"י ד"ה והא ר' הוא וכו' דההוא ג"ש:

א) נראה דל"ל ולאמא מהכא מימים ימימה תלכנה בנות ישראל וגו' ארבע ימים בשנה. ב) שייך לע"ב.

וּבַר פַּדָּא אָמַר לָךְ: לֵיכָּא חַד מִינַּיְהוּ דְּלָאו לְדָרְשָׁא? אֶלָּא, מִדְּהַהוּא לְמִנְיָינָא — כּוּלְּהוּ נַמִי לְמִנְיָינָא. תְּנַן: סְתַם נְזִירוּת שְׁלֹשִׁים יוֹם. בִּשְׁלָמָא לְרַב מַתָּנָא — נִיחָא, אֶלָּא לְבַר פַּדָּא קַשְׁיָא! אָמַר לָךְ בַּר פַּדָּא: אַיְּידֵי דְּאִיכָּא יוֹם תְּלָתִין, דִּמְגַלֵּחַ וּמֵבִיא קָרְבְּנוֹתָיו — מִשּׁוּם הָכִי תְּנָא שְׁלֹשִׁים. *תְּנַן: מִי שֶׁאָמַר "הֲרֵינִי נָזִיר" — מְגַלֵּחַ יוֹם שְׁלֹשִׁים וְאֶחָד. בִּשְׁלָמָא לְרַב מַתָּנָא — נִיחָא, אֶלָּא לְבַר פַּדָּא קַשְׁיָא! אָמַר לָךְ בַּר פַּדָּא, אֵימָא סֵיפָא: אִם גִּילַּח לְיוֹם שְׁלֹשִׁים — יָצָא! אֶלָּא, סֵיפָא מְסַיְּיעָא לֵיהּ, רֵישָׁא — נַעֲשָׂה כְּאוֹמֵר "שְׁלֵימִין". וּלְרַב מַתָּנָא קַשְׁיָא סֵיפָא! קָסָבַר: *מִקְצָת הַיּוֹם כְּכוּלּוֹ. (א) תְּנַן: "הֲרֵינִי נָזִיר שְׁלֹשִׁים יוֹם", אִם גִּילַּח יוֹם ל' — לֹא יָצָא! בְּאוֹמֵר "שְׁלֵימִין". *תְּנַן: מִי שֶׁנָּזַר ב' נְזִירוּת, מְגַלֵּחַ אֶת הָרִאשׁוֹנָה יוֹם ל' וְאֶחָד, וְהַשְּׁנִיָּה לְיוֹם שִׁשִּׁים וְאֶחָד. בִּשְׁלָמָא לְרַב מַתָּנָא — נִיחָא, אֶלָּא

וּבַר פַּדָּא אָמַר לָךְ. אַטּוּ מִי לֵיכָּא חַד מִינַּיְיהוּ דְּלָא אָתָא לִדְרָשָׁא? אֶלָּא מִדְּהַהוּא לְמִנְיָינָא, הָנְהוּ נַמִי דְּלִדְרָשָׁא אָתֵי לְהוּ לְמִנְיָינָא (ב). תְּנַן מִי שֶׁאָמַר הֲרֵינִי נָזִיר מְגַלֵּחַ (ג) לִשְׁלֹשִׁים וְאֶחָד יוֹם בִּשְׁלָמָא לְרַב מַתָּנָא. דְּאָמַר: שְׁלֹשִׁים — הַיְינוּ דְּקָאָמַר שֶׁמְּגַלֵּחַ [יוֹם] א) שְׁלֹשִׁים וְאֶחָד, דְּהַיְינוּ לְאַחַר מְלֹאת יְמֵי נִזְרוֹ. אֶלָּא לְבַר פַּדָּא. דְּאָמַר: עִיקַּר נְזִירוּת לָא הָוֵי אֶלָּא כ"ט — ב) בִּשְׁלֹשִׁים אִיבָּעֵי לֵיהּ לְגַלֵּחַ! הָכִי גָּרְסִינַן: אֶלָּא רֵישָׁא נַעֲשָׂה כְּאוֹמֵר שְׁלֵימִים. (ד) אָמַר לָךְ בַּר פַּדָּא. רֵישָׁא, דְּתָנֵי שֶׁמְּגַלֵּחַ לִשְׁלֹשִׁים וְאֶחָד. נַעֲשָׂה כְּאוֹמֵר שְׁלֹשִׁים יוֹם שְׁלֵימִים. וּלְכַתְּחִילָּה מְגַלֵּחַ לְיוֹם שְׁלֹשִׁים וְאֶחָד. וְכֵיוָן דְּלָא אָמַר בְּהֶדְיָא "שְׁלֵימִים", אִם גִּילַּח לְיוֹם שְׁלֹשִׁים — יָצָא. ג) דְּקָסָבַר מִקְצָת הַיּוֹם. שֶׁעָבַר מִיּוֹם שְׁלֹשִׁים, כְּמִי שֶׁעָבַר כּוּלּוֹ דָּמֵי. וְהַאי דִּמְגַלֵּחַ לְבָתַר הָכִי — נַעֲשָׂה כְּמִי שֶׁגִּילַּח לְיוֹם שְׁלֹשִׁים וְאֶחָד. וְאִם תֹּאמַר: הוֹאִיל וּלְבַר פַּדָּא נַמִי צָרִיךְ לְהַמְתִּין ד) עַד יוֹם שְׁלֹשִׁים וְאֶחָד, מַאי אִיכָּא בֵּין רַב מַתָּנָא לְבַר פַּדָּא? אִיכָּא, ה) דִּלְבַר פַּדָּא אִם נִטְמָא בְּיוֹם שְׁלֹשִׁים — "אַחַר מְלֹאת" קָרֵינָא בֵּיהּ וְשׁוּב אֵינוֹ סוֹתֵר אֶת (ה) נִדְרוֹ, וּלְרַב מַתָּנָא דְּאָמַר: אֵין עִיקַּר נְזִירוּת פָּחוֹת מִשְּׁלֹשִׁים יוֹם — "תּוֹךְ מְלֹאת" קָרֵינָא בֵּיהּ, וְצָרִיךְ לִמְנוֹת פַּעַם שְׁנִיָּה. אִי נַמִי, הַיְינוּ דְּאִיכָּא בֵּינַיְיהוּ: שֶׁאִם אָמַר "הֲרֵינִי נָזִיר ו) כ"ט יָמִים" מְגַלֵּחַ לְכַתְּחִילָּה לְיוֹם שְׁלֹשִׁים אַלִּיבָּא דְּבַר פַּדָּא. וּלְרַב מַתָּנָא הוֹלֵךְ וּמַשְׁלִים כָּל ל', שֶׁאֵין שׁוּם נְזִירוּת פָּחוֹת מִל' יוֹם, וְאֵינוֹ מְגַלֵּחַ עַד ל' וְא'. וְהָא ז) תְּנַן גִּילַּח (ו) יוֹם ל' לֹא יָצָא בְּאוֹמֵר שְׁלֵימִים. (מַמָּשׁ) דְּצָרִיךְ לוֹ לְהַשְׁלִים כָּל מַה שֶּׁנָּזַר ח) וּלְגַלֵּחַ אַחַר מְלֹאת. דַּהֲוָה לֵיהּ כְּמִי שֶׁנּוֹדֵר לְגַלֵּחַ מֵאָה יוֹם, דְּמוֹנֶה מֵאָה יוֹם מִיּוֹם לְיוֹם וַהֲדַר מְגַלֵּחַ. אִיכָּא דְּגָרְסִי לָהּ בְּלִישָּׁנָא אַחֲרִינָא: רֵישָׁא בְּאוֹמֵר שְׁלֵימִין. וּמְפָרֵשׁ לָהּ: רֵישָׁא לְבַר פַּדָּא לָא קַשְׁיָא — כְּגוֹן דְּאָמַר "הֲרֵינִי נָזִיר שְׁלֹשִׁים יוֹם", דְּצָרִיךְ לִמְנוֹת ט) לְכַתְּחִילָּה שְׁלֹשִׁים וּלְגַלֵּחַ בְּיוֹם שְׁלֹשִׁים וְאֶחָד. הָא סְתָמָא אִם גִּילַּח יוֹם שְׁלֹשִׁים — יָצָא. וְסֵיפָא דְּקָתָנֵי: י) לֹא יָצָא — בְּאוֹמֵר שְׁלֵימִין. וּפָרוּשֵׁי מְפָרֵשׁ לָהּ לְרֵישָׁא; מִי שֶׁאוֹמֵר "הֲרֵינִי נָזִיר" מְגַלֵּחַ לִשְׁלֹשִׁים וְאֶחָד, וְאֵימָתַי אָמְרוּ שֶׁצָּרִיךְ לְגַלֵּחַ בְּיוֹם שְׁלֹשִׁים וְאֶחָד כ) — בִּזְמַן שֶׁאָמַר "הֲרֵינִי נָזִיר שְׁלֹשִׁים יוֹם". וְאִם אָמַר "שְׁלֹשִׁים יוֹם שְׁלֵימִין" — אִם גִּילַּח בְּיוֹם שְׁלֹשִׁים לֹא יָצָא. תְּנַן מִי שֶׁנָּזַר שְׁתֵּי נְזִירוּת מְגַלֵּחַ אֶת הָרִאשׁוֹנָה לְיוֹם שְׁלֹשִׁים וְאֶחָד וְהַשְּׁנִיָּה לְיוֹם ס"א. דְּלְכִי גִּילַּח בְּיוֹם שְׁלֹשִׁים וְאֶחָד לָרִאשׁוֹנָה — לְאַלְתַּר נִכְנְסָה לוֹ נְזִירוּת שְׁנִיָּה בְּאוֹתוֹ יוֹם עַצְמוֹ, וְנִמְצָא דְּכִי מְגַלֵּחַ נַמִי בַּשְּׁנִיָּה ל) בְּיוֹם ס"א — קָאֵים לֵיהּ בְּיוֹם שְׁלֹשִׁים וְאֶחָד. בִּשְׁלָמָא לְרַב מַתָּנָא נִיחָא אֶלָּא לְבַר פַּדָּא. לָמָּה לִי כּוּלֵּי הַאי? בְּשִׁשִּׁים חָסֵר אֶחָד סַגִּי! אָמַר לָךְ בַּר פַּדָּא אֵימָא סֵיפָא אִם גִּילַּח (ז) מ) בְּיוֹם שְׁלֹשִׁים כו'. אַלְמָא דְּלָא הָוֵי עִיקַּר נְזִירוּת אֶלָּא שְׁלֹשִׁים חָסֵר אֶחָד. אֶלָּא סֵיפָא מְסַיְּיעָא לֵיהּ. לְבַר פַּדָּא, מִדְּקָאָמַר: שֶׁאִם גִּילַּח אֶת הָרִאשׁוֹנָה לְיוֹם שְׁלֹשִׁים שַׁפִּיר דָּמֵי, וְרֵישָׁא דְּקָתָנֵי שְׁלֹשִׁים וְאֶחָד — נַעֲשָׂה כְּאוֹמֵר "שְׁלֵימִין". אֲבָל הֵיכָא דְּפָרֵישׁ "הֲרֵינִי נָזִיר שְׁלֹשִׁים יוֹם חָסֵר אֶחָד" — מְגַלֵּחַ לְכַתְּחִילָּה לְיוֹם שְׁלֹשִׁים, דְּעִיקַּר נְזִירוּת אֵינוֹ אֶלָּא שְׁלֹשִׁים חָסֵר אֶחָד, אֲבָל

סתם נזירות כ"ט יום. אע"ג דתמלא שלשים וכשאתה יורד למניינם, יש לומר ד"נזר אלהיו על ראשו" לא הוי ממניינא, דהוא לשון כתר כדמתרגמינן: כלילא. **הנהו** לדרשא. וכיון דאתיין לדרשא לא מצטרפין למניינא ומנינן להו כ"ט. **מלמד** שהנזירות חל על הנזירות. ודאי נראה דאם אמר "הריני נזיר ונזיר" לא איצטריך, דמישתמע שפיר כשישלים נזירותו הראשון דמתחיל ומונה נזירות שני. וכי איצטריך קרא להיכא *דאמר "הריני נזיר היום ונזיר", דהוה לן למימר לא חייל עליה אלא חד נזירות כיון דאמר "היום", להכי איצטריך קרא מיותר שהנזירות חל על הנזירות. **הואיל** ואיכא חד מינייהו דלאו לדרשא או אחד או עשרה, ולאו דוקא חד. מדההוא למניינא. כולהון למניינא ונהי דאיכא בהו דרשא, מכל מקום אתו למניינא. **תנן** סתם נזירות שלשים יום וכו' **אלא לבר פדא** קשיא. דמשמע שהתנא מֶשֶׁך נזירות דאורייתא אתא לאשמועינן. ומשני: כיון דאיכא יום תלתין דמגלח ומייתי קרבנות ואסור לשתות ביין וליטמא למתים עד שמביא קרבנותיו — משום הכי [תני] תלתין יומין. דמשך הנזירות עד תלתין יומי, כי לכתחילה אי אפשר להביא קרבנותיו בכ"ט אפילו לבר פדא אלא ביום שלשים (הויא ליה [כפרה], דאפילו נזיר טהור קלת חוטא הוא שליער עצמו מן היין). **מגלח** לשלשים וא' יום כו' **אלא לבר פדא** קשה. דהוה ליה לגלח ביום [ל'], דשלמו נזירות בכ"ט יום. **אמר** לך בר פדא אימא סיפא **ואם גילח ביום שלשים יצא אלא סיפא מסייעא** ליה. ורישא דקאמר – לכתחילה. כשיאמר "שלשים יום שלימין להיות נזיר" אי אפשר לו לגלח ביום שלשים, וגזרו חכמים כשאומר "נזיר" סתם דלכתחילה לא יגלח אלא ביום שלשים וא'. אבל בדיעבד אם גילח ביום ל' יצא, שכן דינו דאורייתא דסתם נזיר יגלח ביום שלשים. ואם תאמר: אמאי איצטריך למימר גזירה אטו היכא דאמר "שלימים"? לימא גזירה אטו היכא דאמר "שלשים יום" בלא "שלימים". דהכי מוכח בסמוך בפירקא שניה, דלבר פדא דלית ליה מקצת היום ככולו, כי אמר "שלשים" דמדאורייתא צריך לגלח ביום ל' ואחד! יש לומר: דמשום דשני לקמן לרב מתנא באומר "שלימים" – דהתם ליכא לשנויי בלישנא אחרינא דאשמועינן כשאמר לשון מיותר "ל' יום" כאילו אמר "שלימין" [דבזה] מקצת היום ככולו, ואיצטריך דאומר "שלימים" – קמשני נמי בהא לישנא לבר פדא. **ולרב** מתנא קשיא **סיפא** קסבר מקצת היום ככולו. הילכך, אם גילח ביום שלשים – יצא, כיון שעשה מקצת היום בנזירות. ומיהו לכתחילה לא יגלח אלא ביום שלשים ואחד. ולבר פדא לית ליה מקצת היום ככולו, דא"כ אפילו ביום כ"ט אם גילח יצא, א] והתנא אמר ביום שלשים "אם גילח יום שלשים יצא". **תנן** הריני נזיר שלשים יום אם גילח יום שלשים לא יצא. בשלמא ב] אי דוקא "יום שלשים" – לבר פדא דלית ליה מקצת היום ככולו, ניחא; אע"ג דלעיל קאמר: אם גילח יום שלשים יצא – התם הוא דסתם נזירות קביל עליה דהוי כ"ט, אבל הכא דאמר "שלשים יום" – משך נזירות כל שלשים יום, הלכך אם גילח ביום שלשים לא יצא, דלית ליה מקצת היום ככולו. אלא לרב מתנא קשה, דאע"ג דאמר ל' יום, הא סבירא ליה [דאמרינן] מקצת היום ככולו, ואם גילח ביום שלשים אמאי לא יצא! ומשני: באומר "שלימים". פירוש: אף על גב דמתניתין סתמא קתני "[שלשים] יום", אפילו הכי כיון דאמר "שלשים יום" לישנא יתירא הוא, דאפילו סתם לרב מתנא הוי שלשים יום, וכי אמר "הריני שלשים יום" הוי כאילו אמר "שלימים" וליכא למימר מקצת היום ככולו, ולכך אם גילח ביום שלשים לא יצא. **ואת** השניה ביום ס"א **בשלמא לרב מתנא ניחא**. כשיגלח הראשונה ביום שלשים ואחד נגמר נזירות, ומתחיל נזירות שני בו ביום. מידי דהוי אאדם שמקבל עליו נזירות בחצי היום שעולה לו אותו יום ליום שלם. הלכך ביום ס' כלו ב' נזירות ובס"א מגלח על השניה, ונמצא דכל תגלחת ביום שלשים וא'. וכ"ת: סוף סוף מאי קמ"ל מתני' לרב מתנא? הא ברישא קתני בהדיא דלכתחילה צריך לגלח ביום ל' ואחד! הא לא קשיא, דסיפא אתא לאשמועינן דיום ל' עולה לכאן ולכאן, כדמסיק לקמן בשינויא אליבא דרב מתנא, והא לא שמעינן מרישא. אלא לבר פדא קשה מרישא שמגלח על הראשונה ביום ל' [ואחד] ועל השניה ביום ס' [ואחד]. ואע"ג דאוקמינן לבר פדא מרישא כי האי, וכבר שני ליה: מדרבנן גזרו דלכתחילה צריך לגלח ביום ל' ואחד, ואם כן מאי [הדר] פריך ליה! דרך התלמוד כן להקשות כעין קושיא ראשונה ולתרלו כעין תירוץ ראשון, ובלבד שישמיענו קצת חידוש מה שלא שמענו ברישא. וה"נ איכא קצת חידוש בסיפא לבר פדא שאין ברישא, כדנפקא לן לקמן במסקנא דתירוצא, דמשמיענו דמקצת היום ככולו לבר פדא בתחילת הנזירות, כאדם שמקבל עליו נזירות בחצי היום. אע"פ שאותו חידוש לא נתפרש בסיפא לבר פדא, נריכין אנו למימר שהתלמוד סומך על כך. עוד סיגנון אחר: בשלמא לרב מתנא ניחא (הא). כלומר: הא דקתני שמגלח כל נזירות ביום שלשים ואחד, דהיינו הראשונה ביום שלשים ואחד והשניה ביום ס"א. ואע"ג דשמעינן מרישא דמגלח ביום שלשים ואחד – סיפא איצטריכא ליה לאשמועינן דיום שלשים עולה לכאן ולכאן לב' נזירות כדמסיק לקמן. אלא לבר פדא קשיא. אף על גב דלבר פדא נמי צריך לגלח ביום שלשים ואחד מדרבנן כדשני לעיל, מכל מקום תיקשי לבר פדא מייתור

המשניות

אלא לבר פדא קשיא. דל' חסר א' סגי א) דמגלח ומביא קרבנותיו ואסור ביין ובטומאה עד שיביא קרבנותיו והויא ליה כפרה דנזיר טהור נמי בעי כפרה על שציער עצמו מן היין משום הכי קתני ל' לפי שגם ביום ל' אסור עד שיגלח ויביא קרבנותיו והשתא לבר פדא סתם נזירות כ"ט יום ומגלח ביום ל' ובמסקנא לא קאי הכי: בשלמא לרב מתנא ניחא כיון דסתם נזיר ל' יום אינו מגלח עד שישלים כל ימי נזירותו. אלא לבר פדא קשיא דמיום כ"ט שלימו ימי נזירותו וביום ל' יגלח והוה מצי לשנויי לאלתר נעשה כאומר שלימים אלא ניחא ליה לאקשויי מסיפא ולאוכוחי דע"כ אמרינן הכי: אם גילח יום ל' יצא. ואם איתא דנזיר ל' יום אמאי יצא כיון דאכתי לא שלים נזירותיה. אלא סיפא ע"כ מסייע ליה לבר פדא. הילכך רישא אית לך לפרושי דנעשה כאומר שלימים. כלומר אע"ג דסתם נזירות כ"ט יום גזרו חכמים בין שאמר הריני נזיר סתם ובין שאמר הריני נזיר כ"ט יום שיהא נזיר ל' יום לפי שמנהג הזה הוא בבני אדם מאחר שסתם נזיר הוא סותר למניין ל' רק חסר יום א' הנודר נזירות מפרש ל' יום שהוא מנין שלם לכך גזרו בכולן ל' יום ויגלח ביום ל' וא'. אבל אם גילח ביום ל' יצא. והאי דקאמר באומר שלימים לאו דוקא דלבר פדא לית ליה מקצת היום ככולו אלא הכי קאמר נעשה כאומר דבר שמשמע שלימים והיינו ל' יום: קסבר [illegible] מקצת היום ככולו וכיון שנהג נזירות מקצת ביום ל' אם גילח בו ביום יצא. ומי' לכתחילה אמרו חכמים שלא יגלח בו ביום כיון שהוא ממנין נזיר והשתא ליכא מידי בעיקר נזיר בין רב מתנא לבר פדא דלתרוייהו מדאורייתא מגלח ביום ל' ומדרבנן אינו מגלח אלא עד יום ל"א אלא בהא פליגי דלבר פדא מיום כ"ט שלמו ימי נזירותו ואם נטמא יום ל' קודם הבאת קרבנותיו אינו סותר מדאורייתא אלא מדרבנן ואינו מביא קרבן. ולרב מתנא יום שלשים מן המנין אלא דמקצת היום ככולו ואם נטמא קודם הבאת קרבנותיו סותר מדאוריי' וי"מ דוקא קאמר בר פדא נעשה כאומר שלימים היינו דוקא היכא דקאמר הריני נזיר בסתם אבל היכא דאמר הריני נזיר כ"ט יום מגלח ביום ל' ואיכא בינייהו טובא. אם גילח יום ל' לא יצא. בשלמא לרב מתנא ניחא אלא לבר פדא קשיא ומשני הכא ודאי דאמר שלימים. פי' כיון דאמר ל' יום הוי כאילו אמר שלימים. אית ספרים דגרסי הכי ולא נהירא הא גירסא דהיאך קאמר לרב מתנא ניחא דהא הך מתני' סיפא דהך מתני' דאוקי לה רב מתנא דסבר מקצת היום ככולו. והאיך ניחא ליה דסיפא פליגא ארישא וסברה דלא אמרי' מקצת היום ככולו. הילכך נראה כגירסת הספרים דגרסי' בשלמא לבר פדא ניחא דכיון דאמר הריני נזיר ל' יום אם גילח ביום ל' לא יצא דלית ליה מקצת היום ככולו אלא לרב מתנא דסבר דסתם נזירות ל' יום ואפ"ה אם גילח ביום ל' יצא משום דמקצת היום ככולו מה לי אמר הריני נזיר סתם ומה לי אם אמר הריני נזיר ל' יום כיון דמקצת היום ככולו ומשני באומר שלימים שאמר בפירוש הריני נזיר שלשים יום שלימים דהשתא לא מצי למימר מקצת היום ככולו כיון שפירש שלימים. ואית ספרים דגרסי נעשה כאומר שלימים. פי' כיון דסתם נזיר ל' יום למה לו לפרש ל' יום אלא ודאי כיון שאמר ל' יום נעשה כאומר שלימים: מי שנזר ב' נזירות: כגון שאמר הרי עלי ב' נזירות: והשניה ליום ששים וא' דהיינו ביום שלשים וא' דאדר שגילח ביום ל"א והתחיל בו ביום לנהוג נזירות אותו מקצת היום נעלה לו למנין שלשים:

א) נראה דצ"ל איידי דאיכא יום תלתין דמגלח ומביא קרבנותיו וכו'.

מסורת הש"ס

לקמן טז.

ולקמן ו: טז: יט. פסחים [illegible] ד. נה. מ"ק [illegible] בכורות כ: כה. נדה לג.]

לקמן טז.

הגהות מהר"ב רנשבורג

א] תוס' ד"ה ולרב מתנא קשיא סיפא וכו' והתנא אמר ביום שלשים אם גלח יום שלשים יצא עכ"ל. נ"ב אם גלח ביום שלשים יצא כצ"ל. ב] ד"ה תנן הריני נזיר שלשים יום אם גלח יום שלשים לא יצא בשלמא אי דוקא יום שלשים. נמחק תיבות אי דוקא יום שלשים:

נוסחת הריב"ן

א) שמגלח לל"א יום: ב) כ"ט יום: ג) ולרב מתנא קשיא סיפא [illegible] ד) שלא יגלח עד: ה) הא: ו) כ"ט ימים) ז) דתניא: [illegible] י) דקתני: [illegible] כ) כגון: ל) ביום ס"א: [illegible]

הגהות הב"ח

(א) גמ' מקצת היום ככולו והא תנן הריני נזיר וכו' אם גילח ליום: (ב) רש"י ד"ה אלא וכו' למניינא וכו' [illegible] הס"ד: (ג) ד"ה תנן וכו' ולאחד בשלמא: (ד) ד"ה הכי גרסי' הס"ד ואח"כ מ"ה אמר לך וכו': (ה) ד"ה כאומר וכו' [illegible] (ו) ד"ה דקסבר אינו סותר את נדרו ולרב מתנא: (ז) ד"ה והא תנן גילח וכו' [illegible] (ח) ד"ה אמר וכו' אם גילח הראשונה ביום שלשים:

גליון הש"ס

תום' ד"ה מלמד. דאמר הריני נזיר היום ונזיר צ"ל ונזיר היום.

אלא

אֲבָל לִשְׁתֵּי נְזִירוּת לָא אָמְרִינַן דְּלֶיהֱוֵי יוֹם אֶחָד עוֹלֶה לְמִנְיַן נְזִירוּת רִאשׁוֹנָה וּנְזִירוּת שְׁנִיָּה, קָמַשְׁמַע לָן דְּעוֹלֶה לְכָאן וּלְכָאן. תְּנַן אִם גִּילֵּחַ לְס' חָסֵר אֶחָד יָצָא. שֶׁיּוֹם שְׁלֹשִׁים עוֹלֶה א) לְכָאן וּלְכָאן. בִּשְׁלָמָא לְרַב מַתָּנָא. דְּאָמַר: אֵין נְזִירוּת פְּחוּתָה מִל' יוֹם, וְאֵינוֹ מְגַלֵּחַ עַד יוֹם ל"א –

אֶלָּא לְבַר פַּדָּא קַשְׁיָא! אָמַר לָךְ בַּר פַּדָּא, אֵימָא סֵיפָא: וְאִם גִּילֵּחַ אֶת הָרִאשׁוֹנָה לְיוֹם שְׁלֹשִׁים — מְגַלֵּחַ אֶת הַשְּׁנִיָּה לְיוֹם שִׁשִּׁים. אֶלָּא, סֵיפָא — מְסַיְּיעָא לֵיהּ, רֵישָׁא (א) בְּאוֹמֵר "שְׁלֵימִים". וּלְרַב מַתָּנָא קַשְׁיָא סֵיפָא! אָמַר לָךְ רַב מַתָּנָא, כִּדְקָתָנֵי סֵיפָא: יוֹם שְׁלֹשִׁים עוֹלֶה לְכָאן וּלְכָאן. מַאי הִיא — *מִקְצַת הַיּוֹם כְּכוּלּוֹ? הָא אֲמָרָהּ חֲדָא זִימְנָא! מַהוּ דְּתֵימָא: ה"מ מִילֵּי לְעִנְיַן חֲדָא נְזִירוּת, אֲבָל לִשְׁתֵּי נְזִירוּת — לָא, קמ"ל. *תְּנַן: אִם גִּילֵּחַ יוֹם שִׁשִּׁים חָסֵר אֶחָד יָצָא, שֶׁיּוֹם שְׁלֹשִׁים עוֹלֶה לוֹ מִן הַמִּנְיָן. בִּשְׁלָמָא לְרַב מַתָּנָא — נִיחָא, אֶלָּא לְבַר פַּדָּא לָמָּה לִי? הָא אֲמַר שְׁלֹשִׁים חָסֵר אֶחָד! אָמַר לָךְ: אֲנָא נַמִי אַהָא סָמְכִי. *תְּנַן: מִי שֶׁאָמַר "הֲרֵינִי נָזִיר", נִטְמָא יוֹם שְׁלֹשִׁים — סוֹתֵר אֶת הַכֹּל. בִּשְׁלָמָא לְרַב מַתָּנָא — נִיחָא, אֶלָּא לְבַר פַּדָּא קַשְׁיָא!
אָמַר

לְהָכִי אִיצְטְרִיךְ לָן הָא מַתְנִיתִין – ג) דְּיוֹם שְׁלֹשִׁים עוֹלֶה לוֹ מִן הַמִּנְיָן לְכָאן וּלְכָאן, דְּכִי גִּילֵּחַ הָרִאשׁוֹנָה בְּיוֹם שְׁלֹשִׁים עוֹלֶה לוֹ אוֹתוֹ ג) יוֹם לְכָאן וּלְכָאן וְנִתְחַלָּה ד) מְנוֹי בַּיּוֹם נְזִירוּת שְׁנִיָּה, וְכִי עָבְרוּ עָלָיו ס' חָסֵר אַחַת נַעֲשָׂה עָלָיו יוֹם ה) כ"ט בְּתַשְׁלוּם ל' ו) מִקְצָת הַיּוֹם כְּכוּלּוֹ. אֶלָּא לְבַר פַּדָּא. לָמָּה לִי לְמִיתְנָא שֶׁיּוֹם שְׁלֹשִׁים עוֹלֶה לוֹ מִן הַמִּנְיָן? הָא הָוֵי נְזִירוּת מִשְּׁלֹשִׁים חָסֵר אֶחָד! אָמַר לָךְ בַּר פַּדָּא. אֲנָא דְּאָמֵינָא דְּאֵין עִיקַּר נְזִירוּת אֶלָּא כ"ט יוֹם – אַהָא סָמְכִי, דִּגְמִירְנָא לְהָא מַתְנִיתִין, וְחָזֵינָא בֵּיהּ דְּתָנֵי: שֶׁאִם גִּילֵּחַ יוֹם שִׁשִּׁים חָסֵר א' יָצָא – שֶׁיּוֹם שְׁלֹשִׁים עוֹלֶה לוֹ מִן הַמִּנְיָן, וּמִשּׁוּם דְּבַתְּחִילָּה כִּי גִּילֵּחַ בְּיוֹם שְׁלֹשִׁים עוֹלֶה לוֹ לְכָאן וּלְכָאן, ז) וְלָא מִשּׁוּם דְּאָמְרִינַן מִקְצָת הַיּוֹם כְּכוּלּוֹ וְנַעֲשָׂה כְּמִי שֶׁגִּילֵּחַ בְּיוֹם שְׁלֹשִׁים וְאֶחָד. אַלְמָא דִּסְתָם נְזִירוּת לָא הָוֵי אֶלָּא כ"ט, ח) וּמִשּׁוּם הָכִי אָמֵינָא לְעֵיל שֶׁאִם גִּילֵּחַ בְּיוֹם ל' יָצָא. אֲבָל טַעְמָא דְּהָא מַתְנִיתִין לָא הָוֵי כְּדְאָמְרַתְּ מִשּׁוּם דְּמִקְצָת הַיּוֹם כְּכוּלּוֹ. תְּנַן מִי שֶׁאָמַר הֲרֵינִי נָזִיר נִטְמָא יוֹם שְׁלֹשִׁים סוֹתֵר אֶת הַכֹּל בִּשְׁלָמָא לְרַב מַתָּנָא. דְּאָמַר דְּאֵין נְזִירוּת פָּחוֹת מִשְּׁלֹשִׁים – מִשּׁוּם הָכִי כִּי נִטְמָא בְּיוֹם שְׁלֹשִׁים, "בְּתוֹךְ מְלֹאת" קָרֵינָא בֵּיהּ, וְסוֹתֵר אֶת הַכֹּל. וְאִי קַשְׁיָא לָךְ: הָא תָּרֵיץ רַב מַתָּנָא לְעֵיל, דְּאָמַר מִקְצָת הַיּוֹם כְּכוּלּוֹ, (ב) הָכָא נַמִי נֵימָא מִקְצָת הַיּוֹם כְּכוּלּוֹ, וְאִם נִטְמָא בְּיוֹם שְׁלֹשִׁים לֹא יְהֵא סוֹתֵר כְּלוּם! הָא לָא קַשְׁיָא, דְּאָמַר לָךְ רַב מַתָּנָא: הָא תַּנָּא קַמָּא דְּרַבִּי אֱלִיעֶזֶר סָבַר לָא אָמְרִי' מִקְצָת הַיּוֹם כְּכוּלּוֹ. דְּהָכִי קָא מְתָרְלִינַן: קָסָבַר רַבִּי אֱלִיעֶזֶר מִקְצָת הַיּוֹם כְּכוּלּוֹ – מִכְּלָל ט) דְּתַנָּא קַמָּא דְּר' אֱלִיעֶזֶר סָבַר לָא אָמְרִינַן מִקְצָת הַיּוֹם כְּכוּלּוֹ. אֶלָּא לְבַר פַּדָּא. דְּאָמַר: אֵין עִיקַּר נְזִירוּת אֶלָּא כ"ט יוֹם, אַמַּאי סוֹתֵר? הָא י) נִיטְמָא אַחַר מְלֹאת יְמֵי נִזְרוֹ!
אָמַר

המשניות, דאע"ג [דחדשה] בסיפא, דקתני: ואם גילח הראשונה ליום שלשים מגלח השניה לכתחילה ליום ששים – אלמא דסוף יום שלשים עולה לו למנין נזירות שני, ומקצת יום חשיב כיום שלם, והא לא שמעינן מרישא, דאדרבה, ס"ל לבר פדא דלא אמר מקצת יום ככולו בסוף נזירות, וחשבינן ליה כאדם המקבל נזירות בחצי היום – הא לא חשיב חידוש למקשה, דפשיטא שאדם מקבל נזירות בחצי היום. [ומשני: סד"א ה"מ] שלא היה עסוק בנזירות תחילה, וניכר לכל נזירותיו. אבל הכא דנהג נזירותיו עד חצי היום – אימר לא יעלה לו, דאינו ניכר נזירותו, קמשמע לן דאפי' הכי עולה לו לכאן ולכאן. **הגה"ה אמר לך סיפא מסייעא ואם גילח הראשונה ליום שלשים מגלח השניה ליום ששים.** אלמא דמשך הנזירות כ"ט יום, [לכך אמר] דבדיעבד אם גילח הראשונה ביום שלשים – יצא. ורישא דלכתחילה צריך לגלח ביום שלשים ואחד – נעשה כאומר "שלימים", ומדרבנן בעלמא, דגזרינן סתם נזירות אטו היכא דאמר "שלימים", דאז צריך לגלח לשלשים ואחד, כדשני נמי ארישא.

ולרב מתנא **קשיא סיפא.** דקתני: אם גילח ראשונה ליום שלשים – אלמא דביום שלשים מצי לגלוחי! אמר לך רב מתנא: סיפא יום שלשים עולה לכאן ולכאן. פירוש: משום א] הכי דיום שלשים יש לומר הראשונה שלשים יום דילא – משום דמקצת היום ככולו, ועולה לו מקצתו לנזירות ראשונה, הלכך נזיר בדיעבד יצא. ולכתחילה בעינן ל"א יום (שלימים), דמשך נזירות שלשים יום, כדשני נמי ארישא. ומה שמגלח השניה לכתחלה ליום ששים – משום דסוף סוף עולה להתחלת נזירות שני, מידי דהוה אאדם דמקבל נזירות בחצי היום, ונמצא דיום שלשים הויא להתחלת נזירות שני – להכי מגלח השניה לכתחילה ליום ששים. ופריך לרב מתנא: מאי קמ"ל תנא דאמר מקצת היום ככולו? הא מרישא שמעינן ליה, דקתני: מי שאמר "הריני נזיר" מגלח יום שלשים ואחד, ואם גילח ביום שלשים – יצא, מטעם דמקצת היום ככולו, לרב מתנא! ומשני: דמרישא לא שמעינן אלא דמקצת היום שלשים עולה לו לנזירות אחת שנדר, אבל לב' נזירות כמו בסיפא, שעולה תחילת שלשים יום לסוף נזירות ראשון, לכאן ולכאן – [לא]. ואם תאמר: ולבר פדא נמי תקשה: מאי קא משמע לן? דאי אתא לאשמועינן דאם גילח הראשונה יום שלשים דילא – הא ברישא קתני לה בהדיא: אם גילח יום שלשים יצא! וצריך לומר: לבר פדא נמי איכא חידוש בסיפא מאי דלא שמעי' מרישא דקתני: אם גילח הראשונה ליום שלשים דמגלח השניה ליום ששים לכתחילה – דנזירות שני התחיל ליום ל' אחר תגלחת ראשונה. וקמ"ל דאותו סוף היום עולה למנין נזירות שני, נמצא כי יום ששים הוי שלשים ואחד להתחלת נזירות שני, ואע"ג דלא אמרי' מקצת היום ככולו לבר פדא ביום שלשים להשלים נזירות שעבר – מודה הוא דמקצת היום מהני להתחיל נזירות שני, מידי דהוה אקיבל נזירות עליו בחצי היום, דפשיטא דעולה לו ליום שלם, והא לא שמעינן מרישא. ואיכא קצת חידוש בדבר, דס"ד כשאינו עסוק בנזירות וניכר לכל נזירותיו – אז הוי מקצתו ככולו בתחילת נזירות, אבל הכא דנהג נזירות עד חצי היום – אימא לא יעלה, דאינו ניכר, [קמ"ל]: ב] אם גילח ליום ששים חסר אחד – יצא, שיום ל' עולה לו מן המנין, כלומר לכאן ולכאן. **תנן אם** גילח יום ששים חסר **אחד יצא בשלמא לרב מתנא ניחא.** פירוש: שהתנא צריך לאשמועינן ולומר דיום ל' עולה לכאן ולכאן, שהרי תגלחת ראשונה היתה ביום ל' וכן תגלחת שניה שהיתה ביום ששים חסר אחד היא ביום ג] שתמלא הנזירות יום ל' שגילח בו בראשונה. ולכך צריך ליתן טעם לדבריו, ולומר שיום ל' עולה לו מן המנין – כלומר לכאן ולכאן. אלא לבר פדא, למה לי? הא אמרי' משך נזירות כ"ט יום, ולמה לו לתנא להאריך וליתן טעם לדבריו *)[שיום ל'] עולה לו מן המנין? הא ודאי כל תגלחת היתה ביום שלשים, ופשיטא דילא בדיעבד, כיון דלא בעינן מדאורייתא אלא כ"ט יום! **אמר** לך בר פדא [אנא נמי] **אהא סמכי.** כלומר, מכאן אני מדקדק דמשך נזירות כ"ט יום, דקתני דיום שלשים עולה לו מן המנין, דמשמע דעולה לו למנין אחרון – אלמא דאין עולה לו למנין ראשון כנזכר לעיל, דכיון דתנא מיקל בו כל כך להחשיב יום לכאן ולכאן. **נטמא** יום ל' סותר הכל **בשלמא לרב מתנא ניחא.** פירוש: שנטמא בתוך נזרו. וקשה: ולרב מתנא מי ניחא? הא אמרינן לעיל ולרב מתנא אליבא דתנא קמא דמקצת היום ככולו, אם כן כי עשה מקצת יום – נשלם יום נזירותו, ולא יסתור אלא [ז']! ויש לומר: כי אמרי' מקצת היום ככולו – היינו לענין תגלחת והבאת קרבנותיו, דאם גילח ביום שלשים בדיעבד יצא, אם לא נטמא. אבל נטמא ביום שלשים קודם תגלחת והבאת קרבנותיו – לא אמרינן מקצת היום ככולו להחשיב כנטמא ביום שלשים ואחד, אלא ודאי נטמא נזרו וסותר הכל, כיון דלא השלים כל נזירותיו בטהרה. ואם תאמר: תקשי לרב מתנא נמי הא דלקמן בההוא פרקא, דתנן: "הריני נזיר מאה", אם נטמא יום מאה – סותר הכל, מאה ואחד – סותר ל' יום. ואמאי? והא נשלם נזרו אפי' לרב מתנא לא יסתור אלא ז'! ויש לומר: דה"נ קאמר; בשלמא לרב מתנא ניחא, בין רישא דנטמא ביום שלשים דסותר הכל מדין תורה, וסיפא דקתני: נטמא יום מאה ואחד דקאמר דסותר שלשים יום, אע"ג דכבר נשלם נזרו – הוי דרבנן, מפני שיום מאה ואחד, שהוא יום הבאת קרבנותיו, גזרינן אטו יום שלשים דסתם נזירות שהוא (תגלחת) מן התורה, דהתם סותר כל שלשים יום למפרע מדין תורה. ומהשתא לרב מתנא ניחא בין רישא ובין סיפא, כדפרישית. ⊕ונראה דיום שלשים ואחד נמי סותר כל שלשים אטו יום שלשים, והכי משמע לקמן, דקאמר: נטמא לל' ואחד סותר הכל. ד] אלא לבר פדא קשה בין רישא בין סיפא, אמאי סותר שלשים יום, בין [שנטמא [ביום] שלשים ובין] שנטמא ביום מאה ואחד? הרי נשלם נדרו לגמרי! ודוחק לו לומר דכי נטמא ביום שלשים סותר מדרבנן, דמדרבנן צריך לנהוג נזירות ל' יום, כדאמרי' לעיל לבר פדא. דסוף סוף נטמא יום **)ס"א לא היה ראוי לגזור אטו נטמא יום ל', כיון דהיא גופא דרבנן! ומשני: אמר לך בר פדא: סיפא כוותי, דקתני: ר"א אומר אינו סותר אלא [שבעה]. פי': אינו סותר כלל למפרע נזרו, דהא השלים נזרו בכ"ט יום וכי נטמא ביום ל' – סותר מיהא ז', שאין יכול להביא קרבנותיו עד שיטהר מטומאה זו, שצריך להזות שלישי ושביעי להביא קרבנותיו בטהרה. והיינו סותר שבעה – שאסור לשתות ביין וליטמא למתים עד שיביא קרבנותיו. ואם תאמר: אכתי בר פדא שביק רבנן ועביד כר' אליעזר? ויש לומר דבר פדא סבירא ליה דמדרבי אליעזר משך נזירות כ"ט יום – הכי נמי לרבנן. דבמשך נזירות לא אשכחן דפליגי, אלא בסתירה, דלר' אליעזר אינו סותר אלא שבעה, ולרבנן שלשים. והאי דסותר שלשים לרבנן – אינו אלא מדרבנן בעלמא, דגזירה מדרבנן היכא דאמר נזירות סתם אטו היכא דאמר "שלשים יום שלמים", דאז ודאי סותר הכל לכו"ע, דהא נטמא בתוך ימי נזרו. ורבי אליעזר לא גזר, לכך אינו סותר אלא שבעה. והיא דלקמן נטמא יום מאה ואחד דסותר שלשים – צריך לדחות לבר פדא, ולומר דהא נמי דרבנן היא. וכולה חד גזירה היא, דאי לא הא לא קיימא הא, דאם לא יסתור שלשים כשנטמא יום ק"א – יבואו לומר כמו כן שלא יסתור שלשים כשנטמא ביום שלשים.
קסבר

*) נ"א שאמאי לא **) נ"א ק"א

אלא לבר פדא קשיא יגלח את הראשונה ביום שלשים והשניה ביום ס' וכי היכי דפריך לה מרישא ומשני לה הכי נמי פריך ומשני מסיפא והכי אורחא דתלמודא בכמה דוכתי דפריך מכמה משניות אע"ג דחד שינויא לכולהו: מאי היא מקצת היום ככולו הא אמרה רב מתנא חדא זמנא דרישא דמתני' שני לה הכי דסברא מקצת היום ככולו ותימה לבר פדא (לב"ר) נמי תקשי לך מאי קמ"ל דאמרינן נעשה כאומר שלמים הא אמר חדא זמנא וי"ל דלבר פדא ניחא דשמעי' מינה דאותו יום שהוא מגלח לנזירות ראשונה עולה לו למנין נזירות שניה וקמ"ל דאע"ג דאין תחלת היום עולה לו בסוף הנזי' סוף היום עולה לו בתחי' הנזי'. אלא לרב מתנא כיון דשמעינן דמקצת היום עולה לו בסופו כ"ש שסוף היום עולה לו בתחלתו ולא שמעינן שום חידוש מהך סיפא מהו דתימא ה"מ לענין חדא נזירות כגון שיעלה תחלת היום בסוף הנזירות או סוף היום בתח' נזי' אבל יום ל' שגילח (לא יעלה) [שעולה] לו תחילת היום לסוף נזי' ראשונה אימא לא יעלה לו סוף היום לתחלת נזי' אחרונה דחד יומא לתרתי נזי' לא מפלגי' קמ"ל שיום ל' עולה לו מן המנין: אלא לבר פדא למה לי הא אמר ל' חסר אחד דס"ד דה"ק שיום ל' עולה לו לכאן ולכאן כדפריש לה רב מתנא לעיל ולבר פדא מה צריך יום ל' למנין הראשון הא אמר ל' חסר אחד אמר לך בר פדא אנא נמי אהא (סמכינן) [סמכי] מכאן אני לומד דסתם נזירות כ"ט יום מדקאמר שיום ל' עולה למנין הב' אלמא נשלמה נזירות הא' [דאל"כ] תו לא מצי למהוי מחשבון נזי' הב' דלא אמרינן מקצת היום ככולו ונמצא שכל היום כולו צריך להשלים נזי' א': בשלמא לרב מתנא ניחא כיון דסתם נזי' ל' יום אם נטמא ביום ל' קודם הבאת קרבנותיו סותר הכל דהא דאמר רב מתנא מקצת היום ככולו היינו לאחר הבאת קרבנותיו אבל קודם הבאת קרבנותיו אכתי הוי נזיר מדאורייתא וסותר הכל אלא לבר פדא דאמר סתם נזי' כ"ט יום מדאורייתא אמאי סותר דפשיטא דנזיר שהשלים נזירותו ואחר מלהביא קרבנותיו שאינו סותר אם נטמא:

הגהות הב"ח

(א) גמ' רישא (כאומר שלמים) תא"מ ונ"ב גי' רש"י נעשה כאומר שלמים: (ב) רש"י ד"ה תנן וכו' והכא נמי וכו' מכלל דתנא קמא לא סבירא ליה הס"ד:

[לעיל ה: וש"נ]

לקמן טז.

ג"ז שם

נוסחת הריב"ן

א) עולה מן המנין ב) דמשמע לן דיום: ג) היום: ד) בו ביום: ה) כ"ט: ו) ומקצת ז) (ולא משום כו' ככולו) ליתא בכ"י: ח) כ"ט יום: ט) דת"ק לא ס"ל הס"ד ואח"כ מה"ד אלא כו': י) איטמי:

גליון הש"ס

תום' ד"ה נטמא יום שלשים. ונראה דיום ל"א וכו'. עי' לקמן י"ד ע"ב תד"ה לוקה ודף טז ע"ב תד"ה נטמא:

הגהות מהר"ב רנשבורג

א] תום' ד"ה ולרב מתנא קשיא סיפא וכו' מש"ה וכו' בדיעבד יצא עכ"ל. מן תיבת משום עד תיבת יצא נמחק. ונ"ב מש"ה אם גלח בראשונה יום ל' דיצא משום דיום ל' י"ל מקצת יום ככולו ועולה מקצתו לנזירות ראשונה הלכך בדיעבד יצא כצ"ל א"מ: ב] בא"ד בסופו אם גילח ליום ס' חסר א' יצא שיום ל' עולה לו מן המנין כלומר לכאן ולכאן. נ"ב כ"ז נמחק א"מ: ג] תום' ד"ה תנן אם גלח יום ששים חסר אחד יצא וכו' שתמלא. נמחק תיבת שתמלא ונ"ב שתמו: ד] ד"ה נטמא יום ל' סותר הכל וכו' ונראה דיום שלשים ואחד נמי סותר כל שלשים אטו יום שלשים והכי משמע לקמן דקאמר נטמא לל' ואחד סותר הכל עכ"ל מן תיבת והכי עד תיבת הכל נמחק. ונ"ב דבריהם תמוהים לכאורה דלא נמצא לקמן הכי. ועוד דמאי משמע אם נמצא כך להדיא ול"ל להתום' לפ"ז כולי הך מילתא. ובאורח מישור ראיתי שהגיה כאן בזה"ל והמ"ל לקמן דקאמר נטמא לל' סותר הכל נטמא לשלשים ואחד סותר הכל כצ"ל והס"ד ואח"כ מה"ד אלא לבר פדא עכ"ל הא"מ. וגם דבריו סתומים וקיצר במובן. ואולם אחרי העיון הדק היטב הבנתי דטעות נפל כאן בדפוס דבספרים היה כתוב והמ"ל לקמן וכו' והוא ראשי תיבות והוה מצי למימר וכו' והכוונה דלקמן דף טז ע"א דקאמר במתני' נטמא יום שלשים סותר הכל הוי מצי למתני נמי נטמא יום שלשים ואחד סותר הכל וכמ"ש גם התום' לקמן דף טז ע"ב בסוף ד"ה נטמא ביום ק"א וכו' והמדפיס טעה בראשי תיבות של והמ"ל והיה סבור שיהיה והכי משמע לקמן וחשב לתקן ותקנתו קלקלתו ולפיכך האריכתי לבאר הדבר באר היטב והשתא הגהתו דבעל א"מ הנ"ל מובנת ודו"ק:

אָמַר לָךְ בַּר פַּדָּא, אֵימָא סֵיפָא: רַבִּי אֱלִיעֶזֶר אוֹמֵר: אֵינוֹ סוֹתֵר אֶלָּא שִׁבְעָה. (א) אִי סָלְקָא דַּעְתָּךְ שְׁלֹשִׁים בָּעֵינַן — נִסְתּוֹר כּוּלְּהוּ! קָסָבַר רַבִּי אֱלִיעֶזֶר: *מִקְצָת הַיּוֹם כְּכוּלּוֹ. *תְּנַן: "הֲרֵינִי נָזִיר מֵאָה יוֹם", נִטְמָא יוֹם מֵאָה — סוֹתֵר אֶת הַכֹּל, רַבִּי אֱלִיעֶזֶר אוֹמֵר: אֵינוֹ סוֹתֵר אֶלָּא שְׁלֹשִׁים יוֹם. וְאִי סָלְקָא דַּעְתָּךְ סָבַר רַבִּי אֱלִיעֶזֶר מִקְצָת הַיּוֹם כְּכוּלּוֹ — נִסְתּוֹר שִׁבְעָה, וְאִי לָא סָבַר מִקְצָת הַיּוֹם כְּכוּלּוֹ — לִיסְתּוֹר כּוּלְּהוּ! לְעוֹלָם לָא אָמְרִינַן מִקְצָת הַיּוֹם כְּכוּלּוֹ. אִי הָכִי לִיסְתּוֹר כּוּלְּהוּ! אָמַר רֵישׁ לָקִישׁ: הַיְינוּ טַעְמָא דְּרַבִּי אֱלִיעֶזֶר: אָמַר קְרָא °"זֹאת תּוֹרַת הַנָּזִיר בְּיוֹם מְלֹאת יְמֵי נִזְרוֹ" *הַתּוֹרָה אָמְרָה: נִטְמָא בְּיוֹם מְלֹאת — תֵּן לוֹ תּוֹרַת נָזִיר. לֵימָא כְּתַנָּאֵי: °"עַד מְלֹאת הַיָּמִם", שׁוֹמְעַנִי מִיעוּט "יָמִים" שְׁנַיִם — ת"ל "קָדוֹשׁ יִהְיֶה גַּדֵּל פֶּרַע", אֵין גִּידּוּל שֵׂעָר פָּחוֹת מִשְּׁלֹשִׁים, דִּבְרֵי רַבִּי יֹאשִׁיָּה. רַבִּי (ג) יוֹנָתָן אוֹמֵר: אֵינוֹ צָרִיךְ, הֲרֵי הוּא אוֹמֵר "עַד מְלֹאת הַיָּמִם", אֵי אֵלּוּ הֵן יָמִים שֶׁצְּרִיכִין לְמַלְּאוֹת — הֱוֵי אוֹמֵר שְׁלֹשִׁים. מַאי לָאו, רַב מַתָּנָא דְּאָמַר כְּרַבִּי יֹאשִׁיָּה, וּבַר פַּדָּא דְּאָמַר כְּרַבִּי יוֹנָתָן? אָמַר לָךְ רַב מַתָּנָא: כּוּלֵּי עָלְמָא שְׁלֹשִׁים בָּעֵינַן, וְהָכָא *בְּ"עַד" וְעַד בִּכְלָל פְּלִיגֵי; רַבִּי יֹאשִׁיָּה סָבַר: "עַד" וְלֹא עַד בִּכְלָל, וְרַבִּי יוֹנָתָן סָבַר: "עַד" וְעַד בִּכְלָל. אָמַר מָר: אֵי אֵלּוּ הֵן יָמִים שֶׁצְּרִיכִין לְמַלְּאוֹת — הֱוֵי אוֹמֵר שְׁלֹשִׁים. וְאֵימָא שַׁבָּת! מִי אִיכָּא חַסִּירוּתָא? וְאֵימָא

תורה אור: במדבר ו; שם

קסבר רבי אליעזר מקצת היום ככולו. השתא חוזר לרב מתנה, ולייסב דברי רבי אליעזר אליבא דתנא קמא; כי היכי דלרבנן משך נזירות שלשים יום – ה"נ לרבי אליעזר, דאדרבה, מדרבנן [נשמע] לר' אליעזר, דבמשך נזירות לא פליגי. וכ"ת: א"כ לר' אליעזר נסתור כל שלשים יום! קסבר רבי אליעזר מקצת היום ככולו, ואפילו נטמא קודם הבאת קרבנותיו. דאחרי שעשה מקצת נזירות ביום שלשים ואח"כ נטמא – חשיב כנטמא ביום שלשים ואחד, על כן אינו סותר אלא ז'. תימה: דאמרינן לקמן "והימים הראשונים יפלו" – מכלל דאיכא אחרונים, וזה אין לו אחרונים! וי"ל: דהאי סברא לא מהניא אלא דלא סתר מאה, אבל שלשים מיהא סותר. ורבנן סברי: לא אמרינן מקצת היום ככולו היכא דנטמא קודם הבאת קרבנותיו, ולהכי סותר כל שלשים יום. ובהא פליגי רבנן ור' אליעזר אליבא דרב מתנא. **תנן** הריני נזיר מאה יום נטמא יום מאה סותר את הכל רבי אליעזר אומר אינו סותר אלא שלשים ואי ס"ד סבר ר' אליעזר מקצת היום ככולו לסתור ז'. לרב מתנא פריך. א] ואי ס"ד [לאו] מקצת היום ככולו – כלומר לבר פדא – ליסתור כולהו, כל ק' יום! **אמר** ריש לקיש. ב] כבר פדא, ולא אמרינן מקצת היום ככולו. וכ"ת: אמאי אינו סותר כולהו – אמר ר"ל כו' אמרה תורה נטמא ביום מלאת – דהיינו ביום ק', שהוא יום מלאת נזרו – תן לו תורת נזרו, כלומר שיעשה עוד תורת סתם נזירות שלשים יום, וגזירת הכתוב שלא יסתור כולו. וא"ת: לבר פדא, לרבי אליעזר כי נטמא יום ל' אמאי אינו סותר אלא ז'? נסתור שלשים כדריש לקיש "תן לו תורת נזיר"! וי"ל: דהתם אחר מלאת הוה לבר פדא, שהרי סתם נזירות הוי כ"ט לבר פדא. ואם תאמר: התינח לבר פדא, אלא לרב מתנא דקאמר לרבי אליעזר מקצת היום ככולו, אף בנטמא קודם הבאת קרבנותיו ביום ק' לא נסתור אלא ז'! וצריך לדחות ולומר, דעתה איירי בשאמר "הריני נזיר מאה יום שלמים", דהשתא ליכא למימר מקצת היום ככולו כיון דאמר "שלמים", ומ"מ אינו סותר כולם – מדרשא דריש לקיש, דכי נטמא ביום מלאת – גזירת הכתוב שלא יסתור אלא שלשים. וקשה: דבמתני' סתמא קתני ק' יום, ולא קתני "שלמים". ועוד: אדמפלגי לר' אליעזר בין נטמא ביום שלשים דאינו סותר אלא ז', לנטמא ביום ק' דסותר שלשים – ליפלוג לעולם בנטמא ביום ק' עצמו: במה דברים אמורים – כשאמר "שלמים" שלשים, אבל לא אמר "שלמים" – לא סתר אלא ז', דמקצת היום ככולו! ונראה למהר"ף דמתניתין איירי דאמר מאה יום ולא אמר "שלמים". ודקשיא לך: לרב מתנא אליבא דר' אליעזר, כיון דאמרינן דמקצת היום ככולו אף בנטמא ביום ק' לא נסתור אלא ז'! לא תיקשי, דאמר ר"ל. ותירוץ זה מסיק לשניהם, דגזירת הכתוב הוא לסתור שלשים, דע"כ ביום מלאת קאי. כי נטמא ביום ק', אע"ג דמקצת היום ככולו – לא נימא כאילו נטמא יום ק"א אחר מלאת, דאינו סותר אלא ז', דהא אם לא נטמא היה צריך להשלים נמי כל יום ק', אם כן יום מלאת הוא, וגזירת הכתוב כי נטמא ביום מלאת שיסתור ל' יום. ואם תאמר: ברישא נמי, כי נטמא ביום ל' לר' אליעזר אמאי אינו סותר אלא ז'? יסתור כל שלשים, שהרי נטמא ביום מלאת! ויש לומר דמשמעות דקרא משמע דאיירי בדמפרש נזירותו, ולא בסתם נזיר; מדקאמר: נטמא ביום מלאת תן לו תורת נזיר – פירוש סתם נזירות – מכלל דעד השתא לאו בסתם נזירות קיימא. אבל כי נדר נזירות סתם – בהא לא איירי כלל, שאם נטמא ביום מלאת שנתן לו עוד תורת סתם נזיר – דודאי לא יהבינן ליה שלשים, כיון דאיתא לרב מתנא. ג] ולבר פדא דנזירות הוי כ"ט – להכי אינו סותר אלא ז' (בו) לר' אליעזר. אבל בסיפא איירי כשנדר בפירוש שלשים, דהא פירש שלשים יום, אז לא הוי נמי סתם נזיר, ובההיא מודה רבי אליעזר כי נטמא ביום שלשים דסותר שלשים, דבדידיה נמי איירי קרא ד"זאת תורת הנזיר". **שומע** אני מיעוט ימים שנים. ויהיה סתם נזירות ב' ימים. תלמוד לומר "קדוש יהיה גדל פרע" ואין גידול פחות משלשים יום, כמנין ["יהיה"]. **שהן** צריכין למלאות הוי אומר [שלשים]. כלומר: חדש, שפעמים שלשים יום ופעמים חסר א'. **מאי** לאו רב מתנא כרבי יאשיה. דדריש "יהיה", ובר פדא כר' יונתן דדריש מ"עד מלאת" ולא עד בכלל, דהיינו כ"ט יום. אמר לך רב מתנא: דכו"ע שלשים כוותיה, דרבי יאשיה סבר בכל דוכתין עד ולא עד בכלל, הילכך ["יהיה"] איבעי למימר. ורבי יונתן סבר בכל דוכתין עד ועד בכלל, ולא איצטריך דרשא ד"יהיה", אלא מ"עד מלאת" נפקא. ולבר פדא צריך לומר תנאי היא. **ואימא** שבת. שהשבת ממלא השבוע. **מי** איכא חסירותא. הא כל ימי השבועות שלמים בשבת, אבל החדשים יש מלאים ויש חסרים. ואימא

אָמַר לָךְ בַּר פַּדָּא אֵימָא סֵיפָא ר' אֱלִיעֶזֶר אוֹמֵר אֵינוֹ סוֹתֵר אֶלָּא ז'. כְּנֶגֶד אוֹתָן יָמִים שֶׁמּוֹנֶה בָּהֶן שְׁלִישִׁי וּשְׁבִיעִי מֵחֲמַת טוּמְאָה. וְאִי ס"ד דְּבָעֵינַן שְׁלֹשִׁים נִיסְתּוֹר כּוּלְּהוּ. אֶלָּא לָאו, א) דְּאֵין עִיקַּר נְזִירוּת [לר"א] אֶלָּא כ"ט יוֹם. וּמַאי טַעְמָא דְּר' אֱלִיעֶזֶר דְּאָמַר דְּסוֹתֵר ז' – מִשּׁוּם דְּצָרִיךְ לְגַלֵּחַ לְאַחַר שֶׁהִזָּה עָלָיו שְׁלִישִׁי וּשְׁבִיעִי מֵחֲמַת טוּמְאָה, כִּדְמְפָרֵשׁ בֵּיהּ קְרָא "בַּיּוֹם הַשְּׁבִיעִי יְגַלְּחֶנּוּ". וּבְדִין הוּא דְּאֵינוֹ צָרִיךְ לִסְתּוֹר מֵהֶן כְּלוּם, שֶׁהֲרֵי עָבְרוּ עָלָיו כ"ט יוֹם בְּטָהֳרָה, אֶלָּא מִשּׁוּם דְּהַשְׁתָּא נִתְגַּלַּח עַל הַטּוּמְאָה, וְקִים לְהוּ לְרַבָּנַן דְּאֵין שֵׂיעָר מִתְגַּדֵּל כְּדֵי לָכוֹף רֹאשׁוֹ שֶׁל זֶה בְּצַד עִיקָּרוֹ שֶׁל זֶה בְּפָחוֹת מִז' יָמִים, וּלְהָכִי אָמַר רַבִּי אֱלִיעֶזֶר דְּצָרִיךְ שֶׁיְּהֵא סוֹתֵר ז' וּמוֹנֶה ז' אֲחֵרִים כְּנֶגְדָּן. וְהָכִי נַמִי מְפָרֵשׁ טַעְמָא דְּרַבִּי אֱלִיעֶזֶר לְקַמָּן. וְאִי קַשְׁיָא: אַמַּאי לָא מְתָרֵץ בַּר פַּדָּא הָכִי ב) כְּרֵישָׁא: מַאי טַעְמָא סוֹתֵר אֶת הַכֹּל – מִשּׁוּם דְּנַעֲשָׂה כְּאוֹמֵר "שְׁלֵמִין"? הַיְינוּ טַעְמָא דְּלָא מְתָרֵץ לָהּ הָכִי: דְּקָסָבַר, דְּכֵיוָן דְּנִטְמָא לְאַחַר כ"ט יוֹם, לָא מַדְחִינַן לֵיהּ מִקָּרְבָּן כּוּלֵּי הַאי עַד שְׁלֹשִׁים אַחֲרִינֵי, דִּילְמָא אָתֵי לְמֶיעֱבַר עַל נִזְרֵיהּ וְאָתֵי לִידֵי תַּקָּלָה. ג) ל"א: רַבִּי אֱלִיעֶזֶר אוֹמֵר אֵינוֹ סוֹתֵר אֶלָּא ז' – דְּבָעֵי הַזָּאָה שְׁלִישִׁי וּשְׁבִיעִי וְאַח"כ יָבִיא קָרְבַּן נָזִיר בְּטָהֳרָה. אַלְמָא קָסָבַר דְּעִיקַּר נְזִירוּת שְׁלֹשִׁים חָסֵר א', וּבְדִין הוּא דְּאֵינוֹ סוֹתֵר כְּלָל, וְהַאי דְּסוֹתֵר ז' – כְּדֵי שֶׁיָּבִיא קָרְבָּנוֹ בְּטָהֳרָה. לָא, לְעוֹלָם אֵימָא לָךְ דְּסָבַר רַבִּי אֱלִיעֶזֶר שְׁלֹשִׁים בָּעֵינַן כו'. וְרַב מַתָּנָא אָמַר לָךְ: לְעוֹלָם אֵימָא לָךְ לְר' אֱלִיעֶזֶר לָא הָוֵי נְזִירוּת פָּחוֹת מִשְּׁלֹשִׁים יוֹם. וְהַאי דְּאָמַר: אִם כֵּן נִיסְתּוֹר לְהוּ לְכוּלְּהוּ – הַיְינוּ טַעְמָא דְּלָא סָתַר לְהוּ, דְּקָסָבַר מִקְצָת יוֹם שְׁלֹשִׁים שֶׁעָבַר עָלָיו בְּטָהֳרָה כְּכוּלּוֹ דָּמֵי. תְּנַן הֲרֵינִי נָזִיר מֵאָה יוֹם נִטְמָא יוֹם מֵאָה סוֹתֵר אֶת הַכֹּל. וַאֲפִי' לְבַר פַּדָּא, הוֹאִיל ד) דְּקָאָמַר מֵאָה יוֹם – שְׁלֵמִים מַשְׁמַע. וְאִי ס"ד דְּסָבַר ר' אֱלִיעֶזֶר מִקְצָת הַיּוֹם כְּכוּלּוֹ לִסְתּוֹר ז'. וְתוּ לָא, כִּי נִטְמָא בְּיוֹם ק', שֶׁהֲרֵי כְּבָר עָבַר נְזִירוּתוֹ כְּשֶׁנִּטְמָא. ה) וְלִדְבָרֶיךָ, אִי לָא סָבַר מִקְצָת הַיּוֹם כְּכוּלּוֹ – לִיסְתּוֹר לְהוּ לְכוּלְּהוּ, וְאַמַּאי קָאָמַר אֵינוֹ סוֹתֵר אֶלָּא שְׁלֹשִׁים? לְעוֹלָם לָא סָבַר מִקְצָת הַיּוֹם כְּכוּלּוֹ. וְהַאי דְּקָאָמַר: אֵינוֹ סוֹתֵר אֶלָּא שְׁלֹשִׁים יוֹם – מְסַיֵּיעַ לֵיהּ לְבַר פַּדָּא. וְהַאי דְּקָאָמַר: אִי לָא סְבִירָא לֵיהּ דְּמִקְצָת הַיּוֹם כְּכוּלּוֹ וְאַכַּתִּי לָא ו) שְׁלֵימִין, אַמַּאי לָא סָתַר לְכוּלְּהוּ? אָמַר רֵישׁ לָקִישׁ: הַיְינוּ טַעְמָא דְּרַבִּי אֱלִיעֶזֶר כו'. **זאת** תּוֹרַת הַנָּזִיר בְּיוֹם **מְלֹאת** יְמֵי נִזְרוֹ ז). בֵּין לִנְזִירוּת שְׁלֹשִׁים בֵּין לִנְזִירוּת מֵאָה – תֵּן לוֹ תּוֹרַת נָזִיר, דְּהַיְינוּ שְׁלֹשִׁים. וְהַיְינוּ דְּקָאָמַר: אֵינוֹ סוֹתֵר אֶלָּא שְׁלֹשִׁים. ח) אֵלּוּ הֵן יָמִים שֶׁצְּרִיכִין לְמַלְּאוֹת הֱוֵי אוֹמֵר ל'. דְּחָדְשָׁהּ שֶׁל לְבָנָה אֵינוֹ אֶלָּא כ"ט וָחֵצִי, וּפְעָמִים שֶׁהוּא צָרִיךְ לְהַשְׁלִים לְמִנְיַן שְׁלֹשִׁים. לְאַפּוּקֵי שְׁאָר יָמִים שֶׁל עֶשְׂרִים וְשֶׁל אַרְבָּעִים שֶׁאֵינָן צְרִיכִין לְמַלֹּאת. ט) דְּמַשְׁמַע דְּתֶיהֱוֵי נְזִירוּת בְּאוֹתָן יָמִים שֶׁצְּרִיכִין לְמַלֹּאוֹת, כַּמָּה הֵן – (הֲרֵי) כ"ט. רַבִּי יֹאשִׁיָּה סָבַר. דְּהַאי דִּכְתִיב "עַד מְלֹאת" – עַד ל' מַשְׁמַע, וְלֹא י) שְׁלֹשִׁים בִּכְלָל. לְהָכִי אִיצְטְרִיךְ "גַּדֵּל פֶּרַע" – שֶׁאֵין גִּידּוּל שֵׂעָר פָּחוֹת מִשְּׁלֹשִׁים. וְרַבִּי (ג) יוֹנָתָן סָבַר עַד וְעַד בִּכְלָל. וְלָא אִיצְטְרִיךְ לָן מִ"גַּדֵּל פֶּרַע", כ) דְּהָא מֵ"עַד מְלֹאת הַיָּמִים" נָפְקָא. **אָמַר מָר אִי אֵלּוּ** הֵן יָמִים שֶׁצְּרִיכִים לְמַלְּאוֹת הֱוֵי **אוֹמֵר** שְׁלֹשִׁים. דְּמַשְׁמַע דְּתֶהֱוֵי נְזִירוּת סְתָם שְׁלֹשִׁים יוֹם. **וְאֵימָא** שַׁבָּת. כְּדֵי שָׁבוּעַ הָוֵי סְתָם נְזִירוּת, דְּהָוֵי ל) שִׁשָּׁה יָמִים, מ) אָתֵי יוֹם שְׁבִיעִי וּמְמַלֵּא לָהּ נ) לְשָׁבוּעַ, וְאֵימָא דְּ"עַד מְלֹאת הַיָּמִים" – עַד מְלֹאת ס) שָׁבוּעַ קָאָמַר! ע) **מַאי חַסִּירוּתָא אִיכָּא**. דְּבָעֵי הַשְׁלָמָה? כּוּלְּהִי שָׁבוּעֵי כִּי הֲדָדֵי נִינְהוּ, וּמִשּׁוּם הָכִי לֵיכָּא לְמֵימַר דְּאַיְירֵי בְּהוּ קְרָא. אֲבָל חֹדֶשׁ דְּאִיכָּא חַסִּירוּתָא, דְּאִיכָּא חָסֵר וְאִיכָּא מָלֵא, פ) אִיכָּא לָךְ לְמֵימַר: הַאי לְחֹדֶשׁ הוּא דְּאָתָא קְרָא. וְאֵימָא

פי' הרא"ש

אמר לך בר פדא אימא סיפא וכו' ואי ס"ד ל' יום בעינן נסתור כולהו: אינו סותר אלא שבעה. כלומר אינו סותר כלל אלא ממנין ז' ימי טומאתו ואז יביא קרבנותיו ואע"ג דטמא משלח קרבנותיו שאני נזיר דכתי' [ונתן] על כפי הנזיר וכיון דסבר ר"א סתם נזי' כ"ט יום מסתמא רבנן לא פליגי עליה בעיקר משך ימי נזירות אלא דבהא קמפלגי דרבנן סברי סותר ביום ל' נזירות אטו היכא דאמר הריני ל' יום דסותר הכל מדאורייתא ומביא קרבן טומאה והיינו דפרישי' לעיל דליכא מידי בין רב מתנא לבר פדא אלא דלרב מתנא אם נטמא ביום ל' קודם הבאת קרבנותיו סותר מדאורי' ומביא קרבן. ולבר פדא אינו סותר אלא מדרבנן: ואי ס"ד קסבר ר"א מקצת היום ככולו נסתור ז' פי' לא לסתור כלל ופריך ואי לא סבר מקצת היום ככולו ניסתור כולהו כיון שנטמא ביום אחרון של נזירותו: אמרה תורה נטמא ביום מלאת תן לו תורת נזרו. כלומר לעולם לית ליה מקצת היום ככולו אלא גזירת הכתוב הוא דאם נטמא ביום אחרון של נזירותו אפי' אם נזר נזירות מרובה אינו סותר אלא ל' יום כתורת סתם נזירות לכאורה איתותב רב מתנא דלא משני תלמודא אלא אליבא דבר פדא ואיכא למימר דרב מתנא מוקי לה באומר שלמים: שומע אני מיעוט ימים ב' דסתם נזירות אינו אלא ב' ימים ת"ל גדל פרע ואין גידול פרע פחות מל' יום דהכי משמע כמנין יהיה גדל פרע: אלו הן ימים שצריכין מלאת אלו ימי החודש שפעמי' הם כ"ט ופעמי' מלאים את החודש ועושים אותו מל' יום. ובר פדא כרבי וה"ק עד מלאת עד אותו היום שממלאים את החודש ולא יום מלאת בכלל. ור' יאשיה נמי אית ליה עד ולא עד בכלל ולהכי דריש ליה מקדוש יהיה ומשני תרוייהו סברי ל' יום: ואימא (מה) שבת שהוא משלים ששת ימי המעשה להיותם נקראים שבוע: מי איכא חסרונא לישנא דמלאת משמע שפעמים בא למלאת החסרון כגון חודש שפעמים הוא מכ"ט אל בימי השבוע ליכא חסרון:

הגהות הב"ח

(א) גמ' ואי סלקא דעתך שלשים: (ב) שם דברי ר' יאשיה ר' יונתן אומר אינו צריך וכו' ורבי סבר עד כל"ה: (ג) רש"י ד"ה ורבי סבר וכו' מגדל פרע דאפילו מעד מלאת:

מסורת הש"ס

[לעיל ה: וש"נ] לקמן טז.

[לקמן כ.]

[ברכות כו: עירובין פב: פסחים קיז: ר"ה כ: סוכה מח. מנחות סח: חולין מו. נג: ערכין יח. נדה נח.]

נוסחת הריב"ן

א) ש"מ דאין עיקר נזירות אלא כו' ותיבת לר"א ליתא: ב) כרישא: ג) מן ל"א ר"א עד שלשים בעינן כו' ליתא בכ"י: ד) וקאמר: ה) ולטעמיך: ו) לא שלימי להו ק' אמאי כו': ז) התורה אמרה נטמא ביום מלאת בין לנזירות כו': ח) וליתו: ט) למלאות הס"ד ואח"כ מה"ד מאי לאו רב מתנא דאמר כר' יאשיה דאמר בכולהו אין גילות פחות מל' יום ובר פדא דאמר עד ימים שצריך למלאות דהוו כמה הם הרי כ"ט ואח"כ מה"ד ר' יאשיה כו': י) יום ל': כ) דהא: ל) שבת: מ) ואתי: נ) לשבוע: ס) יומי שבוע: ע) איכא חסירותא לדבר השלמה: פ) אית לך למימר משום האי לחודש הוא דאתא קרא:

הגהות מהר"ב רנשבורג

א] תוס' ד"ה תנן הריני נזיר וכו' לרב מתנא פריך. נ"ב כאן הס"ד ואח"כ מה"ד ואי ס"ד לאו מקצת היום ככולו וכו' עכ"ל וכל"ל: ב] ד"ה אמר ר"ל כבר פדא. נ"ב כבר פדא: ג] בא"ד בסופו כיון דאיתא לרב מתנא. נ"ב מקצת היום ככולו:

וְאֵימָא שָׁנָה! מִי מָנֵינַן לְיוֹמֵי? וְהָא *רַבָּנַן דְּקֵיסָרִי אָמְרִי: אמִנַּיִן שֶׁאֵין מוֹנִין יָמִים לְשָׁנִים — שֶׁנֶּאֱמַר °"לְחָדְשֵׁי הַשָּׁנָה" — חֳדָשִׁים מְחַשְּׁבִין לְשָׁנִים, וְלֹא יָמִים לְשָׁנִים.§ **מתני'** באָמַר "הֲרֵינִי נָזִיר אַחַת גְּדוֹלָה" "הֲרֵינִי נָזִיר אַחַת קְטַנָּה", אֲפִילּוּ "מִכָּאן וְעַד סוֹף הָעוֹלָם" — נָזִיר שְׁלֹשִׁים יוֹם.§ **גמ'** אַמַּאי? וְהָא "מִכָּאן וְעַד סוֹף הָעוֹלָם" קָאָמַר! הָכִי קָאָמַר: אֲרִיכָא לִי הָדָא מִילְּתָא כְּמִכָּאן וְעַד סוֹף הָעוֹלָם. תְּנַן: *ג"הֲרֵינִי נָזִיר מִכָּאן עַד מָקוֹם פְּלוֹנִי" — אוֹמְדִים כַּמָּה יָמִים מִכָּאן וְעַד מָקוֹם פְּלוֹנִי; פָּחוֹת מִשְּׁלֹשִׁים יוֹם — נָזִיר שְׁלֹשִׁים יוֹם, וְאִם לָאו — נָזִיר כְּמִנְיַן הַיָּמִים. וְאֵימָא הָכָא נַמִי: אֲרִיכָא לִי הָא מִילְּתָא כְּמִכָּאן וְעַד מָקוֹם פְּלוֹנִי! אָמַר רָבָא: דשֶׁהֶחֱזִיק בַּדֶּרֶךְ. וְלֶיהֱוֵי כָּל פַּרְסָה וּפַרְסָה! אָמַר רַב פָּפָּא: בְּאַתְרָא דְּלָא מָנֵי פַּרְסֵי. וְלֶיהֱוֵי כָּל אַוָּונָא וְאַוָּונָא. מִי לָא תְּנַן: *"הֲרֵינִי נָזִיר כַּעֲפַר הָאָרֶץ" וְ"כִשְׂעַר רֹאשִׁי" וּ"כְחוֹל הַיָּם" — הֲרֵי זֶה נָזִיר עוֹלָם, וּמְגַלֵּחַ אֶחָד לִשְׁלֹשִׁים יוֹם! כָּל מִילְּתָא דְּאִית בֵּיהּ קִיצוּתָא לָא קָתָנֵי. וְהָתַנְיָא: *ה"הֲרֵינִי נָזִיר כָּל יְמֵי חַיַּי" "הֲרֵינִי נְזִיר עוֹלָם" — הֲרֵי זֶה נְזִיר עוֹלָם. אֲפִילּוּ "מֵאָה שָׁנָה" אֲפִילּוּ "אֶלֶף שָׁנִים" — אֵין זֶה נְזִיר עוֹלָם (א) אֶלָּא נָזִיר לְעוֹלָם. רַבָּה אָמַר: שָׁאנֵי שְׂעָרוֹת, הוֹאִיל וּמוּבְדָּלוֹת זוֹ מִזּוֹ. גַּבֵּי יוֹמֵי נַמִי, הָא כְּתִיב °"וַיְהִי עֶרֶב וַיְהִי בֹקֶר יוֹם אֶחָד"! הָתָם לָאו דְּמִפְסְקִי מֵהֲדָדֵי הוּא. מַאי קָאָמַר — יְמָמָא וְלֵילְיָא חַד יוֹמָא הוּא, וּלְעוֹלָם לָא מִפְסְקִי מֵהֲדָדֵי. רָבָא אָמַר: לָמָּה לָךְ אַקְשׁוּיֵי כּוּלֵּי הַאי? שָׁאנֵי הָתָם, דְּהָא קָתָנֵי "הֲרֵינִי נָזִיר אַחַת".§ **מתני'** ו"הֲרֵינִי נָזִיר וְיוֹם אֶחָד", "הֲרֵינִי נָזִיר וְשָׁעָה אַחַת", "הֲרֵינִי נָזִיר אַחַת וּמֶחֱצָה" — ה"ז נָזִיר שְׁתַּיִם.§ **גמ'** לָמָּה לִי לְמִיתְנָא כָּל הָנֵי? צְרִיכִי; דְּאִי תְּנָא "הֲרֵינִי נָזִיר וְיוֹם אֶחָד" — הָכָא הוּא דְּאָמְרִי' אֵין נְזִירוּת לְיוֹם א', אַמְּטוּ לְהָכִי קָמָנֵי תַּרְתֵּין. אֲבָל "הֲרֵינִי נָזִיר וְשָׁעָה אַחַת" — לִימְנֵי ל' וְאֶחָד יוֹם, קמ"ל. וְאִי

שמות יב — בראשית א

וְאֵימָא שָׁנָה. שֶׁצְּרִיכָה לְמַלֹּאוֹת, דִּפְעָמִים א) יִהְיֶה שנ"ג, וּפְעָמִים שנ"ד, וּפְעָמִים שנ"ה. מִי מָנֵינַן. שָׁנָה לְיָמִים? ב) הָכָא כְּתִיב "עַד מְלֹאת (ב)יְמֵי" – חֹדֶשׁ הוּא דְּמָנֵינַן לְיָמִים, וּמִשּׁוּם הָכִי אָמְרִינַן דְּבִשְׁלֹשִׁים שֶׁל חֹדֶשׁ אַיְירֵי קְרָא. אֲבָל לֹא לְשָׁנָה, שֶׁאֵין מוֹנִין לָהּ לְיָמִים אֶלָּא לָחֳדָשִׁים. מַתְנִי' אָמַר הֲרֵינִי נָזִיר אַחַת קְטַנָּה. לֹא תְּהֵא פְּחוּתָה מִשְּׁלֹשִׁים יוֹם. (ג) וַאֲפִילּוּ אָמַר "הֲרֵינִי נָזִיר יוֹם אֶחָד" – הֲרֵי זֶה נָזִיר ל' יוֹם, לְפִי שֶׁאֵין נְזִירוּת פְּחוּתָה מִשְּׁלֹשִׁים. אוֹ שֶׁאָמַר "הֲרֵינִי נָזִיר אַחַת גְּדוֹלָה", אֲפִילּוּ אָמַר שֶׁתְּהֵא גְּדוֹלָה מִכָּאן וְעַד סוֹף הָעוֹלָם – הֲרֵי זֶה אֵינוֹ נָזִיר אֶלָּא שְׁלֹשִׁים יוֹם, כִּדְאָמַר בַּגְּמָ', דְּאִי אָמַר הָכִי – מַשְׁמַע דְּאָמַר: אֲרִיכָא עֲלֵיהּ הָדָא נְזִירוּת דִּשְׁלֹשִׁים ג) כְּמִכָּאן עַד סוֹף הָעוֹלָם. גְּמָ' ד) אִם יֵשׁ מְהַלֵּךְ עַד אוֹתוֹ מָקוֹם פָּחוֹת מִשְּׁלֹשִׁים יוֹם הֲרֵי זֶה נָזִיר שְׁלֹשִׁים יוֹם. דִּלְעוֹלָם אֵין נְזִירוּת פְּחוּתָה מִשְּׁלֹשִׁים. וְאִם יֵשׁ מִשָּׁם עַד מָקוֹם פְּלוֹנִי יוֹתֵר מִמַּהֲלַךְ ל' יוֹם, כְּגוֹן אַרְבָּעִים יוֹם אוֹ נ' יוֹם – הֲרֵי זֶה נָזִיר כְּמִנְיַן הַיָּמִים, דְּהָוֵי כְּמַאן דְּאָמַר "הֲרֵינִי נָזִיר עַד מ' יוֹם אוֹ עַד נ'". וְאַמַּאי אֵימָא הָכָא נַמִי. כִּי אָמַר "מִכָּאן וְעַד מָקוֹם פְּלוֹנִי", ה) דְּמַשְׁמַע כְּמַאן דְּאָמַר: אֲרִיכָא לִי הָדָא מִילְּתָא דִּנְזִירוּת דִּשְׁלֹשִׁים יוֹם כְּמַהֲלַךְ נ' דְּמִכָּאן וְעַד מָקוֹם פְּלוֹנִי! אָמַר ו) רָבָא. הָתָם לֵיכָּא לְמֵימַר הָכִי, דִּכְשֶׁהֶחֱזִיק בַּדֶּרֶךְ כְּבָר עַסְקִינַן. דְּהוֹאִיל וְהֶחֱזִיק בַּדֶּרֶךְ, וְקָאָמַר "מִכָּאן וְעַד מָקוֹם פְּלוֹנִי" – מוֹכַח מִילְּתָא לְדַעְתָּא דְּלֶיהֱוֵי נָזִיר כָּל זְמַן שֶׁיְּהֵא בַּדֶּרֶךְ קָאָמַר. וְעוֹד, כֵּיוָן דְּהֶחֱזִיק בַּדֶּרֶךְ, לֵיכָּא לְמֵימַר דַּאֲרִיכָא לֵיהּ מִילְּתָא ז) כְּמִכָּאן וְעַד מָקוֹם פְּלוֹנִי, דְּהָא חָזֵינַן ח) דְּלָא אֲרִיכָא לֵיהּ דֶּרֶךְ, דְּהֶחֱזִיק בַּדֶּרֶךְ כְּבָר. וְקַפְרִיךְ אַמַּתְנִי' גּוּפָא דְּ"מִכָּאן וְעַד מָקוֹם פְּלוֹנִי": וְלֶהֱוֵי כָּל פַּרְסָה וּפַרְסָה חַד נְזִירוּת! דִּלְמָא הַאי דְּקָאָמַר "מִכָּאן וְעַד מָקוֹם פְּלוֹנִי" – כָּל מִנְיַן פַּרְסָאוֹת ט) מִכָּאן וְעַד מָקוֹם פְּלוֹנִי קִבֵּל עָלָיו נְזִירוּת שֶׁל (ד) י) שְׁלֹשִׁים, וִיהֵא מְגַלֵּחַ בְּסוֹף כָּל שְׁלֹשִׁים כ) וְיָבִיא שְׁלֹשָׁה בְּהֵמוֹת, וְאִי הָוֵי עַד הָתָם מֵאָה פַּרְסָאוֹת לֶיהֱוֵי נָזִיר מֵאָה נְזִירוּת! וְלֶיהֱוֵי כָּל אַוָּונָא וְאַוָּונָא. דְּאִיכָּא מִמָּקוֹם פְּלוֹנִי עַד כָּאן, אֲפִילּוּ קִבֵּל עָלֵיהּ חֲדָא נְזִירוּת לְכָל אֲוָונָא; דְּאִי הָווּ עֶשְׂרִים אֲוָונוֹת – לִיחַיַּיב בְּכָל עֶשְׂרִים שֶׁל שְׁלֹשִׁים שְׁלֹשִׁים! דְּמִילְּתָא דַּעֲבִידָא הִיא דְּמָנוּ אֱינָשֵׁי אֲוָונֵי, "כַּמָּה אֲוָונוֹת יֵשׁ מִכָּאן וְעַד מָקוֹם פְּלוֹנִי", דִּבְכָל מָקוֹם מָנוּ אֲוָונֵי = מָחוֹז שֶׁל כְּרַךְ, שֶׁכּוּלָּן תְּלוּיִין לִכְרַךְ, וּלְשָׁם הַשַּׂר תָּדִיר, וּלְשָׁם פּוֹרְעִין הַמַּס. וַאֲוָונָא – לוֹעֲזִין בְּנֵי אָדָם קוֹנְטוֹרד"א, וּכְמוֹ "תַּאֲנַת שִׁילֹה" (יהושע טז), וּכְמוֹ "תַּאֲנָתָהּ מִי יְשִׁיבֶנָּה" (ירמיה ב): ל) מִי לָא תְנַן. בְּכִי הַאי גַּוְונָא. הֲרֵינִי נָזִיר כַּעֲפַר הָאָרֶץ וּכְשֵׂעַר רֹאשִׁי הֲרֵי מ) (ה) נָזִיר לְעוֹלָם. וּמְגַלֵּחַ אַחַת לִשְׁלֹשִׁים יוֹם, דְּמַשְׁמַע דְּאָמַר: הֲרֵי עָלַי נְזִירוּת כְּמִנְיַן שֵׂעַר רֹאשִׁי נ). כָּל מִילְּתָא דְּאִית בֵּיהּ קִיצוּתָא. כְּגוֹן "מִכָּאן עַד מָקוֹם פְּלוֹנִי" לָא קָתָנֵי, דְּלֶיהֱוֵי כְּמַאן דִּמְקַבֵּל עֲלֵיהּ נְזִירוּת שֶׁיְּהֵא מְגַלֵּחַ בְּסוֹף כָּל שְׁלֹשִׁים וּשְׁלֹשִׁים, אֶלָּא כְּמַאן דִּמְקַבֵּל עָלָיו חֲדָא נְזִירוּת אֲרִיכְתָּא ס) עַד מָקוֹם פְּלוֹנִי. וְהָתַנְיָא. דִּמְסַיֵּיעַ: "הֲרֵינִי נָזִיר כָּל יְמֵי חַיַּי" וכו', (ו)ע) [וְאִם] אָמַר "הֲרֵינִי נָזִיר עַד מֵאָה שָׁנָה" אוֹ "עַד אֶלֶף שָׁנִים" – אֵין זֶה נְזִיר עוֹלָם שֶׁיְּהֵא מְגַלֵּחַ בְּסוֹף פ) הַשְּׁלֹשִׁים. אֶלָּא נָזִיר לְעוֹלָם. דְּכַחֲדָא נְזִירוּת אֲרִיכְתָּא דָּמֵי, וְאֵינוֹ מוּתָּר בְּתִגְלַחַת כָּל יָמָיו. אֲבָל הֵיכָא דְּלֵית בֵּיהּ קִיצוּתָא, כְּגוֹן "כְּשֵׂעַר רֹאשִׁי" וּ"כְחוֹל הַיָּם", דְּאֵין לַדָּבָר קִיצְבָה, אִיכָּא לְמֵימַר דִּלְהָכִי אָמַר הָכִי – דִּנְזִירוּת הַרְבֵּה קִבֵּל עָלָיו כְּמִנְיַן שֵׂעַר רֹאשׁוֹ, צ) וְהוּא מְגַלֵּחַ אַחַת לִשְׁלֹשִׁים יוֹם. ק) רַבָּה אָמַר שָׁאנֵי שְׂעָרוֹת הוֹאִיל וּמוּבְדָּלוֹת זוֹ מִזּוֹ. אִיכָּא לְמֵימַר דִּלְמִנְיַן שְׂעָרוֹת קִיבֵּל עָלָיו נְזִירוּת הַרְבֵּה, וּלְכָךְ מְגַלֵּחַ אַחַת לִשְׁלֹשִׁים. אֲבָל ר) אֲוָונָא וּפַרְסֵי לֵיכָּא לְמֵימַר הָכִי, דְּהָא לֵיתְנְהוּ מוּבְדָּלוֹת זוֹ מִזּוֹ, דִּסְדָנָא דְּאַרְעָא חַד הוּא, אִיכָּא לְמֵימַר: חַד נְזִירוּת אֲרִיכְתָּא קִיבֵּל עָלָיו כְּשִׁיעוּר הַיָּמִים שֶׁמִּיכָּן עַד מָקוֹם פְּלוֹנִי. גַּבֵּי יוֹמֵי נַמִי. כִּי אָמַר "כְּמִכָּאן עַד מָקוֹם פְּלוֹנִי", אֵימָא נַמִי כְּמִנְיַן הַיָּמִים קִיבֵּל עָלָיו נְזִירוּת שֶׁל ש) שְׁלֹשִׁים, דְּהָא יוֹמֵי מִיפְסְקֵי מֵהֲדָדֵי, כִּדְכְתִיב "וַיְהִי עֶרֶב וַיְהִי בֹקֶר יוֹם אֶחָד"! הָתָם. דִּכְתִיב קְרָא "יוֹם אֶחָד" לָאו מִשּׁוּם ת) דְּאִיפְסְקוּ מֵהֲדָדֵי, אֶלָּא הַאי דְּקָאָמַר שֶׁהוּא יוֹם אֶחָד א) – דְּקַיְימָא לָן דְּלֵילְיָא וִימָמָא חַד הוּא, שֶׁהַלַּיְלָה הוֹלֶכֶת אַחַר הַיּוֹם, וּלְעוֹלָם לָא מִיפְסְקֵי מֵהֲדָדֵי. וּמִשּׁוּם הָכִי לֵיכָּא לְמֵימַר כִּדְאָמְרִינַן, אֶלָּא חֲדָא נְזִירוּת אֲרִיכְתָּא כְּמִיכָּן וְעַד מָקוֹם פְּלוֹנִי קִיבֵּל עָלָיו. רָבָא אָמַר לָמָּה לָךְ לְאַקְשׁוּיֵי כּוּלֵּי הַאי שָׁאנֵי הָתָם. טַעְמָא מַאי אָמַר כְּמ"ד "אֲרִיכָא לִי מִילְּתָא (ז) ב) מִיכָּן וְעַד סוֹף הָעוֹלָם", וְאֵינוֹ נָזִיר אֶלָּא שְׁלֹשִׁים – דְּהָא קָאָמַר "אַחַת", דְּמַשְׁמַע חֲדָא נְזִירוּת הִיא בִּלְבַד הוּא דְּקָאָמַר, וְהוֹאִיל דְּקָאָמַר חֲדָא – לָא אֶפְשָׁר דְּלָא ג) אָמְרִינַן דְּהָכִי מַשְׁמַע הַאי דְּקָאָמַר "מִיכָּן וְעַד סוֹף הָעוֹלָם". (ח) ד) אֲבָל הֵיכָא דְּקָאָמַר "מִיכָּן וְעַד מָקוֹם פְּלוֹנִי" וְלֹא אָמַר "אַחַת" – לָא אֶפְשָׁר דְּאָמֵינָא לָךְ דְּקִבֵּל עִילָּוֵיהּ בְּלִיר ה) דִּמְהַלֵּךְ הַיָּמִים מֵאוֹתוֹ מָקוֹם עַד אוֹתוֹ מָקוֹם פְּלוֹנִי. מַתְנִי' אָמַר הֲרֵינִי נָזִיר וְיוֹם אֶחָד. (ט) נָזִיר שְׁתֵּי נְזִירוּת. דְּכֵיוָן דַּאֲמַר "הֲרֵינִי נָזִיר" – חָיְילָא עֲלֵיהּ נְזִירוּת רִאשׁוֹנָה, וְכִי הֲדַר וַאֲמַר ו) "יוֹם אֶחָד" אוֹ "שָׁעָה אַחַת" אוֹ "אַחַת וּמֶחֱצָה שֶׁבִּנְזִירוּת" – חָיְילָא עֲלֵיהּ נְזִירוּת שְׁנִיָּה וְחַיָּיב שְׁתַּיִם, ז) דְּקָאָמַר "וְעוֹד מֶחֱצָה". דְּכִי אָמַר "הֲרֵינִי נָזִיר אַחַת" חָל עָלָיו נְזִירוּת אַחַת, וְכִי חָזַר וְאָמַר "וּמֶחֱצָה" חָל עָלָיו נְזִירוּת שְׁנִיָּה. אֲבָל אִם אָמַר "הֲרֵינִי נָזִיר שְׁלֹשִׁים וְאֶחָד" אוֹ "שְׁלֹשִׁים וּשְׁתַּיִם", כֵּיוָן שֶׁפֵּירֵשׁ – אֵינוֹ נָזִיר שְׁתַּיִם, אֶלָּא כְּמִנְיַן הַיָּמִים שֶׁקִּבֵּל עָלָיו. גְּמָ' לָמָּה לִי לְמִיתְנָא כָּל הָנֵי. דְּמִתְחַיֵּיב בָּהּ בִּנְזִירוּת שְׁתַּיִם? לִיתְנֵי חֲדָא וּמִינַּהּ יָדְעָנָא לְאַחֲרִינֵי! צְרִיכִי. דְּאִי הֲוָה תָּנֵי "הֲרֵינִי נָזִיר וְיוֹם אֶחָד", הֲוָה אָמֵינָא: הָכָא הוּא דְּאָמְרִינַן דְּמִתְחַיֵּיב בִּשְׁתֵּי נְזִירוּת, דְּכִי אָמַר "הֲרֵינִי נָזִיר" חָיְילָא עֲלֵיהּ נְזִירוּת, ח) וְהַאי דַּהֲדַר וַאֲמַר "וְיוֹם אֶחָד" – אַדַּעְתָּא דִּנְזִירוּת אַחֲרִיתִי קָאָמַר לֵיהּ, לְפִי שֶׁאֵין נְזִירוּת לְיוֹם אֶחָד, דַּהֲוֵי כְּמַאן דְּאָמַר "הֲרֵינִי נָזִיר יוֹם אֶחָד", דְּחָיְילָא ט) עֲלֵיהּ נַמִי נְזִירוּת שְׁלֹשִׁים. אֲבָל כִּי אָמַר הֲרֵינִי נָזִיר וְשָׁעָה אַחַת, אֵימָא דְּלֶיהֱוֵי כְּמ"ד "שְׁלֹשִׁים וְאֶחָד", קמ"ל. וְאִי

ואימא שנה. דיש שנים מלאים ומרובים בימים – כשהחדשים מלאים, ויש פחותין – כשהם חסרים. **שנים** מי מונין לימים. בתמיה. א] *(וסיטה הוא וכו') חדשים אתה מחשב לשנים, וכשהן מעברין – מוסיפין חדש ולא ימים, כ' או ט"ו. והכא כתיב "עד מלאת הימים" – הלכך ודאי בחדש איירי.

הריני נזיר אחת גדולה הריני נזיר אחת קטנה. כלומר, לא שנא כי אמר "גדולה" ולא שנא כי אמר "קטנה", ואפילו אמר "מכאן ועד סוף העולם" – לא הוי נזיר אלא שלשים יום. ו"גדולה" דקאמר – כלומר: גדול עלי הנזירות, דטריחא עלי. "או קטנה" – כלומר: דלא טריחא עלי כלל. ואפי' "מכאן ועד סוף עולם" – בגמרא מפרש: דטריחא ואריכא לי מלתא כמכאן ועד סוף העולם.

ואמאי והא מכאן ועד סוף העולם קאמר. פירוש: וליהוי נזיר לעולם! ומשני, הכי קאמר: הריני, כלומר אריכא לי האי מילתא כו'. לעולם חד נזירות קביל עליה לקולא, דהכי משתמע טפי. דאם הוא ר"ל מכאן ועד סוף העולם – היה לו להזכיר מנין סוף העולם, דיודע הוא שפיר דהעולם יש בו חמש מאות מהלך, והיה לו לומר חמש מאות שנים, ולפיכך אזלינן לקולא כ"נ.

מכאן ועד מקום פלוני אומדים כמה ימים עד מקום פלוני פחות משלשים יום נזיר שלשים יום. פי': דלא גרע מקיבל נזירות יום אחד דהוי נזיר שלשים יום, ואם לאו – הוי נזיר כמנין הימים, או מ' או נ' יום. ואמאי? ה"נ נימא: אריכא לי מילתא כמכאן ועד מקום פלוני, ולא יהיה אלא ל' יום, ואפילו יהיה נ' יום עד מקום פלוני! [ומשני]: כשהחזיק בדרך וקבל עליו. דמסתמא מפני אונסי הדרך קבל עליו נזירות, להנצל מסכנת הדרך, לסך מהלך הימים עד מקום פלוני.

וליהוי

פי' הרא"ש

ואימא שנה. שפעמים צריכין למלאות חסרון השנה בימים יש פעמים השנה היא שנ"ג ימים ופעמים שנ"ד ופעמים שנ"ה והוה מצי לשנויי תפשת מרובה לא תפשת שנה מי מנינן לימים אין משלימין השנה בימים כי החדש פעמים ממלאין אותו ופעמים מחסרין ומתוך זה יגיעו ימי השנה לשנ"ג או לשנ"ד או לשנ"ה אבל משלימים אותה בחדש שפעמים מעברין אותה ומוסיפין עליה חדש כדאמרי רבנן התם דקסברי דחדשים אתה מונה להשוות שנת הלבנה לשנת החמה וממתינים עד שיגיע מותר ימי החמה על ימי הלבנה לחדש אחד ומוסיפין חדש א'. ואי אתה מונה בכל שנה ימים להוסיפן על שנת הלבנה להשוותן לשנת חמה. א"נ חדשים אתה מונה לשנה שפעמים יש בשנה שתים עשרה חדשי' ופעמי' י"ג א) ואם אמר קונם פירות האלו על שנה מונה מחדש שעומד בו עד חדש זה לשנה האחרת בין שהיא פשוטה בין שהיא מעוברת ואינו מונה ימים לשנה להוסיף על יב"ח עד שס"ה ימים: ואמאי והא עד סוף העולם קאמר ומשמע שקיבל עליו נזירות עד סוף עולמו: אריכא לי כו'. נזירות אחת שקבלתי עלי כבד עלי ודומה לי כאילו הוא עד סוף העולם וכיון דמצינא לתרוצה דבוריה הכי הוה דסתם נזיר להקל: פחות מל' יום. אם יש עד אותו מקום פחות ממהלך ל' יום אין נזיר פחות [מ]ל' יום ואם יש יותר הרי הוא נזיר כמנין הימים: הכא נמי אריכא לי מלתא נזיר' שקבלתי עלי נראה לי ארוך וכבד כמכאן ועד מקום פלוני: שהחזיק בדרך ומסתמא כדי להשמר מסכנת הדרך קיבל עליו נזירות כמנין ימי הדרך: ולימא כל פרסה ופרסה הוי נזיר אמכאן ועד מקום פלוני קפריך דנימא דקיבל עליו מנין נזירות דמנין פרסאות עד מקום פלוני ואמתני' דכשער ראשי קא סמיך ונטר לאיתויי עד קושיא דבסמוך: להוי כל ב) אוונא ואוונא חד נזיר דנהי דלא מנו פרסי מ"מ מנו שיעור מהלך הימים ונימא שקיבל עליו נזירות כמנין הימים הריני נזיר כשער ראשי ה"ז נזיר עולם שקבל עליו נזירות כמנין שער

לד א מיי' פ"א מהלכות קדוש החדש הל' ב:

לה ב מיי' פ"ג מהל' נזירות הלכה א סמג לאוין רמג:

לו ג ד מיי' שם הל' ה:

לז ה מיי' שם הל' יא:

לח ו מיי' שם הל' ח:

[עי' היטב מגילה ה.]

[לקמן ח.]

הגהות מהר"ב רנשבורג

א] בתוס' ד"ה שנים מי מונין לימים בתמיה (וסיטה הוא וכו') נ"ב וסיטות הוא כצ"ל ועי' ת"מ:

לקמן ח.

[תוספתא פ"א לקמן ח:]

נוסחת הריב"ן

[illegible]

הגהות הב"ח

(א) גמ' אין זה נזיר עולם (אלא נזיר לעולם) תא"מ ונ"ב זו היא גי' רש"י אבל מדברי הרמב"ם פ"ג דנזיר משמע דל"ג ליה: (ב) רש"י ד"ה מי מונין וכו' [illegible]

ראשו ומגלח כל ל' יום ומביא קרבנותיו: כל מלתא דאית ליה קיצותא לא קתני. [illegible]

[illegible]

ואי תנא "שעה אחת" — משום דלא נחית לדוקא, אבל "אחת ומחצה" דנחית לדוקא — אימא לא לימני תרתי, קמשמע לן: כולהו נזיר שתים.§

מתני' א"הריני נזיר שלשים יום ושעה אחת" — נזיר שלשים ואחד יום, שאין נזירות לשעות.§

גמ' אמר רב: ב"לא שנו אלא דאמר "שלשים ואחד יום" אבל אמר "שלשים [יום] ויום אחד" — נזיר שתים. רב סבר לה כרבי עקיבא, דדריש לישנא יתירא. *דתנן: לא את הבור ולא את הדות, אע"פ שכתב לו "עומקא ורומא"; גוצריך ליקח לו דרך, דברי ר"ע. וחכ"א: א"צ ליקח לו דרך. ומודה רבי עקיבא בזמן שאמר לו "חוץ מאלו" דשאינו צריך ליקח לו דרך.§

מתניתין

ולידהוי כל פרסה ופרסה. אמתני' פריך, כי אמר "מכאן ועד סוף העולם" נחשוב כמה פרסה עד סוף העולם, למנין שהעולם מהלך חמש מאות שנה, ושמא דמנין נזירות קביל עליה כמנין פרסאות לחומרא, א] ולא מלינן לפרושי להקל! ואין להקשות: אם כן היה לו [לומר] "מנין סוף העולם". דניחא ליה טפי שיהא כל פרסה ופרסה בפני עצמו, שיוכל לגלח עצמו בסוף כל שלשים יום. אבל אין לפרש ולומר דקאי ופריך למאי דמסיק מיניה, דכיון דטעמא הוי משום דהחזיק בדרך – אין בדעתו להיות נזיר כי אם בהיותו בדרך. לכך צריך לפרש דקאי אמתני'. ומשני: באתרא דלא מני פרסה, דליכא למימר דכמנין פרסה קביל עליה. ופריך: ולהוי כל אונא ואונא כמנין מהלך ימים שעד סוף העולם קביל עליה נזירות. מי לא תנן "הריני נזיר כשער ראשי" כו' הרי זה נזיר לעולם כו' – אלמא נזירות הרבה קביל עליה, ולא מפרשינן למילתיה לקולא, למימר: "הריני נזיר" – שלשים יום, ו"כשיער ראשי" דקאמר – כלומר: אריכא לי האי מילתא (דקאמר) כאילו אמרתי הריני נזיר כמנין שיער ראשי. ומשני: כל מילתא דאית ליה קצבתא לא קתני, פירוש: האומר "הריני עד סוף העולם" – אית להו קצבתא, דמהלך העולם חמש מאות שנה, [ואם] נזירות במנין קביל עליה ה"ל לפרש להדיא, אחרי שיש להם מנין, ולכך י"ל דחד נזירות קביל עליה. אבל "שיער ראשי" ו"עפר הארץ" ו"חול הים" אין להם קצבה ומנין, [רוצה] לומר דבמנין שיער ראשו קביל עליה נזירות, ומה שלא פירש – לפי שלא ידע מנין השיער. **והתניא** • בניחותא, שיש חילוק בין קיצבתא ובין לא קיצבתא. "כל ימי חייו" או "נזיר לעולם" – אין לו קיצבה, שאינו יודע ימי חייו, וה"ז נזיר לעולם כאבשלום, ומיקל ומביא ג' בהמות למר כדאית ליה, ולמר כדאית ליה, לעיל (דף ד:). אפי' ק' שנה ואפילו אלף שנה, ומסתמא לא יחיה כל כך, וה"ל כל ימי חייו – [ואפ"ה] חלוק בדינו, דאין זה נזיר לעולם כאבשלום להקל, אלא נזיר עולם – נזיר ארוך עד יום מותו. וא"ת: ב] כיון [דמחלק] מתניתא [בין דלית ליה] קיצבתא, לאלף שנים דאית להו קצבתא – א"כ גם במתניתין יהיה נזיר ארוך עד יום מותו כמו באלף שנים! וי"ל: דשאני הכא, דאמר "הריני נזיר אלף שנים" ולא אמר "מכאן" – משמע נזירות ארוך קביל עליה. אבל במתניתין אמר "מכאן ועד סוף העולם", דמשמע טפי: אריכא ליה מילתא כמכאן ועד סוף העולם, [מלומר] דנזירות ארוך קביל עליה, מדלא אמר "הריני נזיר עד סוף העולם". ולא מייתי מהך ברייתא אלא דאיכא חילוק בין מילתא דאית ליה קיצבתא [למילתא דלית ליה קיצבתא]. דשלשה עניני נזיר [יש]: אמר "כשיער" "כעפר" "כחול" – נזיר לעולם, נזירות אחר נזירות, ומגלח כל שערו בין *נזירות, ומביא קרבנותיו. אמר "כל ימי חייו" "נזיר לעולם" – [הרי זה] נזיר לעולם כאבשלום, ולא לגלח לגמרי אלא להקל, למר כדאית ליה ולמר כדאית ליה, ומביא ג' בהמות. אמר "מאה שנה" או "אלף שנה" – הרי זה נזירות ארוך עד יום מותו, ואינו לא מגלח ולא מיקל ולא מביא קרבן כל ימיו: ג] **הואיל** כו'. ואינו יומי מובדל זו מזו. וי"ל דנזירות קביל עליה, שאין אוונות מובדלות זו מזו. ופריך: גבי כו' "יום אחד" מדקרי ליה יום אחד – משמע להבדילו מ"יום" קאתי, א"כ מהלכין הימים ומובדלים גם הם! ומשני: הכי קאמר: יממא ולילא חד יומא, פי': הערב שלפני היום לענין שבת ויו"ט. ולא לאפוקי מיומא דבבריה קאתי, אלא כל הימים נוגעים זה בזה. **שאני** התם דקתני הריני נזיר אחת. דמשמע ליה דקאי ארישא, דקתני: "הריני נזיר אחת גדולה", או אם אמר "הריני נזיר אחת מכאן ועד סוף העולם", כיון דאמר "הריני נזיר" ו"אחת" – *אריכא ליה. ואמרינן דאריכא ליה מילתא כמכאן ועד סוף העולם. ואמוראי קמאי לא משמע להו דקאי "מכאן ועד סוף העולם" א"אחת". **הריני** נזיר ויום אחד. וסמך "נזיר" בדיבורו אכל היום ואכל השעה, הוי כאילו אמר "הריני נזיר ונזיר יום אחד", או "נזיר שעה" *או "נזיר מחצה". שלא היה יכול לקרב תיבת "נזיר" יותר אצל "מחצה", שלא היה יכול לומר "הריני נזיר ומחצה", דלא משמע מידי על מה מחצה, על כן אמר "נזיר אחת ומחצה", וחשוב כאילו פירש "ונזיר ומחצה" פירוש – חצי נזירות. ואם אמר בפירוש: "הריני נזיר יום אחד" ואפילו "שעה אחת" – הוי נזיר שלשים יום, שאין נזירות ליום אחד וכל שכן לשעה, הלכך הוי נזיר שתים. **הריני** נזיר ויום א' הכא הוא דאין נזירות ליום א'. פי': דחשבינן ליה כאילו אמר "הריני נזיר ונזיר יום א'", ואילו אמר "הריני נזיר ונזיר יום אחד" ואין נזירות ליום אלא ל' יום – להכי מני תרתי נזירות. אבל אמר "הריני נזיר ושעה אחת" כאילו אמר נזיר שעה אחת למנין ל' (ואחד), דס"ד דדי לנו מאותה שעה לעשות יום, ומצרפינן בהדי ל' יום, ויהיה ל"א יום, קמ"ל: כיון דיש להוסיף על דבורו נוסיף נזירות שלם. **ואי** תנא שעה אחת משום דלא נחית לדוקא. פי': דבר שאינו יכול להיות, שאין נודרין שעות. וכיון שיש להוסיף על דבורו – נוסיף נזירות שלם. אבל "אחת ומחצה", דנחית לדוקא, שיכול להיות נזיר, אימא לא לימני תרתי אלא מ"ה הוי, קמ"ל דבכולהו נזיר שתים. **הריני** נזיר שלשים [יום] ושעה אחת. ומעתה לא קיימא דבור ד"נזיר" א"שעה", והוי נזירות ל"א יום, שאין הנזירות לשעות, ומאותה שעה נעשה יום, והוי כאילו אמר "הריני נזיר שלשים ואחד יום", דודאי חייל עליה ל"א יום, דיום אחד מצטרף שפיר בהדי שלשים יום למיהוי נזיר כל ל"א יום. והוא הדין אם אמר "הריני נזיר שלשים (יום) ויום אחד", דלא הוה נזיר אלא ל"א יום, כיון שהפסיק בתיבת "ל'", דארישא קאי, אלא דנקט אחד מן הדינין, וממאי דסליק חילק, דהיינו דקאמר לעיל "הריני נזיר ושעה אחת", והוא הדין שיש לחלק ארישא דמתניתין, דקאמר "הריני נזיר ויום אחד". **לא** שנו אלא דאמר ל"א יום. פי': [אז] לא הוי נזיר אלא ל"א יום. אבל אמר "שלשים יום ויום אחד" – נזיר שתים, לפי שייתר בלשונו ב' פעמים "יום", וכדמפרש ואזיל דסבר לה כר"ע. וק"ק, דבמתניתין לא קתני האי "לישנא ל"א יום", אלא "ל' ושעה אחת"! וי"ל: דבמתניתין פירש לישנא דסליק, היינו "הריני נזיר [ושעה] אחת" (יום), והוא הדין דברישא נמי כי אמר "הריני נזיר ויום אחד" דהוי נזיר שתים, [אי אמר] "הריני נזיר [ל'] ויום אחד", דהפסיק בתיבת "שלשים" בינתיים – דלא הוי נזיר אלא שלשים ואחד יום. והא קאמר רב "לא שנו", שאינו מפרש להדיא ודייק ליה מדיוקא. **לא** את הבור כו'. שאינו בכלל בית, וצריך מוכר זה ליקח לו דרך לבור מן הלוקח, שמכר לו בעין יפה ולא שייר לעצמו. **אין** צריך ליקח לו דרך. דבעין רעה מוכר, ושייר לעצמו דרך. **חוץ** מאלו וכו'. שייתר בלשונו. שבלאו הכי לא מכר את הבור, אלא לשייר לעצמו דרך קמיכוין: *) **הריני** נזיר כשער ראשי ובעפר הארץ ובחול הים הרי זה נזיר לעולם ומגלח אחת לשלשים יום. פירוש: נזירות הרבה קיבל עליו כעפר הארץ וכחול הים, ומגלח ביום שלשים ומביא קרבנותיו. **אין** זה מגלח אחת לשלשים יום. פירוש: רבי סבירא ליה דנזירות מרובה קביל עליו עד יום מותו, עד שיאמר בפירוש "נזירות". כדמסיק: ואי זהו מגלח אחת לשלשים יום – האומר "הרי עלי נזירות כשער ראשי וכעפר הארץ וכחול הים".

*) שייך לדף ח.

הריני

ואי תנא שעה אחת. התם הוא נמי הואיל דלא נחית לנזירות דווקא למהוי שלשים יום ושעה אחת, לפי שאין א) נודרין לשעות – להכי הוא דאמר דמחייב בשתי ב) נזירות. אבל היכא דאמר "נזירות אחת ומחצה", דנזירות נחת לדווקא – אימא דלא לימני תרתי, אלא מ"ה ימים בלבד. קמ"ל דבכולהו חייב תרתי, (א) והיכא דאמר ברישא "הריני נזיר" סתמא – חיילא עליה נזירות, ג) וכי הדר ואמר, או יום אחד או שעה אחת או נזירות ומחצה, כיון דקיבל מקצתה ד) כמי שקיבל את כולה דמי, וחייב בב' ה) נזירות. **מתני'** האומר הריני נזיר שלשים יום ו) ושעה אחת. נעשה כאומר ל"א יום, ואינו חייב אלא ל"א יום בלבד. **גמ' אמר רב.** ז) האי דדייקי' מתני' דכי אמר שלשים יום ושעה נעשה כמי שאמר ל"א, ואינו חייב בנזירות אלא ל"א בלבד. **לא שנו אלא דאמר ל"א יום.** אבל אמר "הריני נזיר שלשים יום ויום אחד", כיון דאמר לישנא יתירא – הוי נזיר שתים. דרב סבר לה כר"ע דדריש לישנא יתירא. **דתנן:** המוכר ח) בית לחבירו והיה לו שם בור ודות – לא מכר את הבור ואת הדות, אע"פ שכתב לו "עומקא ורומא". **וצריך.** לו למוכר ליקח לו דרך לילך לבור ודות שלו, או יפרח באויר, דברי רבי עקיבא. דקסבר: (ב) בעין יפה הוא מוכר, ולא שייר דרך לעצמו. **וחכמים אומרים אינו צריך ליקח לו דרך.** דאמרינן: כשם ששייר את הבור ואת הדות לעצמו – כך שייר לו דרך. **בזמן שאמר לו.** מוכר בפירוש: חוץ מאלו בור ודות, כיון דאמר לישנא יתירא. דהא אפילו לא אמר "חוץ" לא הוו מכורין, להכי אמר "חוץ" – לשייר לו את הדרך.

מתני'

לט א מיי' פ"ג מהל' נזירות הלכה ז:
מ ב מיי' שם הל' ח:
מא ג ד מיי' פכ"ה מהל' מכירה הלכה ג סמג עשין פב טוש"ע ח"מ סי' ריד סעיף ב וסעיף יח:

פי' הרא"ש

יום כיון דאין נזירות פחו' מל' יום וכן נמי הריני נזיר ושעה א' וכן נמי הריני נזיר א' ומחצה מפרשי' לה הריני נזיר א' והריני נזיר מחצה: [מתני'] הריני נזיר ל' יום ושעה אחת נזיר ל"א יום. שאין נוזרים שעות דכיון דהזכיר ל' הוי כאילו אמר ל' וא' יום דלא אמרי' דיום א' הוי נזיר בפני עצמו כיון דבעי לצרפו למנין ל' שהזכיר תחלה ושעה א' הוי כיום א' דאין נודרין שעות אבל אמר הריני נזיר ושעה אחת לא רצה להוסיף [רק] נזירות אחרת שאין מונין נזירות לשעות אלא לימים ולא בא להוסיף כי אם יום א' (פי' ימים לשעות) והוי כאילו אמר ל"א יום: לא שנו אלא [דאמר] ל"א יום כלומר הא דאמר במתני' אם אמר הריני נזיר ל' יום ושעה שהוא נזיר ל"א יום לפי שאין נודרים שעות והוי כאילו אמר ל"א יום דווקא דאמר ל' ואחד יום דומיא דל' יום ושעה אבל אמר ל' יום ויום א' מייתור לשונו דאמר יום יתירא קאמר רב הכי: לא את הבור ולא את הדות אם מכר לו בית סתם לא מכר את אלו. בור בחפירה ודות בבנין א) ושניהם לבינו שמים ושוין. וצריך ליקח לו דרך דמוכר בעין יפה מוכר ולא שייר לו דרך ורבנן סברי מוכר בעין רעה מוכר: בזמן שא"ל חוץ מאלו א"צ ליקח לו דרך דכיון דלא הוה צריך לשייר אלו ושייר לישנא יתירא לשייר לו דרך קא אתי וה"ה דרבנן סברי דלישנא יתירא לשיורי קאתי אלא דליכא מידי לשיורי ונקט ר"ע דאיהו בפי' קאמר דלטפויי קאתי ואע"ג דרב פסיק התם הלכה כחכמים דמוכר בעין רעה מוכר מ"מ בלישנא יתירא לא פליגי כדפרישית

א) אולי צ"ל ושניהם לאו בידי שמים עשויין.

הגהות הב"ח

(א) רש"י ד"ה קמ"ל וכו' דהיכא דאמר: (ב) ד"ה וצריך וכו' דקסבר מוכר בעין יפה:

ערכין יט. ב"ב סד. קלח:

נ"ל כל

נ"ל עריכא

נ"א אבל

נוסחת הריב"ן

א) נודרין: ב) נזירויות: ג) נזירות ל': ד) כאילו קבל כולה: ה) נזירויות: ו) ל' יום ויום א' ושעה כו': ז) דהאי: ח) שדה:

הגהות מהר"ב רנשבורג

א] תוס' ד"ה ולהוי כל פרסה ופרסה וכו' לחומרא ולא מלינן נמחקו תיבות ולא מלינן. ונ"ב ומנא לן כצ"ל א"מ: ב] ד"ה והתניא בניחותא שיש חילוק וכו'. וא"ת כיון [דמחלק] מתניתא [בין דלית ליה] קילבתא עכ"ל. מן תיבת כיון עד תיבת קילבתא נמחק ונ"ב וא"מ גריס כיון דמדמי מתני' קצבתא: ג] ד"ה הואיל וכו' ואינו יומי מובדל זו מזו וי"ל דנזירות קביל עליה שאין אוונות מובדלות זו מזו עכ"ל כל זה נמחק. נ"ב הואיל ומובדלות זו מזו וי"ל לנזירות הרבה קביל עליה משא"כ אוונות שאין מובדלות זו מזו כצ"ל א"מ:

מתני' *א"הֲרֵינִי נָזִיר כִּשְׂעַר רֹאשִׁי", וְ"כַעֲפַר הָאָרֶץ" וּ"כְחוֹל הַיָּם" – הֲרֵי זֶה נְזִיר עוֹלָם, וּמְגַלֵּחַ אַחַת לִשְׁלֹשִׁים יוֹם. רַבִּי אוֹמֵר: אֵין זֶה מְגַלֵּחַ אַחַת לִשְׁלֹשִׁים יוֹם. וְאֵיזֶהוּ מְגַלֵּחַ אַחַת לִשְׁלֹשִׁים – הָאוֹמֵר "הֲרֵי עָלַי נְזִירוּת כִּשְׂעַר רֹאשִׁי" וְ"כַעֲפַר הָאָרֶץ" וּ"כְחוֹל הַיָּם". *ב"הֲרֵינִי נָזִיר מְלֹא הַבַּיִת" אוֹ "מְלֹא הַקּוּפָּה" – בּוֹדְקִין אוֹתוֹ; אִם אָמַר: אַחַת גְּדוֹלָה נָזַרְתִּי – נָזִיר ל' יוֹם, וְאִם אָמַר: סְתָם נָזַרְתִּי – רוֹאִין אֶת הַקּוּפָּה כְּאִילּוּ הִיא מְלֵאָה חַרְדָּל, וְנָזִיר כָּל יָמָיו. *ג"הֲרֵינִי נָזִיר מִכָּאן עַד מָקוֹם פְּלוֹנִי" – אוֹמְדִין כַּמָּה יָמִים מִכָּאן עַד מָקוֹם פְּלוֹנִי, אִם פָּחוֹת מִל' יוֹם – נָזִיר ל' יוֹם, וְאִם לָאו – נָזִיר כְּמִנְיַן הַיָּמִים. "הֲרֵינִי נָזִיר כְּמִנְיַן יְמוֹת הַחַמָּה" – דמוֹנֶה נְזִירוֹת כְּמִנְיַן יְמוֹת הַחַמָּה. אָמַר רַבִּי יְהוּדָה: מַעֲשֶׂה הָיָה, כֵּיוָן שֶׁהִשְׁלִים – מֵת.§

גמ' "רוֹאִין אֶת הַקּוּפָּה כְּאִילּוּ מְלֵאָה חַרְדָּל וְנָזִיר כָּל יָמָיו". וְאַמַּאי? וְלִיחַזְיֵיהּ כְּאִילּוּ מְלֵאָה קִישׁוּאִין וּדְלוּעִין, וְתֶיהֱוֵי לֵיהּ תַּקַּנְתָּא! אָמַר חִזְקִיָּה: בְּמַחֲלוֹקֶת שְׁנוּיָה, ור"ש הִיא, דְּאָמַר: אָדָם מַכְנִיס אֶת עַצְמוֹ לְדָבָר שֶׁסְּפֵיקוֹ חָמוּר מִוַּדָּאִי. דְּתַנְיָא: *"הֲרֵינִי נָזִיר ע"מ שֶׁיְּהֵא בִּכְרִי זֶה מֵאָה כּוֹר" וְהָלַךְ וּמְצָאוֹ שֶׁנִּגְנַב אוֹ שֶׁאָבַד, ר"ש אוֹסֵר, *שֶׁסְּפֵק נְזִירוּת לְהַחְמִיר. ר' יְהוּדָה הַמַּתִּיר, שֶׁסְּפֵק נְזִירוּת לְהָקֵל. רַבִּי יוֹחָנָן אָמַר: אֲפִילּוּ תֵּימָא רַבִּי יְהוּדָה, הָתָם – לָא נָחֵית לֵיהּ לִנְזִירוּת, הָכָא – נָחֵית לֵיהּ לִנְזִירוּת, בְּמַאי לְסַלּוּקֵיהּ מִינֵּיהּ! אַמַּאי לָא? לִיחַזְיֵיהּ לַקּוּפָּה כְּאִילּוּ מְלֵאָה קִישׁוּאִין וּדְלוּעִין, וְתֶיהֱוֵי לֵיהּ תַּקַּנְתָּא, *הָא ס"ד נְזִירוּת הוּא דְּקַבֵּיל עִילָּוֵיהּ! דר'

מתני' הָאוֹמֵר הֲרֵינִי נָזִיר כִּשְׂעַר כו'. א) [דְּאָמְרִינַן] נְזִירוּת כִּשְׂעַר רֹאשׁוֹ קִבֵּל עָלָיו, וַהֲרֵי זֶה נְזִיר עוֹלָם, לְפִי שֶׁשַּׂעֲרוֹת רֹאשׁוֹ מְרוּבִּין מִשְּׁנֵי חַיָּיו. וִיהֵא מְגַלֵּחַ כָּל יָמָיו אַחַת ב) בְּסוֹף שְׁלֹשִׁים וְיָבִיא קָרְבָּן. רַבִּי אוֹמֵר אֵין זֶה מְגַלֵּחַ אַחַת ג) לִשְׁלֹשִׁים. וְהַאי דְּקָאָמַר (א) "כִּשְׂעַר רֹאשִׁי" – חֲדָא נְזִירוּת אֲרִיכָא קִבֵּל עָלָיו כְּשִׁיעוּר שְׂעַר רֹאשׁוֹ, וְאֵינוֹ יָכוֹל לְהַשְׁלִימָהּ, וְאֵינוֹ מְגַלֵּחַ לְעוֹלָם. אֶלָּא אֵיזֶהוּ שֶׁמְּגַלֵּחַ אַחַת לִשְׁלֹשִׁים יוֹם זֶה שֶׁאָמַר הֲרֵי עָלַי נְזִירוּת כִּשְׂעַר רֹאשִׁי. דְּהוֹאִיל וְאָמַר (ב) "עָלַי נְזִירוּת", מַשְׁמַע דְּקָא מַפְלִיג בֵּין נְזִירוּת לִנְזִירוּת, וִיהֵא מְגַלֵּחַ בְּסוֹף כָּל שְׁלֹשִׁים וּמֵבִיא קָרְבָּן. בּוֹדְקִין אוֹתוֹ אִם אָמַר אַחַת גְּדוֹלָה נָזַרְתִּי הֲרֵי זֶה נָזִיר שְׁלֹשִׁים יוֹם. וְתוּ לָא. וְהָא דְּאָמַר "מְלֹא הַבַּיִת", מַשְׁמַע כְּאִילּוּ אָמַר: אֲרִיכָא לִי מִילְּתָא כִּמְלֹא הַבַּיִת אוֹ כִּמְלֹא קוּפָּה. וְאִם אָמַר סְתָם נָדַרְתִּי. נַעֲשָׂה כְּאִילּוּ אָמַר "מְלֹא חַרְדָּל", וְנַעֲשָׂה כָּל יָמָיו נָזִיר – דְּאָמְרִינַן: נְזִירוּת כְּמִנְיַן גַּרְעִינֵי חַרְדָּל שֶׁבּוֹ קִבֵּל עָלָיו, וְאֵין לָהֶם הַפְסָקָה כָּל יָמָיו. **גמ'** וְאַמַּאי וְלִיחַזְיֵיהּ. לְהַאי קוּפָּה כְּאִילּוּ מְלֵאָה קִישׁוּאִין, וְאִי מַחְזְקָא מִינַּיְיהוּ י' – נֵימָא דִּי' ד) נְזִירוּת שֶׁל שְׁלֹשִׁים שְׁלֹשִׁים קִבֵּל עָלָיו. וְתֶיהֱוֵי לֵיהּ תַּקַּנְתָּא. אַחַר אוֹתָם עֲשָׂרָה ה) נְזִירוּת, לִשְׁתּוֹת בְּיַיִן. אָמַר חִזְקִיָּה בְּמַחֲלוֹקֶת שְׁנוּיָה. דְּאִיכָּא מַאן דִּסְבִירָא לֵיהּ (ג) ו) כְּוָותֵיהּ, וּמַתְנִי' ז) לָא תָּנֵי הָכִי. ר"ש הִיא דְּאָמַר אָדָם מַכְנִיס עַצְמוֹ לְדָבָר שֶׁסְּפֵקוֹ חָמוּר ח) מִוַּדַּאי. דְּאִילּוּ נָזִיר וַדַּאי – מְגַלֵּחַ וּמֵבִיא קָרְבָּן וְאוֹכֵל, וְאִילּוּ עַל סְפֵיקוֹ לָא מָצֵי ט) מְגַלֵּחַ. דְּהָכִי מְפָרֵשׁ בְּ"אֵלּוּ מוּתָּרִים" בְּמַסֶּכֶת נְדָרִים. הֲרֵינִי נָזִיר כו' ר"ש אוֹסֵר. שֶׁחַיָּיב בִּנְזִירוּת. י) דְּהוֹאִיל דַּהֲוֵי סָפֵק אִי הָווּ בֵּיהּ מֵאָה כּוֹר, אָמְרִינַן דַּהֲוֵי בֵּיהּ וַדַּאי מֵאָה כּוֹר וְלֶיהֱוֵי נָזִיר, שֶׁכָּל סְפֵק נְזִירוּת לְהַחְמִיר. א] דִּסְפֵיקוֹ בְּנָזִיר חָמוּר מִוַּדָּאוֹ, ב] דְּאִילּוּ וַדַּאי שֶׁלֹּא הָיוּ בּוֹ מֵאָה כּוֹר – לָא הֲוֵי נָזִיר, הַשְׁתָּא דַּהֲוֵי סָפֵק אָמְרִינַן דְּנָזִיר הוּא. הָכִי נַמִּי בְּמַתְנִיתִין, כ) דְּהוֹאִיל דְּסַפֵּקָא הוּא – דְּלָא יָדְעִינַן אִי אַדַּעְתָּא דִּמְלֵאָה קִשּׁוּאִין אִי ל) בְּחַרְדָּל קָאָמַר – אָמְרִינַן בֵּיהּ סְפֵק נְזִירוּת לְהַחְמִיר, וּכְמַאן דִּמְלֵאָה חַרְדָּל קָאָמַר וְאֵין לוֹ תַּקָּנָה. אֲבָל אַלִּיבָּא מ) דְּמ"ד שֶׁכָּל סְפֵק נְזִירוּת לְהָקֵל – לְדִידֵיהּ אָמְרִינַן: רוֹאִין אוֹתָהּ כְּאִילּוּ מְלֵאָה קִשּׁוּאִין. ר' יוֹחָנָן אָמַר אֲפִילּוּ תֵּימָא כְּר' יְהוּדָה. דְּהָתָם טַעְמָא מַאי אָמַר ר' יְהוּדָה דִּסְפֵק נְזִירוּת לְהָקֵל – דִּדְלְמָא לָא הָווּ בֵּיהּ מֵאָה כּוֹרִין וְלָא נָחֵית לֵיהּ לִנְזִירוּת כְּלָל, וּמִסַּפֵּיקָא לָא אָמְרִינַן לֵיהּ דְּלֶיהֱוֵי נָזִיר, כִּי הֵיכִי דְּלָא לַיְיתֵי חוּלִּין לָעֲזָרָה לְכִי מַשְׁלִים נְזִירוּתוֹ (ד). אֶלָּא הָכָא כֵּיוָן דְּנָחֵית לֵיהּ לִנְזִירוּת. אִי מִשּׁוּם מְלֵאָה קִישּׁוּאִין אִי מִשּׁוּם מְלֵאָה חַרְדָּל – נְזִירוּת נ) חָיְילָא עֲלֵיהּ מִמָּה נַפְשָׁךְ, וְכֵיוָן דְּנָחֵית לִנְזִירוּת בְּמַאי לְסַלְּקֵיהּ ס) – מש"ה אִית לָן לְמֵימַר דִּנְזִירוּת כְּמִנְיַן גַּרְעִינֵי חַרְדָּל קִיבֵּל עָלָיו, וּלְעוֹלָם כָּל יָמָיו יְהֵא אָסוּר בְּיַיִן. אַמַּאי לָא לִיסַלְּקֵיהּ נֵימָא דְּלִיחַזְיֵיהּ כְּאִילּוּ מְלֵאָה קִישׁוּאִין. וּלְכִי מַשְׁלִים לֵיהּ נְזִירוּת כְּמִנְיַן קִישּׁוּאִין שֶׁיְּכוֹלִין לִיכָּנֵס בְּתוֹךְ הַקּוּפָּה וּמַיְיתֵי לֵיהּ קָרְבָּן ע) – הָוֵי כִּמְסוּלָּק וְעוֹמֵד, דִּכְלָא נָחֵית לֵיהּ לִנְזִירוּת דָּמֵי, וְתֶיהֱוֵי לֵיהּ תַּקַּנְתָּא. הָא. לָא מָצֵית אָמְרַתְּ פ) דִּנְזִירוּת קִבֵּל עָלָיו. דְּרַבִּי –

הריני נזיר מלא הבית מלא הקופה. פירוש: בית ריקנית או קופה ריקנית *לפניו. בודקין אותו, אם אמר "אחת גדולה נדרתי" – נזיר שלשים יום. פי': נזירות אחת נדרתי. והא דקאמר מלא הבית – דאריכא ליה מילתא [כו'], ואינו נזיר אלא שלשים יום. [ואם אמר "סתם] נדרתי" – רואין הקופה כאילו מלאה חרדל, ונזיר כל ימיו; לרבנן דלעיל – נזירות אחר נזירות, ולרבי – נזירות ארוך. **מכאן** ועד מקום פלוני פחות מל' יום נזיר שלשים יום. מידי דהוה אאומר "הריני נזיר יום אחד" דהוי נזיר ל' יום. ואם לאו נזיר כמנין הימים – וכדפרישי' לעיל, דמיירי כשהחזיק בדרך. **כמנין** ימות השנה מונה נזירות כמנין ימות השנה. דהיינו שס"ה חדשים יהיה נזיר, נזירות אחר נזירות, ומגלח בינתיים ומביא קרבן. כיון דקאמר "כמנין" – משמע נזירות, ולא נזירות ארוך. **אמר** רבי יהודה מעשה היה וכיון שהשלים מת. רבי יהודה לסיועי' לתנא קמא קאתי, וקאמר: מעשה היה וחייבוהו חכמים נזירות הרבה, וכיון שהשלים כולו מת. **וליחזייה** כאילו היא מלאה קישואין ודילועין ותהוי ליה תקנתא. אמתני' קא פריך, דקאמר: רואין כאילו היא מלאה חרדל, ואין לו תקנה. והוא הדין דמצי למיפרך: וליחזי כמאן דמלי בלק, ולא נתכוון זה אלא לנזירות אחד, [וניקל] עליה. וקצת קשה: דהיאך ניקל עליה מספק? ויש לומר: דהתם תנן במסכת טהרות (פ"ד מ"ז): ספק נזירות להקל. וא"ת: והא לעיל, גבי "מכאן ועד סוף העולם", פריך לחומרא! ויש לומר: דהתם לא ידע שום צד דמצי למימר לקולא בלישנא ד"מכאן עד סוף העולם", ולפום ריהטא משמע דנזירות קבל עליה מכאן ועד סוף העולם, ולכך פריך לחומרא ממשמעות לשונו. אבל הכא קס"ד דאין אדם מכניס עצמו לדבר דספקו חמור מודאי – שעל ידי ספק יהיה חמור לו מאילו קבל עליו נזירות ודאי. כמו שאם בבירור לחרדל נתכוין – מונה נזירות אחר נזירות לעולם, ומגלח בין כל אחת ואחת, ומביא קרבן. והשתא דאיכא לספוקי [דלקישואין או] לבלק נתכוין, משיגלח פעם אחת שוב לא יוכל עד שיביא קרבן. וקרבן אינו יכול להביא – דשמא לבלק נתכוין, לחד נזירות, וקמייתי חולין בעזרה. **שיהא** בכרי זה מאה כור ומצאו שנגנב. ואין אנו יודעין אם היו בו מאה כור אם לאו. ר"ש אוסר, דספק נזירות להחמיר, דחיישינן דלמא היו בו מאה כור. *ולקמן מפרש תקנתא ג] לר"ש, דאומר קודם שיתחיל למנות ימי נזירותו: אם היו בו מאה כור והריני נזיר מדבורי הראשון – הנה אשלים נדרי, ומביא קרבנותיו. ואם לא היו בו מאה כור, ואם כן בדבורי לא היה בו ממש – הריני נודר בנזיר מעכשיו, ויהיה נזיר שלשים יום, ויביא קרבנותיו. ואין כאן חולין בעזרה, כי הוא נזיר שלשים, או מכח דיבור הראשון או מכח דיבור השני. ואם תאמר: ומאי ספקו חמור מודאי? הרי הוא נפטר בנזירות אחת ובקרבן אחד כאילו בודאי היו בו מאה כור! ויש לומר: דיכול לבא לידי חומרא – כגון אם נטמא קודם שהתנה, דהשתא הוי ספק נזיר טמא, ואין לו תקנה. דלא יוכל להביא אשם טמא – על הספק שלא היו בו מאה כור וקא מייתי חולין בעזרה, ואסור ביין ובתגלחת לעולם – [דשמא] נזיר הוא, ואינו יכול לפטור מנזירותו אם לא בהבאת אשם טומאה, וזה אין בא על התנאי. אבל נטמא אחר שהתנה – אז הוה ודאי נזיר טמא, ומייתי אשם טומאה והדר משלים נזירותו. **רבי** יהודה מתיר שספק נזירות להקל. דהוא לא קיבל עליו אא"כ ימצא בו מאה כור. וכן במתני' רואין אותה כאילו מלאה בלק, ויפטר בנזירות אחת. **אפי'** תימא רבי יהודה התם לא נחית לנזירות בלל. כלומר, אין להטיל עליו נזירות, דשמא לא היו בו מאה כור. **הכא** נחית לנזירות במאי לסלוקיה מיניה. כלומר, במתניתין על כרחין חייב לנזירות אחת, ואפילו אי בלק אמר. וכיון שירד לנזירות – אינו יכול להסתלק, כמו שמפרש והולך. ופריך: אמאי אינו יכול להסתלק? ליחזי כאילו היא מלאה קישואין או מלאה בלק ותיהוי ליה תקנתא! דסלקא דעתך דנזירות קביל עליה. כלומר, יגלח ממה נפשך לסוף שלשים ויביא קרבן, דאי חדא נזירות קביל עליה – שפיר קמגלח, ואי נמי חרדל קביל עילויה – מצי לגלוחי אחר שלשים יום. דקא סלקא דעתך אי אמר חרדל – לנזירות קביל עליה, כלומר הרבה נזירות ולא נזירות אחת ארוך. וכיון שיגלח לסוף שלשים – שוב לא תטיל עליה נזירות לרבי יהודה, דמאן לימא לן דחרדל קביל? דלמא בלק, והשלים נדרו. והשתא דמי להיא דכרי, דאמר: רבי יהודה מתיר. ואמאי אינו יכול להסתלק? ומשני: רבי יהודה סבר לה כרבי ד] דהאמר *) חרדל הך נזירות ארוך קביל עליה, ועד יום מותו לא מצי לגלח. הלכך, הכא ע"כ נחית לחד נזירות אפילו אי בלק קביל, וכיון שאתה מורידו לנזירות – אפילו לרבי יהודה תו לא מצי להסתלק, דשמא חרדל קביל עליה, ונדון עד יום מותו נזירות חד וארוך. ולא דמי להיא כלל דאינו יורד לנזירות לרבי יהודה. ורבי

*) נ"ל חד נזירות

פי' הרא"ש

הריני נזיר כשער ראשי וכו'. הרי זה נזיר עולם ומגלח א' לשלשים יום. כי קיבל עליו נזירות כמנין שער ראשו וכל ל' ול' הוי נזיר בפני עצמו ומגלח בכל יום ל"א ומביא קרבנותיו ובו ביום מתחיל נזירות ואינו שותה יין ואינו מטמא למתים לעולם ולא כנזיר עולם דלעיל דנזיר אבשלום דמיקל בתער דווקא ולא במספרים ופליגי לענין אם מגלח לשנה או לל' יום או לז' ימים ואם רצה אינו מגלח ואינו מביא קרבן אבל נזיר עולם (בתרא) [דהכא] צריך לגלח ולהביא קרבנותיו משלשים לל'. והא מספקא לי אם ירצה לעמוד בנזירותו בלא הבאת קרבן זמן גדול ורק שלא יעבור בבל תאחר על קרבנות שנתחייב אם הרשות בידו מידי דהוה הנזירות שהשלים ימי נזירותו שיכול להשהות קרבנותיו ובלבד שלא יעבור בבל תאחר. או דלמא כיון שקבל עליו נזירות כל ימיו חייב הוא להשלים נזירות זו מיד ולהתחיל אחרת והדעת נוטה כך כיון שכל ימיו הוא מחייב נזירות אין לו לאחר מלהשלים כל מה שיוכל. ועוד יש דין ג' לנזיר עולם אם אמר הריני נזיר ק' שנה או אלף שנים הוא נזיר לעולם ונזירות א' יש לו כל ימי חייו ואינו מגלח לעולם אם לא נטמא כדקתני בברייתא בגמ' אין זה נזיר עולם אלא נזיר לעולם: ר' אומר אין זה מגלח א' לשלשים יום דסבר ר' דנזיר אחד ימים כמנין שער ראשו קבל עליו ואיכא לא יסתפוקי אם יש לו דין נזיר עולם דאבשלום או דין נזיר לעולם ואין נ"ל ספק כיון דנזיר אחת כמנין שערות קבל עלויה חד נזיר הוה כאומר ק' שנה: האומר עלי נזירות כשער ראשי. דנזירות מופסקות קבל עליו כשער ראשו: אם אמר א' גדולה נזרתי. כלומר נזירות א' קבלתי עלי ונראה לי גדולה כמלא הבית. ואם אמר סתם נזרתי לא היה בלבי אלא מה שידונו חכמים לשוני. ונזיר כל ימיו בגמ' מפרש לה. עד מקום פלוני מפורש למעלה: מונה נזירות כמנין ימות (השנה) [החמה] שס"ה נזירות כמנין ימות החמה ודוקא דאמר כמנין ימות החמה אבל אם אמר כימות החמה חד נזירות קבל עילוהי שנה א' כיון דאית ליה קצותא כדדייקינן לעיל מברייתא דאלף שנה והא דלא דייק מהך מתני' דאמר כמנין הא לאו הכי לא אמרינן נזירות קבל עליה כיון דאית ליה קצותא. משום דאיכא למימר דאתיא (הוא) כרבי או כר' יהודה דסברי דאפילו כשער ראשו חד נזירות קבל עליו אבל לרבנן לא שאני להו בין איכא קצותא לליכא קצותא: ואמאי וליחזייה כאילו היא מלאה קשואים ודלועין. דספק נזירות להקל ולא ימנה אלא אחת כמנין קשואים מלא הקופה ואם היא מחזקת פחות מל' ימנה נזיר א' ואם היא מחזקת מ' או חמשים ימנה נזירות כמנינם: אדם מכנים עצמו לדבר שספקו חמור מודאי. דסבר ספק נזיר' להחמיר ואפילו בדבר שספקו חמור מודאי מכנים עצמו לכל חומר הספק כגון בהך מתני' שאם ודאי כחרדל היה מגלח מל' לל' ועכשיו שהוא ספק שמא מלאה קשואים קאמר אינו מגלח אלא פעם אחת א' נזירו' ראשונה אם מחזקת הקופה פחות מל' מגלח ביום ל"א ואם מחזקת יותר משלשים מגלח סוף ששים וא' ושוב אינו מגלח כל ימיו דשמא כחרדל קאמר ונזיר עולם הוי ואינו יכול לגלח מל' לל' דשמא בקשואים קאמר ואינו מביא קרבן דהוי חולין בעזרה ואע"ג דעולה ושלמים מצי לאתויי ולהתנות בנדבה חטאת אינה באה נדבה ואינו יכול לגלח בלא הבאת קרבן: ר"ש אוסר שספק נזירות להחמיר ואע"ג דספקו חמור מודאי דאילו היה בו ק' כור היה נזיר ומגלח לשלשים יום ועכשיו אינו מגלח לעולם שאינו מביא קרבנותיו בספק ותימה ולמה ספקו חמור מודאי שאומר אם לא היה בו ק' כור הריני נזיר וי"ל דמ"מ הוא חמור קודם שאמר תנאי שאם נטמא קודם שאמר תנאי זה אינו יכול להביא קרבן טומאה וכן במתני' יכול לקבל עליו נזירות כמנין חרדל אלא שאם נטמא אחר שהשלים נזירות של קשואים קודם שקיבל עליו נזירות כחרדל אינו יכול להביא קרבן טומאה: ר' יהודה מתיר שספק נזיר' להקל דלא מעייל נפשיה לספק חמור ואינו נזיר כלל שכך היה דעתו שאם לא יוכל לברר הדבר שלא יהיה כדבורו: התם לא נחית לנזירות. כלומר התם לא נחית ליה לנזירות דשמא לא היה בו ק' כור ומספק לא מחתינן ליה לנזיר כי לא היה דעתו ליכנס לספק חמור: הכא נחית ליה לנזירות או של קשואים או של חרדל במאי לסלוקיה מיניה הרי כל ימיו עומד בספק זה והיאך נוכל לסלקו: אמאי לא לחזייה כאילו היא מלאה קשואים ותהוי ליה תקנתא. למה אתה אומר שעומד כל ימיו בספק זה ואין לו תקנה הרי אחר שעברה נזירות של קישואים יכול לגלח דס"ד נזירות של חרדל קבל עילויה ואחר שגילה לנזירות של קשואים נסתלק מספק קישואים ואין עליו עתה אלא ספק חרדל ולא נחת אכתי לנזיר ומספיקא לא מחתינן ליה דספק נזירות להקל.
סבר

מב א מיי' פ"ג מהל' נזירות הלכה יח:
ל"ל לפניו
מג ב מיי' שם הלכה יז:
מד ג מיי' שם הל' ט:
מה ד מיי' שם הלכה ה:
מו ה מיי' שם פ"ב הלכה ט:

לעיל ז.
(ג"ז שם)
[תוס' פ"ב] לקמן לד. נדרים יט. ע"ש
[לקמן יג.]

נוסחת הריב"ן
א) אומרים: ב) לל' יום: ג) לל' יום: ד) נזירות: ה) נזירות: ו) כותך: ז) דלא: ח) מודאי: ט) מגלח: י) הוא: כ) הואיל: ל) חרדל: מ) דמאן דמתני: נ) דחיילא עליה כמאי דתסלקיה: ס) דתסלקיה מיניה: ע) הכא אית לן למימר כו': ומייתי ליה קרבן תיהוי ליה תקנתא כנ"ל והשאר ליתא: פ) דנזירות:

הגהות הב"ח
(א) רש"י ד"ה רבי אומר וכו' והאי דקאמר הריני נזיר כשער ראשי: (ב) ד"ה אלא זה שאמר הריני וכו' כשער ראשי: (ג) ד"ה אמר חזקיה וכו' דסבירא ליה כותיה ומתניתין דלא תני הכי: (ד) ד"ה ר' יוחנן וכו' לכי משלים נזירותו אבל הכא כצ"ל והד"א:

גליון הש"ס
תוס' ד"ה שיהא בכרי ולקמן מפרש. דף יג ע"א ולב ע"ב:

הגהות מהר"ב רנשבורג
א] רש"י ד"ה הריני נזיר וכו' ר"ש אוסר וכו' שכל ספק נזירות להחמיר דספיקו עכ"ל. נ"ב ואע"ג דספיקו: ב] בא"ד חמור מודאו דאילו ודאי. נ"ב ואילו ודאי עיין: ג] תוס' ד"ה שיהא בכרי וכו' ולקמן מפרש תקנתא. ר"ל לקמן דף יג ע"א מפרש במתני' תקנתא לר"ש להתנות והך תקנתא קאי נמי הכא. אורח מישור: ד] ד"ה הכא נחית לנזירות וכו' ומשני רבי יהודה סבר לה כרבי דהאמר חרדל נמחקו תיבות דהאמר חרדל ונ"ב דאמר הך כנ"ל:

מז א מיי' פ"ג מהל' נזירות הלכה יא:

גירסת א"מ ה"ע

מח ב מיי' שם הל' ח:
מט ג מיי' פי"ד מהל' צרעת הלכה ו:

דר' יְהוּדָה סָבַר לָהּ כְּרַבִּי. דִּתְנַן, רַבִּי אוֹמֵר: אֵין זֶה מְגַלֵּחַ אַחַת לִשְׁלֹשִׁים יוֹם. וְאֵיזֶהוּ שֶׁמְּגַלֵּחַ אַחַת לִשְׁלֹשִׁים יוֹם – הָאוֹמֵר ["הֲרֵי] עָלַי נְזִירוּת כִּשְׂעַר רֹאשִׁי" וְ"כַעֲפַר הָאָרֶץ" וּ"כְחוֹל הַיָּם". וְרַבִּי יְהוּדָה מִי סָבַר לָהּ כְּרַבִּי? וְהָתְנַן: "הֲרֵינִי נָזִיר כְּמִנְיַן יְמוֹת הַחַמָּה" (א) וכו', א"ר יְהוּדָה: מַעֲשֶׂה הָיָה וְכֵיוָן שֶׁהִשְׁלִים מֵת. אא"ב נְזִירוּת קָא מְקַבֵּל עֲלֵיהּ – הַיְינוּ טַעֲמָא דְּכֵיוָן דְּהִשְׁלִים מֵת. אֶלָּא א"א חֲדָא נְזִירוּת קַבֵּיל עִילָּוֵיהּ – מִי הָוֵי הַשְׁלָמָה כְּלָל? וְעוֹד, מִי סָבַר לָהּ כְּרַבִּי? וְהָא תַּנְיָא, רַבִּי יְהוּדָה אוֹמֵר: "הֲרֵינִי נָזִיר מִנְיַן הֶילְקְטֵי קַיִץ" וּ"מִנְיַן שִׁבֳּלֵי שְׁמִיטָּה" – מוֹנֶה נְזִירוּת כְּמִנְיַן הֶילְקְטֵי קַיִץ, וּכְמִנְיַן שִׁבֳּלֵי שְׁמִיטָּה! "מִנְיָן" שָׁאנֵי. וּמִי שָׁאנֵי לֵיהּ לְרַבִּי "מִנְיָן"? וְהָתַנְיָא: *"הֲרֵינִי נָדַר כְּמִנְיַן יְמוֹת הַחַמָּה" – מוֹנֶה נְזִירוּת כְּמִנְיַן יְמוֹת הַחַמָּה, "כִּימֵי הַלְּבָנָה" – מוֹנֶה כִּימֵי הַלְּבָנָה, רַבִּי אוֹמֵר: עַד שֶׁיֹּאמַר "נְזִירוּת עָלַי כְּמִנְיַן יְמוֹת הַחַמָּה" וּ"כְמִנְיַן יְמוֹת הַלְּבָנָה"! רַבִּי יְהוּדָה סָבַר לָהּ כְּוָתֵיהּ בַּחֲדָא, וּפָלֵיג עֲלֵיהּ בַּחֲדָא. סָבַר לָהּ כְּוָתֵיהּ בַּחֲדָא – (ג) *נְזִירוּת קַבֵּיל עִילָּוֵיהּ, וּפָלֵיג עֲלֵיהּ בַּחֲדָא – דְּאִילּוּ רַבִּי יְהוּדָה שָׁנֵי לֵיהּ מוֹנֶה, וְרַבִּי לָא שָׁנֵי לֵיהּ מוֹנֶה.§ *ת"ר: א"הֲרֵינִי נָזִיר כָּל יְמֵי חַיַּי" "הֲרֵינִי נְזִיר עוֹלָם" – הֲרֵי זֶה נְזִיר עוֹלָם, אֲפִילּוּ "מֵאָה שָׁנָה" אֲפִילּוּ "אֶלֶף שָׁנִים" – אֵין זֶה נְזִיר עוֹלָם אֶלָּא נָזִיר לְעוֹלָם.§ ת"ר: "הֲרֵינִי נָזִיר וְאַחַת" – במוֹנֶה שְׁתַּיִם, "וְעוֹד" – מוֹנֶה שָׁלֹשׁ, "וָשׁוּב" – מוֹנֶה אַרְבַּע. פְּשִׁיטָא! מַהוּ דְּתֵימָא: "וָשׁוּב" כִּי כּוּלְּהוּ, וְהָוְיָא לֵיהּ שִׁית, קמ"ל דְּלָא.§ *ת"ר: "הֲרֵינִי נָזִיר", סוּמָכוֹס אוֹמֵר: "הֵן" – אַחַת, "דִּיגוֹן" – שְׁתַּיִם, "טְרִיגוֹן" – שָׁלֹשׁ, "טֶטְרָגוֹן" – אַרְבַּע, "פּוּנְטִיגוֹן" חָמֵשׁ.§ *ת"ר: גבַּיִת עָגוֹל, דִּיגוֹן, טְרִיגוֹן, פּוּנְטִיגוֹן – אֵינוֹ מִטַּמֵּא בִּנְגָעִים. טֶטְרָגוֹן מִטַּמֵּא בִּנְגָעִים. מ"ט? לְמַטָּה הוּא אוֹמֵר °"קִיר" "קִירוֹת", לְמַעְלָה הוּא אוֹמֵר "קִיר" "קִירוֹת" – הֲרֵי כָּאן אַרְבַּע.§ (ויקרא יד)

הדרן עלך כל כנויי

ורבי יהודה מי סבר ליה כרבי. דהאמר חרדל, והתנן הריני נזיר (מן החרלן) כמנין וכו', אמר רבי יהודה מעשה וכו'. אי אמרת בשלמא נזירות הרבה קביל עליה, *דכיון שהשלים מת – כלומר, נראה נופל בו לשון השלמה, שהרבה נזירות שחייבוהו חכמים, כיון שהשלים אותם – מת. אלא אי אמרת חדא נזירות ארוך קביל עליה – מי הויא השלמה כלל? פי', מי שייך ביה לשון השלמה כלל? והרי הוא נזיר נזירות אחת שלא יגלח כמנין ימות החמה, ואין שייך בו לשון השלמה כלל! א] (אלא מאי) לרבי יהודה נזירות הרבה קביל עליה – היינו טעמא, מכיון שהשלים ב] מת – [שאחר] שלשים יום מת, כמו מילתא דת"ק, דאמר: מונה מנין נזירות כמנין ימות החמה. אלא אי אמרת חדא נזירות – מי הויא השלמה דידיה [כהשלמה דת"ק]? ואם כן הוא מעשה לסתור, ומדמייתי ר' יהודה בתר מילתא דת"ק ומעשה וכו' – מכלל דמייתי ראיה למילתיה דת"ק, ג] כמו שכתבתי. (הגה"ה). **מנין** הילקטי. כשמייבשין התאנים עושין תילין תילין מתאנים ליבש עד אין מספר. ומנין שבילי שמיטה – וכן בשמיטה, אין השדות זרועות ומרבין בהן שבילים. **מונה** נזירות מנין הילקטי קיץ. אלמא נזירות הרבה קביל עלויה לר' יהודה! ומשני: מנין שאני. פי': ודאי כי אמר "מנין" – נזירות קביל עליה, אבל כי אמר "כחרדל" או "כהילקטי" ולא הזכיר "מנין" – חד נזירות ארוך קביל עליה כרבי. **ומי** שאני לרבי מנין. היה סובר, כיון דר' יהודה כרבי סבר ליה, ושני ליה בין אמר "מנין" בין לא אמר "מנין" – ה"נ שני ליה לרבי, ומש"ה פריך: רבי אומר עד שיאמר "נזירות עלי כמנין ימות החמה", אלמא דלשון "כמנין" בלא "נזירות" לא משמע לרבי אלא חד נזירות ארוך! ומשני: ר' יהודה סבר לה כוותיה בחדא, דחד נזירות קביל עליה כי אמר "חרדל", ופליג בחדא; דר' יהודה שני ליה "מנין", ורבי לא שני ליה "מנין". **הרי** זה נזיר. כאבשלום. ומיקל, למר כדאית ליה ולמר כדאית ליה כו'. וכדפירשנו לעיל. **אמר** מאה שנה או אלף שנה נזיר לעולם. ואינו מגלח ואינו מיקל עד יום מותו. **נזיר** ואחת מונה שתי נזירות. לפי שהוסיף לומר "ואחת ועוד" – מוסיף ומונה שלשה. כשאמר "נזיר ואחת ועוד ושוב" – [ארבע]. ומקשה: פשיטא. מהו דתימא: "ושוב" כי כולהו, ומני שית – קמ"ל דלא. **[הריני]** נזיר סומכוס אומר הן אחת. פי' אם אמר "הן" הוא אחת, כדאמרן בעלמא (שבת דף לא:): שכן בלשון יוני אחת קורין הינ"א. **דיגון** שתים. בלשון יון: טריגון – שלש, טטרגון – ד', פונטיגון – ה', כמו בלשון יון. **בית** עגול. דהואיל ואין לו ד' זויות אין מטמא בנגעים, כדמסיק מ"קיר" "קירות", והיינו טעמא דכולהו.

הדרן עלך כל כנויי

תורה אור

דְּרַבִּי יְהוּדָה סָבַר לָהּ כְּרַבִּי. דְּקָאמַר בְּמַתְנִי' כִּי אָמַר "הֲרֵינִי נָזִיר כִּשְׂעַר רֹאשִׁי" אֵין זֶה מְגַלֵּחַ אַחַת לִשְׁלֹשִׁים יוֹם, מִשּׁוּם דִּנְזִירוּת אֲרִיכְתָּא קַבֵּיל עִילָּוֵיהּ, וּלְעוֹלָם אֵין לוֹ תַּקָּנָה, שֶׁהֲרֵי שַׂעֲרוֹת רֹאשׁוֹ מְרוּבִּין מִשְּׁנֵי חַיָּיו. ה"נ "הֲרֵינִי נָזִיר מְלֹא הַקּוּפָּה" – נְזִירוּת אֲרִיכְתָּא קַבֵּיל עִילָּוֵיהּ, וְאֵינוֹ מְגַלֵּחַ וּמֵבִיא קָרְבָּן בְּסוֹף כָּל שְׁלֹשִׁים. א) וְכֵיוָן דְּהַהוּא חַד נְזִירוּת מָשֵׁיךְ כִּמְלֹא הַקּוּפָּה – לָא מָצֵית אָמְרַתְּ דְּלִיחַזְיֵיהּ כְּאִילּוּ הִיא מְלֵאָה קִישּׁוּאִים, וּלְכִי מַשְׁלִים נְזִירוּת כְּמִנְיַן קִישּׁוּאִים שֶׁיְּכוֹלִין לִיכָּנֵס לְתוֹכָהּ לַיְיתֵי קָרְבָּן. דְּהוֹאִיל וְעָיֵיל נַפְשֵׁיהּ לִנְזִירוּת, וְאִיכָּא לְמֵימַר דַּחֲדָא נְזִירוּת אֲרִיכְתָּא כְּמִנְיַן חַרְדָּל קִיבֵּל עָלָיו – לָא מַיְיתֵי קָרְבָּן מִסְּפֵיקָא, דִּדְלְמָא פָּגַע לְאֵיתוּיֵי חוּלִּין לָעֲזָרָה. וְהִלְכָּךְ לְרַבִּי יְהוּדָה נַמִי לָא מָצֵי לְסַלּוּקֵי נַפְשֵׁיהּ מִנְּזִירוּת דְּלַיְיתֵי קָרְבָּן, ומש"ה לֵית לֵיהּ תַּקַּנְתָּא. וּמִי סָבַר לָהּ ר' יְהוּדָה כְּרַבִּי (ג) וְהָתַנְיָא הֲרֵינִי נָזִיר כְּמִנְיַן יְמוֹת הַחַמָּה מוֹנֶה ב) נְזִירוּת כְּמִנְיַן יְמוֹת הַחַמָּה. שֶׁיְּהֵא מוֹנֶה שס"ה נְזִירוּת שֶׁל שְׁלֹשִׁים, ג) וְנִמְצָא שֶׁיְּהֵא נוֹהֵג נְזִירוּת שְׁלֹשִׁים שָׁנָה. אָמַר רַבִּי יְהוּדָה מַעֲשֶׂה. בְּאֶחָד שֶׁאָמַר "הֲרֵינִי נָזִיר כְּמִנְיַן יְמוֹת הַחַמָּה", וְכֵיוָן שֶׁהִשְׁלִים ד) נְזִירוּתוֹ לְסוֹף שְׁלֹשִׁים שָׁנָה מִיָּד מֵת. אִי אָמְרַתְּ בִּשְׁלָמָא נְזִירוּת שֶׁל שְׁלֹשִׁים ה) קִיבֵּל עָלָיו כְּמִנְיַן יְמוֹת הַחַמָּה – מַשְׁכַּחַתְּ לָהּ דְּכֵיוָן שֶׁהִשְׁלִים מֵת. אֶלָּא אִי אָמְרַתְּ. דַּחֲדָא נְזִירוּת שֶׁל שס"ה ו) קִיבֵּל עָלָיו, וְכָל חֲדָא וַחֲדָא תֶּהֱוֵי שס"ה יָמִים, וְצָרִיךְ ז) דְּיֶהֱוֵי נָזִיר שס"ה פְּעָמִים שס"ה יָמִים כְּמִנְיַן יְמוֹת הַחַמָּה, וּכְדִבְרֵי רַבִּי דְּאָמַר דְּאֵין זֶה נָזִיר שֶׁיְּהֵא מְגַלֵּחַ בְּסוֹף שְׁלֹשִׁים, אֶלָּא כָּל שס"ה יָמִים יְהֵא נוֹהֵג ח) נְזִירוּתוֹ. מִי הָוֵי הַשְׁלָמָה כְּלָל. בִּשְׁנֵי דְּרַבִּי יְהוּדָה? מִי הָוֵי אִינִישׁ דְּחַיֵּי כּוּלֵּי הַאי (ד) כְּשס"ה יָמִים [שס"ה פְּעָמִים] שֶׁצָּרִיךְ לִנְהוֹג נְזִירוּת בְּעַצְמוֹ? אֶלָּא מִדְּקָאָמַר ר' יְהוּדָה: כֵּיוָן שֶׁהִשְׁלִים מֵת – ש"מ ט) לָא ס"ל כְּרַבִּי. לִישָּׁנָא אַחֲרִינָא: וְהָתַנְיָא הֲרֵינִי נָזִיר כְּמִנְיַן יְמוֹת הַחַמָּה. כְּלוֹמַר, כָּל זְמַן שֶׁהַחַמָּה זוֹרַחַת, דְּהַיְינוּ עַד סוֹף הָעוֹלָם. מוֹנֶה נְזִירוּת כְּמִנְיַן יְמוֹת הַחַמָּה. כְּלוֹמַר, כָּל יָמָיו יְהֵא מוֹנֶה נְזִירוּת שֶׁל ל', י) וּמְגַלֵּחַ וּמֵבִיא קָרְבָּן. וְא"ר יְהוּדָה: מַעֲשֶׂה בְּאֶחָד שֶׁהִזִּיר בְּכָךְ וְכֵיוָן שֶׁהִשְׁלִים מֵת. אִי אָמְרַתְּ בִּשְׁלָמָא נְזִירוּת שֶׁל שְׁלֹשִׁים כ) קִיבֵּל עָלָיו – הַיְינוּ דְּקָאָמַר: כֵּיוָן שֶׁהִשְׁלִים מֵת, דְּכָל קָרְבָּן וְקָרְבָּן דְּמַיְיתֵי לְסוֹף תִּגְלַחַת חֲשִׁיבֵי לֵיהּ כְּמַשְׁלִים. אֶלָּא אִי אָמְרַתְּ דַּחֲדָא נְזִירוּת קִיבֵּל עִילָּוֵיהּ ל) עַד יְמוֹת עוֹלָם וְאָסוּר לְגַלֵּחַ כָּל יָמָיו, מַאי הַשְׁלָמָה אִיכָּא הָכָא? הָא אַכַּתִּי אִילּוּ הֲוָה קַיָּים הֲוָה מִיבָּעֵי לֵיהּ לְמֵיקַם בִּנְזִירוּת! וְעוֹד, מִי סָבַר לָהּ כְּרַבִּי? וְהָתַנְיָא בְּהֶדְיָא רַבִּי יְהוּדָה אוֹמֵר הֲרֵינִי נָזִיר בְּמִנְיַן הֶילְקְטֵי קַיִץ. כְּמִנְיַן שְׁבִילִים שֶׁעוֹשִׂים מ) קַיָּילֵי תְּאֵנִים בֵּין הַקְּלִיעוֹת, נ) כְּדֵי שֶׁיְּהוּ מְהַלְּכִים בֵּינְתַיִים וְלֹא יְהוּ נִדְרָכִים בָּרֶגֶל. וּבְמִנְיַן שִׁבֳּלֵי שְׁמִיטָּה. דִּבִשְׁנַת הַשְּׁמִיטָּה אֵין הַשָּׂדוֹת נִזְרָעוֹת, וּמַנִּיחִין בָּהֶן שְׁבִילִים שֶׁל אֶשְׁתַּקַד. וּלְפִי שֶׁהֵן מוּעָטִין וְנוֹחַ לְמוֹנָתָן קָאָמַר הָכִי. וְאִית דְּגָרְסִי: כְּמִנְיַן שְׁבִילֵי שְׁמִיטָּה – שֶׁהַשָּׂדוֹת הֶפְקֵר, וְכָל ס) הָעָם עוֹשֶׂה שְׁבִילִים בְּתוֹכוֹ וְאֵין בַּעַל הַשָּׂדֶה מְעַכֵּב עַל יָדוֹ. מוֹנֶה נְזִירוּת בְּמִנְיַן הֶילְקְטֵי קַיִץ וּשְׁבִילֵי שְׁמִיטָּה. וִיהֵא מְגַלֵּחַ כָּל ל' וְל' ע) לְמִנְיַן הֶילְקְטֵי קַיִץ, פ) אע"ג דְּלָא אָמַר "נְזִירוּת עָלַי". אַלְמָא לֵית לֵיהּ לְרַבִּי יְהוּדָה הָא דְּרַבִּי, דְּאִי לְרַבִּי אִי הָוֵי הָתָם מֵאָה לְקִיטֵי קַיִץ צָרִיךְ לִהְיוֹת מוֹנֶה נְזִירוּת אֲרִיכָא, מֵאָה פְּעָמִים צ) מֵאָה יוֹם, אוֹ נְזִירוּת אֲרִיכָא מֵאָה יוֹם. מִנְיָן שָׁאנֵי. דְּהֵיכָא דְּאָמַר "כְּמִנְיַן יְמוֹת הַחַמָּה" אוֹ "כְּמִנְיַן הֶילְקְטֵי קַיִץ" אֲפִילּוּ רַבִּי מוֹדֶה דִּנְזִירוּת קַבֵּיל עֲלֵיהּ וּמְגַלֵּחַ אַחַת לִשְׁלֹשִׁים, וְהַיְינוּ נַמִי דְּקָאָמַר רַבִּי יְהוּדָה לְעֵיל: כֵּיוָן שֶׁהִשְׁלִים מֵת. אֲבָל גַּבֵּי קוּפָּה, דִּנְזִירוּת אֲרִיכָא קַבֵּיל עֲלֵיהּ – אֲפִילּוּ רַבִּי יְהוּדָה מוֹדֶה דִּסְפֵק נְזִירוּת לְהַחְמִיר, וְכִדְפָרֵישְׁנָא. רַבִּי אוֹמֵר עַד שֶׁיֹּאמַר נְזִירוּת עָלַי כְּמִנְיַן יְמוֹת הַחַמָּה. לֹא יְהֵא מְגַלֵּחַ אַחַת לִשְׁלֹשִׁים. הָא ק) לֹא אָמַר "נְזִירוּת", אֶלָּא "הֲרֵינִי נָזִיר כְּמִנְיַן יְמוֹת הַחַמָּה" – חֲדָא נְזִירוּת ר) הוּא קַבֵּיל כְּלֵיהּ כְּמִנְיַן יְמוֹת הַחַמָּה עַד עוֹלָם כִּדְלְעֵיל, אוֹ לְאִידָךְ לִישָּׁנָא שס"ה פְּעָמִים שס"ה יָמִים. שָׁנֵי לֵיהּ מוֹנֶה. דְּ"מִנְיָן" שָׁנֵי לֵיהּ, וְהָוֵי כְּמ"ד "נְזִירוּת כְּלַי". אֲפִילּוּ מֵאָה שָׁנָה אֵין זֶה נְזִיר עוֹלָם אֶלָּא זֶה נָזִיר לְעוֹלָם. דַּחֲדָא נְזִירוּת אֲרִיכְתָּא הוּא דְּהָוְיָא, מִשּׁוּם דְּלֵית לֵיהּ קִיצּוּתָא, כִּדְאָמְרִינַן לְעֵיל. (ה) ש) כִּי אָמַר "וְאַחַת" – כְּמַאן דְּאָמַר "וּנְזִירוּת אַחֶרֶת" דָּמֵי. הָאוֹמֵר הֲרֵינִי נָזִיר וְאַחַת וְעוֹד. מוֹנֶה שָׁלֹשׁ נְזִירוּת. אָמַר "הֲרֵינִי נָזִיר וְאַחַת וְעוֹד וָשׁוּב" – מוֹנֶה אַרְבַּע. מַהוּ דְּתֵימָא. (ו) הָא הַאי דְּקָאָמַר "וָשׁוּב" מַשְׁמַע כְּאִילּוּ אָמַר: וָשׁוּב לֶיהֱוֵי עָלַי נְזִירוּת כִּי הָנָךְ דְּאָמְרִינַן, יָהֳוְיָן לְהוּ שִׁית, קָמַשְׁמַע לָן. סוּמָכוֹס אוֹמֵר. "הֲרֵינִי נָזִיר הֵן" – חַיָּיב בִּנְזִירוּת אַחַת. וְאִם אָמַר "הֲרֵינִי נָזִיר דִּיגוֹן" – מוֹנֶה ב'. "טְרִיגוֹן" – מוֹנֶה ג'. "טֶטְרָגוֹן" – מוֹנֶה ד'. "פּוּנְטִיגוֹן" – מוֹנֶה ה'. שֶׁכֵּן מוֹנִין בִּלְשׁוֹן יָוָן. וְאַשְׁמוּעִינַן דִּבְכָל לָשׁוֹן יָכוֹל אָדָם לְקַבֵּל עָלָיו נְזִירוּת ת). בַּיִת עָגוֹל. שֶׁאֵין לוֹ זָוִיּוֹת, אוֹ בַּיִת דִּיגוֹן שֶׁאֵין לוֹ אֶלָּא שְׁתֵּי זָוִיּוֹת, אוֹ א) טְרִיגוֹן שֶׁאֵין לוֹ אֶלָּא שְׁלֹשָׁה, אוֹ פּוּנְטִיגוֹן שֶׁיֵּשׁ לוֹ חָמֵשׁ זָוִיּוֹת – אֵין מִטַּמֵּא בִּנְגָעִים. טֶטְרָגוֹן שֶׁיֵּשׁ לוֹ אַרְבַּע זָוִיּוֹת – מִטַּמֵּא. מ"ט לְמַטָּה הוּא אוֹמֵר קִירוֹת. "וְאִם פָּשָׂה הַנֶּגַע בְּקִירוֹת הַבַּיִת". וּלְמַעְלָה הוּא אוֹמֵר. "וְהִנֵּה הַנֶּגַע בְּקִירוֹת הַבַּיִת". מִדַּהֲוָה לֵיהּ לְמִיכְתַּב בִּתְרַוַּיְיהוּ "קִיר" דְּמַשְׁמַע חַד, (ז) וְכָתַב "קִירוֹת" דְּמַשְׁמַע תְּרֵי – אַלְמָא ד' בָּעֵינַן, כִּדְמַדְּבַר לְהוּ בִּלִישָּׁנָא דִּקְרָא. "וּמַרְאֵיהֶן שָׁפָל מִן הַקִּיר" לָא קָא חָשֵׁיב, אֶלָּא הָנֵי דִּכְתִיב בְּהוּ לִישָּׁנֵי יְתֵירֵי קָחָשֵׁיב. **הדרן עלך כל כנויי**

הֲרֵינִי

פי' הרא"ש

סבר לה כרבי דאמר נזיר א' קבל עליה הלכך לא יצא מספק קישואים שאינו יכול לגלח א) לסוף דשמא כמלא חרדל קאמר וכל ימיו היה נזיר ומכאן מוכח דלרבי אינו מגלח כל ימיו דאל"כ פסיק מניה נזירות דקישואים: אא"ב נזירות קבל עליה היינו טעמא דכיון דהשלים מת כלו' ניחא דמייתינן ליה מלתיה דר' יהודה על מלתיה דרבנן דהשלמה דידי' כהשלמה דרבנן: מי הוי השלמה כלל וא"כ הוי מעשה לסתור דבכל אתר דמייתי מעשה לסיועי מעשה ולא לסתור: הלקטי קיץ. מיבשי תאנים עושין שבילין בין הקציעות כמו בשלהי שבת כמין הלקטי קטנה היתה פי' שביל ור"ת פי' הלקטי קיץ כמו תל המתלקט כמין כלים של קציעות ושבילי שמטה בשביעית השדות הפקר והכל נכנסין בהם ומלאה שבילין: מונה נזירות כמנין הלקטי קיץ והוי נזיר כל ימיו: מנין שאני כיון שאמר כמנין ימות החמה כמנין הלקטי ודאי נזיר קבל עילויה: אבל אם אמר כימות החמה או כהלקטי קיץ חדא נזירות אריכתא קביל עליה: ס"ל כותיה בחדא וכו' ושלשה מחלוקות בדבר לרבנן בין אמר כמנין בין לא אמר כמנין נזירות קבל עליו היכא דלית ליה קיצותא ולר' לעולם חדא נזיר ולר' יהודה שני ליה בין מונה בין לא מונה: הריני נזיר ואחת מונה שנים וכו' א' ועוד מונה ג' א' ועוד ושוב מונה ד' ומגלח בכל א' ומביא (קרבנו) קרבן: מהו דתימא ושוב כבולהו נ"ל דה"ה דהוה מצי למימר מהו דתימא ועוד כי כולהו ומונה ד' אלא אבתראה נקט: דיתון ב' אם אמר הריני דיתון ב' דיתון שאין לו אלא ב' זויות טריתון ג' זויות פרטיתון ד' זויות: קיר קירות הוה מצי למכתב קיר וכתיב קירות והנה הנגע בקירות הבית והנה פשה הנגע בקירות הבית ומראהו שפל מן הקיר לא דריש דלגופא איצטריך ותימה דהא דרשינן מקירות איזה קיר שהוא בקירות הוי אומר זה קרן זויות וי"ל דאי לא אתא אלא לדרשא דהכא לכתוב ד' פעמים קיר ומדכתיב קירות דרשי' מניה איזהו קיר שהוא בקירות וליכא למימר דכולא להך דרשא איצט' וי"ל דא"כ בחד קירות סגי:

סליק פרקא

א) ר"ל שאינו יכול לגלח אחר נזירות דקישואין.

[תוספ' פ"א ע"ש ערכין ט: ע"ש]

גי' א"מ חדא נזירות

לעיל ז. תוספתא פ"א

[תוספ' רפ"א ע"ש] ב"ב קסד: ע"ש

נגעים פי"ב מ"א [ב"ב שם ע"ש תוספתא דנגעים פ"ו]

נוסחת הריב"ן

א) שלשים יום: ב) נזיריות: ג) שלשים שלשים: ד) נזירותיו: ה) שלשים שלשים: ו) שס"ה ימים: ז) דליהוי: ח) נזירות: ט) דלא: י) שלשים שלשים: כ) שלשים שלשים: ל) כל: מ) מקיילי: נ) תיבת כדי ליתא בכ"י: ס) אדם: ע) מנין: פ) ואע"ג: צ) שלשים יום: ק) הא אם לא: ר) נזירות אריכא הוא דקביל עליה: ש) דכי: ת) לקבל עליו נזירות מלתני הין מונה אחת דיגון מונה שתים וכו' מפי רבי הס"ד: א) או בית טריגון:

הגהות הב"ח

(א) גמ' כמנין ימות החמה מונה נזירות כמנין ימות החמה אמר רבי יהודה: (ב) שם סבר לה כוותיה בחדא חדא נזירות וכו' שאני ליה וכו' לא שאני ליה: (ג) רש"י ד"ה ומי סבר וכו' והתנן הריני: (ד) ד"ה מי הוי וכו' כשס"ה פעמים שס"ה ימים שצריך וכו' לישנא אחרינא והתנן הריני כצ"ל והד"א עם ד"ה מונה וכו' למיקם בנזירות הס"ד ואח"כ מ"ה ועוד וכו' כרבי והתניא הד"א: (ה) ד"ה הריני וכו' דכי אמר: (ו) ד"ה מהו דתימא האי כצ"ל ותיבת הא נמחק: (ז) ד"ה ולמעלה וכו' דמשמע חד כדמדבר להו בלישנא דקרא ומראהן שפל מן הקיר וכתב קירות וכו' ד' בעינן הס"ד ואח"כ מ"ה לא קא חשיב וכו' לישני יתירי הוא דקחשיב:

הגהות מהר"ב רנשבורג א] תוס' ד"ה ור"י מי סבר ליה כרבי וכו' ואין שייך בו לשון השלמה כלל. נ"ב כן הס"ד ואח"כ מה"ד הג"ה. אח"כ ד"ה ור"י וכו' והוא פי' אחר על אח"כ א"מ: ב] בא"ד היינו טעמא מכיון שהשלים מת [שאחר] שלשים נמחקו תיבות מת שאחר ונ"ב שם ס"ה כצ"ל א"מ: ג] בא"ד בסופו מכלל וכו' כמו שכתבתי נ"ב אבל נראה כמו שכתבתי עי' א"מ:

[לקמן י.] מנחות פא: קג.
[ערכין ה. וש"נ]
[פסחים נג: וש"נ]
[לקמן יב: מנחות פא: קג.]
[נדרים עח. ב"ב קכ:]
פסחים נג: מנחות קג. [ערכין כ.]

הריני נזיר מן הגרוגרות וכו' בש"א נזיר. דכיון דאמר "הריני נזיר" חל עליה נזירות, וכי הדר ואמר "מן הגרוגרות ומן הדבילה" – לא אמר כלום. ובה"א אינו נזיר. דכיון דאמר "מן הגרוגרות" – לא שייך שום נזירות בגרוגרות ודבילה. א"ר יהודה אף ב"ש לא אמרו. שיהיה בו שום נזירות כלל. (ב) אלא לפי מה שאמרו שחוששין א) לדבריו בזמן שאומר ב) "הריני נזיר מן הגרוגרות ומן הדבילה והרי הן עלי קרבן", כלומר ג) שאסורין עליו כקרבן, שיהיה נדור מלאכול מהן, אבל משום נזירות אין חוששין בו כל עיקר. גמ' ולדברי ב"ש אמאי הוי נזיר. בתמיה: "מכל אשר יעשה מגפן היין" אמר רחמנא דליהוי נזיר, אבל מגרוגרות ודבילה דלאו מגפן היין הוא, לא! ב"ש אית להו כר"מ דאמר אין אדם מוציא דבריו לבטלה (ג). "ערך ד) כלי עלי", אדם יודע שאין ערך ה) לכלי, וחייב בכל ו) דמי ערכו. אף ה"נ, כי אמר "הריני נזיר מן הגרוגרות", יודע הוא שאין נוזרין מן הגרוגרות, ואין מוציא דבריו לבטלה, ומקבל עליו נזירות גמורה. וב"ה. דאמרי: אינו נזיר – סבירא להו כרבי יוסי, דאמר במס' תמורה בפ' "כילד מערימין" (דף כה:) דבגמר דבריו אדם נתפס, וכיון דאמר בגמר דבריו "מן הגרוגרות ומן הדבילה" – תפוס לשון אחרון, ולא חיילא עליה כלל. וא"ת: הא אמר ר' יוסי דאף בגמר דבריו אדם נתפס, ומדקאמר "אף" ליהוי נזיר משום דתפוס לשון ראשון! הא ל"ק, דהיכא א"ר יוסי אף בגמר דבריו אדם נתפס – כגון שהיתה לו בהמת חולין ורוצה להמיר אותה על שתי בהמות קדשים שלפניו, אחת עולה ואחת שלמים, ואמר "זו תמורת עולה ותמורת שלמים", דכיון דאפשר לקיים דבריו הראשונים והאחרונים – תמכר ויביא בדמי חציה עולה ובדמי חציה שלמים – (ד) אמרינן דאף בגמר דבריו אדם נתפס, שכן היתה כוונתו מתחלה לכך לשם עולה ולשם שלמים, אלא שלא היה יכול להוציא את שניהם מפיו בבת אחת, ואמר בזו אחר זו. אבל גבי נזירות ליכא למימר הכי, הוה ליה האי נדר ופתחו עמו. שלא הזיר אלא מן הגרוגרות, והואיל דלא חייל עליה נזירות בגרוגרות – אין בדבריו כלום, ואינו נזיר כלל. ולב"ש נמי. כיון דהאי נדר פתחו עמו, (ה) אמאי הוי נזירות כלל? הא פתחו עמו, דאינו רוצה להיות נזיר אלא מן הגרוגרות, וכל היכא דפתחו עמו אפילו ר"מ מודה! אלא ב"ש סברי לה כר"מ. ז) ומש"ה כיון דאמר "הריני נזיר" הוה ליה נזיר ודאי, והאי דלבתר הכי אמר "מן הגרוגרות" – לאיתשולי הוא דקאתי, דקאמר: כשנזרתי לא נזרתי אלא מן הגרוגרות, ומיהו *אפ"ה מותר ביין. דב"ש סברי אין שאלה בטעות להקדש ולא לטעות בנזירות, דכהקדש דמי, כדכתיב "קדוש יהיה גדל פרע" (במדבר ו). וב"ה סברי. כיון דלא הזיר כשאר הנוזרין שאין נוזרין אלא מן היין – אין שום נזירות חל עליו, דאית להו כר"ש דתנן כו' ח) לבסוף קתני לה: (ו) ט) מתני' דקתני לב"ה דאפי' נדור לא הוי. *ב"ש דסברי נדור מן הגרוגרות ונזיר מן היין סברי להו כר"מ דאמר: אין אדם מוציא דבריו לבטלה, וכיון דאמר "הריני נזיר" – ה"ז נזיר, והוי נמי נדור מן הגרוגרות, דסברי לה כר' יהודה דאמר: י) שאוסרין עליו כקרבן. ומתני' קתני דב"ש סברי נזיר ותו לא. ובה"א נדור. מן הגרוגרות ודבילה, ואינו נזיר מן היין, משום דנדר ופתחו עמו הוא. ומתניתין קתני דבית הלל אומרים אינו נזיר, דבין לרבי יהודה בין לתנא קמא דידיה אליבא דבית הלל אינו נדור ואינו נזיר. לישנא אחרינא אמרי לה כו'. (ז) נדור ואינו נזיר. ותנא קמא דר' יהודה אמר דנזיר אליבא דב"ש. והיינו דלא כרבי נתן. אמר

"הֲרֵינִי *נָזִיר מִן הַגְּרוֹגְרוֹת וּמִן הַדְּבֵילָה", בש"א: נָזִיר, ובה"א: אאֵינוֹ נָזִיר. אָמַר רַבִּי יְהוּדָה: אַף כְּשֶׁאָמְרוּ ב"ש – לֹא אָמְרוּ אֶלָּא בְּאוֹמֵר "הֲרֵי הֵן עָלַי קָרְבָּן". § גמ' "הֲרֵינִי נָזִיר מִן הַגְּרוֹגְרוֹת וּמִן הַדְּבֵילָה", ב"ש אוֹמְרִים: נָזִיר. וְאַמַּאי? "מִכֹּל אֲשֶׁר יֵעָשֶׂה מִגֶּפֶן הַיַּיִן" (במדבר ו) אָמַר רַחֲמָנָא! ב"ש סָבְרִי לָהּ כר"מ, דְּאָמַר: *אֵין אָדָם מוֹצִיא דְּבָרָיו לְבַטָּלָה. וב"ה סָבְרִי לָהּ כְּרַבִּי *יוֹסֵי, דְּאָמַר: בִּגְמַר דְּבָרָיו אָדָם נִתְפָּס. וְהַאי *נֶדֶר וּפִתְחוֹ עִמּוֹ הוּא. (א) וּבֵית שַׁמַּאי נַמִי, נֶדֶר וּפִתְחוֹ עִמּוֹ הוּא! אֶלָּא, ב"ש סָבְרִי לָהּ כְּרַבִּי מֵאִיר, דְּאָמַר: אֵין אָדָם מוֹצִיא דְּבָרָיו לְבַטָּלָה. וְכֵיוָן דְּאָמַר "הֲרֵינִי נָזִיר" – הֲוָה לֵיהּ נָזִיר, כִּי קָאָמַר "מִן הַגְּרוֹגְרוֹת וּמִן הַדְּבֵילָה" – לְאִיתַּשּׁוּלֵי הוּא דְּקָאָתֵי. וב"ש לְטַעֲמַיְיהוּ, דְּאָמְרִי: *אֵין שְׁאֵלָה בְּהֶקְדֵּשׁ. וְכֵיוָן דְּאֵין שְׁאֵלָה בְּהֶקְדֵּשׁ – אֵין שְׁאֵלָה בִּנְזִירוּת. וּבֵית הִלֵּל סָבְרִי כר"ש, דִּתְנַן: *ור"ש פּוֹטֵר, שֶׁלֹּא הִתְנַדֵּב כְּדֶרֶךְ הַמִּתְנַדְּבִים.

מַתְנִי'

הריני נזיר מן הגרוגרות ומן הדבילה בש"א נזיר. כל דין נזירות עליו. ונהי דנחית לפרושי, ולא פירש מיולא מגפן היין. ובגמ' מפרש טעמא. בתוספתא (ריש פ"ב): כינויי כינויין, בש"א: נזיר, ובה"א: אינו נזיר. איזה כינויי כינויין? האומר "הריני נזיר מן הדבילה". ולמה קרי ליה כנויי, מה שייך דבילה בנזירות? וי"ל: דבירוש' קרי לדבילה תירוש. אמר ר' יהודה אף כשאמרו ב"ש לא אמרו אלא באומר הרי עלי קרבן. רבי יהודה פליג אתנא דמתניתין אליבא דב"ש, וקאמר דלא הוי נזיר לדין נזירות, כיון דלא נדר מאשר יוצא מגפן היין, אלא נדור הוי מן הגרוגרות ומן הדבילה, כאילו אמר "הרי הן עלי כקרבן". וא"ת: והא איהו "נזיר" קאמר, ואיך יהיה נזיר? וי"ל: ד"נזיר" לשון הפרשה, וכאילו אמר: הריני פרוש מן הגרוגרות. וא"ת: והא בנדרים (דף יג.) מוכח לרבי [יהודה] אמר "קרבן" – לא הוי נדר בקרבן, עד שיאמר "כקרבן" בכ"ף! וי"ל: דה"מ כשלא אמר "עלי", אלא "ככר זה קרבן", אבל כי אמר "ככר זה עלי קרבן" – א"צ לומר כ"ף. אין אדם מוציא דבריו לבטלה. נחלקו בערכין (דף כ. ע"ש) בהאומר "ערך כלי עלי" דאין ערכין לכלי, רבנן פטרי ליה מכלום, ור"מ פליג ואמר: אדם יודע שאין ערך לכלי, וגמר ואמר לשם דמים, ונותן דמי הכלי להקדש, לפי שאין אדם מוציא דבריו לבטלה. וה"נ אדם יודע שאין נזירות בגרוגרות, וגמר ואמר לשם נזירות יין. וב"ה סברי לה כר' יוסי, דאמר: בגמר דבריו אדם נתפס, והאי נדר ופתחו עמו הוא. דר' יוסי בהאומר "הרי זו תמורת עולה תמורת שלמים" – תרעה עד שתסתאב, ותמכר, וחצי דמיה לעולה, וחצי דמיה לשלמים. ה"נ, בגמר דבריו שאמר "גרוגרות", נתפס, וכיון שאין נזירות בגרוגרות – לא הוי נזיר. ואע"ג דבתחלה אמר "הריני נזיר" – חזר בתוך כדי דבור ואמר "מגרוגרות", ובגמר דבריו אדם נתפס. כאילו נדר ובתוך כדי דבור מצא פתח לו וחרטה, דכיון שנדרו ופתחו עמו – לא חל כלל. וא"ת: והאמר ר' יוסי בגמר דבריו אדם נתפס הוי פי' – אף בגמר דבריו אדם נתפס, והוי תמורת עולה ותמורת שלמים. וה"נ, נתפוס לשון ראשון נמי דקאמר "נזיר", ויהיה נזיר מיין *ונזיר מן הגרוגרות! וי"ל: דהכי מפורש בתמורה (דף כו.) היכא דדבריו סותרין זה את זה, וליכא למימר דסיפא לפרושי תחלת דבריו קאתי – הלכך חיילי ב' הלשונות לר' יוסי, והוי תמורת עולה ותמורת שלמים. אבל במתני' איכא למימר דסיפא לפרושי רישא, כלומר (כיון) האי דקאמר "נזיר" – לאו מיין קאמר, אלא מגרוגרות. והלכך גמר דבריו עיקר הן ליתפס בהן, ולא בתחילת דבריו. והכי מתיישב לי דלא תקשה מדר' יהודה אדר' יהודה. דר' יהודה אית ליה במתני' דנזיר הוי מגרוגרות ולא נזיר מיין, אפי' לב"ש, ואמאי? והא שמעינן ליה לרבי יהודה דפליג אדרבי יוסי בההיא דתמורה (ג"ז שם), וקאמר: תפוס לשון ראשון – ה"נ נתפוס לשון ראשון, וליהוי נזיר מיין! אלא ודאי דוקא בתמורה פליגי, דהדברים סותרין זה את זה, וליכא למימר דדיבור האחרון מפרש. אבל הכא, ודאי דאיכא למימר דלפרושי קאתי, י"ל דודאי דלפרש בא ולומר: לאו מיין נדרתי. וניחא נמי דלא קאמר דב"ש סברי כר' יהודה דאמר: תפוס לשון ראשון עיקר, להכי הוי נזיר מיין. אלא ודאי לא שייכא ההוא פלוגתא להכא. וא"ת: ואמאי קאמר ב"ה כר' יוסי? לימא דסברי ב"ה כרבנן דר"מ בערכין (דף כ.), דאמרי: אדם מוציא דבריו לבטלה! וי"ל: דלא ניחא ליה לאוקמי ההיא פלוגתא דר"מ ורבנן בפלוגתא דב"ש וב"ה, דא"כ ר"מ כב"ש. להכי קאמר ב"ה כר' יוסי, ומעתה אפילו א] דערכין יכול לסבור דב"ה דמתני' מטעמא דקאמר דבגמר דבריו אדם נתפס. וא"ת: ולר"מ מ"ש דבערך כלי מתחייב דמים מטעם דאין אדם מוציא דבריו לבטלה לעולם! וי"ל: דלא דמי, דהתם נהי דאין שייך ערך לכלי – דמים מיהא שייכא ביה, ואדם זה נתכוון ליתן להקדש מה שיוכל – הלכך נותן דמיו, וקרי להו "ערך" לדמי הכלי, משום דערך האדם נמי הוי דמים, להכי קרי דמי כלי "ערך". אבל גרוגרות לא שייך בהן לשון נזירות כלל, וע"כ הוציא דבריו לבטלה, וה"ק: הריני נזיר ולא מיין אלא מגרוגרות, וסיפא לפרושי תחילת דבריו קאתי, הלכך לאו כלום קאמר. לאיתשולי קאתי. לאו דוקא לאיתשולי, דהא לא בא לשאלה. אלא מתחרט וחוזר בו, כאדם שבא לשאול לחכ' על נדרו מחמת חרטה, שהחכם מוצא לו פתח וחרטה, והוי נדר טעות ובטל. אין שאלה לנזירות. דנזירות כהקדש, דכתיב "קדוש יהיה גדל פרע". וא"ת: תיפוק ליה ב] דאין בו חרטה! ותירץ (דשניהם) [דס"ל] דשני הכא דתוך כדי דיבור הוא, ואין צריך חרטה. וב"ש –*) דהקדש טעות הוי הקדש, ולהכי לב"ש לא מהני ביה שאלה. וה"נ לא מהני שאלה בנזיר, דאקרי קדושה, דכתיב "קדוש יהיה". וא"ת: ומה לו להאריך כל כך, ולחזור ולומר ב"ש כר"מ סבירא להו? כי פריך ליה מעיקרא: ולב"ש נדר ופתחו עמו הוא – לישני ליה לאלתר: ב"ש לטעמייהו דאין שאלה כו'! וי"ל: דסד"א דלא אמרינן ב"ש כר"מ ס"ל, וחזר בו משום האי קושיא שהקשה התלמוד, וא"כ שוב אין יכול לתרץ ולומר דקסבר דאין שאלה, דלא אמרינן אין שאלה אלא היכא דחל הקדש רגע אחד שוב אין מועיל בו שאלה, אבל הכא נדרו ופתחו עמו הוא ולא חל עליה נזירות אפילו רגע אחד. להכי חוזר ואומר: בית שמאי כרבי מאיר דאמר אין אדם מוציא דבריו לבטלה, והרי חל הנדר רגע אחד, וכי אמר "מגרוגרות" הוה ליה כבא לאישתולי **) (וכל שכן), דאין שאלה להקדש. ובית הלל כרבי שמעון דפוטר שלא התנדב כדרך הנודבים. לקמן מייתי פלוגתא, "הרי עלי מנחה מן השעורין" – יביא מן החיטין, ור"ש פוטר

*) גירסת א"מ לטעמייהו. **) גירסת א"מ וב"ש ס"ל.

א א מיי' פ"א מהלכות נזירות הלכה י:

פי' הרא"ש

הריני נזיר מן הגרוגרות בש"א ה"ז נזיר בגמ' מפרש טעמא אמר ר"י אף כשאמרו ב"ש לא אמרו אלא באומר (הריני לי) [הרי הן עלי] קרבן דלא נחלקו ב"ש וב"ה לענין נזיר דמודה ב"ש דלא הוי נזיר ולא נחלקו אלא באומר בלבי היה שיהיו הגרוגרות עלי קרבן ב"ש סברי דהוי נדור מן הגרוגרות וב"ה סברי דלא הוי נדור ות"ק סבר א) אפילו אם אמר בלבו היה הוי נזיר כיון שהוציא נזיר מפיו ונדור לא הוי אע"ג דאמר דלהא איכוין דדברים שבלב אינם דברים הואיל והוא משנה מה שהוציא מפיו ולב"ה לא הוי לא נזיר ולא נדור. ואמאי בני הישיבה היו תמיהים היאך הוי נזיר לב"ש הא כתי' מכל אשר יעשה מגפן היין: כר"מ דאמר אין אדם מוציא דבריו לבטלה בערכין פ' האומר משקלי עלי קא' ר"מ האומר ערך כלי זה עלי או ערך פחות מבן חדש נותן דמים ומפרש טעמיה משום דאין אדם מוציא דבריו לבטלה יש לנו לומר שטעה וכסבור היה שיש נזיר בכה"ג: כר' יוסי דאמר אף בגמר דבריו אדם נתפס גבי ה"ז תמורת עולה תמורת שלמים דקאמר ר' יוסי תרעה עד שתסתאב ויביא בדמיה חציה עולה וחציה שלמים דכיון דמתחלה היה בדעתו לומר שתיהן חייל שתיהן הכא נמי מתחלה היה דעתו לומר הריני נזיר מן הגרוגרות והוי נדר ופתחו עמו עם הנדר אמר פתח של היתר וגלה לנו שאין בדעתו לידור כלל כי אמר דברי' שאינן כי אין נזיר מן הגרוגרות: ולב"ש נדרו ופתחו עמו. דנהי דאית להו דאין אדם מוציא דבריו לבטלה מ"מ מה שהוציא מפיו מן הגרוגרות מאי קא עבדת ובמאי דיינת ליה דלא דמי לאומר ערך כלי ופחות מבן חדש עלי דהתם מתוך שאין אדם מוציא דבריו לבטלה מתרצינן לדיבוריה דערך דקאמר היינו דמים אבל הכא מן הגרוגרות דקאמר דיינינן (דמאס) [דסתר] לי' ומשני מתוך שאין אדם מוציא דבריו לבטלה מראשית דבריו דאמר הריני נזיר הוי נזיר ומה שאמר מן הגרוגרות דיינינן ליה בחזרה שרצה למצוא פתח שאלה לנדרו כאדם המתחרט על נדרו ובא לפני חכם ופותח בפתח של חרטה לשאל על נדרו גם זה נתחרט בתוך כדי דיבור ואמר דבר שהוא ניכר בזה שסותר מה שאמר הריני נזיר ולא אזלינן בתר סיפא דמילתי' דב"ש לטעמייהו דאמר לקמן [ברפ"ה] דהקדש בטעות הקדש דילפינן מתמורה הלכך לא שייך בה שאלה וה"ה חזרה וכן נמי בנזיר דכתיב ביה קדוש יהיה ואף בתוך כדי דיבור אין יכול לחזור בו הלכך הוי נזיר: וב"ה סברי כר"ש גבי הרי עלי מנחה מן השעורים דקאמר פוטר שלא התנדב כדרך המתנדבים הכא נמי לא

א) נראה דל"ל ות"ק סבר ואפילו אם אמר דבלבו היה לקרבן מ"מ הוי נזיר כיון שהוציא וכו'.

נוסחת הריב"ן

א) בדבריו: ב) (הריני כו' הדבילה) ליתא בכ"י: ג) שאוסרן: ד) זה: ה) לזה: ו) (דמי) ליתא בכ"י: ז) ומיהו: ח) ובסוף: ט) (מתניתין כו' לא הוי) ליתא בכ"י: י) שאוסרן עליו כקרבן הס"ד ואח"כ מה"ד מתניתין קתני לב"ה דאפי' נדור לא הוי ולישנא אחרינא אמרי לה ר' נתן אומר כו' והס"ד ואח"כ מ"ה אמר הרי עלי והשאר ליתא:

נ"ל שאלה

שייך לע"ב

הגהות הב"ח

(א) גמ' ולבית שמאי נמי: (ב) רש"י ד"ה א"ר יהודה וכו' שום נזירות כלל בזמן שאומר הריני נזיר מן הגרוגרות ומן הדבילה אלא שאמרו שחוששין לדבריו לפי מה שאומר הרי הן עלי קרבן נ"ב פי' שאומר עתה בלבי היה אז שיהיו הגרוגרות עלי קרבן: (ג) ד"ה ב"ש אית להו וכו' דבריו לבטלה דהאומר ערך זה עלי וכו' וחייב בכל דמיו אף ה"נ נ"ב ועי' ערכין דף ה ע"א ת"ר המעריך פחות מבן חדש ר"מ אומר נותן דמיו וחכ"א לא אמר כלום במאי קמפלגי ר"מ סבר אין אדם מוציא דבריו לבטלה וכו' ופליגי נמי התם בכלי וע"ש עוד דף כ ע"א: (ד) ד"ה וב"ה דאמרי וכו' חציה שלמים התם אמרינן וכו' דליכא למימר: (ה) ד"ה ולב"ש נמי וכו' עמו הוא אמאי: (ו) ד"ה וב"ה סברי וכו' קתני לה הס"ד ואח"כ מ"ה ב"ש סברי נדור: (ז) ד"ה לישנא אחרינא אמרי לה כו' ב"ש סברי נדור ואינו נזיר וכו' והיינו דלא כר' נתן ומתניתין קתני לב"ה אינו נזיר אבל נדור מיהא הוה ולישנא אחרינא

הגהות מהר"ב רנשבורג א] תוס' ד"ה אין אדם מוציא דבריו לבטלה וכו' וי"ל דלא ניחא ליה וכו' ומעתה אפילו ר"מ דערכין יכול לסבור כב"ה דמתני' מטעמא דקאמר וכו' כצ"ל: ב] ד"ה אין שאלה לנזירות וכו' וא"ת תיפוק ליה דאין בו חרטה ותירץ דשניהם ס"ל נמחק מתיבת דאין עד תיבת ס"ל וכ"ב דאין פותחין בחרטה וי"ל דאיכא מ"ד דפותחין ותירץ דשניהם ועוד י"ל דשאני הכא דתוך כדי דבור הוא ואין צריך חרטה כצ"ל ועי' א"מ שהגיה כך על פי התוס' דמנחות דף קג ע"א ועוד הגיה שם בדרך אחר אבל זה נראה בעיני:

ב א מיי' פ"א מהלכות נזירות הלכה י ועיין שם בכ"מ:
ג ב ג מיי' פי"ז מהלכות מעשה קרבנות הלכה ט וע"ש בכ"מ:

מַתְנִי' דְּלָא כִּי הַאי תַּנָּא. דְּתַנְיָא, רַבִּי נָתָן אוֹמֵר: בש"א: נָדוּר וְנָזִיר, וב"ה אוֹמְרִים: אנָדוּר וְאֵין נָזִיר. ב"ש סָבְרִי לָהּ כר"מ וכר' יְהוּדָה, וב"ה סָבְרִי לָהּ כְּרַבִּי יוֹסֵי. לִישָּׁנָא אַחֲרִינָא אָמְרִי לָהּ: רַבִּי נָתָן אוֹמֵר, בֵּית שַׁמַּאי אוֹמְרִים: נָדוּר וְאֵינוֹ נָזִיר, וּבֵית הִלֵּל אוֹמְרִים: לֹא נָדוּר וְלֹא נָזִיר. ב"ש – כְּרַבִּי יְהוּדָה, וב"ה – כר"ש. תְּנַן הָתָם: *הָאוֹמֵר "הֲרֵי עָלַי מִנְחָה לְהָבִיא מִן הַשְּׂעוֹרִים" – יָבִיא מִן הַחִטִּים, "קֶמַח" – יָבִיא סוֹלֶת, "שֶׁלֹּא בְּשֶׁמֶן וּלְבוֹנָה" – יְבִיאֶנָּה בְּשֶׁמֶן וּלְבוֹנָה, "חֲצִי עִשָּׂרוֹן" – יָבִיא עִשָּׂרוֹן שָׁלֵם, "עִשָּׂרוֹן וּמֶחֱצָה" – יָבִיא שְׁנַיִם. ר"ש בפּוֹטֵר, שֶׁלֹּא הִתְנַדֵּב כְּדֶרֶךְ הַמִּתְנַדְּבִים. מַאן תַּנָּא, דְּכִי אָמַר "הֲרֵי עָלַי מִנְחָה מִן הַשְּׂעוֹרִים" – מֵבִיא מִן הַחִטִּים? *אָמַר חִזְקִיָּה: בְּמַחֲלוֹקֶת שְׁנוּיָה, °וב"ש הִיא. לָאו אָמְרִי ב"ש כִּי אָמַר "מִן הַגְּרוֹגָרוֹת וּמִן הַדְּבֵילָה" הָוֵי נָזִיר – הָכִי נַמִי, כִּי אָמַר "מִן הַשְּׂעוֹרִין" – מֵבִיא מִן הַחִיטִּים. וְרַבִּי יוֹחָנָן אָמַר: אֲפִילּוּ תֵּימָא דִּבְרֵי הַכֹּל, גבְּאוֹמֵר "אִילּוּ הָיִיתִי יוֹדֵעַ שֶׁאֵין נוֹדְרִין כָּךְ – לֹא נָדַרְתִּי כָּךְ אֶלָּא כָּךְ". אָמַר חִזְקִיָּה: לֹא שָׁנוּ אֶלָּא שֶׁאָמַר "מִן הַשְּׂעוֹרִים", אֲבָל אָמַר "מִן הָעֲדָשִׁים" – לָא מַיְיתֵי וְלָא כְּלוּם. מִכְּדֵי חִזְקִיָּה כְּמַאן מוֹקִים לָהּ לְמַתְנִי' – כְּבֵית שַׁמַּאי, וְהָא עֲדָשִׁים לְגַבֵּי מִנְחָה כִּגְרוֹגָרוֹת לְגַבֵּי נָזִיר דָּמוּ, וְקָאָמְרִי בֵּית שַׁמַּאי הָוֵי נָזִיר! – הֲדַר בֵּיהּ חִזְקִיָּה. וְאַמַּאי הֲדַר בֵּיהּ? אָמַר רָבָא: מַתְנִי' קְשִׁיתֵיהּ, מַאי אִירְיָא דְּתָנֵי "מִן הַשְּׂעוֹרִים"? לִיתְנֵי "מִן הָעֲדָשִׁים"! אֶלָּא סָבַר חִזְקִיָּה: כִּי קָאָמְרִי ב"ש הָתָם – כְּרַבִּי יְהוּדָה. וְרַבִּי יוֹחָנָן אָמַר: אֲפִילּוּ מִן הָעֲדָשִׁים. וְהָא רַבִּי יוֹחָנָן הוּא דְּאָמַר: בְּאוֹמֵר "אִילּוּ הָיִיתִי יוֹדֵעַ שֶׁאֵין נוֹדְרִין כָּךְ – לֹא נָדַרְתִּי כָּךְ אֶלָּא כָּךְ"! לְדְבָרָיו דְּחִזְקִיָּה הוּא דְּקָאָמַר: אַתְּ מ"ט קָא הָדְרַתְּ בָּךְ – מִשּׁוּם דְּלָא קָתָנֵי "מִן הָעֲדָשִׁים", דִּלְמָא לָא מִיבַּעְיָא קָאָמַר; לָא מִיבַּעְיָ' כִּי אָמַר "מֵעֲדָשִׁים" – דְּמַיְיתֵי מִנְחָה מַעַלְיְיתָא, דְּאִיכָּא לְמֵימַר מִיהֲדַר הוּא דַּהֲדַר בֵּיהּ, וּתְפוֹס לָשׁוֹן רִאשׁוֹן. אֶלָּא (א) כִּי אֲמַר "מִן הַשְּׂעוֹרִין" וַדַּאי דְּהָכִי קָאָמַר: אִי קָדְשָׁה כְּמִנְחַת הָעוֹמֶר, אוֹ

פוטר. וא"ת: למה הוצרך לומר ב"ה כר"ש? לימא ב"ה לטעמייהו, דאמרי: יש שאלה להקדש! וי"ל: משום דאכתי לב"ה, נהי דנזיר מיין לא הוי – נדור מיהא ליהוי מן הגרוגרות. להכי קאמר כר"ש, דפוטר לגמרי, שלא התנדב כדרך המתנדבים. שאם בא להיות נדור מן הגרוגרות הל"ל בלשון קונס, כדרך הנודרים.

ב"ש סברי כר"מ. דאמר: אין אדם מוציא דבריו לבטלה, להכי הוי [נזיר. וכרבי יהודה] דמתני', דאמר: נדור הוי. וב"ה סברי כר' יהודה דמתני', דנדור מיהא הוי, ודלא כר"ש דפטר לגמרי. **ב"ש** כר' יהודה. ונדור מיהא הוי. וב"ה כר"ש, ואפילו נדור לא הוי. **יביא** מן החיטין. שאין מנחה באה שעורין אלא א] דחוטא ומנחת קנאות. **יביא** עשרון שלם. שאין מנחה פחותה מעשרון. והוי טעמא דכולהו. **לאו** אמרי ב"ש מן הגרוגרות ומן הדבילה הוי נזיר. אע"ג דגרוגרות לא שייכי לנזירות כלל, מטעמא דפרישית לעיל, משום דאין אדם מוציא דבריו לבטלה. ה"נ מן השעורין, אע"ג דלא שייכי שעורין למנחה – יביא חיטין, דאין אדם מוציא דבריו לבטלה.

באומר אילו הייתי יודע כו'. בבי"ת גרסי': באומר. כלו', באומר בפירוש: אילו הייתי יודע שאין נודרים שעורין כו', אבל טעיתי לומר דנודרין שעורין כמנחת חוטא ב] וקנאות, ולולי זה הייתי נודר חטים. להכי מייתי חטין. וכן בקמח – טעה במנחת קנאות ג] ובשמן ולבונה. וכן בחצי עשרון – לא ידע שצריך להביא עשרון שלם. **לא** שנו אלא מן השעורים. דמצי למיתלי בטעות, כיון דאיכא אוחרי דהויין משעורים. אבל מן עדשים – לא מייתי כלום, דליכא למיתלי בטעותא, דליכא של [עדשים].

מכדי חזקיה כמאן מוקי לה מתני'. דמנחות – כב"ש כו', ואומרים ב"ש דהוי נזיר מטעם דאמרי' אין אדם מוציא דבריו לבטלה, א"כ אפי' עדשים נייתו חיטין! **הדר** ביה חזקיה מההיא. פי': ממאי דאוקי לה מתני' דמנחות כב"ש, ומוקי לה כרבי יוחנן ובאומר. **מתניתין** קשיתיה כו' ליתני מן העדשים. כלומר, אי מתניתין כבית שמאי, ומטעם דאין אדם מוציא דבריו לבטלה – ליתני עדשים, דהוי רבותא טפי.

*אלא התם כצ"ל

***התם** משום טעותא הוא ובאומר אילו הייתי יודע. הלכך, כי אמר שעורים – איכא למימר דטעה, דיש מנחה באה שעורים. אבל בעדשים ליכא למיטעי, דאין מנחה באה מהם כלל. ולא גרס הכא בספר: קסבר חזקיה בית שמאי כר' יהודה. ובמנחות פ' "המנחות והנסכים" (דף קג.) לא גרסינן ליה. והתם גרים: אלא ש"מ משום דהוא בשעורים טעי, בעדשים לא טעי. ורבי יוחנן אמר [כו']. ד] דאיכא למימר מיהדר הוא דקמיהדר ביה, דדיבור האחרון סותר הראשון. דכשאמר "מנחה" – משמע מנחה כשרה מסולת, וכי הדר אמר "מעדשים" – הדר מדיבור ראשון, ותפוס לשון ראשון. **אלא** כי קאמר מן השעורין, ה"ק: לא בא לסתור דבריו ראשונים דאמר "הרי עלי מנחה", [אלא] לפרש ולומר (כיון) שאמר מן השעורין ואפשר ליקדוש *) במנחת העומר ובמנחת סוטה – תיקדוש, ואי לא אפשר לה ליקדוש במנחה – לא יתחייב במנחה אחרת, קמשמע לן דמייתי חיטין. ולעולם כבית שמאי, ומשום דאין אדם מוציא דבריו לבטלה.

פרה

*) נ"ל כמנחת העומר וכמנחת

אָמַר הֲרֵי עָלַי מִנְחָה לְהָבִיא קֶמַח מֵבִיא סוֹלֶת. אוֹ שֶׁאָמַר "הֲרֵי עָלַי מִנְחָה בְּלֹא שֶׁמֶן וּלְבוֹנָה" כו'. **מִי לָא אָמְרֵי ב"ש**. דְּאע"ג דְּלָא קַבֵּיל לִהְיוֹת נָזִיר אֶלָּא מִן הַגְּרוֹגָרוֹת הָוֵי נָזִיר מִן הַיַּיִן – הָכָא נַמִי כִּי אָמַר "מִן הַשְּׂעוֹרִין" מַיְיתִי לָהּ מִסּוֹלֶת שֶׁל חִיטִּים כְּהִלְכָתָהּ. וְר' יוֹחָנָן **אָמַר אֲפִילּוּ תֵּימָא** דִּבְרֵי הַכֹּל. דַּאֲפִי' ב"ה מוֹדוּ בְּהָא דְּיָבִיא מִן הַחִיטִּים אע"פ שֶׁלֹּא הִתְנַדֵּב אֶלָּא מִן הַשְּׂעוֹרִים, כְּגוֹן שֶׁאָמַר: לְכָךְ הִתְנַדַּבְתִּי שְׂעוֹרִין – שֶׁהָיִיתִי סָבוּר שֶׁמְּבִיאִין מִנְחָה מֵהֶן, אֲבָל אִילּוּ הָיִיתִי יוֹדֵעַ שֶׁאֵין נוֹדְרִין אֶלָּא חִיטִּין לֹא נָדַרְתִּי שְׂעוֹרִין. הִלְכָּךְ א) (ב) גָּמַר בְּנַפְשֵׁיהּ לְאֵיתוּיֵי מִידֵי דְּבַר חִיּוּבָא, לְהָכִי יָבִיא מִן הַחִיטִּין. **אֶלָּא** בִּזְמַן שֶׁהִתְנַדֵּב מִן הַשְּׂעוֹרִין. דְּהָתָם הוּא הוֹאִיל וּמִנְחַת סוֹטָה וּמִנְחַת הָעוֹמֶר מִן הַשְּׂעוֹרִים קַמַּיְיתִי לְהוּ, דְּמִמִּינוֹ קָרֵיב לְגַבֵּי מִזְבֵּחַ, לְהָכִי הוּא דְּאָמַר דְּחָל עֲלֵיהּ נִדְבַת מִנְחָה וְיָבִיא מִן הַחִיטִּים. **אֲבָל אָמַר** מִנְחָה מִן הָעֲדָשִׁים. שֶׁאֵין בְּמִינוֹ קָרֵיב לְגַבֵּי מִזְבֵּחַ – לָא מַיְיתִי וְלָא כְּלוּם. מִכְּדֵי חִזְקִיָּה כְּמַאן מוֹקֵי לָהּ לְמַתְנִיתִין. דִּמְנָחוֹת, כְּבֵית שַׁמַּאי. **וְהָא** עֲדָשִׁים לְגַבֵּי מִזְבֵּחַ כִּגְרוֹגָרוֹת לְגַבֵּי נָזִיר דָּמוּ. וְכִי הֵיכִי דְּהָתָם אָמְרֵי בֵּית שַׁמַּאי דְּהָוֵי נָזִיר – הָכָא נַמִי כִּי אָמַר "מִן הָעֲדָשִׁים" יָבִיא מִן הַחִיטִּין. הֲדַר בֵּיהּ חִזְקִיָּה. דְּאָמַר לְעֵיל: ב"ש הִיא דְּלָא אָמְרֵי ב"ש מִן הַגְּרוֹגָרוֹת הָוֵי נָזִיר. ב) אֶלָּא טַעְמָא דְּמוֹקֵי לָהּ כְּב"ש – דְּסָבַר לָהּ כְּרַבִּי נָתָן כְּלִישָּׁנָא בַּתְרָא, דְּאִית לְהוּ לְב"ש דְּנָדוּר וְאֵינוֹ נָזִיר, כְּר' יְהוּדָה דְּאָמַר: בְּאוֹמֵר "הֲרֵי הֵן עָלַי כְּקָרְבָּן", דִּגְרוֹגְרוֹת וּדְבֵילָה כּוּלְּהוּ בְּנֵי נֶדֶר נִינְהוּ. וְכִי הֵיכִי דִּלְהַלָּן אָמְרֵי ב"ש דְּהָוֵי נָדוּר מִשּׁוּם דִּבְנֵי נֶדֶר נִינְהוּ – הָכָא נַמִי כִּי אָמַר "מִן הַשְּׂעוֹרִין", הוֹאִיל דִּבְנֵי הַקְרָבָה נִינְהוּ בְּמִנְחַת הָעוֹמֶר וּבְמִנְחַת סוֹטָה – לְהָכִי הוּא דְּאָמְרִינַן דְּמֵבִיא מִן הַחִיטִּין. **וְאַמַּאי** הֲדַר בֵּיהּ. חִזְקִיָּה מֵהַהִיא? לוֹקְמָא כִּמְעִיקְּרָא כְּת"ק, דְּאָמַר: הָאוֹמֵר "מִן הַגְּרוֹגָרוֹת" הָוֵי נָזִיר גָּמוּר, אע"ג דְּנָזִיר אֵין אָסוּר בִּגְרוֹגָרוֹת, וְלוֹקְמָא לְמַתְנִיתִין דִּמְנָחוֹת בְּאוֹמֵר "הֲרֵי עָלַי עֲדָשִׁים" (ג) מֵבִיא מִן הַחִיטִּין, אע"ג דַּעֲדָשִׁים אֵינָן רְאוּיִם לְגַבֵּי מִזְבֵּחַ – מִידֵי דְּהָוֵי אַגְּרוֹגָרוֹת לְגַבֵּי נָזִיר דְּהָוֵי נָזִיר גָּמוּר! **מַתְנִיתִין**. דִּמְנָחוֹת קְשִׁיתֵיהּ. (ד) אִם אִיתָא דְּלֵית לְהוּ לְב"ש נָדוּר וְאֵינוֹ נָזִיר, דְּלָא סְבִירָא לְהוּ כְּר' יְהוּדָה דְּאָמַר בְּאוֹמֵר "הֲרֵי הֵן עָלַי קָרְבָּן" דִּגְרוֹגָרוֹת וּדְבֵילָה בְּנֵי נֶדֶר נִינְהוּ, אֶלָּא נָזִיר הָוֵי, וְכִי הֵיכִי דִּלְהַלָּן אָמְרֵי ב"ש דְּכִי אָמַר "הֲרֵינִי נָזִיר מִן הַגְּרוֹגָרוֹת" הָוֵי נָזִיר מִן הַיַּיִן, גַּבֵּי מְנָחוֹת מַאי אִירְיָא דְּאָמַר "מִן הַשְּׂעוֹרִין" דְּהָוֵי דָּבָר הָרָאוּי לְגַבֵּי מִזְבֵּחַ? לִיתְנֵי "מִן הָעֲדָשִׁים", דְּהָא עֲדָשִׁים לְגַבֵּי מִזְבֵּחַ כִּגְרוֹגָרוֹת לְגַבֵּי נָזִיר דָּמֵי! אֶלָּא מַתְנִי' דִּמְנָחוֹת כְּב"ש וְלָא תָּנֵי בָּהּ "מִן הָעֲדָשִׁים", אַלְמָא דְּלָא הָוֵי טַעְמָא דְּיָבִיא מִן הַחִיטִּין אֶלָּא מִשּׁוּם דְּהִתְנַדֵּב מִן הַשְּׂעוֹרִין דִּבְנֵי הַקְרָבָה נִינְהוּ – וּלְכַוָּונָתֵהּ נַמִי גַּבֵּי נָזִיר כִּי אָמַר "הֲרֵינִי נָזִיר מִן הַגְּרוֹגָרוֹת" לָא הָוֵי נָזִיר אֶלָּא נָדוּר מִשּׁוּם דִּבְנֵי נֶדֶר נִינְהוּ. ג) לְב"ש אִית לְהוּ ד) כְּר' יְהוּדָה, וּמַתְנִי' דִּמְנָחוֹת כְּב"ש וְלָא כְּב"ה כְּלָל (כלל), דְּאִי כְּב"ה הָא אָמְרֵי דַּאֲפִילּוּ נָדוּר לָא הָוֵי, מִשּׁוּם דִּבְלָשׁוֹן נְזִירוּת קָא נָדַר. הָכָא נַמִי כִּי אָמַר "מִן הַשְּׂעוֹרִים" לָא יָבִיא מִן הַחִיטִּין, שֶׁלֹּא הִתְנַדֵּב כְּדֶרֶךְ הַמִּתְנַדְּבִין. וְר' יוֹחָנָן **אָמַר אֲפִילּוּ** מִן הָעֲדָשִׁים. יָבִיא מִן הַחִטִּין. **וְהָא א"ר** יוֹחָנָן כו'. וְכִדְמוֹקִים לָהּ בִּכְגוֹן דְּקָא טָעֵי. אַלְמָא דִּבְמִידֵי דְּטָעֵי בָּהּ, כְּגוֹן שְׂעוֹרִין, מִשּׁוּם דִּבְנֵי הַקְרָבָה נִינְהוּ, (ה) ה) [קָא מוֹקֵי] מַתְנִי' דִּמְנָחוֹת, אֲבָל לָא בַּעֲדָשִׁים. דְּאע"ג דְּאָמַר "אִילּוּ הָיִיתִי יוֹדֵעַ שֶׁאֵין נוֹדְרִין כָּךְ" לָא מַשְׁגְּחִינַן בֵּיהּ, דִּסְתָמָא דְּמִילְּתָא דִּבְשְׂעוֹרִין הוּא דְּקָא טָעֵי אֲבָל לָא בַּעֲדָשִׁים. **לְדִבְרָיו** דְּחִזְקִיָּה. ו) קא"ל ר' יוֹחָנָן וְהָכִי קא"ל: מ"ט הָדְרַתְּ בָּךְ – מִשּׁוּם דְּלָא קָתָנֵי בֵּיהּ עֲדָשִׁים. **דִּלְמָא לָא מִיבַּעְיָא קָאָמַר**. (ו) דְּלָא תֵּימָא דְּכִי אָמַר "מִן הָעֲדָשִׁים" דְּמַיְיתִי מִנְחָה מַעַלְיְיתָא, מִשּׁוּם דְּאִיכָּא לְמֵימַר דְּכִי אָמַר "הֲרֵי עָלַי מִנְחָה" מִנְחָה מַעַלְיְיתָא קַבֵּיל עִילָּוֵיהּ, וְהָא דַּאֲמַר בָּתַר הָכִי "מִן הָעֲדָשִׁים" – מִשּׁוּם דְּקָא בָּעֵי לְמֵיהְדַּר בֵּיהּ קָאָמַר, דְּמֵידַע יָדַע דְּמִן הָעֲדָשִׁים אֵין מְבִיאִים כְּלוּם, וַהֲרֵי לִפְטוֹר עַצְמוֹ קָאָמַר. וּתְפוֹס לָשׁוֹן רִאשׁוֹן, וְיָבִיא מִן הַחִיטִּין: (ז) **אֶלָּא כִּי אֲמַר** מִן הַשְּׂעוֹרִין. וַדַּאי דְּלֵית לָךְ לְמֵימַר הָכִי דְּהוֹאִיל וּבְמִינוֹ קָרֵיבִין דְּלְהַקְרִיב קָאָמַר, וְהָכִי קָאָמַר: אִם אֶפְשָׁר דְּקָדְשָׁה כְּמִנְחַת הָעוֹמֶר וּכְמִנְחַת

מנחות קג.

[עס כל הסוגיא ע"ש]

פי' הרא"ש

לא נדר כדרך הנודרים שאין נזיר מן הגרוגרות: בש"א נדור ונזיר פי' נדור או נזיר אם אמר לא היה בלבי לנזיר' אלא שיהו עלי קרבן הוי נדור ואם לא אמר כלום הוי נזיר דסבר כר"מ וכר' יהודה וב"ה סברי כרבי יהודה דמתיר אליבא דב"ש והיינו דלא כת"ק ודלא כר' יהודה: קמח יביא סולת קמח שאינו מנופה יביא סולת מנופה. יביא שמן ולבונה שאין מנחת נדבה בא בלא שמן ולבונה: חצי עשרון יביא עשרון שאין מנחה בא פחות מעשרון חוץ ממנחת חביתין: באומר אילו הייתי יודע שאין נודרים כך וכו' ואיכא למימר שטעה לפי שיש מנחה באה שעורים מנחת העומר ומנחת קנאות אבל במתני' במאי איכא למטעי דלא שייך כלל גרוגרות לנזיר: אבל אמר מן העדשים לא אמר כלום דבהא לא טעי איניש דאין מנחה באה עדשים: הדר ביה חזקיה לגבי ר' יוחנן ה"ג לתני מן העדשים ול"ג קסבר חזקיה ב"ש כר' יהודה ובמנחות פ' המנחות ל"ג ליה והכי גרים התם אלא ש"מ משום דטעי הוא בשעורים טעי בעדשים לא טעי ויש ליישב גירסת הספרים דגרסי אלא קסבר חזקיה כר' יהודה ומוקי למתני' כר"ש והכי פי' הדר ביה חזקיה ממאי דאוקי מתני' כב"ש אליבא דת"ק דאמר הוי נזיר דא"כ אפי' מן העדשים נמי: אלא סבר כר' יהודה דאמר א) פליגי וכי היכי דמן הגרוגרות ומן הדבילה הוי נדור ומפרשי' דבעי למימר שיהא מופרש מהן משום דשייך בהו איסור נדר ה"ה נמי הרי עלי מנחה מן השעורים יביא חטים כיון דיש מנחה דבאה שעורי' אבל אמר מן העדשים לאו כלום קאמר דאין מנחה באה עדשים אבל לב"ה כי היכי דמן הגרוגרות לא הוי נדור ה"ה מן השעורים לא יביא חיטים והא דר' יוחנן הוא דאמר באומר אילו הייתי יודע וכו' ובעדשים לא טעו אינשי כי היכי דלב"ה מן הגורגרות לא הוי נדור ונזיר אפילו אי אמר אילו הייתי יודע וכו': לא מיבעיא מן העדשים דמייתי מנחה מעלייתא דליכא למימר שהיה דעתו לומר מתחלה מן העדשים אלא ודאי מתחלה נתכוון לומר מנחה מעלייתא והדר קא הדר ביה: א) נ"ל דאמר דכאומר הרי הן עלי קרבן פליגי:

נוסחת הריב"ן

א) הלכך הואיל דגמר: ב) הוי נזיר דלית ליה לחזקיה האי סברא דהוי נזיר אלא טעמא כו': ג) דב"ש: ד) דרבי יהודה: ה) קאמר למתניתין: ו) קאמר:

הגהות הב"ח

אחרינא אמרי לה ר' נתן אומר כו' דאפילו נדור לא הוי הס"ד ואח"כ מ"ה אמר הרי עלי: (א) גמ' ותפוס לשון ראשון אלא אפי' כי אמר מן השעורין אימא ודאי דהכי קאמר: (ב) רש"י ד"ה ור' יוחנן וכו' הלכך כיון דגמר נפשיה: (ג) ד"ה ואמאי הדר וכו' דמביא מן החיטין: (ד) ד"ה מתני' וכו' דאם איתא וכו' גבי מנחות נמי כי אמר מן העדשים מייתי מן החיטים מאי איריא דתני מן השעורין דהוי דבר וכו' דבני נדר נינהו לב"ש דאית להו: (ה) ד"ה והא אמר וכו' דבני הקרבה נינהו קתני למתניתין: (ו) ד"ה דלמא לא מיבעיא קאמר דלא מיבעיא כי אמר: (ז) ד"ה אלא אפילו כי אמר מן השעורין דלית לך למימר הכי הואיל ובמינו קריבין ודאי להקריב כצ"ל והד"א עם ד"ה וכמנחת סוטה:

גליון הש"ס

גמ' וב"ש היא. קשה לי הא טעמא דב"ש דאין שאלה בהקדש [illegible]

הגהות מהר"ב רנשבורג א] תוס' ד"ה יביא מן החטין וכו' אלא לחוטא. מלת לחוטא נמחק וכ"ב זה טעות דמנחת חוטא ג"כ באה מן החטין דוקא אלא כצ"ל אלא דעומר ומנחת קנאות או צ"ל אלא דסוטה ומנחת עומר. אורח מישור: ב] ד"ה באומר [illegible] ג] בא"ד וכן בקמח טעה במנחת קנאות ובשמן ולבונה טעה במנחת חוטא [illegible] ד] ד"ה התם משום טעותא הוא וכו' ור' יוחנן אמר וכו' נ"ב כאן הס"ד ואח"כ מה"ד דאיכא:

וּכְמִנְחַת סוֹטָה – תִּקְדּוֹשׁ, וּמַיְיתִינַן לָהּ מִן הַשְּׂעוֹרִין, וְאִי לָא – לָא מַיְיתִינַן כְּלָל. קמ"ל. דְּאַפ"ה יָבִיא מִן הַחִטִּין. וּלְעוֹלָם לָא מָצֵית לְמֵידַק מַתְנִי' דְּכִי אָמַר "מִן הָעֲדָשִׁים" לָא מַיְיתִי וְלָא כְלוּם. **מתני'** א) אָמְרָה פָּרָה. בַּגְּמָרָא מְתָרְצִינַן: כְּגוֹן שֶׁהָיְתָה פָּרָה רְבוּצָה לְפָנָיו וְאָמַר "כִּמְדוּמֶּה לִי כִּסְבוּרָה פָּרָה ב) שֶׁאֵינָהּ עוֹמֶדֶת לְעוֹלָם ע"י אָדָם, הֲרֵינִי נָזִיר מִמֶּנָּה מִבְּשָׂרָהּ אִם ג) (ג) נִתְקַיֵּים מַחֲשַׁבְתָּהּ שֶׁתְּהֵא עוֹמֶדֶת מֵאֵלֶיהָ, אֶלָּא אֲנִי אֵלֵךְ וְאַעֲמִידֶנָּה". ד) ב"ש לְשִׁיטָתָן דְּאָמְרִי כִּי אָמַר "מִן הַגְּרוֹגָרוֹת" הָוֵי נָזִיר, הָכָא נַמִּי כִּי אָמַר "הֲרֵינִי נָזִיר" הָוֵי נָזִיר, וְכִי אָמַר "מִבְּשָׂרָהּ" לְאִיתְּשׁוּלֵי קָאָתֵי, וְאֵין שְׁאֵלָה בְּנָזִיר. וּב"ה אָמְרִי: ה) אִי אָמַר "מִבְּשָׂרָהּ" – כִּגְרוֹגָרוֹת דָּמֵי, וְלָא הָוֵי נָזִיר. וּלְגַבֵּי דֶּלֶת – כְּגוֹן שֶׁהָיָה דֶּלֶת נָעוּל לְפָנָיו וְאָמַר "כִּמְדוּמֶּה אֲנִי שֶׁסָּבוּר הַדֶּלֶת הַזֶּה שֶׁאֵין נִפְתָּח ע"י אָדָם, הֲרֵינִי נָזִיר מִנְּכָסָיו אִם תִּתְקַיֵּים מַחֲשַׁבְתּוֹ שֶׁיִּפָּתַח מֵאֵלָיו", וְנִפְתַּח מֵאֵלָיו. וּב"ש הָלְכוּ לְשִׁיטָתָן דְּכִי אָמַר "הֲרֵינִי נָזִיר" הָוֵי נָזִיר, דְּאֵין אָדָם מוֹצִיא דְּבָרָיו לְבַטָּלָה, וְכִי אָמַר "מִנְּכָסָיו" לְאִיתְּשׁוּלֵי הוּא דְּאָתֵי, וְאֵין שְׁאֵלָה בְּנָזִיר. א"ר יְהוּדָה. לֹא אָמְרוּ ב"ש שֶׁיְּהֵא נָזִיר [כְּלָל, שֶׁהֵן] לֹא דִּבְּרוּ אֶלָּא לְעִנְיַן נֶדֶר, שֶׁאִם אָמַר "הֲרֵינִי ו) נָדוּר מִבְּשָׂרָהּ וַהֲרֵי פָּרָה זוֹ עָלַי קָרְבָּן אִם עוֹמֶדֶת הִיא מֵאֵלֶיהָ" (ג ז) וְעוֹמֶדֶת מֵאֵלֶיהָ, דְּהָוֵי נָדוּר הֵימֶנָּה וְאֵינוֹ נָזִיר. **גמ'** כִּסְבוּרָה פָּרָה זוֹ. הַיְינוּ דְּקָתָנֵי "אָמְרָה פָּרָה", שֶׁכֵּן מָצִינוּ (ד) מֵהַמַּחֲשָׁבָה ח) שֶׁהוֹצִיא הַכָּתוּב בִּלְשׁוֹן אֲמִירָה, כְּגוֹן "וְדוֹבֵר אֱמֶת בִּלְבָבוֹ" (תהלים טו) "וַיֹּאמֶר עֵשָׂו בְּלִבּוֹ" (בראשית כז) ט). הֲרֵינִי נְזִירָה. ה"א יְתֵירָה מַשְׁמַע: הֵימֶנָּה. הָא אֲמָרוּהָ ב"ש חֲדָא זִימְנָא. י) דְּאִם אָמַר "הֲרֵינִי נָזִיר מִן הַגְּרוֹגָרוֹת" דְּהָוֵי נָזִיר, וה"ה נַמִּי לְכִי אָמַר "הֲרֵינִי נָזִיר מִבְּשָׂרָהּ", ל"ל לְמִתְנְיֵיהּ? תַּרְתֵּי תְּלָת. קָתָנֵי: פָּרָה דֶּלֶת כ) וּגְרוֹגָרוֹת, וְכוּלְּהוּ צְרִיכֵי וכו'. ל) מִשּׁוּם דְּמִיחַלְּפָן בַּעֲנָבִים. דְּפֵירָא בְּפֵירָא מִיחַלַּף, וְאִית לְהוּ לְבֵית שַׁמַּאי דְּכִינּוּיֵי כִינּוּיִין נְזִירוּת כִּנְזִירוּת, (ה) מִדְּתָנֵי בַּבָּרַיְיתָא. וְאִי אִיתְּמַר בָּשָׂר. לְהוֹדִיעַ, ה"א: הָכָא הוּא דְּאָמְרִי ב"ש דְּהָוֵי נָזִיר, דְּבִישְׂרָא וְחַמְרָא אוֹרְחַיְיהוּ דְּאִינָשֵׁי דְּאָמְרִי בַּהֲדֵי הֲדָדֵי. וְאַמְטוּ לְהָכִי אִיכָּא לְמֵימַר, כִּי אָמַר "מִבְּשָׂרָהּ" – כְּמ"ד *"מִיַּיִן" דָּמֵי. אֲבָל גְּרוֹגָרוֹת וּדְבֵילָה. דְּלָאו בַּהֲדֵי יַיִן נִינְהוּ, אֵימָא דְּלָא תֶּיהֱוֵי לְהוּ שֵׁם כִּינּוּי, קמ"ל. וּמִי קָתָנֵי אִם עָמְדָה מֵאֵלֶיהָ. "אִם עוֹמֶדֶת" סְתָם קָאָמַר, בֵּין מֵאֵלֶיהָ בֵּין ע"י אֲחֵרִים. אֶלָּא אָמַר רָבָא כְּגוֹן שֶׁהָיְתָה פָּרָה רְבוּצָה לְפָנָיו וְאָמַר הֲרֵי עָלַי קָרְבָּן. כְּלוֹמַר, שֶׁהָיְתָה פָּרָה רְבוּצָה לְפָנָיו, וְאָמַר: כִּסְבוּרָה פָּרָה זוֹ שֶׁאֵינָהּ עוֹמֶדֶת, (ו) מְעַכֶּבֶת אֲנִי כָּאן שֶׁלֹּא אֶעֱמוֹד לְעוֹלָם, וַאֲפִילּוּ עַל יְדֵי אָדָם. וְאָמַר הֲרֵי עָלַי קָרְבָּן. כְּלוֹמַר, שֶׁהִזִּיר עַצְמוֹ מִמֶּנָּה אִם לֹא יַעֲמִידֶנָּה, מ) וְעָמְדָה מֵאֵלֶיהָ א]. ב"ש

ס"א מענבים

אוֹ כְּמִנְחַת סוֹטָה — תִּקְדּוֹשׁ, אִי לָא — לָא, קמ"ל דְּמַיְיתֵי מִן הַחִיטִּים.§ **מתני'** אָמַר: "אָמְרָה פָּרָה זוֹ הֲרֵינִי נְזִירָה אִם עוֹמֶדֶת אֲנִי", "אוֹמֵר הַדֶּלֶת הַזֶּה הֲרֵינִי נְזִירָה אִם נִפְתָּח אֲנִי", בש"א: נָזִיר, ובה"א: אֵינוֹ נָזִיר. אָמַר רַבִּי יְהוּדָה: אַף כְּשֶׁאָמְרוּ ב"ש לֹא (א) אוֹמְרִים אֶלָּא בְּאוֹמֵר "הֲרֵי פָּרָה זוֹ עָלַי קָרְבָּן אִם עוֹמֶדֶת הִיא".§ **גמ'** פָּרָה מִי קָא מִישְׁתַּעְיָא? אָמַר רָמִי בַּר חָמָא: הָכָא בְּמַאי עָסְקִינַן — כְּגוֹן שֶׁהָיְתָה פָּרָה רְבוּצָה לְפָנָיו, וְאָמַר: כִּסְבוּרָה פָּרָה זוֹ אֵינָהּ עוֹמֶדֶת — הֲרֵינִי נָזִיר מִבְּשָׂרָהּ אִם עָמְדָה מֵאֵלֶיהָ. וְעָמְדָה מֵאֵלֶיהָ. וְהָלְכוּ ב"ש לְשִׁיטָתָן, וב"ה לְשִׁיטָתָן. בֵּית שַׁמַּאי דְּאָמְרִי:* "מִן הַגְּרוֹגָרוֹת וּמִן הַדְּבֵילָה" הָוֵי נָזִיר — הָכָא נַמִּי, כִּי אָמַר "מִבְּשָׂרָהּ" — הָוֵי נָזִיר. וב"ה אוֹמְרִים: לָא הָוֵי נָזִיר. וְהָא אֲמָרוּהָ ב"ש חֲדָא זִימְנָא! אָמַר רָבָא: תַּרְתֵּי תְּלָת. וְכֵן תָּנֵי ר' חִיָּיא תַּרְתֵּי תְּלָת. וְכֵן א"ר אוֹשַׁעְיָא תַּרְתֵּי תְּלָת. וּצְרִיכִי; דְּאִי אִיתְּמַר בְּהָא, גְּרוֹגָרוֹת וּדְבֵילָה — הָתָם הוּא דְּאָמְרִי ב"ש הָוֵי נָזִיר, מִשּׁוּם דְּמִיחַלְּפָן בַּעֲנָבִים. אֲבָל בָּשָׂר בַּעֲנָבִים — לָא מִיחַלַּף. וְאִי אִיתְּמַר בָּשָׂר — הָכָא הוּא דְּאָמְרִי ב"ש הָוֵי נָזִיר בְּבִישְׂרָא וְחַמְרָא, אֲבָל גְּרוֹגָרוֹת וּדְבֵילָה — לָא, קמ"ל. וְאִי אִיתְּמַר הָנֵי תַּרְתֵּי — הָנֵי הוּא דְּקָאָמְרִי בֵּית שַׁמַּאי, אֲבָל דֶּלֶת — אֵימָא מוֹדוּ לְהוּ לְבֵית הִלֵּל. וְאִי תְּנָא דֶּלֶת — בְּהָא קָאָמְרִי ב"ה, אֲבָל בְּהָךְ תַּרְתֵּי — אֵימָא מוֹדוּ לְהוּ לְבֵית שַׁמַּאי, קָמַשְׁמַע לָן דְּלָא. אָמַר רָבָא: מִי קָתָנֵי "אִם עָמְדָה מֵאֵלֶיהָ"? אֶלָּא אָמַר רָבָא: כְּגוֹן שֶׁהָיְתָה פָּרָה רְבוּצָה לְפָנָיו, וְאָמַר "הֲרֵי עָלַי קָרְבָּן". בִּשְׁלָמָא פָּרָה — בַּת קָרְבָּן הִיא, אֶלָּא דֶּלֶת בַּת קָרְבָּן הִיא? אֶלָּא אָמַר רָבָא: כְּגוֹן שֶׁהָיְתָה פָּרָה רְבוּצָה לְפָנָיו, וְאָמַר

פרה זו. כגון שהיתה פרה רבוצה לפניו. משמע ליה דהיתה רבוצה, מדקתני "אם עומדת אני". לשנויא דרמי בר חמא יש לפרש לישנא דמתני' הכי: אמר – פי': אמר אדם הרואה הפרה הרבוצה (הא מדקתני "הריני עומדת" – מכלל דרבוצה היא). ב] אמר: אמרה פרה זו (פי': סבורה פרה זו), כלומר סבורה פרה זו בלבה מה שהיא רבוצה, ומסתמא מחשבה זו בלבה, מחמת שרבוצה כ"כ, שאינה יכולה לעמוד מאליה. ולא שהפרה עצמה מחשבת כן, שהרי אין לה דעת לסבור ולחשב, אלא כלומר בני אדם העוברים ורואים אותה רבוצה כל כך בכח סבורים בלבם לומר כן. ולפי שהרואה הפרה חושב כן בלבו על הפרה, לפיכך תולה המחשבה בפרה עצמה, כמו "והאניה חשבה להשבר" (יונה א) ולא שהאניה חשבה כן, אלא האדם הרואה האניה חושב עליה להשבר, ותולה הפסוק המחשבה באניה, ה"נ תולה המחשבה בפרה. "הריני נזיר אם עומדת" – "הריני" מוסב על האדם המקבל עליו הנזירות. להכי קאמר הריני נזירה מפיק ה"א – הריני נזיר מבשרה אם עומדת. ורמי בר חמא מוסיף על לשון המשנה "אם עומדת מאליה", כי "מאליה" אינו מלשון המשנה. "אני" – צריך לדחוק ולפרש שמוסב על האדם המקבל הנזירות. וה"ק: אם עומדת מאליה – אני נזיר מבשרה. ואע"ג דכבר אמרה "הריני נזירה" – כפל מלה הוא על האדם המקבל הנזירות. לכן נראה למהר"ף נ"ע דלפום ריהטא דמתני' משמע שהפרה עצמה אמרה "הריני נזירה אם עומדת אני" – היה נופל בטוב בלשון, ולכך נשנית במשנה לשון "אני". אבל לשנויא דרמי בר חמא לא היה צריך לשנות "אני", שכבר אמרה "הריני נזירה", ויתור לשון הוא, אלא שהמשנה שנויה כאילו הפרה מדברת. וכי היכי דמיירי לישנא דמתני' אפרה – ה"נ יש לפרש אדלת. והר"ר יוסף איש ירושלים פירש דה"פ דמתני': אמר – פירוש: אמר האדם כשראה פרה רבוצה: כמדומה אני דאמרה פרה זו "הריני נזירה אם עומדת" – שהיא תואבת לעמוד ואינה יכולה, וברצון תדור נזירות אם תעמוד. אני אשלים לה דבריה, כי הריני נזיר מבשרה אם תעמוד. וכולה מתניתין אמלתא דפרה, והתלמוד מוסיף בה מילתא דאמר האדם. וקצת לתמוה על שטה זו: דאי איירי שהאדם אומר בפירוש "הריני נזיר מבשרה אם היא עומדת" – א"כ הוי כוליה ענינא דאמרה פרה בכדי, דאין דיבורה מועיל כלום! ונראה לפרש: שאין האדם אומר כלום, רק שהיה מספר מילתא דפרה, ולא שייך בה נזירות, רק שתהא מופרשת לאיסורא שלא יהנה מבשרה. הלכך, כשאדם מספר לפנינו כך – בדעתו לקיים עליו שיהיה נזיר מבשרה, ופליגי ב"ש וב"ה כאילו אמר האדם בפירוש "אני נזיר מבשרה אם תעמוד". ומיהו, צ"ע, דמאי פריך "והאמרי ב"ש חדא זימנא" – [הא] איצטריך לאשמועינן אע"ג דלא הזכיר כלל נזירות. ג] והלכו בית שמאי לשיטתן, דכי היכי דלא שייכי גרוגרות לנזירות, ואפ"ה נזיר – הכי נמי לא שייך בשר לנזיר. **תרתין** תלת. כלומר בב' בג' מקומות: בגרוגרות, ובפרה ובדלת. וצריכי, כדמפרש ואזיל. דאי איתמר בגרוגרות – משום דמחלפי בענבים, דתרווייהו פירי נינהו, ושמא בדעתו היה לומר ענבים ועלה בפיו גרוגרות. ובשר וחמרא – זו היא עיקר הסעודה, ומיחלף בלשון בני אדם זה לזה. וא"ת: וליפלוג בבשר [וחמרא] בלא עמידת הפרה *(ולא לומר) לשיטתו! וי"ל דאה"נ, אלא אגב אורחיה קמ"ל דכוונתו שעמדה – ר"ל מאליה. ד] לקמן מפרש שזהו בכלל קושית התלמוד דפריך אשינויא דרמי בר חמא. **מי** קתני מאליה. "אם עומדת" קתני! דודאי אי הוה "מאליה" במתני' מפורש – הייתי מודה לדבריך, אך מדלא קאמר "מאליה" – ש"מ דליכא לפרושי בדידך. דאי בדידך – ליתני "הריני נזיר מבשרה", ולא ליתלי נזירות בהעמדה. [ולכן הקשה] לו, שמוסיף על הלשון המשנה "מאליה". [אבל] הא לא קשיא מאי דמוסיף רמי בר חמא "ועמדה מאליה", שזה הלשון אין צריך להוסיף אלשון המשנה, אלא עיקר הדבר במה שתולה נדרו צריך לשנות התנא, ומה שעשתה הפרה אחרי כן א"צ לשנות, אלא בעל פה אומר איך נעשה המעשה אחרי כן. דודאי שתלה נדרו בעמדה הפרה מאליה, דלא הוי נזיר אם לא עמדה מאליה. ולכך הוצרך לפרש ועמדה. וליכא לפרש בין מאליה בין מאחרים, שאין דרך בני אדם לתלות בדבר שיודע שיעשה, שאם דעתו להיות נזיר – למה תלה בשום דבר? וא"ת: ומאי קשיא ליה "מי קתני מאליה"? והא כמה משניות דמשנינן "חסורי מיחסרא והכי קתני"! וי"ל, דה"מ היכא דמוכח החיסרון – אז יש כח להוסיף על לשון המשנה. אבל לפי' דרמי בר חמא לא מוכח כלום דמשנה חסר "מאליה", כיון דאינה תולה מחלוקת התנאים כלל בעמידת הפרה, אלא כל המחלוקת בנודר מן הבשר, אי חייל עליה נזירות לכל מילי אי לא. לכך פריך "מי קתני מאליה" דאין לו להוסיף על לשון המשנה, כיון דלא מוכח מפלוגתא דתנאי דחסר כלום. **הרי** עלי בקרבן. פי': הפרה, ור"ל: ה] אם עמדה אם לא עמדה, כדמסיק לקמן. אלא דלא שבקיה לסיומי למילתיה עד דפריך ליה. *)**ב"ש** סברי תורפיה דההוא גברא משום [אוקמה] בידיה הוא. ואם לא עמדה, ר"ל אם לא אעמידה, (והכא) [והא] לא אוקמה – וחייב להביא קרבן. וב"ה [סברי]: אם לא עמדה כלל, משום דרבוצה, והא קמתה. וכיון דקמתה – אינו חייב להביא קרבן. וא"ת: והא בלישנא דמתני' קתני "הריני נזירה", והיכי משתמע קרבן? וי"ל, דה"ק: הריני מביאה בקרבן נזירות אם לא עמדה. ואע"ג דקרבנות נזיר אינם באים מבהמה גסה – [ה"מ] חובותיו של נזיר, אבל היו רגילים להביא נדרים ונדבות עם קרבנות נזירות, ואותם באים אף מבקר וצאן, הכל לפי נדרו ונדבתו. ואמר

נ"ל ולהזו

*) שייך לע"ב

דאי לנזר מן הענבים נמי לא להוי נזיר דליכא למיגזר גבי בשר הכי דבשר בענבים לא מחלף ואי איתמר בשר הכא הוא דליכא למגזר משום בשרא וחמרא ואי אתמר הני תרתי בגרוגרות ובשר דהאי פירא דפירא גרוגרות ובשרא וחמרא דמתכלי ביחד להכי גזרי ב"ש בהני תרתי דהוי נזיר אבל דלת כו': וכן תני ר' חייא בתוספ' דידיה דבתרתי תלת בכל אלו גרוגרות ודבילה ופרה ודלת נוהג טעם זה. תוספות משום דמחלפן כו' כן איתא בכ"י: מ) אם לא יעמידנה הס"ד:

הדר ביה: ה"ג אמר אמרה פרה זו הריני נזירה אם עומדת אני אמרה הדלת הזו הריני נזירה אם נפתחת אני הדלת לשון נקבה כדכתיב הדלת תסוב על צירה ובגמ' מפרש לכולה מתני': ואמר כסבורה פרה זו אינה עומדת כמו והאניה חשבה להשבר כלומר לפי ענינה אינה יכולה לעמוד והיינו אמר אמרה פרה זו דמתני' שאמר האדם סבורה פרה זו שאינה עומדת ואני אומר הריני נזיר מבשרה אם עומדת אני (אומר כן) ועמדה מאליה ופליגי בית שמאי וב"ה בפלוגתא דרישא מן הגרוגרות ור' יהודה קאמר דלא פליגי בנזיר אלא כשפירש דבריו ואמר שלא נתכוון אלא לאסור הפרה עליו כקרבן ותימ' וליתני הריני נזיר מבשר פרה זו וי"ל דנקט פרה רבוצה לאשמועינן כשהוא אומר בלשון הזה יש במשמעות שתעמוד מאליה אבל אם בעמידת אדם לא הוי נזיר לב"ש וכן בדלת אם אמרה לפי ענינה של דלת שלא תהא נפתחת הריני נזיר ממנה אם נפתחה היא ונפתחה על ידי הרוח כן פי' המפרשים והלשון דחוק דמשמע דלישנא דמתני' דכל מתני' מאמר הפרה הוא ופי' ר' יוסף קלצון אמר האומר כסבורה פרה זו שאינה יכולה לעמוד ותאיבה היא לעמוד וברצון תדור נזיר אם תעמוד בלשון משל אדם הנודר בעת צרה ואני משלים חפצה הריני נזיר מבשרה אם עומדת היא וכל לישנא דמתניתין מאמר הפרה הוא והתלמיד הוסיף בה פ' מאמר אדם וקצת קשה אם אמר האדם בפירוש הריני נזיר מבשרה א"כ כל מאמר הפרה דמתני' בכדי נקטינן דאין דיבורה מועיל כלום ועוד דבור האדם חסר במתני' ונראה לפרש שהאדם לא קבל עליו נזירות בפי' אלא מספר מאמר הפרה שמתוך שתאיבה לעמוד ברצון קאמרה הריני נזירה אם עומדת אני ונזירות לא שייך בה אלא שתהא מופרשת ואסורה שלא יהנו ממנה וכשהוא מספר דברים הללו הוי כאילו אמר הוא הריני נזיר מבשרה דבענין אחר למה לו לאמר דברים הללו אלא שבלבו לקיים מה שהוא מספר מאמר הפרה. ומיהו תימה מאי פריך והא אמר ב"ש חדא זימנא הא טובא איצטריך הך דפרה לאשמועינן דהוי נזיר אע"ג דלא הזכיר נזירות ושמא קשה לו למה הוצרכו ב"ה לחלוק כיון דהוה פלוגתא דרישא: תרתי תלת הוצרך להשמיענו מחלוקתן בג' בבות הללו כדמפרש ואזיל: משום דמחלפי בענבים ואיכא למימר שהיה סבור לומר מן הענבים ונפל בפיו גרוגרות: בשרא וחמרא מצוין הן ביחד זוללי בשר וסובאי יין ועבדי אינשי דטעו ומחלפו להו: אמר רבא מי קתני עמדה מאליה הא אמרת דעיקר חידושא דמתניתין הא דתנן רבוצת פרה לאשמועינן דוקא עמדה מאליה וא"כ ה"ל למתני בפי' עומדת מאליה וליכא לפרש בין עמדה מאליה בין עמדה ע"י אחרים דא"כ אמאי תנא כלל רביצת פרה ליתני האומר הריני נזיר מבשר פרה ועוד דבר ברור הוא שתעמוד ע"י עצמה או ע"י אחרים ומה לו לתלות נזירותו במאי שהוא יודע בבירור אם הוא רוצה להיות נזיר יאמר בלא תנאי הריני נזיר: כגון שהיתה פרה רבוצה לפניו ואמר הרי עלי קרבן וה"פ דמתני' סבורה פרה שאינה יכולה לעמוד ותאבה לידור שאם תעמוד בין מאליה בין ע"י אחרים שתכנס לעזרה ויקריבוה לקרבן נזיר ואע"פ שאין מביא פרה לקרבן חובה [illegible] ולאידך פירושא הוי כאילו אמר הרי עלי קרבן נזיר [illegible] שיך בה למימר שיעשה קרבן הריני

הגהות הב"ח
(א) במשנה כשאמרו ב"ש לא אמרו אלא: (ב) רש"י ד"ה אמרה פרה וכו' אם תתקיים מחשבתה וכו' ולעמידנה והכלכו ב"ש לשיטתן דאמרי כי אמר הריני נזיר מן הגרוגרות: (ג) ד"ה א"ר יהודה וכו' היא מאליה ועמדה מאליה דהוי: (ד) ד"ה כסבורה וכו' שכן מצינו מחשבה כצ"ל ותיבת מה נמחק: (ה) ד"ה משום דמיחלפן וכו' נזירות כנזירות כדתני בברייתא כצ"ל: (ו) ד"ה אלא וכו' שאינה עומדת מתעכבת אני:

[לעיל ט.]

הגהות מהר"ב רנשבורג
א] רש"י ד"ה ואמר הרי עלי קרבן וכו' אם לא יעמידנה ועמדה מאליה. [illegible]

נוסחת הריב"ן
[illegible]

וְאָמַר "הֲרֵינִי נָזִיר מִיַּיִן אִם לֹא עָמְדָה", וְעָמְדָה מֵאֵלֶיהָ; בֵּית שַׁמַּאי סָבְרִי: תּוּרְפֵּיהּ דְּהַאי גַּבְרָא מִשּׁוּם אוּקְמָהּ בִּידֵיהּ הוּא, וְהָא לָא אוּקְמָהּ. וּבֵית הִלֵּל סָבְרִי: (א) מִשּׁוּם דִּרְבִיעָא הוּא, וְהָא קָמַת. אִי הָכִי, אֵימָא סֵיפָא: אָמַר רַבִּי יְהוּדָה: אַף כְּשֶׁאָמְרוּ בֵּית שַׁמַּאי לֹא אָמְרוּ אֶלָּא בְּאוֹמֵר (ב) "הֲרֵי הֵן עָלַי קָרְבָּן", פָּרָה מִי קָא מַתְפִּיס בָּהּ מִידֵי? אֶלָּא, כְּגוֹן דְּאָמַר "הֲרֵינִי נָזִיר מִבְּשָׂרָהּ אִם לֹא עָמְדָה" וְעָמְדָה מֵאֵלֶיהָ; בֵּית שַׁמַּאי סָבְרִי: תּוּרְפֵּיהּ דְּהַהוּא גַּבְרָא מִשּׁוּם אוּקְמָהּ בִּידֵיהּ הוּא, וְהָא לָא אוּקְמָהּ. וּבֵית הִלֵּל סָבְרִי: תּוּרְפֵּיהּ דְּהַאי גַּבְרָא מִשּׁוּם דִּרְבִיעָא, וְהָא קָמַת. וּב"ה סָבְרִי: אִי לָא קָמַת הָוֵי נָזִיר. וְהָאָמְרִי "מִבְּשָׂרָהּ" לָא הָוֵי נָזִיר! לְטַעֲמַיְיהוּ דב"ש קָאָמְרִי: לְדִידָן – אֲפִי' לָא קָמַת נַמִי לָא הָוֵי נָזִיר, לְדִידְכוּ דְּאָמְרִיתוּ הָוֵי נָזִיר – אוֹדוּ לָן מִיהַת דְּתוּרְפֵּיהּ דְּהָדֵין גַּבְרָא מִשּׁוּם דִּרְבִיעָא, וְהָא קָמַת. וּבֵית שַׁמַּאי: לָאו תּוּרְפֵּיהּ דְּהַאי גַּבְרָא מִשּׁוּם אוּקְמָהּ בִּידֵיהּ הוּא – וְהָא לָא אוּקְמָהּ.§

מתני'

ואמר הריני נזיר מיין אם לא וכו'. מתני' דקתני "הריני נזירה" – פי': הריני נזיר מיין כך בשבילה. ועמדה מאליה – זה אינו מוסיף על לישנא דמתני', אלא "לא" בלבד, דבלשון המשנה "אם עמדה", והוא מוסיף תיבת "לא". אלא ממילא אמר, שכך נעשה המעשה שעמדה מאליה.

ב"ש א] תורפי' דההוא גברא משום אוקמה ב] בידיה והא לא אוקמה. פי': תורפיה – גילוי דעתו. כלומר, ב"ש סבירא להו כי אמר האדם כי האי לישנא, דעתו לומר כן: העולם סבורים שהפרה רבוצה כל כך בחוזק שאין אדם יכול להעמידה. הריני נזיר – כלומר, אע"פ שאין רצוני להיות נזיר, דטריחא לי – הריני נזיר. אם לא עמדה – פי': ג] אין כח בידי להעמידה בכח, ואם לא עמדה משם – לא כ"ש אם יעמידנה. ולבסוף נעשה מעשה שלא טרח בה ולא יגע בה להעמידנה, ועמדה מאליה. ב"ש סברי: אם לא יעמידנה קאמר, והא לא אוקמה – הלכך חייל נזירות, דהא מדין נזיר. *וב"ה סברי: אם לא עמדה משום דרבוצה היא בכח, כלומר: אהא נזיר אם [לא] תעמוד – והיא קמתה, הלכך לא חייל עליה נזירות. וא"ת: והשתא נמי תקשי "מידי אם לא עמדה קתני"? וי"ל: דכמה משניות משובשות, ומשנינן להו ב"חסורי מחסרא". ד]דהכי תולה רבא פלוגתא דתנאי בעמידת הפרה, וא"א לו לפרש פלוגתא דתנאי בעמידת הפרה אם לא יוסיף "לא" בגירסת המשנה, והוי מוכח דחסר "לא" כאן, דאי אפשר לו לפרש פלוגתייהו בע"א. אבל לשנויא דרמי בר חמא – אינו תלוי מחלוקת התנאים (כלומר) [כלום] בעמידה, אלא בנודר מן הבשר, אי חייל עליה נזירות אי לא, ולדידיה ודאי קשה "מידי מאליה קתני" דלא מוכח מפלוגתא דתנאי דחסר "מאליה", ולכך אין לו כח להוסיף על לשון המשנה. וא"ת: וליפרוך ליה בהדיא: למה לי פרה רבוצה לתנא זה אם עמדה מאליה – ליפלוג בהדיא בנודר בנזיר מן הבשר, אי חייל עליה נזירות, וליזלו ב"ש לשיטתן וב"ה לשיטתן! וי"ל: דה"נ פריך "מידי מאליה קתני", ולא הוקשה לו עיקר קושיא זו אלא לגלגל עליו, ולומר כיון דאינה פלוגתא דתנאי כלל בעמידת הפרה – אין לך כח להוסיף על לשון המשנה "מאליה", וכיון דתנאי לא פליגי בעמידת הפרה – א"כ תקשי לך טפי (א"כ) למה לתנא להזכיר כלל בעמידת הפרה, ליפלגו בנודר מן הבשר וליזלו לשיטתן. ולא הזכיר קושיא ד"מאליה" אלא להזכיר לו דפלוגתא דתנאי לא תליא בעמידת הפרה כלל, ומעתה תקשי לך קושיא חזקה טפי, דליפליגו בבשר להדיא, וליזלו לשיטתן. **אימא** סיפא. מי קא מתפיס בה מידי. כלומר, אמאי פליג רבי *את"ק, דהפרה לא הויא אלא כקרבן בעלמא? הרי לא התפיס בלשונו קונס, לומר "פרה זו כקונס" או "כקרבן", אלא נזיר מיין להדיא "אם לא עמדה" כו'! ה] אלא ה"ג: כגון דאמר "הריני מיר [מבשרה] אם לא עמדה" ועמדה מאליה וכו'. והשתא נחלקו בלשון, כדפרישית לעיל, ונחלקו נמי כי נדר מן הבשר אי הוי נזיר לכל מילי. וא"ת: והשתא, כיון דאוקי רבא פלוגתייהו בעמידת הפרה – למה לו להגיה ולהוסיף תיבת "לא" על לשון המשנה? והא יכול לפרש בלא הגהה ותוספת, כגון דאמר "הריני נזיר מבשרה אם עמדה" והעמידה, ב"ש משמע להו "אם עמדה" – אם אעמידנה בכח ידי. וכן עשה, טרח ויגע להעמידנה בכח – הלכך הוי נזיר מבשרה, וכיון דחייל נזירות אבשרה – חייל נמי אכל מילי, דב"ש לשיטתן. וב"ה סברי "אם עמדה" – מאליה משמע, והוא העמידה ולא עמדה מאליה, ולא חייל נזירות אפי' אבשרה! י"ל: דהה"נ, אלא *) ודאי לא הוו פליגי ב"ה לומר דלא ליהוי נזיר, דכיון דקאמר יהיה נזיר "אם (אמר) עמדה" – משמע בכל ענין שתעמוד, בין ע"י עצמה בין ע"י אחרים, הוי נזיר. ועי"ל: דאין דרך הנודרין לומר בהאי לישנא לב"ש שתלה נזירותו "אם עמדה", פירוש: אם אעמידנה, דטרח בה בעל כרחו להעמידה כדי שיחול עליו נזירות. דכיון דהפי' להיות נזיר – [לימא] בהדיא "הריני נזיר", למה תלה נדרו בעמידת הפרה? אבל בלשון זה דרך העולם לידור: "אהיה נזיר אם לא עמדה" פירוש: אם לא אעמידנה, כלומר, אע"פ שאיני נזיר ברצון – הריני מקבל עלי נזירות אם לא יהיה לי כח להעמידנה ו] אהיה נזיר, לא שאני חפץ בנזירות. להכי מוסיף על לשון המשנה "לא" כדי לפרש בלשון שרגילות לומר ולידור. וא"ת: ומאי קא עביד לריכותא לעיל מתרתין תלת? והא בהא נחלקו כאן מחלוקת חדש ב"אם לא עמדה ז] מאליה"! ח] י"מ: דשמא כל התירוצים שתירץ התלמוד בשם רבא – לא תירץ מעולם, ולית ליה בתרי ותלת. ולא תירץ רבא כ"א תירוץ אחרון: מבשרה אם לא עמדה. אבל תירוצי קמאי – לא רבא תירץ, אלא משום דהקשה ארמי בר חמא – הוזכר בתלמוד בשמו. דה"נ אשכחנא ביבמות פרק "החולץ" (דף לה:) דקאמר: מיתיבי הכונס, ובביאה לא פליג כלל עליה, דהא קאמר בתר הכי: בביאה דכ"ע לא פליגי. וכן לקמן פ"ג (דף יז.). ובלישנא דבית שמאי סברי תורפיה דההוא גברא וכו', לא שמעינן הא פלוגתא מגרוגרות! ויש לומר: דע"כ פליגי נמי בנודר מן הבשר, דאם לא כן – ליפלגו מן היין בהדיא בעמידת הפרה. ומדרבי יהודה מוכיח דלא בנודר מן היין פליגי, דהא לא הוה פליג רבי יהודה. אלא על כרחך הנודר מבשרה, והלכו לשיטתן, והשתא קא עביד צריכותא לעיל. ומכל מקום גם בעמידת הפרה פליגי, דאם כן ליפלוג בבשר להדיא, למה לי להזכיר פרה אם עמדה במתני'? אלא ע"כ גם בעמידת הפרה נחלקו. ואם תאמר: ומאי דוחקיה למימר: ובית הלל סברי תורפיה דההוא גברא כו', וצריך לומר דבית הלל לטעמייהו דבית שמאי קאמרי? לימא דב"ה [סברי] דלא הוי נזיר במה דנזיר מן הגרוגרות! וי"ל: דע"כ ב"ה אתי לפלוגי נמי בעמידת הפרה. דאי בנודר מן הבשר, ולטעמייהו – ליפלגו בבשר לחודיה. דליכא למימר שנה עמידת הפרה לאשמועינן טעמא דבית שמאי דהוי נזיר מבשר כי תלה נדרו בעמידת הפרה, וכי *טעמא דב"ש לחוד אתא לאשמועינן? אלא על כרחך טעמא דב"ה אתא לאשמועינן, כי תלה נדרו בעמידת הפרה – דלא חל נדרו אפילו על הבשר. וא"ת: סוף סוף מאי נפקא מינה לבית הלל? והלא אפי' כשנזר זה ט] [מן] הבשר לא חייל אכל מילי דנזירות, כדמשמע להו בגרוגרות! וי"ל: דנפקא מינה היכא דנדר מן היין בפי', ותלה נדרו בעמידת הפרה – דלא חייל עליה נזירות, דלבית הלל משמע להו משום דרבוצה היא, והא קמתה.

*) נ"א דלא

הריני

ב"ש סָבְרִי תּוּרְפֵּיהּ דְּהַאי גַּבְרָא כו'. כִּדִלְקַמֵּיהּ מוֹקֵי לָהּ. וְאָמַר לָנוּ הַמּוֹר"ה: אע"ג דְּלָא (ג) תָּנֵי לָהּ רָבָא בְּהֶדְיָא בְּהַךְ קַמַּיְיתָא בְּ"אִם לֹא עָמְדָה" וְעָמְדָה מֵאֵלֶיהָ, דִּבְדִין הוּא דַּהֲוָה לֵיהּ לְמִיתְנֵי הָכִי, כִּדְקָאָמַר לָהּ נַמִי בְּאִידָךְ תֵּירוּצָא דִּמְתָרֵץ לָהּ. אֶלָּא א) אָמוֹרָא דִּמְסַדֵּר הַתַּלְמוּד, כֵּיוָן דִּשְׁמָעֵיהּ לְרָבָא דְּאָמַר מִילְּתָא דְּאִית בָּהּ פִּירְכָא – לָא ב) אַנִּיחַ לְסִיּוּמֵיהּ לְמִילְּתֵיהּ, וּפָרֵיךְ לֵיהּ כִּדְפָרֵיךְ: בִּשְׁלָמָא פָּרָה בַּת קָרְבָּן הִיא. וַהֲדַר מַחֲלִיף שִׁיטָתוֹ ג) דִּמֵעִיקָּרָא דְּמוֹקֵי לָהּ בִּכְגוֹן דְּאָמַר "הֲרֵי עָלַי קָרְבָּן", ד) וַהֲדַר מוֹקִים לָהּ בִּכְגוֹן דְּאָמַר "הֲרֵינִי נָזִיר מִיַּיִן", וּמְסַיֵּים לְמִילְּתָא. *בִּשְׁלָמָא פָּרָה בַּת קָרְבָּן הִיא. בִּשְׁלָמָא לְגַבֵּי פָּרָה מָצֵית מוֹקְמַתְּ לָהּ בִּכְגוֹן דְּקָאָמַר "הֲרֵי עָלַי קָרְבָּן" דְּהָוֵי נָזִיר, (ד) דְּהוֹאִיל דְּבַת קָרְבָּן הִיא – כְּלוֹמַר דְּקָא שַׁיְיכָא בִּכְלַל קָרְבָּן, אע"ג דִּבְקָרְבַּן נָזִיר לָא שַׁיְיכָא – אִיכָּא לְמֵימַר כְּאוֹמֵר "הֲרֵי עָלַי קָרְבַּן נְזִירוּת" דָּמֵי, וְהָוֵי נָזִיר. אֶלָּא לְגַבֵּי דֶּלֶת – הֵיכִי קִים לְהוּ לב"ש הָכִי? בִּשְׁלָמָא גַּבֵּי גְּרוֹגָרוֹת אִיכָּא לְמֵימַר: הוֹאִיל וּפֵירֵי הוּא, מִיחַלְּפִי בַּעֲנָבִים, וְיֵשׁ בַּלָּשׁוֹן הַזֶּה לְשׁוֹן נְזִירוּת. אֶלָּא לְגַבֵּי דֶּלֶת, כִּי קָאָמַר "הֲרֵי הִיא עָלַי קָרְבָּן אִם לֹא נִפְתָּח" – מִי שַׁיָּיךְ בְּקָרְבַּן נְזִירוּת כְּלָל? **אֶלָּא אָמַר רָבָא** כְּגוֹן שֶׁהָיְתָה פָּרָה רְבוּצָה לְפָנָיו. וְאָמַר: כִּסְבוּרָה פָּרָה זוֹ שֶׁאֵינָהּ עוֹמֶדֶת לְעוֹלָם, לֹא מֵאֵלֶיהָ וְלֹא ע"י אָדָם. **וְאָמַר** הֲרֵינִי נָזִיר מִיַּיִן **אִם לֹא** עָמְדָה. וּמַתְנִי' דְּקָתָנֵי "אִם עוֹמֶדֶת", הָכִי מַשְׁמַע: הִיא סְבוּרָה שֶׁאַתְּ מִתְעַכֶּבֶת שָׁם, הֲרֵינִי נָזִיר אִם תִּתְקַיֵּים מַחֲשַׁבְתָּהּ שֶׁאַתְּ עוֹמֶדֶת שָׁם, אֶלָּא אֲנִי אַעֲמִידֶהָ. וְעָמְדָה מֵאֵלֶיהָ. וּמַתְנִי' לֵיכָּא לְאַקְשׁוּיֵי הַשְׁתָּא כִּדְמַקְשִׁינַן לְעֵיל "מִידֵי אִם עָמְדָה מֵאֵלֶיהָ קָתָנֵי", דְּהָא רָבָא גּוּפֵיהּ לָא שָׁנֵי לֵיהּ הָכָא בֵּין עָמְדָה מֵאֵלֶיהָ בֵּין עָמְדָה ע"י אֲחֵרִים. וּבְהָא **פְּלִיגֵי** דב"ש סָבְרִי תּוּרְפֵּיהּ דְּהַאי **גַּבְרָא**. עִיקָּר שֶׁל זֶה, לֹא הֲוַת אֶלָּא אַדַּעְתָּא דְּאִיהוּ לוֹקִים לָהּ בְּעַל כָּרְחָהּ. וְהַאי דְּקָאָמַר "אִם לֹא עָמְדָה" – אִם לֹא אַעֲמִידֶהָ בְּמַשְׁמַע, וְהִלְכָּךְ כֵּיוָן דְּלָא אוֹקְמָהּ – הָוֵי נָזִיר ה). **וְאָמַר** הֲרֵינִי נָזִיר מִיַּיִן כו'. לָא אִיצְטְרִיךְ (ה) לְמֵימַר אֶלָּא "הֲרֵינִי נָזִיר", אֶלָּא מִשּׁוּם דִּמְשַׁנֵּי לְעֵיל "מִבְּשָׂרָהּ" – אֲמַר הָכָא "מִיַּיִן", לְאַפּוּקֵי מִשִּׁנּוּיָא קַמַּיְיתָא. ו) א] וְקָא מְהַדַּר לֵיהּ רַבִּי יְהוּדָה לְתַנָּא קַמָּא: לֹא כְּשֶׁאַתָּה סָבוּר דִּבְמַתְפִּיס בְּפָרָה לֶיהֱוֵי נָזִיר כָּךְ אָמְרוּ ב"ש, אֶלָּא אַף כְּשֶׁאָמְרוּ ב"ש דְּמִיתְפַּס בָּהּ – לֹא אָמְרוּ אֶלָּא בְּאוֹמֵר "הֲרֵי פָּרָה זוֹ עָלַי קָרְבָּן", דְּהָוֵי נָדוּר וְאֵינוֹ נָזִיר. אֲבָל בְּדֶלֶת לָא פָּלֵיג ר' יְהוּדָה, דְּהָא לָא שַׁיְיכָא לִישָּׁנָא דִּנְדָרִים גַּבֵּי דֶּלֶת כְּלָל. וב"ה **אָמְרִי**. (ו) ז) טַעַם מִשּׁוּם דְּקָמַת לָא הָוֵי נָזִיר, הָא אִם לֹא קָמַת – הָוֵי נָזִיר. **וְהָאָמַרְתְּ**. לב"ה, דְּכָל הֵיכָא דְּאָמַר "הֲרֵינִי נָזִיר מִבְּשָׂרָהּ" לָא הָוֵי נָזִיר, דּוּמְיָא דְּמ"ד "הֲרֵינִי נָזִיר מִן הַגְּרוֹגָרוֹת" דְּלָא הָוֵי נָזִיר! לְטַעֲמַיְיהוּ דב"ש קָאָמְרִי לְהוּ: לְדִידָן כו'.

מתני'

פי' הרא"ש

הריני נזיר מיין אם לא עמדה וה"פ סבורה פרה זו שאינה עומדת לא ע"י עצמה ולא ע"י אחרים ואמר הריני נזיר מיין אם לא תעמוד ותימה אם עומדת קתני וי"ל דהא לא קשיא ליה דזמנין שמדלג התנא א) או האח' אבל עמדה מאליה שהוא עיקר החידוש ה"ל למתני' ולפי' בתרא א"צ להגיה המשנה וה"פ סברה פרה זו שאינה עומדת שאינה רוצה לעמוד ודומה הוא שתאמר ברצון הריני נזיר אם עומדת אני ולשון משל כאדם המסרב לעשות דבר ואמר אהא נזיר אם אעשנו וסברי בית שמאי דהמספר דברי פרה הוי כאילו הוא אומר הריני נזיר אם לא אעמידנה לפי שהוא כועס עליה לפי שאינה רוצה לעמוד ואומר בלבו אדרבה אני אעמידנה ואם לאו אהא נזיר ועמדה ע"י עצמה או שהעמידה אחר וזה קורא מאליה כיון שהוא לא העמידה ב"ש סברי תורפיה דההוא גברא אוקמא בידיה גלוי דעתו כמו מניחה במקום התורפה ותורף שהוא גלוי השטר ועיקרו והא לא אוקמה דמעצמה עמדה או אחרים העמידוה וב"ה [סבר] לא היה דעתו אלא שתקום והא קמת ולא הוי נזיר: מי קמתפים בה מידי מה שייך לומר בדעתו היה שתאסר הפרה עלי כקרבן הא לא מתפים בה מידי אלא אמר בפירוש הריני נזיר מיין: אלא כגון דאמר הריני נזיר מבשרה אם לא עמדה וה"פ ב) פרה זו בלבד שאינה עומדת לא מעצמה ולא ע"י אחר הריני נזירה מפיק הי נזיר מבשרה אם לא עמדה ולאידך פירושא כסבורה פרה זו שאינה עומדת שאינה חפצה לעמוד ומסרבת ואומרת אהא נזיר מופרשת ואסורה שלא יהנו ממנה וכשהוא מספר דבר זה בדעתו שיהא נזיר מבשרה אם לא יעמידנה א"נ מיירי שאמר בפי' הריני נזיר מבשרה אם לא עמדה ואין לתמוה כיון דאמר בפי' הכי אמאי תנא כלל רביצת הפרה דמשום דפליגי ביה ב"ש וב"ה במאי תורפי דההוא גברא נקטיה והשתא פליגי נמי בפלוגתא דהריני נזיר מן הגרוגרות ופריך לב"ה הא לא קמת הוי נזיר והא מבשרה קאמר ומשני לטעמייהו דבית שמאי קאמר

א) נראה דצ"ל שמדלג התנא תיבת לא אבל עמדה וכו' ועי' בתוס' ד"ה ב"ש. ב) נראה דצ"ל כסבורה פרה זו שאינה עומדת וכו' הריני נזיר מבשרה וכו'.

הגהות הב"ח

(א) גמ' וב"ה סברי תורפיה דהאי גברא משום דרביעא: (ב) שם אלא באומר הרי פרה זו עלי קרבן וכו' מי קא מתפיס בה מידי נ"ב פי' הלא לא מתפיס בפרה אלא שנדר מן היין וא"כ קשה אמאי פליג ר' יהודה דשפיר קאמר ת"ק דלב"ש הוי נזיר ומהדרינן אלא דמתפיס בפרה דקאמר לאו הריני נזיר מבשרה וכו' כדלעיל אלא דקאמר אם לא עמדה: (ג) רש"י ד"ה ב"ש סברי וכו' אע"ג דלא קאמר לה רבא בהדיא בהך קמייתא אם לא וכו' מאליה בדין הוא דהוה ליה למימר הכי וסי' קרבן היא וכו' והדר מאליה: (ד) ד"ה בשלמא וכו' דהוי נזיר הואיל כצ"ל ואות ד' נמחק: (ה) ד"ה ואמר הריני וכו' לא איצטריך מיה למימר וכו' קמייתא [illegible] אלא כגון דאמר הריני נזיר מבשרה וכו' וקא מהדר ליה וכו' ליהוי נזיר לא כך אמרה: (ו) ד"ה וב"ה אמרי טעמא:

נוסחת הריב"ן

א) תנא דמסדר תלמודא כיון כו': ב) אנחיה: ג) (למעיקרא) ליתא בכ"י: ד) הרי עלי קרבן שמוקים: ה) בכ"י כתוב כאן בזה"ל גליון ואי קשיא הא לא קתני מתני' אם לא עמדה אלא אם עומדת אני הא לא קשיא בין עומדת אני לאם לא עמדה ליכא דוקיא כ"כ אבל בתר עמדה לאוסופי מאליה היכא דלא קתני במתניתין לא מוספינן וב"ה סברי תורפיה דהאי גברא משום לחזא דרבצה קמיה ולא היה סבור דתיקום מהתם לעולם וכי נדר בנזירות אדעתא דקיימה רביעה קאמר ואילו היכא דקמת לא חייל עליה נזירות. תורפיה כגון מקום הזמן ומקום התורף כלומר שהוא עקרו של שטר ואית דגרסי תורפיה דהאי גברא גילוי דעתו של זה ומשמע כגון אם היתה מונחת במקום המוצנע יניחנה במקום התורפה. אי הכי דבמזיר עצמו מן היין אימא סיפא אמר ר' יהודה אף כשאמרו ב"ש לא אמרו אלא באומר הרי עלי קרבן שנודר הימנה אם עומדת למ"ל לר' יהודה למהדר לת"ק ממידי דפרה דאילו ת"ק מי קא מתפים בה מידי בפרה דקא מהדר ליה ר' יהודה לא כשאתה סבור שנזר הימנה אלא שנודר הימנה והא ת"ק אמר דהאי מתפים ביין וכל היכא דמתפים ביין מי איכא למ"ד דלא הוי נזיר אלא כגון דאמר הריני נזיר מבשרה כו' הס"ד ואח"כ מה"ד ואמר הריני נזיר כו': ו) משנויא קמייתא מפי המורה: ז) טעמא:

גליון הש"ס

תום' ד"ה אימא סיפא וכו' טעמא דב"ש אתי לאשמועינן. ק"ל הא לפי קושית התוספות ליכא פלוגתא ביסוד זה דאם לא העמידה ועמדה מאליה דמיקרי נתקיים התנאי גם לב"ה ואם היה אומר הריני נזיר מיין הוי נזיר א"כ הך חידוש הוא להלכתא ולא שייך בזה טעמא דב"ש לחוד אתי לאשמעינן וצ"ע:

הגהות מהר"ב רנשבורג

א] רש"י ד"ה ואמר כו' וקמהדר ליה נ"ב עיין א"מ: ב] תום' ד"ה ב"ש סברי תורפיה דהאי גברא משום [אוקמוה] בידים הוא עכ"ל נ"ב עיין א"מ לעיל ע"א בתום' ד"ה הרי עלי והכל הוא דבור אחד לפי הגהתו עם זה הדבור יעו"ש: ג] בא"ד פי' אם אין כח בידי להעמידה בכח ואם לא עמדה משם לא כל שכן אם יעמידנה מן תיבת אם לא עד תיבת יעמידנה נמחק ונ"ב ואם לא עמדה משמע לב"ש אם לא יעמידנה כצ"ל א"מ: ד] בא"ד ומשנינן להו חסורי מיחסרא דהכי נמחק תיבת דהכי ונ"ב דהא: ה] בד"ה אימא סיפא וכו' אם לא עמדה וכו' נ"ב נלע"ד דכאן הס"ד ואח"כ מה"ד אלא ה"ג וכו': ו] בא"ד כלומר אע"פ שאיני נזיר ברצון הריני מקבל עלי נזירות אם לא יהיה לי כח להעמידנה ואם יהיה לי כח להעמידנה לא אהיה נזיר כצ"ל א"מ: ז] בא"ד והא בהא נחלקו כאן מחלוקת חדש באם לא עמדה ועמדה כצ"ל: ח] בא"ד י"מ דשמא כל התירוצים עד וכן לקמן פ"ג דף יז נ"ב מן תיבות י"מ עד לקמן פ"ג דף יז כ"ז מוסגר והוא הגה"ה מחכם אחר שלא מדברי התוספות הללו וקודם תיבות י"מ נ"ל הג"ה ואחרי תיבות לקמן פ"ג דף עז ויז נ"ל עד כאן הג"ה א"מ: ט] בא"ד וא"ת סוף סוף מאי נפקא מינה לבית הלל על הבשר לא חייל אכל מילי דנזירות נ"ב ר"ל בין נזירות מיין בין נדור מבשר כמו שס"ל גבי גרוגרות וא[illegible] דתלה בעמידת הפרה א"מ:

מתני' מזגו לו את הכוס, ואמר "הריני נזיר ממנו" — ה"ז נזיר. מעשה באשה אחת שהיתה שיכורה, ומזגו לה את הכוס, ואמרה "הריני נזירה ממנו". אמרו חכמים: ג'לא נתכוונה זו אלא לומר "הרי הוא עלי קרבן".§ גמ' מעשה לסתור?! אמרת רישא "הרי זה נזיר", והדר תני "מעשה באשה אחת", אלמא בהאי הוא דאסור, הא יינא אחרינא — שרי! חסורי מיחסרא והכי קתני: מזגו לו את הכוס ואמר "הריני נזיר ממנו" — הרי זה נזיר. ואם שיכור הוא, ואמר "הריני נזיר ממנו" — אינו נזיר; מ"ט — כמאן דאמר "הרי עלי קרבן" הוא. וכי תימא: לימא הכי — סבר: מייתין לי אחרינא ומצערן לי, אימא להו הא מילתא דפסיקא להו; ומעשה נמי באשה אחת.§

מתני' ג'"הריני נזיר על מנת שאהא שותה יין ומיטמא למתים" — הרי זה נזיר, ואסור בכולן. "יודע אני שיש נזירות אבל איני יודע שהנזיר אסור ביין" — ד'הרי זה אסור, ור' שמעון מתיר. "יודע אני שהנזיר אסור ביין, אבל סבור הייתי שחכמים מתירין לי מפני שאין אני יכול לחיות אלא ביין" או "מפני שאני קובר את המתים" ה' — הרי זה מותר, ור' שמעון אוסר.§ גמ' ולפלוג נמי רבי שמעון ברישא! אריב"ל: חלוק היה ר"ש אף ברישא. רבינא אמר: ברישא לא פליג ר"ש; מאי טעמא ו' — משום דהוה ליה מתנה על מה שכתוב בתורה, *וכל המתנה על מה שכתוב בתורה — תנאו בטל. ור' יהושע בן לוי אמר לך: [האי] "על מנת" — כ"חוץ" דמי. תניא כוותיה דרבינא: *אמר "הריני נזיר על מנת שאהא שותה יין ומיטמא למתים" — ה"ז נזיר, ואסור בכולן, מפני שהוא מתנה על מה שכתוב בתורה, וכל המתנה על מה שכתוב בתורה — תנאו בטל.§ "יודע אני שהנזיר אסור ביין".§ והאמרת רישא: אסור, ור"ש מתיר! אימא נמי: הרי זה אסור, ור"ש מתיר. ואיבעית אימא: לעולם לא תיפוך, התם

רישא

רש"י

מתני' אמרו חכמים. כיון דשיכורה היא ואינה זקוקה לשתיה, נראין הדברים שלא נתכוונה זו לקבל עליה א) זה לשם נזירות, אלא לומר: יאסר עלי כוס זה כקרבן, ואינה אסורה אלא בכוס יין זה בלבד. גמ' וכ"ת. אי לאו (א) דנתכוונה לקבל עליה נזירות אלא להיות נידורה ממנו, לימא הכי בהאי לישנא: ב) "הרי הוא עלי קרבן" — להכי הוא דלא אמרה הכי, דסברה: אי אמינא הכי — סבירא להו שלא אסרתי עלי אלא כוס זה בלבד, ומייתו לי כוס אחרינא ואמרי לי "אשתי" וקא מצערין לי, ג) דשתויי אנא ולא מצינא למשתי לי. אימא להו בהאי לישנא דפסיקא להו מילתא דהואי אסירא נמי בכסא אחרינא, ותו לא מייתין לי ומעשה נמי באשה כו'.

מתני' הריני נזיר על מנת שאהא שותה יין ד). וקיבל עליו את השאר. הרי זה נזיר ואסור בכולן. שכל דקדוקי נזירות עליו. אבל אם אמר: יודע אני שיש נזיר בעולם ואיני יודע שנזיר אסור ביין. ואמר "הריני נזיר" — הרי זה אסור בכולן. והיינו רבנן (ב) דאמרי: אפילו לא ה) נדר אלא אחד מיניהו הוי נזיר בכולם. ורבי שמעון מתיר. דהואיל שלא קיבל עליו אלא חלי נזירות, שלא היה יודע שהנזיר אסור ביין — הרי זה מותר בכולן. ור' שמעון לטעמיה דאמר: אינו אסור עד שיזיר מכולן. ואם אמר: יודע אני שנזיר אסור ביין אבל סבור הייתי. כשהזרתי מן היין, שיהו חכמים מתירין לי, מפני שאיני יכול לחיות בלא יין. או יודע אני שהנזיר אסור לקבור מתים, וכשקבלתי עלי נזירות סבור הייתי שיהו חכמים מתירין לי מפני שאומנתי לקבור מתים — הרי זה מותר, דאיגלאי מילתא למפרע דמעיקרא לא קביל עילויה נזירות מיין ומטומאת מתים, ולא קיבל עליו אלא חלי נזירות. ור"ש אוסר. וטעמא ו) מפרש בגמ'. גמ' וליפלוג נמי ר"ש ברישא. כי היכי דפליג ר"ש ז) א"יודע אני שיש נזירות" דלא חייל עליה נזירות משום דלא קיבל כל דקדוקי נזירות. חלוק היה ר"ש אף בראשונה. (ג) ח) דראשונה נמי קאמר ר"ש: ט) כיון דאמר "על מנת שאהא שותה ביין ומיטמא י) למת" — לא נדר אלא בתגלחת לבד. ור"ש לטעמיה דאמר: אינו נזיר עד שיזיר מכולן. רבינא אמר ברישא ודאי לא פליג ר"ש. דאילו התם כיון דאמר "הריני נזיר" — קיבל עליו כל תורת נזיר, והאי דאמר "על מנת" הוי ליה כ) מתנה על מה שכתוב בתורה, (ד) ואין בתנאו כלום, והוה ליה נזיר גמור. דהוי ליה כמי שאמר "על מנת שאין לך עלי שאר כסות ועונה", שאין בתנאו כלום ל) ויתחייב לה בכולן. וריב"ל אמר לך. ברישא נמי פליג ר"ש, דהאי "על מנת" כ"חוץ" דמי, כיון דקבל עליו נזירות במקצת לא הוי מתנה על מה שכתוב בתורה. דאילו לגבי מאן דאמר "על מנת שאין ליך עלי מ) לא שאר ולא כסות ולא עונה" לא קיבל עליו כלום, אבל הכא קבל עליו במקצת, ומשום הכי הוי תנאו קיים. ואינו נזיר לפי שאין דבריו הראשונים כלום, משום דלרבי שמעון לא הוי נזיר עד שיזיר בכולן. תניא כוותיה דרבינא. דאפילו במקצת (ה) נ) קא חשיב ליה מתנה. ור"ש אוסר והאמרת רישא ר"ש מתיר. דהאי נזירות קיבל עליו, ואין ס) נודרין לאלאין.

רישא

תוספות

הריני נזיר ממנו. פי': נזיר מן הכוס, הרי זה נזיר — פי': כל דין נזירות עליו. מעשה באשה אחת ואמרו חכמים לא נתכוונה זו אלא לומר הרי עלי כוס זה כקרבן. ולא נאסרה אלא באותו כוס בלבד. ובגמ' פריך: מעשה לסתור? ואם שכור הוא הוה כאומר עלי בקרבן. פי': שדרך בני אדם להפציר בשכור שישתה, ועתה אינו רוצה לשתות, ואומר נזיר הוא — לסלקם מעליו. שאם לא יאמר נזיר הוא — ירא שיביאו לו כוס אחר, לכך אומר נזיר — לסלקם לגמרי מעליו. אבל כשאינו שכור אין דרך להפצירו, ולכך אומר דנזיר מכולהו, ומעשה נמי באשה אחת וכו'. על מנת שאשתה ביין כו' ה"ז נזיר ואסור בכולן. איכא למ"ד בגמ' משום דהוי מתנה על מה שכתוב בתורה, [דכי אמר] "הריני נזיר" — הוי נזיר לכל מילי, וכי מטיל בה תנאי — אין בתנאי כלום. ואפי' ר"ש מודה ברישא כההוא לישנא דתניא כוותיה. אבל איני יודע שנזיר אסור ביין. כלומר, שאר הלכות קבלתי עלי לבד מאיסור יין שלא קבלתי, לפי שלא ידעתי שנזיר אסור ביין. לרבנן הוי נזיר, לטעמייהו דלעיל, דאפי' לא נדר אלא אחד — הוי נזיר. ור"ש מתיר, ואזיל לטעמיה דאמר (לעיל דף ג:): עד שיזיר מכולן. יודע אני שהנזיר אסור ביין אבל אני סבור הייתי שהחכמים מתירין מפני שאיני יכול לחיות אלא ביין או מפני שאני קובר את המתים. כלומ', שאני צריך לטמאות בהם וליטפל בהן בשכר מחמת דוחקי, ולכך לא היה בדעתי לקבל איסור יין או טומאת מתים (ה"ז מותר), וכן הוא אומר שלא קיבל עליו איסור יין או טומאת מתים — ה"ז מותר, ור"ש אוסר. ובגמ' פריך דאיפכא הוה ליה למיתני. אף בראשונה. והא דקתני ר"ש [מתיר] קאי א) בתרי [בבי].

דהוי מתנה על מה שכתוב בתורה. דכשאמר "הריני נזיר" — חייל עליו נזירות לכל מילי, וכי אמר "ע"מ" — מטיל התנאי על מה שכתוב בתורה, ובטל התנאי. וא"ת: ⊕ותיפוק ליה דנזירות אי אפשר לקיים ע"י שליח, דאמר ב"המדיר" (כתובות עד.) דבעינן תנאי דומיא דבני גד ובני ראובן, שנתקיים המעשה ע"י יהושע שהיה שליח משה, והתם מהני תנאה לבטל המעשה, ולא בעלמא! וי"ל: ⊕אחרי שאחרים יכולים להביא קרבנות תחתיו נחשב כאילו כל המעשה יכול לעשות ע"י שליח. וא"ת: הא אמרינן (במנחות קט.) "הריני נזיר לגלח בבית חוניו" — יגלח בבית המקדש, גילח בבית חוניו — יצא. ואמאי? הא הוי מתנה על מה שכתוב בתורה, והל"ל בחוניו לא יצא! וי"ל: דמשמעות לשונו הרי הוא שנים: משמע ב] מקדש, ואז גילח בחוניו — לא יצא, ומשמע נמי שאינו מכוין כי אם לצעורי, ואז גילח בחוניו — יצא, ובמקדש הוי חולין בעזרה. ונזירות מתלא תליא וקאי; אי מגלח במקדש — גליא מלתא דלנזירות מעלייתא איכוין, ו"על מנת" דאמר — לא כלום הוא, ואם גילח בחוניו — גליא מילתא דלצעורי מכוין. האי ע"מ כחוץ דמי. כאילו אמר "הריני נזיר מכל מלתא חוץ מן היין" דלא הוי נזיר לר"ש, דבעינן עד שידור מכולן. וא"ת: והא מקדש את האשה ע"מ שאין לה עליו שאר כסות ועונה — הויא מקודשת והתנאי בטל (קדושין דף יט:), ולא אמר כ"חוץ" דמי! וי"ל: דגבי קדושין שאני, דאפילו אמר בפירוש "חוץ משאר" לא מהניא ליה דבורו, דאין קדושין לחצאין. וכי אמר "הרי את מקודשת" — [מקודשת], וכי אמר "חוץ משאר" — לאו מידי קאמר, ולכך חייב בכולן. אבל גבי נזיר ילפינן לעיל (דף ג:) מקראי דצריך שיזיר מכולן, דאם נדר מאחד מהם לא הוי נזיר. תניא כוותיה דרבינא. *)דהא אמר "על מנת" חשבינן ליה תנאי ולא כאומר "חוץ". *)סיפא דנדר מכולהו ואיתשיל מחדא. והיינו דקתני: אבל סבור הייתי שחכמים מתירין לי (ויתירו לו) היין או לטמאות למתים, שאינו יכול לחיות בלא יין או שלא יטפל בשכר למתים, שזהו פרנסת ביתו. לרבנן כיון דנשתרי ליה חדא משום הכי מישתריא ליה לכולהו, דלאיסורו כך היתירו, כשם שנאסר בתחילת הנזירות באחד מענייני נזירות — כן ניתר בסוף הנזיר באחד. וכמו דפליגי התם פ"ג דנדרים (דף כה:) גבי מנא אוכלים תאנים, ונמצא אביו אחד מהן והתיר נדרו, ופליגי אי הותרו כולן או לא — ה"נ סברי רבנן. ואפילו למ"ד לא הותרו כולן — משום דהוי ג] נדר ושבועה. אבל הכא כיון דתחילה הוי נזירות ד] על אחד — ה"נ סוף נזירות. ור"ש ס"ל: אפי' למ"ד הותרו כולן, מ"מ הכא כיון דאין נזירות ה] בא לו עד שיפרש מכולן — כמו כן צריך שאלה לכולן, והי דנשאל האחד — לא הותר השני.

ולרבי

*) נ"ל דכי אמר א"מ **) שייך לעי"ב

עין משפט נר מצוה

ד א מיי' פ"א מהלכות נזירות הלכה יא סמג לאוין רמג:
ה ב מיי' שם הל' יב:
ו ג מיי' שם הלכה יג:
ז ד מיי' שם הלכה יד:
ח ה מיי' שם הל' טו:
ט ו מיי' שם הלכה יג:

פי' הרא"ש

מזגו לו את הכוס ואמר הריני נזיר ממנו ה"ז נזיר ואפי' לר"ש דאמר עד שיזיר מכולן הכא מודה כיון דלא הזכיר בהדיא יין דלא גרע מידות נזירות: וכ"ת לימא הכי סבר מייתי' [לי] אחרינא ומצערו לי שכן דרך להפציר בשיכור להוסיף על שכרותו. אבל אין דרך להפציר כ"כ באדם שאינו שכור הלכך אם אין דעתו לנזיר [הו"ל] לומר הרי עלי קרבן: ה"ז נזיר ואסור בכולן. רבנן לטעמיהו דאמרי לעיל אפילו לא נדר אלא מן החרצנים נזיר מכולן: אבל איני יודע שהנזיר אסור ביין ואיני מקבל עלי ליאסור ביין. ונ"ל דלא זו אף זו קתני דרישא שהוא יודע שנזיר אסור ביין ודאי אמרינן דאין נזיר לחצאין ואסור בכולן אבל בסיפא הוי כמו נדר בטעות דאילו היה יודע שהנזיר אסור ביין לא היה מקבל נזירות: אבל סבור הייתי שחכמים מתירים וכו'. ס"ד דה"ק סבור הייתי שחכמים מתירים לי אף אם הייתי מקבלו ולכך אינו מקבלו עליה ולהכי פריך בגמ' והא אמרת רישא [אסור ור"ש מתיר] משום דהוי מתנה על מה שכתוב בתורה כיון שאמר בלשון על מנת דמיד כשאמר הריני נזיר חל עליו כל דין נזיר וכי קאמר תו על מנת ומטיל תנאי בנזירותו לא מהני א) דמתנה על מה שכתוב בתורה הוא [האי] ע"מ כחוץ דמי וכי היכי דבחוץ לא הוי נזיר בע"מ נמי לא הוי נזיר: תניא כותיה דרבינא וכו' מפני שמתנה על מ"ש בתורה והיינו כר"ש דאי לרבנן אפילו אמר חוץ מן יין הוי נזיר: והא אמרת רישא אסור ור"ש מתיר פי' ס"ד שבשעת נזירותו לא קיבל עליו יין.

א) כתוב מן הצד הגה"ה ז"ל משמע שמלשון לא בלקדוק וכך הי' מתחלה *) הריני נזיר ע"מ וכו' וכו' ונ"ע לפלוני מה שכתב הרא"ש ז"ל בפ"ק לנדרים וכו' ביו"ד סימן ר"ל לגבי נדרים ושבועות טוקא משפט התנאים א"כ אמאי נקט תנאי משום דהוא מתנה על מ"ש בתורה ותיפוק ליה מעשה קודם לתנאי. ע"ש

*) איט מוכרח ועיין היטב במ"מ בפ"ב מהל' אישות ה"ד:

מסורת הש"ס

א) [בתוספתא פ"ב]

[ב"מ נא. קדושין יט: וש"נ]

[תוספתא פ"ב]

גליון הש"ס

תוס' ד"ה דהוי מתנה כו' וא"ת ותיפוק ליה. לא ידעתי מאי קושיא דאי לאו טעמא דמתנה על מה שכתוב בתורה הוי מהני תנאה כאן דאינו יכול לקיים ע"י שליח לא כיון דאין מעשה גמור דלא מצי עשה ע"י שליח. קי"ל לעיל כן ולא אמרינן כלל שלא הכא באו כפי מאי שלא גמור שמתנה את עצמו שקיים אף על תנאי פי"ע:

הגהות מהר"ב רנשבורג

א] תוס' ד"ה אף קאי בתרי בבי תיבות בתרי בבי נמחקו וצ"ל בתרוייהו: ב] ד"ה דהוי וכו' שנים משמע נזירות מעליא ומקדש: ג] ד"ה לרבנן וכו' ואפילו למ"ד לא הותרו כולן משום דהוי נדר ושבועה: ד] בא"ד הוי נזירות על אחד: ה] בא"ד מ"מ הכא כיון דאין נזירות חלה עד שיפרש מכולן:

נוסחת הריב"ן

א) עליה שום נזירות: ב) לישנא דאמרה: ג) וקא מצערין לי: ד) וקבל עליו שאר דקדוקי נזירות או ע"מ שאטמא למתים וקבל עליו כו': ה) נדר: ו) מפרש: ז) ביודע: ח) דלראשונה: ט) כיון: י) למתים: כ) מתנה: ל) ונתחייב בכולן: מ) ע"מ שאין ליך עלי שאר כסות ועונה: נ) כי הא: ס) נודרין:

הגהות הב"ח

(א) רש"י ד"ה וכ"ת תימא אי לאו דנתכוון לקבל עליו נזירות אלא להיות נידור ממנו לימא בלשון הכי: (ב) ד"ה אבל וכו' והיינו רבנן דפ"ק סוף דף ג דאמרי אפי' לא נדר: (ג) ד"ה חלוק וכו' דלראשונה נמי: (ד) ד"ה רבינא וכו' ואין בתנאו: (ה) ד"ה תניא וכו' במקצת נמי קא חשיב:

י א ב מיי' פ"ג מהלכות שבועות הלכה ה ופ"ד מהלכות נדרים הלכה ג ופ"ב מהלכות נזירות הל' ח סמג לאוין רמב טוש"ע יו"ד סימן רלב סעיף ה:

יא ג ד ה מיי' פ"ח מהל' נזירות הל' יט:

רישא — כגון דנזר מחדא; לרבנן *דאמרי דאפי' לא נזר אלא מאחת מהן — הוי נזיר, ואסור. *לר' שמעון דאמר עד שיזיר מכולם — מותר. סיפא — דנדר מכולהו ואיתשיל מחדא; לרבנן דאמרי אפילו לא נזר אלא מאחת מהן הוי נזיר, כי מתשיל מחדא מינייהו — אישתרי. לרבי שמעון דאמר עד שיזיר מכולם, כי מתשיל נמי מההוא — עד דמתשיל מכולהו, משום הכי קתני: ור"ש אוסר. ואב"א: בנדרי אונסין קא מיפלגי, ובפלוגתא דשמואל ורב אסי. דתנן: *א ארבעה נדרים התירו חכמים: נדרי זירוזין, נדרי הבאי, נדרי שגגות, נדרי אונסין. *ואמר רב יהודה אמר רב אסי: ארבעה נדרים הללו צריכין שאלה לחכמים. כי אמריתה קמיה דשמואל, אמר לי: תנא קתני ב"התירו חכמים", ואת אמרת צריכין שאלה לחכמים?! רבנן סברי כשמואל, ור"ש כרב אסי.§ **מתני'** ג"הריני נזיר ועלי לגלח נזיר", ושמע חבירו ואמר "ואני ועלי לגלח נזיר", אם היו פקחים — מגלחין זה את זה, ואם לאו — מגלחין נזירים אחרים.§ **גמ'** איבעיא להו: שמע חבירו ואמר "ואני", מהו? "ואני" אכוליה דיבורא משמע, או דלמא אפלגיה דדיבורא משמע? את"ל אפלגיה דדיבורא משמע, ארישא או אסיפא? תא שמע: "ואני ועלי לגלח נזיר" אם היו פקחים — מגלחין זה את זה. מדקאמר "ואני ועלי" ד ש"מ "ואני" אפלגיה דדיבורא. (א) אמרי: אין, אפלגיה דדיבורא משמע, מיהו ארישא או אסיפא? מינה, מדקאמר "ועלי לגלח" ה — ש"מ "ואני" על תחילת דיבורא משמע. א"ל רב הונא בריה דרב יהושע לרבא: ממאי דהכי? (ב) לעולם אימא לך "ואני" אכוליה דדיבורא, ואי משום "ועלי", מאי קאמר — ועלי בהא מילתא. דאי לא תימא הכי, דקתני סיפא: *"הרי עלי לגלח חצי נזיר" ושמע חבירו ואמר "ואני עלי לגלח חצי נזיר", התם מי איכא תרתין מילי? אלא מאי קאמר "עלי" — בהא מילתא, הכא נמי כי קאמר "עלי" — בהא מילתא. א"ל רבא: הכי השתא?! אי אמרת בשלמא רישא צריכא סיפא לא צריכא, תני סיפא דלא צריכא משום רישא דצריכא. אלא אי אמרת רישא לא צריכא סיפא לא צריכא, תני רישא דלא צריכא ותני סיפא דלא צריכא?! אמר ר' יצחק בר יוסף אמר רבי יוחנן: *האומר לשלוחו צא

צא

ולרבי שמעון. כי היכי דבתחלת הנזירות צריך שיזיר, גם בסוף הנזירות צריך לשאול ולהתיר כולו. **ואי** בעית אימא בנדרי אונסין. זה חשיב אונס, שאינו יכול לחיות בלא יין. **נדרי** זירוזין. כגון שהמוכר אומר "קונם ככר זה עלי אם אתן לך חפץ זה בפחות מד' דינרין" — ה"ז נדרי זירוזין, או "קונם ככר זה עלי אם אתן לך יותר משני דינרים" ורצון שניהם לקנות בג' דינר — ה"ז נדרי זירוזין, ג] ואין צריכין עוד שאלה, למ"ד מדרבנן. **נדרי** שגגות. "קונם ככר זה אם אכלתי היום", ושכח שאכל היום. **נדרי** אונסים. מפרש בנדרים (דף כז.): כגון שהדירו חבירו שיאכל אצלו ביום פלוני, ואירע לו אונס שלא יכול לבא אצלו, אם צריך לשאול על אותו נדר מדרבנן — פליגי בה אמוראי התם. **נדרי** הבאי. מפרש התם, פי': בנדרים (כד:). וא"ת: ומי דמי? התם בשעת הנדר לא ידע האונס, דהא סבור ליילך ולאכול, וגמר ונדר — ולהכי צריך לשאול מדרבנן, למ"ד. אבל הכא — בשעת הנדר ידע האונס, ומסתמא לא גמר ונדר, ואיכא למימר דלכ"ע לא בעי שאלה! ומפ' ר"ת: דמתניתין נמי איירי שהאונס בא אחרי כן, כגון דבשעת הנדר היה בריא וחזק ויכול לחיות בלא יין, ולבסוף החלים. או תחלה היה עשיר ולא היה צריך ליטפל למתים, ולבסוף העני. אי נמי, מייתי ליה דין זה ד] היכא דאין פיו ולבו שוין, דפליגי בהא התם אמוראי אי בעי שאלה מדרבנן, והכי נמי פליגי הכא. הגה"ה: וכמו כן במתניתין פיו היה להיות נזיר מיין, אבל לבו לא היה. ומה דאמר "אבל" — כסבור הייתי ה] בלבי כשעשיתי הנדר. **הריני** נזיר ועלי לגלח נזיר. כי "הריני נזיר" — בעצמו חייב בנזירות ולהביא קרבנותיו, "ועלי לגלח נזיר" — אחר, ולהביא קרבנותיו. השתא נזירות חייל עליה, ועתה צריך לגלח נזיר אחר ולהביא קרבנותיו. ושמע חבירו ואמר: ואני, פירוש: ואני ועלי לגלח נזיר אחר — חייל עליה [נזירות] וגם תגלחת של נזיר אחר. **ואם** היו פקחין מגלחין זה את זה. פירוש: כל אחד ואחד יעשה נזירותו שלשים יום, ומביא קרבן בעבור חבירו, ומפטרי. מידי דהוה אאיניש בעלמא אם היה מביא קרבן עבורו שפטר. וגם זה נפטר ממה שנדר לגלח לאחר, שהרי גלח לאחר. נמצא כי כל אחד לא יביא אלא קרבן א' ואפ"ה [יצא] נמי ידי ו] נדריה, שהרי בלאו אחר עשה נזירות שלשים יום וגילח לחבירו. **ואם** לאו. שאין להם פקחות זה, אלא כל אחד הביא קרבן לעצמו — צריך לגלח לנזיר אחר, ולהביא קרבנותיו תחתיו. **ושמע** חבירו ואמר ואני. ולא [אמר] עוד, [מהו]? על כוליה דיבור של הראשון משמע, וחייב השני להיות נזיר ולגלח, או דלמא על פלגיה דיבורא משמע, ולא קבל עליו השני אלא או נזירות או תגלחת לאחר. **מדקאמר** ואני ועלי ש"מ. אם לא אמר שני הדבורים, דפלגא דדיבור' משמע. **ומינה.** כלומר, גם זה תיפשוט ממתניתין — מדקאמר "ועלי לגלח" — ש"מ "ואני" — על תחילת דיבורו משמע. **לעולם** ואני אכוליה דיבוריה משמע ואי משום ועלי מאי קאמר ועלי בהך מילתא. כלומר, ומה שקבלתי כבר נזירות תגלחת לאחר, כמו דרך בני אדם לכפול (על) לשונן. והוא הדין דאם לא אמר "ועלי" דמחייב בנזיר ותגלחת אדיבור קמא. **ושמע** חבירו ואמר ואני ועלי לגלח חצי נזיר, מי איכא תרתי מילי? והרי הראשון לא קבל עליו אלא דבר אחד.
משום רישא דצריכא. דאיצטריך למיתני "ועלי" לאשמועינן ד"ואני" לא קאי אלא אפלגא דדיבוריה, ותנא סיפא ד"עלי" אע"ג דלא

רישא כגון דנזר מחדא כו'. א] ואילו (ג) א) לרבנן ברישא דרישא מודה ר"ש דאסור אע"ג דלא נדר בכולהו, משום דהוי ליה מתנה על מה שכתוב בתורה ותנאו בטל. **ואיתשיל מחדא.** דקאמר: אבל סבור הייתי שחכמים מתירין. ב) ולרבנן דאמרי: אפילו כי לא נזר אלא באחת מהן הוי נזיר, הכי נמי כי מיתשיל אחד מינייהו — אישתרי נמי אכולהו, והלכך הוא מותר. (ד) ולר"ש דאמר. לעולם אינו נזיר עד שיזיר מכולן בבת אחת, כגון דאמר "הריני נזיר" סתם — הכי נמי לכי מיתשיל לחכם אחדא מינייהו — לא מפקע נזירותיה מיניה עד דמיתשיל אכולהו. והלכך הואיל דלא איתשיל אלא חדא, משום הכי אוסר ר"ש. **איבעית אימא בנדרי אונסין קא מיפלגי.** במתניתין, (ה) הואיל דנדרי אונסין הן, הואיל דאין יכול לחיות בלא יין, או שאין קוברין באותו מקום אלא זה. ל"א: דבמתני' להכי קרי להו אונסין — דלבו אונסו, שהוא סבור שיתירו לו חכמים, דבכה"ג קרי ליה אונס, כדאמרי' נמי במס' שבועות (דף כו.) דרב כהנא ורב אסי מר משתבע דהכי אמר רב ומר משתבע דהכי אמר רב, וכי הוה אתי רב ואמר כחד מינייהו, א"ל אידך: ואנא בשיקרא אישתבעי? א"ל רב: לבך אנסך, ומיפטרת. **וקמיפלגי בפלוגתא דשמואל ורב אסי.** דתנן בפרק "ארבעה נדרים" במסכת נדרים: ד' נדרים התירו חכמים וכו', והתם מפרש להו. **רבנן סברי.** דאין צריך שאלה כשמואל, ומשום הכי שרי. **ור' שמעון** ג) **כרב אסי.** דאוסר בלא שאלה לחכם, ומשום הכי מיתסר כל זמן שלא התירו לו. **מתני'** אמר הריני נזיר ועלי לגלח נזיר. ואני במקומו של נזיר אחר להביא קרבנותיו ביום תגלחתו. **אם היו פקחין מגלחין זה את זה.** מביא זה קרבנותיו של זה וזה קרבנותיו של זה, ויהו פטורים מלהביא קרבן אחר ואם לאו — כל אחד ואחד מביא קרבנותיו שלו, וצריכין להביא כל אחד ואחד קרבנות של נזיר אחר. **גמ' איבעיא להו.** אמר "הריני נזיר ועלי לגלח נזיר" ושמע חבירו ואמר "ואני" ולא אמר תו מידי. **מהו.** מי אמרי': האי דאמר "ואני" אכוליה דיבורא משמע, והוי נזיר ומיחייב לגלח נזיר אחר. **או דלמא הא דאמר ואני אפלגא דדיבוריה משמע.** דחדא מינייהו הוא דקביל עילויה — או נזירות או לגלח, אבל תרווייהו לא משמע. **ארישא או אסיפא.** ארישא משמע: ואני בנזירות כמותך, או אסיפא משמע: ואני ד) אגלח נזיר כמותך. **מדאמר ואני ועלי.** מדקתני לתרוייהו — ש"מ דהאי דאמר "ואני" לא קאי אלא אפלגא ה) דיבוריה. **ומינה,** מדקאמר "עלי לגלח" — ש"מ "ואני" אתחלת דיבוריה קאי. והכי משמע: ואני בנזירות כמותך, ועלי לגלח נזיר כמותך. **וממאי דהכי הוא.** כדקאמרת, ד"ואני" אפלגא דדיבוריה קאי? דלמא אכוליה דיבוריה קאי. ואי אמרת לי: כיון (ו) ד"אני" אכוליה דיבוריה ו) משמע, "עלי" למה לי? איהו ודאי לא ז) מילטריך, אלא פירושי קמפרש למילתא, דמשמע כמו דאמר: עלי בהא מילתא. **דאי לא תימא הכי.** דפירושי קא מפרש לה, אלא ד"ואני" קאי אדיבורא דרישא, ו"עלי" אדיבורא דסיפא, סיפא דמתניתין דקתני: "הרי עלי לגלח" כו' התם למה לי כו'. **אי אמרת בשלמא רישא.** דתני "ועלי" צריכא לך למימר משום דקא מקבל בה בדיבורה ב] (דסיפא) — אהכי תנא בסיפא (ז) אידך מתניתין "עלי" דלא צריך. אלא אי אמרת ד"עלי" דרישא לא צריכא, דהא קאי "ואני" אכוליה דיבוריה, השתא איכא למימר: מי עבידת כי הא מילתא ח) למיתני תנא "עלי" ברישא דלא צריכא וסיפא דלא צריכא?! אלא לאו שמע מינה: "ואני" אפלגא דדיבוריה קאי, שמע מינה.

לא

פי' הרא"ש

סיפא דנזר מכולהו ואיתשיל מחדא קיבל עליו נזירות בסתם ואח"כ בא לפני חכם ונתחרט על איסור היין או על טומאת מתים ואמר כסבור הייתי שחכמים מתירים לי שא"א לי להיות בלי יין או בלי לטמא למתים לרבנן סוף נזיר כתחילת נזיר כמו בקבלת נזירות אם קיבל עליו דבר אחד חל עליו כל תורת נזיר ה"ה נמי סוף נזיר אם נשאל על א' הותר הכל הכא א) מודה מטעמא דפרישי' דסוף נזיר כתחלת נזיר ור"ש נמי סבר סוף נזיר כתחלת נזיר ואפילו למאן דאית לי' נדר שהותר מקצתו הותר כולו הכא מודה כי היכי דבתחלת נזיר אינו נזיר עד שיזיר מכולן ה"נ לענין חרטה לא הותר עד שיתחרט על כולו: ד' נדרים התירו חכמים נדרי זירוזים מפרש התם היה מוכר חפץ ואמר קונם שאיני פוחת לך מן הסלע והלה אומר קונם שאיני מוסיף לך על השקל ושניהם רוצי' בג' דינרים שניהם מותרים שכל אחד נתכוון לזרז חבירו ולא היה פיו ולבו שוין לשם נדר: נדרי שגגות כגון קונם אם אכלתי ושתיתי ונזכר שאכל ושתה לא הוי נדר דאמרינן האדם בשבועה פרט לאנוס ובשעה שנדר היה סבור שלא אכל ולא היה בדעתו לידור ואנוס הוא מחמת שכחה: נדרי הבאי קונם אם לא ראיתי בדרך הזה כעולי מצרים אם לא ראיתי נחש כקורת בית הבד אינו נדר שכן דרך אנשים כשרואים דבר מופלג ומשונה מוסיפין עליו שפת יתר ומדברי' לשון הבאי וגוזמא: נדרי אונסים הדירו חבירו שיאכל אצלו וחלה הוא או שחלה בנו או שעכבו נהר כיון שעכבו אונס לא הוי נדר דאדעתא דהכי לא נדר: ד' נדרים הללו צריכים שאלה לחכם ולא בפתח חרטה דכל נדר נמי ניתר ע"י חרטה אלא אע"ג דלא נדרים נינהו צריך לילך לחכם ויתיר לו שלא יקיל ראשו בנדרים ובמתני' נמי אונס הוא שאינו יכול לחיות בלא יין ושלא לטמא למתים רבנן סברי כשמואל דלא בעי שאלה ור"ש אוסר עד שיתיר לו כרב אסי וק"ק דלא דמי לנדרי אונסי' דהתם בשעה שנדר לא ידע באונס שאירע לאחר מכאן אבל הכא בשעה שנדר ידע זה האונס ותירץ הר"מ דמ"מ טעמא דמתני' כמו טעמא דנדרי אונסים דהתם בשעה שנדר הוי טעמא משום דאין פיו ולבו שוין דאדעתא דאונס לא נדר. במתני' נמי בשעה שקיבל עליו נזירות לא היה בדעתו לאסור עצמו ביין כי אם שאר דברים ולא היה פיו ולבו שוין הלכך לרבנן לא בעי שאלה ואע"ג דאי הוה אמר בהדיא חוץ מן היין דהוי נזיר הני מילי היכא דלא אנים בקבלת יין אבל הכא דמחמת אונס אינו מקבל עליו יין לא הוי נזיר כלל ובשם ר' יצחק מצאתי דמתני' מיירי כשקבל עליו נזירות סתם והיה דעתו לכל דין נזירות ואירע לו מקרה או חולה שצריך לשתות יין או שהוצרך ליטמא למתים ועתה הוא אומר יודע אני שהנזיר אסור ביין אבל הייתי סבור שאפילו היה בדעתי להיות נזיר בכל ענין הוו חכמים מתירים לי מחמת האונס כ"ש דהוא שיתירו לי כי ודאי לדעת אלו האונסים לא קבלתי עלי ונ"ל שצריך להוסיף על דבריו דאכתי לא דמי לגמרי לנדרי אונסים דהתם אימא דהאונס קודם שחל הנדר הלכך יש לפרש דהכא מיירי כגון

א) אולי צ"ל ואפילו למ"ד דנדר שהותר מקצתו לא הותר כולו הכא מודה.

[לעיל ג:]

[לעיל שם וש"נ]

נדרים כ: [שבועות כח:]

[נדרים כח:]

[לקמן יב:]

גיטין סד. ע"ש

נוסחת הריב"ן

א) לרבינא: ב) מתירים לי: ג) ור"ש אוסר כלו: ד) לגלח: ה) אפלגא ומינה: ו) קאי: ז) אנטריך: ח) לאיתני:

הגהות מהר"ב רנשבורג

א] רש"י ד"ה רישא וכו' ואילו וכו' נ"ב עיין א"מ: ב] ד"ה א"ב וכו' דקא מקבל בה בדיבורה (דסיפא) נ"ב עי' א"מ: ג] תוס' ד"ה נדרי זרוזין וכו' ה"ז נדרי זרוזין ואין נ"ב הכן נמחק מלת ואין וכו' כצ"ל א"מ: ד] ד"ה נדרי הבאי וכו' אי נמי מייתי ליה דין זה הכא כצ"ל: ה] בא"ד הג"ה וכמו כן וכו' אבל כסבור הייתי היינו בלבי כשעשיתי הנדר כצ"ל וכ"ב בתוס' הרא"ש על המשנה: ו] ד"ה ואם היו פקחין מגלחין וכו' ואפ"ה יצא נמי ידי נדריה כצ"ל:

הגהות הב"ח

(א) גמ' ואני אפלגיה דדיבורא משמע אמרי וכו' או אסיפא ומינה: (ב) שם ממאי דהכי הוא לעולם וכו' אכוליה דדיבורא משמע ואי משום: (ג) רש"י ד"ה רישא וכו' ואילו כרישא מודה ר"ש לרבנן דאסור: (ד) ד"ה ולר"ש וכו' אלא אחת: (ה) ד"ה איבעית אימא בנדרי אונסין במתניתין דנדרי כצ"ל ותיבת הואיל נמחק: (ו) ד"ה וממאי וכו' כיון דואני אכוליה דיבורא משמע ועלי וכו' דאמר ועלי: (ז) ד"ה אי אמרת וכו' איכא למימר מי עביד תנא כי הא מילתא למיתני עלי ברישא כצ"ל:

"צֵא וְקַדֵּשׁ לִי אִשָּׁה" סְתָם — (א) אאָסוּר בְּכָל הַנָּשִׁים שֶׁבָּעוֹלָם; *חֲזָקָה שָׁלִיחַ עוֹשֶׂה שְׁלִיחוּתוֹ, וְכֵיוָן דְּלָא פָּרֵישׁ לֵיהּ — הָא לָא יָדַע הֵי נִיהוּ קַדֵּישׁ לֵיהּ. אֵיתִיבֵיהּ ר"ל לְרַבִּי יוֹחָנָן: *בקֵן סְתוּמָה שֶׁפָּרְחָה גּוֹזָל אֶחָד מֵהֶן לַאֲוִיר הָעוֹלָם, אוֹ שֶׁפָּרְחָה לְבֵין חַטָּאוֹת הַמֵּתוֹת, אוֹ שֶׁמֵּת אֶחָד מֵהֶן — יִקַּח זוּג לַשֵּׁנִי. וְאִילּוּ קֵן מְפוֹרֶשֶׁת — אֵין לוֹ תַּקָּנָה. וְאִילּוּ שְׁאָר קִינִּין בְּעָלְמָא — מִיתַּקְּנָן. וְאַמַּאי? לֵימָא כָּל חֲדָא וַחֲדָא דִּלְמָא הַאי נִיהוּ! אֲמַר לֵיהּ: קָאמִינָא אֲנָא אִשָּׁה דְּלָא נַיְידָא, וְאָמְרַתְּ לִי אַתְּ אִיסּוּרָא דְּנַיֵּיד? וכ"ת: הָכָא נַמִי נַיֵּיד, אֵימוּר בְּשׁוּקָא אַשְׁכַּח וְקַדֵּישׁ — הָתָם הָדְרָא לְנִיחוּתָא, גַּבֵּי קֵן מִי הָדְרָא? אֲמַר רָבָא: גוּמוֹדֶה רַבִּי יוֹחָנָן בְּאִשָּׁה שֶׁאֵין לָהּ לֹא בַּת, וְלֹא בַּת בַּת, וְלֹא בַּת בֵּן, וְלֹא אֵם, וְלֹא אֵם אֵם, וְלֹא אֲחוֹת, וְאַף עַל פִּי שֶׁהָיְתָה לָהּ אֲחוֹת וְנִתְגָּרְשָׁה לְאַחַר מִכָּאן — דְּהַהִיא שַׁרְיָא. מַאי טַעְמָא — דִּבְהַהִיא שַׁעְתָּא דקא"ל, הֲוָה (ב) נְסִיבָן לְגַבְרֵי. כִּי מְשַׁוֵּי שָׁלִיחַ — בְּמִילְּתָא דְּקַיְימָא קַמֵּיהּ, בְּמִילְּתָא דְּלָא קַיְימָא קַמֵּיהּ — לָא מְשַׁוֵּי שָׁלִיחַ. תְּנַן: "הֲרֵינִי נָזִיר וְעָלַי לְגַלֵּחַ נָזִיר" וְשָׁמַע חֲבֵירוֹ וְאָמַר "וַאֲנִי, וְעָלַי לְגַלֵּחַ נָזִיר", אִם הָיוּ פִּקְחִין — מְגַלְּחִין זֶה אֶת זֶה, וְאִם לָאו — מְגַלְּחִין נְזִירִים אֲחֵרִים. בִּשְׁלָמָא בַּתְרָאָה אִיכָּא קַדְמָאָה קַמֵּיהּ, אֶלָּא קַדְמָאָה — מִי אִיכָּא בַּתְרָאָה קַמֵּיהּ? אֶלָּא

רש"י

צא וְקַדֵּשׁ לִי אִשָּׁה סְתָם. שֶׁלֹּא פֵּירֵשׁ לוֹ בְּאֵיזוֹ עִיר וְאֵיזוֹ אִשָּׁה. חֲזָקָה שָׁלִיחַ עוֹשֶׂה שְׁלִיחוּתוֹ. וְהָלַךְ וְקִידֵּשׁ לוֹ אִשָּׁה. וְכֵיוָן שֶׁלֹּא פֵּירֵשׁ לוֹ הֵי מִינַּיְיהוּ קַדֵּישׁ לֵיהּ וְלֹא יָדַע אֵיזוֹ קִידֵּשׁ לוֹ, וְאִי הֲדַר אוֹתוֹ הָאִישׁ וְנָסֵיב אִיתְּתָא — דִּלְמָא זוֹ הִיא אִמָּהּ אוֹ בִּתָּהּ אוֹ אֲחוֹתָהּ שֶׁל אוֹתָהּ הָאִשָּׁה שֶׁקִּידֵּשׁ לוֹ שְׁלוּחוֹ, וְהֵן כּוּלָּן אֲסוּרוֹת לוֹ, כִּדְאָמַר הָתָם *(קדושין דף עו): הַמְקַדֵּשׁ אֶת הָאִשָּׁה אוֹסֵר עָלָיו שֶׁבַע עֲרָיוֹת. קֵן סְתוּמָה. אֶחָד מֵחַיָּיבֵי קִינִּין, כְּגוֹן הַזָּב וְהַזָּבָה יוֹלֶדֶת וּמְצוֹרָע, שֶׁהִפְרִישׁוּ לָהֶן שְׁתֵּי תוֹרִין אוֹ שְׁנֵי בְנֵי יוֹנָה, וַעֲדַיִין לֹא קָרְאוּ לָהֶן שֵׁם אֵיזוֹ לְחַטָּאת וְאֵיזוֹ לְעוֹלָה, וּפָרַח גּוֹזָל אֶחָד מֵהֶן לַאֲוִיר הָעוֹלָם. א] אוֹ שֶׁפָּרְחָה לְבֵין חַטָּאוֹת מֵתוֹת — כְּגוֹן שֶׁהָיוּ שָׁם א) מֵה' חַטָּאוֹת הַמֵּתוֹת, כְּגוֹן חַטָּאת שֶׁכִּיפְּרוּ בְּעָלֶיהָ כו', וְנִתְעָרְבָה בֵּינֵיהֶן וְאֵין יָדוּעַ אֵיזוֹ הִיא, דְּאֵין לָהּ שׁוּב תַּקָּנָה. יִקַּח גּוֹזָל לַשֵּׁנִי. וְאַחַ"כ יַפְרִישׁ אֶחָד לְחַטָּאת וְאֶחָד לְעוֹלָה. (גִּלָּיוֹן: לְהָכִי קָאָמַר בֵּין חַטָּאוֹת הַמֵּתוֹת — דְּאִילּוּ נִתְעָרְבָה בֵּין חַטָּאוֹת חַיּוֹת וְהָנָךְ חַטָּאוֹת דִּידֵיהּ נִינְהוּ — מָצֵי לְמֵיסַב חַד מִינַּיְיהוּ וְעָבֵיד לֵיהּ זוּג לְהַאי, וְהָא דְּלָא נִתְעָרֵב הָוֵה ג) קָרֵיב לָהּ עוֹלָה). וְאִילּוּ קֵן מְפוֹרֶשֶׁת. שֶׁפָּרַח אֶחָד מֵהֶן וְאֵינוֹ יוֹדֵעַ אֵיזוֹ ג) הִיא — אֵין לוֹ תַּקָּנָה, לְפִי שֶׁאֵין יוֹדֵעַ אֵיזוֹ לְחַטָּאת וְאֵיזוֹ לְעוֹלָה. ד) וְאַעַ"ג דְּפֵירֵשׁ, כֵּיוָן דְּלָא הָוֵי תַּרְוַיְיהוּ קַמֵּיהּ — לֵית בְּהוּ הֶיכֵּרָא, דְּלָא יָדַע אִי הַאי שֵׁנִי הָוֵי חַטָּאת אוֹ עוֹלָה. וְאִילּוּ שְׁאָר קִינִּין דְּעָלְמָא מִתַּקְּנָן וְאַמַּאי לֵימָא. לְכָל מַאן דְּמַיְיתֵי קִינִּין: הַיְינוּ הַאי דְּפָרַח לִפְלוֹנִי אֶתְמוֹל, וְנִמְצָא מִתְכַּפֵּר בְּקָרְבַּן חֲבֵירוֹ, דְּהָא אָמַרְתְּ שֶׁהוּא אָסוּר בְּכָל הַנָּשִׁים שֶׁבָּעוֹלָם! אֲמַר לֵיהּ אָמִינָא לָךְ אֲנָא אִשָּׁה דְּלָא נַיְידָא. ד"כָּל כְּבוּדָּה בַת מֶלֶךְ פְּנִימָה", וְהוֹאִיל דִּקְבִיעָה הָוֵה לֵיהּ כְּמֶחֱצָה עַל מֶחֱצָה וְאָסוּר. וְאַתְּ מוֹתְבַתְּ לִי מֵאִיסּוּרָא דְּנַיֵּיד, דְּאִיכָּא לְמֵימַר דְּהָתָם בְּדִין הוּא דְּלִישְׁתְּרוּ, מִשּׁוּם דְּאִית בָּהּ טַעְמָא ד"כָל דְּפָרֵישׁ מֵרוּבָּא דְּהֶיתֵּירָא פָּרֵישׁ". וְכִי תֵּימָא גַּבֵּי אִשָּׁה נַמִי אֵימוּר. הַאי בַּעַל אַשְׁכְּחֵיהּ לְהַהִיא אִיתְּתָא בְּשׁוּקָא, דְּנַיְידָא וְלִישְׁתְּרֵי בָּהּ — דְּכָל דְּפָרֵישׁ מֵרוּבָּא פָּרֵישׁ — אַכַּתִּי לָא דָּמֵי. דְּאִילּוּ אִיתְּתָא הָדְרָא לְנִיחוּתָא, כֵּיוָן דְּעָיְילָא לְבֵיתָהּ — הָוְיָא לָהּ קְבוּעָה, אֲבָל גַּבֵּי קֵן — לְעוֹלָם הָוְיָא לָהּ אִיסּוּרָא דְּנַיְידָא. וּמוֹדֶה ר' יוֹחָנָן בְּאִשָּׁה שֶׁאֵין לָהּ בַּת כו' וְלֹא אָחוֹת. פְּנוּיָה. וְאַעַ"פ ה) וכו' — דִּלְאַחַר מִכֵּן הָוְיָא לָהּ חֲדָא מֵהָנֵי קְרוֹבוֹתֶיהָ פְּנוּיָה. כֵּיוָן דִּבִזְמַן שֶׁשִּׁילַּח זֶה שְׁלוּחוֹ הָיְתָה הָאַחַת נְשׂוּאָה וְהָאַחַת פְּנוּיָה, וּבָא זֶה ו) וְקִידֵּשׁ אֶת הַפְּנוּיָה — אֵין חוֹשְׁשִׁין לוֹמַר: שֶׁמָּא שְׁלוּחוֹ בָּא לְכָאן וְקִידֵּשׁ אֶת אֲחוֹתָהּ לְאַחַר שֶׁנִּתְגָּרְשָׁה, וְנִמְצָא זֶה פּוֹגֵעַ בַּאֲחוֹתָהּ וְיֵשׁ בּוֹ מִשּׁוּם אִיסּוּר שְׁתֵּי אֲחָיוֹת. דִּסְתָמָא דְּמִילְּתָא כִּי מְשַׁוֵּי אִינִישׁ שָׁלִיחַ — בְּמִילְּתָא דְּקַיְימָא קַמֵּיהּ בְּלֹא אִיסּוּרָא, אֲבָל בְּמִלְּתָא דְּלָא קַיְימָא קַמֵּיהּ, כְּגוֹן זוֹ דִּבְהַהִיא שַׁעְתָּא דְּקָא מְשַׁוֵּי שָׁלִיחַ לְהַאי הֲוָה מִינַּסְבָא לְגַבְרָא — לָא מְשַׁוֵּי אִינִישׁ שָׁלִיחַ. בִּשְׁלָמָא בַּתְרָא. לְהָכִי מְגַלֵּחַ אֶת הָרִאשׁוֹן ז) — דְּזֶה קָאֵים קַמֵּיהּ הָאֵיךְ נָזִיר קַדְמָאָה, וְאִיכָּא לְמֵימַר דְּהוֹאִיל וְקָאֵים קַמֵּיהּ מִיחַיֵּיב בְּקָרְבַּן תִּגְלַחְתּוֹ (ג). אֶלָּא קַדְמָאָה. אַמַּאי מְגַלֵּחַ אֶת הַשֵּׁנִי? וְהָא בְּהַהוּא שַׁעְתָּא לָא הֲוָה הַאי נָזִיר קַמֵּיהּ, וְאַתְּ הוּא דְּאָמְרַתְּ: ח) מִילְּתָא דְּלָא קָאֵים קַמֵּיהּ דְּאִינִישׁ לָא מַסֵּיק אַדַּעְתֵּיהּ לְקַבּוּלֵי עִילָּוֵיהּ, ט) וְאַמַּאי אָמְרַתְּ דִּמְגַלְּחִים זֶה אֶת זֶה? הָכִי

תוספות

דלא נריכא, אטו רישא. אסור בכל הנשים שבעולם. וא"ת: וכ"ע יאסרו לישא נשים, דשמא זאת היא שנתקדשה ע"י שליח! ולר"ת, דהנשים נאמנות לומר "לא נתקדשתי" – תינח גדולות, קטנות שאינן יודעות אם אביהם קבל עבורן קדושין מאי איכא למימר? וכבר מת אביה! וי"ל: דמדאורייתא אפילו הוא שרי לישא, דאזלינן בתר רובא [מלומר] מקרובות המקודשת היא. ואינו אלא קנסא בעלמא – שעשה שליח סתם ולא פירש לו "קדש לפלונית", ולדידיה קנסו ולאחריני לא קנסו. [וא"ת]: וליהוי איסורא דאורייתא, דהויא ליה קבוע, וכל קבוע כמחצה על מחצה דמי! וי"ל: דלא אמרינן קבוע כמחצה דמי אלא כשהאיסור ניכר לעצמו וההיתר ניכר לעצמו, אבל כשאין האיסור ניכר לעצמו לא אמרינן קבוע*.

קן סתומה. דזב וזבה ויולדת שמביאין חטאת העוף ועולת העוף. וסתומה – פירוש: זב וזבה שהבעלים לא פירשו בשעת לקיחת בעלים איזהו לעולה. ומש"ה נקט סתומה, *דאי מפורשת – היה צריך להאריך ולפרש איזהו פרח, העולה [או] החטאת, ולהכי קיצר בלשונו ואמר דפרח אחד מהם.

ואילו שאר קינין בעלמא מתקנן ואמאי לימא כל חדא וחדא הוא. [דלמא] אותו שפרח, כלומר והוקבע כבר לראובן, ואיך יצא שמעון בו ידי חובתו? וא"ת: והא כבר פירשנו דלעלמא לא קנסו! ויש לומר: דמשמע ליה דשאר קינין דעלמא, אפי' לראובן מיתקן אם יצטרך לקן אחד [לזיבה אחרת], אמאי? הא קנסו לדידיה – ה"נ יקנסוהו שלא שמר קיניה, ולומר שזה פרח מקן ראשון והוקבע לזיבות ראשון!

אשה דלא ניידא. ונהי דלא קבוע לגמרי כדפ"ל, מ"מ דמיא קצת לקבוע, ויש להחמיר. **בשוקא** אשכח וקדיש. ◎כלומר היכא דמצא אותה בשוקא היה לנו לומר שיוכל לקדשה, דלא קביעה הויא, וא"כ לא הוה קבוע. **התם** הדרא לניחותא. ודמי לקבוע.

באשה שאין לה בת כו'. פי': כגון *[שמצאו] שליח בר"ח ניסן. אבל כל קרובותיה, שראויה רחל זו לאסור מקדושיה, הוו נשואות בר"ח ניסן כשעשהו שליח. ואע"פ שנתגרשו קודם יום הקדושין – מותרת רחל זו למשלח, כדמפרש טעמא – דמשעה דקאמר הויין נסיבן.

כי משוי איניש שליח במילתיה דקיימא קמיה. כלומר, [אין] דעתו שיקדש לו אשה שנתגרשה אחרי כן. הלכך, אפילו אם קידש אחת מקרובותיה של רחל – לא נאסרה רחל בקידושין שהוא ב] עשאו שליח, לכך לא חלו קדושי קרובי רחל. והשתא קס"ד דאין דעת האדם אלא במידי דקאי קמיה, לכך פריך אמתני': בשלמא ג] מתני' בתראה איכא קדמאה קמיה – שנדר כבר, ואיכא למימר דדעתיה עליה, ולכך פוטר עצמו בקרבנות הראשון. אלא קדמאה – מי איכא בתראה כשנדר הראשון? וא"כ לא היה בדעתו עליו להביא קרבנות, ואיך יפטר מנדרו בהבאת קרבנותיו של שני? **מ"ט**. כלומר, היכי דמי שלא היה לה אחות ועתה יש לה? ומן הדין הוה ליה לומר "היכי דמי", אלא משום דלשון נזיר משונה. ויש ליישב הלשון ד"מאי טעמא", דלעולם הוה ידע שפיר דמיירי כגון דנסיבן לגברי, מכל מקום עתה שנתגרשו – יש לנו לספק ולאסור מספק! *ומשני: כי משוי איניש שליח במילתיה דאיהו מצי עביד וכו'. פי': ודאי דעת האדם אפילו במידי דלא קאי קמיה, והלכך הראשון נפטר בגילות השני. אבל שליחותא* (בעא) דלא מצי איניש משוי שליח אלא במילתיה דמצי עביד נפשיה בשעה שעושה שליח – דהא נסיבי' – לא מצי לשוויה שליח לקדש לו אף כשתתגרש, ואף קדשה השליח – אינה מקודשת. ואם תאמר: דהא מעשים בכל יום שהאשה אומרת לחבירתה: לושי לי קמח והפרישי חלה בעבורי, וגם תלמידים של בית רבן אומרים כן, ואיך נעשה שליח בדבר הזה? הא בשעה שעושה אותה שליחות – לא היתה יכולה בעצמה להפריש חלה מקמח זה שאינו בר חיובא, שאין מפרישין חלה מקמח! ואומר רבינו תם: דיש בידה להביא עיסה מגולגלת, ולומר: עיסה זו תהא חלה על קמח לכשיהיה נילוש, ודברים שבידה קיימים, דאין זה דבר שלא בא לעולם. כיון שבידה ללוש ולגלגל העיסה – קרוי שפיר בא לעולם, כיון שבידה לעשות. כדאמר פרק "האומר לחבירו" (קדושין דף סב:): "פירות ערוגה זו תלושה יהא תרומה על פירות ערוגה זו מחוברת לכשיתלשו" ונתלשו – דבריו קיימין, דכל שבידו לעשות – לאו כמחוסר מעשה דמי, ובידו לתולשם. ומכל מקום בהאי טעמא לחודא לא סגי לן למימר דמצי למיעבד שליח כאן, כיון דבידו ללוש ולגלגל. ◎מדאמר פרק "רבן גמליאל" (יבמות דף נב.): האומר לחבירו "כתוב גט לארוסתי לכשאכניסנה אגרשנה" – הרי זה גט, מפני שבידו לגרשה מיהא אם ירצה. ובעי התם: ליבמתו מהו? ומאי קא מיבעיא ליה? והא בידו לבא עליה ולגרשה! אלא ודאי, כיון דהשתא לא מצי לגרשה – לא מצי משוי שליח, כיון דמחוסר מעשה לבא עליה. הכא נמי, כיון דהשתא איהו לא מצי להפריש – אינו קרוי "בידו" מה שבידו ללוש ולגלגל לענין זה שיכול לעשות שליח, כיון דמחוסר לישה וגילגול. טעמא

פי' הרא"ש

כגון שאמר הריני נזיר לזמן ידוע שאז יתחיל נזירותי וקודם הגעת הזמן אירע לו אונס: אסור בכל הנשים שבעולם דשמא קדש שלוחו אחת מקרובותיה: קן סתומה שלא פירש איזו לעולה ואיזו לחטאת או שפרח לבין חטאות המתות כגון שמתו בעליהן או נתכפרו באחרות דהלכה למשה מסיני שימותו וה"ה דהוה מצי למתני קן מפורשת כגון שפירש איזו לעולה ואיזו לחטאת אלא שהיה צריך לפרש ובלבד שיכיר הנשארת אם היא חטאת או עולה דאם אינו מכירה אינו [י]כול ליקח לה זוג דאינה ראויה להקרבה שהעולה נעשית למעלה והחטאת למטה ולא רצה להאריך ותנא קן סתומה וגם אורחא דמלתא שאינו מכיר אם עולה אם חטאת כשנאבד זוגה אלא כשהם ביחד אז נקיל להכירם א"נ נקט קן סתומה משום סיפא פרח לבין הקרבנות פסול ופוסל א' כנגדו ואם היה מפורש היה פוסל שנים ועשר: ואילו שאר קינין דעלמא מתקנין ולא פסלינן כל קינין שבעולם דדלמא זו שפרחה היא אחת מהן ונמצא מתכפר בקרבן חבירו: אמינא לך איסור דניחא דבשעה שקדשה השליח היתה נחה וקבועה בביתה הלכך היתה חשובה בין כל הנשים שבעולם כמחצה על מחצה ואילו עשאו שליח לקדש לו נשים הרבה וקידש חצי הנשים שבעולם היו נאסרות כל הנשים משום ספק קרובות אפילו אי ניידי משום דרוב כל הנשים אסורות עליו משום ספק קורבה השתא נמי נאסרות כל הנשים כיון שהאוסר קבוע אע"פ שאין הנאסר קבוע: ואת אמרת לי איסורא דנייד העוף הפורח הוא נד בעולם וכיון דלא הוי קבוע אין לו כח לאסור דבטל הוא ברוב קנין שבעולם אבל אי הוי קבוע חשבינן כאילו חצי קנין שבעולם אסורים כדחשבינן האשה המקודשת כאילו קדש חצי הנשים שבעולם וכי תימא הכא נמי דנייד דאימר בשוקא אשכח וקדיש דחומרא יתירא היא לאסור כל הנשים שבעולם והיה לנו לתלות שמא בשעה שקדשה לא היתה קבועה ולא היתה כחצי הנשים שבעולם הדרה לניחותא אחר שקדשה וכיון דקבועה היא השתא חשובה כחצי הנשים אבל עוף אין לו קביעות אפילו כשחוזר לקנו דתדיר נודד ממקומו ופורח מקן לקן ואין לו קביעות מקום: שאין לה לא בת דניחוש לחמות וגם לא בת בת וגם לא בת בן דניחוש לאם חמיו ואם חמותו ולא אם דניחוש לבת אשתו וגם לא אם אם ולא אם אב דניחוש לבת בתה ולבת בנה ואע"פ שהיתה לה אחות והיתה נשואה בשעה שמנה את שלוחו לקדש לו אשה ונתגרשה לאלתר לאחר מינוי השליחות מותרת היא ולא חיישינן שמא קדשה שלוחו אחר שנתגרשה: במילתא דלא קיימא קמיה לא משוי איניש שליח וקס"ד דמקשה [ממתני'] דלא מסיק איניש אדעתא למנותו שליח למה שאין בידו לעשות עתה הלכך לא הוי שלוחו לקדש לו אותה אשה שנתגרשה אחר מינוי השליחות ואם קידשה לו אינה מקודשת ומותר בקרובותיה אבל אם פירש בפירוש שעשאו שליח אפילו לנשים שהן עתה אסורות אם יהיו מותרות הוי שלוחו לפי מאי דס"ד השתא: בשלמא בתראה שאמר ואני ועלי לגלח נזיר איכא קדמאה קמיה (שהם ניכר) [שכבר] נזר בנזירות ויכול השני לפוטרו אלא קדמאה בשעה שקיבל עליו לגלח נזיר אכתי לא נזר השני והיאך נאמר שדעתו היה לפוטרו אם יקבל עליו נזירות הא לא מסיק איניש אדעתיה במה

מסורת הש"ס

[ריש מסכת דרך ארץ]

[עירובין לא: גיטין סד. חולין יב.]

קינין פ"ב מ"א

נוסחת הריב"ן

א) מאותן חמש: ב) קרי: ג) לשני: ד) לעולה הס"ד ואח"כ מה"ד ואלו: ה) ואע"פ שלאחר מיכן הויא לה אחות פנויה כיון כו': ו) המשלח: ז) דהוה: ח) דממילתא: ט) אלא אמאי קא אמרת כו' זא"ז הס"ד ומ"ה דהכי קאמר:

הגהות הב"ח

(א) גמ' אשה סתם ומת השליח אסור בכל הנשים: (ב) שם הוה נסיבא לגברא כי משוי: (ג) רש"י ד"ה בשלמא בתרא הד"א עם ד"ה אלא וכו' זה את זה אלא הכי קאמר כצ"ל והד"א:

גליון הש"ס

תוס' ד"ה בשוקא אשכח וכו' כלומר. עי' כתובות דף טו ע"א תוס' ד"ה דלמא אזלא: **ד"ה** מ"ט וכו' מדאמר פרק ר"ג. קשה לי כיון דנקטו דבידו לייבם אם כן עדיין קשה הא הוא בעצמו יכול לגרשה עתה לכשתתייבם דלא הוי דבר שלא בא לעולם וא"כ מצי משוי שליח כמו בחלה וצ"ע:

הגהות מהר"ב רנשבורג

א] רש"י ד"ה קן סתומה וכו' או שפרחה לבין חטאות מתות נ"ב עיין לקמן דף כא ע"ב רש"י ד"ה והיינו טעמא וכו' ובשער המלך פ"ד הלכה א' מהל' פסמ"ק: ב] תוס' ד"ה כי משוי וכו' בקידושין שהוא לא עשאו שליח לכך וכו' ולא כצ"ל: ג] בא"ד לכך פריך אמתני' בשלמא מתני' נמחק מלת מתני':

שייך לע"ב

נ"ל בענין אחר

עין משפט נר מצוה

יב א מיי' פ"ט מהלכות אישות הלכה ו סמג עשין מח טור ש"ע אה"ע סימן לה סעיף יא:

יג ב מיי' פ"ט מהלכות פסולי מוקדשין הל' א:

יד ג מיי' פ"ט מהלכות אישות ה"ז סמג עשין מח טוש"ע אה"ע סימן לה סעיף יא [וברי"ף פ"ב דקדושין דף רל ע"א וברא"ש שם סימן יח]:

[וע"ע בתוס' גיטין סד. ד"ה אסור]

[כתב התי"ע במס' קינין פ"ב משנה א' נראה להתוס' לא גרסו בגמ' הך דאילו קן מפורש אין לו תקנה עכ"ל]

גי' א"מ שמינה כו' אבל כל כו'

עין משפט נר מצוה

טו א מיי' פי"ג מהלכות נדרים הלכה ט סמג לאוין רמב טוש"ע י"ד סימן רלד סעיף ל:
טז ב ג מיי' שם טור ש"ע שם סעיף כח:
יז ד מיי' פ"ח מהלכות נזירות הלכה כ:
יח ה מיי' שם הל' יח:
יט ו מיי' שם פ"א הל' יז:

אלא הכי קאמר: אי משכחנא דהוי נזיר – אגלחיה. הכא נמי הכי קאמר ליה: אי משכחת דמיגרשה – קדיש לי. אמרי: לא משוי איניש שליח אלא במילתא דמצי עביד השתא, במילתא דלא מצי עביד ליה השתא – לא משוי. (א) ולא?! ת"ש: *האומר לאפוטרופוס שלו "כל נדרים שתדור אשתי מכאן עד שאבוא ממקום פלוני הפר לה" והפר לה, יכול יהו מופרין? – ת"ל °"אישה יקימנו ואישה יפרנו" דברי ר' יאשיה, ור' יונתן אומר: מצינו בכל מקום *ששלוחו של אדם כמותו. טעמא דאמר רחמנא "אישה יקימנו ואישה יפרנו", הא לאו הכי – אפוטרופוס מיפר. ואילו גבי דידיה *תניא: בהאומר לאשתו "כל נדרים שתדורי מכאן ועד שאבא ממקום פלוני יהו קיימין" – לא אמר כלום. "הרי הן מופרין", ר"א אומר: מופר, וחכ"א: גאינו מופר. קס"ד: כי אמר רבי יאשיה – אליבא דרבנן דאמרי: לא מצי מיפר. ואי לאו דאמר רחמנא "אישה יקימנו ואישה יפרנו" – אפוטרופוס הוה מיפר! ודלמא אליבא דרבי אליעזר, דאמר: מצי מיפר. אי הכי למה לי לשוויי שליח? ליפר לה איהו! קסבר: דלמא משתלינא, או רתחנא, או מיטרידנא.§ מתני' *"הרי עלי לגלח חצי נזיר", ושמע חבירו ואמר "ואני עלי לגלח חצי נזיר" – זה מגלח נזיר שלם, וזה מגלח נזיר שלם, דברי רבי מאיר. וחכמים אומרים: דזה מגלח חצי נזיר, וזה מגלח חצי נזיר.§ גמ' אמר רבא: ההכל מודים כל היכא דאמר "חצי קרבנות נזיר עלי" – חצי קרבן מייתי, "קרבנות חצי נזיר עלי" – כוליה קרבן בעי איתויי; מאי טעמא – דהא לא אשכחן נזירות לפלגא. וכי פליגי – בלישנא דמתני' פליגי, ר"מ סבר: כיון דאמר "הרי עלי" – איחייב אכוליה קרבן נזירות, וכי קאמר חצי נזירות – לאו כל כמיניה. ורבנן סברי: אנדר ופתח עמו הוא.§ מתני' ו"הריני נזיר לכשיהיה לי בן" ונולד לו בן – הרי זה נזיר. נולד לו בת, טומטום, ואנדרוגינוס – אינו נזיר. אם אמר ב"כשיהיה לי ולד" – אפילו נולד לו בת, טומטום, ואנדרוגינוס – הרי זה נזיר. הפילה

א) לעיל ע. מנחות פא: קג. ב) נ"א כשאראה

פירוש (בגיליון השמאלי של הגמרא):

הכי קאמר. אי משכחנא כו'. דמצי עבד ליה איהו גופיה השתא. כגון בפלוגתא דשריא ליה, לאפוקי היכא דבההיא שעתא לא משתריא ליה: (הפר לה והיפר לה. שלוחו של אדם כמותו). שתדורי מכאן עד שאבא כו'. קס"ד דכי א"ר יאשיה אין אפוטרופוס מיפר – אליבא דרבנן, דאמרי גבי דידיה דבעל דאיהו נמי לא מצי מיפר. ואי לאו דאמר רחמנא ואישה יפרנו אפוטרופוס הוה מיפר. ואע"ג דבעל לא מצי מיפר השתא. אלמא במילתא דלא מצי איניש למיעבד השתא משוי ליה שליח א). אי הכי. דמצי מיפר, למה ליה לשוויי שליח? ליפר לה בעל לאלתר! סבר. האי בעל: לא צריכנא להפר לה אלא בשעה שאלך לדרך, דלמא בההוא שעתא מישתלינא או מטרדינא או רתחנא. הלכך קאמר לאפוטרופוס דליעבד איהו. מתני' הרי עלי לגלח חצי נזיר. דאמר: הרי עלי להביא חצי קרבנותיו של גילוח נזיר אחד. זה מגלח נזיר שלם וזה מגלח נזיר שלם. שלא מצינו ב) נזיר לחצאין ג) ולא קרבן לחצאין. והוא סבר: אין אדם מוציא דבריו לבטלה. וחכ"א. ד) יביאו שניהן קרבנותיו של נזיר אחד ויהיו פטורין, שהרי לא ה) נזרו כל אחד אלא חצי נזיר. (ב) גמ' אמר רבא ה"ג: הכל מודים כל היכא דאמר חצי קרבנות נזיר עלי וכו' כוליה קרבן בעי לאיתויי. מ"ט – דהא לא אשכחן נזירות לפלגא. כי פליגי בלישנא דמתני', היכא דאמר הרי עלי לגלח, דר"מ סבר כיון דאמר הרי עלי לגלח איחייב אכוליה קרבן דנזיר, והאי דהדר אמר חצי נזיר לאו כל כמיניה, ורבנן סברי כל כה"ג – נדר ופתחו עמו הוא, ובין שניהם מביאין קרבן, דנדר אחד הוא. ואיכא ספרים דלא כתיב בהו הך "אמר רבא", אלא הכי כתיב בהו: קרבן בעי איתויי. כלומר, נזיר מיהא לא מיפטר בקרבנותיהן דהנך, הואיל דכל חד וחד קיבל עילוייה פלגא דנזירות ותו לא ו) אשכחן נזירות לפלגא, והאי דקא ז) מייתי ליה אינהו – לייתי ליה משום נדבה. כי פליגי בלישנא דמתני', כגון דאמר "הרי עלי לגלח", ולא אמר בסתם "חצי נזירות עלי", דר"מ סובר: כיון דאמר "הרי עלי לגלח" – ח) אכוליה קרבן נזירות, ומיפטר ביה נזיר בהאי קרבן נזירות, והאי דהדר אמר "חצי נזירות" – מיהדר הוא דקא בעי, ולאו כל כמיניה. ורבנן סברי: נדר ופתחו עמו הוא, א] ולא מיפטר נזיר בקרבנותיו דהאיך. ט) ושניהם מיהא קרבן אחד בעי איתויי. [ל"א]: אילו אמר אחד בלבד "הרי עלי לגלח חצי נזיר" – אפילו רבנן מודו דקרבן שלם בעי איתויי. מ"ט – דהא לא אשכחן נזירות לפלגא. כי פליגי י) אלישנא דמתני' דאיכא תרי, דבין שניהם מביאין קרבן שלם; ר"מ סבר: כי אמר "הרי עלי" מיחייב אכוליה קרבן, וכי הדר אמר "חצי נזיר" לאו כל כמיניה, דתפוס לשון ראשון. הלכך זה מגלח נזיר שלם וזה מגלח נזיר שלם. ורבנן סברי: כיון דתרי אינון – לא הוי קרבן לחצאין, והוי נדר ופתחו עמו, דכי אמר "לגלח חצי נזיר" כ) פירוש "עלי" דאמר לכתחלה. הלכך זה מגלח חצי נזיר וזה מגלח חצי נזיר, דכיון דבין שניהם מביאין קרבן שלם לא הוי קרבן לחצאין ל). מתני' נולד לו בת או טומטום ואנדרוגינוס הרי זה נזיר. דולד מיהא מיקרי. הפילה

תוספות:

טעמא דכתב רחמנא אישה יפירנו. ניחא ליה לאותובי גם לר' יאשיה, דמדר' יונתן מצי לאותובי [בההיא] הרי הן קיימין לא אמר כלום. דהקמה בטעות הוא, דשמא [תדור] בדבר שא"א ליה להקים. ליפר לה הוא. פירוש כשילא מביתו. דלמא מישתלינא. לשון שגגה, או מיטרידנא – מן הדרך. ולכך רוצה למנות אפוטרופוס, ואותו אפוטרופוס יהיה מיושב בדעתו. וא"ת: ואכתי ליפר לה איהו מעכשיו, שהרי הוא זוכר עתה ומיושב בדעתו! וי"ל: דאינו רוצה לומר שיהא מופר אלא נדרים שתדור מכי יסע ואילך, אבל לא נדרים שלפני נסיעתו, שזה קלא קשה. אבל קשה: דלימא לה השתא "כל נדרים שתדורי מכשאסע עד שאשוב יהו מופרין"! ב] וי"ל: דמתוך כך תפול קטטה ביניהם, שזה קשה לה לעולם. ובנדרים מיבעיא לן אי בעלה מצי מיפר בלא שמיעת קול, וגם הפרה דשליח [אינה] מועלת עד דשמע הבעל הנדר, דהכי מוקי לה התם (דף עג:). ולפי' זה נפרש: ליפר לה איהו – פירוש: כשיסע יפר לה בעלה, ותועיל ההפרה לכשיבא הבעל וישמע הנדר. ואם ימתין להפר עד שישוב וישמע – שמא יהיה טרוד לכשישמע, וישתוק מלהפר, ולכך פריך: ליפר לה מהשתא, ותועיל ההפרה כשישמע. ובשלמא אי סבר כרבנן – ניחא, [דלא] מצי מיפר. ומשני: דלמא טרידנא כשירצה ליסע, כדפרישית. ע"כ הגה"ה.

ושמע חבירו ואמר ואני. בכדי נקט, דהא בראשון נמי פליגי.

אמר רבא הכל מודים באומר חצי קרבנות נזיר עלי חצי קרבן מייתי. כיון שתלה החצי בקרבן, שאמר "חצי קרבנות" – ודאי פלגא דקרבן, ג] שיחד [תיבת] "חצי" מתיבת "נזיר". "קרבנות חצי נזיר עלי" – קרבן שלם בעי ליה לאתויי. מאי טעמא דלא אשכחן נזירות לפלגא. דכיון דסמך תיבת "חצי" אצל ד] "נזיר" (מתיבת) משמע מדיבורו ד"חצי" אנזירות קאי, ואין חייב שום חצי נזיר בעולם. כי פליגי בלישנא דמתני'. ה] [באומר] "הריני נזיר" וכיון דאמר "הרי עלי לגלח" – ומיחייב בכוליה קרבן לר"מ, דתפוס לשון ראשון, וכי אמר "חצי נזיר" – לא כל כמיניה, והוי כאומר "קרבנות חצי נזיר עלי" דמייתי קרבן שלם. וקשה: אמאי קאמר האי לישנא "כיון דאמר עלי איחייב [בכוליה]"? לימא להדיא דדמי ו] [כאומר] "קרבנות חצי נזירות", רבנן סברי: נדרו ופתחו, דהוי כאומר חצי קרבנות נזיר עלי! וי"ל: דהא דאמר רבא "קרבנות חצי נזיר עלי", דכולה בעי איתויי – משום ד"חצי" קאי א"נזיר", אבל משמע להו במתני' דלישנא ד"חצי" קאי א"עלי", וכמי שאמר "חצי קרבנות נזיר עלי".

הריני נזיר כשיהיה לי בן. פירוש: הודאה ושבח להקב"ה שחנני וזיכני ונולד לי בן – *הריני נזיר. בגמרא פריך: פשיטא.

בת טומטום ואנדרוגינוס אינו נזיר. דזה לא מחשיבו. אהא נמי פריך בגמ': פשיטא. אבל אמר בלשון זה: "כשאראה לי ולד", אפי' טומטום ואנדרוגינוס – הרי זה נזיר. אהא נמי פריך בגמרא: פשיטא:

*)הפילה אשתו. ולא ידעינן אי נפל הוא, או בן קיימא הוא וכלו לו חדשיו, או שמת במעי אמו – אינו נזיר. ובגמ' מוקי לה כר' יהודה, דסבר: לא מחית איניש נפשיה לספיקא, ז] וספק נזיר הוי – דלמא בן קיימא מה שהפילה. הלכך טוב להתנות ולומר: אם בן קיימא – הריני נזיר חובה מדבורי הראשון, ואם אינו בר קיימא, כגון דלא כלו לו חדשיו, ולא היה בדיבורי הראשון כלום – הריני נזיר נדבה, כלומר, מעתה הריני מקבל עלי נזירות. [ומונה] נזירות ומביא קרבנותיו, ומותר ביין ומגלח. שאם לא התנה כן – כל ימיו היה מקולקל לר"ש, דמספיקא לא מצי לגלח, ויאסר כל ימיו ביין ובתגלחת ובטומאה. ור"ש לא פליג אהא דנולד לו בן טומטום וכו' – דליכא לספוקי, דכשאמר "כשיהיה לי בן" ודאי לא היה דעתו אלא לבן ודאי, ולא לטומטום. ולא פליג ר"ש אלא היכא דהפילה בן זכר, דמספקא ליה דשמא הוה בן קיימא, והוי בן גמור. וה"א הדין דמילתיה דר"ש קאי ארישא, היכא דאמר "הריני נזיר כשיהיה לי בן" והפילה כו'.

*) שייך לדף יג.

פי' הרא"ש

במה דלא קיים קמיה אלא מאי קאמר אי משכחנא דהוי נזיר מגלחנא ליה אפילו אם ידור אחר קבלת נדרו דמסיק איניש (שפירש) אדעתיה במאי דלא קיים קמיה א) השתא במילתיה דלא מצי עביד לא משוי שליח ולעולם מסיק איניש אנפשיה במאי דלא קיים קמיה ואפ"ה לא הוי שלוחו אפי' אם פירש לו בפירוש דכל מילתא דלא מצי איהו למעבד השתא שאם היה אומר לה הרי את מקודשת לי לאחר שיגרשך בעליך לא הויא מקודשת דאין אדם מקנה דבר שלא בא לעולם הלכך אי אמר נמי לשלוחו קדשנה לי לאחר שתתגרש לא הוי שלוחו: ת"ל אישה יקימנו ואישה יפירנו מיתורא דקרא דריש דלא מצי משוי שליח טעמא דאמר רחמנא אישה יקימנו ואישה יפירנו [הא] לאו הכי וכו' הוה מצי לאקשויי ממלתיה דרבי יונתן אלא דניחא ליה לאקשויי מתרווייהו: יהון קיימין לא אמר כלום דאנן סהדי דלא אמר בלבו לקיים לה כל נדריה דשמא תדור דבר שהוא גנאי לו וקשה בעיניה אם יתקיים: הרי הם מופרים. ר' אלעזר אומר מופר דאין אדם חפץ באשה נדרנית וניחא ליה שכל נדריה יהיו מופרים וחכ"א אינו מופר מפ' בנדרים טעמייהו משום דכתיב אישה יקימנו ואישה יפירנו כל שאינו בכלל הקמה אינו בכלל הפרה קס"ד דבני הישיבה שרצו להקשות מכאן דכי אמר רבי יאשיה אליבא דרבנן דאמרי לא מצי מיפר דאי אליבא דר' אלעזר אמאי משוי שליח להפר יפיר לה הוא בעצמו אלמא מלתא דלא מצי איהו למעבד משוי שליח ומשני לעולם ר' יאשיה אליבא דר"א והא דקשיא לך אמאי אינו מיפר לה בשעה שמחזיק בדרך דלמא משתלינא או ריתחנא או מטרידנא הלכך ממנה שליח יום או יומיים קודם הליכתו והא ליכא למימר אמאי לאי יפיר לה באותה שעה כל נדרים שתידור מאותה שעה עד שישוב מן הדרך לפי שכל זמן שישנו בעיר אינו רוצה שיהו מופרים עד שישמע את נדרה דשמא תדור נדר שהוא חפץ [בו] ומיהו קשה יפיר לה משעת הליכתו עד שישוב כמו שאומר לשליח טרם לכתו להפר לה משיחזיק בדרך עד שישוב וי"ל דלא משו' שליח אלא בשעת הליכתו דלא מסיק אדעתיה קודם לכן ואותה שעה דלמא מטריד ולא יוכל להפר בפניה וא"ג דמשמע בנדרים שיכול להפר אפילו שלא בפניה מ"מ הוא ירא שמא תעבור על נדרה ואע"פ שהפר לה כיון שלא ידעה יש לה עונש כנתכוון לאכול בשר חזיר ועלה בידו בשר טלה הלכך ניחא ליה טפי שיפר לה השליח בפניה: היכא דאמר חצי קרבנות נזיר חצי קרבנות בעי אתויי כיון דאמר חצי קרבנות יפרע לשיר אחד דמי חצי קרבנותיו אבל אם אמר קרבנות חצי נזיר כיון דלא אשכחן חצי נזיר הוי כאילו קבל עליו קרבנות נזיר שלם. רבי מאיר סבר כיון דאמר הרי עלי איחייב בכוליה קרבן נזירותיה דרבי מאיר לטעמיה דאית ליה תפוס לשון ראשון וכי אמר הרי עלי לגלח הוי כאילו אמר תגלחת שלימה של נזיר וכי אמר תו חצי נזיר דמשמע דמגלח קאי אחצי נזיר עליה לאו כל כמיניה דתפוס לשון ראשון דמשמע תגלחת שלימה אבל אם אמר הרי עלי חצי קרבנות נזירות לא שייך הכא למימר תפוס לשון ראשון דהרי עלי לא כלום קאמר בלא סיום דבריו ורבנן סברי נדר ופתחו עמו והוי כאומר חצי קרבנות נזיר עלי והכי קאמר הרי עלי חצי תגלחת נזיר ולא דמי לקרבנות חצי נזיר דקרבנות משמע

חזרה

א) נראה דצ"ל אלא במילתא דמצי עביד השתא במילתא דל"מ עביד וכו'.

מסורת הש"ס

נדרים עב: [ב"מ נו.]

נוסחת הריב"ן

א) בכ"י כתוב כאן בזה"ל גליון מצינו בכאן מקום ששלוחו של אדם כמותו שנאמר ושחטו אותו כל עדת ישראל וכי כל הקהל שוחטין אותו אלא מכאן ששלוחו של אדם כמותו אף בהפרה נמי יהא שלוחו של אדם כמותו דמצי מיפר ואפי' לרבי יאשיה טעמא דאמר רחמנא כו': דלמא היכא דאמרת השתא דאי לאו דכתיב אישה יפרנו הוי אמר ר' יאשי' דאפוטרופוס מיפר דלמא אליבא דר' אליעזר קאמר דבעל מצי מיפר מהשתא ומשום דבעל מיפר מהשתא מצי נמי לשוויה שליח הס"ד ואח"כ מה"ד מתני' זה מגלח כו': ב) שלא מצינו שיהא אדם נזיר: ג) ולא קרבן לחצאין ליתא בכ"י: ד) יבואו שניהם ויביאו קרבנותיו של נזיר אחר ויהיו: ה) נדרו: ו) ואנן לא אשכחן: ז) מייתו ליה אינהו לייתו: ח) מחייב אכוליה: ט) דהיאך ושניהם מפי המורה ל"א קרבן בעי אתויי אילו אמר אחד בלבד הרי עלי כו': י) בלישנא דמתני' כו' דר"מ סבר: כ) פרש: ל) בכ"י כתוב כאן בזה"ל גליון ואי לא הוי חד לאמר עלי לגלח חצי נזיר ילך לנזיר אחר ויביא בעבורו חצי קרבנותיו ויהא קרבן שלם בין שניהם ואי קשיא הא אמרינן לעיל היכא דאמר הריני נזיר מן הגרוגרות דאמרי בית הלל נדר ופתחו עמו הוא ופטור מכולן והכי אמרי רבנן נדר ופתחו עמו חייב להביא חצי קרבן תריץ התם להכי פטור משום דפתח הוא במידי דלא שייך בנזיר כגון גרוגרות דלא שייכי בנזירות אבל הכא דשייך הפתח בנזיר כגון הכא מודו כולהו לחייב מפי רבי:

הגהות הב"ח

(א) גמ' השתא לא משוי שליח ולא: (ב) רש"י ד"ה וחכמים וכו' נזיר הס"ד ואח"כ מ"ה ה"ג אמר רבא הכל מודים וכו' פלגא דנזירות ולא אשכחן וכו' הרי עלי לגלח איחייב אכוליה קרבן וכו' בעי אתויי ליפנא אחרינא קרבן בעי איתויי אילו אמר אחד בלבד וכו' לכתחלה הוא הלכך וכו' לחצאין הס"ד ואח"כ מ"ה אפילו נולד:

הגהות מהר"ב רנשבורג א] רש"י ד"ה אמר רבא וכו' ולא מיפטר נזיר בקרבנותיו דהאיך ושניהם כ"ב עיין תורת מישור: ב] תוס' ד"ה דלמא וכו' וי"ל דמתוך כך תפול קטטה ביניהם שזה וכו' נ"ב עיין א"מ: ג] ד"ה אמר רבא וכו' ודאי פלגא דקרבן שיחד תיבת חצי מתיבת נזיר וכו'. מן תיבת שיחד עד נזיר נמחק ונ"ב שיחוד חייב מצי מחייב בנדר כצ"ל א"מ: ד] ד"ה מאי טעמא וכו' דכיון דסמך תיבת חצי אצל נזיר מתיבת וכו' תיבות נזיר מתיבת נמחקו ונ"ב אצל תיבת נזיר משמע מדיבורו דחצי כצ"ל: ה] ד"ה כי פליגי בלישנא דמתני' דהוי כאומר כצ"ל: ו] בא"ד לימא להדיא דדמי לאומר כצ"ל: ז] ד"ה הפילה וכו' לספיקא ור"ש חייש לספיקא כצ"ל א"מ:

הפילה אשתו – אינו נזיר. ר"ש אומר: יאמר "אם היה בן קיימא – הרי אני נזיר חובה, ואם לאו – הרי אני נזיר נדבה". אחזרה וילדה – ה"ז נזיר. ר"ש אומר: יאמר "אם הראשון בן קיימא – הראשון חובה, וזו נדבה. ואם לאו – הראשון נדבה, וזו חובה". § **גמ'** האי מאי למימרא? משום סיפא: בת, טומטום, ואנדרוגינוס – אינו נזיר. פשיטא! מהו דתימא: "לכשאבנה" הוא דקאמר, קמ"ל דלא. § "ואם אמר כשיהיה לי ולד" כו'. § פשיטא! מהו דתימא: ולד דמיחשב ביני אינשי בעינן, קמ"ל. § "הפילה אשתו אינו נזיר". § מאן קתני לה? *רבי יהודה דכרי הוא. § "ר"ש אומר: יאמר "אם היה בן קיימא הריני נזיר חובה ואם לאו הריני נזיר נדבה". § בעא מיניה רבי אבא מרב הונא: "הריני נזיר לכשיהיה לי בן" והפילה אשתו, והפריש קרבן, וחזרה וילדה, מהו? אליבא דמאן? אי אליבא דר"ש – מאי תיבעי ליה? הא *אמר ר"ש: ספק נזירות להחמיר. ואלא אליבא דרבי יהודה, דאמר ספק נזירות להקל, מאי? קדוש או לא קדוש? מאי נ"מ? לגיזתו ולעבוד בו. בתיקו. בעא מיניה בן רחומי מאביי: "הריני נזיר לכשיהא לי בן", ושמע חבירו ואמר *"ועלי", מהו? אדיבוריה משמע, או אגופיה משמע? גאת"ל אגופיה משמע, אמר "הריני נזיר לכשיהא *לי בן", ושמע חבירו ואמר "ואני", מהו? אנפשיה קאמר, או דילמא ה"ק*: רחימנא לך כוותיך? דאת"ל כל באנפיה כסיפא

הפילה אשתו אינו נזיר. דדילמא האי דהפילה לא הוה בן קיימא, שלא כלו לו חדשיו, ולא ולד הוי, וספק נזירות – להקל. ר' שמעון אומר. אין דרך זו מוליאתו מידי נזירות. אלא (א) אם היה בן קיימא הריני נזיר חובה ואם לאו הריני נזיר נדבה. דקסבר: ספק נזירות להחמיר. חזרה וילדה. לאחר שהפילה. הרי זה נזיר. דהשתא מיהא ולד הוא דאית ליה, וחיילא עליה נזירות. ר"ש אומר. שמא הראשון הוה בן קיימא וחל עליו נזירות, והשתא כי ילדה לא חייל נזירות, ואם כדרכו יעשה – נמצא זה מביא חולין לעזרה. אלא, יחזיר וימנה נזירות שנייה, ויאמר: אם הראשון שהפילה היה בן קיימא – נזירות הראשונה חובה וזו נדבה, ואם לא היה בן קיימא – נזירות הראשונה נדבה וזו חובה. **גמ'** האי מאי למימרא. דכי נולד לו בן הרי זה נזיר. מהו דתימא. האי דקאמר לאו משום בן דוקא, והאי דאמר "בן" – לכשאבנה ממנה הוא דמשמע, כגון "ואבנה גם אנכי ממנה" (בראשית ל), וכי נולד בת או טומטום ואנדרוגינוס נמי ליהוי נזיר, קמ"ל דלא. ולד דמיחשב ביני אינשי קאמינא. דהיינו בן ותו לא, קמ"ל דבת וטומטום ואנדרוגינוס נמי איקרו "ולד". ר' יהודה. דאמר לעיל דספק נזירות להקל, כדאמרי' בפ"ק (לעיל ד' ח.), דתניא: "הריני נזיר ע"מ שיש בכרי זה ק' כור", והלך כו' ר' יהודה מתיר, דספק נזירות להקל. והפריש קרבן וחזרה וילדה מהו. מי הוי קדוש או לא. אליבא דמאן. קמיבעיא לך. אי אליבא דר"ש – פשיטא דהוי קדוש, דהאמר ספק נזירות להחמיר, וקודם שילדה אשתו נמי הוי נזיר. אלא אליבא דר' יהודה דאמר ספק נזירות להקל מאי. מי אמרינן: כיון שהפרישו בשעה שהפילה ולא חיילא עליה (א) נזירות כלל – לא הוי קדוש כלל, ומיבעי ליה למיהדר ולקדושי. מאי נפקא לך מינה. (ב) אי הוה קדוש או לא, דהא ילדה וחיילא עליה נזירות. נפקא מינה לגיזתו ולעבוד בו. והכי קא מיבעיא ליה: אי אמרת משעה שהפריש תחילה כשהפילה הוה ליה קדוש – הוה ליה אסור בגיזה ועבודה. אלא אי אמרת דלא חיילא עליה נזירות אלא משעה שחזרה וילדה – הוה ליה מותר בגיזה ובעבודה. מאי? תיקו. ושמע חבירו ואמר ועלי מהו אדיבוריה. דההוא גברא קאי, ומשמע: ועלי להיות נזיר כשיהיה לך בן. או (ג) דילמא אגופיה משמע, אנפשיה, דהכי משמע: ועלי נמי להיות נזיר כשיהיה' לי בן. (ד) ושמע חברו ואמר ואני מהו אנפשיה קאמר. ומשמע כי קאמר: ואני נזיר כשיהא לי בן. או דילמא. אדיבורא דחבריה קאי, ומשמע כאילו אמר: ואני רחימנא ליה לאותו בן כוותיך, ואהא נזיר לכשיהא לך בן. (ג) (ה) ואהא לעיל נמי, כי קא מיבעיא ליה "ועלי", מאי טעמא לא מיבעיא ליה (ו) בהאי לישנא? הא לא אפשר, דלאו לישנא מתרלתא היא (ז) דלימא "ועלי" לאוהבו כמותך. ואם תימצי לומר כל באנפיה. בין אמר "ועלי" בין אמר "ואני" – כסיפא ליה מילתא להדורי ליה למימר: (ח) לכשיהא לי בן אהא נזיר, דאי אדעתא לקבל עליו נזירות כשיהא לו בן – למה לו להזיר בפני זה, יזיר בינו לבין עצמו. אלא מדקאמר ליה באנפיה, איכא למימר דהכי אמר ליה: אף אני אהא נמי נזיר כשיהא לך בן. *) אמר הריני נזיר לכשיהא לפלוני בן ושמע חבירו ואמר ואני. וה"ה דקא מיבעיא ליה "ועלי" (ג) (ט) ול"א מ"ה. מאי. מי (י) אמר כיון דשלא בפניו דאבי הבן קא מהדר ליה – לא כסיפא

*) שייך לע"ב

חזרה וילדה. פי': מהריון אחר. ולד קיימא – הרי זה נזיר ודאי לרבי יהודה א] וילדה זו ולד קיימא, דממה שהפילה תחילה – אפי' ספק נזיר לא, וכאילו לא הפילה כלל. **רבי** שמעון אומר יאמר וכו'. דלר"ש מעת שהפילה הוי ספק נזיר. הילכך יתנה עתה בלידה זו, ויאמר: אם היה הראשון בן קיימא – נמלא שילא נדרו מנזירות ראשון, ונזירות של לידה אחרונה – נדבה. או שמא הראשון נפל היה, והנזירות הראשון נדבה היתה, ועכשיו בלידה זו מוטלת עליו נזירות של חובה שנדר בנזיר שיהיה לו ולד. לכך צריך להתנות, דלא סגי ליה בנזירות הראשון, דשמא נדבה היתה. **לכשאבנה** הוא דקאמר. ולא בן ממש קאמר, אלא ל' בנין, כמו "ואבנה גם אנכי", ובכה"ג בנוי. **ולד** דחשיב ביני אינשי. דבת נמי לא מיחשבא, וכל שכן טומטוס ואנדרוגינוס, קמשמע לן. **לר'** יהודה ב]. בברייתא דאיתניא לעיל פ"ק (דף ח.), דקאמר: נגנב – אינו נזיר, הוא דקאמר לעיל דנזיר דכרי דלא הוי נזיר כלל לר' יהודה. אבל לא רצה לומר ר' יהודה דהפלאה הוא, דאם כן אפילו היה הולד בן קיימא אינו נזיר, כיון דבשעת הנדר לא היה הולד בעולם. כנ"ל. **והפילה** אשתו והפריש קרבן. פי': לנזירותו, וילדה – פירוש מאותו הריון עצמו, ולד קיימא. דהשתא יש הוכחה גדולה, מדהאי בר קיימא – הנפל [הוה] נמי בר קיימא, וכלו לו חדשיו, דטיפה היא נחלקת לשתים. הילכך חלה קדושה על קרבן שהפריש כשהפילה, ששוב לא ג] הקדיש אותם הבהמות. דאפילו לר' יהודה, דאמר: לא מחית איניש נפשיה לספיקא, הכא דאיכא הוכחה גדולה – קדוש הקרבן ליאסר בגיזה ובעבודה. או דילמא ד] כי ה"ג דאיכא הוכחה, לר' יהודה דלא מחית איניש לספיקא – לא חלה הקדושה על הקרבן כלל מכח הפרשה ראשונה, דשמא מקלת הטיפה נקלטה מיד, ומקלת הטיפה השניה לא נקלטה עד אחר שני ימים או ביום ג', וההוא נפל (כך מסיק התלמוד ואזיל דלר"י קמבעיא ליה, ה] דאי אליבא דר' שמעון – הא אמר ספק נזירות להחמיר, דבלא ילדה נמי הוי קדוש מספק, והשתא נמי כי ילדה – אינו אלא ספק. אלא אליבא דר' יהודה, דאי לא ילדה – חולין הוא, והשתא כי ילדה ליה, מי הוי קדוש מספק? וכדפי'. **ונפקא** מינה לגיזתו ועבודתו [ולא] דלילקי אהאי, משום דליכא ו] כי הך סברא דולד אחרון משוי ליה בספק. דאי מספקא ליה להתלמוד דשמא לילקו בודאי, מדשני בר קיימא הראשון אינו נפל – א"כ לר' שמעון נמי מצי למיבעי למלקות, דאי לא ילדה – ליכא קדושה ודאית, אלא הוי ספק לר' שמעון, והשתא דילדה – יקדש בודאי. אלא ש"מ דלא משמע ליה להתלמוד דלקי, דקדושה ודאית אין בו, כי נמי ילדה, אפי' לר"ש. ע"כ הגה"ה). **ושמע** חבירו ואמר *ועלי. היכא דאמר "ואני ועלי" – מדבוריה משתמע כלומר: גם אני נודר בנזיר כשיהיה לי ז] בן. **את"ל** הך אגופיה משתמע. הואיל ואמר "עלי", היכא דאמר "ואני" מהו? אנפשיה קאמר – כלומר אפי' בשאמר "ואני" – אגופיה מישתמע, או דילמא: רחימנא לך כוותך לכשיהיה בן קיימא. **את"ל** כל באנפיה כסיפא ליה מילתא. דילמא מסתמא ה"ק: דרחימנא לך כוותך. א] **אמר** ראובן הריני נזיר כשיהיה ללוי בן. ושמע שמעון ואמר "ואני", מי ב] שאמר שלא בפניו – אנפשיה קאמר, או דילמא ה"ק: רחימנא ליה לפלוני כוותך. **הריני** נזיר ונזיר כשיהיה לי בן. דהשתא [כשקיבל] נזירות דנפשיה ברישא, והתחיל ומונה את שלו, שהרי קבלו מתחילה קודם נזירות דבנו, ובמלאת ימי נדרו מגלח ומביא קרבנות לנזירות דנפשיה, ואחר כך מונה את של בנו. וכן כשישלים את נזירות בנו – יגלח, ויביא קרבן לנזירותו. **הריני** [נזיר] כשיהיה לי בן ונזיר. דהשתא קבל נזירות דבנו ברישא, ונזיר – מלבד נזירות דבנו קיבל עוד נזירות אנפשיה. התחיל מונה את שלו ונולד לו בן, פי': עד שלא השלים מניינו, מניח את שלו ומונה את של בנו – כיון דקבל עליו תחילה נזירות של בנו הוא זקוק למנותם מיד כשיוולד, ואחר שהשלים נזירות בנו ישלים נזירות של עצמו, ואחר כך יגלח על שתיהם, ומביא שתי קרבנות, אחד לנזירות בנו ואחד לנזירות עצמו. אבל לא יגלח אחר שהשלים נזירות [בנו] – דאם כן היאך ישלים נזירותו? נמלא כי לא יוכל לגלח בהשלמת נזירותו, דאין גידול שיער פחות משלשים יום. ונהי דאם נדר נזיר מרובה, שהיה נשאר אחר נזירות דבנו שלשים יום, דאז היה יכול לגלח לנזירות בנו ולהשלים נזירותו ולשוב ולגלח – מ"מ במתניתין דמיירי בסתם נזירות, דהוי שלשים יום, הילכך אם יגלח ח] לנזירות בנו – לא יוכל לקיים מצות גילוח אנזירות דנפשיה. לכך לא יגלח עד שישלים שתי הנזירות ויביא שתי קרבנות.

א] שייך לע"ב. ב] נ"ל אמרינן.

הריני

עין משפט נר מצוה

כ א מיי' פ"א מהל' נזירות הל' ז:

כא ב מיי' פ"ט מהל' נזירות הלי"ג:

כב ג ד מיי' שם פ"ב הל' ה:

פי' הרא"ש

חזרה וילדה אחר שקיבל עליו נזיר והביא קרבן הרי זה נזיר שמחמת הנפל לא חל עליו נזיר ולר"ש צריך להתנות כבראשונה שמא הא' היה בן קיימא. ומודה ר"ש בילדה טומטום דלא הוי נזיר אע"ג דהוי ספק זכר ספק נקיבה דלספק' כזו לא מחית נפשיה שלא היה דעתו על טומטום כלל: מהו דתימא לכשאבנה קאמר. כלומר בן דקאמר לשון בנין כמו ואבנה גם אנכי ממנה: דחשובי ביני אינשי ובת וטומטום ואנדרוגינוס לא חשיב: ר' יהודה דכרי הוא. ברייתא דאייתינן לעיל. והפילה אשתו והפריש קרבן וחזרה וילדה. פי' בו ביום ומסיק דמבעי' ליה אליבא דר' יהודה דאמר על נפל לא הוי א) נזיר. והיא לא חזרה וילדה פשיטא דלא הוי קדושי. אבל השתא דילדה בו ביום איכא הוכחה דהוי בן קיימא שאין אשה מתעברת וחוזרת ומתעברת וטפה אחת נחלקת לשנים. או דלמא זה נגמרה צורתו לז' והראשון נגמרה צורתו לט' ולא כלו חדשיו ולא קדיש והגוזז ועובד בו פטור. אבל לר' שמעון כיון דממה נפשך חייב למנות נזירות ולהביא קרבן קדוש. ואע"ג דאי בעי לא יקבל עליו נזירות ויעמוד בספק זה לעולם ולא יגלח ולא יביא קרבן נמצא שאין בהפרשה זו כלום. מ"מ כיון שהפריש קרבן עלה ברעתו שרוצה לקבל עליו נזירות והוי כאומר הרי אלו בהמות קדושים לקרבן נזיר שאקבל עלי דמסתבר דקדשי. א"נ כמו שחייב להיות נזיר מספק כמו כן חלה קדושה על קרבן מספק ואסור בגיזה ועבוד': אדיבוריה משמע. כלומר ועלי נמי להיות נזיר כשיהי' לך בן גם אני מקבל עלי נזירות כשיהיה לי בן. ואת"ל דועלי ודאי אגופי משמע. דמשמע על גופי נדר כמו שקבלת עליך ואני מהו דואני איכא לפרושי אני דומה בנדר זה. כל באנפיה כסיפא ליה מילתא. אם לא יעשה לו נחת רוח להראות שהוא חפץ בטובתו:

א) נ"ל על נפל לא הוי נזיר ואם לא חזרה וילדה פשיטא דלא קדיש.

נוסחת הריב"ן

א) (נזירות) ליתא בכ"י: ב) מינה השתא מיהא קדוש הוא דהא ילדה כו': ג) או בגוף המעשה ומשמע דקאמר ועלי להיות נזיר: ד) (ושמע חבירו כו' לי בן) ליתא בכ"י: ה) וא"ת: ו) מיבעי ליה הכי דלמא ועלי אדבוריה משמע הא כו': ז) דדלמא: ח) למימר ליה: ט) ולא מפי המורה: י) אמרינן:

הגהות הב"ח

(א) רש"י ד"ה אלא ימנה נזירות ויאמר אם היה בן קיימא: (ב) ד"ה או דילמא וכו' לך בן וא"ת לעיל נמי: (ג) ד"ה אמר הריני וכו' וה"ה דקא מיבעיא ליה ועלי אלא חדא מהם נקט הס"ד:

גליון הש"ס

גמ' ר"י דכרי הוא. עי' לקמן דף לד ע"א תד"ה אלא ר"י וצ"ע:

ס"א ואני

ס"א לך

הגהות מהר"ב רנשבורג

א] תום' ד"ה חזרה וילדה פי' מהריון וכו' ודאי לר' יהודה וילדה. תיבת וילדה נמחק וכ"ב מלידה זו וכו' אפי' ספק נזיר לא הוי וכו' כנ"ל: ב] ד"ה לר' יהודה וכ"ב רבי יהודה דכרי וכו' כנ"ל: ג] ד"ה והפילה אשתו והפריש קרבן וכו' הלכך חלה קדושה על קרבן שהפריש כשהפילה ששוב לא הקדיש אותם הבהמות. מלות הקדיש אותם הבהמות נמחקו וכ"ב יקדיש אותה בהמה כנ"ל. א"מ: ד] בא"ד או דילמא אפי' כי האי גוונא כנ"ל: ה] בא"ד ומקלת הטפה לא נקלטה עד אחר שני ימים או ביום ג' וההוא נפל כך מסיק הש"ס ואזיל דלר"י קמבעיא ליה עכ"ל. נ"ב כאן הס"ד ואח"כ מה"ד אי אליבא דר"ש: ו] ד"ה ונפקא מינה לגיזתו ועבודתו [ולא] דלקלי אהאי משום דליכא כי הך סברא דולד אחרון משוי ליה בספק. מן תיבות כי עד בספק נמחק וכ"ב כח בהך סברא דולד אח"כ למשוי ליה כודאי כנ"ל. א"מ: ז] ד"ה ושמע חברו ואמר ועלי וכו' גם אני נודר בנזיר כשיהיה לי. מלת לי נמחק וכ"ב לך בן כנ"ל לענ"ד וכפרש"י ובא"מ הגיה לו: ח] תוד"ה הריני נזיר וכו' הילכך אם יגלח כשישלים כנ"ל:

שייך לדף טו.

כג א מיי' פ"ב מהלכות נזירות הלכה ז:

כד ב מיי' שם פ"ד הל"ג סמג עשין קכז:

כה ג מיי' שם הל"ו:

נ"ל ולכן אמרינן

כְּסִיפָא לֵיהּ מִילְּתָא, אָמַר "הֲרֵינִי נָזִיר לִכְשֶׁיְּהֵא לִפְלוֹנִי בֵּן", וְשָׁמַע חֲבֵירוֹ וְאָמַר "וַאֲנִי", מַהוּ? מִי אָמְרִינַן שֶׁלֹּא בְּפָנָיו — אַנַּפְשֵׁיהּ קָאָמַר, אוֹ דִילְמָא הָכִי קָאָמַר לֵיהּ: רַחֲמָנָא לֵיהּ כְּוָותֵיךְ? אתִּיבָּעֵי.§ **מתני'** ב"הֲרֵינִי נָזִיר, וְנָזִיר כְּשֶׁיִּהְיֶה לִי בֵּן" הִתְחִיל מוֹנֶה אֶת שֶׁלּוֹ, ואח"כ נוֹלַד לוֹ בֵּן — מַשְׁלִים אֶת שֶׁלּוֹ, ואח"כ מוֹנֶה אֶת שֶׁל בְּנוֹ. "הֲרֵינִי נָזִיר כְּשֶׁיִּהְיֶה לִי בֵּן, וְנָזִיר" הִתְחִיל מוֹנֶה אֶת שֶׁלּוֹ, וְאַחַר כָּךְ נוֹלַד לוֹ בֵּן — מַנִּיחַ אֶת שֶׁלּוֹ וּמוֹנֶה אֶת שֶׁל בְּנוֹ, וְאַחַר כָּךְ מַשְׁלִים אֶת שֶׁלּוֹ.§ **גמ'** בָּעֵי רָבָא: אָמַר "הֲרֵינִי נָזִיר לְאַחַר עֶשְׂרִים יוֹם וּמֵעַכְשָׁיו מֵאָה יוֹם" מַהוּ? גכֵּיוָן דְּהָלֵין מֵאָה בְּעֶשְׂרִין לָא שָׁלְמִין — לָא חָיְילִין, אוֹ דִילְמָא כֵּיוָן דְּאִית לֵיהּ גִּידּוּל שֵׂעָר לְבַסּוֹף — חָיְילִין? וְתִיבָּעֵי לֵיהּ נְזִירוּת מוּעֶטֶת! חֲדָא מִגּוֹ חֲדָא קָא מִיבַּעְיָא לֵיהּ; את"ל

כְּסִיפָא לֵיהּ מִילְּתָא. וְאַנַּפְשֵׁיהּ קָאָמַר, דְּ"אֱהֵא נָזִיר כְּשֶׁיְּהֵא לִי בֵּן". **אוֹ** דִילְמָא הָכִי א"ל **רַחֲמָנָא** לֵיהּ לִפְלוֹנִי כְּוָותֵיךְ. לִכְשֶׁיְּהֵא לוֹ בֵּן אֱהֵא נָזִיר כְּמוֹתְךָ, תֵּיקוּ. **מתני'** אָמַר הֲרֵינִי נָזִיר. מֵעַכְשָׁיו וְנָזִיר לִכְשֶׁיְּהֵא לִי בֵּן הִתְחִיל מוֹנֶה אֶת שֶׁלּוֹ. וְעַד שֶׁלֹּא הִשְׁלִים אֶת שֶׁלּוֹ נוֹלַד לוֹ בֵּן, וְחָלָה עָלָיו נְזִירוּת שֶׁהִזִּיר עַל בְּנוֹ א] לִכְשֶׁיְּהֵא לוֹ (א). מַשְׁלִים אֶת שֶׁלּוֹ. לְפִי שֶׁקִּיבְּלוֹ עָלָיו תְּחִילָּה, וְאח"כ מוֹנֶה נְזִירוּת שֶׁהִזִּיר עַל בְּנוֹ. *דְּכֵיוָן שֶׁחָל עָלָיו שֶׁל בְּנוֹ עַד שֶׁלֹּא הִשְׁלִים נְזִירוּת שֶׁלּוֹ — נַעֲשָׂה כִּנְזִירוּת אַחַת, וּלְכָךְ אֵינוֹ יָכוֹל לְגַלֵּחַ א). אֲבָל אִם אָמַר: הֲרֵינִי נָזִיר כְּשֶׁיְּהֵא לִי בֵּן וְנָזִיר. דְּמַשְׁמַע (ב) ל' מֵעַכְשָׁיו, הִתְחִיל לִמְנוֹת אֶת שֶׁלּוֹ וְאח"כ נוֹלַד לוֹ בֵּן, הוֹאִיל וְקִבֵּל נְזִירוּת שֶׁל בְּנוֹ תְּחִילָּה — מַנִּיחַ אֶת שֶׁלּוֹ, וּמוֹנֶה אֶת שֶׁל בְּנוֹ, וְאֵינוֹ מְגַלֵּחַ. וְאח"כ מַשְׁלִים אֶת שֶׁלּוֹ לַמָּקוֹם שֶׁפָּסַק ב) מַתְחִיל: (גליו"ן ג) ומ"ה: (ג) דְּהוֹאִיל וְקִיבֵּל עָלָיו נְזִירוּת שֶׁלּוֹ תְּחִילָּה — מַשְׁלִים אֶת שֶׁלּוֹ, שֶׁיְּהֵא מְגַלֵּחַ בֵּינְתַיִם. וְאִילּוּ בְּסֵיפָא דְּקִבֵּיל נְזִירוּת שֶׁל בְּנוֹ תְּחִילָּה — מוֹקֵי לָהּ הַמּוֹרֶה כְּגוֹן דִּנְזִירוּת שֶׁלּוֹ הָווּ שֶׁל חֲמִשִּׁים. וּמשה"ה מוֹקֵי לָהּ ד) הָכִי, דְּאִי לָא תֵּימָא הָכִי ב] — לָא הָוֵי נְזִירוּת כְּלָל, כֵּיוָן דְּהִפְסִיק אֶת שֶׁלּוֹ וְהִתְחִיל אֶת שֶׁל בְּנוֹ וְגִלֵּחַ — תּוּ לָא פָּשׁוּ לֵיהּ כְּדֵי גִּידּוּל שֵׂעָר, וְקַיְימָא לָן בְּבָבָא דְּסֵיפָא דְּסוֹתֵר אֶת הַכֹּל אִם אֵין שָׁם כְּדֵי גִּידּוּל שֵׂעָר. וְא"ת: דְּבָתַר שֶׁמּוֹנֶה שֶׁל בְּנוֹ לָא לִיגַלַּח! הָא וַדַּאי מִילְּתָא דְּלָא אֶפְשָׁר, חֲדָא — דְּקִיבְּלוֹ, וַהֲוָה לֵיהּ כְּמִי שֶׁאָמַר "הֲרֵינִי נָזִיר וְנָזִיר", שֶׁצָּרִיךְ לְגַלֵּחַ בֵּין זוֹ לְזוֹ. וְעוֹד: מִדְּקָאָמַר דְּמַנִּיחַ אֶת שֶׁלּוֹ וּמוֹנֶה אֶת שֶׁל בְּנוֹ, לְמַאי מִילְּתָא הוּא ה) קָא מַתְחִיל ו) אֶת שֶׁל בְּנוֹ — אִי לָאו דְּלַיְיתֵי קָרְבְּנוֹתָיו וּלְגַלֵּחַ בֵּינְתַיִים. וְכִי תֵּימָא: אִי הָךְ בָּבָא לָא מַיְירֵי בִּנְזִירוּת סְתָם, אֶלָּא בְּנָזִיר כ', לָמָּה לֵיהּ דְּמַיְיתֵי אִידָךְ בָּבָא דִּנְזִירוּת מֵאָה? ז) (אִם) מִשּׁוּם דְּאָתָא לְאַשְׁמוּעִינַן דְּעַד ע' לֹא הִפְסִיד כְּלוּם, דִּלְאַחַר ע' סוֹתֵר. ע"כ גליו"ן. **גמ'** בָּעֵי **רָבָא** הֲרֵינִי נָזִיר כו'. כְּלוֹמַר, הָא וַדַּאי פְּשִׁיטָא לִי שֶׁאִם אָמַר "הֲרֵינִי נָזִיר לְאַחַר ל' יוֹם וּמֵעַכְשָׁיו נָזִיר סְתָם", כֵּיוָן (ד) ח) דְּבִנְזִירוּת זוֹ שֶׁאָמַר "מֵעַכְשָׁיו" ט) יָכוֹל לְהַשְׁלִים קוֹדֶם שֶׁיַּתְחִיל אוֹתוֹ נְזִירוּת שֶׁאָמַר "לְאַחַר שְׁלֹשִׁים יוֹם", דְּהָא י) דְּאָמַר "נָזִיר" סְתָם — דְּהַיְינוּ ל' יוֹם, הִילְכָּךְ חָלָה כ) לִנְזִירוּת דְּ"מֵעַכְשָׁיו" לְאַלְתַּר, וּמְגַלֵּחַ לְיוֹם ל', וְשׁוּב מוֹנֶה נְזִירוּת ל) שֶׁנָּדַר לְאַחַר שְׁלֹשִׁים", וּמְגַלֵּחַ לְסוֹף ל'. אֶלָּא הָא בָּעֵי רָבָא: *כֵּיוָן דְּאָמַר הֲרֵינִי כו'. כֵּיוָן דְּהָלֵין ק' בְּעֶשְׂרִין **לָא** שָׁלְמִין **לָא** חָיְילִין. מֵעַכְשָׁיו, וּמוּתָּר לִשְׁתּוֹת יַיִן. אֶלָּא מוֹנֶה ל' לְאַחַר כ' יוֹם, וּמְגַלֵּחַ, וְאח"כ מוֹנֶה ק' יוֹם. **אוֹ דִילְמָא** כֵּיוָן. דְּאִילּוּ מַתְחִיל לְמִימְנֵי נְזִירוּת ק' מֵעַכְשָׁיו, אַכַּתִּי מִיַּיתְרֵי לְהוּ כְּדֵי גִּידּוּל שֵׂעָר, דְּהָא פָּשׁוּ לְהוּ תְּמָנִין דְּאִית בְּהוּ גִּידּוּל שֵׂעָר טוּבָא. וְהִילְכָּךְ מַתְחִיל מֵעַכְשָׁיו וּמוֹנֶה כ' יוֹם, וְאַחַר כָּךְ מוֹנֶה ל' יוֹם, וְאח"כ מוֹנֶה פ' יָמִים כְּדֵי לְהַשְׁלִים נְזִירוּת רִאשׁוֹנָה. וְתִיבָּעֵי לֵיהּ נְזִירוּת מוּעֶטֶת. כְּגוֹן דְּאָמַר "הֲרֵינִי נָזִיר לְאַחַר כ' יוֹם וּמֵעַכְשָׁיו נָזִיר סְתָם", דְּל' נַמִי בְּכ' לָא שָׁלְמִי מ) וְלָא חָיְילֵי, אוֹ דִילְמָא לְאַלְתַּר נ) חָיְילִין, [וּמְגַלֵּחַ] אַחַת עַל כּוּלָּן. **אִין הָכִי קָמִיבַּעְיָא** לֵיהּ **אֶלָּא חֲדָא** מִגּוֹ **חֲדָא** קָא **מִיבַּעְיָא** לֵיהּ. כְּלוֹמַר, נְזִירוּת מִתּוֹךְ נְזִירוּת קָא מִיבַּעְיָא לֵיהּ, וְהָכִי קָא מִיבַּעְיָא לֵיהּ. את"ל

*הריני נזיר כשיהיה לי בן. פירוש: דסתם נזירות דהוי שלשים יום, ונזיר מאה יום נזירות דנפשיה. והשתא נמי קבל נזירות דבנו ברישא, והתחיל למנות נזירות דנפשיה ק' יום, ונולד לו בן עד שבעים, ויום שבעים נמי בכלל. לא הפסיד כלום. פירוש: ג] אחרי שנזירות בנו של שלשים יום מובלעים תוך ק' יום עדיין דפירש, *ולא הני ק' יום עולים לנזירות דבנו וגם למאה יום דנפשיה. דאף ע"ג דמיד כשיוולד בנו צריך להניח את שלו ולמנות של בנו, שהרי קיבלו תחילה כדאמר לעיל, אפ"ה כיון דשל בנו מובלעין בתוך המאה יום — עולים לשל בנו ולשלו, וישלים מאה יום ויגלח על שניהם, ויביא שני קרבנות. וה"ה לעיל, כי אמר "הריני נזיר כשיהיה לי בן ונזיר", והתחיל למנות את שלו, אם נולד לו הבן למניינו ביום א' דאותן שלשים יום — עולין היו לבנו ולעצמו, כיון דשל בנו מובלע בשל עצמו, דאידי ואידי ל' יום. ודוקא כי קבל נזירות דבנו ברישא, דמיד שנולד הוי זקוק למנות אותו — מהני הבלעה. אבל קבל נזירות דמאה יום ברישא, אפי' נולד לו הבן קודם ע' יום — צריך להשלים המאה יום ברישא כשקיבל עליו תחילה, דלא חייל נזירות בנו עליו [עד] השלמת נזירותו. אלא משלים נזירות ק' ויגלח, ויביא קרבן לנזירותו, ושוב יעשה נזירות דבנו ל' יום, ויגלח לל' יום, ויביא קרבן. *לאחר שבעים. היינו ע"א, סותר. ול"ג "סותר שבעים יום", דהא אינו סותר ע'. וה"פ: מניח את שלו ומונה את של בנו, ולאו דוקא סותר, כלומר מניח את מניינו ומונה שלשים דבנו. שאין תגלחת פחות משלשים יום. פי': לכך אין עולין שאר הימים שעד ק' ימים לנזירות דבנו, לפי שאין נזירות דבנו פחות משלשים יום, וליכא ל' יום עד גמר השלמת מאה. ולכך זקוק להפסיק מניינו, הואיל דנמשך דבנו על ימי נזירותו. ולשון תגלחת אינו מכוון, דטפי ה"ל למימר: שאין נזירות פחות משלשים יום. ונקט "שאין תגלחת" — למימר: מכשישלים ד] של בנו יחזור למניינו, וישלים נזירות הק' יום, ויגלח בסוף כל המנין את' לכולן. אבל בסוף מנין דבנו אינו מגלח, דאם כן לא יוכל להשלים אחר נזירות שלו, דליכא שלשים יום מנזירות. הגה"ה: לכאורה משמע כדמפרש דאחר שישלים של בנו יחזור וישלים את שלו, כי ימי בנו אין עולין לנזירות מאה יום שלו, כמו ברישא ה] דקתני מניח את שלו. מיהא, יש בירושלמי: נולד ביום שמונים — סותר עשרה, נולד ביום תשעים — סותר את עשרים. ולפי שיטת הירושלמי מיד שנולד הבן מונה של בן ו] לגמרי, ואותו מנין בן עולה לו לנזירות דק' יום. ושמא י"ל הירושלמי דסותר כ' — כלומר בשביל בנו קאמר, דמונה עשרה של מאה, וכ' אחר המאה, ולעולם ה"נ קאמר — שאין עולה לנזירות דמאה כלל, וחוזר וישלים המאה כמו שהיה לו למנות בלידת הבן. ובגמרא מוכחא דאם נולד ע"א דסותר, אע"ג דאיכא שלשים יום עד המאה מיום לידת הבן. והטעם: דיום לידת הבן נימנית ממנין שלו, ולא תחשב לימי הבן, וליכא אלא כ"ט עד יום ק'. ז] ול"ע, שפירש לעיל שאם נולד הבן ביום ראשון שהתחיל בו נזירותו — שימנה ל' ועולין לשניהם! וצריך ליתן חילוק בדבר: דרישא, הואיל וביום לידת הבן התחיל למנות נזירות של עצמו — ימנה לשניהם. אבל הכא, שהתחיל זה ימים רבים של עצמו — לא ימנה יום הלידה לבנו כי אם לעצמו. ע"כ הגה"ה. **בעי** רבא **אמר** הריני נזיר **לאחר** כ' יום ומעכשיו מאה יום מהו, כיון דהלין **מאה** יום **לא** שלמי בהנך **עשרים** יום **לא חיילא**. נזירות של מאה יום עליה מעכשיו, דמסתמא אין דעת זה האיש להפסיק נזירות, שימנה עתה עשרים יום מן המאה יום. ואחר עשרים יום ימנה נזירות שלשים יום שקבל עליו לאחר עשרים יום, ושוב ימנה שמנים יום להשלים המאה יום. אלא אחרי שאינו יכול להשלים נזירות של ק' יום בהלין כ' — דעתו שאלו כ' יום יהיו פנויים, ויהיה מותר ביין ובתגלחת בהנך כ' יום, ואחר כך ימנה ל' יום לגלח, ויביא קרבן, ושוב מונה ק' יום רצופין, ויגלח ויביא קרבן. ומה שאמר "מעכשיו מאה יום", ר"ל: ומעכשיו כמו כן אני מקבל ק' יום, אחר שעשה סתם הנזירות לאחר כ' יום. וא"ת: ואמאי לא פשיט ממתני', דקתני: מניח את שלו ומונה של בנו, ושוב משלים את שלו — אלמא לא חייש האי גברא אהפסקת נזירותו! דאיכא למימר: שאני מתני', כשהתחיל למנות נזירותו סבור היה לתשלומין, שלא ידע שיוולד לו בן תוך ימי נזרו. וגם אפשר להיות שפעמים ישלים נדרו קודם שיוולד לו הבן, הילכך גמר ונדר, ואפי' יוולד הבן מפסיק נזירותו ומניח ח] נדרו ומונה את של בנו, ולא קפיד בהפסק נזירותו. אבל הכא דלא אפשר כלל, אם יתחיל נזירות של מאה יום לאלתר. **או** דילמא כיון **דאית** ליה גידול שיער לבסוף חיילא. פי': כיון שנשארו לו ל' ימים לאחר סתם נזירות, כדי גידול שיער, היינו נזירות שלם — חיילא, ולא חייש בהפסקת נזירותו. והכא נשארו לו אפי' פ' יום, הלכך מונה עשרים יום הללו לנזירות דמאה יום, ויפסיק, וימנה ל' יום ויגלח ויביא קרבן, ואחרי כן ימנה פ' יום להשלמת מאה יום. וה"נ אמרינן בברייתא דמייתי לקמן: אחר שמנה ל' יום אינו מונה רק פ' יום להשלים המאה יום על העשרים שמנה קודם שלשים יום. ואע"ג דתגלחת סותר — היינו כדי שיהיה לאחר התגלחת שלשים יום, כדי גידול שיער. אבל אם נשארו אחר התגלחת שלשים יום עד כלות נזירותו — אינו סותר כלום, כיון דאית ליה גידול שיער דתגלחת טהרה. והכי אמרינן בפ' "ג' מינין" (לקמן מד.). והכא נשארו לו פ' יום כדי גידול שיער ויותר. ואע"ג דאמרינן במתניתין: נולד לו בן עד ע' לא הפסיד כלום, דימי בנו עולים למנין הק' יום, ט] והכי אמרינן לקמן בברייתא דאחר שמנה נזירות של ל' יום מונה פ' יום להשלים הראשונים, ולא סלקי הנך ל' יום, אע"ג דמובלעין הם תוך הפ' יום. דלא דמיא למתניתין, דבמתניתין לא נדר נזירות אלא אם יוולד אחר ע', אבל אם יוולד תוך הע', שיוכל להבליע נזירות דבנו תוך הק' — אין דעתו למנות נזירות לבנו, אלא ל' אחרונים יעלו לשניהם, דהיינו ק' יום בין הכל. ומה שלא אמר בפי' "הריני נזיר כשיהיה לי בן ומעכשיו ע' יום" — היינו משום שדעתו להיות נזיר ק' יום אם לא יוולד לו בן, לבר מנזירות דבנו. אבל מ"מ אם יוולד לו בן קודם ל' — חפץ הוא להבליעו בנזירות דידיה. אבל הכא, שקיבל נזירות אחר כ' — בדעתו למנות לו מנין שלא יעלה למנין המאה יום. דאם איתא דחפץ להבליע, והרי הוא יודע בברור דבהנך כ' לא [שלמי] ק' — לימא בפי': "הריני נזיר אחר כ' ומעתה", פי': י] בין הכל ק'. אלא ודאי חפץ לעשות ק' יום בלא הנזירות. ע"כ הגה"ה. **ותבעי** ליה נזירות מועטת. פי': סתם נזירות, דהוא שלשים יום. וכגון דאמר "הריני נזיר לאחר עשרים יום ונזיר מעתה", אי חיילא השתא וימנה עשרים יום, ויניח מנין זה וימנה שלשים יום, וימנה עשרה ימים להשלים נזירות ראשונה, ולא יגלח עד [ששים] השלמת שניהן. **חדא** מגו חדא קמיבעי' ליה

פי' הרא"ש

הריני נזיר כשיהיה לי בן ונזיר קבל עליו ונזירות בנו תחלה התחיל מונה את שלו אלו ישלמו שלשים יום [קודם] שילד לו בן ואח"כ נולד לו בן קודם ששלמו מניח את שלו ומונה את של בנו. דכיון שקבל נזירות בנו תחילה מיד כשנולד לו בן צריך להניח את שלו ולמנות את של בנו ואח"כ ישלים את שלו ונפקא מינה בהפסקה זו שאינו מגלח כי אם פעם אחת דאם היה מגלח על של בנו היה צריך למנות ל' לנזירותיו דאין תגלחת פחות מל' יום ולא שייך למתני ואח"כ משלים את שלו דאין זו השלמה כיון שצריך למנות ל' יום משלם אבל אם היה משלים שלו בלא הפסקה ואח"כ היה מונה של בנו היה צריך ב' תגלחות. אבל השתא מביא על תגלחת א' שני קרבנות ונ"ל דלרב דאם נטמא ביום גידול שער אינו סותר אפי' דמגלח על של בנו ואח"כ מונה ל' על נזירותו ודאי דקרי ליה השלמה לפי שאם נטמא אחר ששלמו הל' שלו אינו סותר כיון שאינו מונה מאז והלאה אלא גידול שער. ונפקא מיניה בהך הפסקה שצריך להשלים יותר על ב' נזירות כדי גידול שער. ועוד נפקא מינה לרב דאמר נטמא בשל בנו אינו סותר את שלו דאם מנה עשרים והפסיק והתחיל למנות את בנו ונטמא בתוך עשרה ימים אינו סותר אלא נזירות בנו ואם היה משלים את שלו בלא הפסקה היה סותר הכל. ולר' יוחנן דאמר סותר את הכל. נפקא מינה דאם מנה עשרים לנזירותו והפסיק ומנה עשרים לשל בנו ונטמא סותר הכל ואלו היה משלים את שלו תחלה לא היה סותר כ"א עשרה ימים: הריני נזיר כשיהיה לי בן ונזיר ק' קבל עליו נזירות של ל' יום כשיולד לו בן ועוד קבל עליו נזירות של ק' יום. נולד לו בן עד שבעים יום לא הפסיד כלום כיון שנשארו מנזירות ק' ל' יום דמשלם ימי נזירות בנו בהדי נזירותו וה"ה קודם שבעים יום. וה"ה אם אמר איפכא הריני נזיר ק' יום. ונזיר כשיהיה לי בן אם נולד לו בן עד ע' לא הפסיד כלום דלעולם כשישלים ימי בנו להיות מובלעים בתוך ימי נזירותו וא"צ למנות מנין אחר בשביל בנו. והא דאמרינן הריני נזיר ונזיר כשיהיה לי בן דמונה שתיהן היינו משום דלא שלמי כהדדי. אבל אם נולד לו בן ביום ראשון למנין נזירותו מנין אחד פוטר את שתיהן. ור"ת פי' דדוקא הריני נזיר כשיהיה לי בן ונזיר ק' יום הוא דאמרי' לא הפסיד כלום משום דמיד כשנולד לו בן צריך להפסי' נזירותו ולמנות נזירות בנו. הלכך אותו מנין עולה גם למנין ק' יום שהתחיל כבר למנות. אבל אם אמר הריני נזיר ק' יום ונזיר כשיהיה לי בן כיון דאינו צריך להפסיק נזירותו כשיולד לו בן לא חיילא עליה נזירות בנו עד שישלים נזירותו. והכי מסתברא דבהפסקה שצריך להפסיק גורמה שעולים לכאן ולכאן. א) דהא אם קבל עליו נזיר של ל' יום ונזיר של ק' יום צריך למנות שתיהן ולא אמרי' דמתחלה היה בדעתו דק' להיות נזיר ל' יום ושוב נמלך להיות נזיר ק' יום אבל אם רוצה הוא שיהא מובלעים הל' בתוך הק' אלמא דווקא

א) נראה דצ"ל אבל הכא דקיבל נזירות שלו בתחילה אינו עולה לכאן ולכאן דהא אם קבל עליו וכו':

נוסחת הריב"ן

א) כב"י כתוב כאן הגליון למטה במשנה: ב) יתחיל: ג) ומפי המורה: ד) מוקי לה בהאי טעמא דאי אמרת דלא הוי אלא נזירות סתם כיון דהפסיק כו': ה) דקא: ו) למנות את: ז) יום: ח) דנזירות: ט) יכולה: י) קאמר: כ) נזירות: ל) שנדר: מ) (ולא חיילי) ליתא בכ"י: נ) חיילא נזירות דמעכשיו ואינו מגלח וכל עשרים יום אסור לגלח לשתות יין ולטמאה למתים ולאחר כ' מונה נזירות ל' ואינו מגלח וחוזר ומונה י' להשלים כ' ראשונים ומגלח תגלחת אחת על כולן הס"ד:

הגהות הב"ח

(א) רש"י ד"ה אמר הריני וכו' לכשיהא לו בן מגלים: (ב) ד"ה אבל וכו' דמשמע של ל': (ג) ד"ה גליון ומ"ה הואיל וקיבל וכו' ומשום הכי מוקי לה בהאי טעמא דאי אמרת דמיירי בנזירות סתם לא הוי נזירות כלל דכיון דהפסיק וכו' את של בנו למאי מילתא הוא קא מתחיל וכו' מאה יום משום וכו' לאחר ע': (ד) ד"ה בעי רבא וכו' כיון דבנזירות זו וכו' דהא אמר נזיר וכו' אלא הא בעי רבא כגון דאמר הריני כו' כצ"ל ותיבת כיון נמחק:

גי' א"מ כגון

הגהות מהר"ב רנשבורג

א] רש"י ד"ה אמר הריני נזיר וכו' שהזיר על בנו. נ"ב עי' א"מ: ב] ד"ה גליון ומפי המורה דהואיל וכו' דאי לא תימא הכי סותרת ולא כצ"ל: ג] תוד"ה הריני וכו' אחרי שנזירות בנו של ל' יום מובלעים תוך הק' יום עדיין דפירוש ולא. כ"ז נמחק נ"ב פי' אמרינן כיון דל' יום מובלעים תוך הק' לחסרו עדיין ל' לגילוי ק' יום. א"מ: ד] ד"ה לאחר שבעים וכו' ונקט שאין תגלחת למימר מכשישלים שלשים כצ"ל: ה] בא"ד הגה"ה לכאורה משמע וכו' דקתני מניח את שלו. נ"ב עיין ביאור דברי הגה"ה הזאת באריכה בתורת מישור: ו] בא"ד מונה של בן ומניח שלו כצ"ל: ז] בא"ד וליכא אלא כ"ט עד יום ק' ול"ע. נ"ב עי' לקמן טו ע"א תוס' ד"ה אבל לאחר ממש מאי: ח] ד"ה בעי רבא אמר וכו' ואפי' יולד הבן מפסיק נזירותו ומניח נדרו. מלת נדרו נמחק ונ"ב נזרו כצ"ל א"מ: ט] ד"ה או דלמא כיון דאית ליה וכו' דימי בנו עולין למנין הק' יום והכי. מלת והכי נמחק ונ"ב והיכי כצ"ל: י] בא"ד והרי הוא יודע בבירור דבהנך כ' לא שלמי ק' לימא בפי' הריני נזיר אחר כ' ומעתה פי'. כצ"ל נ"ב ר"ל כך יאמר להדיא פי' בין הכל ק':

את"ל נְזִירוּת מוּעֶטֶת, כֵּיוָן דַּעֲשָׂרָה יוֹמִין הוּא דְּיָתְרִין – לָא סָלֵיק לֵיהּ הָלֵין עֲשָׂרָה; וַדַּאי נָזִיר מֵאָה יוֹם, כֵּיוָן דְּאִית לֵיהּ תְּמָנִין יוֹמִין לְבַסּוֹף – סָלְקִין לֵיהּ, אוֹ לָא? ואת"ל חָיְילִי, אָמַר "הֲרֵינִי נָזִיר לְאַחַר כ' יוֹם וּמֵעַכְשָׁיו נְזִיר עוֹלָם" מַהוּ? מִי חָיְילָא עֲלֵיהּ א אוֹ לָא? את"ל, הָכָא כֵּיוָן דְּאֶפְשָׁר לְאִיתְשׁוּלֵי – חָיְילָא, אָמַר "הֲרֵינִי נְזִיר שִׁמְשׁוֹן לְאַחַר עֶשְׂרִים יוֹם וּמֵעַכְשָׁיו נָזִיר סְתָם" מַהוּ? הָכָא לָא אֶפְשָׁר לְאִיתְשׁוּלֵי – מִי חָיְילָא ב אוֹ לָא? אָמַר "כְּמֹשֶׁה בְּשִׁבְעָה בַּאֲדָר", מַאי? פְּשׁוֹט מִינַּיְיהוּ קַדְמַיְיתָא: *"הֲרֵינִי נָזִיר לְאַחַר עֶשְׂרִים יוֹם וּמֵעַכְשָׁיו מֵאָה יוֹם" – ג מוֹנֶה עֶשְׂרִים, ואח"כ מוֹנֶה שְׁלֹשִׁים, ואח"כ מוֹנֶה שְׁמוֹנִים, כְּדֵי לְהַשְׁלִים נְזִירוּת רִאשׁוֹנָה. נִטְמָא בִּימֵי בְּנוֹ, רַבִּי יוֹחָנָן אָמַר: ד סוֹתֵר, רֵישׁ לָקִישׁ אָמַר: אֵינוֹ סוֹתֵר. רַבִּי יוֹחָנָן אָמַר: סוֹתֵר, ה חֲדָא נְזִירוּת אֲרִיכְתָּא הִיא. רֵישׁ לָקִישׁ אָמַר: אֵינוֹ סוֹתֵר, נְזִירוּת דִּידֵיהּ לְחוּד, וְדִבְרֵיהּ לְחוּד. נִטְמָא

את"ל נְזִירוּת מוּעֶטֶת בָּיָן. דְּאִילּוּ מַתְחִיל מֵעַכְשָׁיו לִמְנוֹת לָא מִיַּיתְרֵי לֵיהּ מֵהָאֵיךְ נְזִירוּת אֶלָּא עֲשָׂרָה יָמִים, וְלָא הָוֵי בָּהֶן כְּדֵי גִידּוּל שֵׂיעָר, דְּאֵין תִּגְלַחַת פָּחוֹת מִשְּׁלֹשִׁים. לָא סָלְקִין לֵיהּ הָלֵין עֲשָׂרָה. לְמִנְיַן נְזִירוּת, דְּהָא לֵית בְּהוּ גִּידּוּל שֵׂיעָר – הִילְכָּךְ לָא חָיְילֵי לֵיהּ מֵעַכְשָׁיו, אֶלָּא לְאַחַר עֶשְׂרִים יַתְחִיל לִמְנוֹת שְׁתֵּי נְזִירוּת, וִיהֵא מְגַלֵּחַ בֵּינְתַיִם. וְאִי אָמְרַתְּ: תִּפְשׁוֹט מִמַּתְנִי', דְּקָתָנֵי: מַנִּיחַ אֶת שֶׁלּוֹ וּמוֹנֶה אֶת שֶׁל בְּנוֹ, וְאח"כ מַשְׁלִים אֶת שֶׁלּוֹ, וְאע"ג דְּלָא מִיַּיתְרֵי מִשֶּׁלּוֹ אֶלָּא עֲשָׂרָה, וַאֲפִי' הָכִי חָיְילֵי! הָא לָא (א) דָּמֵי, דְּאִילּוּ הָתָם כֵּיוָן דְּאָמַר: הֲרֵינִי נָזִיר סְתָם לִכְשֶׁיְּהֵא לִי בֵּן – לָא נָחֵית לְמִנְיָינָא, דְּלָא קָאָמַר אֵימַת (אִי לְאַחַר עֶשְׂרִין וַחֲמִשָּׁה). (א) הִילְכָּךְ, הַאי דַּהֲדַר וַאֲמַר "הֲרֵינִי נָזִיר" – דִּינָא הוּא דְּלֵיחוּל עֲלֵיהּ לְאַלְתַּר, דְּדִילְמָא לֹא יְהֵא לוֹ בֵּן עַד לְאַחַר שְׁלֹשִׁים, דְּלָא מִיַּיתְרֵי כְּלָל, וְאִישְׁתַּכַּח דִּמְלְאַלְתַּר הֲוָה לֵיהּ לְמִימְנֵי נְזִירוּת שֶׁלּוֹ. א"כ, זִמְנִין דְּלָא יַסְפִּיק לְמִימְנֵי אֶת שֶׁלּוֹ קוֹדֶם שֶׁנּוֹלַד לוֹ בֵּן, כֵּיוָן דְּאִי אֶפְשָׁר לֵיהּ בְּגִילּוּחַ, כִּדְפָרִישִׁי' לְעֵיל גַּבֵּי מַתְנִי' – כִּנְזִירוּת אַחַת דָּמֵי. אֶלָּא הָכָא, דְּקָא נָחֵית לֵיהּ לְמִנְיָינָא, דְּאָמַר "לְאַחַר עֶשְׂרִים" – אִיכָּא לָךְ לְמִיבָּעֵי בְּהָכִי בְּעַיָּין, כֵּיוָן דְּעֶשְׂרִים יוֹמִין כו'. ואת"ל. הֵיכָא דְּאָמַר (ב) "מֵעַכְשָׁיו ב) מֵאָה", כֵּיוָן דְּאֶפְשָׁר לְמִימְנֵי מֵעַכְשָׁיו עֶשְׂרִים, וּלְאַחַר דְּמוֹנֶה לֵיהּ שְׁלֹשִׁים אֶפְשָׁר לְמֶיהֱדַר וּלְמִימְנֵי תְּמָנִין, מִשּׁוּם דְּאִיכָּא גִּידּוּל שֵׂיעָר לְבַסּוֹף חָיְילֵי לְהוּ מֵהָשְׁתָּא, אַכַּתִּי תִּיבָּעֵי לָךְ הָא: אָמַר "הֲרֵינִי נָזִיר לְאַחַר עֶשְׂרִים וּמֵעַכְשָׁיו נְזִיר עוֹלָם" מַהוּ? ג) כֵּיוָן דְּלִנְזִירוּת עוֹלָם לֵית לֵיהּ הֶפְסֵק, דְּהֵיכָא דְּאָמַר "מֵעַכְשָׁיו מֵאָה יוֹם" הוּא דְּאִיכָּא לְמֵימַר דְּמוֹנֶה עֶשְׂרִים, וְאח"כ מוֹנֶה שְׁלֹשִׁים, וְאח"כ מוֹנֶה שְׁמוֹנִים – דְּוַדַּאי חָיְילָא עֲלֵיהּ לְאַלְתַּר מִכִּי אָמַר "מֵאָה יוֹם", מִשּׁוּם דְּכֵיוָן דְּאִית לְהוּ הֶפְסֵק לְסוֹף מֵאָה – הִילְכָּךְ הָכָא נַמִי אֶפְשָׁר לְמִפְסְקִינְהוּ מִתּוֹכָן. אֲבָל הָכָא דְּאָמַר "מֵעַכְשָׁיו נְזִיר עוֹלָם", דִּנְזִיר עוֹלָם אֵין לוֹ הֶפְסֵק, וְהַאי דִּמְגַלֵּחַ מִשְּׁלֹשִׁים לִשְׁלֹשִׁים – הַיְינוּ טַעְמָא מִשּׁוּם כּוֹבֶד, וְלָא מִשּׁוּם דְּלֶיהֱוֵי הֶפְסֵק, וְכֵיוָן דְּאֵין לוֹ הֶפְסֵק לָא פָּסְקִינַן לְהוּ מִתּוֹכָן, וְכֵיוָן דְּלָא אֶפְשָׁר בְּלֹא הַפְסָקָה – לָא תֵּיחוּל עֲלֵיהּ נְזִירוּת כְּלָל עַד לְאַחַר עֶשְׂרִים, דְּלִימְנֵי שְׁלֹשִׁים שֶׁל נְזִירוּתוֹ בְּרֵישָׁא. ואת"ל. לְעִנְיַן כּוּלְּהוּ שְׁאֵילָתָא – לְעִנְיַן נְזִירוּת מוּעֶטֶת, ד) לִנְזִירוּת מֵאָה, אוֹ לִנְזִירוּת עוֹלָם (ג). כֵּיוָן דְּאֶפְשָׁר לֵיהּ לְאִיתְשׁוּלֵי. אַהַהוּא נְזִירוּת שֶׁקִּבֵּל עָלָיו לְאַחַר עֶשְׂרִים – לֵיחֲלוּ לְהוּ כּוּלְּהוּ מֵהָשְׁתָּא, אַכַּתִּי תִּבָּעֵי לָךְ: אָמַר "הֲרֵינִי נְזִיר שִׁמְשׁוֹן לְאַחַר עֶשְׂרִים יוֹם וּמֵעַכְשָׁיו נָזִיר סְתָם" מַהוּ? הָכָא. בִּנְזִיר שִׁמְשׁוֹן, דְּלָא אֶפְשָׁר לְאִיתְשׁוּלֵי עֲלֵיהּ, מִשּׁוּם דְּשִׁמְשׁוֹן לָא הֲוָה נָדוּר, אָמְרִינַן: כֵּיוָן דְּלָא אֶפְשָׁר לְאִיתְשׁוּלֵי עֲלֵיהּ אַנְּזִיר שִׁמְשׁוֹן – לָא חָיְילָא הַהוּא נְזִירוּת סְתָם, (ד) ה) דְּהוֹאִיל דְּסוֹף עֶשְׂרִים לָא שָׁלְמִי, אוֹ דִּילְמָא חָיְילָא? אָמַר הֲרֵינִי כְּמֹשֶׁה בְּשִׁבְעָה בַּאֲדָר. דְּמַשְׁמַע: כְּמֹשֶׁה שֶׁנִּפְטַר בְּשִׁבְעָה בַּאֲדָר, א] וְשׁוּב לָא שָׁתָה יַיִן. מִי הָוֵי לְשׁוֹן נְזִירוּת אוֹ לָא? נִטְמָא בִּימֵי בְּנוֹ. הַאי דְּאָמַר "הֲרֵינִי נָזִיר כְּשֶׁיְּהֵא לִי בֵּן וְנָזִיר סְתָם", הִתְחִיל מוֹנֶה אֶת שֶׁלּוֹ, וְעַד שֶׁלֹּא הִשְׁלִים אֶת שֶׁלּוֹ נוֹלַד לוֹ בֵּן – מַנִּיחַ אֶת שֶׁלּוֹ וּמוֹנֶה אֶת שֶׁל בְּנוֹ. וְאִם נִטְמָא בְּתוֹךְ יָמִים הַלָּלוּ ו) שֶׁמָּנָה לִבְנוֹ. ר' יוֹחָנָן אָמַר סוֹתֵר. אַף אוֹתָן יָמִים שֶׁמָּנָה כְּבָר עַל שֶׁלּוֹ. ב] דְּכֵיוָן ז) דַּאֲפִילּוּ מָנָה אֶת שֶׁלּוֹ אֵינוֹ מְגַלֵּחַ בֵּינְתַיִם – כִּנְזִירוּת אֲרִיכְתָּא דָּמֵי, וְסוֹתֵר אֶת הַכֹּל. וְרֵישׁ לָקִישׁ אָמַר אֵינוֹ סוֹתֵר. אֶת שֶׁלּוֹ, דִּנְזִירוּת דִּידֵיהּ לְחוּד, וְדִבְנוֹ לְחוּד.
נִטְמָא

ליה. כלומר, תחילה שאל בנזירות מועטת, ושוב שאל בנזירות מרובה ב"אם תמצא לומר". דאפילו את"ל דנזירות מועטת לא חיילא, כיון דעשרה יומין לבד הוא – לא סלקי הנך עשרה שישלים אחר עשרים לאיצטרופי לעשרים שספר מתחילה, משום דהנך עשרה לא חזו לנזירות לחודייהו, ולהכי לא ניחא ליה להפסיק נזירותו, אלא אלו עשרים יום רוצה שיהיו פנויים, ויהיה מותר ביין ובתגלחת וליטמאות למתים. אכתי מיבעי ליה לנזירות מרובה דמאה יום, כיון דאי חיילא השתא כ' יום אכתי פשו להו פ' יום אחר נזירות דל' יום, דחזו לנזירות לחודייהו, ומצטרפי שפיר להני עשרים יום להשלמת ק' יום. וימנה [כ'] יום, ושוב מונה ל' יום, ומגלח ויביא קרבן, ושוב מונה פ' יום להשלים המאה יום, ויגלח שנית ויביא קרבן. ולא קפיד אהפסקת נזירות. או דילמא אפ"ה לא חיילי, כיון דלא שלמי מאה יום בהנך [כ'] יום, ואין רצונו להפסיק נזירותו, ומסתמא בשעת קבלה היה בדעתו [דכ'] יום קמאי יהיה מותר ביין ובתגלחת ובטומאה, ואחרי כן יעשה שלשים יום ויגלח ויביא קרבן, ושוב יעשה מאה יום רצופין ויגלח ויביא קרבן. הגה"ה: וצ"ע אי מצי למיבעי היכא דאמר "הריני נזיר מאה יום ונזיר לאחר עשרים יום", דהשתא הקדים המאה יום [אי אמרת] חיילי מהשתא אי לא. [ושמא] דה"ה דמצי למיבעי הכי, וחדא מנייהו נקט. הגה"ה.

אמר הריני נזיר לאחר עשרים יום ומעכשיו נזיר לעולם. דדינו אם הכביד שערו – דמיקל ומביא שלש בהמות.

מי חיילא. נזירות עליה מהשתא או לא. את"ל דבין נזירות מועטת ובין נזירות מרובה מהשתא חיילא, משום דכי מטו עשרים ויחול נזירות לא הוי הפסק כולי האי, שהרי דמי הוא לנזירות דמאה. אבל הכא, אי חיילא מהשתא נזיר עולם – נזירות דאחר עשרים אינו כיוצא בו כלל, והוי הפסק. הילכך לא הוי נזיר עולם כלל עד שישלים נזירותיו, ובהנך עשרים קמאי יהיה מותר ביין ובתגלחת ובטומאה. או דילמא דמ"מ יחול מהשתא נזיר לעולם, וכי אתו עשרים – ימנה נזירות שלשים יום ומגלח, למ"ד נזיר עולם מיקל אחר שלשים יום, או אחר *[ש"א], למר כדאית ליה ולמר כדאית ליה (לעיל דף ה.). ג] דחזיא לנזירות עולם שהתחיל, ולא חשיב הפסקת נזירותו – כיון שבידו לשאול על נזירות של שלשים יום, והיה עושה נזירות עולם לפניו בלי הפסק – הילכך ד] אסר אפילו לא שאל על נזירות [דל' יום] יחול עליו נזיר עולם מהשתא. וה"ה דמצי ה] למיבעי אי אמר "הריני נזיר לאחר כ' נזיר עולם ומעכשיו נזיר סתם". **ואת"ל**, הכא ודאי כיון דאפשר לאתשולי אנזירות שיחול לאחר עשרים יום – הכא ו] חיילא נזיר עולם, ומהשתא יכול לשאול אנזירות דבתר עשרים, ולא תהיה הפסק כלל בתוך נזירות דנזיר עולם.

אמר הריני נזיר כשמשון לאחר עשרים יום ומעכשיו נזיר סתם. הכא ודאי לא אפשר לאתשולי אנזירות שמשון שיחול עליו אחר [עשרים], הילכך לא יחול עליו סתם נזירות בהנך עשרים כלל, הואיל ולא מצי להשלים בהנך עשרים סתם נזירות, דהויין שלשים יום. ויהיה מותר ביין ולטמאות למתים בהנך עשרים, ואח"כ יתחיל נזירות שמשון, ז] [וידמה] סתם נזירות, כיון דלא אפשר להשלימו – קפיד אהפסקת נזירותו. או דלמא סוף סוף חייל עליה סתם נזירות בתוך עשרים יום, ונהי דלא מצי לגלח לסוף עשרה דלאחר עשרים, דהא חל נזירות שמשון – מ"מ כל דין נזירות שיכול לנהוג ינהוג, כגון איסור יין וטומאת מתים, ח] ואחר עשרים יפסיק נזירות זה ויתחיל נזירות שמשון, דלא קפיד ט] אפי' אהפסקת נזירותו. אבל לא מצי למיבעי היכא דאמר "הריני י] סתם לאחר [כ'] ומעכשיו נזיר שמשון", דודאי חייל עליה לאלתר נזיר שמשון. דכיון דמצי לאתשולי אסתם נזירות לאחר עשרים – ישאל עליו, ולא יהיה הפסק בנזירות שמשון. והך בעיא לא מצי בעי בנזיר עולם, כגון דאמר "הריני נזיר עולם לאחר [עשרים] ומעכשיו נזיר [סתם]", דודאי חייל עליה נזיר סתם מהשתא, כיון דאפשר איתשיל אנזיר עולם הבא לחול עליו אחר עשרים – שישאל עליו, וישלים סתם נזירות. דדוקא אנזיר שמשון מיבעיא, דלא אפשר לאיתשולי עליה. וה"נ משמע בפ"ג דמכות (דף כב.) אמתני' דיש חורש תלם אחד, דנזיר שמשון לא אפשר לאתשולי, נזיר עולם אפשר אתשולי. **אמר** כמשה בז' באדר מהו. דביום הוולדו, דהיינו בז' באדר, שמחו שמחה גדולה, וביום מותו בז' באדר מסתמא רבים נדרו בנדר, ורבו נזירים בישראל, מחמת צער. והוא אמר בסתם "אהא", היינו כמו שהיה דורו של משה בז' באדר ביום מותו, ונזירות קבל עליה. או כיום הוולדו קאמר, ושמחה קבל עליה. וק"ק למ"ד (זבחים דף קיז.) נדרים ונדבות לא קריבין בבמה: א"כ אותם שנדרו בנזיר בפטירת משה רבינו – הא היו נזירים כל ימיהם, ולא יכלו להקריב קרבנות, דקרבן נזיר נידר ונידב הוא, ולא היה היתר גם בשילה. וכן קשה מן נזירות דאבשלום*. **פשוט** מיהא קמייתא הריני נזיר וכו'. נטמא בימי בנו. אמתני' קאי, דתנן: מניח את שלו ומונה של בנו. לריש לקיש נפקא מינה לענין דאם נטמא בימי בנו – אינו סותר את שלו. ולר' יוחנן נמי דסותר – היינו דוקא כשפוסק מניינו, כ] והניח את שלו ומונה את של בנו, ועומד באמצע מניינו, אז דסותר את של בנו – סותר נמי את של מניינו, לפי שלא השלים מניינו. ואילו היה מונה שני מניינים, אחד לו מסויים לעצמו, ושוב היה מונה לבנו לעצמו, ונטמא בימי בנו – לא היה סותר מנין של עצמו ל] לגמרי עד שלא התחיל מנין של בנו. וריש לקיש אמר: אינו סותר אלא נזירות של בנו, אבל מה שמנה משלו תחילה – אינו סותר. אבל ברישא דמתני', דקתני "הריני נזיר ונזיר כשיהיה לי בן" דמונה את שלו ואח"כ את של בנו, דאם נטמא בימי בנו – ד"ה אינו סותר אלא של בנו, דכבר נסתלק לגלח את שלו. **חדא** נזירות אריכתא היא. שהרי אינו מגלח [אלא] לאחר שישלים שלו ושל בנו, ובאמצע נזירותו הוא עומד. אבל ודאי נטמא בימי השלמה שלו – אינו סותר אלא אותו שלו, ולא של בנו. ב"ש הג"ה.
נטמא

כו א מיי' פ"ד מהל' נזירות הל' ח וע"ש בכ"מ:
כז ב מיי' שם הל"ט וע"ש:
כח ג מיי' שם הל' ו ז:
כט ד ה מיי' שם הל"ג:

פי' הרא"ש

דוקא ההפסקה גורמת: ה"ג אמר הריני נזיר לאחר [כ'] יום ומעכשיו נזיר עולם מי חיילא עליה או לא. את"ל הריני נזיר לאחר [כ'] יום ומעכשיו ק' יום חיילי שאני התם דאע"ג דחיילי ק' יום מעכשיו אפשר לו לקיים כל משפט נזיר' שלאחר כ' יום כי אחרי ההשלמה של נזירות ק' יגלח ויביא קרבנותיו של ק' ושל נזיר שלאחר כ'. או לאידך פי' יגלח אחר נזירות שלאחר כ' ויביא קרבן ויגלח שנית אחר השלמת הק' אבל הכא אי חייל נזיר עולם מיד שוב לא יגלח לעולם. ומיירי כגון דאמר ומעכשיו נזיר לעולם דאותו אינו מגלח לעולם. אבל נזיר עולם מיקל בתער. למר כדאית ליה ולמר כדאית ליה לעיל בפ"ק. ואת"ל כיון דאפשר לאתשולי חיילא. כלומר לא תמנע נזיר לעולם מלחול לאלתר משום בטול נזירות שלאחר כ' אמרי' כשאמר ומעכשיו נזיר לעולם היה בדעתו שיחול מיד ועל נזירות שלאחר כ' ילך אצל חכם ויתיר לו והרי הוא כאילו קיים אמר הריני נזיר שמשון לאחר כ' יום ומעכשיו נזיר סתם מהו מי אמרי' יתחיל למנות מעכשיו נזיר סתם ולאחר כ' יפסיק נזירותו ויתחיל נזיר שמשון ולא יגלח לעולם או דלמא כיון דאינו יכול להשלים נזירותו וגם אין שאלה לנזיר שמשון כדאיתא פ' בתרא דמכות לא חיילא עלי' כלל נזיר של ל' יום. וי"מ הריני נזיר לאחר כ' יום ומעכשיו נזיר עולם דדינו דהכביד שערו מיקל בתער ומביא ג' בהמות מי חיילי. את"ל דבין נזיר מרובה בין נזיר מועטת חיילי. וכי מטו כ' יום מפסיק. שאני התם דלא הוי הפסק כולי האי דדומה הוא לנזיר א' דבני חדא בקתא אינון. אבל הכא אי חייל מהשתא נזיר עולם כיון דנזיר [עולם] אינו כיוצא בו כלל הוי הפסק א): כולי דדומה הוא לנזיר א' הילכך לא חייל נזיר עולם עד אחר שישלים נזירותו שלאחר כ' יום או דלמא אפ"ה חייל מהשתא וכי מטו כ' יום יפסיק וימנה נזירותו ויגלח ויחזור לנזיר עולם כיון דאפשר לאתשולי' אנזיר דלאחר כ' ולא הוי הפסק כלל. וה"ה דהוי מצי למבעי הריני נזיר עולם לאחר כ' יום ומעכשיו נזיר סתם דמצי נמי לאתשולי אנזיר עולם: אמר כמשה בז' באדר מהו. מי אמרינן דהוי קבלת נזירות דמסתמא ביום שנפטר משה רבינו רבו

א) נראה דל"ל הוי הפסק הלכך לא חייל נזיר עולם וכו' וכ"ה בתוס' ד"ה מי חיילא.

[תוספתא פ"ב]

ס"א אינו

נוסחת הריב"ן

הגהות הב"ח

גליון הש"ס

[וע' היטב תוס' זבחים קיז. סד"ה ר' שמעון ותוס' תמורה יד: ד"ה שמי מכאן]

הגהות מהר"ב רנשבורג א] רש"י ד"ה אמר הריני כמשה בז' באדר וכו' ושוב לא שתה. מלת שתה נמחק ונ"ב שתו יין כצ"ל וכוונתו כהתוס' ד"ה אמר כמשה א"מ: ב] ד"ה ר' יוחנן וכו' דכיון דאפילו מנה. נמחקו ונ"ב דאילו מניח את שלו וכו' כצ"ל א"מ: ג] תוס' ד"ה מי חיילא וכו' דחזיא. מלת דחזיא נמחק ונ"ב דדמיא כצ"ל א"מ: ד] בא"ד בלי הפסק הלכך אסר. מלת אסר נמחק ונ"ב אמרינן כצ"ל: ה] בא"ד וה"ה דמצי למבעי נ"ב עי' א"מ: ו] בד"ה ואת"ל הכא וכו' חיילא נזיר עולם דמהשתא כצ"ל: ז] ד"ה אמר הריני נזיר כשמשון וכו' ואח"כ יתחיל נזירו' שמשון וידמה. מלת וידמה נמחק ונ"ב מדלא מצי להשלים כצ"ל ור"ל דאותן כ' יום יהא מותר ביין וטומאה וגילוח ולאחר כ' יתחיל סתם נזירות ל' יום ומדלא הסתם נזירות אח"כ יחול נזירות שמשון וכמ"ש תוס' לעיל ד"ה בעי רבה ובד"ה תלה מגו תלה א"מ: ח] בא"ד ואח"כ יפסיק נזירות זה כצ"ל: ט] בא"ד ויתחיל נזירות שמשון דלא קפיד אפי' אהפסקת. תיבות אפי' אהפסקת נמחקו ונ"ב גילוח בהפסקת כצ"ל ור"ל לאחר כ' ימים יסיים סתם [illegible]

עין משפט
נר מצוה

ל א מיי' פ"ז מהל' נזירות הל' י:
לא ב מיי' פ"ו מהל' נזירות הל"ה:
לב ג מיי' שם פ"ח הל' ה:
לג ד (מיי' שם פ"ו הל"ז):

תורה אור

נִטְמָא בִּימֵי צָרַעְתּוֹ, ר' יוֹחָנָן אָמַר: אסוֹתֵר, רֵישׁ לָקִישׁ אָמַר: אֵינוֹ סוֹתֵר. רַבִּי יוֹחָנָן אָמַר: סוֹתֵר, דְּהָא בִּנְזִירוּת קָאֵי. רֵישׁ לָקִישׁ אָמַר: אֵינוֹ סוֹתֵר, צָרַעַת לְחוּד וּנְזִירוּת לְחוּד. וּצְרִיכָא, דְּאִי אִיתְּמַר בְּהָךְ קַמַּיְיתָא – בְּהַהִיא א"ר רַבִּי יוֹחָנָן סוֹתֵר, שֵׁם נְזִירוּת אַחַת הִיא, אֲבָל בְּהָא – אֵימָא מוֹדֶה לֵיהּ לְרֵישׁ לָקִישׁ, דְּנָזִיר לְחוּד וְצָרַעַת לְחוּד. וְאִי אִיתְּמַר בְּהָא – בְּהָא קָאָמַר ר"ל, אֲבָל בְּהָךְ – אֵימָא מוֹדֶה לֵיהּ לְר' יוֹחָנָן, צְרִיכָא. נִטְמָא בְּיוֹם גִּידּוּל שֵׂעָר, רַב אָמַר: באֵינוֹ סוֹתֵר; אֲפִי' לְר' יוֹחָנָן דְּאָמַר סוֹתֵר – הָנֵי מִילֵּי הֵיכָא דְּקָאֵי בִּנְזִירוּת, גִּידּוּל שֵׂעָר – מִישְׁלָם נְזִירוּת הוּא. וּשְׁמוּאֵל אָמַר: סוֹתֵר; אֲפִי' לְרֵישׁ לָקִישׁ דְּאָמַר אֵין סוֹתֵר – הָתָם שְׁתֵּי נְזִירוּת, הָכָא חֲדָא נְזִירוּתָא. אָמַר רַב חִסְדָּא: הַכֹּל מוֹדִים שֶׁאִם קִדֵּשׁ שֵׂעָר בַּדָּם – אֵין לוֹ תַּקָּנָה. אַלִּיבָּא דְּמַאן? אִי אַלִּיבָּא *דְּרַבִּי אֱלִיעֶזֶר, כֵּיוָן דְּאָמַר תִּגְלַחַת מְעַכֶּבֶת – תּוֹךְ מְלֹאת הִיא, וְלִסְתּוֹר! אֶלָּא אַלִּיבָּא דְּרַבָּנַן – גהָאָמְרִי תִּגְלַחַת לֹא מְעַכֶּבֶת! לְעוֹלָם אַלִּיבָּא דְּרַבָּנַן, וּמַאי "אֵין לוֹ תַּקָּנָה" – דאֵין לוֹ תַּקָּנָה לְמִצְוַת גִּילּוּחַ. אָמַר ר' יוֹסֵי בְּרַבִּי חֲנִינָא: נָזִיר שֶׁכָּלוּ לוֹ יָמָיו – לוֹקֶה עַל הַטּוּמְאָה, וְאֵינוֹ לוֹקֶה עַל הַתִּגְלַחַת וְלֹא עַל הַיַּיִן. מַאי שְׁנָא טוּמְאָה דְּלָקֵי – דְּאָמַר קְרָא °"כָּל יְמֵי הַזִּירוֹ לַה'" (במדבר ו) לְרַבּוֹת יָמִים שֶׁלְּאַחַר מְלֹאת כַּיָּמִים שֶׁלִּפְנֵי מְלֹאת. אִי הָכִי אִתְגַּלַּחַת נַמִי לִיחַיֵּיב, דְּהָא אָמַר רַחֲמָנָא °"כָּל יְמֵי נֶדֶר נִזְרוֹ תַּעַר לֹא יַעֲבֹר עַל רֹאשׁוֹ" (שם) – לַעֲשׂוֹת יָמִים שֶׁלְּאַחַר מְלֹאת כַּיָּמִים שֶׁלִּפְנֵי מְלֹאת! וְתוּ, °"כָּל יְמֵי נִזְרוֹ מִכֹּל אֲשֶׁר יֵעָשֶׂה מִגֶּפֶן הַיַּיִן" (שם) – לַעֲשׂוֹת יָמִים שֶׁלְּאַחַר מְלֹאת כַּיָּמִים שֶׁלִּפְנֵי מְלֹאת!

שָׁאנֵי

נטמא בימי צרעתו. אמר "הריני נזיר מהיום" והתחיל למנות נזירות. א] [שימי] חלוטו אינו עולה לנזירות, וגם אינו סותר, כדלקמן בפרק "מי שאמר" (דף יז:). ונטמא במת בימי חלוטו. לר"ל אינו סותר הימים הראשונים שמנה לנזירותו קודם ימי צרעתו, וכשיטהר מצרעתו – יגלח ויביא קרבנות מצורע, ויחזור וישלים מנין נזירות כמו שפסק. ור' יוחנן אומר: סותר, דהא בנזירות קאי, ועדיין לא מנה המאה, ולכשיטהר מצרעתו – צריך למנות כל ימי נזירותו. וצריכא. לאשמועינן פלוגתייהו בבנו ובצרעתו. **נטמא** ביום גידול שיער. פי': אמר "הריני נזיר שלשים יום", וכשמנה כ' מנזירותו גילחוהו ליסטים על כרחו. דהשתא לא יוכל לגלח ביום שלשים לנזירות ולהביא קרבנותיו עד אחר שלשים יום מיום שגילחוהו הליסטים, דאין גידול פחות משלשים יום. והתחיל הל', וכשמנה עשרה סיים נזירותו, שהרי תחילה מנה עשרים טרם שגילחוהו הליסטים, ואלו העשרים יום האחרונים אינם רק לגדל שיער, שיוכל לגלח אחר נזירותו ולהביא קרבנותיו, ובהם נטמא. והאי דנקט "ביום גידול שיער" ולא נקט "בימי" כדנקט לעיל בימי צרעתו – לפי [שאי] אפשר שלא יהו נמשכים ימי צרעתו טפי מיום אחד. אבל גידול שיער אפשר שלא יצריך עליו אלא יום אחד, כגון שגילחוהו ליסטים יום שני לנזירותו, דהשתא אינו מוסיף על שלשים אלא יום שלבסוף בעבור גידול שיער. **התם** שני נזירות. של בנו ושלו. וכן נטמא בימי צרעתו – נזירות לחוד וצרעת לחוד. הכא חדא נזירות הוא, וכן נטמא ביום שהוא טהור – חד נזירות הוא. **אמר** רב חסדא הכל מודים שאם קידש שיער בדם. פירוש: אם לאחר שנזרק הדם נטמא, קודם שגילח, וקורא קידוש שיער – שלא גילח, כדכתיב "וקידש ראשו", שפירושו: יתחיל לגדל ראשו. אין לו תקנה. קס"ד שלא יוכל עולמית לשתות ביין ולגלח, כיון שהביא כבר קרבנותיו, וכיון דנטמא קודם שגילח, ובלא הבאת קרבן – לא יוכל לגלח. אליבא [דמאן] אי אליבא דר' אליעזר כיון דאמר תגלחת מעכבו. לשתות יין – "תוך מלאת" הוא, כלומר, הרי הוא כאילו נטמא קודם הבאת קרבנותיו שהוא בתוך מלאת. ולסתור. כלומר: יחזור ויביא קרבנות, כדתנן פרק "ג' מינין" (לקמן דף מז.): מי שנזרק עליו אחד מן הדמים ונטמא, ר' אליעזר אומר: סותר את הכל. ופריך בגמרא: והאמר ר' אליעזר כל אחר מלאת – [שבעה] סותר! ומשני: מאי סותר – קרבנותיו, ולאחר [שיטהר] יביא קרבנותיו. והאי ב] "יסתור" דהכא – ע"כ לאו דווקא דנטמא ביום שלשים, דהא א"ר אליעזר בפירקין לקמן (דף טז:) דאינו סותר [אלא שבעה]: אלא אליבא דרבנן דאמרי דתגלחת לא מיעכבא. לשתות ביין, וכיון שהביא קרבנות – מותר לטמאות ולשתות בלא תגלחת כלל. **לעולם** אליבא דרבנן ומאי אין לו תקנה למצות גילוח. דכיון שהביא כבר קרבנותיו – שוב לא יביא, ונסתלק, ומיד מותר לשתות ביין בלא תגלחת כלל. ו"הכל מודים" דקאמר רב חסדא – קאי אפלוגתא דרב ושמואל, דפליגי דנטמא ביום גידול שער אם סותר. והכא דנטמא קודם תגלחת – מודים דאינו סותר, דהוי כמי שגילח כבר. **נזיר** שכלו לו ימיו. שמנה כל ימי נזירות, ועומד ביום הבאת קרבנותיו.

לוקה על הטומאה. אם נטמא קודם הבאת קרבנותיו. אבל אינו סותר נזירות שמנה אחר שכלו ימיו כבר. והיינו דאשכחן בפירקא דלקמן (דף טז.) ואייתי לעיל: נטמא יום מאה ואחד סותר שלשים – היינו דוקא יום ק"א, וגזרינן אטו יום שלשים, דהוי יום תגלחת דאורייתא, כדתנן פרק קמא (לעיל דף ה:), אבל ביום מאה ושנים – אינו סותר, °או ביום שלשים ואחד אינו סותר. *)**שאני** הכא דאמר. לענין טומאה, דאמר רחמנא "וטמא ראש נזרו" – מי שנזרו תלוי לו בראשו, שכבר שלמו, אלא אין לו עדיין נזירות אלא בראשו, שלא גילח – אז לוקה על הטומאה, דכתיב "וטמא [ראש נזרו]". ומיהא, כשנטמא אחר שהביא קרבנותיו – לא מחייב למ"ד תגלחת לא מעכבא. דהך דרשא לא מתוקמא אלא קודם הבאת קרבן, הבאת קרבן ומיקרי שפיר נזירות תלוי בראשו, אע"פ שעדיין לא הביא קרבנותיו – לפי שאין בגופו לעשות אלא תגלחת, אבל אם שתה יין או גילח – לא מחייב, דהא ליכא בהו קרא כמו גבי טומאה.

*) שייך לדף טו ע"א

נטמא בימי צרעתו. היה נזיר, ונצטרע, ובימי צרעתו נטמא למתים. ר' יוחנן אמר סותר. את הקודמין, דהא אכתי קאי בנזירות, הואיל א) דכי נתרפא מצרעתו משלים מה ב) שכבר מנה קודם שנצטרע. ריש לקיש אמר אינו סותר. דימי צרעת לחוד, הואיל ואין עולין לו למנין ימי נזרו. והימ"ן שונה להני תרתי דרבי יוחנן וריש לקיש בטעמא אחרינא, ואף המורה חז"ר ג) להיו"ת כדברי הימ"ן, דבין כי נטמא בצרעתו ובין בנזירות בנו, דההוא איידך נזירות נזיר מאה מיירי, לפי שלא מלינו גידול (א) פחות משלשים, והואיל ובתרווייהו צריך לגלח. דלכי נתרפא מצרעתו נמי צריך לגלח, הילכך לא מיתוקם אלא בנזירות מאה: ד) נטמא ביום גידול שער. כגון שקיבל עליו נזירות מאה יום, וכי מנה שבעים נצטרע, וכי נטהר גילח תגלחת לצרעת, ואכתי פשו מן המאה שלשים יום דאית בהו גידול שיער, ונטמא ביום גידול שער – היינו ביום מאה, שבו שלם גידול שיער שלו – דברי הכל סותר השלשים שאחר הצרעת. אבל באם סותר שבעים שלפני הצרעת פליגי. רב אומר אינו סותר. דאפי' לרבי יוחנן דאמר נטמא בימי בנו דסותר כל נזירות – התם בנזירות קאי, להכי מצי סתר לנזירות נמי. אבל הכא, כיון דנטמא ביום מישלם גידול שיער, ה) כבר שילם נזירותו, ולית ליה כח למסתר דלפני צרעת. ושמואל אמר סותר. את הכל, אפי' ע' קמאי (ב). שם נזירות אחת היא. ו) [אבל] מנין שלו ומנין של בנו ז) – תרי נזירות מיתקרו. ל"א: נטמא ביום גידול – כגון דאמר "הריני נזיר" והתחיל ומנה עד עשרים יום, ונטמא, וסתר את הכל, והתחיל למנות נזירות אחרת, ומנה עשרה ימים בטהרה, ואח"כ נטמא באחד מכל עשרים יום הסותרין להשלים לנזירות. רב אמר אינו סותר. הללו עשרה. דאפילו לרבי יוחנן דאמר סותר – הני מילי היכא דקאי בנזירות גמור, אבל האי דלא איטמי אלא בימי גידול שיער, דמשלם נזירות הוא, דלכי ח) מצרפי הני עשרה לעשרים קמאי – הוו להו שלשים, והילכך האי דאהדר איטמי מעשרה ואילך – לא הוי אלא תשלומי נזירות. ואפי' ר' יוחנן מודה דאינו סותר להנך עשרה, אלא כיון דהויה שלישי ושביעי מתחיל למנות מעשרה ואילך עד שלשים. ושמואל אמר סותר אפילו לר"ל כו'. אבל הכא חדא נזירות. והא דאמרינן מישלם נזירות הוא – לא איריא, דכיון דסתרו הראשונים שוב אי אתה יכול לצרף עמהן הללו ט) ולומר שלשים הן. הכל מודים שאם קידש שיער בדם. י) ביום ל"א, צריך להביא קרבנותיו ולהתגלח אחר קרבנותיו, אם כבר נזרק הדם כשנטמא ועדיין לא גילח – שאין לו תקנה להתירו. כ) כיון דלמנות פעם אחרת ולהביא קרבן אחר – אי אפשר, דקרבן אחד הוא מביא ולא שני קרבנות, וכבר הביא קרבן אחד ואין עולה לו – דהא כבר נטמא, לפיכך אין לו תקנה. והא דקתני קידש – לישנא דקרא נקיט, דכתיב "וקדש את ראשו" (במדבר ו). כיון דאמר תגלחת מעכבת. לשתות ביין – בתוך מלאת קרינא ביה, ל) לסתור מה שמנה, ולייתי קרבן אחר. אלא אליבא דרבנן. דפליגי עליה בפרק "שלשה מינין" (לקמן דף מז.), ואמרי: כיון שנזרק עליו אחד מן הדמים נטהר מ). למצות גילוח. דלא יהא תגלחת בטהרה כמצותו (ג) לעולם, שהרי אינו יכול לסתור ולמנות נזירות אחרת, שהרי לאחר מלאת נטמא, הילכך אין לו תקנה לגלח בטהרה, אלא מגלח בטומאה. נזיר שכלו לו. ימי שלשים (ד) נזירות סתם, ולנזירות מרובה – כל ימים שהזיר, ולאחר מלאת, שצריך להביא קרבנותיו, נטמא – לוקה על הטומאה. ואינו לוקה על התגלחת – אבל אינו לוקה אם גילח קודם שהביא קרבנותיו, או שתה יין קודם שהביא קרבנותיו. דאמר קרא כל ימי הזירו לה'. דכתיב "כל" דלא צריך, וכתביה, ואמר "כל ימי הזירו לה' על נפש מת לא יבא" – לרבות ימים כו'. כל ימי נדר נזרו תער וגו' כל ימי נזרו מכל אשר יעשה מגפן היין וגו'. ולילקי נמי אתרווייהו!

שאני

אסור

פי' הרא"ש

רבו נודרים נזירות מחמת צער. או דלמא לא שהרי גם בז' באדר נולד וכמו כן הוא יום משתה ושמחה. פשוט מיהא קמייתא אמר הריני נזיר ברייתא היא א) והא דאמרי' במתני' נולד לו בן עד ע' לא הפסיד כלום. והכא לא אמרי' דמיבלע נזיר של כ' בתוך נזיר ק'. וי"ל דהכא אם איתא דכוונתו להבליע א"כ בחנם אמר הריני נזיר לאחר כ' יום דלעולם מובלע בתוך נזיר ק' אבל במתני' בדעתו היה שיהיה נזיר מיד אולי ישלמו נזירותו קודם שיולד לו בן. ואם יולד לו בן קודם שישלימו שיהו מובלעים זה בתוך זה: נטמא בימי בנו. אסיפא דמתני' קאי דקתני מניח את שלו ומונה את של בנו: ר' יוחנן אומר סותר אף שלו דכיון דהפסיק באמצע נזירות והתחיל למנות את של בנו כוליה נזירות אריכתא היא וקרינן בכוליה והימים הראשונים יפלו. אבל ברישא מודה ר' יוחנן דאינו סותר הכל כיון דכבר השלים את שלו וכן בסיפא ב) אם נטמא בימי השלמה שלו: נטמא בימי צרעתו. אמר הריני נזיר ק' יום והתחיל למנות ונצטרע ואמרי' לקמן דימי חלוטו אינן עולים וגם אינן סותרים וכשיטהר מצרעתו יגלח ויביא קרבן מצרעתו וישלים ימי נזירות שהפסיק ר' יוחנן אומר סותר כיון שנטמא קודם שהשלים ימי נזירות [נזירות] אריכתא היא: וצריכא לאשמועינן פלוגתייהו בתרווייהו: נטמא ביום גידול שער כגון סתם נזיר שנצטרע וביום טהרתו מגלח ומביא קרבנותיו וצריך למנות עוד ל' יום לגדול שער מלבד הימים הראשונים שמנה קודם שנצטרע לפי שאין תגלחת פחות מל' יום. וכן אם גלחוהו לסטים אחר שמנה קצת צריך למנות ל' יום לגדול שער אם נטמא אחר שהשלים ל' יום נזירותו קודם שהשלים ימי גידול שער פליגי רב ושמואל. והא דנקט ביום גידול שער. ולעיל נקט בימי צרעתו לפי שא"א שלא יהיה בצרעת יותר מיום א' אבל הכא אפשר שאין גידול שער אלא יום א' כגון שנצטרע או שגלחוהו לסטים ביום הראשון: התם שתי נזירות שלו ושל בנו. וכן נזיר לחוד וצרעת לחוד: הכל מודים שאם קדש שער בדם אין לו תקנה הכל מודים רב ושמואל דפליגי בנטמא ביום גידול שער שאם (גדל) [קדש] שער בדם. כלומר שנזרק עליו בעוד שערו קדוש דהיינו קודם גילוח כדכתיב וקדש ראשו ביום ההוא דגידול שער מקרי קדושה: אין לו תקנה. קס"ד שלא יוכל לגלח וליטמא למתים לעולם. דכיון שניטמא אחר זריקת הדם קודם שגילח לא יוכל לגלח קודם ג) הבאת קרבן אי ר' אליעזר כיון דאמר תגלחת מעכבת דאפי' הביא קרבנותיו אסור לשתות יין וליטמא למתים עד שיגלח דאמרי' לקמן פ' ג' מינין אם משנזרק עליו א' מן הדמים נטמא ר"א אומר סותר הכל ופריך לקמן והא אמר ר' אליעזר כל לאחר מלאת אינו סותר ומשני מאי סותר קרבנותיו ולאחר ז' יביא קרבנותיו: תוך מלאת הוא ולסתור ולאו דוקא תוך מלאת אלא הוי כמו נטמא קודם הבאת קרבנותיו שסותר ז': הא אמרי' תגלחת לא מעכבא. ואחר הבאת קרבנותיו מותר לשתות יין וליטמא למתים מיד אפי' לא גלח: אין לו תקנה למצות גילוח [illegible] גילוח בטהרה ובהא מודו רב ושמואל: נזיר שכלו לו ימיו שהשלים ימי נזירותו ועדיין לא הביא קרבנותיו לוקה על הטומאה אע"פ שאינו סותר [illegible] לוקה. דאמר קרא כל ימי הזירו לה' על נפש [illegible]

נוסחת הריב"ן

א) דלכי: ב) שמנה כבר: ג) להורות: ד) בכ"י כתוב כאן ענין אחר גליון וכי נטמא במת בימי צרעתו פליגי בה ר' יוחנן אמר סותר כל ימי נזירותו דאע"ג דבימי צרעתו הוא מ"מ הא בנזירות קאי הלכך סותר כי היכי דסתר כשנטמא במת בלא צרעת ור"ל אמר אינו סותר כלום דהא בימי צרעתו קאי ואע"ג דהוי נזיר כיון דבימי צרעתו נטמא צרעת לחוד שהרי יש לו גילוח לבדו שאין עולה לו לגלחות נזיר הלכך דינו משונה מדנזיר שאם נטמא בימי צרעתו אינו סותר כלום ונזירות לחוד שאם נטמא כשהוא (מצורע) [נזיר] סותר נזירותו: ה) הא כבר: ו) אחת היא דמנין: ז) תרווייהו: ח) מצרפת: ט) הללו י' ימים ולומר: י) אם ביום ל"א שצריך: כ) להתירו ביין לטמאות: ל) ולסתור: מ) ותגלחת לא מעכבא ה"ל מותר לגמרי: לעולם אליבא דרבנן ומאי אין לו תקנה דקאמר לאו לענין היתר יין אלא למצות גילוח דלא יהא כו':

הגהות הב"ח

(א) רש"י ד"ה ריש לקיש וכו' גידול שער פחות משלשים והואיל ובתרווייהו נ"ב זהו ע"פ דעת הגליון לעיל במתניתין: (ב) ד"ה ושמואל וכו' ע' קמאי דשם נזירות אחת היא אבל מנין שלו וכו' מיתקרו ל"א נטמא ביום גידול שער כגון דאמר וכו' להשלים לנזירות רב אמר כצ"ל והד"א: (ג) ד"ה למצות גילוח וכו' כמצותו שהרי כצ"ל ותיבת לעולם נמחק: (ד) ד"ה נזיר וכו' לנזירות סתם:

גליון הש"ס

תום' ד"ה לוקה כו' או ביום ל'. ע' לעיל דף ו ע"א תד"ה נטמא ולקמן דף טז ע"ב ד"ה נטמא:

הגהות מהר"ב רנשבורג

א] תוד"ה ניטמא בימי צרעתו וכו' והתחיל למנות נזירות ונצטרע כצ"ל: ב] ד"ה אליבא דמאן וכו' ומשני מאי סותר קרבנותיו ולאחר שיטהר יביא קרבנותיו והאי יסתור. מלת יסתור נמחק וצ"ב סותר כצ"ל:

שָׁאנֵי הָכָא. גַּבֵּי טוּמְאָה, טַעְמָא מַאי הוּא דְּלוֹקֶה — דִּכְתִיב "וְטִמֵּא רֹאשׁ נִזְרוֹ", מִי שֶׁנִּזְרוֹ תָּלוּי לוֹ בְּרֹאשׁוֹ, דְּמַשְׁמַע שֶׁתָּלָה הַכָּתוּב אֶת הַטּוּמְאָה בְּמִי שֶׁעֲדַיִין לֹא נִתְגַּלַּח, וַאֲפִי' לְאַחַר שֶׁכָּלוּ לוֹ יָמָיו, א) כָּל זְמַן שֶׁלֹּא גִּילַּח שְׂעָרוֹ, שֶׁנִּזְרוֹ עַל רֹאשׁוֹ. מִי שֶׁכְּבָר כָּלוּ יְמֵי נְזִירוּתוֹ, וְאֵין נִזְרוֹ תָּלוּי אֶלָּא בְּרֹאשׁוֹ. אִם גִּילַּח וְשָׁתָה יַיִן וְנִטְמָא לַמֵּתִים סוֹפֵג אֶת הָאַרְבָּעִים. אַלְמָא דְּגָמְרִי "יְמֵי" "יְמֵי" לְרַבּוֹת יָמִים שֶׁלְּאַחַר מְלֹאת, וּתְיוּבְתָּא לְר' יוֹסֵי בְּר' חֲנִינָא. מתני' הֲרֵינִי נָזִיר כְּשֶׁיִּהְיֶה לִי בֵּן וְנָזִיר מֵאָה יוֹם. וְהִתְחִיל לִמְנוֹת אֶת שֶׁלּוֹ. אִם נוֹלַד לוֹ בֵּן עַד ע' יוֹם — ב) צָרִיךְ לְהַנִּיחַ אֶת שֶׁלּוֹ וְלִמְנוֹת אֶת שֶׁל בְּנוֹ. לֹא הִפְסִיד כְּלוּם. דִּשְׁלֹשִׁים יוֹם הוּא דְּמִיַּיתְרֵי לֵיהּ מִמֵּאָה. אֶלָּא מַנִּיחַ אֶת שֶׁלּוֹ, וּמוֹנֶה אֶת שֶׁל בְּנוֹ וּמְגַלֵּחַ, וּמוֹנֶה שְׁלֹשִׁים כְּדֵי לְהַשְׁלִים מֵאָה שֶׁלּוֹ וּמְגַלֵּחַ, דְּבִשְׁלֹשִׁים אִית בְּהוּ כְּדֵי גִידּוּל שֵׂעָר. אֲבָל אִם נוֹלַד לוֹ לְאַחַר ע'. דְּלָא מִיַּיתְרֵי לְהוּ שְׁלֹשִׁים, ג) דְּלֵית בְּהוּ גִּידּוּל שֵׂעָר, שֶׁאֵין תִּגְלַחַת פָּחוֹת מִל' יוֹם — הִלְכָּךְ סוֹתֵר אֶת הַכֹּל וּמַתְחִיל לִמְנוֹת אֶת שֶׁל בְּנוֹ וּמְגַלֵּחַ, וְאַחַר כָּךְ מוֹנֶה מֵאָה שֶׁלּוֹ. וְה"מ בִּנְזִירוּת מְרוּבָּה, אֲבָל בִּנְזִירוּת מוּעֶטֶת — אֵינוֹ סוֹתֵר כְּלָל, כִּדְתְנַן לְעֵיל: מַנִּיחַ אֶת שֶׁלּוֹ וּמוֹנֶה אֶת שֶׁל בְּנוֹ, וְאַחַר כָּךְ מַשְׁלִים אֶת שֶׁלּוֹ, וְאֵינוֹ סוֹתֵר. וְטַעְמָא מַאי — כִּדְאָמְרַן, שֶׁאֵין תִּגְלַחַת בֵּינְתַיִם, וְכַחֲדָא נְזִירוּת אֲרִיכָא הוּא. גמ' אָמַר רַב. נוֹלַד לוֹ בֵּן בְּיוֹם ע' — עוֹלֶה לוֹ לְכָאן וּלְכָאן. אוֹתוֹ יוֹם עוֹלֶה לוֹ לְמִנְיַן ע', וּלְמִנְיַן שֶׁל בְּנוֹ, ד) דִּשְׁלֹשִׁים דִּלְבְנוֹ נַמִי מַתְחִיל לִמְנוֹת בּוֹ בַּיּוֹם. וְכֵן כְּשֶׁבָּא לְהַשְׁלִים מֵאָה שֶׁלּוֹ שֶׁלְּאַחַר נְזִירוּת שֶׁל בְּנוֹ — אֵין צָרִיךְ לִמְנוֹת אֶלָּא כ"ט: ה) אִיתַּגּוּרֵי מִיתְגַּר. דְּעוֹלֶה לוֹ לְכָאן וּלְכָאן, שֶׁאֵינוֹ צָרִיךְ לְהַשְׁלִים (א) אֶלָּא לְמֵאָה בִּלְבָד, וְעוֹד: ו) שֶׁנְּזִירוּת שֶׁל בְּנוֹ מַתְחִיל מִבּוֹ בַּיּוֹם, צְרִיכָא לְמֵימַר דְּלָא הִפְסִיד כְּלוּם? אֶלָּא בְּדִין הוּא דְּלָא לִיתְנֵי עַד שִׁבְעִים וּמִשּׁוּם דְּקָתָנֵי סֵיפָא כו'. הָךְ "אֶלָּא" נִשְׁתַּנָּה מִכָּל "אֶלָּא" שֶׁבַּתַּלְמוּד. וְהָכִי מַשְׁמַע: אֶלָּא מִשּׁוּם דְּקָתָנֵי סֵיפָא "אַחַר שִׁבְעִים", תָּנָא לֵיהּ רֵישָׁא "עַד שִׁבְעִים", וּבְדִין הוּא דְּלָא לִיתְנְיֵיהּ כְּלָל, דְּהָא אָמְרִינַן דַּאֲפִילּוּ אִיתַּגּוּרֵי מִיתְגַּר. וְאִית סְפָרִים דִּכְתִיב בְּהוּ: ז) בְּדִין לִיתְנֵי עַד ע' כו', אֶלָּא מִשּׁוּם דְּקָתָנֵי סֵיפָא לִישָּׁנָא דְּהִפְסִיד, דְּקָתָנֵי "אַחַר ע' סוֹתֵר", תָּנָא נַמִי רֵישָׁא [עַד ע'] דְּאֵינוֹ סוֹתֵר ח). ת"ש נוֹלַד אַחַר שִׁבְעִים סוֹתֵר ע'. וְאִי אִיתָא כִּדְקָאָמְרַתְּ — ט) אַמַּאי סוֹתֵר? כֵּיוָן דְּמַתְחִיל לִמְנוֹת מִבּוֹ בַּיּוֹם לִבְנוֹ, וְיוֹם שְׁלֹשִׁים דִּבְנוֹ עוֹלֶה לוֹ לְכָאן וּלְכָאן — אַכַּתִּי פָּשׁוּ לְהוּ שְׁלֹשִׁים יוֹם כְּדֵי גִידּוּל שֵׂיעָר! מַאי אַחַר. דְּקָתָנֵי — אַחַר אַחַר, דְּהַיְינוּ ע"ב. דַּאֲפִילּוּ י) אִי אָמְרַתְּ דְּעוֹלֶה לְכָאן וּלְכָאן — אַכַּתִּי לָא פָּשׁוּ לְהוּ אֶלָּא כ"ט יוֹם, וְאֵין תִּגְלַחַת פָּחוֹת מִשְּׁלֹשִׁים יוֹם. מַאי אִירְיָא דְּקָתָנֵי. רֵישָׁא: עַד ע' לֹא הִפְסִיד כְּלוּם? אֲפִילּוּ לְאַחַר ע', בְּיוֹם ע"א נַמִי לֹא הִפְסִיד, דְּהָא אָמְרַתְּ דְּלָא סָתַר! אֶלָּא ש"מ אַחַר מַמָּשׁ, בְּיוֹם ע"א, דְּקָתָנֵי סוֹתֵר מִשּׁוּם דְּלָא אָמְרִינַן שֶׁהוּא עוֹלֶה לוֹ לְכָאן וּלְכָאן. א] וְכֵן מַתְנִיתִין לְרַב. כ) וְכֵן לְעִנְיַן זֶה קַשְׁיָא מַתְנִיתִין לְרַב, ש"מ. וְרַב כְּמַאן אֲמָרָהּ לִשְׁמַעְתֵּיהּ. וְאִי קַשְׁיָא: לָמָּה לִי ל) מִיבַּעְיָא הָכִי? הָא אַשְׁכְּחַן בְּפ"ק דְּתָנֵי "יוֹם שְׁלֹשִׁים עוֹלֶה לְכָאן וּלְכָאן"! דִּילְמָא מַתְנִי' דְּהָתָם לָא מִתְּרְצָא כְּרַב מַתְּנָא אֶלָּא כְּבַר פַּדָּא, דְּאָמַר אֵין סְתָם נְזִירוּת אֶלָּא כ"ט מ). ג' יָמִים קוֹדֶם לָרֶגֶל בָּטְלָה מִמֶּנּוּ גְּזֵירַת שִׁבְעָה. שֶׁאֵין צָרִיךְ לְהַשְׁלִים אַחַר הָרֶגֶל ז' יְמֵי אֲבֵילוּת. דְּכֵיוָן דְּעִיקַּר הָאֲבֵילוּת, דְּהַיְינוּ ג' יָמִים רִאשׁוֹנִים, כִּדְאָמְרִינַן בְּמוֹעֵד קָטָן, הָווּ קוֹדֶם לָרֶגֶל — בִּיטֵּל הָרֶגֶל אֶת הָאַחֲרוֹנִים. וְאִם קְבָרוֹ ח' יָמִים נ) לִפְנֵי הָרֶגֶל. כֵּיוָן דְּיוֹם אֶחָד שֶׁל שְׁלֹשִׁים הָיָה קוֹדֶם הָרֶגֶל — בִּיטֵּל הָרֶגֶל מִמֶּנּוּ גְּזֵירַת שְׁלֹשִׁים. וּמוּתָּר לְסַפֵּר עֶרֶב הָרֶגֶל. מִשּׁוּם כְּבוֹד הָרֶגֶל. אָסוּר לְסַפֵּר אַחַר הָרֶגֶל. עַד שְׁלֹשִׁים.
אַבָּא

תורה אור

שָׁאנֵי הָכָא, דְּאָמַר רַחֲמָנָא °"וְטִמֵּא רֹאשׁ נִזְרוֹ" (במדבר ו) — מִי שֶׁנִּזְרוֹ תָּלוּי לוֹ בְּרֹאשׁוֹ. מֵיתִיבֵי: אנָזִיר שֶׁכָּלוּ לוֹ יָמָיו — אָסוּר לְגַלֵּחַ וְלִשְׁתּוֹת יַיִן וְלִטַּמֵּא לַמֵּתִים, וְאִם גִּילַּח וְשָׁתָה יַיִן וְנִטְמָא לַמֵּתִים — ה"ז סוֹפֵג אֶת הָאַרְבָּעִים! תְּיוּבְתָּא.§

מתני' ב"הֲרֵינִי נָזִיר לִכְשֶׁיְּהֵא לִי בֵּן, וְנָזִיר מֵאָה יוֹם", נוֹלַד לוֹ בֵּן, עַד שִׁבְעִים — לֹא הִפְסִיד כְּלוּם, לְאַחַר שִׁבְעִים — סוֹתֵר שִׁבְעִים, שֶׁאֵין תִּגְלַחַת פָּחוֹת מִשְּׁלֹשִׁים יוֹם.§

גמ' אָמַר רַב: יוֹם שִׁבְעִים עוֹלֶה לְכָאן וּלְכָאן. תְּנַן: נוֹלַד לוֹ עַד שִׁבְעִים לֹא הִפְסִיד כְּלוּם. וְאִי סָלְקָא דַּעְתָּךְ עוֹלֶה לְכָאן וּלְכָאן — אִיתַּגּוּרֵי מִיתְגַּר! אֶלָּא, בְּדִין הוּא דְּלָא לִיתְנֵי "עַד שִׁבְעִים", וּמִשּׁוּם דְּקָתָנֵי סֵיפָא "אַחַר שִׁבְעִים סוֹתֵר שִׁבְעִים", קָתָנֵי רֵישָׁא שִׁבְעִים. ת"ש מִסֵּיפָא: נוֹלַד אַחַר שִׁבְעִים — סוֹתֵר שִׁבְעִים. מַאי "אַחַר" — אַחַר אַחַר. אֲבָל אַחַר מַמָּשׁ מַאי — הָכִי נַמִי דְּלָא סָתַר? אִי הָכִי, מַאי אִירְיָא דְּתָנֵי "נוֹלַד עַד שִׁבְעִים לֹא הִפְסִיד כְּלוּם"? אֲפִי' אַחַר שִׁבְעִים נַמִי, הָא אָמְרַתְּ לֹא סָתַר! אֶלָּא, ש"מ: אַחַר מַמָּשׁ. וְכֵן מַתְנִי' לְרַב, שְׁמַע מִינָּהּ. וְרַב, כְּמַאן אֲמָרָהּ לִשְׁמַעְתֵּיהּ? אִילֵימָא כְּאַבָּא שָׁאוּל, *דִּתְנַן: גהַקּוֹבֵר אֶת מֵתוֹ שְׁלֹשָׁה יָמִים קוֹדֶם לָרֶגֶל — בָּטְלָה מִמֶּנּוּ גְּזֵירַת שִׁבְעָה, דשְׁמוֹנָה יָמִים קוֹדֶם לָרֶגֶל — בָּטְלָה מִמֶּנּוּ גְּזֵירַת שְׁלֹשִׁים, וּמוּתָּר לְסַפֵּר עֶרֶב הָרֶגֶל. וְאִם לֹא סִיפֵּר עֶרֶב הָרֶגֶל — אָסוּר לְסַפֵּר אַחַר הָרֶגֶל.
אַבָּא

אסור לגלח. פי': קודם זריקת דמים, שהרי מצותו לגלח על הדמים. ואם גילח על אחד משלשתן — אמרינן לקמן דילא.

אמר רב יום שבעים עולה לו לכאן ולכאן. פי': נולד לו בן ביום ע' — מקצת היום שקודם הלידה עולה למנין המאה, והרי עשה ע' יום מן המאה, (שהוא יום ל"א), ומקצת היום שאחר הלידה עולה לתחילת הנזירות, ולא ימנה נזירות בנו אלא עד כ"ט יום. הרי ביום ל"ט דשלו ל' לבנו. וכ"מ השתא שיום ע' עולה לכאן ולכאן — שיוכל לגלח ביום המאה, שהוא יום ל"א לבנו. מתוך שאותו תגלחת עולה לנזירות בנו מן הדין, שהוא יום [ל"א] לבנו — עולה נמי אותו תגלחת גם לנזירות דנפשיה שהוא מאה יום. אע"פ שאם לא נולד לו הבן לא היה יכול לגלח על נזירתו אלא ביום ק"א — השתא כשנולד הבן יכול לגלח ביום [ק'], כדפרישית. וא"ת: ומאי סברא היא, כיון דאם לא נולד לו בן — לא יכול לגלח עד יום ק"א, דהא לא מצי לגלח עד יום ק"א לנזיר נזירות דנפשיה, השתא נמי לא יגלח עד יום ק"א! ויש לומר: דהא [דלא] מצי לגלח ביום ק' — לא הוי אלא מדרבנן, כדפירשנו בפ"ק (דף ו.), דמדאורייתא מצי לגלח ביום ק', דמקצת היום ככולו, אלא דרבנן גזרו דלא מגלח עד יום ק"א אטו היכא דאמר "שלימים". והכא אוקמיה אדין תורה, כשנולד לו בן, שיוכל לגלח ביום מאה. כיון דלנזירות ב] דבנו קא הוי יום ל"א, ויכול לגלח לנזירות דבנו ביום [ק'] — הלכך גם לנזירות דנפשיה עולה התגלחת של יום ק'.

נולד הבן עד ע'. עד ועד בכלל.

לא הפסיד כלום. ואי ס"ד עולה לו לכאן ולכאן איתגורי מיתגר, והוי ליה למיתני במתניתין "הרויח" ג]בריות הבן. דאי לא נולד לו הבן — לא מגלח אלא עד יום ק"א, והשתא לפי דברי רב מגלח ביום ק'. נמצא שהרויח בלידת הבן, ומאי קאמר "לא הפסיד"? **אלא** בדין הוא דלא ליתני עד ע' לא הפסיד כלל. כלומר, מן הדין לא היה לו לשנות בזה הלשון "לא הפסיד", אלא אדרבה ה"ל למיתני "הרויח", ומשום דקתני סיפא "לאחר שבעים סותר", פי': כי מפסיד בלידת הבן — תני נמי רישא: עד שבעים לא הפסיד כלום. וה"ה אפי' ברישא הרויח בלידת הבן. ובמקצת ספרים אין כתוב אלא רק: בדין הוא דלא ליתני עד שבעים, ולא הפסיד, ד] והוי כמו וכו'.

ת"ש מסיפא נולד לו לאחר שבעים סותר. פי': מפסיד. וסבירא ליה ד"אחר שבעים" הוי פי' ביום שבעים ואחד. ואמאי מפסיד כלום לרב בלידת הבן? והא יום הלידה עולה לכאן ולכאן, עולה נמי לתחילת הנזירות דבן, נמצא כי ל' יום דבן כלים ביום ק', ויכול השתא לגלח ביום ק"א, והשתא כי נולד הבן ביום ע"א יגלח ביום ק"א. הרי לא הפסיד כלום! **מאי** אחר דמתני' דקתני סותר אחר אחר. פירוש: שנולד ביום ע"ב, דהשתא לא יכול לגלח אלא ביום ק"ב, והפסיד בלידה. **אבל** אחר ממש מאי, דהיינו ביום ע"א — הכי נמי לא סתר כו'. אלא ש"מ אחר ממש. **וכן** מתני' לרב ש"מ. פי': ממתני' יש להוכיח דלא כרב. דסבירא ליה למתני' דיום הלידה אינו נחשב לנזירות הבן כמו דנחשב לנזירות דידיה למאה יום, שהוא נגרר ונחשב אחר ימים שעברו דהיינו לנזירות דידיה. ולא דמי למאי דפרשינן במתני' דאי נולד הבן ביום ראשון לנזירות דעולה לשניהם, דודאי כיון שהוא תחילת נזירות לזה כמו לזה — למה יעלה לאחד טפי מלשני? אבל הכא, דהוא התחיל לנזירותו כבר זה ימים רבים — סברא הוא דיום לידה יהיה נחשב ונגרר אחר ימים שעברו, דהיינו לנזירות דנפשיה, ונזירות הבן יתחיל מיום שאחר הלידה. ואם תאמר: והא תנן לקמן, ומייתינן לה בפ' קמא (לעיל דף ו.), דיום שלשים עולה מקצתו לראשון ומקצתו לנזירות שני, אלמא דיום ל' עולה לכאן ולכאן! וי"ל: דשאני התם, דאותו יום בין שתי נזירות, וראוי להחשיבו תחילתו (לו) לנזירות ראשון וסופו לנזירות שני, משום דכיון דהביא קרבנותיו — א"כ נגמר נזירתו — דין הוא שיתחיל נזירות השני מיד, דהוה אמקבל נזירות בחצי היום, דאותו יום עצמו עולה למנין נזירות. אבל הכא, דיום לידה דהיינו ע"א עומד באמצע נזירות דידיה ובהתחלת נזירות דבריה — ראוי להחשיבו כולו לנזירות דידיה אחר ימים שעברו, משום דגם הוא מחשבון ק' יום. וכיון שאותו יום ע"א נחשב אחר ק' — שוב אין למנותו שיהיה חשוב כיום שלם להיות נחשב נזירות אחד, לכך אינו עולה לבנו לתנא דמתני'. **ורב** כמאן אמרה. כיון דתנא דמתניתין לא סבר לה כוותיה.

אילימא כאבא שאול כו' בטלה הימנו גזרת שבעה. ה] תוך ז', שיהיה אסור בנעילת סנדל ובתשמיש המטה. ומיהו, לאו הילכתא הכי, דבמ"ק (דף כ.) הכי מסקינן: אפי' שעה אחת קודם לרגל בטלה הימנו [גזירת] שבעה, [שמונה] ימים קודם לרגל — בטלה הימנו גזירת שלשים לענין תספורת, הואיל ומתחיל יום אחד מדין שלשים קודם לרגל, ומותר לספר ערב הרגל משום כבוד הרגל. ואי לא סיפר ערב הרגל — אסור לספר אחר הרגל, דלא ניתן לדחות אלא מפני כבוד הרגל, והואיל ולא חילק כבוד לרגל — לא יועיל לו הרגל להפסיק, וישלים אחר הרגל.
אבא

פי' הרא"ש

אמר רב יום שבעים עולה לכאן ולכאן. אם נולד לו בן עד יום ע' ויום ע' בכלל יום לידת הבן עולה לכאן ולכאן. כיצד נולד לו בן יום ע' אותו היום עולה לו לשנים ותחלתו קודם שנולד לו הבן עולה לנזי' כאלו השלי' ע'. וסופו עולה לו לנזירות בנו ומונה ל' יום עד יום (זה) [ק'] ומגלח ביום ק' דהיינו ל"א לנזירות בנו ויום ק' לנזירותו הוי כמו יום ק"א דכיון דיום ע' עולה גם לנזי' בנו חשוב כשני ימים לענין נזירותו. והיינו טעמא משום דמדאורייתא מותר לגלח ביום ק' דמקצת היום ככולו. ומדרבנן הוא דאצטריך לאמתוני [עד] יום ק"א והכא אוקמו' אדאורייתא ולאידך פירושא יום ע' מתחיל נזי' בנו ומגלח יום ק' שהוא יום ל"א לנזי' בנו ומשלים ל' לנזירותו נמצא שהרויח יום א'. ולפי' קמא תימא הוא שיום א' באמצע עולה לו לשנים: אתגורי אתגור. וה"ל למתני הרויח יום א'. בדין הוא דלא ליתני עד ע' לא הפסיד אלא הו"ל לשנות עד ע' הרויח. אלא משום דקתני סיפא אחר ע' סותר שהוא מפסיד קתני רישא נמי לא הפסיד ולאו דוקא אלא אף מרויח הוא: ת"ש מסיפא נולד לו אחר ע' סותר. ולרב אם נולד לו ביום ע"א אמאי סותר הרי מובלע נזי' בנו בתוך הק'. ותימה לרב לא היו מובלעים ימי נזירות בנו בתוך ימי נזירותו דימי נזירותו שלמי ביום צ"ט כיון דיום ע"א עולה לב' ימים לנזירותו וימי נזירות בנו לא שלמי עד יום ק'. וי"ל דמ"מ נזי' בנו מובלע בתוך מאה יום שהזכיר בנזי'. ועי"ל הא דאמר רב דעולה לשנים א) אז לא יהיו מובלעים ימי נזירות בנו בימי נזירותו. ועל כרחיך אז לא יעלו לשנים. ולכך אמרי' דאינו עולה לשנים ואז יהיו מובלעים. ולאידך פירושא פריך שאם נולד ביום ע"א אינו מפסיד כלום: מאי אחר אחר אחר כגון שנולד לו ביום ע"ב: אלא ש"מ אחר ממש ומתני' ליתא לדרב כלו' לית לה להא דרב: ורב כמאן אמרה לשמעתיה דאית ליה דיום א' עולה לב' ימים אליבא דמאן (א"ר) [אילימא] כאבא שאול דתנן הקובר את מתו ג' ימים קודם הרגל בטלה הימנו גזרת ז' דאמ' במ"ק ג' לבכי וז' להספד ול' לגיהוץ. וכיון שמנה ג' ימים החמורים קודם הרגל
מ"ט

עין משפט נר מצוה

לד א מיי' פ"ד מהל' נזירות הל' יב:
לה ב מיי' שם הל' יז:
לו ג (מיי' פ"ו מהל' אבל הל' ג סמג עשין דרבנן ב טוש"ע יו"ד סי' שצט סעי' א וטוש"ע או"ח סי' תקמח סעי' ז):
לז ד (מיי' שם הל' ה סמג שם טוש"ע יו"ד שם סעי' ג וטוש"ע או"ח שם סעי' ח):

נוסחת הריב"ן

א) שכלו לו ימיו הואיל ולא הביא קרבנותיו חייב אבל אם נתגלח שאין נזירות בראשו ונטמא אין לוקה על הטומאה וכ"ש אם נתגלח קודם שהביא קרבנותיו דאין לוקה דהא לא מפרש ביה קרא כי היכי דקא מפרש בטומאה הס"ד והשאר ליתא: ב) וצריך: ג) וליתא: ד) לשלשים של בנו: ה) (אתגורי כו' למאה בלבד) ליתא בכ"י: ו) שנזירותו: ז) אלא בדין הוא דלא לתני עד שבעים לא הפסיד כו' אלא כו': ח) לא הפסיד הס"ד: ט) כדקאמר מאי אחר דקתני אמאי סותר כו': י) כי אמרת: כ) ובשמונין: ל) כי מיבעיי: מ) כ"ט יום ואח"כ כתוב גליון ג' ימים: נ) קודם הרגל:

מ"ק יט: [נ"ל דתניא]

הגהות הב"ח

(א) רש"י ד"ה אתגורי וכו' שאינו צריך להשלים למאה אלא כ"ט בלבד ועוד:

גליון הש"ס

גמ' מאי אחר. כזה נדה דף י"ד ע"ב:

הגהות מהר"ב רנשבורג

א] רש"י ד"ה וכן מתניתין לרב. כ"ב עיין תוס' ב"מ: ב] תוס' ד"ה אמר רב כו' יום שבעים וכו' שיוכל לגלח ביום מאה כו' לנזירות קמא כצ"ל: ג] ד"ה לא הפסיד כלום וכו' והוי ליה כריות. מלת כריות נמחק ונ"ב בלידת כצ"ל: ד] ד"ה אלא בדין הוא וכו' עד שבעים לא הפסיד והוי כמו וכו'. תיבות והוי כמו וכו' נמחקו: ה] ד"ה אילימא כו' בטלה הימנו גזרת שבעה תוך. מלת תוך נמחק ונ"ב תורת ז' כצ"ל:

בטלה הימנו גזרת ז' ח' ימים בטלה הימנו גזרת ל' דכיון דנהג יום א' דין ל' יום קודם הרגל נתבטלו. ומותר לספר ערב הרגל מפני כבוד המועד: ואם לא ספר ערב הרגל. לא חש לכבוד המועד אסור לספר אחר הרגל עד מלאת לו ל' יום:

א) נראה דצ"ל הא דאמר רב דעולה לשנים דוקא דיהיו מובלעים בין כך וכך אבל אם יהיה עולה לשנים אז לא יהי'.

לח א ב מיי' פ"ו מהלכות אבל הלכה ה סמג עשין דרבנן ב טוש"ע י"ד סי' שצט סעיף ג וטוש"ע א"ח סי' תקמח סעיף ח:

לט ג מיי' פ"ה מהל' משכב ומושב הל"ט:

מ ד מיי' פ"ו מהל' קרבן פסח הלכה ג: (עמוס ח)

מא ה מיי' פ"ג מהל' מחוסרי כפר' הל"ח:

גמרא

אַבָּא שָׁאוּל אוֹמֵר: אאֲפִי' לֹא סִיפֵּר קוֹדֶם הָרֶגֶל – מוּתָּר לְסַפֵּר אַחַר הָרֶגֶל, שֶׁכְּשֵׁם שֶׁמִּצְוַת שְׁלֹשָׁה מְבַטֶּלֶת גְּזֵירַת שִׁבְעָה – כָּךְ במִצְוַת שִׁבְעָה מְבַטֶּלֶת גְּזֵירַת ל'. מ"ט דְּאַבָּא שָׁאוּל – לָאו מִשּׁוּם דְּקָסָבַר שְׁבִיעִי עוֹלֶה לְכָאן וּלְכָאן? דִּלְמָא עַד כָּאן לָא קָאָמַר אַבָּא שָׁאוּל אֶלָּא בַּאֲבֵילוּת ז' דְּרַבָּנַן, אֲבָל בְּנָזִיר דְּאוֹרַיְיתָא – לָא. אֶלָּא, רַב דְּאָמַר כְּר' יוֹסֵי. *דְּתַנְיָא, ר' יוֹסֵי אוֹמֵר: שׁוֹמֶרֶת יוֹם כְּנֶגֶד יוֹם שֶׁשָּׁחֲטוּ וְזָרְקוּ עָלֶיהָ בַּשֵּׁנִי שֶׁלָּהּ, וְאַחַ"כ רָאֲתָה – הֲרֵי זוֹ אֵינָהּ אוֹכֶלֶת, וּפְטוּרָה מִלַּעֲשׂוֹת פֶּסַח שֵׁנִי. מ"ט דְּרַבִּי יוֹסֵי – לָאו מִשּׁוּם דְּקָסָבַר *מִקְצָת הַיּוֹם כְּכוּלּוֹ?[א] מִמַּאי? וְדִלְמָא מִשּׁוּם דְּקָסָבַר מִכָּאן וּלְהַבָּא הוּא מְטַמֵּא? וּמִי סָבַר רַבִּי יוֹסֵי הָכִי? *וְהָתַנְיָא, רַבִּי יוֹסֵי אוֹמֵר: זָב בַּעַל שְׁתֵּי רְאִיּוֹת שֶׁשָּׁחֲטוּ וְזָרְקוּ עָלָיו בַּשְּׁבִיעִי, וְכֵן שׁוֹמֶרֶת יוֹם כְּנֶגֶד יוֹם שֶׁשָּׁחֲטוּ וְזָרְקוּ עָלֶיהָ, וְאַחַ"כ רָאוּ, אע"פ גשֶׁמְּטַמְּאִין מִשְׁכָּב וּמוֹשָׁב לְמַפְרֵעַ – דפְּטוּרִין מִלַּעֲשׂוֹת פֶּסַח שֵׁנִי! מַאי לְמַפְרֵעַ – מִדְּרַבָּנַן. הָכִי נַמִי מִסְתַּבְּרָא, דְּאִי ס"ד מִדְּאוֹרַיְיתָא – אַמַּאי פְּטוּרִין מִלַּעֲשׂוֹת פֶּסַח שֵׁנִי? לְעוֹלָם אֵימָא לָךְ טוּמְאָה דְּאוֹרַיְיתָא, תְּהוֹם דְּזִיבָה הִתִּירוּ. *וְאַף רַבִּי אוֹשַׁעְיָא סָבַר לְמַפְרֵעַ מִדְּרַבָּנַן. *דְּתַנְיָא, רַבִּי אוֹשַׁעְיָא (א) אָמַר: ה(אֲבָל) הָרוֹאֶה זָב בַּשְּׁבִיעִי שֶׁלּוֹ סוֹתֵר אֶת שֶׁלְּפָנָיו, וְאָמַר לֵיהּ ר' יוֹחָנָן: לָא נִסְתּוֹר אֶלָּא יוֹמוֹ. מַה נַּפְשָׁךְ; אִי סָתַר – כּוּלְּהוּ סָתַר, אִי לָא סָתַר – לָא נִסְתּוֹר וְלָא יוֹמוֹ! אֶלָּא אֵימָא: לָא נִסְתּוֹר וְלָא יוֹמוֹ. וא"ל

פסחים פ: · [לעיל ה: וש"נ נסמן] · פסחים פח. · ר"ה לא מתמול

רש"י

אַבָּא שָׁאוּל אוֹמֵר כו'. מִצְוַת אֲבֵילוּת הַנּוֹהֶגֶת שְׁלֹשָׁה יָמִים הָרִאשׁוֹנִים, כֵּיוָן שֶׁעֲשָׂאָם קוֹדֶם הָרֶגֶל – בָּטֵל הֵימֶנּוּ גְּזֵירַת ז' לְגַמְרֵי. כָּךְ מִצְוַת ז', כֵּיוָן שֶׁנַּעֲשׂוּ קוֹדֶם הָרֶגֶל – שׁוּב הָרֶגֶל מְבַטֵּל גְּזֵירַת ל' לְגַמְרֵי. גְּזֵירַת ל' גִּלּוּחַ וְכִיבּוּס. מ"ט דְּאַבָּא שָׁאוּל. דְּקָאָמַר דְּיוֹם ז' מְבַטֶּלֶת גְּזֵירַת ז' וְל'? וְהָא לֹא שִׁימֵּר עֲדַיִין מִיּוֹם ל' כְּלוּם קוֹדֶם הָרֶגֶל, אֲפִי' יוֹם אֶחָד! דִּבִשְׁלָמָא לְת"ק דְּאָמַר שְׁמֹנָה – הַיְינוּ מִשּׁוּם דְּיוֹם שְׁמִינִי עוֹלֶה לְמִנְיַן ל', אֶלָּא לְאַבָּא שָׁאוּל מ"ט? לָאו מִשּׁוּם דְּקָסָבַר (א) דְּיוֹם שְׁבִיעִי עוֹלֶה לְכָאן וּלְכָאן – לְמִנְיַן ז' וּלְמִנְיַן ל', וּכְמַאן דְּעָבַר עָלָיו יוֹם אֶחָד מִגְּזֵירַת ל' דָּמֵי, וּמש"ה מִתְבַּטֶּלֶת? ב) אֶלָּא בַּאֲבֵילוּת (ב) דְּרַבָּנַן. דְּעִיקַּר אֲבֵילוּת אֵינוֹ אֶלָּא יוֹם אֶחָד, דִּכְתִיב (עמוס ח) "וְאַחֲרִיתָהּ כְּיוֹם מָר". אֶלָּא רַבָּנַן תִּקְנוּ ז', דְּסָמְכוּ אַקְּרָא ג) כִּדְכְתִיב (בראשית נ) "וַיַּעַשׂ לְאָבִיו אֵבֶל שִׁבְעַת יָמִים". אֲבָל נְזִירוּת דְּאוֹרַיְיתָא בְּחוּשְׁבְּנָא דְּיוֹמֵי ד) דְּל' יוֹם בָּעֵינַן, כִּדְכְתִיב (במדבר ו) "יִהְיֶה" – לֹא אָמַר דְּיוֹם אֶחָד עוֹלֶה לְכָאן וּלְכָאן. שֶׁשָּׁחֲטוּ וְזָרְקוּ עָלֶיהָ בַּשֵּׁנִי שֶׁלָּהּ. שֶׁכְּבָר רָאֲתָה בַּיּוֹם שְׁמִינִי, (ג) ה) עַד שֶׁלֹּא רָאֲתָה בַּיּוֹם תְּשִׁיעִי שֶׁהִיא שׁוֹמֶרֶת כְּנֶגְדּוֹ, לֵידַע אִם תִּרְאֶה בְּג' יָמִים ג' רְאִיּוֹת וּתְהֵא זָבָה. וְאַחַ"כ רָאֲתָה הֲרֵי זוֹ אֵינָהּ אוֹכֶלֶת. בַּפֶּסַח, דִּטְמֵאָה הִיא. וְאע"ג דְּאֵינָהּ אוֹכֶלֶת – פְּטוּרָה מִלַּעֲשׂוֹת פֶּסַח שֵׁנִי, דַּאֲכִילַת פְּסָחִים לָא מְעַכְּבָא. מ"ט דְּר' יוֹסֵי. דִּפְטוּרָה מִלַּעֲשׂוֹת פֶּסַח שֵׁנִי – לָאו מִשּׁוּם דְּקָסָבַר מִקְצָת הַיּוֹם כְּכוּלּוֹ? דְּיוֹם שֵׁנִי שֶׁהוּא תְּשִׁיעִי כְּכוּלּוֹ דָּמֵי, וְהָוְיָא לַהּ טְהוֹרָה בְּשָׁעָה שֶׁשָּׁחֲטוּ וְזָרְקוּ עָלֶיהָ. וְהָכָא נַמִי לֵימָא דְּעוֹלֶה לוֹ לְכָאן וּלְכָאן, מִשּׁוּם דְּמִקְצָת הַיּוֹם כְּכוּלּוֹ. דִּילְמָא. הַאי דְּקָאָמַר ר' יוֹסֵי דִּפְטוּרָה – לָאו מִשּׁוּם דְּקָסָבַר דְּמִקְצָת הַיּוֹם כְּכוּלּוֹ, אֶלָּא מִשּׁוּם דְּקָסָבַר דִּכְשֶׁהִיא רוֹאָה – מִכָּאן וּלְהַבָּא הִיא מְטַמְּאָה, אֲבָל לְמַפְרֵעַ לֹא. וּמִשּׁוּם הָכִי פְּטוּרָה, דִּבְהַהִיא שַׁעְתָּא דְּשָׁחֲטוּ וְזָרְקוּ עָלֶיהָ – טְהוֹרָה הֲוַאי, וּלְהָךְ דְּבָתַר ו) נִטְמֵאת לָא חָיְישִׁינַן. וּמִי סָבַר ר' יוֹסֵי. דְּמִכָּאן וּלְהַבָּא הִיא מְטַמְּאָה, אֲבָל לְמַפְרֵעַ לֹא? ז) זָב בַּעַל שְׁתֵּי רְאִיּוֹת. בֵּין בְּיוֹם אֶחָד בֵּין בִּשְׁנֵי יָמִים, כִּדְאָמְרִי' הָתָם (ב"ק דף כד.): תָּלָה הַכָּתוּב אֶת הַזָּב בִּרְאִיּוֹת, דִּכְתִיב "וְזֹאת תִּהְיֶה טוּמְאָתוֹ בְּזוֹבוֹ", וְאֶת הַזָּבָה בְּיָמִים, דִּכְתִיב "וְאִשָּׁה כִּי יָזוּב זוֹב דָּמָהּ יָמִים רַבִּים", מִיעוּט יָמִים – שְׁנַיִם, רַבִּים – ג'. בַּשְּׁבִיעִי שֶׁלּוֹ. שֶׁאֵין בֵּין זָב רוֹאֶה שְׁתַּיִם לְרוֹאֶה ג' אֶלָּא קָרְבָּן; שֶׁבַּעַל ג' מוֹנֶה ז' וּמֵבִיא קָרְבָּן, וּבַעַל ב' מוֹנֶה ז' וְאֵין מֵבִיא קָרְבָּן. ח) לְהָכִי נָקַט בַּעַל שְׁתֵּי רְאִיּוֹת וְשׁוֹמֶרֶת יוֹם – מִשּׁוּם דְּלָאו בְּנֵי קָרְבָּן נִינְהוּ. דְּעַל הָנָךְ דִּבְנֵי קָרְבָּן לָא מָצֵי לְמִשְׁחַט עֲלַיְיהוּ בַּשְּׁבִיעִי, מִשּׁוּם דְּלָא מָצוּ אָכְלֵי פֶּסַח בָּעֶרֶב, דְּכַפָּרַת קָרְבָּן דְּבָעוּ לְאֵיתוּיֵי בַּשְּׁמִינִי מְעַכֶּבֶת לְהוּ, כִּדְקי"ל (יבמות דף עד:) הֵבִיא כַּפָּרָתוֹ אוֹכֵל בַּקֳּדָשִׁים. (ד) ט) אַלְמָא מִיהָא, מִדְּקָתָנֵי מְטַמֵּא מִשְׁכָּב וּמוֹשָׁב לְמַפְרֵעַ – דְּלָא הָוֵי טַעְמָא דְּר' יוֹסֵי מִשּׁוּם דְּמִכָּאן וּלְהַבָּא הוּא מְטַמֵּא, וְטַעְמָא מִשּׁוּם דְּמִקְצָת הַיּוֹם כְּכוּלּוֹ קָא פָּטַר מִלַּעֲשׂוֹת פֶּסַח שֵׁנִי, דְּה"ל כְּכָל מִידֵי דְּתָלֵי בְּמִנְיָינָא, דְּאָמְרִי' בֵּיהּ מִקְצָת הַיּוֹם כְּכוּלּוֹ, וּמש"ה פְּטוּרִין: לְעוֹלָם אֵימָא לָךְ דְּמִכָּאן וּלְהַבָּא הוּא מְטַמֵּא. וְלָאו טַעְמָא דְּר' יוֹסֵי מִשּׁוּם דְּמִקְצָת הַיּוֹם כְּכוּלּוֹ. (ה) י) וּדְקָאָמַר לְמַפְרֵעַ מְטַמֵּא – מִדְּרַבָּנַן הוּא דְּקָאָמַר, וּמִשּׁוּם דְּלֵית בְּהוּ טוּמְאָה אֶלָּא מִדְּרַבָּנַן – פְּטוּרִין מִלַּעֲשׂוֹת פֶּסַח שֵׁנִי. דְּאִי ס"ד מִדְּאוֹרַיְיתָא. מְטַמְּאִין לְמַפְרֵעַ, אֲפִי' אָמְרַתְּ מִקְצָת הַיּוֹם כְּכוּלּוֹ – אַכַּתִּי אַמַּאי פְּטוּרִין? וְהָא אִיגַּלַּאי מִילְּתָא לְמַפְרֵעַ דִּבְהַהוּא שַׁעְתָּא דְּשָׁחַט וְנִזְרַק הַדָּם טְמֵאָה מִדְּאוֹרַיְיתָא הֲוַאי. לְעוֹלָם אֵימָא לָךְ. דִּטְמֵאִין לְמַפְרֵעַ מִדְּאוֹרַיְיתָא, וְכָל הֵיכָא דְּתָלֵי מִילְּתָא בְּמִנְיָינָא, כְּגוֹן בִּשְׁתֵּי נְזִירוּת שֶׁצָּרִיךְ לִמְנוֹת לָזוֹ ל' וְלָזוֹ ל' – הָוֵי מִקְצָת הַיּוֹם כְּכוּלּוֹ. וְהָכָא, אע"ג דְּמִדְּאוֹרַיְיתָא מְטַמֵּא לְמַפְרֵעַ, (ו) אַמַּאי הֵקִילּוּ בָּהּ – הַיְינוּ טַעְמָא: דְּטוּמְאָה דִּתְהוֹם דְּזִיבָה הִתִּירוּ, דְּכֵיוָן דִּבְהַהִיא שַׁעְתָּא דְּנִשְׁחַט אַכַּתִּי הֲוָה קַיְימָא טִיפַּת דָּם בַּמָּקוֹר שֶׁל אִשָּׁה, וְלֹא כ) יָצָא לַחוּץ – אַהֲנֵי בָּהּ מִקְצָת הַיּוֹם כְּכוּלּוֹ, דִּכְמַאן דְּנִשְׁחַט עָלֶיהָ בִּשְׁעַת טָהֳרָה דָּמֵי. וְאִית דִּמְפָרְשֵׁי טוּמְאַת הַתְּהוֹם בְּזִיבָה – הַיְינוּ דִּבִשְׁעַת שְׁחִיטָה וּזְרִיקָה עֲדַיִין לֹא הָיְתָה יוֹדַעַת אִם תֵּהֵא רוֹאָה בּוֹ בַּיּוֹם וְאִם לָאו, מִשּׁוּם הָכִי קָרֵי לָהּ "טוּמְאַת תְּהוֹם", דְּהָוְיָא טְמֵאָה לְמַפְרֵעַ בִּשְׁעַת שְׁחִיטָה וּזְרִיקָה, וְאִיהִי לָא הֲוַת יָדְעָה בְּהַהִיא שַׁעְתָּא. וְדָמֵי לְעוֹבֵר בִּרְשׁוּת הָרַבִּים וְטוּמְאַת הַתְּהוֹם תַּחְתָּיו. וְאַף רַבִּי אוֹשַׁעְיָא סָבַר. דְּרַבִּי יוֹסֵי לֹא אָמַר דִּמְטַמֵּא לְמַפְרֵעַ אֶלָּא מִדְּרַבָּנַן. וּמְהַדַּר הָכָא דְּקָאָמַר לְעֵיל מַאי לְמַפְרֵעַ – מִדְּרַבָּנַן. אִי סָתַר. דִּלְמַפְרֵעַ טְמֵאָה – כּוּלְּהוּ לִסְתּוֹר, דְּהָא לָא הָווּ לְהוּ שִׁבְעָה נְקִיִּים כְּלָל. אֶלָּא אֵימָא וְלָא לִסְתּוֹר אֲפִילּוּ יוֹמוֹ. מִשּׁוּם דְּמִכָּאן וּלְהַבָּא מְטַמְּאָה, וּלְמַפְרֵעַ הָוְיָא טְהוֹרָה מַמָּשׁ. וַאֲמַר לֵיהּ(ז). רַבִּי יוֹחָנָן רַבִּי

תוספות

אבא שאול אומר אפילו לא סיפר ערב הרגל מותר לספר אחר הרגל. פליג את"ק דסבר דרגל מבטל בכל [ענין], ופליג באחריתי, שכשם שמצות [ג'] מבטלת גזירת ז' – כך מצות ז' מבטלת גזירת ל'. ופליג את"ק דמצריך ח'. א] לאו משום דקסבר יום ז' עולה לו למנין שבעה, ומקצתו עולה למנין ל', אע"פ שעומד באמצע אבילות. אלא באבילות דרבנן. דמן התורה אינו אבל אלא יום ראשון, כדכתיב *"ואחריתה כיום מר". אבל בנזירות דאורייתא, דדרשינן מקרא דבעינן ל' יום – לא אמרי' דמקצת יום עולה לו לכאן ולכאן. ששחטו וזרקו עליה בשני. שחל בערב פסח, ושחטו עליה הפסח, ואח"כ ראתה – הרי זו אינה אוכלת בלילה בפסח, לפי [שהיא] נטמאה. ב] ופטורה מלעשות פסח שני – דבשעת שחיטה טהורה היתה. מאי טעמא דר' יוסי (הגלילי) לאו משום מקצת היום ככולו. ומכאן ולהבא היא מטמאה. *(דאתמול). נמצא כי בשעת שחיטה וזריקה היתה טהורה גמורה, דמכאן ולהבא היא מטמאה ולא למפרע. וכי הדרא חזיא – מטמאינן לה מכאן ולהבא, ולמחר תעשה שימור גמור למקצת יום זה שנטמאת. אלמא דיום שני זה מקצת יום חשבינן ליה יום טהור, דליהוי שימור ליום שאתמול – הילכך, שחיטה וזריקה בטהרה היה. ומקצתו חשבינן ליה יום טומאה – דליהוי יום של מחר שימור להאי מקצת יום. אבל רבנן פליגי, ומטמאי למפרע, וחשבינן זה היום כולו טמא [כיום] של אתמול. ורב דאמר כר' יוסי. ואע"ג דהכא נמי היה סברא לחשיבת יום כולו טמא כיום שלפניו כסברא דרבנן – אפ"ה ר' יוסי מחשיבו לכאן ולכאן, והיינו כסברת רב. וזו שכתוב בספרים: ודילמא משום דקסבר – לא גרסינן ליה, דאי לאו הכי – מה מהני שאינו מטמא למפרע? זב בעל שתי ראיות. דאילו בעל שלשה לא חזי למיכל ג] [לאחר דראה שלישית] עד יום ח', שיביא קרבנותיו. וביום ח' לא מצי למינקט: ואח"כ ראה מטמא משכב ומושב למפרע – דמיום ז' ואילך פסק מסתירה. ומשכב ומושב דמאתמול שאחר הטבילה עד הנה טהורין, ואפי' ראה היום ביום ח' – לא מטמא למפרע. אע"פ שמטמאין משכב ומושב למפרע. ואפילו טבל בשביעי, משכבות דלאחר טבילה טמאין, ד] סתר מניינו והרי הוא כתחילתו, דכתיב "וספרה לה שבעת ימים" – והרי אין כאן ז' ימים. ומדקתני בשמירת יום למפרע טומאה – אלמא לא אמר מקצת יום ככולו, וקשיא דר' יוסי אדר' יוסי! ומשני: למפרע מדרבנן, אבל מן התורה טהורה. הכי נמי מסתברא וכו'. ודחי: אימא לך טומאת התהום דזיבה התירו. כלומר, אימא לך שמטמאין למפרע מדאורייתא, ופטורין לעשות פסח שני, דהלכה למשה מסיני ה] דטומאה דמת הותרה לעושי פסח. והאי תנא ס"ל דאפי' טומאת התהום דזיבה הותרה לעושי הפסח. התהום. פי': דבשעת שחיטה ישב על אבן אחת, ולא נודע כלל שקבר תחתיו עד אחר שחיטה, נודע לו שניטמא בקבר התהום. וכן הכא, לא ידע אדם בשעת שחיטה אם אחרי כן תראה ותסתור להיות טמאה. וטומאת התהום [התירו] לעושי הפסח ונזיר. ואף רבי אושעיא. קאי אשינויא דלמפרע דרבנן. אבל הרואה זוב. פי' [רש"י] ב"כיצד צולין" (פסחים ד' פא.): ו] לא ידעינן אהיכא קאי. סותר את שלפניו כו'. ספוריה שספר, וצריך למנות ז' ימים אחרים: [א"ל ר"י לא נסתור אלא יומו] יחזור ויספור יום אחד. והוינן בה במילתא דר' יוחנן: אי סתר – כולהו בעי למיסתר, דכתיב "וספרה לה ז' ימים לטהרתה" – שלא תהא טומאה מפסקת בינתים. ז] בפרק "כיצד צולין" גרס: [אי קסבר למפרע הוא מטמא אפילו כולהו נסתור] ואי מכאן ולהבא הוא מטמא יומו נמי לא נסתור. דהרי היא כראיה ראשונה של זיבה אחרת ואין בה אלא טומאת ערב, ויטבול לערב ויטהר, דקי"ל ראיה ראשונה של זב קרי בעלמא הוא. ה"ק לא יסתור ולא יומו. כלומר, אפי' יומו, לפי שכבר עלה לו מקצת היום, ושלמו לו ספוריה שלו, ויצא מכלל הזיבה. *) א"ל. פי': ר' אושעיא לר' יוחנן: רבי יוסי סבר כוותך. השתא מסיק דרבי אושעיא ס"ל אליבא דר' יוסי דמטמא למפרע, היינו מדרבנן.

*) שייך לדף עז.

זבה

פי' הרא"ש

מ"ט דאבא שאול. דבשלמא מצות ג' מבטלת גזרת ז' משום דנהג מצות ג'. אלא מצות ז' אמאי מבטלת גזירת ל' הא אכתי לא נהג דין ל': משום דקסבר ז' עולה לכאן ולכאן תחלתו עולה למנין ז' וסופו עולה למנין ל'. הרי נהג דין ל' (ובכו"ש) דייקינן כיון דז' עולה לכאן ולכאן לא ימנה אלא כ"ט כדאמר הכא בנולד לו בן ביום ע' דמגלח ביום ק' א) ולא משא מידי. ולי נראה דלא קשה דל' יום לגיהוץ ולתספורת אסמכוה אקרא במ"ק דיליף פרע פרע מנזיר. ואי אמרת דיום ז' עולה לב' ימים לא משכחת לה ל' לעולם: אבל בנזיר דאורייתא לא. ואע"ג דפרישית לעיל דרב לא בא לעקור נזיר' דאורייתא אלא לאוקמי אדאורייתא מ"מ נזי' יש לו עיקר מן התורה וראוי להחמיר בו יותר מבאבלות שאין לו עיקר מן התורה: הרי זו אינה אוכלת דטמאה היא. מ"ט דר' יוסי דכיון דראתה סותרת ואיגלאי מלתא דטמאה היתה בשעת שחיטת הפסח ואמאי פטורה מלעשות פסח שני: לאו משום דקסבר מקצת היום ככולו. ומכאן ולהבא מטמא משעת ראיה ואילך ולא סתרה למפרע וחשוב יום ב' כב' ימים ותחלת היום עולה לה לשיעור וכשראתה אח"כ הוי ביום א': ומי סבר ר' יוסי. דמכאן ולהבא מטמא: אע"פ שמטמאין משכב ומושב למפרע וכו' אלמא קסבר למפרע הוא מטמא: מדרבנן. רבנן החמירו לסתור למפרע אבל מדאורייתא מכאן ולהבא הוא מטמא: לא דטומא' זיבה בתהום התירו. כלו' ה"נ מסתברא דקאמר ליתא דמצינא לדחויי דלעולם מדאורי' מטמא למפרע ואפ"ה פטורה מלעשות פסח שני משום דבשעת שחיטת הפסח היה הדבר עומד בספק אם תראה ואמרי' בכיצד צולין דטומאת התהום התירו בפסח. כל טומאת ספק קרי ליה טומאת התהום כמו שהתהום מכוסה ואין אדם יודע מה יש בו. ומי' מסקי' התם דלא התירו טומאת התהום אלא למת בלבד וכך היא הלכה למשה מסיני: א"ל ר' יוחנן ולא לסתור אלא יומו. פי' יום הראיה. מתמה תלמודא אי סותר יומו ליסתור כולהן כדאיתא בנדה ואחר תטהר שלא תהא טומאה מפסקת ביניהם: ה"ק ולא לסתור ולא יומו. כלו' אף יומו לא ליסתור דס"ל מקצת היום ככולו ומכאן ולהבא הוא מטמא א"ל ר' אושעי[א](ה) [ר"י] סבר כותיך:

א) נ"ל ולא מתרץ מידי.

נוסחת הריב"ן

א) (דיום) ליתא בכ"י: ב) בכ"י כתוב כאן גליון: ג) דכתיב: ד) תלויה מלתא לל': ה) ועד: ו) דכתר הכי: ז) ומשום הכי פטורה הס"ד: ח) בכ"י כתוב כאן גליון: ט) (אלמא) ליתא בכ"י: י) והאי דקאמר: כ) ילתא.

נ"א דאמר ר"א אבל

הגהות הב"ח

(א) גמ' דתניא ר' אושעיא אומר זב הרואה בשביעי שלו כו' כצ"ל: (ב) רש"י ד"ה אלא באבילות דרבנן וכו' אלא דרבנן תקנו וכו' דחושבנא דיומי ל' יום וכו' לא אמרינן דיום: (ג) ד"ה ששחטו וכו' ועד שלא וכו' ותהא זבה שחטו הפסח וזרקו עליה ואח"כ ראתה הרי זו כו' והד"א: (ד) ד"ה בשביעי שלו וכו' אוכל בקדשים אלא מיהא וכו' אלא מיהא: (ה) ד"ה לעולם וכו' דמקצת היום ככולו וכו' דקאמר למפרע הוא מטמא מדרבנן: (ו) ד"ה לעולם וכו' מטמא למפרע והיינו טעמא הקילו בה והיינו טעמא כצ"ל ותיבת אמאי נמחק: (ז) ד"ה ואמר ליה ר' יוחנן ר' יוסי קאי טוהיר הס"ד:

הגהות הגר"א

[א] גמ' מקצת היום ככולו ומכאן ולהבא כו' כצ"ל (ושבירותא לג"ב וכמ"ש התוס'):

הגהות מהר"ב רנשבורג

א] תוס' ד"ה אבא שאול אומר וכו' למלריך ח' כאן הס"ד ואח"כ מה"ד לאו משום וכו' ואע"פ שעומד באמצע אבילות מבטלות כצ"ל: ב] ד"ה ששחטו וזרקו עליה בשני וכו' שהיא נטמאה כאן הס"ד ואח"כ מה"ד ופטורה וכו' טהורה היתה כאן הס"ד ואח"כ מה"ד מ"ט דר' יוסי וכו' ומכאן ולהבא היא מטמאה וכו' והוא מקצת יום שימור לאתמול כצ"ל ה"מ: ג] ד"ה זב בעל שתי ראיות. לא חזי למיכל לאחר דראה שלישית. מלות לאחר דראה שלישית נמחקו ונ"ב לאחרונה בקדשים כצ"ל א"מ: ד] ד"ה אע"פ וכו' דלאחר טבילה טמאין וסתר כצ"ל: ה] ד"ה ה"נ מסתברא וכו' דהלכה למשה מסיני דטומאת התהום כצ"ל: ו] ד"ה אבל הרואה זוב וכו' לא ידענא. נ"ב עיין א"מ: ז] ד"ה א"ל ר"י וכו' טומאה מפסקת בינתיים כאן הס"ד ואח"כ מה"ד בפ' כילד צולין וכו':

רַבִּי יוֹסֵי קָאֵי כְּוָותֵיךְ. וְרַבִּי יוֹסֵי מִכְּדִי סָבַר מִקְצָת הַיּוֹם כְּכוּלּוֹ. דְּכָל הַאי דְּקָא מְשַׁנֵּינַן לְעֵיל דְּמִכָּאן וּלְהַבָּא מְטַמְּאָה – שִׁינּוּיֵי דְּחִיקֵי נִינְהוּ, וּמִיהוּ שְׁמַעְתִּין אִיתָא כְּרַב. זָבָה גְּמוּרָה. דְּבָעֵינַן ג' יָמִים רְצוּפִים, כְּדְאָמַר א) מִי: תָּלָה הַכָּתוּב אֶת הַזָּבָה בְּיָמִים, הֵיכִי מַשְׁכַּחַתְּ לָהּ? (ד) וְהָא כֵּיוָן דְּחַזְיָא בְּפַלְגֵּיהּ דְּיוֹמָא. בְּיוֹם שֵׁנִי מֵחֲצוֹת וְאֵילָךְ – אִידָךְ פַּלְגָּא דְּמִבֹּקֶר עַד חֲצוֹת עוֹלֶה לָהּ לְשִׁימּוּר כְּאִילּוּ נִשְׁמַר יוֹם אֶחָד בְּטָהֳרָה, וַהֲוָה לָהּ הֶפְסֵק. ע"א: א] וְר' יוֹסֵי מִכְּדִי. שׁוֹמֶרֶת יוֹם כְּנֶגֶד יוֹם, ב) כֵּיוָן דְּקָאָמַר דְּטַעְמָא הָוֵי מִשּׁוּם דְּמִקְצָת הַיּוֹם כְּכוּלּוֹ. ג) וְכָךְ שָׁמַעְנוּ כָּאן מִפִּ"י הַמּוֹרֶ"ה. ב] אֲבָל בְּ"כֵּיצַד צוֹלִין" בְּמַסֶּכֶת פְּסָחִים שָׁמְעִינַן דְּמִכָּאן וּלְהַבָּא קָמִיבָּעֲיָא לָן, דִּלְר' יוֹסֵי זָבָה גְּמוּרָה הֵיכִי מַשְׁכַּחַתְּ לָהּ. וְלֹא מִפִּ"י הַמּוֹרֶ"ה. אִיבָּעֵית אֵימָא בְּשׁוֹפַעַת. כָּל ד) הַיּוֹם [תְּלָתָא יוֹמֵי] בַּהֲדֵי הֲדָדֵי. וְאִיבָּעֵית אֵימָא. שְׁלֹשָׁה יוֹמֵי בֵּין הַשְּׁמָשׁוֹת סָמוּךְ לִשְׁקִיעַת הַחַמָּה. דְּכִי רָאֲתָה בְּשַׁבָּת אַחַר שְׁקִיעַת הַחַמָּה – הָוֵי טְמֵאָה כָּל יוֹם רִאשׁוֹן, וְכִי חָזְרָה וְרָאֲתָה בְּיוֹם רִאשׁוֹן שֵׁנִית סָמוּךְ לִשְׁקִיעַת הַחַמָּה – הָוְיָא טְמֵאָה כָּל יוֹם שֵׁנִי, וְכֵן שְׁלִישִׁי, דְּלָא הָוְיָא שָׁהוּת דְּטָהֳרָה בֵּינֵי וּבֵינֵי כְּלָל. וְלָא הֲוֵי סָלֵיק לְמִנְיָינָא דְּשׁוֹמֶרֶת יוֹם כְּנֶגֶד יוֹם, דְּהָא לָא הֲוַאי שָׁהוּת.

הדרן עלך הריני נזיר

מִי שֶׁאָמַר הֲרֵינִי נָזִיר מְגַלֵּחַ יוֹם שְׁלֹשִׁים וְאֶחָד. לְרַב מַתָּנָא כִּדְאִית לֵיהּ ה) – דְּאַנְּזִירוּת סְתָם קָאֵי, וְאֵין נְזִירוּת פָּחוּת מִל' יוֹם. וּלְבַר פַּדָּא כִּדְאִית לֵיהּ – דְּמוֹקֵי לָהּ (ה) כְּגוֹן דְּנַעֲשָׂה כְּאוֹמֵר "שְׁלֵימִים". וְכוּלָּהּ מַתְנִי' ו) הָכִי מְפוֹרָשׁ בְּפ"ק, לְרַב מַתָּנָא כִּדְאִית לֵיהּ וּלְבַר פַּדָּא כִּדְאִית לֵיהּ. **גמ'** ר"א אוֹמֵר אֵינוֹ סוֹתֵר אֶלָּא שִׁבְעָה. כְּדֵי שֶׁיָּבִיא קָרְבָּנוֹ בְּטָהֳרָה, וְכִדְפָרְשִׁינַן בְּפֶרֶק קַמָּא לְבַר פַּדָּא כִּדְאִית לֵיהּ, דְּקָסָבַר

זבה גמורה היכי משכחת לה. דמכאן ולהבא מטמינן לה; וכל יומא טומאה באפי נפשה היא. וכיון דחזיא היא בפלגא דיומא – אידך פלגא דיומא הוא קא סליק לה לשימור, ואע"פ שלא טבלה בינתים. ג] מכי ראתה ביום י"א וביום י"ג וביום ט"ו דלא הויא זבה, ואע"ג שלא טבלה בינתים, דבעינן שתראה ג' ימים רצופים. הלשון ק"ק: אמאי קאמר אידך פלגא דיומא? דבקילור הוה מצי למימר: אידך יומא סליק ליה שימור! ובדוחק יש לפרש: ד] ראתה י"א, דכיון דחזיא ביום ב' בפלגא דיומא – אידך פלגא דיומא שהיה לפני שראתה סליק ליה שימור. וקשה: ואמאי לא משכחת לה דרואה שלשה לילות, דהשתא היא טמאה בתחילת היום! ופי' בקונטרס ב"כילד צולין" (פסחים דף פא.) לפי הדברים למ"ד מקצת היום ככולו, ותחילת הלילה תהא נמי ככולה לספירה, ובתחילת הלילה סליק לה שימור, ואין צריך עלות השחר. *ולי נראה דמשנה שלימה היא בפרק "תינוקת" (נדה דף עב.): ושוין ברואה ה] יום י"א וטבלה לערב [ושמשה] שמטמאין משכב ומושב למפרע. ומוכח התם דתחילת הלילה לא הוי שימור. ונראה לר"ת: דכי היכי דלר' יוסי תחילת יום הוי שימור – ה"נ ראתה בלילה, סוף היום דלמחר שאינה רואה, עולה לשימור, דכך לי סוף היום כתחילת היום. ובהכי ניחא לישנא: כיון דחזאי בפלגא דיומא ו] אידך פלגא – דאותו יום עצמו בסופו – הוה ליה שימור. וצ"ל דודאי בזבה גדולה לא אמר ר' יוסי דיום שלישי יהיה ממנין של ז' של טהרה, דהא בפרק "תינוקת" (שם ד' סט. ושם) קאמר דכותאי יום שפוסקת בו מונה אותו למנין ז'. והטעם – דמצינו דבסוף הספירה מקצת היום ככולו, דזב וזבה טובלין ביום – הילכך בזבה קטנה ז] דתחילת הספירה מקצת היום ככולו. אבל בתחילת ספירת זבה גדולה, שזקוקה לספור ז' – אז לא אמרי' בתחילת ספירת' ז' נקיים מקצת היום ככולו. והא

וא"ל: רַבִּי יוֹסֵי קָאֵי כְּוָותֵיךְ, דְּאָמַר: מִכָּאן וּלְהַבָּא מְטַמֵּא. וְהָא רַבִּי יוֹסֵי לְמַפְרֵעַ הוּא דְּאָמַר! מַאי לְמַפְרֵעַ – מִדְּרַבָּנַן. וְרַבִּי יוֹסֵי, מִכְּדִי סָבַר *מִקְצָת הַיּוֹם כְּכוּלּוֹ, זָבָה גְּמוּרָה דְּמַיְיתָא קָרְבָּן הֵיכִי מַשְׁכַּחַתְּ לָהּ? כֵּיוָן דְּחַזְיָא בְּפַלְגֵּיהּ דְּיוֹמָא – אִידָךְ פַּלְגֵּיהּ דְּיוֹמָא סָלֵיק לָהּ לְשִׁימּוּר! אב"א: דְּקָא שָׁפְעָה תְּלָתָא תְּלָתָא (א) יוֹמֵי בַּהֲדֵי הֲדָדֵי, ואב"א דְּחַזְיָא תְּלָתָא יוֹמֵי סָמוּךְ לִשְׁקִיעַת הַחַמָּה, דְּלָא הֲוַאי שָׁהוּת (ג) דְּסָלֵיק לֵיהּ לְמִנְיָינָא.§

הדרן עלך הריני נזיר

מִי *אשֶׁאָמַר "הֲרֵינִי נָזִיר" – מְגַלֵּחַ יוֹם שְׁלֹשִׁים וְאֶחָד, וְאִם גִּילַּח לְיוֹם שְׁלֹשִׁים – יָצָא. "הֲרֵינִי נָזִיר שְׁלֹשִׁים יוֹם", אִם גִּילַּח לְיוֹם שְׁלֹשִׁים – לֹא יָצָא. *מִי בשֶׁנָּזַר שְׁתֵּי נְזִירוֹת – מְגַלֵּחַ אֶת הָרִאשׁוֹנָה יוֹם שְׁלֹשִׁים וְאֶחָד, וְאֶת הַשְּׁנִיָּה יוֹם שִׁשִּׁים וְאֶחָד, *וְאִם גִּילַּח אֶת הָרִאשׁוֹנָה יוֹם שְׁלֹשִׁים – מְגַלֵּחַ אֶת הַשְּׁנִיָּה יוֹם שִׁשִּׁים, וְאִם גִּילַּח יוֹם שִׁשִּׁים חָסֵר אֶחָד – יָצָא. וְזוֹ עֵדוּת הֵעִיד רַבִּי פַּפְּיָיס עַל מִי *שֶׁנָּזַר שְׁתֵּי נְזִירוֹת, שֶׁאִם גִּילַּח אֶת הָרִאשׁוֹנָה יוֹם שְׁלֹשִׁים – מְגַלֵּחַ אֶת הַשְּׁנִיָּה (ג) לְיוֹם שִׁשִּׁים, וְאִם גִּילַּח לְיוֹם שִׁשִּׁים חָסֵר אֶחָד – יָצָא, שֶׁיּוֹם שֶׁל שְׁלֹשִׁים עוֹלֶה לוֹ מִן הַמִּנְיָן. מִי שֶׁאָמַר "הֲרֵינִי *נָזִיר", גנִטְמָא יוֹם שְׁלֹשִׁים – סוֹתֵר אֶת הַכֹּל, רַבִּי אֱלִיעֶזֶר אוֹמֵר: אֵינוֹ סוֹתֵר אֶלָּא שִׁבְעָה. "הֲרֵינִי נָזִיר שְׁלֹשִׁים יוֹם", נִטְמָא יוֹם שְׁלֹשִׁים – סוֹתֵר אֶת הַכֹּל. "הֲרֵינִי נָזִיר *מֵאָה יוֹם", נִטְמָא יוֹם מֵאָה – סוֹתֵר אֶת הַכֹּל. ר"א אוֹמֵר: אֵינוֹ סוֹתֵר אֶלָּא שְׁלֹשִׁים. נִטְמָא יוֹם מֵאָה וְאֶחָד ד סוֹתֵר שְׁלֹשִׁים יוֹם, רַבִּי אֱלִיעֶזֶר אוֹמֵר: אֵינוֹ סוֹתֵר אֶלָּא שִׁבְעָה.§ **גמ'** "מִי שֶׁאָמַר "הֲרֵינִי נָזִיר" וְנִטְמָא יוֹם שְׁלֹשִׁים סוֹתֵר אֶת הַכֹּל, רַבִּי אֱלִיעֶזֶר אוֹמֵר: אֵינוֹ סוֹתֵר אֶלָּא שִׁבְעָה". קָסָבַר

דעביד ק"ו (ר"ה דף י.): ומה נדה שאין תחילת יום ח] כסופו, דטבלה בלילה, מהני סוף יום כתחילתו, דלא בעיא כ"א ט] ז' ימים, ויום שפוסקת בו. [שנה], שתחילתו עולה בסופו – אינו דין שסופו עולה בתחילתו. לימא: זבה גדולה תוכיח, דתחילת יום כסופו, דטובלת ביום, וסופו לאו כתחילתו! אלא, ודאי רבא לא עביד הקל וחומר אליבא דר' יוסי. י] ומיהו, לפירוש רש"י ניחא, דלא מצי למימר זבה תוכיח*).

ומשני דחזיא שלשה יומין סמוך לשקיעת החמה דלא הוי שהות דסליק לה למניינא. לפי [שהם] מסובבין בטומאה בתחילת היום ובסופו, וליכא בהם שימור כלל. וכן יום שלישי טמא בתחילתו, והרי שלשה ימים רצופין טמאין, דמקצת יום שלישי ככולו, ואין בהן שימור בינתים.

הדרן עלך הריני נזיר

מי שאמר הריני נזיר מגלח יום שלשים ואחד. בפרק קמא (לעיל דף ה:) מייתינן ליה, ופי' רב מתנא ובר פדא כדאית להו. **שיום** ל' עולה לו מן המנין. לרב מתנא עולין למנין ימי נזירות דראשון, דמדאורייתא ל', וכן למנין שני עולה לו מדאורייתא, דבעינן שלשים דאורייתא. ולבר פדא אין צריך למנות נזירות ראשון, שכבר נשלם מיום כ"ט, ותגלחת ראשונה נעשית ביום ל' כדין תורה. ודקאמר במתניתין דיום ל' עולה לו מן המנין – היינו לענין נזירות שני, כדי שגם תגלחת שניה תהיה ביום ל', שהרי גילח ביום [ששים] חסר אחד. **הריני** נזיר נטמא יום ל' סותר הכל. לרב מתנא סותר מן התורה, ומביא קרבן טומאה, וחוזר ומונה שלשים יום נזירות טהרה. ולבר פדא סותר הכל מדרבנן, דיום כ"ט נשלם הנזירות. וסותר מדרבנן, גזירה להיכא דאמר "הריני נזיר ל' יום", ואינו מביא קרבנות נזיר טמא. **רבי** אליעזר אומר אינו סותר אלא שבעה. לבר פדא לא גזרינן. ולרב מתנא אליבא דר"א ס"ל מקצת היום ככולו, ואפילו נטמא קודם הבאת קרבנותיו. ורבנן אית להו דלא אמרי' מקצת היום ככולו אלא היכא דהביא קרבנותיו בטהרה ביום ל', דילא, כאילו הביאם ביום ל' ואחד. **הריני** נזיר ל' יום נטמא יום ל' סותר את הכל. ולא פליג ר"א לרב מתנא דאמר דסתם נזירות ל' יום, והכא מיתורא דלישנא דקאמר, "ל'" – הוי כאילו אמר "שלימים". הילכך, אפי' לר"א דאמר דמקצת היום ככולו – סותר הכל (ולבר פדא דלית ליה מקצת היום ככולו). דהכא אמר "ל'" – הוי ממנין הנזירות, כיון שפירש ל' יום. וא"ת: מ"מ אמאי סותר הכל לר"א? הא לר"א דריש לקמן בברייתא ד"הריני נזיר מאה יום" ונטמא יום מאה, יכול יסתור הכל – ת"ל "והימים הראשונים יפלו" – מכלל דאיכא אחרונים, וזה אין לו אחרונים. וה"נ כי נטמא ביום ל' – אין לו אחרונים, והל"ל דלא סתר הכל! וי"ל: דכיון דאמר "ל'" – א"כ יום ל' הוי יום מלאת, ודרשינן "וזאת תורת הנזיר ביום מלאת" – נטמא ביום מלאת תן לו תורת נזיר. ולקמן נמי בברייתא גבי נטמא בסוף מאה לא קממעיט להו מ"והימים יפלו" אלא דאינו סותר כל מאה, אבל שלשים יום ודאי סותר, כדקתני בסמוך במתני': נטמא יום מאה, דלר"א סותר שלשים. אבל ברישא, כי אמר "הריני נזיר" סתמא, דקאמר ר"א אינו סותר אלא שבעה, כי נטמא ביום שלשים – לבר פדא ניחא, משום דמיום כ"ט פסק מנין נזירותו, ויום שלשים אינו יום מלאת, כיון דלא אמר שלשים בפירוש. וגם לת"ק דסותר – אינו אלא מדרבנן לבר פדא, ולא מייתי קרבן טומאה. ולרב מתנא נמי דקאמר מקצת היום ככולו, הילכך יום ל' אינו יום מלאת, דהוי כאילו כלה כל אותו יום [כיון] דעשה מקצת בנזירות. אבל בסיפא מחשב כאילו אמר "שלימים", לרב מתנא לא אמרינן מקצת היום ככולו – הילכך הוי שפיר יום שלשים מלאת, דלכך סותר לר' אליעזר מדרשא ד"זאת תהיה תורת הנזיר", ולתנא

*) [ועי' תוס' פסחים פא. ד"ה א"נ וכו' ומש"כ שם על הגליון]

לעיל ה: וש"נ
לעיל ה:
שם
שם ו.
גם זה שם
גם זה שם
שם:

א א מיי' פ"ד מהל' נזירות הל"א סמג עשין קכז:
ב ב מיי' שם הל"ב סמג שם:
ג ג מיי' פ"ו שם הל"ג:
ד ד מיי' שם הל"ד:

פי' הרא"ש

ור' יוסי מכדי קסבר מקצת היום ככולו זבה גמורה היכי משכחת לה. כיון דחזאי בפלגא דיומא סליק לה שימור כשראתה ביום א' וביום ב' תחלת יום ב' הוי שימור ליום ראשון וטהרה מאותה ראיה וכשרואה אח"כ מכאן ולהבא היא מטמא ולא מצטרף בהדיה יום ראשון להיותה זבה: כגון ששפעה ג' ימים ולא היה לה טהרה בינתיים לשימור: ואי בעית אימא כגון דחזאי ג' יומי סמוך לשקיעת החמה. שהתחילה קצת מבעוד יום וראתה עד הלילה נמצאת בכל יום טמאה תחלתו וסופו ולא סליק לה שיעור:

סליק פירקא

מי שאמר הריני נזיר מגלח ליום ל"א. לרב מתנא דאמר סתם נזי' ל' יום הילכך מגלח יום ל"א. ולבר פדא סתם נזי' כ"ט יום והיה לו לגלח יום ל' אלא כדמפרש לעיל נעשה כאומר שלימים: ואם גלח יום ל' יצא לבר פדא ניחא דמדאורייתא דינא הכי לגלח יום ל' ולרב מתנא מפ' לעיל משום דמקצת היום ככולו. הריני נזיר ל' יום אם גילח יום ל' לא יצא. אף בר פדא מודה בהא כיון דאמר ל' יום דבעי' ל' יום שלימים: מי שאמר הריני נזיר ונטמא יום ל' סותר את הכל. לרב מתנא סותר מן התורה ומביא קרבן טומאה לבר פדא סותר מדרבנן אטו היכא דאמר ל' ואינו מביא קרבן טומאה: ור' אליעזר אומר אינו סותר אלא ז' דלא גזר. ולרב מתנא משום דסבר מקצת היום ככולו. ורבנן לית להו מקצת היום ככולו אלא אחר שהביא קרבנותיו: הריני נזיר ל' יום ונטמא יום ל' סותר הכל דכיון דאמר ל' יום בעי' שלימים ולא אמרי' מקצת היום ככולו: ר"א אומר אינו סותר אלא ל' כדדריש לעיל נטמא ביום מלאת תן לו תורת נזי': נטמא יום ק' וא' סותר ל'. מדרבנן גזרו שיסתור יום תגלחת אטו יום ק' ולא גזרו שיסתור אלא כסתם נזיר. וה"ה א) סתם נזיר שנטמא ביום ל"א הוי כנטמא יום ק"ב שאינו סותר: [ר"א אומר] אינו סותר אלא ז' ר"א לטעמי' דאפי' ביום ל' לא גזרי':

א) אולי צ"ל וה"ה בנזיר ל' יום שנטמא ביום ל"א שסותר את הכל אבל סתם נזיר שנטמא וכו'.

נוסחת הריב"ן

א) מר: ב) בין: ג) היום ככולו א"נ משום דקסבר דמכאן ולהבא היא מטמאה זבה דמתייא קרבן היכי משכחת לה וה"נ מיבעיא לן בכילד צולין דאליבא דר' יוסי דאמר דמכאן ולהבא היא מטמאה זבה גמורה דמתייא קרבן היכי משכחת לה הס"ד והשאר ליתא: ד) כל שלשה גבי הדדי ואב"א דחזאי כל תלתא יומי סמוך לבין השמשות לשקיעת החמה דכי ראתה בשבת בסמוך לשקיעת החמ' הויא טמא' כל יום ראשון וכן כי ראתה ביום ראשון בסמוך לשקיעת החמה וביום שני בשקיעת החמה הויא לה טמאה כל הלילה וכל היום דהיום הולך אחר הלילה והויא לה זבה גמורה משום דלא הוה לה שהות דטהרה ביני וביני כלל וסלקי לה למניינא דשומרת יום כנגד יום וכ"ן שמענ"ו כא"ן מפ"י המור"ה אבל בכילד צולין במסכת פסחים שמעו דהואיל ובין השמשות ספק יום ספק לילה ואינו יודע אם בין השמשות יום הוא הלכך הואיל וראתה כל בין השמשות בג' ימים בין אם אתה אומר שבין השמשות לילה או אתה אומר שהוא יום הוו להו תלתא יומין רצופין שלא היתה לה שעת הטהר כלל הס"ד והשאר ליתא בכ"י: ה) דבנזירות: ו) דהכא:

הגהות הב"ח (א) גמ' תלתא יומי. נ"ב עיין בנדה דף לג: (ב) שם דלא הואי שהות דלהוי סליק ליה למניינא: (ג) במשנה מגלח את השניה יום ששים ואם וכו' שיום שלשים עולה כצ"ל ותיבת של נמחק: (ד) רש"י ד"ה זבה וד"ה והא הד"א: (ה) רש"י ד"ה מי שאמר וכו' דמוקי לה לנעשה כאומר וכו' מתניתין הכא מפורש בפ"ק כצ"ל ותיבת כגון נמחק:

הגהות מהר"ב רנשבורג א] רש"י ד"ה והא כיון וכו' ור"י מכדי שומרת יום כנגד יום. נ"ב וכוונתו כזו לפר"ת בתוס' כאן: ב] בא"ד אבל בכילד צולין במס' פסחים שמעינן דמכאן ולהבא. נ"ב ר"ל כיון דבפסחים שם מפורש להדיא דפריך לר"י למאי דסבר מכאן ולהבא וכו' א"כ גם כאן הפירוש כן ואין צורך הטעם למ"ש רש"י בד"ה ור"י מכדי וכו' שדבריו שם הם רק לפירוש המורה ולכן חזר בו רש"י עכשיו ודו"ק: ג] תוס' ד"ה זבה גמורה וכו'. ואע"פ שלא טבלה בינתיים מכי ראתה ביום י"א וביום י"ג וביום ט"ו. מן תיבת מכי עד ט"ו נמחק. ונ"ב כמו ראתה ביום א' וביום ג' וביום ה' ר"ל תוך אחד עשר יום שבין נדה לנדה ראתה כן עכ"ל א"מ: ד] בא"ד ובדוחק יש לפרש ראתה י"א. ראתה י"א נמחק ונ"ב לראתה למימר ראתה יום א' כצ"ל א"מ: ה] בא"ד ושוין ברואה יום. מלת יום נמחק. ונ"ב תוך י"א כצ"ל: ו] בא"ד אידך פלגא לאותו יום עצמו. נ"ב וזהו ג"כ כוונת הענין אחר שפרש"י בשם המורה יעו"ש ודו"ק: ז] בא"ד הלכך בזבה קטנה בתחילת וכו' כצ"ל: ח] בא"ד ומה נדה שאין תחלת יום עולה בסופו דטבילה כצ"ל: ט] בא"ד דלא בעי' כ"א ז'. נמחק אות ז'. ונ"ב ו' ימים כצ"ל: י] בא"ד ומיהו לפי' רש"י. נ"ב עי' על דבריהם בזה בארוכות בא"מ:

קָסָבַר ר"א: *כָּל אַחַר מְלֹאת — שִׁבְעָה סוֹתֵר. "הֲרֵינִי נָזִיר שְׁלֹשִׁים יוֹם" וְנִטְמָא יוֹם שְׁלֹשִׁים — סוֹתֵר אֶת הַכֹּל. לָא פָּלֵיג ר"א*, דְּאָמַר "שְׁלֵימִין". "הֲרֵינִי נָזִיר מֵאָה יוֹם" וְנִטְמָא יוֹם מֵאָה — סוֹתֵר אֶת הַכֹּל. ר"א* אוֹמֵר: אֵינוֹ סוֹתֵר אֶלָּא שְׁלֹשִׁים. א ב ג ד וְכוּלָּהּ כִּדְהָוֵינַן בָּהּ אַלִּיבָּא דְּבַר פַּדָּא וְרַב מַתָּנָא.§ **מתני'** אמִי שֶׁנָּזַר וְהוּא בְּבֵית הַקְּבָרוֹת, אֲפִי' *הָיָה שָׁם ל' יוֹם — אֵין עוֹלִין לוֹ מִן הַמִּנְיָן, וְאֵינוֹ מֵבִיא קָרְבַּן טוּמְאָה. ביָצָא וְנִכְנַס — עוֹלִין לוֹ מִן הַמִּנְיָן, וּמֵבִיא קָרְבַּן טוּמְאָה. ר"א* אוֹמֵר: לֹא בּוֹ בַּיּוֹם, שֶׁנֶּאֱמַר °"וְהַיָּמִים הָרִאשֹׁנִים יִפְּלוּ" — עַד שֶׁיִּהְיוּ לוֹ יָמִים רִאשׁוֹנִים.§ (במדבר ו) **גמ'** אִיתְּמַר, מִי שֶׁנָּזַר וְהוּא בְּבֵית הַקְּבָרוֹת, ר' יוֹחָנָן אָמַר: *גנְזִירוּת חָלָה עָלָיו, (נדרים ד.) וְר"ל אָמַר: אֵין נְזִירוּת חָלָה עָלָיו. ר' יוֹחָנָן אָמַר: נְזִירוּת חָלָה עָלָיו, סָבַר: מִיתְלָא תַּלְיָא וְקַיְימָא, כֵּיוָן דְּמַשְׁכְּחָא טָהֳרָה — חָיְילָא. וְר"ל אָמַר: אֵין נְזִירוּת חָלָה עָלָיו, אִי הָדַר וְאָמַר — חָיְילָא עֲלֵיהּ, וְאִי לָא — לָא. אֵיתִיבֵיהּ ר' יוֹחָנָן לר"ל: מִי שֶׁנָּזַר וְהוּא בְּבֵית הַקְּבָרוֹת, אֲפִי' הָיָה שָׁם שְׁלֹשִׁים יוֹם — אֵין עוֹלִין מִן הַמִּנְיָן, וְאֵינוֹ מֵבִיא קָרְבַּן טוּמְאָה. קָרְבַּן טוּמְאָה הוּא דְּלָא מַיְיתֵי, הָא מֵיחַל חָיְילָא עֲלֵיהּ! א"ל: אֵינוֹ בְּתוֹרַת טוּמְאָה וְאֵינוֹ בְּתוֹרַת קָרְבָּן. אֵיתִיבֵיהּ: *דמִי שֶׁהָיָה טָמֵא וְנָזַר — אָסוּר לְגַלֵּחַ וְלִשְׁתּוֹת יַיִן וְלִיטַּמֵּא לַמֵּתִים. וְאִם גִּילֵּחַ וְשָׁתָה יַיִן וְנִטְמָא לַמֵּתִים — ה"ז סוֹפֵג אֶת הָאַרְבָּעִים. (תוספתא פ"ב) אִי אָמְרַתְּ בִּשְׁלָמָא חָיְילָא — הַיְינוּ טַעְמָא דְּסוֹפֵג אֶת הָאַרְבָּעִים, אֶלָּא אִי אָמְרַתְּ לָא חָיְילָא — אַמַּאי סוֹפֵג אֶת הָאַרְבָּעִים?
הָכָא

תורה אור

דְּקָסָבַר ר' אֱלִיעֶזֶר אַחַר מְלֹאת הוּא, שֶׁאֵין נְזִירוּת אֶלָּא כ"ט, וּלְכָךְ אֵינוֹ צָרִיךְ לִסְתּוֹר אֶלָּא ז'. א) וְכִדְאָמְרִינַן נַמִי קִים לְהוּ לְרַבָּנַן דְּאֵין תִּגְלַחַת כְּדֵי לָכוּף רֹאשׁוֹ לְעִיקָּרוֹ בְּפָחוֹת מִז' יוֹם. וּלְרַב מַתָּנָא כִּדְאִית לֵיהּ, דְּטַעְמָא דְּר' אֱלִיעֶזֶר מִשּׁוּם דְּמִקְצָת הַיּוֹם כְּכוּלּוֹ. **נִטְמָא** יוֹם שְׁלֹשִׁים סוֹתֵר אֶת הַכֹּל **וְלָא פָּלֵיג** ר' אֱלִיעֶזֶר דְּהָא קָאָמַר שְׁלֵימִין. וַאֲפִילּוּ לְבַר פַּדָּא, דְּהַשְׁתָּא "תּוֹךְ מְלֹאת" קָרֵינָא בֵּיהּ. **נִטְמָא** בְּיוֹם מֵאָה סוֹתֵר אֶת הַכֹּל. דְּתוֹךְ "מְלֹאת" קָרֵינָא בֵּיהּ. **רַבִּי אֱלִיעֶזֶר** אוֹמֵר לֹא סוֹתֵר אֶלָּא שְׁלֹשִׁים. כְּדַאֲמַר ר"ל בְּפ"ק (לעיל ד' ו:) דְּטַעְמָא דְּר' אֱלִיעֶזֶר מִשּׁוּם דְּקָאָמַר קְרָא "זֹאת תּוֹרַת הַנָּזִיר בְּיוֹם מְלֹאת" — הַתּוֹרָה אָמְרָה: נִטְמָא בְּיוֹם מְלֹאת — תֵּן לוֹ תּוֹרַת נָזִיר, וַאֲפִי' בִּנְזִירוּת מְרוּבָּה. **וְכוּלָּהּ**. טַעְמָא דְּמַתְנִיתִין עַד הַשְׁתָּא, כִּדְהָוֵינַן בָּהּ אַלִּיבָּא דְּבַר פַּדָּא וְרַב מַתָּנָא בְּפ"ק (ד' ה וד' ו) ב). **מתני'** מִי שֶׁנָּזַר וְהוּא בְּבֵית הַקְּבָרוֹת **אֲפִי'** הוּא עוֹמֵד שָׁם שְׁלֹשִׁים יוֹם אֵינָן עוֹלִין לוֹ מִן הַמִּנְיָן. כְּלוֹמַר, אֵין עוֹלִין לְכָךְ ג) שֶׁתְּהֵא חָלָה עָלָיו אוֹתוֹ נְזִירוּת שֶׁקִּיבֵּל כְּשֶׁנִּטְמָא, וְאֵין מֵבִיא קָרְבַּן טוּמְאָה. ד) **יָצָא וְנִכְנַס**. כְּגוֹן שֶׁהִזָּה וְשָׁנָה וְטָבַל, כִּדְמְפָרֵשׁ בַּגְּמָרָא, וְאַח"כ נִכְנַס — עוֹלִים לוֹ לְמִנְיַן נְזִירוּת. דְּכֵיוָן [שֶׁהִזָּה] וְשָׁנָה וְטָבַל בְּיוֹם שְׁבִיעִי שֶׁלּוֹ — מֵבִיא קָרְבָּן עַל הַטּוּמְאָה. **רַבִּי אֱלִיעֶזֶר** אוֹמֵר **לֹא** בּוֹ בַּיּוֹם. כְּשֶׁהִזָּה וְשָׁנָה וְטָבַל, אִם נִכְנַס ה) — אֵינוֹ מֵבִיא קָרְבַּן טוּמְאָה עַד ו) שֶׁיַּעֲבוֹר עָלָיו ב' יָמִים ז) בְּטָהֳרָה, שֶׁנֶּאֱמַר: "וְהַיָּמִים הָרִאשׁוֹנִים יִפְּלוּ" אֵימָתַי לִכְשֶׁאֲנִי קוֹרֵא ח) מִקְרָא זֶה — שֶׁיִּהְיוּ לוֹ יָמִים הָרִאשׁוֹנִי' ט) דְּטָהֳרָה, וְאֵין "יָמִים" פְּחוּתִים מִשְּׁנַיִם. **גמ'** אִיתְּמַר מִי שֶׁנָּזַר וְהוּא בְּבֵית הַקְּבָרוֹת ר' יוֹחָנָן **אוֹמֵר** נְזִירוּת חָל עָלָיו. דְּקָסָבַר דְּהַאי מַאן דִּמְקַבֵּל נְזִירוּת בְּבֵית הַקְּבָרוֹת מִיתְלָא תַּלְיָא וְקַיְימָא, וְכֵיוָן דְּמַשְׁכַּחַתְּ טָהֳרָה, דְּהַיְינוּ לְאַחַר שֶׁיָּצָא וְהִזָּה וְשָׁנָה וְטָבַל — חָיְילָא עֲלֵיהּ, אע"ג דְּלָא הָדַר אָמַר "אֲנִי אֲקַבֵּל עָלַי מַה שֶּׁאָמַרְתִּי כְּשֶׁהָיִיתִי עוֹמֵד בְּבֵית הַקְּבָרוֹת". **וְר"ל אָמַר.** אִי הָדַר אָמַר "אֱהֵא כְּמוֹ שֶׁקִּבַּלְתִּי י) בְּבֵית הַקְּבָרוֹת" — חָיֵיל עֲלֵיהּ, וְאע"ג דְּלָא כ) מְפָרֵשׁ "אֱהֵא נָזִיר". וְאִי לָא — לָא, שֶׁאִם נִטְמָא לַמֵּתִים וְשׁוֹתֶה יַיִן — אֵין בְּכָךְ כְּלוּם. **א"ל.** מַסְקָנָא דְּמַתְנִיתִין בְּהָכִי הָוֵי, דְּמִי שֶׁנָּזַר בְּבֵית הַקְּבָרוֹת — אֵינוֹ בְּתוֹרַת טוּמְאָה, וְאֵינוֹ בְּתוֹרַת קָרְבַּן טָהֳרָה לִיסְתּוֹר וּלְהָבִיא קָרְבַּן טָהֳרָה, לְפִי שֶׁאֵין נְזִירוּת חָל עָלָיו כְּלָל. **מִי שֶׁהָיָה טָמֵא וְנָזַר.** דְּהַיְינוּ נַמִי מִי שֶׁעוֹמֵד בְּבֵית הַקְּבָרוֹת.
הָכָא

ולתנא קמא דאמר הכל סותר בנזיר סתמא, לרב מתנא הוי מן התורה, דהוי ממנין הנזירות, ומקצת היום ככולו א] דאמרי רבנן – היכא [דלא] נטמא. הגה"ה: ובסיפא ד"הריני נזיר מאה יום" ונטמא יום מאה סותר [שלשים] לרבי אליעזר, מדרשא ד"זאת תהיה" וגו'. וצ"ל לרב מתנא מאי שנא מרישא כי נדר סתם ונטמא יום שלשים, דחשבינן ליה לרבי אליעזר אליבא דרב מתנא כנטמא אחר מלאת, ומשום מקצת היום ככולו – הכי נמי כי נדר מאה יום נחשביה ליום מאה כאחר מלאת, דנימא מקצת היום ככולו, (הריני נזיר מאה דליכא יתור)! ותירצו התוספות לעיל (דף ו:) דמיירי דאמר "הריני נזיר מאה יום שלימים". ובזה ניחא, דהשתא ליכא למימר מקצת היום ככולו ב] בסיפא. והסוגיא מתיישבת בפ"ק (שם) דמייתי הך דנזיר ג] שלשים ונטמא יום שלשים כו' סותר הכל, בשלמא לרב מתנא אלא כו', א"ל בר פדא אימא סיפא: ר' אליעזר אומר אינו סותר כי אם ז'. והשתא היכי מוכח? לעולם אימא לך משך נזירות ל', והא דאינו סותר כי אם ז' לר"א – [משום] דאין כאן ימים אחרונים! ולרב מתנא נמי, מאי דוחקיה דסבר דמקצת היום ככולו? לימא טעמא דר"א משום דליכא ימים אחרונים! ולמאי דפרישי' ניחא, דאם היה יום שלשים ממנין הנזירות לבר פדא, ולרב מתנא נמי אי לאו דאמרינן מקצת היום ככולו – היה סותר הכל מדרשא ד"זאת תורת הנזיר". ע"ד כא"ן הגה"ה. זאת הגה"ה ממורי רבינו יצחק בהר' יצחק זצ"ל: נראה דלכ"ע בין לרב מתנא ולבר פדא קרא ד"זאת תורת הנזיר" וקרא ד"ימים הראשוני'" איירי במאה שלימים. נראה דלפי הגה"ה זאת ר"ל דלא בנזירות מועטת דרשא ד"זאת", כדפרישי' בפ"ק (גם זה שם) בשם מהר"ף נ"ע. וכן דרשא דקרא דמן הימים הראשונים – מכלל דאיכא אחרונים – [לא] דרשינן בנזירות מועטת, אלא בנזירות ארוך דלמאה יום. ובהכי נמי מתיישב הסוגיא. *)**הריני** נזיר מאה יום **נטמא** יום מאה סותר הכל. שהוא אחרון של נזירותו. ולרבנן לא אמרינן מקצת היום ככולו היכא דנטמא ולא הביא קרבנותיו. **ולרבי אליעזר** אינו [סותר] **אלא** שלשים. מן הדין היה לו לסתור הכל לבר פדא, דלא אמרינן מקצת היום ככולו. ולרב מתנא נמי פרשינן בפ"ק דאמר "שלימים", והיה לו לסתור את הכל. אלא מדרשא ד"זאת תורת הנזיר" – גזירת הכתוב הוא דאינו סותר אלא ל' יום ד]. **נטמא** ביום ק"א סותר שלשים. מדרבנן בעלמא הוא, ולכך אינו סותר אלא שלשים. דהואיל ויום ק"א יום תגלחת ויום הבאת קרבנותיו – גזרי' אטו היכא דנטמא ביום שלשים היכא דאמר "הריני נזיר" סתמא, והוי ה] (כמו) יום שלשים תגלחת מה"ת לרב מתנא, משום דאמר מקצת היום ככולו. ולבר פדא שמיום כ"ט נשלם הנזירות, וביום שלשים מגלח מה"ת, ואם נטמא ביום שלשים סותר לרב מתנא מה"ת, וגזרי' יום ק"א אטו יום שלשים. ולבר פדא ביום שלשים סותר מדרבנן, אטו היכא דאמר "הריני נזיר שלשים". וכן נטמא ביום *אחד ומאה שהוא יום תגלחת גזרו אטו יום ל', דאי לא הא לא קיימא הא, שגם יום ל' הוא יום תגלחת. וה"ה לעיל הוה מצי למיתני הכי גבי "הריני נזיר" נטמא יום ל"א דסותר הכל מדרבנן. [אבל] ודאי נטמא יום ק"ב – אינו סותר שלשים, רק [שבעה], שיטהר ויביא קרבנותיו. **ור"א** אומר אינו סותר **אלא** ז'. דלא גזר יום ק"א אטו יום ל', דביום ל' גופיה לא סתר לר' אליעזר. ו] ואע"ג דלבר פדא דאמר "הריני נזיר" סתמא ונטמא יום *אחד, דנזירותו פסק כבר מיום כ"ט, ויום ל' הוי תגלחת מה"ת. אבל יום ל' ואחד – סוי יום דבתר תגלחת, והוי [כמו] ק"ב. **מי** שנדר והוא בבית הקברות. וה"ה אם היה טמא ונדר, ובגמ' מדמה להו. **ואפי'** היה שם ל' אין עולין לו מן המנין. לענין דמונה והולך, דאינו מביא קרבן טומאה, דרחמנא מיעטיה מקרבן [כדמפרש] בגמרא. אבל הא פשיטא דהימים אין עולין, דאפי' מנה בטהרה ונטמא – סותר את הראשונים. וכ"ש שאין עולין לו כי טמא מעיקרא. **יצא** ונכנס עולה לו מן המנין. מפרש בגמ': יצא ונכנס והזה ושנה, ונכנס בו ביום שטבל בשביעי – עולין מן המנין, לענין זה כשנטמא – סותר אותו מנין ומתחייב (אותו) קרבן טומאה, דאותו יום עצמו מתחיל נזירות טהרה. ובגמרא פליגי ר' יוחנן ור"ל כשנטהר, אם צריך לחזור ולקבל נזירות, או סגי ליה במה שקיבל בימי טומאתו. **ר"א** אומר לא בו ביום. כלומר: אם נכנס בו ביום שנטהר – אין מביא קרבן טומאה עד יום שני שהתחיל הטהרה שנאמר "והימים הראשונים יפלו" – דבעינן בסותר שיסתור ב' ימים דאז מביא קרבן טומאה, וה"ה דמצי למיתני פלוגתייהו בנזיר טהור שנטמא ביום ראשון של קבלת נזירותו. ז] וביום נטמא בתחילה, דלרבנן – מביא קרבן טומאה, ולר"א – אינו מביא קרבן טומאה, אלא מונה ז' ימי טומאה, ומזה ושונה וטובל ומונה כ"ט יום ליום הראשון שמנה, ומגלח ביום ל', שהוא ל' ואחד לנזירותו. ****גמ'** קסבר ר"א כל אחר מלאת ז' סותר. ולכך אומר ד"הריני נזיר" סתם ונטמא יום שלשים [דאינו] סותר, דלאחר מלאת הוא, לרב מתנא משום דאמר מקצת היום ככולו, ולבר פדא מיום כ"ט נשלם נזירותו. **לא** פליג ר"א דאמר שלימים. לרב מתנא חשיב ליה כאילו אמר "שלימים", ולא אמר מקצת היום ככולו – הילכך סותר הכל. ולבר פדא נמי, כי אמר "שלשים" בפירוש – חשיב כאילו אמר "שלימים", דלא אמר מקצת היום ככולו. הילכך לא פליג ר"א כלל. **רבי** יוחנן אמר נזירות חלה עליו. לכל מילי, ולוקה בעודו שם אטומאה אם התרו בו לצאת ממנו (יוצא), ואתגלחת ואשתיית יין, וכשיטהר אין צריך לחזור ולקבל עליו נזירות. **מיתלא** תליא וקאי. ח] ומ"מ נ"ל לאסור: וכי משכחת טהרה חייל. פירוש: דין נזירות טהרה לענין הבאת קרבן. מיתלא תליא וקאי – עד שיצא משם ויטהר, וכי יטהר – חייל ממילא עליה לענין הבאת קרבן. ובקילור הוה מצי למימר דחייל עליה נזירות מהשתא, ולקי על תגלחת ויין וטומאה. **וריש** לקיש אמר אין נזירות חייל עליה. בעודו טמא, עד שיטהר, ואז יצטרך לחזור ולקבל עליו הנזירות. ובקונטרס פי' דבקבלה מועטת סגי ט] לומר יחול עליו הנזירות – אומר "הריני כמו שנדרתי". ובפ"ק דנדרים (דף ד.) אמרי' לר"ל דעובר ב"בל תאחר" אם אינו מקבל נזירות עליו מיד כשיטהר. **קרבן** טומאה הוא דלא מייתי. דמעטיה קרא לקמן. הא מיחל חייל עליה נזירות לענין דלקי אטומאה אתגלחת ואיין. **א"ל** אינו בתורת טומאה. דלא חייל נזירות כלל.
הכא

*) מכאן עד ד"ה מי שנדר שייך לע"א. **) שייך לעיל קודם ד"ה מי שנדר

ח א מיי' פ"ו מהל' נזירות הל"ח:
ו ב מיי' שם הל"י:
ז ג מיי' שם הל' ז ח:
ח ד מיי' שם ה"ז:

פי' הרא"ש

[מתני'] מי שנזר והוא בבית הקברות אפי' שהה שם ל' יום וכו' ואינו מביא קרבן טומאה דכי כתיב קרבן טומאה בנזיר טהור שנטמא כתיב. וה"ה טמא שנזר: יצא ונכנס כלומ' והזו עליו ג' ח' [וטבל] ומיד אחר הזאה וטבילה מתחיל נזירותו. אם נכנס בבית הקברות אפי' בו ביום מביא קרבן טומאה: ר"א אומר לא בו ביום. שנאמר והימים הראשונים יפלו לאשמועינן דסותר כל מה שמנה: איתמר מי שנזר והוא בבית הקברות ר"י אומר נזירו' חלה עליו ליאסר ביין ותגלחת ואם א"ל אל תנזור ונזר או אחר שנזר התרו ביה לצאת ולא יצא לוקה אבל קרבן נזי' לא מייתי כל זמן שלא חלה עליו נזי' טהרה. מיתלא תליא וקיימא. נזירות טהרה תלויה ועומדת ולכשיצא מיד תחול ואינו צריך לקבל עליו שנית. ור"ל אמר אי הדר אמר חיילא עליו לכשיצא ויטהר. ומיהו מוטל עליו לצאת ולקבל כדמוכח פ"ק דנדרים וכן א) לר' יוחנן כדי שיחול עליו נזי' טהרה. ונראה דלר"ל נמי אינו צריך קבלת נזי' גמורה אלא אומר הריני בנזיר: הא מיחל חיילא. דאי לא חיילא מה שייך למתני אינו מביא קרבן טומאה הא לא חלה עליו נזי' כלל: א"ל אינו בתורת טומאה ואינו בתורת קרבן. וה"ק אין עולין לו מן המנין ב) לנזי' כלל שאם נטמא אח"כ אע"פ שטהר לא לקי ואינו מביא קרבן טומאה עד שיטהר ויקבל עליו נזי':

א) נ"ל דגם לר"י איכא לאו דבל תאחר מלבד הלאו דטומאה. ב) אולי נ"ל דלא חייל נזירות כלל שאם נטמא:

נ"ל מאה ואחד

נ"א ל'

גליון הש"ס

גמ' מי שנזר וכו'. עיין נדריס דף ד ע"א: **תוס'** ד"ה נטמא כו' הריני נזיר נטמא יום ל"א. ע' לעיל ו' ע"א תד"ה נטמא ודף יד ע"ב ד"ה לוקה:

לקמן לט: מז. סג:

נוסחת הריב"ן

א) כדי שיביא קרבנו בטהרה וכדאמרן נמי כו': ב) בכ"י כתוב כאן בזה"ל. גליון נטמא יום ק' וא' קודם שיקריב קרבנותיו סותר לפי שצריך לגלח תגלחת טומאה לאלתר ואח"כ מגלח תגלחת טהרה בסוף ל' יום שאין תגלחת טהרה פחות מל' יום הלכך סותר ל' יום ותו לא משום דהוי נזיר שכלו לו ימיו וה"ה כי נטמא יום ל"א סותר את הכל ולר' אליעזר סותר ז' והכי תניין בתוספתא ר' אליעזר אומר אין סותר אלא ז' דקסבר כל אחר מלאת ז' ותו לא כדי שיקריב קרבנותיו בטהרה דקסב' רבי אליעזר כי נטמא אחר מלאת אין צריך לגלח תגלחת טומאה אלא מונה ז' ומגלח תגלחת טהרה: ג) שתהא נזירות חלה עליו כדי להביא קרבן טומאה על שנטמא בבית הקברות הס"ד והשאר ליתא: ד) בכ"י איתא בזה"ל יצא ונכנס אבל אם יצא והוזה ושנה וטבל מיד חלה עליו אף אותו נזירות שקבל כשנטמא שאם לאחר מכאן נכנס עולין לו למנין נזירות מכיון ששנה וטבל ביום שביעי שלו שמביא קרבן על הטומאה הס"ד והשאר ליתא בכ"י: ה) (אינו) ליתא בכ"י: ו) שיעברו: ז) ב' ימים ויהא עומד בשלישי שנאמר והימים כו': ח) קורא כל מקרא: ט) הראשונים הס"ד והשאר ליתא בכ"י: י) עלי: כ) אמר:

הגהות מהר"ב רנשבורג

(בתוס' שמעבר לדף) א] בא"ד ומקצת היום ככולו דאמרי רבנן היכא דלא נטמא. מן תיבת דאמרי עד תיבת נטמא נמחק. ונ"ב לא אמרי רבנן כצ"ל א"מ: ב] בא"ד הגה"ה ובסיפא וכו' ובזה ניחא דהשתא ליכא למימר מקצת היום ככולו בסיפא והסוגיא. מלת בסיפא ואות ו' מן תיבת והסוגיא נמחק ונ"ב ובהכי הסוגיא מתיישבת בפ"ק (שם) כצ"ל: ג] בא"ד דמייתי הך דנזיר שלשים. נמחק מלת שלשים ונ"ב סתם כצ"ל: ד] ד"ה ולר"א אינו סותר וכו' אלא מדרשא דזאת תורת הנזיר גזירת הכתוב הוא דאינו סותר אלא שלשים יום מכי נטמא יום מאה כצ"ל א"מ: ה] ד"ה נטמא ביום ק"א סותר שלשים וכו' היכא דאמר הריני נזיר סתמא והוי נמי כצ"ל: ו] ד"ה ור"א אומר אינו סותר וכו' דביום שלשים גופיה לא סתר לר"א ואע"ג. נמחק ואע"ג ונ"ב ואפי' לבר פדא באמר הריני נזיר סתמא ונטמא יום ל' דנזירותו כצ"ל: ז] ד"ה ר"א אומר לא בו ביום וכו' ביום ראשון של קבלת נזירותו וביום נטמא. תי' וביום נטמא נמחק ונ"ב וכיון דנטמא כצ"ל א"מ: ח] ד"ה מתלי תלי וקאי ומ"מ נ"ל נמחק. ונ"ב ומש"ה ס"ל לאיסור כצ"ל א"מ: ט] ד"ה וריש לקיש אמר כו' ובקונט' פי' דבקבלה מועטת סגי לחול עליו כצ"ל:

הָכָא בְּמַאי עָסְקִינַן — בְּיוֹצֵא וְנִכְנָס. אֵיתִיבֵיהּ: *אאֵין בֵּין טָמֵא שֶׁנָּזַר לְנָזִיר טָהוֹר שֶׁנִּטְמָא, אֶלָּא: טָמֵא שֶׁנָּזַר — שְׁבִיעִי שֶׁלּוֹ עוֹלֶה לוֹ לְמִנְיָן, וְנָזִיר טָהוֹר שֶׁנִּטְמָא — אֵין שְׁבִיעִי שֶׁלּוֹ עוֹלֶה לוֹ לְמִנְיָן. וְאִי ס"ד לָא חָיְילָא — אַמַּאי עוֹלֶה לוֹ מִן הַמִּנְיָן? *אֲמַר מָר בַּר רַב אַשִׁי: מֵיחַל — כ"ע לָא פְּלִיגֵי דְּחָיְילָא, אֶלָּא כִּי פְּלִיגֵי — לְמִלְקֵי; רַבִּי יוֹחָנָן סָבַר: כֵּיוָן דְּחָיְילָא — לָקֵי, ור"ל סָבַר: לָא לָקֵי, וְחָיְילָא. אֵיתִיבֵיהּ ר' יוֹחָנָן לר"ל: מִי שֶׁנָּזַר וְהוּא בְּבֵית הַקְּבָרוֹת, אֲפִילּוּ הָיָה שָׁם שְׁלֹשִׁים יוֹם — אֵין עוֹלִין לוֹ מִן הַמִּנְיָן, וְאֵינוֹ מֵבִיא קָרְבַּן טוּמְאָה. קָרְבַּן טוּמְאָה הוּא דְּלָא מַיְיתֵי, הָא מִילְקֵי לָקֵי עֲלֵיהּ! בְּדִין הוּא דְּלִיתְנֵי "אֵינוֹ לוֹקֶה", אֶלָּא מִשּׁוּם דְּקָא בָּעֵי לְמִיתְנָא סֵיפָא "יָצָא וְנִכְנַס עוֹלֶה לוֹ מִן הַמִּנְיָן, וּמֵבִיא קָרְבַּן טוּמְאָה" — תְּנָא רֵישָׁא "אֵינוֹ מֵבִיא קָרְבַּן טוּמְאָה". ת"ש: אֵין בֵּין טָמֵא שֶׁנָּזַר לְנָזִיר טָהוֹר שֶׁנִּטְמָא, אֶלָּא שֶׁטָּמֵא שֶׁנָּזַר — שְׁבִיעִי שֶׁלּוֹ עוֹלֶה לוֹ מִן הַמִּנְיָן, וְנָזִיר טָהוֹר שֶׁנִּטְמָא אֵין שְׁבִיעִי שֶׁלּוֹ עוֹלֶה לוֹ מִן הַמִּנְיָן. הָא לְמַלְקוֹת — זֶה וָזֶה שָׁוִין! א"ל: לָא, לְתִגְלַחַת — זֶה וָזֶה שָׁוִין. אֲבָל לְעִנְיַן מַלְקוֹת מַאי — זֶה לוֹקֶה וְזֶה אֵינוֹ לוֹקֶה? לִיתְנְיֵיהּ! בְּתַקַּנְתֵּיהּ קָא מַיְירֵי, בְּקִלְקוּלֵיהּ לָא קָא מַיְירֵי. תָּא שְׁמַע: מִי שֶׁהָיָה טָמֵא וְנָזַר — אָסוּר לְגַלֵּחַ וְלִשְׁתּוֹת יַיִן, וְאִם גִּילַּח וְשָׁתָה יַיִן וְנִטְמָא לַמֵּתִים — הֲרֵי זֶה סוֹפֵג אֶת הָאַרְבָּעִים! תְּיוּבְתָּא. *בבָּעֵי רָבָא: (א) נָזִיר וְהוּא בְּבֵית הַקְּבָרוֹת, מַהוּ? בָּעֵי שְׁהִיָּיה לְמַלְקוֹת אוֹ לָא? הֵיכִי דָּמֵי? אִילֵימָא דְּאָמְרִי לֵיהּ "לָא תִּינְזוֹר" — לָמָּה לִי שְׁהִיָּיה? נָזִיר (ב) מַאי טַעְמָא לָא בָּעֵי שְׁהִיָּיה — דְּקָא מַתְרֵי בֵּיהּ, ה"נ — קָא מַתְרֵי בֵּיהּ! אֶלָּא

רש"י

הָכָא בְּמַאי עָסְקִינַן בְּיוֹצֵא וְנִכְנָס. שֶׁיָּצָא וְהִזָּה בַּשְּׁלִישִׁי וּבַשְּׁבִיעִי, וְטָבַל, וְהָדַר אֲמַר "הֲרֵינִי נָזִיר", א) וַהֲדַר נִכְנַס – סוֹפֵג אֶת הָאַרְבָּעִים. וּלְאַפּוּקֵי מִדְּר' אֱלִיעֶזֶר דַּאֲמַר לֹא בּוֹ בַּיּוֹם כו'. אֲבָל אִי לָא הֲדַר וַאֲמַר – אֵינוֹ אָסוּר לְגַלֵּחַ וכו', שֶׁאֵין נְזִירוּת חָלָה עָלָיו. טָמֵא שֶׁנָּזַר. כְּגוֹן שֶׁהָיָה עוֹמֵד בְּבֵית הַקְּבָרוֹת וְנָזַר. שְׁבִיעִי שֶׁלּוֹ עוֹלֶה לוֹ לְמִנְיָן. דְּכֵיוָן דְּטָבַל וַהֲוֵי טָהוֹר – מַתְחִיל לִמְנוֹת מִבּוֹ בַּיּוֹם, לְפִי שֶׁאֵינוֹ מֵבִיא קָרְבָּן. וְנָזִיר טָהוֹר שֶׁנִּטְמָא אֵין שְׁבִיעִי שֶׁלּוֹ עוֹלֶה לוֹ מִן הַמִּנְיָן. אע"פ שֶׁטָּבַל וְהוּא טָהוֹר, עַד יוֹם שְׁמִינִי שֶׁמֵּבִיא בּוֹ קָרְבְּנוֹתָיו. כִּדְאָמְרִינַן בְּפֶ' "שְׁלֹשָׁה מִינִין" (לקמן דף מד:): סֵדֶר תִּגְלַחַת כֵּיצַד: הָיָה מַזֶּה בַּשְּׁלִישִׁי וּבַשְּׁבִיעִי וּמְגַלֵּחַ בַּשְּׁבִיעִי, וּמֵבִיא קָרְבְּנוֹתָיו בַּח'. מֵיחַל דְּכוּלֵּי עָלְמָא לָא פְּלִיגֵי. דְּכֵיוָן דְּמַשְׁכַּחַתְּ טָהֳרָה חָיְילָא מִמֵּילָא. אֶלָּא כִּי פְּלִיגֵי לְמִילְקֵי ר"י סָבַר כֵּיוָן דְּחָיְילָא לָקֵי. אֲפִילּוּ אַטּוּמְאָה דְּמֵעִיקָּרָא, דְּנָזַר בְּבֵית הַקְּבָרוֹת. ור"ל סָבַר: אע"ג דְּחָיְילָא, שֶׁהוּא צָרִיךְ לִשְׁמוֹר מִכָּל דִּקְדּוּקֵי נְזִירוּת – לָא לָקֵי אֲפִילּוּ אַטּוּמְאָה דְּבַסּוֹף, אִי לָא הֲדַר וַאֲמַר. הָא לְמַלְקוֹת זֶה וָזֶה שָׁוִין. שֶׁשְּׁנֵיהֶם לוֹקִין עַל הַטּוּמְאָה וּלְדִקְדּוּקֵי נְזִירוּת. אֵימָא לְתִגְלַחַת זֶה וָזֶה שָׁוִין. שֶׁשְּׁנֵיהֶם מְגַלְּחִין בְּיוֹם שְׁבִיעִי שֶׁלָּהֶן. לִיתַנְיֵיהּ. אֵין בֵּין טָמֵא שֶׁנָּזַר כו' אֶלָּא שֶׁטָּמֵא שֶׁנָּזַר שְׁבִיעִי שֶׁלּוֹ עוֹלֶה לוֹ מִן הַמִּנְיָן וְאֵינוֹ לוֹקֶה, וְטָהוֹר שֶׁנָּזַר אֵין ז' שֶׁלּוֹ עוֹלֶה לוֹ מִן הַמִּנְיָן, וְלוֹקֶה. בְּתַקַּנְתֵּיהּ קָמַיְירֵי. אֵימַת מַתְחִילִין לִמְנוֹת, זֶה מִשְּׁבִיעִי וְזֶה מִשְּׁמִינִי. אֲבָל קִלְקוּלֵיהּ, דְּלוֹקֶה – לָא קָמַיְירֵי. א] ב) וַאֲמַר לָן רַבִּי: דְּהָכִי נַמִי מָצֵי לְמִיתְנֵי: אֶלָּא טָמֵא שֶׁנָּזַר אֵין מְגַלֵּחַ תִּגְלַחַת טוּמְאָה, וְנָזִיר טָהוֹר שֶׁנִּטְמָא מְגַלֵּחַ ג) בְּז', וְטָמֵא שֶׁנָּזַר אֵין מְגַלֵּחַ בַּשְּׁבִיעִי. אֶלָּא תָּנָא שְׁבִיעִי שֶׁלּוֹ וְכָל ד) מִילֵּי, כִּדְמְפָרֵשׁ לְקַמָּן. ת"ש מִי שֶׁהָיָה טָמֵא וְנָזַר אָסוּר לְגַלֵּחַ וְלוֹקֶה. וש"מ, דְּכֵיוָן דְּחָיְילָא עֲלֵיהּ נְזִירוּת, דַּהֲוֵי אָסוּר לְגַלֵּחַ – לוֹקֶה. וּתְיוּבְתָּא דְּר"ל. וּבְיוֹצֵא וְנִכְנָס לָא מָצֵי לְתָרֵץ לֵיהּ כִּדִלְעֵיל, דְּהָא אוֹקִימְנָא דְּמוֹדֵי ר"ל דְּחָיְילָא וְקָאֵי לֵיהּ בְּאִיסּוּרָא, אֲבָל מִילְקֵי לָא לָקֵי. וְאִילּוּ הָכָא ה) מַשְׁמַע דְּכֵיוָן שֶׁאָסוּר – לוֹקֶה, אע"ג דְּלָא הֲדַר וַאֲמַר. בָּעֵי רָבָא. הוֹאִיל דְּאָמַר ר' יוֹחָנָן דְּלוֹקֶה, וּתְנַן בְּמַתְנִיתִין כְּוָותֵיהּ. בָּעֵי שְׁהִיָּיה לְמַלְקוֹת. דְּלָא לִילְקֵי עַד דְּלִישְׁהֵי בֵּיהּ כְּדֵי שִׁיעוּר הִשְׁתַּחֲוָיָה, ו) כִּדְמְפָרֵשׁ בְּמַסֶּ' שְׁבוּעוֹת בְּפֶרֶק "יְדִיעוֹת הַטּוּמְאָה" (דף יז.). נָזִיר. טָהוֹר, הַנִּכְנָס בְּבֵית הַקְּבָרוֹת, מ"ט לָא בָּעֵי שְׁהִיָּיה – דְּקָא מַתְרוּ בֵּיהּ "אַל תִּכָּנֵס לְבֵית הַקְּבָרוֹת", הָכָא נַמִי מַתְרוּ בֵּיהּ "לָא תִּינְזוֹר", וּשְׁהִיָּיה לָמָּה לִי? אֶלָּא

תוספות

הכא במאי עסקינן ביוצא ונכנס. ביולא מן הטומאה, והזה ושנה וטבל, וקיבל עליו נזירות פעם אחרת, ושוב נכנס לטומאה. [והא] קמ"ל ההיא ברייתא: דאע"ג דלא הדר ואמר "הריני נזיר" אלא אמר "יחול עלי נזירות" – דהוי נזיר, ולקי, כדפי' לעיל בקונטרס. אי נמי, י"ל: דקמ"ל ברייתא (דמיירי) [דמיד] כשיטהר מוטל עליו לקבל נזירות מיד, ועובר ב"בל תאחר" אם אינו נזיר מיד.

אין בין נזיר טמא. שנדר בעודו טמא, לנזיר טהור שנטמא, אלא דנזיר טמא שביעי עולה לו מן המנין – כשהזה ג' ושנה בז' וטבל יום ז' ב] – למנין נזירות טהרה, לפי שאין צריך להביא קרבן בא' על טומאתו, ומיד כשהזה ושנה וטבל – ראוי לחול עליו נזירות לאלתר. ונהי דבעי הערב שמש, ואיך יחול עליו נזירות? יש לומר דטבול יום קלישא טומאתיה, ולא מעכב מלחול נזירות עליו. **ונזיר** טהור שנטמא אין שביעי עולה מן המנין. למנין נזירות טהרתו, וצריך להביא חטאת העוף ועולת העוף ואשם בשמיני. וכתיב (במדבר ו) "וקדש ראשו ביום ההוא" – דבאותו יום מתחיל למנות נזירות טהרה, מוקמינן לה ג] דלא חייל עליה נזירות דטהרה עד יום ח'. ואי ס"ד לא חיילא – אמאי עולה לו מן המנין, כיון דלא הדר קביל עליה נזירות? וא"ת: [ולישני] דהדר וקיבל, כדשני לעיל ביולא ונכנס! ויש לומר: דא"כ ה"ל לאיתויי: זה בעי למיהדר ולנדור, וזה לא בעי למיהדר ולנדור. כיון דהאי תנא נחית לפרושי הכא ד] בין זה לזה. וה"ה דמצי למיפרך לר' שמעון ב"ל: [ליתני] זה שותה ביין ומיטמא דלא לקי, וזה לקי, ה] כדפירש הקונטרס. ונראה לומר דלא קשה, דמצי לשנויי דבקלקולא לא מיירי האי דינא, אלא דין דנטמא באונס. ולרבי יוחנן לא קשה [דליתני]: זה מביא קרבן על טומאתו וזה אין מביא קרבן. דהיינו הך, דקתני אין ז' עולה לו מן המנין, משום איתויי קרבן. **הגה"ה** מיחל דכ"ע דחייל. ולכשיטהר אין צריך לחזור לידור בנזיר, דחייל עליו מנזירות ראשון. וניחא השתא דשביעי עולה לו מן המנין, ואפילו לא יחזור ויקבל. והוא הדין נמי דמודה ר' שמעון בן לקיש ו] (נמי אם שותה יין) דלקי תוך ימי טומאתו אשתיה ואתגלחת. וכי פליגי למלקי, פירוש: אטומאה לחוד, אי התרו בו אטומאה. ר' יוחנן סבר: כיון דחיילא נזירות [לשאר] מילי, אשתיית יין ואתגלחת – [חיילא] נמי אטומאה, אם התרו בו לצאת ולא יצא, דרחמנא לא מעטיה אלא מקרבן לחודיה לקמן, ולא ממלקות דטומאה. ור"ש בן לקיש סבר: אע"ג דחיילא לשאר מילי, ליין ולתגלחת – לא לקי אטומאה. דכיון דמיעטיה רחמנא מקרבן טומאה – מיעטיה מכל דין טומאה, אף ממלקות. **קרבן** טומאה הוא דלא מייתי הא מילקי לקי. אטומאה לאלתר, אפילו תוך שבעה שמבקש לטהר ז] לענין ליטהר עלמו ולעשות נזירות דטהרה. דאי [לא] לקי – הוה ליה למיתני במתני': ואינו לוקה. **משום** דקתני סיפא כו' ומביא קרבן טומאה. דהתם לא שייך למיתני דלוקה אטומאה, דתני מביא קרבן טומאה – לכך לא תנא לעיל: ואינו לוקה. **הא** למלקות זה וזה שוין. מדלא תני: זה לוקה וזה אינו לוקה אטומאה, (וזה אינו לוקה). **לא** הא לתגלחת זה וזה שוין. י"מ דלקי אתגלחת. [ולא נהירא, דלימא] לתגלחת ויין זה וזה שוין, כיון דלאיסור תגלחת קמיירי. לכן נראה לי: הא לתגלחת – פירוש למצות תגלחת, לענין שמגלח בשביעי לטהרתו. אע"ג דלקמן בעיא היא, ואיפשיטא, דנזיר טמא דמעיקרא אינו מגלח בשביעי לטהרתו – אפ"ה לא קפיד לשנויי הכי, [דבלא"ה] איתותב רבי שמעון בן לקיש בסוף. **בתקנתא** קמיירי. מתי יתחיל מנין לנזירותו והוא נטמא בשוגג. בקלקולא לא קמיירי – שמקלקל עלמו במזיד, דהיינו קלקול גופיה. ח] דגם לר"ל אסור לטמאות אפילו בתוך [שבעה], דאם לא כן ליתני: זה מותר לטמאות וזה אסור לטמאות, דהא לאו קלקולא הוא. **הגה"ה** מי שהיה טמא ונדר. היינו בנזר והוא בבה"ק. ואם גילח, ושתה יין, ונטמא למתים – סופג הארבעים. ומשמע דאף תוך ז' לוקה. ואם תאמר: ולישני ליה ביולא ונכנס ושנה וטבל, כדשני לעיל אהך גופא! י"ל: דמשמע ליה טומאה דומיא דגלוח ושתיית יין, דחייל עליה בימי טומאה, כדמסיק ליה: מיחל דכ"ע חיילא, דומיא דהכי מלקות דטומאה, אפילו לא נטהר – חייל עליה בימי טומאתו, לכך איתותב. אבל בלשון ראשון הוה משוי להו כולהו ר' שמעון ב"ל, גילוח ושתיית יין לטומאה, לכך הוה שייך לשנויי לעיל ביולא ונכנס.

בעי שהייה למלקות. כי היכי דבעינן שהייה בפ"ב דשבועות (דף יז.) גבי מקדש [או לא]. **אילימא** דאמרי ליה לא תנזור. והוא עומד בבית הקברות, למה לי שהייה? פשיטא דלקי בלא שהייה. דנזיר טהור מאי טעמא דלא בעי שהייה, ולא משכחת ליה [כלל] דבעי שהייה – משום דקמתרין ביה שלא יטמא והוא נזיר טהור. הכא נמי מתרין ביה שלא ידור בו בנזיר, והוא עובר – לקי, כמו היכא דהוה טהור ומתרין ביה שלא יטמא. ולאו האי כלאו שאין בו מעשה הוא – במה שאינו יוצא משם כשנודר בנזיר. ט] דלאו שיש בו מעשה במה שמקבל נזירות. אלא

מסורת הש"ס

[לקמן יח.]

[נדרים ז.]

[שבועות יז. ע"ש ובתוס' שם ד"ה צריך]

עין משפט נר מצוה

ט א מיי' פ"ו מהל' נזירות הל' ז:
י ב מיי' שם הל' ט וע"ש בכ"מ:

פי' הרא"ש

הכא במאי עסקינן ביוצא ונכנס שיוצא מן הטומאה ע"י הזאה וטבילה וקיבל עליו נזירות ונכנס וקמ"ל אע"ג דלא קבל עליו קבלה גמורה אלא אמר הריני נזיר (בנזירות) [הוי נזיר]: אלא טמא שנזר ז' עולה לזמן המנין לפי שאינו צריך להביא קרבן ומתחיל למנות מיד אחר שהזה וטבל אבל נזיר טהור שנטמא אינו מתחיל למנות עד אחר הבאת קרבנותיו דכתיב וקדש ראשו ביום ההוא ואי ס"ד לא חיילא אמאי עולה לו מן המנין הא אין עליו נזירות כלל עד שיקבל. וכ"ת דמיירי בשקבל עליו א"כ ליתני שזה צריך לחזור ולידור וזה אין צריך מיחל כ"ע לא פליגי דחיילא ואינו צריך לקבל עליו שנית וגם לוקה על התגלחת ועל היין: כי פליגי למלקי. פי' על הטומאה: ר' יוחנן סבר כיון דחיילא. ללקות על היין ועל התגלחת לקי נמי על הטומאה כי היכי דאינו מביא קרבן טומאה: והא דאותביה ר"י לר"ל לעיל תלמודא הוא דמותיב לפי מה דהוה ס"ד דפליגי וכהנה רבות בתלמוד: א"ל לא לתגלחת זה וזה שוין. פי' לגלח א"נ ללקות על התגלחת וה"ה על היין: אבל לענין מלקות. פי' על הטומאה. בתקנתא מיירי בקלקולא לא מיירי. פי' להורות לנו תקנתו מתי יתחיל ימי נזירותו. אבל לא מיירי בקלקול להשמיענו הדין אם יעשה עבירה שיטמא למתים אי ישתה יין ויגלח: ה"ז סופג את הארבעים תיובתא. והכא ליכא לשנויי ביוצא ונכנס דמשמע נטמא דומיא דגלח ושתה יין דמיירי אפילו בלא יוצא ונכנס: בעי שהייה למלקות. שיעור שהייה המפורשת (בז') [בשבועות] למי שנטמא באונס בעזרה שאינו חייב כרת אלא אם כן שהה שיעור השתחואה והלכה למשה מסיני הוא: אי דאמרו ליה לא תגזור למה לי שהייה. כיון דבמזיד

נוסחת הריב"ן

א) הריני נזיר ונכנס: ב) בכ"י כתוב כאן גליון ואמר לן רבי: ג) מגלח תגלחת טומאה לנזיר טהור שנטמא מגלח בז' כו': ד) מילה כדמפרשינן: ה) תנן: ו) כדי שיעור השתחויה מוזכרו לסופיה דקרא כדמפרש כו':

הגהות הב"ח

(א) גמ' בעי רבא. נזיר והוא בבית הקברות: (ב) שם נזיר טהור מ"ט לא:

הגהות מהר"ב רנשבורג

א] רש"י ד"ה בתקנתיה קמיירי וכו' ואמר לן רבי דהכי נמי מצי למיתני אלא טמא שנזר. נ"ב עיין א"מ דזה דוקא לפי' קמא בתוס' ד"ה לא הא וכו' ודו"ק: ב] תד"ה אין בין נזיר טמא וכו' כשהזה ג' ושנה בז' וטבל יום ז' עולה כצ"ל: ג] ד"ה ונזיר טהור שנטמא וכו' דבאותו יום מתחיל למנות נזירות טהרה מוקמינן ליה לקמן כצ"ל: ד] בא"ד כיון דהאי תנא נחית לפרושי הכא מאי איכא כצ"ל: ה] בא"ד זה שותה ביין ומטמא דלא לקי וזה לקי כדפי' הקונטרס. מלות כדפי' הקונטרס נמחק ונ"ב כדפירש לקמן כצ"ל ועי' א"מ ודו"ק: ו] ד"ה הגה"ה מיחל דכ"ע דחייל וכו' וה"ה נמי דמודה ר"ש דלא לקי כצ"ל: ז] ד"ה קרבן טומאה הוא דלא מייתי הא מלקי לקי אטומאה לאלתר אפילו תוך שבעה שמבקש לטהר עצמו כצ"ל: ח] ד"ה בתקנתא קמיירי וכו'. דהיינו קלקול גופיה בלאסור ליה וכו' כצ"ל א"מ: ט] ד"ה אילימא דאמרי ליה לא תנזור וכו' דלאו שיש בו מעשה הוא. נ"ב סברא זאת רחוקה קצת דאיך יחשב זה כמעשה ועי' תוס' לשבועות דף יז ע"א ד"ה או וכו' שנדחקו בזה דאזלא סוגיין למ"ד לוקין על לאו שאב"מ או דלאיסור מלקות אמר אבל לדעת הרב המגיד דס"ל כל לאו שאפשר ע"י מעשה לוקה אף היכא דאין בו מעשה יעו"ש בפי"ג מהל' שכירות הל' ב' א"כ א"ש סוגיין ומכאן ראיה והוכחה ברורה לדבריו ודו"ק היטב:

גליון הש"ס

גמ' אמר מר בר רב אשי. עיין נדרים דף ד' ע"א:

אֶלָּא כְּגוֹן *שֶׁנִּכְנַס בְּשִׁידָּה תֵּיבָה וּמִגְדָּל, וּבָא חֲבֵירוֹ וּפָרַע מֵעָלָיו מַעֲזִיבָה. כִּי גְּמִירִין שְׁהִיָּיה — בְּבֵית הַמִּקְדָּשׁ, אֲבָל אַבָּרַאי — לָא, אוֹ דִּלְמָא אלָא שְׁנָא? תֵּיקוּ. בָּעֵי רַב אַשִׁי: נָזַר וְהוּא בְּבֵית הַקְּבָרוֹת, טָעוּן גִּילּוּחַ אוֹ לֹא? כִּי בָּעֵי תִּגְלַחַת — טָהוֹר שֶׁנִּטְמָא, דְּקָא מְטַמֵּא לִנְזִירוּתֵיהּ, אֲבָל טָמֵא שֶׁנָּזַר — לָא, אוֹ דִּלְמָא לָא שְׁנָא? ת"ש: מִי שֶׁנָּזַר וְהוּא בְּבֵית הַקְּבָרוֹת, אֲפִילּוּ הָיָה שָׁם שְׁלֹשִׁים יוֹם — אֵינוֹ עוֹלֶה לוֹ מִן הַמִּנְיָן, וְאֵינוֹ מֵבִיא קָרְבַּן טוּמְאָה. קָרְבַּן טוּמְאָה הוּא דְּלָא מַיְיתֵי, אֲבָל גַּלּוּחֵי — בָּעֵי! מַה טַּעַם קָאָמַר; מַה טַּעַם אֵינוֹ מֵבִיא קָרְבַּן טוּמְאָה — מִשּׁוּם דְּלָא בָּעֵי גַּלּוּחֵי. ת"ש: *אֵין בֵּין טָמֵא שֶׁנָּזַר לְנָזִיר טָהוֹר שֶׁנִּטְמָא, אֶלָּא: טָמֵא שֶׁנָּזַר — שְׁבִיעִי שֶׁלּוֹ עוֹלֶה לוֹ מִן הַמִּנְיָן, וְנָזִיר טָהוֹר שֶׁנִּטְמָא — אֵין שְׁבִיעִי שֶׁלּוֹ עוֹלֶה לוֹ מִן הַמִּנְיָן. מַאי לָאו, הָא לְתִגְלַחַת — זֶה וָזֶה שָׁוִין? לָא, הָא לְמַלְקוֹת זֶה וָזֶה שָׁוִין. אֲבָל תִּגְלַחַת מַאי — זֶה מְגַלֵּחַ, וְזֶה אֵינוֹ מְגַלֵּחַ? לִיתְנְיֵיהּ! תְּנָא שְׁבִיעִי שֶׁלּוֹ, וְכָל מִילֵּי. ת"ש: *אֵין לִי אֶלָּא יְמֵי טוּמְאָתוֹ שֶׁאֵין עוֹלִין לוֹ מִן הַמִּנְיָן, יְמֵי חִלּוּטוֹ מִנַּיִן? וְדִין הוּא: מַה יְּמֵי טוּמְאָתוֹ מְגַלֵּחַ וּמֵבִיא קָרְבָּן — אַף יְמֵי חִלּוּטוֹ מְגַלֵּחַ וּמֵבִיא קָרְבָּן, וּמַה יְּמֵי טוּמְאָתוֹ אֵין עוֹלִין לוֹ מִן הַמִּנְיָן [ב] — אַף יְמֵי חִלּוּטוֹ אֵין עוֹלִין לוֹ מִן הַמִּנְיָן! לֹא, אִם אָמַרְתָּ בִּימֵי טוּמְאָתוֹ — שֶׁכֵּן מְבַטֵּל בָּהֶן אֶת הַקּוֹדְמִין, לְפִיכָךְ אֵין עוֹלִין לוֹ מִן הַמִּנְיָן, תֹּאמַר בִּימֵי חִלּוּטוֹ שֶׁאֵינוֹ מְבַטֵּל אֶת הַקּוֹדְמִין, לְפִיכָךְ עוֹלִין לוֹ מִן הַמִּנְיָן. אָמַרְתָּ: וּמַה נָּזִיר בַּקֶּבֶר, שֶׁשְּׂעָרוֹ רָאוּי לְתִגְלַחַת — אֵין עוֹלִין לוֹ מִן הַמִּנְיָן, יְמֵי חִלּוּטוֹ שֶׁאֵין רָאוּי לְתִגְלַחַת — לֹא כ"ש שֶׁאֵין עוֹלִין לוֹ מִן הַמִּנְיָן? מַאי לָאו תִּגְלַחַת טוּמְאָה? לָא, תִּגְלַחַת טָהֳרָה. הָכִי נַמִּי מִסְתַּבְּרָא, דְּאִי

[לקמן יח.]

אלא כגון שנכנס בשידה תיבה ומגדל. תחילת כניסתו במקום טמא בהיתר, ולא לקי אכניסה. א] [אלא] כי מתרין ביה – שילא בשידה וכו' פרע לו עליו המעזיבה, מספקא ליה דלמא [לא] בעי שהייה, או דלמא ל"ש, דכל היכא דאירעה טומאה – התם בעי שהייה. **ובא** חבירו ופרע מעליו המעזיבה. דווקא באונס. דאי מרצונו, אי נמי אם הוא עצמו פרע – כי האי גוונא לא איבעיא לן אי בעי שהייה. דבפ"ב דשבועות (דף יז.) קאמר אהך בעיא דנזיר טמא: או דילמא באונס גמירי לה שהייה, ל"ש בחוץ ול"ש בפנים. הגה"ה: טעון גילוח או אין טעון גילוח. פי': תגלחת דטומאה ביום שיוצא ויטהר מטומאה. דקרבן ודאי לא בעי, כדתנן במתני' דמיעטיה קרא לקמן. אבל בתגלחת מספקא ליה אי בעי לגלח בלא קרבן טומאה, או לא, דלא בעי גילוח בלא קרבן: הגה"ה. אבל תגלחת של טהרה ודאי בעי, כשימנה נזירות של טהרה – יגלח ויביא קרבנות טהרה כדין נזיר טהור. **קרבן** טומאה הוא דלא מייתי. דמיעטיה קרא לקמן (דף יח.). הא גלוחי בעי, מדלא קאמר: ואינו מגלח בשביעי שלו. **מה** טעם קאמר. כלומר, כיון דתנן אינו מביא – ממילא ידעינן דאינו מגלח, דהא בהא תליא, דהפסוקים קרובים זה לזה. אע"ג דגילוח ביום ז' וקרבן טומאה ביום שמיני, משמע ליה דכיון דאינו מביא קרבן טומאה דאינו מגלח. **הא** לתגלחת זה וזה שוין. פירוש: תגלחת דטומאה, מדלא תנא: זה מגלח וזה אינו מגלח. **תנא** שביעי שלו וכל מילי. וכיון דתנא שביעי שלו עולה לו מן המנין – היינו משום שאינו מביא קרבן, וממילא ידעינן דאינו מגלח, כיון דאינו מביא קרבן. **ימי** טומאה שאין עולין לו מן המנין. פירוש: כשנטמא במת. שהרי אם מנה בטהרה כמה ימים, ונטמא – סותר אפילו מנין הראשון, כדכתיב "והימים הראשונים יפלו", וכ"ש ב] שאותן ימים אין עולין לו. כדכתיב "וכפר עליו" וגו' והיינו כשיטהר – "וקדש ראשו ביום ההוא" שיתחיל מנין נזירות טהרה. ימי חלוטו שיושב מחוץ למחנה והחליטו. ומנה מקצת נזירות שקבל עליו קודם שנצטרע, ושוב נרפא, וגילח לצרעתו, מנין שיחזור למנות להשלים נזירות למנין שמנה קודם צרעת, וימים שבימי חלוטו לא יעלו לו מן המנין נזירות. אבל ימי הסגרו דודאי עולין לו, לפי שאין זקוק לגלח כמו מוחלט, ואין ג] [נחשב] לימי טומאה כמו מוחלט. הגה"ה: **אף** ימי חלוטו. שוין לימי טומאתו. ד] דאין עולין לנזירות – ה"נ ימי חלוטו אין עולין לו לנזירותו. **לא** אם אמרת בימי טומאתו שכן מבטל בו את הימים הקודמים. כדכתיב "והימים הראשונים יפלו". וא"ת: והיא גופא נילף בהאי דינא, דימי חלוטו יבטלו הקודמים! וי"ל: דאיכא מיעוטא לקמן בפ' "שלשה מינין" (דף מד.): על טומאתו סותר, ואינו סותר על תגלחת. הכי נמי נימעוט, ונימא דאינו סותר על החלטו. **נזיר** בקבר ששערו ראוי לתגלחת. ודמי לנזיר, אין עולין לו מן המנין. ימי חלוטו, שאין שערו ראוי לתגלחת, ולכך לא דמי [לנזיר] – לא כל שכן שאין עולין לו מן המנין. **מאי** לאו תגלחת דטומאה [לא תגלחת דטהרה]. והכי קאמר: [ומה נזיר קבר] ששערו ראוי לתגלחת, דשיער שעליו עומד להתגלח לכי ישלים נזירות דטהרה, שהרי אינו מגלח בשביעי – אין עולין. ימי חלוטו, שאין שערו עומד להתגלח לנזירות טהרה, שהרי זקוק לגלח לכשיתרפא מצרעתו – לא כל שכן שאין עולין לו.

אלא. הֵיכִי דָּמֵי שְׁאֵילְתָּא דְּרָבָא. כְּגוֹן שֶׁנִּכְנַס בְּשִׁידָּה תֵּיבָה וּמִגְדָּל. בְּבֵית הַקְּבָרוֹת, שֶׁמַּפְסִיק בֵּינוֹ לְבֵין הַטּוּמְאָה, א) וְנָדַר בְּעוֹדוֹ בַּשִּׁידָּה, שֶׁהוּא טָהוֹר, וְאח"כ בָּא חֲבֵרוֹ וּפָרַע אֶת הַמַּעֲזִיבָה ב) שֶׁהוּא תַּחְתָּיו, שֶׁהָיְתָה הַשִּׁידָּה מֵעַל רֹאשׁוֹ. ה"ג: כִּי גְּמִירִי שֶׁהִיָּה בִּפְנִים **אֲבָל אַבָּרַאי** לָא. כִּי גְּמִירִי שְׁהִיָּיה כְּשֶׁנִּטְמָא בְּבֵית הַמִּקְדָּשׁ, ג) בְּפֶרֶק "יְדִיעוֹת הַטּוּמְאָה": נִטְמָא בְּבֵית הַמִּקְדָּשׁ וְשָׁהָה כְּדֵי הִשְׁתַּחֲוָיָה – חַיָּיב. **אֲבָל אַבָּרַאי.** כְּגוֹן בְּבֵית הַקְּבָרוֹת, לָא בָּעֵי שְׁהִיָּיה. וְכֵיוָן שֶׁפָּרַע מִתַּחְתָּיו אֶת הַמַּעֲזִיבָה, אע"ג דְּלָא שָׁהָה – חַיָּיב. **אוֹ דִּילְמָא לָא שְׁנָא.** דְּהָכָא וְהָכָא בָּעֵי' שִׁיעוּר ד) כְּדֵי הִשְׁתַּחֲוָיָה? תֵּיקוּ. **בָּעֵי רַב אַשִׁי** נָזַר וְהוּא בְּבֵית הַקְּבָרוֹת טָעוּן גִּילּוּחַ. בַּיּוֹם הַשְּׁבִיעִי שֶׁלּוֹ, אוֹ לָא? **קָרְבַּן טוּמְאָה** הוּא דְּלָא מַיְיתֵי. מִשּׁוּם דְּלָא מַיְיתֵי קָרְבָּן אֶלָּא מַאן דִּמְטַמֵּא לֵיהּ לִנְזִירוּתֵיהּ, אֲבָל גִּילּוּחַ – בָּעֵי. **מַה טַּעַם קָאָמַר.** (א) ה) אֵינוֹ מֵבִיא קָרְבָּן – ו) לְפִי שֶׁאֵינוֹ מְגַלֵּחַ. **מַאי לָאו הָא לְתִגְלַחַת זֶה וָזֶה שָׁוִין.** דְּזֶה וָזֶה מְגַלְּחִין בַּשְּׁבִיעִי שֶׁלָּהֶן. **לָא לְמַלְקוֹת זֶה וָזֶה שָׁוִין.** וְכִדְר' יוֹחָנָן לְעֵיל. **לִיתְנְיֵיהּ** תְּנָא שְׁבִיעִי שֶׁלּוֹ וְכָל מִילֵּי. ז) דְּהָכִי מַשְׁמַע: שְׁבִיעִי שֶׁלּוֹ עוֹלֶה לוֹ מִן הַמִּנְיָן, לְפִי שֶׁאֵינוֹ מֵבִיא קָרְבָּן. וּמַה טַּעַם אֵינוֹ מֵבִיא קָרְבָּן – לְפִי שֶׁאֵינוֹ טָעוּן גִּילּוּחַ טוּמְאָה בְּז'. וְזֶה אֵין שְׁבִיעִי שֶׁלּוֹ עוֹלֶה, לְפִי שֶׁיֵּשׁ לוֹ לְגַלֵּחַ בַּשְּׁבִיעִי וּלְהַקְרִיב קָרְבָּן בַּשְּׁמִינִי. וּמֵאוֹתוֹ יוֹם שֶׁמַּקְרִיב קָרְבָּן חָל עָלָיו נְזִירוּת, כִּדְכְתִיב (במדבר ו) "וְכִפֶּר עָלָיו מֵאֲשֶׁר חָטָא עַל הַנָּפֶשׁ וְקִדַּשׁ אֶת רֹאשׁוֹ בַּיּוֹם הַהוּא", ח) דְּמַשְׁמַע: מֵאוֹתוֹ יוֹם וְאֵילָךְ נְזִירוּת דְּטָהֳרָה. **ת"ש אֵין לִי.** שֶׁלֹּא יְהוּ עוֹלִין לוֹ מִן הַמִּנְיָן: **אֶלָּא יְמֵי טוּמְאָתוֹ.** כִּדְכְתִיב "וְהִזִּיר לַה' אֶת יְמֵי נִזְרוֹ וְקִדַּשׁ אֶת רֹאשׁוֹ בַּיּוֹם הַהוּא", דְּמַשְׁמַע: מֵאוֹתוֹ הַיּוֹם וְאֵילָךְ שֶׁהֵבִיא קָרְבְּנוֹתָיו (ב) ט) יִתְכַּפֵּר וְיַתְחִיל לִמְנוֹת לִימֵי נִזְרוֹ. **יְמֵי חִלּוּטוֹ מִנַּיִן.** שֶׁאִם נִצְטָרַע בִּימֵי נְזִירוּתוֹ וְהוּחְלַט, שֶׁלֹּא יְהוּ עוֹלִין לְמִנְיַן נְזִירוּתוֹ. י) מַה יְּמֵי טוּמְאָתוֹ מְגַלֵּחַ. תִּגְלַחַת טוּמְאָה, וּמֵבִיא קָרְבַּן לְכַפָּרִים. **אַף יְמֵי חִלּוּטוֹ.** דִּכְתִיב "וְכִבֶּס הַמִּטַּהֵר אֶת בְּגָדָיו וְגִלַּח אֶת כָּל שְׂעָרוֹ" (ויקרא יד), וּכְתִיב "וּבַיּוֹם הַשְּׁמִינִי יִקַּח שְׁנֵי כְבָשִׂים" וגו' – אֵין עוֹלִין לוֹ. שֶׁכֵּן מְבַטֵּל בָּהֶן אֶת הַקּוֹדְמִין. כִּדְכְתִיב "וְהַיָּמִים הָרִאשֹׁנִים יִפְּלוּ". **תֹּאמַר בִּימֵי חִלּוּטוֹ שֶׁאֵין מְבַטֵּל בָּהֶן אֶת הַקּוֹדְמִין.** כְּגוֹן בִּנְזִירוּת מְרוּבָּה, כְּדִלְקַמָּן בְּפֶרֶק "כֹּהֵן גָּדוֹל וְנָזִיר" (דף נו:) תְּנַן לָהּ. וְהוֹאִיל וְאֵינוֹ מְבַטֵּל אֶת הַקּוֹדְמִין – יְהוּ עוֹלִים לוֹ יְמֵי חִלּוּטוֹ מִן הַמִּנְיָן. **אָמַרְתָּ וּמַה נָּזִיר בַּקֶּבֶר.** נָזִיר וְהוּא בְּבֵית הַקְּבָרוֹת, שֶׁשְּׂעָרוֹ רָאוּי כו'. **מַאי לָאו תִּגְלַחַת דְּטוּמְאָה.** דְּכֵיוָן שֶׁהִזָּה וְשָׁנָה וְטָבַל מְגַלְּחִין אוֹתוֹ, וש"מ דְּטָעוּן גִּילּוּחַ. וְהָכִי מַשְׁמַע: מַה נָּזִיר בַּקֶּבֶר שֶׁשְּׂעָרוֹ רָאוּי לְתִגְלַחַת כ) ז' – אֵין עוֹלִין לוֹ מִן הַמִּנְיָן, יְמֵי חִלּוּטוֹ שֶׁאֵין שְׂעָרוֹ רָאוּי לְתִגְלַחַת טוּמְאָה אֶלָּא לְתִגְלַחַת צָרַעַת – לֹא כָּל שֶׁכֵּן דְּאֵין עוֹלֶה לוֹ. **לָא תִּגְלַחַת דְּטָהֳרָה.** שֶׁאִם לֹא נִכְנַס לַקֶּבֶר, א"נ נִכְנַס לַקֶּבֶר וְנִטְהַר, וְאח"כ הִשְׁלִים יְמֵי נִזְרוֹ, שֶׁהוּא טָעוּן גִּילּוּחַ לְסוֹף שְׁלֹשִׁים. דְּהָכִי מַשְׁמַע: שֶׁשְּׂעָרוֹ רָאוּי לְתִגְלַחַת טָהֳרָה, שֶׁאֵין מְגַלֵּחַ תִּגְלַחַת טוּמְאָה אֶלָּא תִּגְלַחַת לְסוֹף ל) מַיְירֵי. מ) אֲבָל בִּימֵי חִלּוּטוֹ נ) אֵינוֹ מְגַלֵּחַ תִּגְלַחַת טָהֳרָה, אֶלָּא תִּגְלַחַת צָרַעַת לְסוֹף ז'. דְּאִי

ימי

יא א מיי' פ"ו מהלכות נזירות הלכה ח ופ"ה שם הל' יט וע"ש בכ"מ:
יב ב מיי' פ"ז שם הלכה ט:

פי' הרא"ש

טמא עצמו: ופרע עליו המעזיבה. כמו ופרע ראש האשה. שגלהו מתחתיו שהסיר את מעזיבת השידה ולא מצי למימר כגון שנכנס לבית הקברות שוגג והתרו בו לצאת. דאמרינן בשבועות כי גמירי שהייה (באולם) [באונס] הוא דגמירי: קרבן טומאה הוא דלא מייתי אבל גלוחי מגלח. מדלא קתני אינו מגלח דהוי רבותא טפי: מה טעם קאמר. כלומר כיון דתנא אינו מביא טומאה ממילא ידענא דאינו מגלח דהא בהא תליא: תנא ז' וכל מילי. כל דבר שתלוי בטהרת ז' דהיינו תגלחת וקרבן: אין לי אלא ימי טומאה. פי' טומאת מת שאין עולין לו מן המנין דכתיב והימים הראשונים יפלו וכ"ש שאין ימי טומאתו עולים: ימי חלוטו מנין. אם נחלט בצרעת בימי נזירותו: ימי חלוטו מגלח ומביא קרבן לצרעתו: תאמר בימי חלוטו שאין מבטל בהם את הקודמים. והא ליכא למימר דהיא גופה נילף מבנין אב שיהיה סותר הקודמים. דהא אמרינן לקמן פ' ג' מינין [דף מד] [וטמא ראש] נזרו טומאה סותרת ואין תגלחת סותרת. וה"ה נמי דאמרינן טומאת מת סותרת ואין טומאת צרעת סותרת: אמרת ומה נזיר בקבר ששערו ראוי לתגלחת נזיר מאי לאו לתגלחת טומאה. כלומר שיגלח לסוף ז' כדין נזיר שנטמא ומחמת שיש לו דין נזיר אחר לענין תגלחת כדין נזיר: לא לתגלחת טהרה. ששערו ראוי להתגלח אחר שישלים נזי' טהרה וכ"ז אינו מגלח אפ"ה אינן עולים ימי חלוטו שאין שערו ראוי לתגלחת נזיר אלא לתגלחת צרעתו שהוא טעון העברת שער קודם שיתחיל למנות נזי'

לקמן מג.

נוסחת הריב"ן

א) ונזר: ב) המעזיבה מעל הקבר שהוא כו': ג) כדתנן בפרק: ד) (כדי) ליתא בכ"י: ה) מ"ט אינו כו': ו) קרבן טומאה: ז) וכל מילי דטמא שנזר שביעי שלו כו': ח) ביום ההוא ומונה מאותו היום ואילך: ט) ונתכפר לו יתחיל: י) (מה ימי טומאתו כו' אין עולין לו) ליתא בכ"י ומה"ד מה לשבעת ימי טומאתו אין עולין לו שכן מבטל בהן: כ) לגלחת טומאה לסוף ז': ל) לסוף ל' מיירי: מ) תאמר: נ) שאינו:

הגהות הב"ח

(א) רש"י ד"ה מה טעם קאמר. מה טעם אינו מביא: (ב) ד"ה אלא ימי וכו' שהביא קרבנותיו ונתכפר יתחיל למנות:

גליון הש"ס

גמ' אין לי אלא ימי טומאתו. עי' לקמן דף ט ע"א:

הגהות מהר"ב רנשבורג

א] תוס' ד"ה אלא וכו' ולא לקי אכניסה וכי כצ"ל: ב] ד"ה ימי טומאה שאין עולין לו מן המנין וכו' כדכתיב והימים הראשונים יפלו וכ"ש שאותן. מלת שאותן נמחק ונ"ב שמנין אותן כצ"ל: ג] בא"ד לפי שאין זקוק לגלח כמו מוחלט ואין נחשב. מלת נחשב נמחק ונ"ב שוה כצ"ל: ד] ד"ה אף ימי חלוטו שוין לימי טומאתו לאין. מלת לאין נמחק ונ"ב מה ימי טומאתו אין כצ"ל:

יג א מיי' פ"ו מהל' נזירות הלכה ג:
יד ב מיי' שם הלכה ח:
טו ג מיי' שם הל' ז:
טז ד מיי' שם הל' טו וע"ש בכ"מ:

תורה אור

דאי ס"ד תגלחת טומאה — ימי חלוטו מי לא בעי תגלחת? לא, תגלחת דנזירות קתני. ת"ש: (במדבר ו) "וטמא ראש נזרו" — אבטהור שנטמא הכתוב מדבר, שהוא טעון העברת שער והבאת ציפרין, ולפטור את הנזיר בקבר — בשאין טעון העברת שער והבאת ציפרין. והלא דברים קל וחומר: ומה טהור שנטמא — טעון העברת שער והבאת ציפרין, מי שהיה טמא מתחלה אינו דין שיהא טעון העברת שער והבאת ציפרין? ת"ל "וטמא ראש נזרו" — במי שהיה טהור ונטמא הכתוב מדבר, שיהא טעון העברת שער והבאת ציפרין, ולפטור את הנזיר בקבר. ש"מ. מאן תנא הא, דתנו רבנן: *אין בין טמא שנזר לנזיר טהור שנטמא, אלא שטמא שנזר שביעי שלו עולה לו מן המנין, ונזיר טהור שנטמא אין שביעי שלו עולה לו מן המנין? א"ר חסדא: רבי היא, דאמר רבי: אין נזירות טהרה חלה אלא עד שמיני. דאי תימא ר' יוסי בר' יהודה היא — האמר נזירות דטהרה משביעי הוא דחיילא. *מאי רבי ומאי ר' יוסי ברבי יהודה? דתניא: "וקדש את ראשו ביום ההוא" — גביום הבאת קרבנותיו, דברי רבי. ר' יוסי בר' יהודה אומר: ביום תגלחתו. והא דתנן: *דנזיר שנטמא טומאות הרבה אינו מביא אלא קרבן אחד, מאן תנא? אמר רב חסדא: ר' יוסי בר' יהודה היא, דאמר: נזירות טהרה משביעי חיילא. ומשכחת לה כגון שנטמא בשביעי וחזר ונטמא בשביעי, (ומני — ר' יוסי בר' יהודה היא); כיון דלא יצא שעה הראויה להביא קרבן — אינו חייב אלא קרבן אחד. דאי תימא רבי היא, אי דנטמא בשביעי וחזר ונטמא בשביעי, (וחזר ונטמא בשביעי) — כולהו טומאה אריכתא היא. ואי דנטמא בשמיני, וחזר ונטמא בשמיני — הרי יצתה שעה שראויה להביא קרבן. מאי טעמא דרבי? אמר קרא "וכפר עליו מאשר חטא על הנפש" והדר "וקדש את ראשו". ורבי יוסי ברבי יהודה: א"כ לימא קרא "וקדש את ראשו", ביום

דאי סלקא דעתך תגלחת טומאה ימי חלוטו מי לא בעי תגלחת. והכתיב "וכבס המטהר את בגדיו" וגו', והאי דינא דקא מייתי ומה נזיר בקבר כו' היכי קאתי? והא זה וזה ראויין לתגלחת. לעולם אימא לך תגלחת דטומאה א) כיון שהוזה ושנה וטבל מתגלח בשביעי שלו, והאי (א) דקא פריך: ימי חלוטו שאין שערו ראוי לתגלחת – בתגלחת דנזירות קאמר. דאילו נזירות בקבר, כשהוא (ב) מגלח מעכשיו – מתגלח על נזירות. אבל נזיר מלורע, כשמתגלח תחילה – מתגלח על שנתרפא מצרעתו. והכי קתני: ימי חלוטו שאין ראוי לתגלחת טומאה דנזיר, אלא לתגלחת דצרעת – לא כל שכן שאין עולין מן המנין דנזירות דטהרה. ולעולם אימא לך היכא דנזר והוא בבית הקברות – טעון גילוח דטומאה. תא שמע. "וכי ימות מת עליו בפתע פתאום" – בטהור שנטמא כו'. נזיר בקבר. שהיה טמא מתחילת ב) נזירות. אינו דין כו'. (ג) ג) מדקתני: ולפטור את הנזיר בקבר, שאין טעון העברת שער – שמע מינה דאין טעון גילוח ד) שער, ש"מ. אלא (ד) טמא שנזר שביעי שלו. שטובל בו, עולה לו מן המנין. דהואיל ה) ואינו בר קרבן – מתחיל למנות מבו ביום. ונזיר טהור שנטמא אין שביעי שלו עולה לו מן המנין. דאין לו טהרה עד יום שמיני, ו) שמביא קרבנותיו כו'. דתניא וקדש את ראשו. שיתחיל למנות לענין נזירות ביום הבאת קרבנותיו, שהוא שמיני, כדכתיב "וביום השמיני יביא שתי תורים". ביום תגלחתו. שהוא שביעי, כדכתיב "וגילח (ה) את ראשו ביום טהרתו ביום השביעי יגלחנו". והא דתנן נזיר שנטמא כו' מאן תנא. ז) חשיב להו טומאות הרבה, ואפ"ה לא מייתי עלייהו אלא קרבן אחד. אמר רב חסדא ר' יוסי ברבי יהודה היא. דאמר: נזירות טהרה, משביעי, שהוא יום תגלחתו, חיילא עילויה. ומשכחת לה. דתיהוי טומאות הרבה. כגון שנטמא. ומנה ששה כדי להזות ח) עליה בשלישי ובשביעי, א] וחזר ונטמא ביום ז'. דטומאה אחריתי איקרי, הואיל וטבל בו ביום. אבל בקרבן אינו חייב אלא אחד, שכל זמן שלא יצתה שעה שראויה להביא קרבן, שעדיין לא הגיע ליום ח' – אינו חייב אלא קרבן אחד. אבל אם נטמא וחזר ונטמא בששי – אינו קורא לו טומאות הרבה, לפי שעדיין לא חל עליו טהרה כלל, (ו) ודמי ט) לטומאה אריכתא. דאי אליבא דרבי – לא משכחת לה דמיקרי טומאות הרבה, ולא ליחייב אלא קרבן אחד. דאי אמרת משכחת לה, כגון שנטמא בשביעי וחזר ונטמא בשביעי – י) אינו חייב אלא קרבן אחד לסוף ימי טהרתו. כיון דנזירות דטהרה לא חיילא עליה עד יום שמיני – כולה חדא טומאה אריכתא היא, וליכא בהו טומאות הרבה. ואי אמרת כגון דנטמא כ) בשמיני, והויין להו טומאות הרבה – הא נמי לא מיתרצתא, דלא יביא אלא קרבן אחד. דאי אליבא דרבי, כיון דנטמא יום שמיני, שיצתה שעה שראויה להביא בה קרבן – נתחייב על כל ל) אחד. הילכך לא מיתוקמא מ) אלא כרבי יוסי ברבי יהודה, ש"מ. מאי טעמא דרבי. דאמר: לא חיילא עליה נזירות דטהרה עד יום הבאת קרבנותיו. דאמר קרא וכפר עליו מאשר חטא על הנפש וגו'. נ) דמשמע: אימתי "וקדש את ראשו" שיתחיל למנות – בו בזמן שכיפר עליו, דהיינו בשמיני ס).
ורב

ימי חלוטו מי לא בעי תגלחת. בסוף ימי חלוטו, כדכתיב "וכבס המטהר את בגדיו וגלח את כל שערו". אבל תגלחת דטהרה לית ביה במלורע, דגם תגלחת שניה שמגלח אחר ימי ספרו מתוך טומאה הוא מגלחה, שגם בימי ספרו מטמא אדם במגע. לא תגלחת טומאה דנזירות קתני. כלומר, לעולם אימא לך תגלחת דטומאה. ודקאמרת דבימי חלוטו נמי איכא תגלחת דטומאה – לא, תגלחת דנזירות קתני. דנזיר בקבר ראוי שערו לתגלחת מחמת נזירות, ובימי חלוטו לא בעי תגלחת דטומאה מחמת נזירות אלא מחמת צרעתו, וזה אין שייך לנזירות כלל, הילכך לא יעלו לו ימיו לנזירותו. בטהור שנטמא הכתוב מדבר. כלומר, שהתחיל למנות נזירות בטהרה, ואחרי כן נטמא, כדכתיב "והימים הראשונים יפלו". ולפטור את הנזיר בקבר שאין טעון העברת שיער והבאת ציפרים. והוא הדין דממעט ליה מאשם, דכתיב בההוא עניינא. והיינו דקאמר במתני' בנזיר בקבר אינו מביא קרבן טומאה, דמיעטיה קרא, כדדרשינן הכא. והלא דברים ק"ו. פירוש: אי לא מיעטיה קרא. ומה טהור שנטמא טעון כו' – כלומר שטומאתו הזקיקתו לכך, כל שכן היכא דנטמא מתחילתו שטמא ביותר, שהזקיקתו טומאתו לכל. ת"ל "וטמא ראש נזרו" – מיותר, דמצי למימר "וכי ימות מת [עליו] בפתע פתאום וגלח ראשו". ביום הבאת קרבנותיו. דכן כתיב בקרא "ביום השמיני יביא שתי תורים וכו' וכפר עליו מאשר חטא על הנפש וקדש ראשו ביום ההוא", שמעינן: ביום שמיני, שהוא הבאת קרבנותיו, כדמפרש לקמן בסמוך. ביום תגלחתו. הכתוב מדבר, דהיינו בשביעי. בסמוך מפרש טעמא. והא דתנן. פ' קמא דכריתות ב](דף ט.). משביעי הוא דחיילא. משביעי שמתחיל לימנות נזירות משביעי. ומשכחת טומאות הרבה, כגון שנטמא ביום שביעי וחזר ונטמא בשביעי – לסוף שביעי, אחר שהזה ושנה וטבל. דמיד כשהזה וטבל חל עליו באותו יום נזירות טהרה, שיום שביעי הוי ממנין שלשים. כי נטמא ביום שביעי כיון דחל עליה נזירות טהרה – כבר חשיב ליה טומאה אחריתי. ולא הוה כנטמא בששי, דההיא ודאי טומאה אריכתא היא, דהכתי לא חל עליה נזירות טהרה. ומכל מקום פוטר עצמו מקרבן טומאה אחר, כיון שנטמא בשביעי ולא יצא שעה אחת ליום שראוי הוא להביא קרבנות, דהיינו ביום שמיני. דאי רבי. דאמר דאינו מתחיל למנות נזירות טהרה עד יום שמיני – כולה טומאה אריכתא היא, דלא נראה עדיין להתחיל נזירות, והוי כאילו נטמא בששי, ואמאי קרי ליה טומאות הרבה? ואי דנטמא בשמיני כו', כיון דיצא לשעה שראוי להביא קרבנותיו, והוי כנטמא אחר הבאת קרבנותיו, דודאי צריך להביא קרבן טומאה אחר. דכתיב מאשר חטא על הנפש. וכתיב בההוא קרא לאלתר "וקדש ראשו ביום ההוא" – פי': ביום שכיפר עליו, דהיינו בשמיני. אם כן לימא קרא וקדש את ראשו. ופשיטא דאשמיני דקיימינן ביה איירי. "ביום ההוא" למה לי? אם אינו ענין לשמיני – תנהו לשביעי, דאייתור למשדי אשביעי.
ורבי

לעיל יז:
[כריתות ב:]
כריתות ט.

פי' הרא"ש

טהרה: מה טהור שנטמא וכו' אע"פ שתחלתו היה טהור כ"ש טמא שקבל עליו נזי' בטומאה: ביום הבאת קרבנותיו. דהיינו יום ח' אז מתחיל קדוש ראשו דהיינו גידול שער לנזירות טהרה דכתיב קדוש יהיה גדל פרע: רבי יוסי בר' יהודה אומר ביום תגלחתו. היינו בז' ולקמן מפרש טעמייהו: מני ר"י בר' יהודה [היא] דאמר נזיר טהרה מז' הוא דחיילה. הלכך קרי ביה טומאות הרבה כי כבר התחיל למנות נזירו' טהרה ומי' אינו מביא אלא קרבן א' דכיון דעדיין לא יצאת שעה שראוי להביא בה קרבן אבל לרבי דאמר נזי' דטהרה לא חיילא עד ח' אם נטמא בז' חדא טומאה אריכתא היא ואם נטמא בח' הרי ייצאת שעה שראוי להביא בה קרבן וב' קרבנות בעי למיתי: א) אימתי וקדש את ראשו בזמן שכפר. כלומר בזמן הראוי לכפרה אף אם לא כפר: א"כ לימא קרא וקדש את ראשו. ותו לא וממילא ידענא דאוכפר קאי:
א) נראה דכן היה גירסתו בגמ'.

הגהות מהר"ב רנשבורג

א] רש"י ד"ה כגון שנטמא וכו' וחזר ונטמא ביום ז' לטומאה וכו'. נ"ב עי' ת"מ: ב] תום' ד"ה ביום תגלחתו וכו' והא דתנן פ' קמא דכריתות דף ב' נ"ב כצ"ל. ולפנ' כחילופי גרסאות לעיל שהגיהו בתנם. אורח מישור:

נוסחת הריב"ן

א) דכיון: ב) נזירותו אינו דין: ג) כדאמרי': ד) שער ליתא בכ"י: ה) דאינו: ו) שמביא בו קרבן מאן תנא דנזיר טהור שנטמא אין שביעי שלו עולה לו מן המנין אמר רב חסדא רבי היא דאמר אין נזירות טהרה חלה עליו עד יום שמיני שמביא קרבנותיו דתניא וקדש כו': ז) דחשיב: ח) עליו: ט) ודמי ליה כטומאה: י) דאינו: כ) בשמיני כו': ל) אחת ואחת: מ) לא מתוקמא כר' אלא כר' יוסי: נ) (דמשמע) ליתא בכ"י: ס) בשמיני הס"ד ואחר כך מה"ד תניהו ענין לשביעי שהוא יום תגלחתו שחלה עליו נזירות: דאהדר אטמי קודם שהביא קרבנו לחייב אותו בשני קרבנות טומאה: ורב וכו':

הגהות הב"ח

(א) רש"י ד"ה לעולם וכו' והאי דקאמר ימי חלוטו כצ"ל ותיבת פריך נמחק: (ב) בא"ד כשהוא מתגלח מעכשיו: (ג) ד"ה נזיר וכו' נזירות אינו דין כו' הס"ד ואח"כ מ"ה ש"מ כו' מדקתני: (ד) ד"ה אלא שטמא שנזר: (ה) ד"ה ביום תגלחתו וכו' וגילח ראשו כצ"ל ותיבת את נמחק: (ו) ד"ה כגון שנטמא וכו' טהרה כלל וקרי ליה טומאה אריכתא הס"ד ואח"כ מ"ה דאי אליבא וכו' ואינו חייב וכו' אלא קרבן אחד דאליבא דרבי כיון דנטמא ביום שמיני וכו' נתחייב קרבן על כל אחד כצ"ל והד"א ותיבת לאו נמחק:

יז א מיי' פ"ו מהלכות נזירות הלכה טו:
יח ב מיי' שם הל' יב:

"בַּיּוֹם הַהוּא" לָמָּה לִי? אִם אֵינוֹ עִנְיָן לַשְּׁמִינִי, תְּנֵהוּ עִנְיָן לַשְּׁבִיעִי. וְרַבִּי נַמִי, הָכְתִיב "בַּיּוֹם הַהוּא"! אָמַר לָךְ רַבִּי: הַהוּא לְהָכִי הוּא דְּאָתָא, לוֹמַר לָךְ: אע"פ שֶׁלֹּא הֵבִיא קָרְבְּנוֹתָיו. וְרַב חִסְדָּא, מַאי דּוּחְקֵיהּ לְאוֹקְמֵיהּ כר' יוֹסֵי בְּרַבִּי יְהוּדָה? לוֹקְמָהּ כְּגוֹן דְּנִטְמָא דְּחַזְיָא בְּלֵיל שְׁמִינִי, וְרַבִּי הִיא! מִדְּלָא מוֹקִים לָהּ כְּרַבִּי, לֵימָא קָסָבַר *לֵילְיָא לָאו מְחוּסַּר זְמַן הוּא? אֲמַר רַב אַדָּא בַּר אַהֲבָה: *הָא בְּהָא תַּלְיָא; אִי אָמְרַתְּ לֵילְיָא מְחוּסַּר זְמַן, אֵימַת מֶיחֱזֵי לְקָרְבָּן — לְצַפְרָא, נְזִירוּת נַמִי לָא חָיְילָא עַד צַפְרָא. וְאִי אָמְרַתְּ לֵילְיָא אֵינוֹ מְחוּסַּר זְמַן — נְזִירוּת טָהֳרָה חָיְילָא מֵאוּרְתָּא.§

(א) גּוּפָא, נִטְמָא בַּשְּׁבִיעִי וְחָזַר וְנִטְמָא בַּשְּׁבִיעִי — אֵינוֹ מֵבִיא אֶלָּא קָרְבָּן אֶחָד. נִטְמָא בַּשְּׁמִינִי וְחָזַר וְנִטְמָא בַּשְּׁמִינִי מֵבִיא קָרְבָּן עַל כָּל אֶחָד וְאֶחָד. מַתְחִיל וּמוֹנֶה מִיָּד, *דִּבְרֵי ר' [א] אֱלִיעֶזֶר, וחכ"א: אקָרְבָּן אֶחָד עַל הַכֹּל, עַד שֶׁיָּבִיא חַטָּאתוֹ. הֵבִיא חַטָּאתוֹ וְנִטְמָא, וְהֵבִיא חַטָּאתוֹ וְנִטְמָא — מֵבִיא קָרְבָּן עַל כָּל אֶחָד וְאֶחָד. בהֵבִיא חַטָּאתוֹ וְלֹא הֵבִיא אֲשָׁמוֹ — מוֹנֶה. *ר' יִשְׁמָעֵאל בְּנוֹ שֶׁל רַבִּי יוֹחָנָן בֶּן בְּרוֹקָה אוֹמֵר: כְּשֵׁם שֶׁחַטָּאתוֹ עִיכַּבְתּוֹ (ב) — כֵּן אֲשָׁמוֹ מְעַכְּבוֹ. בִּשְׁלָמָא לְרַבִּי [ב] אֱלִיעֶזֶר, אָמַר קְרָא °"וְקִדֵּשׁ אֶת רֹאשׁוֹ בַּיּוֹ' הַהוּא" — אע"פ שֶׁלֹּא הֵבִיא קָרְבְּנוֹתָיו. וְרַבָּנַן: "הַהוּא" — אע"פ שֶׁלֹּא הֵבִיא אֲשָׁמוֹ. אֶלָּא רַבִּי יִשְׁמָעֵאל, "הַהוּא" לָמָּה לִי? אָמַר לָךְ: "הַהוּא" — אע"פ שֶׁלֹּא הֵבִיא עוֹלָתוֹ. וְרַבָּנַן: עוֹלָה לָא בָּעֵי מִיעוּטָא, דּוֹרוֹן בְּעָלְמָא הוּא. מַאי טַעֲמַיְיהוּ דְּרַבָּנַן? דְּתַנְיָא: °"וְהִזִּיר לַה' אֶת יְמֵי נִזְרוֹ וְהֵבִיא כֶּבֶשׂ בֶּן שְׁנָתוֹ לְאָשָׁם" מַה ת"ל? לְפִי שֶׁמָּצִינוּ שֶׁכָּל אֲשָׁמוֹת שֶׁבַּתּוֹרָה שֶׁהֵן מְעַכְּבִין, יָכוֹל אַף זֶה מְעַכְּבוֹ — ת"ל

במדבר ו | שם

רַב חִסְדָּא מַאי דּוּחְקֵיהּ לְאוֹקְמֵיהּ כְּרַבִּי יוֹסֵי בְּרַבִּי יְהוּדָה לוֹקְמָהּ(ג) כְּרַבִּי. וּמַשְׁכַּחַתְּ א) לָהּ דְּאִית בְּהוּ טוּמְאוֹת הַרְבֵּה. כְּגוֹן דְּחַזְיָא בְּלֵיל שְׁמִינִי. כְּלוֹמַר, דְּנִטְמָא בְּלֵיל שְׁמִינִי. וְהַאי דְּקָאָמַר "דְּחַזְיָא" — לָאו דַּוְקָא הָכָא, אֶלָּא אַיְּידֵי ב) דְּנָקִיט לָהּ בְּמַסֶּ' כְּרֵיתוֹת נַקְטֵיהּ לְהָכָא. וְחָזַר וְנִטְמָא בְּלֵיל שְׁמִינִי. דְּטוּמְאוֹת הַרְבֵּה אִיכָּא, מִכֵּיוָן דְּנִטְמָא בְּלֵיל ח' וְחָיְילָא עֲלֵיהּ טָהֳרָה. וְאֵינוֹ חַיָּיב עֲלֵיהֶן אֶלָּא קָרְבָּן אֶחָד, לְפִי שֶׁעֲדַיִין לֹא הִגִּיעַ יוֹם שְׁמִינִי ג) שֶׁהָיְתָה שָׁעָה הָרְאוּיָה לְהָבִיא בָּהּ קָרְבָּן. וּמִדְּלָא מוֹקִים לָהּ. רַב חִסְדָּא בְּכה"ג וְאַלִּיבָּא דְּרַבִּי — תִּיפְשׁוֹט מִינָּהּ דְּאִית לֵיהּ לְרַב חִסְדָּא דְּלַיְלָה לָאו מְחוּסַּר זְמַן הוּא, ד) דְּאִם נִטְמָא בְּלֵיל שְׁמִינִי — הָוֵה כְּנִטְמָא בְּיוֹם שְׁמִינִי, דְּנִטְמָא בְּשָׁעָה שֶׁרְאוּיָה לְהָבִיא קָרְבָּן. אע"ג דְּאֵינוֹ קָרֵב עַד הַיּוֹם א] — דָּמְיָא הַלַּיְלָה לְיוֹם, וְחַיָּיב קָרְבָּן עַל כָּל אַחַת וְאַחַת. אָמַר רַב אַדָּא בַּר אַהֲבָה. אֲפִילּוּ אִי אִית לֵיהּ לְרַב חִסְדָּא דְּלַיְלָה מְחוּסַּר זְמַן הוּא, הָכִּי לָא מְתוֹקְמָא לֵיהּ כְּרַבִּי, דְּהָא בְּהָא תַּלְיָא. דְּאִי אָמְרַתְּ לְרַבִּי מְחוּסַּר זְמַן הָוְיָא אֵימַת מִיתְחֲזֵי לְקָרְבָּן לְצַפְרָא וּנְזִירוּת טָהֳרָה נַמִי לָא חָיְילָא עֲלֵיהּ עַד צַפְרָא. וְהִילְכָּךְ כִּי מִיטַּמֵּי בְּלֵיל שְׁמִינִי כּוּלָּהּ טוּמְאָה אֲרִיכְתָּא הִיא, וְלֵית לָךְ לְמֵימַר בְּהוּ טוּמְאוֹת הַרְבֵּה. וְאִי אָמְרַתְּ דִּלְרַבִּי אֵינוֹ מְחוּסַּר זְמַן, דְּלַיְלָה נַמִי ה) זְמַן הַקְרָבָה וְאִית בְּהוּ טוּמְאוֹת הַרְבֵּה — נְזִירוּת טָהֳרָה נַמִי חָיְילָא מֵאוּרְתָּא, וְחַיָּיב קָרְבָּן עַל כָּל טוּמְאָה וְטוּמְאָה, הִילְכָּךְ לָא מִיתּוֹקְמָא כְּרַבִּי כְּלָל. ה"ג: ת"ר נִטְמָא בַּשְּׁבִיעִי וְחָזַר וְנִטְמָא כו' וְאִית סְפָרִים ו) דְּגָרְסִי בֵּיהּ גּוּפָא: נִטְמָא בַּשְּׁבִיעִי כו', וְשִׁבּוּשָׁא הוּא, דְּקי"ל דְּכָל הֵיכָא דְּכָתַב "גּוּפָא" דְּכְבָר נִשְׁנֵית הַהִיא שְׁמַעְתָּא לְעֵיל, וְאִילּוּ הָכָא לֹא נִשְׁנֵית כְּלָל. מַתְחִיל וּמוֹנֶה. לִנְזִירוּת טָהֳרָה מִיָּד, כֵּיוָן שֶׁהִגִּיעַ שְׁמִינִי, ז) וַאֲפִילּוּ שֶׁלֹּא הֵבִיא קָרְבְּנוֹתָיו. דִּבְרֵי ר' אֱלִיעֶזֶר: ח) וַחכ"א קָרְבָּן אֶחָד עַל הַכֹּל עַד שֶׁיָּבִיא חַטָּאתוֹ הֵבִיא חַטָּאתוֹ וְנִטְמָא מֵבִיא קָרְבָּן עַל כָּל אַחַת וְאַחַת הֵבִיא חַטָּאתוֹ וְלֹא הֵבִיא אֲשָׁמוֹ מוֹנֶה. נְזִירוּת דְּטָהֳרָה. אֲבָל אִם לֹא הֵבִיא חַטָּאתוֹ — אֵינוֹ מוֹנֶה. לְעוֹלָם אֵין מַתְחִילִין לִמְנוֹת לִנְזִירוּת טָהֳרָה עַד שֶׁיָּבִיא חַטָּאתוֹ, אֶחָד מֵהַלָּלוּ ט) שְׁנֵי תוֹרִים שֶׁמֵּבִיא אֶחָד לְחַטָּאת. שֶׁאִם נִטְמָא קוֹדֶם שֶׁהֵבִיא חַטָּאתוֹ — אֵינוֹ מֵבִיא אֶלָּא קָרְבָּן טוּמְאָה אֶחָד, אֲבָל אִם הֵבִיא חַטָּאתוֹ וְלֹא הֵבִיא אֲשָׁמוֹ, כֶּבֶשׂ בֶּן שְׁנָתוֹ לְאָשָׁם — מוֹנֶה לִנְזִירוּת יְמֵי טָהֳרָה. י) כָּךְ אֲשָׁמוֹ מְעַכְּבוֹ. שֶׁלֹּא יַתְחִיל לִמְנוֹת עַד שֶׁיָּבִיא אֲשָׁמוֹ. בִּשְׁלָמָא לְר' אֱלִיעֶזֶר. דְּקָאָמַר: מַתְחִיל וּמוֹנֶה מִיָּד. אע"פ שֶׁלֹּא הֵבִיא קָרְבָּנוֹת. כ) מַתְחִיל לִמְנוֹת מִבּוֹ בַּיּוֹם. וּלְרַבָּנַן אָתָא לֵיהּ "הַהוּא" — אע"פ שֶׁלֹּא הֵבִיא אֶת אֲשָׁמוֹ. אע"פ שֶׁלֹּא הֵבִיא עוֹלָתוֹ. שֶׁהָאֶחָד לְעוֹלָה. וּבִלְבַד שֶׁהֵבִיא אֲשָׁמוֹ וְחַטָּאתוֹ מַתְחִיל לִמְנוֹת. מִשּׁוּם עוֹלָה לָא (ד) ל) מִיבַּעְיָא. דְּהִיא לָא אָתְיָא לֹא מִשּׁוּם עוֹלָה וְלֹא מִשּׁוּם נְזִירוּת, אֶלָּא לְדוֹרוֹן בְּעָלְמָא. מ) כָּל הָאֲשָׁמוֹת שֶׁבַּתּוֹרָה מְעַכְּבִין. כִּדְאָמְרִינַן (יבמות דף עד:): הֵבִיא כַּפָּרָתוֹ — אוֹכֵל בַּקֳּדָשִׁים.
ת"ל

ורבי ביום ההוא למה לי. דממילא ידעינן דאשמיני קאי. אע"פ שלא הביא קרבנותיו. דפשטיה דקרא משמע דלא חייל עליה נזירות עד שיכפר בעולה ובחטאת, דכתיב בקרא [קודם] "וקדש ראשו", והשתא אתי יתורא ד"ביום ההוא" לאשמועינן דחייל עליה נזירות ביום שמיני, אע"פ שלא הביא קרבנותיו. לוקמה כרבי וכגון שנטמא בליל שמיני. דחייל עליה נזירות קודם הבאת קרבנותיו. ול"ג ["דחזא"]. פי': כיון [דמרבינן] לרבי ביום השמיני, אע"פ שלא הביא קרבנותיו – א"כ גם בליל שמיני חייל עליה נזירות, ושייך ליום שמיני. ומעתה נוקי למתני' כרבי, דנטמא בליל ח', דכיון דחייל עליה נזירות – טומאות הרבה יש כאן, ומ"מ פוטר עצמו בקרבן אחד – לפי שלא יצא שעה אחת הראויה להביא קרבנותיו, דאין מקריבין קרבנות בלילה, מ"ביום צוותו". מדלא מוקי לה הכי – נימא קסבר ליליא לאו מחוסר זמן הוא. פי': ולא לענין שיוכל להקריבו בלילה, אלא דחשבינן ליה כילא לשעה שראוי להקריב קרבנותיו, ולא יפטר בקרבן טומאה אחד. הא בהא תליא. ולא מצי אתיא כרבי. ה"ג אי אמרת לילה מחוסר זמן, אימת מייתי קרבן עד צפרא – נזירות נמי לא חייל עד צפרא ד"כפר וקדש" כתיב, בשעה שראויה להביא קרבן חייל נזירות טהרה. כי נטמא בלילה לא הוו טומאות הרבה אלא טומאה אריכתא. ואי קסבר לילה לאו מחוסר זמן, להחשב כשעה שראויה להקריב בלילה – נזירות נמי חייל מאמתה, ומיחייב קרבן טומאה על כל אחת ואחת. אית ספרים דגרסי ביה: גופא נטמא בשביעי כו'. ולא גרסינן, דבכולה התלמוד לא גרסינן "גופא" אלא כשהתלמוד הביא מימרא או ברייתא תחילה ומייתי אותה אגב גררא – אז חוזר ואומר "גופא" לפרש המימרא או הברייתא. אבל ברייתא לא הביא התלמוד כלל לעיל, אלא מלישנא דהתלמוד לעיל דקאמר: אילימא שנטמא בשביעי. אינו מביא אלא קרבן אחד. אע"ג דס"ל דחייל עליה נזירות טהרה משביעי, כיון דנטמא עד שלא האיר השמיני, שעה הראויה להביא קרבנותיו – נפטר בקרבן אחד על טומאות הרבה. אבל כשנטמא בשמיני וחזר ונטמא בח', כיון שיצא לשעה הראויה להביא קרבנותיו – מביא קרבן על כל אחד ואחד. מתחיל ומונה מיד דברי ר' אליעזר וכו'. לכאורה הוה משמע דמתחיל מנין נזירות טהרה שלו בשמיני. ⊕אלא אי אפשר לומר כן, דאי לא חייל עליה נזירות טהרה שלו אלא בשמיני – א"כ כי נטמא בשמיני לא סותר אלא יום אחד, ולא הוה מתחייב קרבן טומאה לרבי אליעזר, [כדתנן] במתני': ר"א אומר לא [בו] ביום. אלא מתחיל ומונה מיד בשביעי, דאז חייל עליה נזירות טהרה מכי הזה וטבל (מכי הזה וטבל), וכי נטמא בשמיני – סותר ב' ימים, ומתחייב שפיר בקרבן ב] ובטומאה לרבי אליעזר. וחכ"א קרבן אחד על הכל עד שיביא חטאתו כו'. רבנן סבירא להו דלא חייל נזירות טהרה עליה עד שיביא חטאתו. הביא חטאתו ולא הביא אשמו – מונה נזירות טהרה. [וטעמייהו] יליף בסמוך. כך אשמו מעכבתו. דלא חייל עליה נזירות טהרה עד שיביא גם אשמו. וטעמיה מפרש בסמוך.

בשלמא לר' אליעזר אמר קרא וקדש ראשו ביום ההוא. מיותר "ביום ההוא" לרבות ביום השביעי, דמשביעי חייל עליה נזירות טהרה כדפרישית לעיל לר"א. ולשון התלמוד דקאמר "אע"פ שלא הביא קרבנותיו" הוי פירושו: אע"פ שלא הגיע יום הראוי קצת להביא קרבנותיו, דהיינו יום ז'. ולא הוי פירושו כההוא דלעיל דקאמר התלמוד אליבא דרבי: "ביום ההוא" מיותר, לומר לך אע"פ שלא הביא קרבנותיו. דההוא ולאי הוי פירושו לרבות יום שמיני דוקא משהאיר הבקר, אבל אליבא דר"א אתא [לרבות] אפילו יום השביעי, כדפי': ולרבנן ההוא אע"פ שלא הביא אשמו. אע"ג שכל אשמות שבתורה מעכבות, הכא מרבינן מ"ההוא" דלא מעכב ליה מלחול עליה נזירות טהרה. אלא לר' ישמעאל "ההוא" מאי אתא לרבויי? אמר לך: אע"פ שלא הביא עולתו. ורבנן עולה לא בעיא מיעוטא דדורון בעלמא הוא. וא"ת: מ"ט דרבי ישמעאל? ספיר קאמרי ליה רבנן! וי"ל: משום דחטאת ועולה כתיבי בחד קרא, והדר כתיב "וכפר עליו וקדש ראשו". דס"ד דאע"ג דעולה דורון הוא, כיון דלקדמיה קרא ל"וקדש ראשו" לא חייל עליה נזירות טהרה עד דמייתי לעולה נמי, קא משמע לן "ההוא" לומר: אע"פ שלא הביא עולתו. ומסתברא לאוקמי לעולה ולא לחטאת, דעיקר כפרה בחטאת. וא"ת: מנא ליה להתלמוד לעיל לומר דפשיטות אליבא דרבי דההוא (מפרש) מרבה אע"פ שלא הביא קרבנותיו, פי': משהאיר השמיני חייל עליה נזירות טהרה? דלמא לא מרבה רבי אלא הביא חטאתו ולא אשמו, או כר' ישמעאל?! וי"ל

ור' סבר דמה"ד הוא דחיילא נזי' טהרה אע"פ שלא הביא קרבן. ורבנן סברי דלא חיילא עד שיביא חטאתו. ור' ישמעאל אומר אפילו אשמו. וא"ת הא דקאמר רב חסדא לעיל אי בנטמא בח' וחזר ונטמא בח' הרי יצאת שעה שראוי להביא בה קרבן מנליה דר' דלא כרבנן ולא כר' ישמעאל. וי"ל דלשנא דמילתיה דר' משמע מדקאמר ביום הבאת קרבנותיו בסתם ולא פירש עד שיביא חטאתו או אשמו. משמע דהיום גורם אע"פ שלא הביא כלל. ורבנן ההוא אע"פ שלא הביא אשמו. ודוקא אשם דבתר ב' תורים או ב' בני יונה כתיב ... ר' ישמעאל ההוא אע"פ שלא הביא עולתו [דמעולה] (דמעילא) סליק דעולה דורון

פי' הרא"ש

ביום ההוא למה לי תנהו ענין לז'. כלומר ביום ההוא של תגלחתו: לוקמה כר' וכגון שנטמא בליל ח' דקרי' ביה טומאות הרבה דמתחיל' ליל ח' חלה עליו נזירות טהרה וחדא קרבן הוא דמייתי דאכתי לא יצאת שעה שראוי להביא קרבן עד למחר. ומדלא מוקי לה הכי ש"מ קסבר לילה לאו מחוסר זמן דכל דבר שזמנו ביום מתחלת הלילה יש לו דין היום אע"פ שאינו מביא קרבן בלילה הילכך מביא ב' קרבנות: הא בהא תליא. כלומר לא מצית למפשט דלילה לאו מחוסר זמן הוא מדלא אוקמא כר' דאפי' אי לילה מחוסר זמן לא מצי לאוקמה כר' דאי אמרת לילה מחוסר זמן אימת מחזי לקרבן נזיר מצפרא טהרה נמי לא חיילא עד צפרא דוכפר וקדש את ראשו בשעה הראויה להביא קרבן חייל עליה נזי' טהרה וכי נטמא בלילה טומאה אריכתא הוא. ואי אמרת לילה לאו מחוסר זמן נזי' טהרה חלה מאורתא וכי נטמא בלילה מביא קרבן על כל א' וא' כמו שנטמא ביום ח': גופא נטמא בז' וכו'. הך גופא לא הוי כשאר גופא שבתלמוד אלא שלשון נזיר משונה שהרי לא הביא זאת הברייתא לעיל אלא משום דרבי ורבי יוסי איירי לעיל בהך ענינא אמרי גופא: מתחיל ומונה מיד. פי' מיד בז' אחר שהזה וטבל דס"ל דנזי' טהרה חיילא בז' כר' יוסי בר יהודה. וכן מוכח לקמן פ' כ"ג דתנן ואינו מתחיל למנות עד שיטהר ומיבעי' ליה בגמ' עד שיטהר בז' ומני ר"א היא. והאי דקים ליה לתלמוד הכי ולא בעי לפרושי מתחיל ומונה מיד בח' אע"פ שלא הביא קרבן לאפוקי מדרבנן דאמרי דאינו מביא קרבן על טומאתו ואינו מתחיל למנות עד שיביא חטאתו משום דר"א הוא דקאמר במתני' לא בו ביום דאם נטמא ביום ראשון לנזירותו אינו סותר א"כ ע"כ מדהביא קרבן על טומאתו שנטמא בח' צ"ל שהתחיל למנות נזירותו מאתמול ולקמן דקאמר ר"א היא הוה מצי למי' ר"י ברבי יהודה היא. וכן לעיל הוה מצי למימר ר"א היא: ביום ההוא אע"פ שלא הביא קרבנותיו כלומר אע"פ שלא הגיע זמן הבאת קרבנותיו דהיינו משביעי וכדדריש ר"י בר' יהודה לעיל. וארבע מחלוקות דר"י בר' יהודה ור"א משביעי הוא דחיילא נזי' טהרה

הגהות הגר"א

[א] גמ' אליעזר נמחק. (ובזה א"ש לכ"מ שהקשו התוס' בזה לגרסת דידן ר"א): [ב] שם אליעזר נמחק:

[חגיגה ט: ושם נסמן]

[שבת קלה: וש"נ]

גליון הש"ס

גמ' הביא חטאתו. עיין לקמן דף מז ע"ב תד"ה וסופרין: תוס' ד"ה מתחיל ומונה מיד כו' אלא א"א לומר כן. ע' לקמן ד' נד ע"א:

[לקמן נו.]

[פסחים נט. ע"ש ערכין כא. ע"ש]

נוסחת הריב"ן

א) להו כרבי: ב) דנקטו בה גבי זיבה במסכת: ג) שהיתה: ד) מחוסר זמן הוא להקרבה דלילי שמיני נמי הוי שעה שראויה להביא קרבן ומשו"ה מחייב קרבן על כל אחת ואחת והשתא ליתא: ה) מחזי לקרבה: ו) דלכתיב כהו: ז) ואע"פ: ח) וחכמים: ט) כגון כהן כתוב כאן בזה"ל וכו' ה"ג ותו חכ"א קרבן א' על הכל עד שיביא חטאתו הביא חטאתו ונטמא מביא קרבן על כל אחת ואחת הביא חטאתו ולא הביא אשמו מונה ואין מתחילין כו': י) וכן: כ) ואע"פ: ל) לא בעיא מיעוטא דהא לא אתיא לא משום טומאה ולא משום נזירות: מ) כב"ב כתוב כאן בזה"ל לפי שמצינו בכל אשמות שבתורה שהן מעכבין כלומר דמעכבין כפרתו אוכל בקדשים אשמו מעכבו

הגהות הב"ח

(א) גמ' חיילא מאורתא תנו רבנן נטמא בשביעי: (ב) שם כך אשמו מעכבו: (ג) רש"י ד"ה רב חסדא וכו' לוקמה כרבי ומשכחת לה לרבי דאית בהו טומאות הרבה כגון וכו' ומשכחת לה בליל שמיני: (ד) ד"ה משום עולה לא מבעיא דהיא לא אתיא לא משום טומאה ולא משום

הגהות מהר"ב רנשבורג א] רש"י ד"ה ומדלא מוקים לה וכו' עד היום רמיא וכו'. אע"ג דאינו קרב עד היום ... ב] תוד"ה מתחיל ומונה מיד דברי ר"א וכו' מכי הזה וטבל וכי נטמא בשמיני וכו' ומתחייב ספיר בקרבן טומאה לר"א כצ"ל:

תורה אור

ת"ל "וְהִזִּיר... וְהֵבִיא" – אע"פ שֶׁלֹּא הֵבִיא – הִזִּיר. רַבִּי יִשְׁמָעֵאל בְּנוֹ שֶׁל רַבִּי יוֹחָנָן בֶּן בְּרוֹקָה אוֹמֵר: "וְהִזִּיר... וְהֵבִיא", *אֵימָתַי הִזִּיר – בִּזְמַן שֶׁהֵבִיא. מַאן תְּנָא לְהָא, *דת"ר: [א]אִשָּׁה שֶׁנָּדְרָה בְּנָזִיר וְנִטְמְאָה, ואח"כ הֵפֵר לָהּ בַּעְלָהּ – מְבִיאָה חַטַּאת הָעוֹף, וְאֵינָהּ מְבִיאָה עוֹלַת הָעוֹף? אֲמַר רַב חִסְדָּא: ר' יִשְׁמָעֵאל הִיא. מַאי קָסָבַר? אִי קָסָבַר *בַּעַל מִיעֲקַר עָקַר – חַטַּאת הָעוֹף נַמִי לָא לַיְיתֵי, אִי קָסָבַר בַּעַל מֵיגַז גָּיֵיז – עוֹלַת הָעוֹף נַמִי לַיְיתֵי! לְעוֹלָם קָסָבַר בַּעַל מִיעֲקַר עָקַר, ור' יִשְׁמָעֵאל סָבַר לָהּ כר' אֶלְעָזָר הַקַּפָּר. *דְּתַנְיָא, ר' אֶלְעָזָר הַקַּפָּר בְּרַבִּי אוֹמֵר: מַה ת"ל °"וְכִפֶּר עָלָיו מֵאֲשֶׁר חָטָא עַל הַנָּפֶשׁ"? וְכִי בְּאֵיזוֹ נֶפֶשׁ חָטָא זֶה? אֶלָּא שֶׁצִּיעֵר עַצְמוֹ מִן הַיַּיִן. וק"ו: וּמַה זֶּה שֶׁלֹּא צִיעֵר עַצְמוֹ אֶלָּא מִן הַיַּיִן – נִקְרָא חוֹטֵא, הַמְצַעֵר עַצְמוֹ מִכָּל דָּבָר – עַל אַחַת כַּמָּה וְכַמָּה. וְהָא בְּנָזִיר טָמֵא כְּתִיב, וַאֲנַן אֲפִילּוּ נָזִיר טָהוֹר קָאָמְרִינַן! קָסָבַר ר' אֶלְעָזָר הַקַּפָּר: נָזִיר טָהוֹר נַמִי חוֹטֵא הוּא, וְהַיְינוּ טַעֲמָא דִּכְתִיב בְּנָזִיר טָמֵא – הוֹאִיל וְשָׁנָה בְּחֵטְא.§ "יָצָא וְנִכְנַס עוֹלִין לוֹ מִן הַמִּנְיָן".§ קָתָנֵי "עוֹלִין לוֹ מִן הַמִּנְיָן", מִשּׁוּם דְּיָצָא חָל עֲלֵיהּ נְזִירוּת? אָמַר שְׁמוּאֵל: [ב]כְּגוֹן שֶׁיָּצָא וְהִזָּה, וְשָׁנָה וְטָבַל. אֶלָּא נִכְנַס הוּא דְּעוֹלִין לוֹ מִן הַמִּנְיָן, לֹא נִכְנַס אֵין עוֹלִין לוֹ מִן הַמִּנְיָן?! לָא מִיבַּעְיָא קָאָמַר; לָא מִיבַּעְיָא יָצָא, אֶלָּא אֲפִילּוּ נִכְנַס – עוֹלִין לוֹ מִן הַמִּנְיָן. אֲמַרוּ לֵיהּ רַב כָּהֲנָא וְרַב אַסִּי לְרַב: *מ"ט לָא מְפָרַשְׁתְּ לָן כְּהָלֵין מִילֵּי? אֲמַר לְהוֹן: אָמִינָא דִּלְמָא לָא צְרִיכִיתוּ.§ "רַבִּי אֱלִיעֶזֶר* אוֹמֵר לֹא בּוֹ בַּיּוֹם שֶׁנֶּאֱמַר °"וְהַיָּמִים הָרִאשׁוֹנִים יִפְּלוּ" עַד שֶׁיִּהְיוּ יָמִים רִאשׁוֹנִים".§ אָמַר עוּלָּא: לֹא אָמַר רַבִּי אֱלִיעֶזֶר אֶלָּא בְּטָמֵא שֶׁנָּזַר, אֲבָל בְּנָזִיר טָהוֹר שֶׁנִּטְמָא, אֲפִילּוּ יוֹם אֶחָד – סוֹתֵר. אֲמַר

במדבר ו | שם

רש"י

ת"ל והזיר. לה' את ימי נזרו והביא א) [כבש בן שנתו לאשם]. לפיכך הקדים הכתוב "והזיר" להבאת אשמו – לומר לך: אע"פ שלא הביא הזיר. **אימתי הזיר.** אימתי מתחיל למנות ימי נזירות – בזמן שהביא. **מאן תנא להא דת"ר האשה שנדרה כו' ואינה מביאה עולת העוף.** למאן איצטריך למיתני דאינה מביאה עולת העוף. **אמר רב חסדא ר' ישמעאל היא.** דלדידיה חשיב ליה עולת העוף. דאי לרבנן – לא איצטריכא ליה למיתני שאינה מביאה עולת העוף, דהא אמרינן עולת העוף לא מיעכבא, דלא אתיא אלא משום דורון בעלמא, ג) ופשיטא שאינה צריכה להביא. **לשון אחר** אמר לנו המורה. **אמר רב חסדא** א] ר' ישמעאל היא ומאי קסבר כו'. **מיגז גייז.** דמהשתא ואילך לא מיחייבא בנזירות – עולת העוף נמי לייתי. **לעולם** ד) **מיעקר עקר. והאי** ה) **דמביאה חטאת העוף** – ו) לא משום נזירות, אלא משום שצערה עצמה מן היין. **וסבר לה כרבי אלעזר הקפר.** אבל עולת העוף לא ז) אתיא ליה אלא משום נזירות. והילכך מיתוקמא לה כר' ישמעאל ולא כרבנן. דאי רבנן, כיון דאמרי משום דורון בעלמא קמייתי ליה, ולא משום נזירות – הכא נמי אמאי מייתי ליה, ולית ביה משום הבאת חולין לעזרה. אבל לרבי ישמעאל, כיון דמשום חובה קמייתי ליה ובעל מיעקר עקר ליה – אי אפשר ליה להביא עולת העוף, דאי מייתי ליה – נמצא שמביא חולין לעזרה. **והא האי קרא בנזיר טמא כתיב ואנן** ח) **אפילו נזיר טהור קאמרינן.** דקרי חוטא, משום שציער עצמו מן היין. לר"א הקפר נזיר טהור נמי הוי חוטא. ט) ודין הוא דהוה ליה למיכתביה להאי "וכפר עליו מאשר חטא על הנפש" בנזיר טהור, והאי דכתביה בנזיר טמא – הואיל ושנה בחטא, שכבר הזיר עצמו מן היין, ועכשיו שונה בחטא, שהיה לו להזהר מן הטומאה, ונטמא. **משום דיצא.** בתמיה, חל עליו נזירות?! והא הוי טמא י) בזמן שעמד בבית הקברות! **אמר שמואל כגון שיצא והזה כו'.** (א) כדמפרש לעיל. **ואלא כי נכנס.** ונטמא, אמרינן דעולין לו מן המנין, וחל עליה נזירות דטהרה. הא לא נכנס והוי טהור – אין עולין לו מן המנין, ולא חיילא עליה נזירות דטהרה?! אדרבה, כי לא נכנס והוי טהור – כ"ש דחל עליה נזירות דטהרה! **אלא אפילו נכנס.** דס"ד, דכיון דנכנס הו"ל כמעיקרו כ) שנזר והוא בבית הקברות, ולא יהו עולין לו מן המנין, ולא חיילא עליה נזירות דטהרה – קמשמע לן, כיון שיצא והזה ושנה וטבל – ל) דהו"ל נזיר טהור, מ) וחיילא עליה נזירות דטהרה. ואי הדר איטמי – מביא קרבן טומאה.

תוספות

וי"ל: משום דרבי לא אדכר במילתיה ב] כ"א דהבאת קרבן הכתוב מדבר, משמע דלא קפיד עליה אלא איום שמיני, ולמעוטי שביעי דבר פלוגתי'. אבל הני תנאי מפרשי דמיחל נזירות תלוי בקרבנות עצמו, למר כדאית ליה ולמר כדאית ליה. **ת"ל והזיר והביא אשמו אע"פ שלא הביא אשמו והזיר.** פירוש: חייל עליה נזירות טהרה, דבהכי משתמעי קרא. וא"ת: אם כן לרבנן "ההוא" למה לי? תיפוק ליה מ"והזיר" ברישא והדר "והביא"? ג] וי"ל: אי לאו "ההוא" הוה דרשינן ["והזיר"] לרבות אע"פ שלא הביא עולתו, ולעולם אשם מעכב – כתב רחמנא "ההוא", ומגלי דאית לן למדרש: והזיר אע"פ שלא הביא. ומש"ה צריכי למיכתב תרתי. **ונטמאה.** והפרישה שתי תורים, אחד לעולה ואחד לחטאת, ואשם בהמה, להביא קרבנות נזיר טמא. ואח"כ היפר לה בעלה, ונמצא שהנדר נעקר למפרע, וכאילו לא היתה נזירה כלל – מביאה חטאת העוף, [ואינה מביאה] עולת העוף, כדמפרש ואזיל. **אמר רב חסדא ר' ישמעאל היא.** דמרבה לעיל מ"ההוא" אע"פ שלא הביא עולתו, אלמא עולת נזיר לאו דורון הוא וכפרה תלויה בה. דאי כרבנן דאמרי לעיל עולה דורון הוא – אמאי לא תביא עולת העוף? אע"פ דהפר לה בעלה ואינה נזירה – אין כאן חולין, דכל אימת *מצי לאיתויי מייתי דורון! [אלא] ודאי רבי ישמעאל היא, דסבירא ליה עולה דנזיר לאו דורון הוא. ואם תאמר: כ"ש דחטאת נמי לאו דורון הוא, והיכי מייתי חטאת כי הפר לה ואין כאן נזירות למפרע? וי"ל: משום דבסמוך מוקמינן לה כר"א הקפר דצריכה כפרה על שהפרישה עצמה מן היין, ואע"ג שהפר לה, הילכך חטאת מייתי, לפי שמצינו בעלמא חטאת ד] באה על הספק – גם כאן בעילה כל דהוא מביאה חטאת העוף. אבל עולת העוף, כיון דלאו דורון הוא, לא מצית לאתויי כיון דהיפר לה בעלה. **[אי קסבר בעל] מיעקר קעקר.** [נמצא] שלא חל עליה נזירות מעולם – חטאת העוף נמי לא תייתי.

ואי בעל מיגז גייז. פירוש: מכאן ולהבא – עולת העוף נמי תייתי, דהא אתמול כי נטמא – נזירה היתה. ולקמן מיבעיא לן באידך פירקין (דף כא:) אי מיעקר קא עקר אי מיגז גייז. **לעולם** קסבר מיעקר קא עקר. דאי מיגז גייז – עולת העוף ואשם בעי איתויי. **סבר** כר"א הקפר. דאף נזיר טהור חוטא הוי. הלכך זאת שנטמאה כמו כן בעיא כפרה, דמצינו חטאת העוף באה על הספק ה]אם כן, עולה לא מייתי. **המצער** עצמו מכל דבר על אחת כמה וכמה. אלמא חוטא הוא, לכך מייתי חטאת העוף. ודוקא אם נטמאה, אבל אם לא נטמאה והפר לה בעלה, נהי נמי דבעיא כפרה על שציערה עצמה – לא תביא כלום. משום שאם לא היפר [לה] ו] – מביאה חטאת בהמה, שאינו בא על הספק, ואם כן עתה, כשהיפר לה – לא תביאנו. וחטאת העוף לא מציא לאתויי, כיון דמעיקרא אי לא היפר לה לא היתה מביאתו, א"כ כשהיפר לה – לא ניתן לה דין חדש. **ואנן** אפילו נזיר טהור קאמרינן. כלומר, אית ליה לר"א הקפר בעלמא, דאפילו נזיר טהור חוטא. דבעלמא מייתי ליה אנזיר טהור, וגם הק"ו שלו שייך גם בנזיר טהור. **והיינו** טעמא דכתיב קרא בנזיר טמא הואיל ושנה בחטא. שלא נזהר מטומאה, והאריך לצער על נערו מלהנות מיין. **קתני** יוצא ונכנס, וקס"ד אפילו תוך שבעה, משום הכי פריך: משום דיצא חייל עליה נזירות? ומשני: כגון שיצא והזה ושנה וטבל. ואיירי אפילו בשביעי, דחייל עליה בשביעי טהרה משום דנדר בטומאה, ולא בעי איתויי קרבן טומאה בשמיני. **לא** נכנס אין עולין. בתמיה: אדרבה, כי לא נכנס – טפי סלקי ליה ממניינא! וצ"ע: דלא סגי למיתני ונכנס, משום דפליג ר"א, ואמר: לא בו ביום! וי"ל: מכל מקום לא הוה צריך למיתני (אינו) עולה מן המנין לאפוקי, וה"ל למיתני: יצא [ונכנס] מביא קרבן טומאה. **הכי** גרסינן: לא מבעיא יצא כל אותו היום אלא אפילו נכנס בו ביום. דסד"א לא סליק ליה (חד) מקצת טהרה משהזה עד שנטמא. **לא** אמר רבי אליעזר. דבעינן שמנה ימים שנים ז] אלא בטמא שנדר, כלפי דאמר קרא "כי טמא נזרו" – משמע דבטומאה נדר, והאי קאמר "והימים הראשונים יפלו" דבעינן ימים שנים. צריך עיון מנלן למידרש הכי אליבא דר"א? דהא דרבנן דלא דרשינן ימים שנים לא מיפלג קרא בין טמא שנדר לטהור שנדר. הכי

פי' הרא"ש

דורון בעלמא היא דאינה מכפרת בשום מקום: מאי טעמא דרבנן. בשלמא א) לר"א אתה ההוא ורבי ישמעאל אמר והזיר והביא אימתי והזיר בזמן שהביא. וההוא אתא למי' אע"פ שלא הביא עולתו דאי לא כתיב אלא והזיר והביא הוה אמרינן אחר שיביא כל קרבנות ואפי' עולה. ואי לא כתיב אלא ביום ההוא הוה אמינא אע"פ שלא הביא כלל מקרבנותיו: האשה שנדרה בנזיר ונטמאה והפרישה ב' תורים ואשם ואח"כ הפיר לה בעלה: ר"י בנו של ר"י בן ברוקה היא. דסבר דעולה מעיק' נזי' הויא הלכך כי הפיר לה בעלה נתבטל נדרה ואינה מביאה עולת העוף. אבל חטאת העוף מביאה כדמסיק דרבי אלעזר הקפר היא דאי כרבנן כיון דאמרי דעולה דורון הוא אף כי הפיר לה בעלה נמי מתיא: בעל מעקר עקר. עוקר הנדר מעיקרו כמו התרת חכם. ובפרקי' דלקמ' מבעיא לן. חטאת העוף נמי לא לייתי דהוי כאילו לא נדרה כלום: בעל מיגז גייז. חותך הנדר מכאן ולהבא ולא דמי להתרת חכם שהוא ע"י פתח חרטה ועושה הנדר טעות מעיקרו: עולת העוף נמי תייתי. וה"ה אשם נמי דהא נטמאה קודם שהפיר לה דקרבנות נזיר טמא על עון טומאה קא אתו ולא לצורך הכשר נזיר טהרה: ס"ל כר"א הקפר דאמר נזיר חוטא הוא מחמת שציער עצמו מן היין. הלכך זאת שנטמאה אע"פ שהפיר לה הבעל ומעקר עקר כיון שנתחייבה חטאת העוף ומצינו בעלמא שבקל מביא' חטאת העוף דחטאת העוף בא על הספק זאת נמי מביאה העוף לכפר עליה וכן מפרש טעמא בפרק בתרא דנדרים [דף פ"ג] משום דחטאת העוף בא על הספק ואנן אפילו בנזי' טהור קאמרינן מדמפרש ר"א הקפר טעמא דחטא בשביל שציער עצמו מן היין. והיינו אף נזי' טהור ג) ואע"פ שלא הזה ושנה וטבל: הא לא נכנס אין עולי' לו כ"ש אם לא נכנס והוא טהור שעולי' לו: לא מבעיא קאמר ג) ומשאמר זה דבר פשוט הוא דמוכחא מתני' משום פלוגת' דר' אלעזר נקטיה דאמר לא בו ביום: אלא בטמא שנזר. בטמא שהתחיל למנות נזיר בטהרה ונטמא בז' שאינו מביא קרבן טומאה: אבל נזי' טהור וכו' טהור שקבל עליו נזי' ונטמא אף ביום א' סותר ד) היכה דכתיב והימים הראשונים יפלו כי טמא נזרו דוק' בטמא שנזר בעי' ימים הראשונים: נטמא

א) נראה דצ"ל בשלמא לר"א מפיק ליה מההוא: ורבי ישמעאל בנו של ריב"ב אומר: ב) נ"ל משום דילא חל עליה נזירות. ואע"פ כו': ג) נ"ל ומה שאמר זה אף דדבר פשוט הוא מוכחא ממתני' דמשום פלוגתא: ד) נראה דצ"ל דכי כתיב והימים כו' כי טמא נזרו בנזיר טמא כתיב והלכך דוקא בטמא וכו'.

מסורת הש"ס

לקמן כב. [נדרים פג.]

[נדרים סח. לקמן כח:]

לעיל ג. לקמן כב. ב"ק לח. נדרים י. תענית יא. שבועות ח. סוטה טו. [כריתות כו.]

[על דבר זה סוכה יד: מגילה כג. סנהדרין יז:]

נוסחת הריב"ן

א) את אשמו לה' וגו': ב) דורון בעלמא ואשם אינה צריכה להביא כדלקמן באידך פרקין שאין אשם בא אלא במקום שיחול עליו נזירות אחרת ל"א אמר רב חסדא כו' והשאר ליתא: ג) על שהיתה נזירה ונטמאת הס"ד: ד) קסבר מיעקר: ה) דמייתי: ו) לאו: ז) לא מתייא דהא לא מתייא ליה משום נזירות: ח) ואנן היכי משמע לן בנזיר טהור: לר"א: ט) ובדין: י) טמא כמו בזמן: כ) כשנזר: ל) הוה ליה: מ) דחיילא:

הגהות הב"ח

(א) רש"י ד"ה אמר שמואל וכו'. כדפרישית לעיל:

גליון הש"ס

גמ' אימתי הזיר בזמן שהביא. כעין זה הוריות דף יב ע"א ובלק משום דוימשחה:

הגהות מהר"ב רנשבורג

א] רש"י ד"ה לשון אחר וכו' ר' ישמעאל היא. נ"ב עי' א"מ: ב] תוס' ד"ה (בלף הקודם) ורבנן עולה לא בעיא מעוט וכו' וי"ל משום דרבי לא אדכר במילתיה כ"א דהבאת מלות כ"א דהבאת נמחק. ונ"ב אלא ביום הבאת כצ"ל א"מ: ג] ד"ה תלמוד לומר והזיר והביא וכו' וי"ל אי לאו ההוא וכו'. נ"ב עי' א"מ: ד] ד"ה אמר רב חסדא ר' ישמעאל היא וכו' לפי שמצינו בעלמא חטאת עוף כצ"ל: ה] ד"ה סבר כר"א הקפר וכו' על הספק א"כ. תיבת א"כ נמחק. ונ"ב אבל: ו] ד"ה המצער עצמו מכל דבר וכו' ודוקא אם נטמאה אבל אם לא נטמאה וכו' משום שאם לא הפר לה תביא וכו' כצ"ל: ז] ד"ה לא אמר כו' שמנה ימים שנים. כאן הס"ד ואח"כ מה"ד אלא בטמא שנדר וכו' והאי קאמר קרא כצ"ל:

כא א ב מיי' פ"ו מהל' נזירות הלכה ו:
כב ג מיי' פ"ב שם הל' כא סמג לאוין רמג:

אמר רבא: מ"ט דר"א* – אמר קרא °"כי טמא נזרו" – משום דבטומאה נזר. איתיביה אביי: "הריני נזיר מאה יום" ונטמא בתחלת מאה, יכול יהא סותר? ת"ל "והימים הראשונים יפלו" – אעד שיהו לו ימים ראשונים, וזה אין לו ראשונים. נטמא בסוף מאה, יכול יהא סותר? ת"ל "והימים הראשונים יפלו" – מכלל דאיכא אחרונים, וזה אין לו אחרונים. נטמא ביום מאה חסר אחת, יכול לא יהא סותר – ת"ל "והימים הראשונים יפלו" – מכלל דאיכא אחרונים, וזה יש לו ראשונים ואחרונים. והא בטמא שנזר לא מצית אמרת, מדקתני "הריני נזיר מאה" ונטמא בתחלת מאה, וקתני: עד שיהו לו ימים ראשונים! תיובתא. א"ל רב פפא לאביי: הלין ימים דקאמרינן, דנפק חד ומתחילין תרין, או דלמא דנפקין תרין ומתחילין תלתא? לא הוה בידיה, אתא שייליה לרבא. א"ל: ב"יפלו" כתיב. ואיצטריך למיכתב "ימים" ואיצטריך למיכתב "יפלו"; דאי כתב רחמנא "ימים" ולא כתב "יפלו", ה"א: (א) עד דנפקין תרין ועיילין תלתא, כתב רחמנא "יפלו". ואי כתב "יפלו" ולא כתב "ימים" הוה אמינא: אפילו חד, כתב רחמנא "ימים".§

מתני' *מי שנזר נזירות הרבה, והשלים את נזירותו, ואח"כ בא לארץ, בש"א: נזיר שלשים יום, ובית הילל אומרים: גנזיר בתחלה. מעשה בהילני המלכה שהלך בנה למלחמה, ואמרה: אם יבוא בני מן המלחמה בשלום – אהא נזירה שבע שנים. ובא בנה מן המלחמה, והיתה נזירה שבע שנים. ובסוף שבע שנים עלתה לארץ, *והורוה ב"ה שתהא נזירה עוד שבע שנים אחרות. ובסוף שבע שנים נטמאת, ונמצאת נזירה עשרים ואחת שנה. אמר רבי יהודה: לא היתה נזירה אלא ארבע עשרה שנה.§

גמ' א] קתני רישא: בית שמאי אומרים נזיר שלשים יום, ובה"א: נזיר בתחלה, לימא בהא קמיפלגי; דבית שמאי סברי: *ארץ העמים משום גושה גזרו עליה, ובית

תורה אור: במדבר ו

אמר רבא מאי טעמא דר' אליעזר. אליבא דעולא. אמר קרא והימים הראשונים מכלל דאיכא אחרונים וזה אין לו אחרונים. לפיכך אינו סותר כולן, אלא שלשים. ורבי אליעזר לטעמיה, כדאמרינן בפירקא קמא (לעיל דף ו:): "זאת תורת הנזיר" (ג א). נטמא ביום מאה חסר אחת. דהשתא איכא תרי, מקצת יום ל"ט וכל יום מאה. ומדקתני הריני נזיר ג) מאה יום (ג) ונטמא בתחילת מאה. דהיינו בו ביום, וקתני שיהו לו ימים הראשונים – אלמא שמעינן מהא דבנזיר טהור שנטמא נמי אמר ר' אליעזר דבעינן ימים הראשונים, ותיובתא דעולא. הלין ימים דבעינן. אליבא דרבי אליעזר. מפיק חד ומתחילין תרין – שעומד ביום שני כשנטמא. או נפקין תרין ומתחילין תלתא. דבעינן שני ימים שלימין. אמר ליה יפלו כתיב. דמשמע דליהוון תרין בנפילה, וכגון דנפקין תרין ועיילין תלת. ג) ואי כתב רחמנא ימים ולא כתב יפלו. אלא "והימים הראשונים יעזוב" – ה"א: האי דכתיב "ימים" – משמע כגון דנפיק חד ועיילין תרין, ד) ואפילו הכי אקיים "ימים", דהא כבר עייל יום שני. כתב רחמנא "יפלו", דמשמע: ימים שלימים. ואי כתב יפלו ולא כתב ימים הוה אמינא אפילו חד. כלומר, הוה אמינא דהאי דכתיב "יפלו", משמע אכולהו ימים שכבר מנה, או ארבעה או תלתא או תרין או חד. ואית דמפרשי: אי כתב "יפלו" ולא כתב "ימים" – ה"א: האי דכתיב "יפלו" – אפילו חד משמע, והאי דכתיב "יפלו" – ה) אנזירים דעלמא קאי, כלומר: ונפיק חד ועיילין תרין, ואיקיים לו "יפלו". לשון אחר: דאי כתב רחמנא "ימים" ולא כתב "יפלו", הוה אמינא: עד דנפקין תרין ועיילין תלת, דב' ימים שלימין בעינן. ואי כתב "יפלו" ולא כתב "ימים" – הוה אמינא דאפילו חד, ד"יפלו" משמע נפילה, והאיכא נפילה דחד יומא. להכי כתב רחמנא "ימים", דבעינן דנפיק חד ועיילין תרין. לימא בהא קמיפלגי דב"ש סברי משום גושה גזרו. ולא משום אוירא, והויא קלישא טומאתה, ומשום הכי סגי לה בשלשים יום.

וב"ה

הכי גרסינן ונטמא בתחילה. פירוש: ביום ראשון. ב] וזה אין לו [ראשונים], הילכך יום שנטמא – ממנין נזירותו הוא, וימנה ל"ט לזה, ויגלח ביום מאה, שהוא יום ק"א למנינו. נטמא בסוף מאה, ביום אחרון, יכול יהא סותר הכל – ת"ל "והימים הראשונים יפלו" מכלל דאיכא אחרונים לבא עליו כשנטמא, ומסתמא שנים בעינן, דומיא דראשונים, ולכך אינו סותר הכל. ואם תאמר והא תנן (לעיל דף טז.) במתניתין (כו'): נטמא ביום מאה – סותר שלשים לר"א! וי"ל: דהכי נמי קאמר: יכול יסתור הכל – ת"ל "והימים הראשונים יפלו" וזה אין לו אחרונים, ולכך לא יסתור הכל, אבל שלשים מיהא סותר, מדרשא דדרשינן בפ"ק (דף ו:) "וזאת תורת הנזיר ביום מלאת", נטמא ביום מלאת – תן לו תורת נזיר. וצריכי הני תרי קראי, דאי לאו "זאת תורת הנזיר" – ה"א דכי נטמא ביום אחרון, שהוא יום מלאת – לא יסתור כלל, ואפילו שלשים יום – כתב רחמנא "זאת תורת הנזיר". וא"ת: א"כ, לכתוב "זאת תורת הנזיר" ולשתוק מ"והימים הראשונים יפלו"! וי"ל: א"כ הוה אמינא דיום מלאת היינו יום ק"א, כמו "ובמלאת ימי טהרה" (ויקרא יב) – דהוי לאחר שמלאו ימי טהרה, שהוא יום התגלחת, שמלאו ימיו כבר, וההוא סותר שלשים יום. אבל נטמא יום מאה – יסתור כולם, כתב רחמנא "והימים הראשונים יפלו" – דאפילו נטמא ביום מאה – [אינו] סותר כולם. ועוד, דלא סגי דלא לכתוב "והימים", לאפוקי תחלת המאה שלא היו לו ראשונים. ה"ג וזה יש לו אחרונים. יום טומאה, ויום מאה שאחריו, שהוא כולו ממנין הנזירות כל כמה שלא הביא קרבנותיו. דאפילו לרב מתנא דאמר מקצת היום ככולו – מצוה עליו להשלים לכתחלה, כדאמר בפ"ק (דף ו.). מדקתני הריני נזיר ק' יום ונטמא. אלמא שנדר בטהרה, והדר נטמא. אמר ליה רב פפא לאביי הלין ימים. הראשונים דקאמר ר' אליעזר, דנפק חד ומתחילין תרין, דהיינו ביום שני לנזירותו. או דלמא דבעינן יום אחד שלם; כי היכי דבימים אחרונים איכא חד יום שלם, דהיינו יום המאה – ה"נ בימים הראשונים כי מתחיל תלת. אבל כי נטמא ביום שני, דפעמים אינו אלא שני חצאי ימים, כגון דקבל נזירות אתמול בחצי היום והיום נטמא בחצי היום. ואם תאמר: ונפשוט ליה ממתניתין, דקתני ר"א [אומר]: לא לבו ביום, מכלל דיום שלאחריו סותר! וי"ל: דלא חש ר' אליעזר להזכיר רק ממה דפליג אדרבנן דאמרי: בו ביום מביא קרבן טומאה, ואמר להו ר' אליעזר: לא לבו ביום. וה"ה נמי לא ביום שני עד שלישי. ואם תאמר: ולפשוט ליה מברייתא דאייתי לעיל גופא, "נטמא בתחילת מאה יכול יהא סותר" וכו', מכלל דכי נטמא ביום שני – ודאי סותר! וי"ל: תחילת מאה ג] היינו נמי יום שני [קרא] תחילת מאה ועי"ל דמשום דלרבנן סותר אפילו ביום ראשון, קאמר להו ר"א [דאינו] סותר. וא"ת: ונפשוט ליה מסיפא, דקאמר כי נטמא ביום מאה חסר אחת דסותר, אלמא דבתרי יומי סגי ליה, וה"ה בתחילת נזירות, דמסתמא אחרונים דומיא דראשונים! וי"ל דאחרונים פשיטא ליה דבתרי יומי סגי ליה, לפי שיש שם יום שלם – דהיינו יום מאה, אבל בתחילת נזירות – פעמים דליכא אלא שני חצאי ימים, כגון אם נדר בחצי יום, לכך מספקא ליה אי לכך בעינן דנפקא תרין וקאי בתלת. אבל קשה: דליפשוט ליה מברייתא דלעיל, דמתחיל ומונה מיד, פי' משביעי, וכי נטמא בשמיני דליכא אלא ב' ימים, מביא קרבן טומאה (לו) לר"א! וצריך לומר: דלא שמיע ליה להההיא ברייתא דלעיל. אי נמי, שמיע ליה, וקבעי טעמא מקרא. א"נ, י"ל כדפרישית לעיל, דהא דבעינן דנפקא תרין וקאי אתלת – משום דבעינן יום שלם שחל עליו נזירות דומיא דאחרונים. אבל לעיל, כיון דנזירות חל עליו משביעי, דנטמא בשמיני – יש כאן שביעי שלם, ולכך כיון דנטמא בשמיני – מביא קרבן טומאה. וקצת קשה: הא שביעי אינו שלם, שצריך להזות ולטבול קודם שיחול הנזירות. לשון הג"ה: פ"ל "יפלו" כתיב, משמע נפילה כל דהו – לרבות *שלא בא נמי יום שלם. ואיצטריך למיכתב "ימים" ואיצטריך למיכתב "יפלו", דמאי למיכתב הכי: "וקדש ראש נזרו ביום ההוא מלבד ימים הראשונים", ולשתוק מ"יפלו". עד דנפקי תרין ועיילי תלת – ד"ימים" משמע הכי, דבעינן דומיא *דאחרון, דאיכא יום שלם – כתב רחמנא "יפלו" דמשמע כל דהו, דנפק חד וקאי בתרין. ואי כתב רחמנא "יפלו הראשונים" ולא כתב "ימים", דמאי למיכתב "והראשונים יפלו" – ה"א: ואפילו לבו ביום, כת"ק, ולשון "יפלו" קאי אנזירות דעלמא, כתב רחמנא "ימים".

מי שנדר בחוצה לארץ נזירות הרבה מל' יום והשלים נזירותו בחוצה לארץ ואח"כ בא לארץ. לאו דוקא במקרה בעלמא, דלא סגי דלא אתי לארץ ישראל להקריב קרבנותיו ולהשלים נזירותו למר כדאית ליה ולמר כדאית ליה. נזיר שלשים יום. בגמרא מפרש דמדרבנן קנסא בעלמא הוא שגזרו בארץ העמים דגזרו עליהם טומאה ומן התורה ודאי טהור ויצא ידי נזירותו. נזיר בתחילה. לחזור ולהתחיל כל מניינו. גם דברי ב"ה קנס, ומדרבנן, והכי מפורש בגמרא. ובסוף שבע שנים באה ואחר כך נטמאת. ד] וי"מ בגמרא דלא נבלעו [אלו] באלו, [מדמנינן] אחת ועשרים שנה. אמר רבי יהודה לא היתה נזירה אלא י"ד שנה. בגמ' מפרש לה.

לימא

פי' הרא"ש

נטמא בסוף מאה יכול יהא סותר פי' הכל. אבל ל' יום סותר כדדרשינן בפ"ק דכתיב ביום מלאת ימי נזרו התורה אמרה ביום מלאת תן לו ימי נזרו. ותרווייהו קראי צריכי דאי לא כתיב אלא ביום מלאת הוה אמינא היום ק' וא' שהוא יום הבאת קרבנותיו קרי' יום מלאת כמו ובמלאת ימי טהרה דכתיב גבי יולדת אבל נטמא יום ק' סותר הכל ת"ל והימים הראשונים ואי לא כתיב אלא והימים הראשונים הוה אמינא נטמא ביום הק' לא יסתור כלום ת"ל ביום מלאת: הלין ימים דנפק חד ומתחלי תרי. פר"ת דהכי מיבעיא ליה מי אמרינן כי היכי דבימים אחרונים לא בעי' אלא שיש עוד עליו נזי' ב' ימים הכי נמי בימים הראשונים לא בעי' אלא שיהא עליו נזירות ב' ימים והיינו דמיפיק חד ועייל תרי או דלמא דומיא דאחרונים לגמרי בעי' שיהא עליו יום א' שלם. דיום אחרון של נזי' שלם הוא דמביא קרבנותיו ביום שאחר השלמת נזירו' ואפ"ה אם ביום ל' [נטמא] כל זמן שלא הביאם לא פסקה נזי' אף ראשון בעי' יום א' שלם והיינו דנפקי ב' ומתחלי ג': א"ל יפלו כתיב דמשמע נפילה כל דהו: ואצטריך למכתב ב' ימים ואצטריך למכתב יפלו. דהוה מצי למכתב וקדש ראשו ביום ההוא מלבד הימים הראשונים: הוה אמינא אפילו חד. (כמת"ק) דיפלו נפילה כל דהו משמע: מתני' מי שנזר נזיר' מרובה יותר מל' יום ואח"כ בא לארץ להביא קרבנותיו: ב"ש אומרים [נזיר] ל' יום דקנסינן ליה למנות נזירות טהרה: וב"ה סברי דקנסינן ליה להשלים כל נזי' דמחשבינן ליה כאילו נדר בבית הקברות. ואינו עובר משום בל תאחר דיש כח ביד חכמים לעקור דבר מן התורה בשב ואל תעשה: קתני רישא ב"ש אומרים וכו'. לא הוה צריך למימר כן דארישא קיימינן אלא דשיט' נזי' משונה: [ה"ג] דב"ש סברי ארץ העמים משום אוירא גזור. דאפילו נכנס לה בשידה תיבה ומגדל טמא שהחמירו על ארץ העמים לטמא אף האויר ולא כדין טומאת מת. הלכך אין טומאתה כטומאת מת ודי בל' יום. וב"ה סברי משום גושה גזור כדין מאהיל על הגוש ואם נכנס בשידה תיבה ומגדל טהור הלכך טור"מ כדין מאהיל על המת והוי כנדר בבית הקברות:

לא

נוסחת הריב"ן

א) הנזיר נטמא ביום מלאת כו' הס"ד: ב) ומנה יום אחד ונטמא כו': ג) לאו: ד) (ואפ"ה כו' ימים שלמים) ליתא בכ"י: ה) אנזיר קאי כלומר כו':

הגהות מהר"ב רנשבורג

א] גמ' קתני רישא וכו'. נ"ב כאן שייך תוס' ד"ה קתני שנדפס בדף הסמוך: ב] תוס' ד"ה ה"ג ונטמא בתחלה פי' ביום ראשון. כאן הס"ד ואח"כ מה"ד וזה אין לו וכו': ג] ד"ה אמר לי' רב פפא לאביי וכו' היינו נמי יום שני. נ"ב עי' א"מ: ד] ד"ה ובסוף שבע שנים וכו' וי"מ בגמ'. נ"ב על תיבות וי"מ בגמ' נ"ב הא"מ מוחק זה:

[עדיות פ"ד מי"א]

כתובות ז.

[לקמן נד: נה.]

הגהות הב"ח

(א) גמ' הוה אמינא (עד דנפקין תרין ועיילין תלתא). תא"מ ונ"ב ס"א דנפק חד ועיילין תרין: (ב) רש"י ד"ה אמר קרא וכו' הנזיר וגו' הס"ד ואח"כ מ"ה נטמא ביום מלאת וכו' נטמא ביום מאה וכו' דהשתא איכא תרי יומי מקלת: (ג) ד"ה ומדקתני הריני נזיר ק' יום ומנה יום אחד ונטמא בתחילת:

נ"ל דלא בעי נמי

נ"ל דלאחרונים

תורה אור

ובית הלל סברי: *משום אוירא גזרו עליה? לא, דכולי עלמא אמשום גושה גזרו עליה, וב"ש סברי: בסתם נזירות קניסנא, וב"ה סברי: כי קניסנא — בתחילת נזירות.§ "מעשה בהילני המלכה" וכו'.§ איבעיא להו: בשנטמאת ואליבא דב"ש, או דלמא בשלא נטמאת ואליבא דב"ה? ת"ש: עלתה לארץ והורוה ב"ה שתהא נזירה עוד שבע שנים אחרות וכו'. ואי ס"ד בשנטמאת ואליבא דב"ש, אי הכי, רבי יהודה אומר לא היתה נזירה אלא י"ד שנה? י"ד שנה ושלשים יום מיבעי ליה! תניא נמי הכי, רבי יהודה אומר משום רבי אליעזר: (במדבר ו) דאמר קרא °"זאת תורת הנזיר" (א) *התורה אמרה: כי נטמא ביום מלאת — תן לו תורת נזיר.§

מתני' *מי שהיו שתי כיתי עדים מעידות אותו, אלו מעידים שנזר שתים ואלו מעידים שנזר חמש, ב"ש אומרים: נחלקה העדות, ואין כאן נזירות. וב"ה אומרים: ביש בכלל חמש שתים, שיהא נזיר שתים.§

גמ' מתני' דלא כי האי תנא. דתניא, *רבי ישמעאל בנו של רבי יוחנן בן ברוקא אומר: לא נחלקו ב"ש וב"ה על שתי כיתי עדים, אחת אומרת שתים ואחת אומרת חמש, שיש בכלל חמש שתים. על מה נחלקו — על כת אחת, אחד אומר שתים ואחד אומר חמש. שב"ש אומרים נחלקה עדותן, ובה"א: יש בכלל חמש שתים. אמר רב: הכל מודים במונה. א"ל רב חמא לרב חסדא: מאי קאמר? אילימא אחד אומר חמש ולא שתים, ואחד אומר שתים ולא חמש — הא קא מכחשי אהדדי. אלא: אחד אומר אחת ושתים, ואחד אומר: שלש ארבע חמש —
הא

וב"ה סברי משום אוירא גזרו. ואמירא טומאתא, ומשום הכי צריכה דתיהוי כבתחלה. לא דכ"ע משום גושה גזרו. דקילא א) טומאה. והאי דאמרו לה דתיהדר לנזירותא — קנסא ב) בעלמא הוא דקנסוה. איבעיא להו. הא דא"ר יהודה דלא היתה נזירה אלא י"ד, ג) כשנטמאת קאמר. ואליבא דב"ש. דכשעלתה לארץ והיתה עושה ל' יום כב"ש, נטמאת בטומאת מת וסתרה את הכל, ועשתה ז' שנים אחרים כבתחלה. או דלמא שלא נטמאת. אלא בשביל שבאת בארץ העמים ועלתה לא"י עשתה ז' שנים כבתחלה, ואליבא דב"ה. ת"ש עלתה לארץ ואי ס"ד כו' ד). ואי ס"ד כשנטמאת, ואליבא דב"ש, אי הכי י"ד שנה ול' יום מיבעיא ליה. שהרי בתוך ל' נטמאת, וסתרה כל שלמפרע ז' שנה ול' יום — א"כ ז' שנים ול' יום היה לה למנות תחתיהן. אלא מדלא תני הכי אלא י"ד שנה — ש"מ דבלא נטמאת (ב) ה) מיירי ר' יהודה, ואליבא דב"ה. ע"א: איבעיא להו הא דא"ר יהודה לא היתה נזירה אלא י"ד שנה — כשנטמאת עוד טומאה אחרת בסוף שבעה ראשונים, אבל לא ו) ביום מלאת, ז) ועדיין יש לה יום אחד או ב' מן הז' שנים, ולבסוף ז' שנים עלתה לארץ ומנתה ז' שנים אחרות, שהרי סותרת ז' שנים ראשונים לד"ה, דהא נטמאת — הרי י"ד שנה. ולהכי לא אמרי ב"ש דצריכה למנות ל' ח) יום בארץ, דהא סגי לה באותן ז' שנים שהיא מונה בארץ. תא שמע עלתה לארץ כו'. ואי ס"ד כשנטמאת, ואליבא דב"ש דנטמאת בסוף ז' ראשונים וחזרה ונטמאת בסוף י"ד, כדאמר ת"ק — אי הכי י"ד שנה ול' יום איבעי ליה לרבי יהודה למימר. דכיון שנטמאת בסוף י"ד ט) דיום מלאת, היתה צריכה למנות עוד ל', דהא ס"ל דכי נטמאת ביום מלאת מונה ל'. י) תניא נמי הכי, דלר' יהודה אית ליה דכי נטמאת ביום מלאת מונה ל'. וכיון דס"ל הכי — ודאי הא דא"ר יהודה לא היתה נזירה אלא י"ד שנה — בשלא נטמאת, וקא פליג אתנא קמא, דסבירא ליה לרבי יהודה דלא נטמאת כלל, אלא לסוף שבע שנים עלתה לארץ, והורוה שתהא נזירה עוד שבע שנים. ובלשון הזה דן ר"א ב"ר יצחק הלוי לפני רבינו וקבלה (כ"ל ז"ה גליו"ן כ). (ג) כת אחת. אחד אומר שתי שנים קיבל עליו נזירות, ואחד אומר חמש שנים. שב"ש אומרים נחלקה העדות. הואיל ואין שם ב' עדים על ב' שנים. וב"ה אומרים. מ"מ שניהם מעידים על ב' שנים, ל) ויש בכלל חמש שתים, ולא נחלקה עדותן. מ) אבל בשני כיתי עדים, אחת אומרת שתים ואחת אומרת חמש — דברי הכל יש בכלל חמש שתים. אמר רב הכל מודים במונה. שנחלקה עדותן. מאי קאמר אילימא באחד אומר חמש ולא שתים ואחד אומר שתים ולא חמש. פשיטא דנחלקה עדותן, דהא קא מכחשי אהדדי. אלא. כגון שהאחד אומר "אחת שתים", והאחד אומר "שלש ארבע חמש".
הא

לימא בהא קמיפלגי דב"ש סברי ארץ העמים משום גושא גזרו וב"ה סברי משום אוירא גזרו. אית ספרים דגרסי הכי, דב"ש סברי ארץ העמים משום גושא גזרו עליה ולא על אוירא, ומותר ליכנס בה בשידה תיבה ומגדל, וב"ה סברי אפילו על אוירא גזרו, ומש"ה החמירו לסתור הכל. וקשה לגירסא זו, דמאי טעמא דב"ש? דנהי דלא גזרו כי אם משום גושא — מ"מ לסתור הכל, מידי דהוה אבית הקברות דאינו מטמא באויר, ואפ"ה סותר הכל! לכן נראה דגרסינן איפכא: ב"ש סברי משום אוירא גזרו, והחמירו בארץ העמים. וב"ה סברי משום גושא גזרו. וא"ת: והשתא נמי, מאי טעמא דב"ש? אטו משום דהחמירו בה יותר מקבר לא יסתור אלא ל'? וי"ל: דאין הכי נמי, דכיון דהחמירו בה לגזור על אוירא — גלוי לכל דאותה טומאה אינה אלא מדרבנן, ולכך סגי לן דיסתור שלשים יום, דלא מיחלפא בטומאה דאורייתא. וב"ה סברי: משום גושא גזרו, וכיון דדינה כקבר — צריך שיסתור הכל, ומשום דמיחלפא ארץ העמים בקברות. וכענין סברא זו איכא בפ' "כהן גדול" (לקמן דף נד:) דקאמר: אי משום אוירא — ל"ל הזאה, אבל אי משום גושא — ניחא, דטעמא דהזאה כשאר טומאות. ולפ"ז ה"ג: לא, דכ"ע משום אוירא גזרו. ולכך ניחא לב"ש דלא קנים אלא ל' יום, וב"ה סברי: א] אע"ג דגלוי לכל דטומאה דרבנן הוא, ואינה כשאר אהל — קנסינן ליה בתחילת נזירות. ובקנסא הוא דפליגי. **בשנטמאת** ואליבא דב"ש. [אמר] רבי יהודה דהוצרכה למנות ל' יום בא"י, ונטמאה בסוף ל' יום בא"י, ומנתה עוד ז' שנים, שהרי הוצרכה לסתור כל נזירות. ונמצא דלר' יהודה היתה י"ד שנים ול' יום. והיינו דוקא לב"ש, דאין צריך למנות בא"י רק ל' יום לבד. דאי לב"ה — זקוקה לחזור ולמנות בא"י ז' שנים אחרים, אי נטמאת בסוף מנין כנטמאת, דלעיל היה כך שנטמאה בסוף מנין של הארץ, וא"כ היתה צריכה להא נזירות כ"א שנה. או דלמא בשלא נטמאת, ודר' יהודה אליבא דב"ה דוקא, דלב"ש לא הוצרכה לי"ד שנים, ובז' שנים ול' יום סגי. **תא** שמע עלתה לא"י וכו' ואי ס"ד בנטמאת ואליבא דב"ש אי הכי ר' יהודה אומר לא היתה נזירה אלא י"ד שנה ול' יום מיבעי ליה. ב] ולא גרסינן מה שכתוב בספרים: ועוד מתניתין. וא"ת: ודלמא ל' יום היו מובלעים בז' שנים הראשונים, כגון שעשתה בחו"ל ז' שנים חסר חדש, ושלשים יום דקנסא בארץ — [הרי] ז' שנים ולא יותר. ונטמאה בסוף ל' יום של הקנס, ועשתה עוד ז' שנים — הרי י"ד בין הכל! ועוד קשה: למה לו להאריך דברי ת"ק? לא יביא אלא דברי ר' יהודה לדקדק מהם! וי"ל: דמש"ה מייתי דברי ת"ק — לאוכוחי דלת"ק לא מיירי בהבלעה, דקתני: ולבסוף שבע שנים נטמאת ונמצאת נזירה כ"א שנה (ול' יום), [א"כ] גם דברי ר' יהודה לא מיירי בהבלעה, וא"כ י"ד שנים ושלשים יום מיבעי ליה. **מי** שהיו שתי כתי עדים מעידות אותו אלו מעידין שנדר שני נזירות ואלו מעידין שנדר חמש נחלקה עדותן. ואין כאן נזירות כלל. וא"ת: היכי דמי? אם שתק הנודר — שתיקה כהודאה דמיא! וי"ל: שהנודר מכחיש כל אחת ואחת. דאי מודה לאחת — למה לא יהיה כהודאתו? א"נ: באומר איני יודע, והשתא צריך לידון לפי העדות. א"נ: כששותק, ובאו שתי הכיתות יחד, דלא הוי שתיקותיה כהודאה, דלאו מודה הוא, דאמר: מה לי להכחישן — הא שתיהן מכחישין זה את זה. וב"ה אומרים: יש בכלל חמש שתים, [ומונה] ב', דהוי כאילו אמרו שתיהן: שתים נדרת.

*)**קתני** רישא ב"ש כו'. כל זה לא היה צריך, דודאי ברישא קיימינן. ולשון נזיר משונה. **מתניתין** · דקתני דפליגי ב"ש וב"ה בשתי כתי עדות — [דלא כהאי] תנא דר' ישמעאל. לרבי ישמעאל, דאמר דפליגי בית שמאי ובית הלל בכת אחת, היינו כשאומר אחד שתים, ואחד אומר חמש. אבל אם מונה, כדמפסיק ואזיל — נחלקה העדות. **מאי** קאמר. כלומר, והיכי דמי מונה דקאמר? אילימא דקא מכחשי אהדדי להדיא, כדקאמר חמש ולא שתים כו' — פשיטא דנחלקה עדותן, ומאי קא משמע לן רב?
אלא

*) ד"ז שייך לעיל יט:

כג א מיי' פ"ח מהל' טומאת מת ה"ח:
כד ב מיי' פ"ג מהל' נזירות הלכה ט:

פי' הרא"ש

לא דכ"ע משום אוירא גזור הלכך לב"ש די בל' וב"ה סברי דאפ"ה קנסוה בעיקר נזירות ולקמן בפ' כ"ג מוכח כי האי גירסא דאמרינן לקמן אי משום אוירא למה לי הזאה אלמא אי משום אוירא אין לה דין טומאת מת ולא בעיא הזאה: איבעיא להו כשנטמאת וה"ק ליה ר' יהודה לת"ק ודאי אמת היה שנטמאת בסוף נזירותה ואפ"ה לא היתה נזירה אלא י"ד שנה דהורו לה כב"ש להיות נזירה ל' יום ונטמאת בסוף ל' יום והוצרכה להיות נזירה עוד ז' שנים: או דלמא כשלא נטמאת ואליבא דב"ה. ולא פליג ר"י את"ק אלא בעיקר המעשה שרבי יהודה אומר שכך היה המעשה שלא נטמאת אבל אם נטמאת היתה צריכה להיות נזירה כ"א שנה: ת"ש עלתה לארץ וכו' לא היה צריך להביא כל זאת המשנה אלא שרוצה לדקדק דכי היכי דלת"ק נטמאה בסוף ימי נזירותה הכי נמי לר' יהודה הלכך פריך אי ס"ד בשנטמאת ואליבא דב"ש א"כ נטמאת בסוף ל' יום של נזירו' א"כ י"ד ול' מבעי ליה. ואית ספרים דגרסינן י"ד שנה ל' מבעי ליה דתניא ר' יהודה אומר משום ר"א זאת תורת הנזיר ביום מלאת אמרה תורה נטמא ביום מלאת תן לו תורת נזיר. ואי ס"ד כשנטמאת ואליבא דב"ש כיון שנטמאה בסוף ל' לא היתה צריכה להיות נזירה אלא ל' יום: מי שהיו ב' כתי עדים מעידים אותו אלו מעידים שנדר ב' שקבל עליו ב' נזירו' ואלו מעידים שנדר ה' באותה שעה שאתם אומרי' שנדר ב' אנו אומרי' שנדר ה'. ומפרי' כגון שהיה מכחיש ואומר שלא נדר כלל. דאי שתיק הוי' שתיקותא כהודאה כדאי' בקידושין פ' האומר גבי נטמאו טהרותיך והלה שותק. ומי' איכא למי' דמיירי אפילו בשותק דכיון דבאו ב' כתות כאחד ומכחישות זו את זו נתבטלו דבריהם והוי כאילו לא העידו ולא שייך הכא למימר שתיקה כהודאה דמיא:

שיש בכלל ה' שתים כיון שיש עדות שלימה בכולה דבר אבל בכת א' בהא קאמרי ב"ש דנחלקה עדותם שהאחד אומר אמת והא' משקר ואין כאן אלא עד אחד אמיתי וב"ה אומר יש בכלל ה' שתים ושניהם מעידים על שניהם. ולתנא דמתני' גם ב"ה מודו בכת אחת דנחלקה עדותם: אמר רב הכל מודים במונה א) אהא' מן העדים נז' א' ועוד שניה והשני אומר נזר ג' נזירות ועוד ד' ועוד ה' כיון דנחת למניינא הוי כאילו מכחישים זא"ז

א) אולי צ"ל במונה אחד מן העדים אומר נזר נזירות א' וכו'.

[לקמן נד: נה.]

[לעיל ו:]

עדיות פ"ד מי"א

[תוספתא פ"ג] ב"ב מא: ע"ש סנהדרין לא. ע"ש

הגהות מהר"ב רנשבורג

א] תוס' ד"ה לימא וכו' וב"ה סברי אע"ג דגלוי לכל דטומאה דרבנן הוא ואינה כשאר אהל מן תיבות אע"ג עד אהל נמחק. ונ"ב אעפ"כ אינו גלוי לכל דטומאה דרבנן הוא כשאר אהל וכו' כצ"ל א"מ: ב] ד"ה ת"ש וכו' ול"ג מה שכתוב בספרים ועוד וכו' נ"ב עי' א"מ:

נוסחת הריב"ן

א) טומאתה: ב) קנסא הוא דקנסוה דב"ש סברי כו' גליון נזירות מרובה של ק' יום ב"ש אומרים נזיר ל' משום דלארץ העמים טמאה היא לא חשיב נזירות דהו"ל להכי ימנה ל' יום דנזירות טהרה בארץ ישראל ודייה וב"ש כו' הס"ד: ג) שנה: ד) כו' גליון ואי ס"ד: ה) בארץ מיירי: ו) ביום: ז) דעדיין: ח) (יום) ליתא בכ"י: ט) ביום: י) ל' יום: כ) ואית ספרים דכתיב בהו תניא נמי הכי ושבקתא היא הס"ד: ל) דיש: מ) בכל מקום שיש שם שתי כתי עדים כו':

הגהות הב"ח

(א) גמ' זאת תורת הנזיר ביום מלאת התורה אמרה: (ב) רש"י ד"ה ת"ש עלתה וכו' ש"מ דבלא נטמאת משבאת לארץ מיירי ר' יהודה וכו' בסוף שבע ראשונים אבל לא ביום מלאת דעדיין הי' לה יום אחד או ב' מן הז' וכו' לדברי הכל דהא נטמאת תוך מלאת הרי י"ד וכו' בסוף י"ד ביום מלאת היתה: (ג) ד"ה על מה נחלקו על כת אחת אחד כצ"ל והד"א עם ד"ה וב"ה וכו' דיש בכלל וכו' אבל בשתי כיתי:

אלא אחד אומר "אחת ושתים" ואחד אומר "שלש וארבע וחמש" ואינם מכחישים בפירוש זה את זה. וקמ"ל רב, דכיון דכל חד וחד נחת למניינא, שזה אינו אומר שתים בבת אחת, אלא אומר "אחת ושתים", וזה "ג' וארבע וה'" ולא "אחת ושתים" – כאילו אמר: לא אחת ושתים נדר, אלא של שלש וארבע וה'. וזה שאמר "אחת ושתים" – כאילו אומר: ולא נדר שלש וארבע וחמש.

ה"ג תו ל"ל השתא י"ל חמירתא אמר קילתא לא כ"ש. ולא גרסינן: אמר רב. וה"פ, דפריך: [אמאי] קאמר דהוי הכחשה – משום דאמרינן כיון דזה [אמר] "שלש ארבע חמש" ולא אמר גם "אחת ושתים" – הוי כאילו אומר בפירוש: ולא אחת ושתים נזר. אמאי? נימא דלא הוי הכחשה, ומה שלא הזכיר "אחת ושתים" – דמה לו להזכיר? חמירתא, דהיינו "שלש וארבע וחמש", אמר, קילתא לא אמר?! הא מלינו למימר ד"אחת ושתים" בכלל דבריו, ומוסיף הוא על האחד. אלא ודאי לא הוי הכחשה.

אמרי במערבא אין הכחשה במונה. דודאי כי אמר אידך "שלש וארבע וחמש" – לא מיעט שלא אמר הנודר "אחת ושתים". ובירושלמי דסנהדרין משמע דמונה הוי הכחשה אפילו טפי, א] כאילו אמר: [לא] אחת ושתים [אלא] שלש וארבע. דקאמר התם: אמר רב: מחלוקת בכלל, אבל בפרט לכ"ע נחלקה עדותן, ואין כאן נזירות. ורבי יוחנן אומר: בפרט נחלקו, אבל בכלל – לכ"ע יש בכלל חמש שתים.

הדרן עלך מי שאמר

הָא ל"ל. לְמֵיהֲדַר וּלְמִיתְנֵי. הָשְׁתָּא י"ל חֲמִירְתָּא אֲמַר רַב. הֵיכָא דְּהָווּ ב' כִּתֵּי עֵדִים, וְאַחַת אוֹמֶרֶת "אַחַת שְׁתַּיִם", וּשְׁנִיָּה אוֹמֶרֶת "שָׁלֹשׁ אַרְבַּע חָמֵשׁ", שָׁמְעִינַן לֵיהּ לְרַב נֶחְלְקָה עֵדוּתָן. בְּקִילְּתָא, דְּלָא הָווּ אֶלָּא חַד וְחַד – לָא אֲמַר דְּנֶחְלְקָה עֵדוּתָן?! פְּשִׁיטָא דְּוַדַּאי אֲמַר! וְהֵיכָא שָׁמְעִינַן לֵיהּ לְרַב דַּאֲמַר הָכִי – בְּמַסֶּ' סַנְהֶדְרִין יְרוּשַׁלְמִית (פ"ה), דְּקָתָנֵי הָתָם לְהָךְ מַתְנִי' דְּהָכָא, וּכְתִיבָא תַּמָּן: הָכִי תָּנֵינַן תַּמָּן, מִי שֶׁהָיוּ שְׁתֵּי כִיתֵּי עֵדִים מְעִידִים אוֹתוֹ, אֵלּוּ מְעִידִים שֶׁנָּזַר שְׁתַּיִם וְאֵלּוּ מְעִידִים שֶׁנָּזַר חָמֵשׁ, ב"ש אוֹמְרִים: נֶחְלְקָה עֵדוּתָן, וְאֵין כָּאן א) נְזִירוּת כְּלָל. וּב"ה אוֹמְרִים: יֵשׁ בִּכְלַל חָמֵשׁ ב', שֶׁיְּהֵא נָזִיר שְׁתַּיִם. וְאָמַר רַב: בִּכְלָל נֶחְלְקוּ, אֲבָל בִּפְרָט – דִּבְרֵי הַכֹּל נֶחְלְקָה הָעֵדוּת. וְר' יוֹחָנָן אוֹמֵר: בִּפְרָט נֶחְלְקוּ, אֲבָל בִּכְלָל – יֵשׁ בִּכְלַל חָמֵשׁ שְׁתַּיִם, ב) יְהֵא נָזִיר שְׁתַּיִם. פְּרָט – כְּגוֹן שֶׁהָאַחַת אוֹמֶרֶת "אַחַת שְׁתַּיִם", וְהַשְּׁנִיָּה אוֹמֶרֶת "שָׁלֹשׁ אַרְבַּע חָמֵשׁ". כְּלָל – שֶׁהָאַחַת אוֹמֶרֶת שְׁתַּיִם, וְהַשְּׁנִיָּה אוֹמֶרֶת ג) ה'. אָמְרִי בְּמַעֲרָבָא אֵין הַכְחָשָׁה בְּמוֹנֶה. שֶׁאִם אֶחָד אוֹמֵר "אַחַת שְׁתַּיִם" וְאֶחָד אוֹמֵר "שָׁלֹשׁ אַרְבַּע חָמֵשׁ" – אֵין זוֹ הַכְחָשָׁה, וְיֵשׁ בִּכְלַל חָמֵשׁ שְׁתַּיִם, וִיהֵא נָזִיר שְׁתַּיִם.

הדרן עלך מי שאמר

הָא לָמָּה לִי? הָשְׁתָּא יֵשׁ לוֹמַר חֲמִירְתָּא אֲמַר רַב, קִילְּתָא לָא אֲמַר?! אָמְרִי בְּמַעֲרָבָא: אֵין הַכְחָשָׁה בְּמוֹנֶה.§

הדרן עלך מי שאמר

מִי אשֶׁאָמַר "הֲרֵינִי נָזִיר", וְשָׁמַע חֲבֵירוֹ וְאָמַר "וַאֲנִי", "וַאֲנִי" – כּוּלָּם נְזִירִים. בהוּתַּר הָרִאשׁוֹן – הוּתְּרוּ כּוּלָּן. הוּתַּר הָאַחֲרוֹן – הָאַחֲרוֹן מוּתָּר, וְכוּלָּם אֲסוּרִין. אָמַר "הֲרֵינִי נָזִיר", וְשָׁמַע חֲבֵירוֹ וְאָמַר "פִּי כְּפִיו וּשְׂעָרִי כִּשְׂעָרוֹ" – גה"ז נָזִיר. ד"הֲרֵינִי נָזִיר", וְשָׁמְעָה אִשְׁתּוֹ וְאָמְרָה "וַאֲנִי" – מֵיפֵר אֶת שֶׁלָּהּ, וְשֶׁלּוֹ קַיָּים. *"הֲרֵינִי נְזִירָה", וְשָׁמַע בַּעְלָהּ וְאָמַר "וַאֲנִי" – האֵינוֹ יָכוֹל לְהָפֵר. "הֲרֵינִי נָזִיר וְאַתְּ", וְאָמְרָה "אָמֵן" – ומֵיפֵר אֶת שֶׁלָּהּ, וְשֶׁלּוֹ קַיָּים. "הֲרֵינִי נְזִירָה וְאַתָּה" וְאָמַר "אָמֵן" – זאֵינוֹ יָכוֹל לְהָפֵר.§ **גמ'** יְתִיב ר"ל קַמֵּיהּ דר' יְהוּדָה נְשִׂיאָה, וִיתֵיב וְקָאָמַר: חוְהוּא שֶׁהִתְפִּיסוּ כּוּלָּן בְּתוֹךְ כְּדֵי דִיבּוּר. וְכַמָּה *תּוֹךְ כְּדֵי דִיבּוּר – כְּדֵי שְׁאֵלַת שָׁלוֹם, וְכַמָּה כְּדֵי שְׁאֵלַת שָׁלוֹם – טכְּדֵי שֶׁאוֹמֵר שָׁלוֹם תַּלְמִיד לָרַב. א"ל: תּוּב לָא שָׁבְקַתְּ רַוְוחָא לְתַלְמִידָא. תַּנְיָא

מִי שֶׁאָמַר הֲרֵינִי נָזִיר וְשָׁמַע חֲבֵירוֹ וְאָמַר וַאֲנִי כו'. וְכֵן חֲבֵירוֹ אָמַר "וַאֲנִי". הוּתַּר (א) רִאשׁוֹן. שֶׁנִּשְׁאַל עַל נְזִירוּתוֹ. הוּתְּרוּ כּוּלָּן – שֶׁכּוּלָּן תָּלוּ נְזִירוּתָן בָּרִאשׁוֹן. **גמ'** יְתִיב ר"ל קַמֵּיהּ דר' יְהוּדָה נְשִׂיאָה וִיתֵיב וְקָאָמַר. כִּי תְּנַן בְּמַתְנִי' "וְכוּלָּן נְזִירִים" – כְּגוֹן שֶׁהִתְפִּיסוּ כּוּלָּן בְּתוֹךְ כְּדֵי דִּבּוּר שֶׁל רִאשׁוֹן, דִּבְכְדֵי שְׁאֵילַת תַּלְמִיד לָרַב, דְּאִית בֵּיהּ שָׁלֹשׁ תֵּיבוֹת "שָׁלוֹם עָלֶיךָ רַבִּי" הִתְפִּיסוּ כּוּלָּן. וּמַתְנִיתִין דְּקָתָנֵי: "וַאֲנִי" "וַאֲנִי", דְּלָא תָּנֵי אֶלָּא תְּרֵין – דַּוְקָא קָתָנֵי. דְּכִי שֶׁקָּלַתְּ לַחֲדָא תֵּיבָה מִקַּמָּא דַּאֲמַר "הֲרֵינִי נָזִיר" וּמְלָרְפַתְּ לֵיהּ לְהָנָךְ דְּאָמְרֵי "וַאֲנִי" "וַאֲנִי", (ב) שֶׁכּוּלָּן שְׁלֹשָׁה נָדְרוּ בְּתוֹךְ כְּדֵי שְׁאֵילַת שָׁלוֹם תַּלְמִיד לָרַב, דְּהָוְיָין נַמִי שְׁלֹשָׁה תֵּיבוֹת. תּוּב לָא שָׁבְקַתְּ רַוְוחָא לְתַלְמִידָא. דְּלֵימָא לֵיהּ אֶלָּא הָנָךְ תְּלָת מִילֵּי. וְלָאו מִשּׁוּם דְּאִית לֵיהּ לְרַבִּי יְהוּדָה נְשִׂיאָה דְּלֵימָא לֵיהּ טְפֵי, אֶלָּא מִילְּתָא בְּעָלְמָא קמ"ל, (ג) ד) וּמְסַיֵּיע לֵיהּ לְרֵישׁ לָקִישׁ. תַּנְיָא

מי שאמר הריני נזיר ושמע חבירו ואמר ואני ואני. כלומר, שנים שמעו לראשון שקבל נזירות, והאחד אומר "ואני", וכן השני אומר "ואני" – כולם נזירים. הותר הראשון, אם הראשון בא לחכם והתיר לו נדרו – גם האחרונים הותרו, לפי שאמרו "ואני כמוהו", ותלו נדריהם בנדרו. הותר האחרון ע"י חכם – הוא מותר וכולן אסורים, אם לא יתירו גם הם נדריהם ע"י חכם. אבל בלא התרה – לא, שלא תלו נדריהם בנדר האחרון. **פי** כפיו שערי כשערו ה"ז נזיר. בגמרא מפרש. **הריני** נזיר ושמעה אשתו ואמרה ואני מיפר את שלה ושלו קיים. דלא תלה כלל נדרו בנדרה. אלא אדרבה, היא אמרה "ואני נזירה כמוך" אחר שהוא כבר נדר בנזיר. **הריני** נזירה ושמע בעלה ואמר ואני אינו יכול להפר. בגמרא בעי לאכותי מינה דבעל מיעקר קא עקר נדר אשתו מעיקרו. ולכך אינו יכול להפר, שאם מיפר לה – א"כ יתבטל גם את שלו, שנדרו תלוי בנדרה, וכדתנן לעיל: הותר הראשון – הותרו כולן שבאו מחמתיה דראשון, ואינו רשאי לגרום דבר להיות נדרו מבוטל, כדכתיב "לא יחל דברו", ודרשינן: הוא אינו מיחל, אבל אחרים מוחלין לו. ודחי בגמרא: דלעולם מיגז גייז מהפרה ואילך מהשתא, ב] אבל כי נמי מיפר את שלה ג] ושלו קיים – מ"מ חל נדרה עד עתה, ונזירותיה אינו יכול להפר, דכיון דאמר "ואני" – קיים לה נדרה. **הריני** נזיר ואת. כלומר, וכי גם את רוצה לידור בנזיר? ואמרה "אמן". פי': קבלה עליה נזירות. מיפר את שלה, ושלו קיים – דלא תלה נדרו בנדרה. אבל אם לא אמרה "אמן" – היא מותרת, שאינו יכול להדירה בע"כ. ודאי מה דאמר לה "ואת" – לא הוי קיום, שאין הנדר חל עליה אלא כשאמרה "אמן", ועדיין אינו יודע אם תקבלנו אם לאו, ולכך לא הוי קיום. **הריני** נזירה ואתה. הכי גרס ר"ת: ושמע בעלה ואמר "אמן" – אינו יכול להפר. אי מיעקר [קא עקר] – ניחא, משום דא"כ יתבטל נזירותו. ואי מיגז גייז – משום דהוי קיום כי אמר "אמן", כמו "ואני" כדלעיל. (עיין לקמן דף כג ע"א) **הרי** זו סופגת את הארבעים. בגמ' (דף כא:) מסיק: שלא היפר לה בעלה. ופשיטא הוא, ומשום דקא בעי למיתני סיפא: ואינה סופגת וכו', דהוי חידושא, אע"ג דנתכוונה לאיסורא, כיון דעלה בידה היתר – אינה סופגת, תנא נמי רישא וסופגת. **רבי** יהודה אומר אם אינה סופגת את הארבעים תספוג מכת מרדות. מדרבנן, שנתכוונה לאיסורא במזיד. ובפ' בתרא דמכות (דף כב.): מכות ארבעים מן התורה, אבל מכת מרדות בלי מנין, אלא מכין עד שתצא נפשו, או עד שמקבל עליו. ומספקא לרבי דהכא דלוקה על שעברה, דשמא דוקא מ' ותו לא. דדוקא כשאין רוצה לקיים אותה המצוה מכין אותו בלי מספר, אבל הכא שכבר עברה – למה תלקה יותר מדאורייתא אם לא הפר? הג"ה גמ' **יתיב** ר"ש בן לקיש קמיה דר' יהודה נשיאה ויתיב וקאמר והוא שהתפיסו כולם בתוך כדי דיבור. כדמפרש והולך: כדי שאילת שלום תלמיד לרב, דהיינו "שלום עליך רבי" ג' תיבות. ה"נ יכולין שלשה אנשים להתפיס עצמן בראשון שנדר בנזיר, שכל אחד אמר "ואני" הם שלש תיבות, דאפילו האחרון תוך כדי דיבור מן הראשון. אבל הרביעי אינו יכול להתפיס עצמו בראשון אפילו אמר "ואני", שכבר שהו כדי דיבור מן הראשון, ולכך לא חייל נזירות ארביעי. **אמר** ליה תו לא שבקת רווחא לתלמידא. כלומר, תלמיד ששמע לאחד שנדר בנזיר, ובקש לומר "ואני" ובתוך כך עובר רבו לפניו, והוא חייב להקדים לו שלום ולומר "שלום עליך רבי" [והם שלש תיבות] – שוב לא יועיל להתפיס בנזיר אם יאמר "ואני", שכבר שהה כדי דיבור. ואין זו סברא, אלא ודאי גם הרביעי נתפס, הואיל ולא שהה כלל לאחר כדי דבור, אלא לאלתר אחר כדי דבור אמר "ואני". אבל החמישי ודאי אינו נתפס, ששהה קצת אחר כדי דיבור. תניא

עין משפט נר מצוה

א א מיי' פ"ב מהלכות נזירות הלכה ד:
ב ב מיי' פ"ד מהל' נדרים הלכה ע סמג לאוין רמב טוש"ע י"ד סי' רכט סעיף ג:
ג ג מיי' פ"ב מהלכות נזירות הלכה ד:
ד ד מיי' פי"א מהל' נדרים הל' יא יב סמג לאוין רמב טוש"ע י"ד סימן רלד סעיף נג:
ה ה מיי' שם טוש"ע שם סעיף נב:
ו ו ז מיי' שם הל' יג יד טוש"ע שם סעיף נד:
ז ח מיי' פ"ב מהל' נזירות הלכה ד:
ח ט מיי' פ"ב מהל' שבועות הלכה יז:

פי' הרא"ש

זא"ז: ה"ג הא למה לי השתא חמירתא אמר קילתא לא כ"ש. ולא גר' חמירתא אמר רב וה"פ אמאי הויא הכחשה. הך דקאמר ג' וד' לא מכחיש כלל הא דקאמר א' וב' דמימר אמרי' א) הא למה לי להזכיר א' וב' מה שאמר חבירו בזה אני מודה לו חמירתא שאני מוסיף ומחמיר עליו זה אומר קילתא שאמר חבירו לא כ"ש שהם אומרים בכלל דברי ומה לי להזכירם דבכלל דברי ישנו דבריו: במערבא אמרינן אין הכחשה במונה כאתקפת' דרמי בר חמא:

סליק פירקא

פ"ד מי שאמר הריני נזיר ושמע חבירו ואמר ואני ושמע חבירו ואמר ואני כולם נזירים הותר הא' ע"י חכם כולם מותרים שכולן תלויין בו: והוא שתפסו בתוך כדי דיבור דהיינו שלום עליך רבי כדמפ' כדי שאלת תלמיד שהם ג' תיבות. הילכך ג' מתפסה בראשון אבל ד' לא שכבר הפסיקו בג' ואני והוי יותר מכדי דיבור: א"ל תו לא שבקת רווחא לתלמודא שאם פגע בו רבו ונתן לו שלום לא יוכל להתפיס באותו שנדר לפניו. הלכך נר' דגם הד' יכול להתפיס המחובר לתוך כדי דיבור כתוך כדי דיבור דמי:

א) נראה דל"ל הא דקאמר א' וב' דמימר אמרינן הא למ"ל להזכיר דמה חמירתא שאני מוסיף וכו' לא כ"ש שהם אמורים בכלל דברי.

הגהות מהר"ב רנשבורג

א] תוס' ד"ה אמרי במערבא וכו' דמונה הוי הכחשה אפילו טפי כאילו אמר לא אחת ושתים אלא שלש וארבע. מן תיבת כאילו עד וארבע נמחק. וצ"ב מאילו אמר אחד שתים ואחד שלש או ארבע כצ"ל א"מ: ב] ד"ה הריני נזירה וכו' מהפרה ואילך מהשתא אבל. מלת אבל נמחק. וצ"ב א"כ: ג] בא"ד כי נמי מיפר את שלה ושלו קיים דמ"מ כצ"ל:

[לקמן כה:] נדרים ע.

[ב"ק עג: מכות ו. שבועות לב.]

נוסחת הריב"ן

א) עלות כלל: ב) ויהא: ג) אומרת ג' ד' ה': ד) בכ"י כתוב כאן בזה"ל ע"א כדי שאילת תלמיד לרב ב' תיבות בלבד וכנגדן קתני מתניתין ואני ואני ב' פעמים בלבד ולא יותר שאם אמר השלישי נמי ואני השלישי מותר דלא התפיס בתוך כדי דבור ובדין הוא דאיבעי ליה למימר כדי שאילת רב לתלמיד דרב קאמר לתלמידו שלום עליך בלבד אלא משום דברייתא מיירי לקמן כדי שאילת תלמיד לרב נקט איהו נמי כדי שאילת תלמיד לרב ולעולם שאילת תלמיד לרב שלום עליך תו לא שבקת רווחא לתלמידא כלומר וכי אין לו לתלמיד לומר לרב אלא ב' תיבות בלבד והלא י"ל ג' שלום עליך רבי וכיון שהן ג' תיבות יכולין להתפיס כנגדן ג' נזירים ומתני' דקתני ואני ואני הכי נמי דקסבר ג' ואני כנגד ג' תיבות אלא דלא בעי למחשב וליזול הס"ד ואח"כ מה"ד מסייע ליה לר"ל תנ"ה כו':

הגהות הב"ח

(א) רש"י ד"ה מי שאמר וכו' הותר הראשון: (ב) ד"ה יתיב וכו' ואני כולן שלשה וכו' שלש תיבות: (ג) ד"ה תוב לא שבקת וכו' קמ"ל הס"ד ואח"כ מ"ה תניא נמי הכי וכו' הרי זה נזיר כמוהו. ומסייע ליה לר"ל הס"ד ואח"כ מ"ה ליתא מסייע: